Teaching Children's Literature in an Era of Standards

Amy A. McClure

Ohio Wesleyan University

Abigail Garthwait

University of Maine

Janice V. Kristo

University of Maine

PEARSON

Boston • Columbus • Indianapolis • New York • San Francisco • Upper Saddle River
Amsterdam • Cape Town • Dubai • London • Madrid • Milan • Munich • Paris • Montréal • Toronto
Delhi • Mexico City • São Paulo • Sydney • Hong Kong • Seoul • Singapore • Taipei • Tokyo

Development Editor: Jeffery Johnston
Acquisitions Editor: Kathryn Boice
Editorial Assistant: Carolyn Schweitzer
Marketing Manager: Christopher Barry and Krista Clark
Production Editor: Mary Beth Finch
Editorial Production Service: Mary Tindle,
  S4Carlisle Publishing Services

Manufacturing Buyer: Linda Sager
Electronic Composition: S4Carlisle Publishing
  Services
Interior Design: Denise Hoffman
Photo Researcher: Jorgensen Fernandes
Cover Designer: Diane Lorenzo
Cover Photos: Fotolia

Credits and acknowledgments borrowed from other sources and reproduced, with permission, in this textbook appear on page 391.

Library of Congress Cataloging-in-Publication Data

McClure, Amy A.
  Teaching Children's Literature in an Era of Standards/Amy A. McClure, Ohio Wesleyan University; Abigail Garthwait, University of Maine; Janice V. Kristo, University of Maine.
    pages cm
  Includes bibliographical references and index.
  ISBN 978-0-13-357124-0 (alk. paper)—ISBN 0-13-357124-6 (alk. paper) 1. Children's literature—Study and teaching—United States. 2. Language arts—Standards—United States. 3. Children—Books and reading—United States. I. Kristo, Janice V. II. Garthwait, Abigail. III. Title.
  PN1008.8.M33 2015
  809′.89282071—dc23

2013047563

10 9 8 7 6 5 4 3 2 1

ISBN 13: 978-0-13-357124-0
ISBN 10:   0-13-357124-6

Contents

Preface   xiii

Part I   Foundations   1

CHAPTER 1

Knowing Children's Literature and the Common Core State Standards (CCSS)   3

What Is Children's Literature?   4

What Is Included in Children's Literature   4

The Role of Literature in the Lives of Children   5

Organizing Children's Literature   7

Forms   7

Picture Books   7   •   *Poetry*   8

Genres   8

Fiction   8   •   *Traditional Literature*   8   •   *Fantasy and Science Fiction*   8   •   *Historical Fiction*   8   •   *Contemporary Realistic Fiction*   8   •   *Nonfiction and Biography*   9*

Series Books   9

Blended Genres   10

Criteria for Choosing High-Quality Children's Literature   11

A Close Look at *Roll of Thunder, Hear My Cry* by Mildred Taylor   11

What Are the Elements of Fiction?   12

Characterization   12   •   *Plot*   13   •   *Theme*   14   •   *Setting*   14   •   *Style*   17   •   *Point of View*   17   •   *Illustration*   18*

Awards for Children's Literature   19

Guiding Principles for Creating and Implementing a Literature Program   19

Principle 1   19

Principle 2   19

Principle 3   20

Principle 4   21

Principle 5   21

Reconciling Our Principles with the Requirements to Meet Standards   21

■ COMMON CORE STATE STANDARD FEATURE #1: Determine Central Ideas or Themes of a Text (CCSS.RL.2)   21

21st-Century Skills   23

Integrating Our Principles, Standards, and Exemplary Literature to Meaningfully and Authentically Connect Children and Books   25

Supporting Culturally Diverse Students with Children's Literature   25

Supporting English Language Learners with Children's Literature   25

Supporting All Students with Technology   26

Controversial Issue: Movies, Commercialization, and Children's Literature   27

Summary   28

Questions/Activities to Invite Thinking, Writing, and Conversation About the Chapter   29

CHAPTER 2

Literature Response and Engagement   31

What Is Response and Engagement?   32

Response and Engagement: The Reader   33

Experiential Background   34   •   *Interests*   34   •   *Preferences*   35
•   *Developmental Characteristics*   39   •   *Literacy Skills*   43

Response and Engagement: The Text   43

Text Characteristics   43   •   *Text Complexity*   44   •   *Text Substantiality*   45

Response and Engagement: The Context   45

Peer Influence on Response/Engagement with Books   46   •   *Teacher Influences on Response/Engagement*   46   •   *Classroom Context Influence on Response/Engagement*   47

Theoretical Perspectives on Reader Response   48

Formal Criticism, Generic Perspective, and Intertextual Criticism   48

Transactional Response Theory   49

Efferent and Aesthetic Response   49   •   *The Critical Stance*   50

Teaching from Transactional and Critical Perspectives   51

Response, Engagement, and the Common Core State Standards   53

Opportunities for Children to Respond to Books   54

Writing   55

Literature Response Journals or Blogs   55   •   *Written Conversations*   56
•   *Writing from Literature Models*   56

Oral Responses   56

Oral Retelling   57   •   *"Say Something"*   57   •   *Book Talks*   57
•   *Book Discussions*   57   •   *Choral Speaking*   57

Drama   58

Puppetry   59   •   *Storytelling*   59   •   *Pantomime*   61   •   *Reader's Theater*   61

Art and Music   61

Explorations of Illustrators' Media and Style 62 • *Comic Strips* 62
• *Sketch-to-Stretch* 62 • *Response Through Music* 62

Responding Through Graphic Organizers   63

Maps and Time Lines   63

Controversial Issue: Are Response Activities Appropriate in the Standards Era?   63

Summary   66

Questions/Activities to Invite Thinking, Writing, and Conversation
About the Chapter   67

CHAPTER 3

Strategies for Sharing Literature   69

Close Reading   71

Close Reading and the CCSS   71

■ COMMON CORE STATE STANDARD FEATURE #1: Asking and Answering
Questions About Texts, Referring to Explicit Evidence (CCSS.RL.1 and RI.1)   71

Key Elements of Close Reading Sessions   72

Short Passages from Complex Text 72 • *Limited Pre-Prereading Discussions* 72
• *Repeated Readings* 73 • *Text-Dependent Questions* 73 • *Annotations* 73

Implementing Close Reading Sessions   73

First Reading: Focus on Key Ideas and Details 76 • *Second Reading: Focus on
Discerning Significant Literary Aspects and Ideas* 76 • *Third Reading: Focus
on Author's Craft and Text Structure* 76 • *Fourth Reading: Interpretation and
Synthesis* 76

Cautions Regarding Close Reading   77

Interactive Read-Aloud   77

Interactive Read-Alouds and the CCSS   79

Implementing Effective Interactive Read-Alouds   80

Selecting Books for Read-Alouds 80 • *A Suggested Read-Aloud Sequence* 81

Shared Book Experience   82

Implementing Shared Book Experiences   84

First Reading 84 • *Shared Rereadings* 84

Extending Shared Reading   85

Literature Circles   88

Literature Circles and the CCSS   89

■ COMMON CORE STATE STANDARD FEATURE #2: Collaborative Conversations
and Oral Presentations (CCSS.SL.1, SL.2, and SL.4)   89

Planning for and Implementing Literature Circles   89

Choosing Books for Literature Circles 89 • *Establishing Ground
Rules* 90 • *Helping Students Prepare for Discussions* 90 • *Book
Extensions* 93 • *Literature Strategy Lessons* 93 • *Structuring Time* 94

A Suggested Literature Circle Planning Guide   94

Independent Reading: Reader's Workshop   **94**

   Reader's Workshop and the CCSS   96

   Implementing Reader's Workshop   96

    Self-Selection of Books   96   •   *Work Time: Reading and Responding to Books*   97   •   *Conferences*   98   •   *Sharing*   98   •   *Literature Strategy Lessons*   98   •   *Structuring Time and Expectations*   98

Literature Across the Curriculum   **100**

Controversial Issue: Book Selection   **101**

   Looking Ahead   103

Summary   **103**

Questions/Activities to Invite Thinking, Writing, and Conversation About the Chapter   **103**

Recommended Book Lists   **104**

Part II   The Forms and Genres of Children's Literature   107

CHAPTER 4

Picture Books   109
(Literary Form)

What Are Picture Books?   **110**

   Elements of Picture Books   111

    The Art of the Picture Book   111

   Looking Closely at the Writing in Picture Books   115

    Well-Written Prose   115   •   *Figurative Language*   118   •   *Voice*   118   •   *Understatement*   118   •   *Plot*   118   •   *Leads*   119   •   *Characters*   119   •   *Dialogue*   119   •   *Setting*   119

The Role of Picture Books in Children's Lives   **120**

Criteria for Evaluating Picture Books   **121**

Types of Picture Books   **121**

   Genre and Thematic Connections   121

   Concept Books   122

   Alphabet Books   123

   Easy-to-Read Books   123

   Wordless and Almost Wordless Picture Books   124

   Predictable Patterned Language Books   124

   Pop-Up Books   125

   Interactive Books   125

   Graphic Novels   126

   Postmodern Picture Books   126

Teaching Strategies   128

    Connecting to the Common Core State Standards   128

■ COMMON CORE STATE STANDARD FEATURE #1: Understanding How Illustrations Interact with Text (CCSS.RL.7)   128

    Supporting Culturally Diverse Learners with Picture Books   132

    Supporting English Language Learners with Picture Books   133

    Controversial Issue Using Picture Books: The Trend of Digital Picture Books   133

Summary   134

Questions/Activities to Invite Thinking, Writing, and Conversation About the Chapter   135

Recommended Picture Books   135

CHAPTER 5

Poetry   139
(Literary Form)

What Is Poetry?   140

    The Literary Elements of Poetry   141

        Sound 141 • *Rhythm* 142 • *Figurative Language* 143 • *Shape* 143 • *Emotional Impact* 144 • *Insight* 144

    Genres and Forms of Poetry for Children   144

The Role of Poetry in Children's Lives   146

    Children's Poetry Preferences   146

Criteria for Evaluating Poetry   147

Categories of Poetry   147

    Thematic Poetry   147

        Humor and Wordplay 148 • *Poetry About Nature and the Seasons* 148 • *Poetry About Children's Everyday Lives* 149 • *Poetry About School* 149 • *Poetry About Animals* 150

    Poetry and Content-Area Studies   151

    Poetry in Different Formats   151

        Comprehensive Anthologies 154 • *Single-Poet Collections* 154 • *Single Poems in Picture Book Format* 154

    Poetry for Young Children   156

Teaching Strategies   156

    Connecting to the Common Core State Standards   156

■ COMMON CORE STATE STANDARD FEATURE #1: Identifying Figurative and Other Nonliteral Language in Poetry Conversations   156

■ COMMON CORE STATE STANDARD FEATURE #2: Developing Fluency with Poetry Performance (CCSS.RF.1, 2)   159

    Supporting Culturally Diverse Students with Poetry   163

    Supporting English Language Learners with Poetry   166

Controversial Issue: Close Reading of Poetry   167

Summary   168

Questions/Activities to Invite Thinking, Writing, and Conversation
About the Chapter   169

Recommended Poetry Books by Themes   169

CHAPTER 6

Traditional Literature   175
(Literary Genre)

What Is Traditional Literature?   176

    Elements of Traditional Literature   177

        Plot   177 • *Setting*   177 • *Characterization*   177 • *Style*   178
        • *Theme*   178 • *Motifs*   178 • *Variants and Versions*   178

The Role of Traditional Literature in Children's Lives   180

Criteria for Evaluating Traditional Literature   181

Categories of Traditional Literature   182

    Folktales   183

    Fables and Learning Stories   185

    Myths   187

    Legends and Epics   188

    Ghost Stories   189

    Tall Tales   190

    Nursery Rhymes   191

    Ballads and Folk Songs   192

    Playground and Other Game-Related Literature   193

Teaching Strategies   193

    Connecting to the Common Core State Standards   194

■ COMMON CORE STATE STANDARD FEATURE #1: Comparing Similar
Traditional Stories Across Cultures (CCSS.RL.9)   194

■ COMMON CORE STATE STANDARD FEATURE #2: Comparing How Visual
Aspects of a Text Contribute to Story Meaning in Traditional Literature
(CCSS.RL.7)   197

    Supporting Culturally Diverse Students with Traditional Literature   199

    Supporting English Language Learners with Traditional Literature   199

Controversial Issue: The Misappropriation of a Culture's Traditional
Literature by Mainstream Cultures   203

Summary   205

Questions/Activities to Invite Thinking, Writing, and Conversation
About the Chapter   205

Recommended Traditional Literature Books   206

CHAPTER 7

Fantasy and Science Fiction   211
(Literary Genre)

What Are Fantasy and Science Fiction?   212

The Role of Fantasy and Science Fiction in Children's Lives   213

Criteria for Evaluating Fantasy and Science Fiction   214

    Characterization   215

    Setting   215

    Plot   215

Categorizing Fantasy and Science Fiction   215

    Literary Fairy Tales: Hans Christian Andersen   216

    Fantasy Novels Based on Traditional Literature   216

    Animal and Toy Fantasy   216

    Ghosts and the Supernatural   219

    Children and Magic   220

    Alternative Worlds   221

    Fantastic Adventures   222

    Time Travel Fantasy   223

    Heroic Fantasy   224

    Science Fiction: Future Worlds   226

    Science Fiction: Space Travel and Beyond   227

Picture Books in Fantasy and Science Fiction   228

Transitional Books in Fantasy and Science Fiction   228

Teaching Strategies   229

    Connecting to the Common Core State Standards   229

■ COMMON CORE STATE STANDARD FEATURE #1: Discerning Theme (CCSS.RL.2)   229

■ COMMON CORE STATE STANDARD FEATURE #2: Discerning Plot Structure (CCSS.RL.5)   230

    Supporting Culturally Diverse Students with Fantasy and Science Fiction   233

    Supporting English Language Learners with Fantasy and Science Fiction   235

Controversial Issue: Are Electronic Media Supplanting Book Reading?   236

Summary   237

Questions/Activities to Invite Thinking, Writing, and Conversation About the Chapter   238

Recommended Fantasy and Science Fiction Picture Books   238

Recommended Fantasy/Science Fiction Novels   241

CHAPTER 8

Historical Fiction 245
(Literary Genre)

What Is Historical Fiction? 246

The Role of Historical Fiction in Children's Lives 248

Criteria for Evaluating Historical Fiction 249

    Setting 249

    Characterization 249

    Writing Style 250

Categorizing Historical Fiction: Historical Eras 250

    Ancient Civilizations (up to A.D. 600) 251

    The Middle Ages (A.D. 600–1500) 252

    North America: Colonial Times and the American Revolution
(1600–1800) 253

    Westward Expansion (1800s) 254

    Slavery and the Civil War (1800s) 254

    Industrialization, Immigration, and Segregation (Late 19th and Early
20th Centuries) 255

    The Great Depression (1930s) 257

    World War II (1940s) 258

    Civil Rights, Political Unrest, and the Vietnam War (1950–1970s) 259

    Picture Books in Historical Fiction 262

    Series and Transitional Books in Historical Fiction 263

Teaching Strategies 263

    Connecting to the Common Core State Standards 263

■ COMMON CORE STATE STANDARD FEATURE #1: Comparing and
Contrasting Books on the Same Theme, Historical Era, or Different Genre
(CCSS.RL.9 and RI.9) 263

■ COMMON CORE STATE STANDARD FEATURE #2: Analyzing the
Connection Between Text and Illustration in Historical Fiction Picture
Books (CCSS.RL.7) 267

    Supporting Culturally Diverse Learners with Historical
Fiction 268

    Supporting English Language Learners with Historical
Fiction 269

Controversial Issue: Should All Aspects of History Be Included
in Historical Fiction for Children? 269

Summary 271

Questions/Activities to Invite Thinking, Writing, and Conversation
About the Chapter 272

Recommended Historical Fiction Picture Books 272

Recommended Historical Fiction Novels 276

CHAPTER 9

Contemporary Realistic Fiction   279
(Literary Genre)

What Is Contemporary Realistic Fiction?   280

The Role of Contemporary Realistic Fiction in Children's Lives   281

Criteria for Evaluating Contemporary Realistic Fiction   282

    Plot   283

    Characterization   283

    Theme   284

    Setting   284

    Style   284

    Point of View   285

Categorizing Contemporary Realistic Fiction   286

    Growing Up: Peer Relationships, Life Changes, and Contending with Problems   287

    Stories About Family Relationships   288

    Animal Stories   289

    Adventure and Survival Stories   289

    Humorous Stories   290

    Mysteries   291

    Sports Stories   292

    School Life   293

    Books About People with Physical and Mental Challenges   293

    Lesbian, Gay, Bisexual, and Transgender (LGBT) Literature   294

    Contemporary Realistic Fiction Picture Books   295

    Contemporary Realistic Fiction Transitional and Series Books   296

Teaching Strategies   297

    Connecting to the Common Core State Standards   297

■ COMMON CORE STATE STANDARD FEATURE #1: Understanding Character   297

■ COMMON CORE STATE STANDARD FEATURE #2: Determining Point of View (CCSS.RL.6)   300

    Supporting Culturally Diverse Learners with Contemporary Realistic Fiction   303

    Supporting English Language Learners with Contemporary Realistic Fiction   303

Controversial Issue: Bibliotherapy: Should Books Be Used to Address Life Issues?   305

Summary   306

Questions/Activities to Invite Thinking, Writing, and Conversation About the Chapter   307

Recommended Contemporary Realistic Fiction Picture Books   307

Recommended Contemporary Realistic Fiction Transitional/Series Books   310

Recommended Contemporary Realistic Fiction Novels   310

CHAPTER 10

Nonfiction   315
(Literary Genre)

What Is Nonfiction?   317

The Role of Nonfiction in Children's Lives   318

Criteria for Evaluating Nonfiction   319

 Quality of Writing   321

  Style 321 • *Clarity* 321 • *Organization* 321 • *Leads
  and Conclusions* 321 • *Language: Sentence Structure and
  Vocabulary* 323 • *Figurative Language* 323 • *Accuracy* 324

 Visual Information   325

  Access Features 325

 Format and Design   326

  Size and Shape 326 • *Book Covers* 326 • *End Pages* 327
  • *Typeface and Distinctive Markings* 327

Categorizing Nonfiction   327

 Biographies   328

  Picture Book Biographies 329 • *Partial Biographies* 330 • *Complete
  Biographies* 331 • *Collective Biographies* 331 • *Autobiographies and
  Memoirs* 331 • *Biography in Poetic Form* 332

 Concept Books   333

  Informational Picture Books 334 • *Photographic Essays* 334 • *Survey Books* 335
  • *Specialized Books* 335 • *Journals, Diaries, Sketchbooks, and Documents* 335
  • *Life Cycle Books* 336 • *Activity, Craft, Experiment, and How-to Books* 336
  • *Identification Books and Field Guides* 337 • *Reference Books* 337
  • *Nonfiction Graphic Novels* 337

Teaching Strategies   338

 Connecting to the Common Core State Standards   338

■ COMMON CORE STATE STANDARD FEATURE #1: Knowing Various
 Text Features   338

■ COMMON CORE STATE STANDARD FEATURE #2: Comparing and Contrasting
 Key Points in Two Tests   344

 Supporting Culturally Diverse Learners with Nonfiction   348

 Supporting English Language Learners with Nonfiction   349

Controversial Issue: Using Blended or Faction Books   350

Summary   351

Questions/Activities to Invite Thinking, Writing, and Conversation
About the Chapter   352

Recommended Nonfiction Books   353

Awards for Children's Literature   358

References   363

Index   374

Credits   391

Preface

We are passionate book lovers. You know those little kids who read all night under the covers with a flashlight? That was us. Maybe it was you. You know those kids who reluctantly closed a freely chosen book they were reading when the teacher announced, "Time for reading groups." That was us. Maybe it was you, too. Books have brought us much pleasure in our lives. We are educators who possess a combined 100+ years of teaching experience during which we communicated our passion for children's literature. We continue to find joy in the literature written for children that has long crowded our home and office bookshelves. We have shared laughter, shed some tears, acquired knowledge, and lingered over the language of these books. This text is our way of giving back, helping teachers bring the pleasures of sharing memorable, high-quality books to the students in their lives.

With the mandates of No Child Left Behind, Race to the Top, the 21st Century Skills Framework, and now the Common Core State Standards (CCSS), we hear teachers worrying that they can no longer spend time with literature and foster the varied responses that students make as they read real books that are engaging and challenging. "My school says I have to prepare students for the state test," "I have to use programmed materials which have short reading passages because that's efficient and that's what students will encounter on the test," or "I have all these standards to teach." We understand these concerns. We also passionately believe that teachers can meet the mandates of testing and standards by sharing engaging, challenging books of fiction, nonfiction, and poetry with their students. In fact, we contend that those students will not only master the skills mandated by standards but also surpass these expectations if given the opportunity to respond thoughtfully to books of substance.

When we agreed to do this book, we were a bit skeptical of the CCSS. Could young children really do literary analysis, finding evidence to support their answers, we wondered? Could students in grades K–8 engage in rich discussions about a character's point of view, make in-depth comparisons across multiple texts from various genres, or engage in other kinds of complex literary analysis? What about our diverse students and those whose first language is not English? We've found that the CCSS are not perfect. They do not address the needs of diverse students. They do not explicitly provide for students who may be struggling with reading and may need some accommodations to be successful. Most important, they focus almost entirely on analysis and acquiring information and ignore the elements of passion and delight in reading that we see as critical to creating lifelong readers.

What the CCSS *do* provide is a blueprint for helping students read closely and learn what distinguishes a book as high literary quality. They emphasize the importance of fiction, nonfiction (informational text), and poetic texts—something we have not seen in many prior standards. They ensure that we are purposeful in our teaching—that we carefully show students what makes a poem so delightful to the ear or a nonfiction book a compelling read. They remind us of the necessity for integrating all the language arts. They also challenge us to make sure that every child learns to read competently. We have added the elements that we believe are missing from the CCSS: how to engage our culturally diverse students, how to support students who are English language learners, and how to develop interest and excitement in reading.

In *Teaching Children's Literature in an Era of Standards*, you will find the tools to instill a lasting love for literature while also building reading and critical thinking skills, thus meeting the mandates of standards. Although we emphasize the CCSS, we also have integrated references to the 21st Century Skills Framework, as they are an important and interrelated set of skills. This text is designed to help you understand how students respond to books, build your knowledge of quality children's literature, and develop teaching strategies that support authentic interactions with books. Thus, it is appropriate for both undergraduate and graduate courses in children's literature and reading or children's literature and language arts.

Mentor Texts

We have organized a significant number of examples around several mentor texts. In general, mentor texts are books that have particular qualities or features that teachers can draw on for class discussions and activities. Rich classroom conversations evolve when students read or listen to the same book. The mentor texts we have selected will help make the examples and lesson plans in this book more meaningful and memorable. The selected mentor texts are the following:

- *Roll of Thunder, Hear My Cry* by Mildred Taylor: a classic historical fiction book that still resonates with today's children.
- *Wonder* by R. J. Palacio: a contemporary book of realistic fiction that we believe will be a classic of the future.
- *The Very Hungry Caterpillar* by Eric Carle: one of the best-known picture books that is also complex enough to generate in-depth discussions about the integration of text and illustration in picture books.
- *Smithsonian: Bug Hunter* by David Burnie: a nonfiction book that offers fascinating information about a variety of insects and includes related activities.

A Content Walk Through This Text

Teaching Children's Literature in an Era of Standards is organized in two sections. Part I emphasizes foundational concepts. Part II features seven chapters devoted to each of the major forms and genres of children's literature. Instructional methods are woven into each chapter. *We strongly believe that the books children have enjoyed for decades should not be lost to future generations.* These books have lasted because children have seen something memorable in them and have passed their passion for these books to friends, siblings, and their own children. Thus, form and genre chapters feature examples of both older titles and those published more recently that we believe will resonate with children in the years to come. We have endeavored to mention only the best. More titles could not be included due to limited space in the book, but we hope you will continue to discover quality books on your own. This book is organized as follows:

Part I: Foundations

Chapter 1: discusses the foundational and philosophical aspects of teaching in classrooms where literature plays a prominent role. We take the perspective that what teachers believe about learners, books, and school will affect how they choose to teach literacy. We also provide an overview of the CCSS and 21st Century literacy skills.

Chapter 2: addresses the concepts of response to literature. We build a framework for how the factors of reader, text, and context interact to drive one's engagement with books. We also discuss theories of literary response, focusing specifically on Rosenblatt's Transactional Response Theory and how the mandates of the CCSS do and do not mesh with this theory. General strategies teachers use to encourage authentic interactions with books are described.

Chapter 3: describes the teaching strategies educators can use to involve children in meaningful reading experiences and how literature can be shared in various ways across the curriculum.

Part II: The Forms and Genres of Children's Literature

Chapters 4 to 10: present detailed information on each of the major forms and genres in children's literature, including picture books, poetry, traditional literature, fantasy/ science fiction, historical fiction, contemporary realistic fiction, and nonfiction, including biography.

Each chapter features sections on defining the form or genre, how it is significant in children's lives, evaluation and selection criteria, discussion of memorable books, and connections to the CCSS. We also discuss how the books in that form or genre can support the needs of culturally and linguistically diverse learners. A controversial issue invites readers to consider the pros and cons of a related important debate topic. We conclude each chapter with an extensive list of notable and representative titles.

We suggest that teacher candidates carefully read Chapters 1 to 3 in their entirety. We also recommend carefully reading the introductory and concluding sections of Chapters 4 to 10. Skimming the sections of these chapters in which specific books are discussed "Categorizing Books Within the Form or Genre" provides an overview of the genre and book suggestions. We hope this provides a strong foundation but also leaves time to read the wonderful books we recommend. We also anticipate that these sections will serve as references when teacher candidates need to find books for their future students who will have wide interests and tastes in what they want to read.

Important Features of This Text

- For the sake of efficiency, we have used abbreviations when we reference standards. A key to these abbreviations and acronyms is provided in Chapter 1.

- In most instances, books within lists are designated as follows: P (primary grades, K–3); I (intermediate grades, 4–6), and M (middle grades, 6–8). Books suitable for preschoolers are marked with an asterisk (*). If these designations do not appear, the list is suitable for one grade level (as noted at the beginning of the list).

- The hash mark (#) designates titles that feature culturally diverse characters, settings, plots, or information. Exceptions are noted.

- We have designated activity/CCSS connections that work particularly well with a specific genre. However, many of the activities can be used with books from multiple genres; thus, we encourage you to adapt activities across genres.

Integration of Technology

Computer technology offers additional tools for research, reading assistance, and media for student response to literature. Throughout the text, we have integrated three types of "Tech Clicks": Information Technology within the context of 21st Century literacy skills, ideas for student responses to books, and a sampling of important Web sites. Due to the likelihood that URLs have changed, we provide the sponsoring organization or the title of the site rather than long and awkward addresses.

As you embark on the journey to use technology in the most meaningful ways to support good literature and mastery of standards, a helpful strategy is to discard the notion that the teacher must know everything. Consider the "voice and choice" of your students when it comes to response to books and, at the same time, be mindful of your purposes and goals.

Acknowledgements

We deeply appreciate the contributions from so many of our colleagues, teacher friends, students, and family who made this book a reality. This was a huge project that could not have been accomplished without the wisdom, expertise, and goodwill of so many people. We sincerely hope that we have not omitted anyone, and if we did, please forgive us.

We first thank and gratefully acknowledge our colleague Dr. Wendy Kasten, who has been an integral part of our journey. We deeply value the years of collaboration and friendship we have shared with you, Wendy, and wish you much rest and happiness in your retirement.

We also wish to acknowledge the expertise, wisdom, and insights from university and author colleagues: Penny Colman, Diane Jackson, Lisa Patrick, Jane Wellman-Little, and Sandip Wilson.

We also thank all the teachers and librarians who have shared their classrooms and libraries, insights about teaching, and remarkable commitment to bringing wonderful books to their students: Mary Bagley, Judy Bouchard, Cynthia Crosser, Marty Cryer, Nora Curtis, Kerri Doyle, Jessica Dunton, Emily Esker, Sharon Esswein, Sarah Holliday, Hilary Larbus, Susan Marantz, Judy Markham, Margaret Mattson, Kelley McDaniel, Liz McMahan, Lynn Mayer, Shelly Moody, Kim Oldenburgh, Peggy Oxley, Tammy Ranger, Franki Sibberson, Candy Staley, Karen Terlecky, Stella Villalba, and Deb White.

Our students also deserve recognition not only for great book suggestions and useful teaching strategies but also for challenging us to think in new ways. Our thanks also go to bookshop owner Cathy Anderson.

Special thanks to friends and family for your unending support, encouragement, and tolerance for spouses and moms who spend considerable time with their noses in books and computers: Rusty McClure; Wayne Garthwait; Dana Smith; Kaci, Haileigh, and Crosleigh McClure; and Seamor and Tory Kristo.

We also extend appreciation to staff and graduate assistants who keep us sane and organized: Joette Kugler and Kim Strain of Ohio Wesleyan University and Amy Cates and Phyllis Thibodeau at the University of Maine.

We are deeply grateful to the authors, illustrators, poets, and editors who supply us with wonderful children's books and generously contribute their own time, talents, and insights about their books. Thanks to you all.

Finally, we would like to thank the reviewers of our manuscript for their helpful insights: Stephanie Affinito, SUNY Albany; Diane Barone, University of Nevada, Reno; Karen L. Bramble, American Indian College; Nancy E. Cardenuto, Kutztown University; Catharine R. Freeman, Hawkeye Community College; Lindsay Persohn, University of South Florida; Erin Reilly-Sanders, The Ohio State University; and Patricia L. Rieman, Carthage College.

Part I
Foundations

Picture-Books in Winter

Summer fading, winter comes—
Frosty mornings, tingling thumbs,
Window robins, winter rooks,
And the picture story-books.

Water now is turned to stone
Nurse and I can walk upon;
Still we find the flowing brooks
In the picture story-books.

All the pretty things put by,
Wait upon the children's eye,
Sheep and shepherds, trees and crooks,
In the picture story-books.

We may see how all things are
Seas and cities, near and far,
And the flying fairies' looks,
In the picture story-books.

How am I to sing your praise,
Happy chimney-corner days,
Sitting safe in nursery nooks,
Reading picture story-books?

—From *A Child's Garden of Verses*,
  Robert Louis Stevenson, 1905 Scribner's.

Knowing Children's Literature and the Common Core State Standards (CCSS)

To provide foundational context for children's literature, we address the following questions in this chapter:

- What is children's literature?

- Why use literature with children?

- What are the forms and genres of children's literature?

- What are the basic criteria for evaluating children's literature?

- What principles guide teachers as they create and implement a literature program?

- How do we integrate our beliefs, standards, and exemplary literature to meaningfully and authentically connect children and books?

The most important thing you learn at school is how to read. It's important because we live in a literate society and in our society it's as important to be able to read as it is to be able to walk and talk—if you can't do these things, your ability to participate in society is restricted. But literature is bounding along ahead like the white rabbit, and before you know where you are, it's over the hills and far away. Because children's literature knows perfectly well that literacy is only a beginning, not an end. It's the starting point, not the goal. (Parkinson, 2011, p. 52)

Siobhán Parkinson, Ireland's first laureate for children's literature, understands the desire to pass along culture to the next generation. Yet in the excerpt on the previous page, she also conveys the exuberant experiences that books can afford readers. She describes the boundless opportunities of literature to construct personal meaning and to show the commonalities of being human. Siobhán points out that "literacy is only a beginning," implying that standards provide educators with starting points, but standards are not the goals, nor do they proscribe a methodology.

Similarly, Robert Louis Stevenson's poem paints with words the emotional enticement of stories, the pull of stepping outside one's everyday life, and the pleasure of learning new things—all feeding the mind and soul. Teachers who know and treasure books will lead their students on wonderful reading adventures, such as traveling to "seas and cities, near and far" or following a white rabbit. Teachers who know quality literature will bring books and children together. This is especially critical in a time when schools must focus on outcome-based learning. *Teaching Children's Literature in an Era of Standards* will help you integrate quality literature with the expectation that your students will meet critical standards.

What Is Children's Literature?

What is children's literature? The obvious answer, *books written for children*, is too simplistic. A working definition is more nuanced, and, oddly enough, children's literature professionals disagree on the details. This section examines the characteristics of children's literature.

What Is Included in Children's Literature

We use the term *children's literature* to encompass the realm of books written for children or read by children, regardless of format: print, audio, or digital. Children's literature can include non-fiction, poetry, magazines, traditional literature, fiction, and picture books. For the purposes of this book, we emphasize literature that is appropriate for children kindergarten through middle school and also suggest books appropriate for preschoolers.

Some experts recognize the literacy value of children's magazines and e-zines, such as *Cobblestone, Cricket,* or *Ranger Rick* (Johnson, 2010; Strickland & Morrow, 1991), as well as acknowledging that many students prefer this format. A 2005 survey of more than 8,200 students found that more than 75% indicated that magazines were on their list of favorite reading materials (Davila & Patrick, 2010, p. 202).

Some professionals eliminate nonfiction, even when written for children. Nancy Anderson (2009) offers her opinion that nonfiction books usually function as a quick reference and were not designed to be read from cover to cover. We politely disagree; in Chapter 10, we provide a strong rationale for viewing nonfiction as literature. Another contended category includes books designed for *sampling* rather than reading cover to cover, such as joke books or poetry anthologies. We include them as children's literature.

Note that many children's literature professionals view the term *kiddie lit* as denigrating to this vital, complex, and rewarding area of study. Children's literature has been discussed in deeply scholarly ways, dissected with passionate precision, and minutely examined under the lens of cultural studies (McGillis, 2011). Thus it should be referred to in a scholarly fashion.

When classrooms are rich with quality literature they engage and captivate students.

Some professors (Atkinson, Matusevich, & Huber, 2009) use the term *trade books* synonymously with children's literature, referring to the types of books found in quality bookstores. In contrast, textbooks, workbooks, and related skill-based resources are considered curriculum materials rather than literature.

By high school, students typically read more advanced books that bridge the divide between adolescence and adulthood. Literature that targets a maturity level between childhood and adulthood is called young adult literature. However, vocabulary and sentence complexity are not the only measures that separate books for children and adolescents. Plato used simple words in *The Cave*, but these metaphysical reflections are not for children.

A healthy discussion flourishes regarding whether books originally written for adults and now read by middle-level students, such as *The Adventures of Huckleberry Finn* (Twain), *The Yearling* (Rawlings), or *The Lord of the Rings* (Tolkien), should be categorized children's literature (Trites, 2007). We also consider a title as children's literature if it is intended for children but boasts a wide adult readership, such as Rowling's *Harry Potter* series.

The Role of Literature in the Lives of Children

Teachers in preschool through grade 8 can prepare a foundation for powerful reading and writing experiences by sharing a variety of children's literature with their students. Quality literature is well written and memorable, with varied writing styles, engaging plots, richly developed characters, beautiful poetic language, and accurate and intriguing information.

Teachers need to make many decisions about teaching reading and writing no matter what grade they teach. Sometimes a school or district requires specific materials, such as basal readers or workbooks, but that should not preclude sharing real books with students. Children long remember books their teacher shared aloud. Access to quality literature for independent reading is not a luxury, but a necessity for reading growth. Be committed to your own literary growth and development; know your students and know books. Wise choices and thoughtful planning and sharing of books are all essential factors in fostering positive attitudes and growth in reading and writing regardless of age or grade level. Whereas reading was once taught as a separate subject in many classrooms, the Common Core State Standards emphasize reading and writing as essential to learning in all disciplines. Researchers continue to examine the best way to motivate students to read, as shown in Figure 1.1.

These are important points to keep in mind: organizing learning around children's literature is an excellent way to accomplish this goal (Galda & Beach, 2004; Wooten & Cullinan, 2009). We should build on what we know about developing positive attitudes toward reading and counteract or avoid the elements that build poor ones. You will create an environment for rich learning and lasting engagement with literature by knowing your students, by reflecting on

FIGURE 1.1 **What We Know About Nurturing Positive and Enduring Attitudes Toward Reading**

- Students read more, with better understanding, if books are plentiful and easily accessible (Guthrie & Humenick, 2004). Because at-risk students are less apt to read during vacations and have less access to books, additional support needs to be provided (Allington et al., 2010).

- Students enjoy reading more when instruction includes literature as opposed to solely using workbooks or other decontextualized materials (Goodman, 2005; Reis et al., 2007). This is also true for struggling readers (Thames et al., 2008).

- Students are motivated to read when they have choice in their reading (Allington et al., 2010; Guthrie & Humenick, 2004; Reis et al., 2007).

- Students who are read to by teachers develop positive attitudes toward reading (Bruckerhoff, 1977).

- Students are motivated when they are able to discuss books with peers (Allington, 2002; Guthrie & Humenick, 2004; Nystrand, 2006).

- Students improve in reading attitudes when they have opportunities to teach and to help younger students, such as in cross-aged tutoring (Leland & Fitzpatrick, 1994; Slavin, Lake, Cheung, & Davis, 2009). On the other hand, research on computerized assessments such as *Accelerated Reader* show mixed results (Smith & Westberg, 2011; What Works Clearinghouse, 2010).

- As students become teenagers, their interest in reading tends to decline (Tunnell, Calder, & Phaup, 1991). Middle school teachers have the weighty responsibility of trying to prevent this.

- Poor reading attitudes are likely when reading instruction is limited to prescribed texts and does not include engaging literature (Allington, 2010; Garan & DeVoogd, 2008; Sweet, Guthrie, & Ng, 1998).

- When students are grouped for reading by ability, lower-ability groups rarely score high on reading attitude surveys, and it is often difficult to motivate them (Schooley, 1994).

your beliefs, and by modeling a love of literature. By becoming familiar with classroom practices that engage readers and writers, you will help to build on their natural curiosity to develop content-area knowledge, reading and writing skills, and a love of books while still addressing standards.

The Common Core State Standards (National Governors Association Center for Best Practices & Council of Chief State School Officers, 2010, p. 7) lists the following strategies that improve students' reading skills by incorporating literature in the curriculum. Through exposure to literature, students will be better able to do the following:

- Demonstrate self-directed and independent reading and build an awareness that reading can be personally useful, satisfying, and powerful

- Build foundational knowledge in a wide range of subjects

- Communicate with attention to various audiences

- Understand and question reading matter

- Recognize and attribute evidence and its source
- Use appropriate digital technology mindfully
- Appreciate and seek to understand multiple cultural perspectives

It's important that children *want* to read, not just know *how* to read.

The Common Core State Standards (CCSS) provide a framework for the literacy skills that lie at the heart of all subjects. Children's literature is the core component in leading children to a lifelong enjoyment and appreciation of reading, and *Teaching Children's Literature in an Era of Standards* presents a fusion of these two essential concepts. We believe that teaching with literature will enhance children's reading across topics in social studies and science as well as other subject areas. Thus, creating a *standards-based, literature-rich* classroom has the potential to increase reading development and promote positive feelings toward books and lifelong reading.

While it is conceivable that almost any text could work with the Common Core Standards, Roger Sutton (2013), editor in chief of *The Horn Book Magazine*, cautions that "the hard part comes in the classroom, where teachers have the task of putting these Standards, at once weirdly specific and uselessly generalized, into effective practice. . . . Librarians, support those books and your teachers by bringing them together. Parents and kids, keep reading" (para. 5).

Our goal is to help you build a solid foundational knowledge of children's literature, the key concepts regarding book response, and ways to thoughtfully design literacy learning incorporating the Common Core State Standards and other standards mandated by governing bodies. Our job as teachers of reading has two parts: to teach students to read. But the second, teaching students to *want to read*, is equally important. Mark Twain is blunt: "The man who does not read good books is no better than the man who can't."

Organizing Children's Literature

Children's literature is primarily organized as *genres*. The term *genre* refers to distinct categories based on defining characteristics, for example the distinguishing attributes that separate fantasy literature from historical fiction or contemporary realistic fiction. We use the term *form* for two other categories—picture books and poetry. These forms are used across genres, such as a historical novel written in verse or a contemporary realistic picture book.

This section provides a brief introduction of the key concepts about form and genre. We also address series books and blended genres—titles that do not neatly fit into one category. Specific form and genre chapters outline the important role literature plays in students' lives and provide greater definitional details and appropriate ways to integrate technology. These chapters discuss how to choose high-quality titles and make teaching connections, including the integration of technology. Each form and genre chapter suggests ways that literature meets the needs of diverse students and the mandates of the Common Core State Standards can support instructional decisions and increase the scope and depth of student learning.

Forms

Picture Books. The picture book is considered a *form* used in all literary genres—for example, poetry, folklore, historical fiction, and nonfiction. A picture book is usually a combination of text and illustration, although some have few or no words. Many picture books specifically target a young audience, but others can be appreciated at any age level. Chapter 4 focuses on the art and writing of picture books, including a discussion of graphic "novels," manga, and anime comics. (Chapter books are referenced throughout but are not examined as a discrete form.) We also discuss the future of picture books and whether animated digital books are likely to take their place.

Poetry. Poetry is also considered a form rather than a genre. Poets love musical language and create patterns with words that please the ear. Words can be arranged playfully with romping rhythms or spun into elegant beauty with verbal images. Chapter 5 describes various poetic elements and forms of poetry. In addition, we explore the controversial issue of asking students to dissect and analyze poems based on critics' opinions.

Genres

Fiction. The genre of fiction encompasses narratives or stories drawn from an author's imagination. Fiction does not make a story "fake" or "untrue." Author Madeleine L'Engle calls fiction "a vehicle for truth," explaining that "truth and story are what connect human beings to each other" (quoted in Schmidt, 1991, p. 11). The three fictional genres—fantasy and science fiction, contemporary realistic fiction, and historical fiction—each have a dedicated chapter.

Traditional Literature. Traditional literature encompasses works that have been handed down orally for generations and therefore have no identifiable author. Some stories preserve the history and mores of a culture; others were intended purely as entertainment. In Chapter 6, readers will learn to distinguish various categories in this genre, such as fables, legends, folktales, and tall tales. We also examine the concern that mainstream authors have misappropriated the stories of other cultures.

Fantasy and Science Fiction. Fantasy fiction contains elements that are not considered possible in our world. These include such disparate components as ghosts, talking animals, magic lamps, or transformations. In science fiction, the main elements are based on reasonable but extrapolated scientific theory. Someone might travel forward or backward in time, live on another planet, or encounter unknown but realistic oceanic creatures. Good science fiction also explores ethical or societal aspects of the future. Chapter 7 delves into various subcategories of fantasy and science fiction, such as alternative worlds and heroic fantasy. We also explore the controversial aspects of this genre as it continues to be one of the most censored types of children's literature.

Historical Fiction. Stories set in the past with believable and realistic elements are called historical fiction. Although main characters are generally fictionalized, the setting is identifiable as a specific time period. Minor characters may be historical figures. In Chapter 8, we classify the genre by time period and explain how significant themes appear regardless of era or geographic location. In addition, we investigate the controversial question of exposing children to all aspects and perspectives of our turbulent history.

Contemporary Realistic Fiction. Contemporary realistic fiction is the term used for stories about people and animals that could realistically occur. Readers often find personal value as they vicariously come to know fictional characters facing realistic issues and challenges. In contemporary realistic stories, animals can be the main character but cannot talk or think as humans do. In Chapter 9, we discuss the many categories of contemporary realistic fiction, such as stories about school life, peer relationships, family life, mysteries, humor, and adventure.

We examine this genre through the lens of critical literacy, focusing on the reader's potential response to stories that reflect social and cultural issues.

Nonfiction and Biography. Nonfiction is "the literature of fact." It is the only literary genre that is named for what it is not ("not fiction") instead of what it is. An important criterion for nonfiction is that content must be factual and accurate (Kristo & Bamford, 2004). Biography is a subtype of nonfiction, documenting a person's lifetime or focusing on a specific time period. Biographies are often popular with intermediate and middle school students who are searching for their own identity and speculating about what their future may hold. Chapter 10 describes many types of nonfiction and biography. We explore how to use blended genres, specifically literature that blurs the line between fiction and nonfiction.

Series Books

College students inevitably list series books among their childhood favorites. When children read a book they like, they commonly beg for "another one just like it!" Child readers, like adult readers, become enamored of an author's style; they may become "friends" with characters, or they enjoy learning about a specific historical era. It is natural to want more of these pleasurable experiences, and series books can provide that anticipated pleasure. Some series are written by multiple people who use either a pseudonym or the original author's name, such as *The Baby-Sitters Club*; the original author was Ann Martin.

Many books become popular because friends recommend them, often from series such as *Clifford the Big Red Dog*, *Magic School Bus*, *Percy Jackson and the Olympians*, *The Princess Diaries*, *The Baby-Sitters Club*, *Time Warp Trio*, *Captain Underpants*, or *Goosebumps Gold*. When reading series books with their friends, children experience the positive aspects of being part of a group (Greenlee, Monson, & Taylor, 1996). Another reason that series are popular is the ease of selecting the next book to read (Greenlee et al., 1996).

Series books are usually formulaic, with little change in characterization or plot structure. R. L. Stine, creator of the *Goosebumps* series, acknowledges this: "Nobody learns and nobody grows. Mostly, they're just running" (quoted in Greenlee et al., 1996, p. 217). A number of years ago, we noticed a boy who was a voracious *Hardy Boys* reader. When he brought the latest one back to the library, he glumly announced that he didn't want to read any more. After a dramatic pause, he complained that he knew exactly what was going to happen and it wasn't exciting anymore! The series had honed his powers of prediction, but he wanted something more challenging.

Ellen Singleton (2006) notes that in a field where most early series books for girls perpetuated the cultural message of restricted physical activities for young women, *The Girls of Central High* was a clear exception. This series promoted sports and other rigorous recreational activities, and Singleton attributes the series with influencing interschool sports for girls.

Not all series are constructed using formulaic plots, and these may fall between cookie-cutter pop fiction and acclaimed award winners. Such books might be called workhorses because they "collectively help move youngsters from word callers to lifetime readers" (Carter, 2010, p. 53). One such example is the *Alice* series (Naylor), which follows the chronological order of a young heroine's typical traumas and delights of growing up.

Tech Click

Loyal readers of Phyllis Reynolds Naylor's *Alice* series freely write on her blog how much they cried when they finished the latest book and knew there were no others to anticipate. Reciprocally, Phyllis acknowledges that her blog helps her learn as

(continued)

much from her fans as they do from her. For instance, her readers taught her delicious details about Spirit Week, Prank Day, and pep rallies (Scales, 2011). Author Rick Riordan's blog shows the "human" behind the popular writer by including pictures of his pets as well as recommending books and posting covers of new books in his *Heroes of Olympus* series.

Series books are frequently criticized as "pernicious," "mind weakening," and "addictive." Interestingly, the features that are typically criticized by adults (plot predictability and one-dimensional characters) are exactly what young readers like about them. The use of familiar characters, stable settings, and predictable plots allows readers to build substantial background knowledge, which, in turn, aids comprehension (Brooks, Waterman, & Allington, 2003).

Series books should not be automatically dismissed as being without literary merit. Arter and Nilsen (2009) suggest vocabulary activities to use with the word-rich *Lemony Snicket* series. Alcatraz Smedry is the fictive author of a recent fantasy series by Brandon Sanderson (*Alcatraz Versus the Evil Librarians* and *Alcatraz Versus the Shattered Lens*). Michele Castleman (2011) draws interesting connections between the humorous "autobiographical" series and how it makes theories about implied readers and implied authors accessible for middle school students. In addition, she found that her in-depth study of this series enabled her to better reflect on her own teaching.

Series books are often the first chapter books for young readers. They minimize the challenges of reading longer books due to consistent characters and predictable plots. They provide a scaffold until readers are ready to make the leap to longer texts. Developing readers need many opportunities for "high-success" reading to become independent, active, and fluent readers (Brooks et al., 2003).

Children who read voraciously by choice and for pleasure are more likely to succeed at school than those who dislike reading (for a seminal work, see Anderson, Wilson, & Fielding, 1988; on intrinsic motivation, see Garan & DeVoogd, 2008). If series provide that practice, they serve a useful purpose. For these reasons, we believe that series should be included in classroom collections and that children should be allowed to read them, particularly during independent reading time.

Blended Genres

Some recent book titles do not fit neatly into the discrete categories we have described, such as nonfiction or contemporary realistic fiction. The definition of *verse novel* is "necessarily elastic, since as a genre it is still evolving. There is the vexed question of distinguishing between a novel told in verse and a series of poems linked in a narrative sequence" (Alexander, 2005, p. 270). For example, teachers might ponder whether to place Hesse's *Out of the Dust* (a verse novel set in Depression-era Oklahoma) in the poetry basket or with historical fiction, or should Koertge's *Shakespeare Bats Cleanup* (a baseball story for middle school readers told in free verse) mingle with sports or poetry? Combining the rich language of poetry with the characteristics of quality verse novels makes this subgenre appealing in an audio book format.

Novels such as the puzzling *When You Reach Me* by Rebecca Stead or mystical *Maniac Magee* by Jerry Spinelli skillfully blend elements of fantasy and realism, causing the reader to ponder what is real. Miranda, the main character in *When You Reach Me*, tries to make sense out of the mysterious notes she receives and a street person who fascinates her. The title of each section of the book demonstrates her need to organize: "Things You Keep in a Box," "Things That Go Missing," and "Things That Turn Upside Down." Spinelli begins *Maniac Magee* with the conventions and cadence normally found in folktales. The main character, whose real name is Jeffery, takes on the hues of a larger-than-life tall-tale hero as he battles homelessness, community unrest, and racism.

A story may unfold in a traditional narrative style but interweave several story lines and hyperlink to alternative versions of the same or related stories in verse (Ward & Day, 2010, p. 63). Combining multiple writing styles, various formats, and differing voices is not surprising in our era of techno-music, "photoshopping," remixing sound tracks, and mash-ups (Knobel & Lankshear, 2008). This blurring of boundaries is also called *blending genres* and may produce a *hybrid work* such as *Black and White* (Macaulay).

Blended books work well when implementing the CCSS because of the complexity of the texts and discernment required from readers. "The Reading standards place equal emphasis on the sophistication of what students read and the skill with which they read" (National Governors Association Center for Best Practices & Council of Chief State School Officers, 2010, p. 8). Students' skills grow when making connections between ideas, genres, textual evidence, prior reading, and life's experiences.

Criteria for Choosing High-Quality Children's Literature

The Common Core State Standards recommend that teachers help children respond deeply and thoughtfully to the literature they read, hear, or otherwise experience. Investigating literary elements is a primary way to implement these standards. This section describes the literary elements of fiction as useful tools in discussing the genres of fantasy, science fiction, contemporary realistic fiction, and historical fiction. We explore one historical fiction title in depth to illustrate what might typically be discussed regarding a fictional work. We examine the unique qualities for picture books, poetry, and nonfiction in their respective chapters.

Book selection guidelines conclude this section.

A Close Look at *Roll of Thunder, Hear My Cry* by Mildred Taylor

The winner of the 1977 Newbery Award was Mildred Taylor's gripping tale of one year in the life of an African American family in *Roll of Thunder, Hear My Cry*. Facing the crushing poverty of the Great Depression of the 1930s, the Logans strive to keep their land. In a time and place of vicious racism, they retain their dignity while finding ways to confront social inequities. The reader experiences events mostly through the eyes of 9-year-old Cassie Logan.

As the novel begins, Cassie is angered at being purposefully splashed by a school bus carrying white children. She sides with her fastidious younger brother as he expresses resentment at the "gift" of dilapidated textbooks no longer "good enough" for white students. But, she also exudes a naïveté nurtured by her close and loving family. All readers alike will feel her stunned reaction, not only when a shopkeeper keeps them waiting to attend to white customers but also, more deeply, when Cassie realizes that some African Americans consciously perpetuate racial inequities. There are currents of tension between the African Americans who see and accept their position and those, like the Logans, who see and refuse to accept. As Cassie's awareness of racial injustice grows, we also see Cassie and her family take risks to stand against these atrocities.

Even as Mrs. Logan desires to shield her own children from life's cruelties, every action of the parents strives to lift the children above their oppressive history, to demonstrate that land stewardship is a route to freedom, and that there are no shortcuts to an ethical life. For example, Mrs. Logan insists that they go with her to visit a friend who has been horrifically burned by the Wallaces. She knows that the valuable lesson about why they are boycotting the Wallace

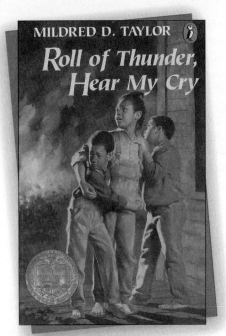

Roll of Thunder, Hear My Cry exemplifies numerous literary elements.

store will not be forgotten. But a boycott is just the beginning, and both mother and father Logan show by example that they have "agency"— power to act positively to address racial and social issues (McDowell, 2002). There are numerous times in which the two older children, Stacey and Cassie, take matters into their own hands, knowing that they are courting trouble but believing in their hearts that they are doing the right thing as shown by their parents' examples. This is explicitly seen as Uncle Hammer chides Stacey for giving away his warm new coat at the same time he drives home the consequences of Stacey's action and the misguided thinking that drove him to lose the coat.

In a powerful example of "showing," not "telling," *Roll of Thunder, Hear My Cry* takes us on a journey to another time and place to experience the gut-wrenching terror of "night riders" and outrage when an innocent man is profoundly burned. In the harrowing final scene, the life of a neighboring boy is apparently and inevitably in danger. Yet the Logans' courage and self-respect, amidst a conflagration of evil, terror, and flames, encourages readers to reflect on love, compassion, and principled stands. The title comes from the defiant song that opens chapter 11, a refusal to be beaten down by those who oppress.

What Are the Elements of Fiction?

Understanding core concepts such as characterization, plot, theme, setting, style, point of view, and illustration can enhance students' appreciation of fiction. Although each element is defined individually in this section, skilled authors weave them into a cohesive whole. A light touch is needed when sharing this information, as too much analysis leads to disengagement. As we discuss each element, we use examples from *Roll of Thunder, Hear My Cry* to illustrate the application to an actual book.

Characterization. Good fiction writers create credible, realistic characters. As we become immersed into the lives of fictional characters, they help us understand plots and themes more deeply. Younger children can be guided into deeper understandings of character, such as a first-grade teacher who uses props, a map, and drama to help her students understand the ethical dilemma faced by the main character in Winthrop's *The Castle in the Attic* (Roser, Martinez, Fuhrken, & McDonnold, 2007).

The *protagonist* is the main character, and the problems or situations facing this person drive the plot. For example, in *Roll of Thunder, Hear My Cry* the reader watches Cassie's innocence sweep away and her sense of outrage grow. Cassie's actions are clearly the focus, but nearly every main character also faces a private struggle. Cassie's mother clashes with the school board, her father strives to find sufficient money to keep their land, and her brother faces confrontations with a bully. (Similarly, we share the agonies of the little mouse with the big ears in Kate DiCamillo's *The Tale of Despereaux* as he strives to be brave and loyal).

An *antagonist* appears in many stories as a foil for the protagonist. Sometimes, this character attempts to thwart the goals of the protagonist or is on the opposing side of a controversy. An antagonist might have another point of view or may provoke a dilemma through which we come to understand the main character. For example, in *The Lord of the Rings*, (Tolkien) Gollum is alternatively portrayed as an obsessed, wicked creature and a creature to be pitied.

Cassie and her family face a number of antagonists: the Wallaces, who own the sole local store and viciously discriminate against African Americans. Poor whites who attempt to steal their land and the racist school board that fires Mrs. Logan are among the tribulations faced by the Logans. T.J., a contemporary of the children, serves a complex function. At his core, he is lonely but attempts "friendship" with Cassie's brother Stacey in a misguided way. By subterfuge, T.J. wrangles Stacey's new coat; he implicates Stacey in a cheating scheme and endangers all of their lives. Readers can see right through him even when Stacey does not. But as poorly as T.J. acts, he does not deserve a near lynching, and the Logan family risks everything to save his life.

Another author writing about the Great Depression who is also an expert in characterization is Christopher Paul Curtis. He uses all these techniques to breathe life into his main character in *Bud, Not Buddy*. Because the story is written in the first person, readers come to know Bud's thoughts and feelings intimately: his longing for a father and a permanent home. Readers understand why he travels on foot from Detroit to Flint, Michigan, and why he is cautious around unfamiliar people. They also know him through the eyes of the "Dusky Devastators of the Depression," members of a jazz band who alternately tease and comfort him as he searches for his identity.

Writers sometimes develop characters in subsequent books, exemplified by J. K. Rowling's *Harry Potter*. As the story opens, Harry is presented as an intelligent but frightened 11-year-old boy, ignorant of his heritage and oblivious to his powers. Readers of the many volumes watch as he becomes more courageous and able to face the numerous challenges he faces. Authors must maintain internal consistency of a story or a series; they do so by ensuring that everything characters say or do fits with prior thoughts and actions. As Mildred Taylor does so well, the characters' behavior should also be consistent with their ages and the cultural context of the story.

Children develop an understanding of characterization as they mature (Roser et al., 2007). Younger readers focus on actions or external qualities, such as appearance. Older readers are more attuned to the inner qualities, such as feelings, motives, and relationships. Readers can empathize with Bud's desire for family and a permanent home in *Bud, Not Buddy* (Curtis). In quality fiction, main characters are highly developed. Through the course of the story, readers come to know their gifts as well as their flaws and struggles. This is true even if the protagonist is a stuffed toy, such as Winnie-the-Pooh (Milne), or an animal, as in *Babe the Gallant Pig* (King-Smith).

Plot. The plan of action, the manner in which events unfold, and the resolution of the central conflict are all aspects of plot. Plots in children's books tend to be linear, with an identifiable beginning, middle, and end. Younger children often have trouble following flashbacks, multiple interwoven plotlines, or other complex plot structures. Often, the story focuses on one main struggle or pivotal event. This is true even for the nearly wordless plot in the 2012 Caldecott winner *A Ball for Daisy* (Raschka), which shows what happens to a puppy's new toy.

A well-constructed plot develops logically, even if the events are presented in a flashback or flash-forward. The story usually features a conflict in which the main characters struggle with a problem or overcome an obstacle. Children's literature typically features four main types of conflict: (a) person against person, (b) person against society, (c) person against nature, and (d) person against self (Lukens, Smith, & Coffel, 2012).

Some stories focus on one conflict, whereas others have evolving layers of conflict. In *Roll of Thunder, Hear My Cry* several plotlines are interwoven. The reader wants to know whether Jeremy, a neighboring white boy, will succeed with his overtures of friendship; whether T.J. will ever understand loyalty; and how the Logans will survive when their mother is unfairly fired. However, these are minor threads in the larger fabric of 1930s racism, where property rights and life itself appear to have little value.

Good plots are not predictable. Rather, authors strive to make their plots believable yet fresh and original. In *Roll of Thunder, Hear My Cry* readers have multiple opportunities to make predictions. Will the Logan children's plan for revenge on the bus that purposefully splashed them be successful? Can the family resist sustained efforts to steal their land? The plot reveals answers to some questions. However, deeper, more systemic problems have no easy answers and are left percolating in the reader's mind.

In another example, in *Crispin: The Cross of Lead*, author Avi crafts an intriguing mystery set in medieval times. Crispin must fend for himself after his mother dies. To complicate matters, he is falsely accused of murder and must flee for his life. His many adventures keep readers intrigued. As one child described the most enjoyable part about Crispin's adventures she explained that nothing was predictable and she was always surprised. Children are drawn to books that feature action scenes with minimal dialogue or description. They raptly turn pages to conclude cliffhangers or experience the breathtaking action that characterize plots such as Avi's *Beyond the Western Sea*, an exciting story of three children emigrating from Ireland.

Theme. Theme refers to the dominant idea of a story: an insight about life or society. One way to think about "theme" is by relating it to music. When we watch a movie with theme music, such as *The Lord of the Rings* or *Titanic*, the increasingly familiar melody surfaces time and again as the movie progresses. Themes in literature work the same way as these connecting musical threads: characters and their actions form patterns that resurface as the plot progresses.

Themes in books for young children are frequently based on common childhood experiences. For example, the theme of *Frog and Toad Are Friends* (Lobel) is the importance of friendship. *Me . . . Jane* (McDonnell) shines with the themes of following your dreams and being a steward of nature.

In contrast, themes in books for older readers often focus on the journey to adulthood and the consequences of one's choices (Norton & Norton, 2010). Along with the powerful themes of racism injustice and striving for an honorable life, *Roll of Thunder, Hear My Cry* offers additional complexities. The Logan family exhibits *agency*: the self-perception that one has power over how one lives regardless of social context. Cassie's little brother gets into trouble when he pastes over the offensive list of textbook borrowers that shows that only white children used the books. Not only does Mrs. Logan refuse to punish the children, but, at the same time, she acknowledges inequities and the existence of evil.

Many well-written books feature themes that function on multiple layers. Gary Paulsen's *Hatchet* conveys a theme of person versus the environment as Brian struggles to survive in the wilderness. However, his experiences transformed him from an inexperienced boy to one who is independent and responsible. Because the struggle for basic survival has forever changed Brian, *Hatchet* is also a coming-of-age story.

Sometimes, themes are directly stated, but in some books, readers must think critically to discern deeper meaning. Writers must be careful that a theme does not override the story, making the message too didactic or preachy. Jack Gantos, in *Dead End in Norvelt*, conveys complex and challenging themes with just the right amount of dark humor and comic relief. The 12-year-old protagonist must wend his way between his quarreling parents (coming of age) and coming to grips with the history and future of his town (reflections on utopian ideals). Jack struggles to solve the mystery of the growing number of deaths as he records the history of the town through assisting an elderly neighbor type the obituaries she composes.

Figure 1.2 lists some common themes found in children's literature, matched with recommended titles.

Setting. Setting includes both where and when a story takes place. It can be a real place within a real time period, an invented place in real time, or an invented place in manipulated time. Setting is an important element in fiction; Mildred Taylor's setting of the Deep South of the 1930s in *Roll of Thunder, Hear My Cry* with its stifling poverty and overt racism, remains vivid in readers' minds decades later. She does not baldly state that her story takes place during the Depression; she shows us Mrs. Logan placing cardboard inside her shoes because the soles are worn through. Readers observe the Logans mixing cornbread, forced to use less flour and less baking powder than required.

Similarly, Lois Lowry, in *The Giver*, introduces a utopian setting, but the reader gradually understands that a seemingly perfect world is severely restricted by authoritarian rules. The

FIGURE 1.2 Common Themes in Children's Fiction

Theme	Sample Books Featuring the Theme
Conflict: person vs. environment (physical and cultural)	Hiaasen, Carl. *Hoot.* (M) Law, Ingrid. *Savvy.* (M) Lowry, Lois. *The Giver.* (M) Staples, Suzanne Fisher. *Shabanu: Daughter of the Wind.* (M) Taylor, Mildred. *Roll of Thunder, Hear My Cry.* (M)
Conflict: person vs. self	Brooks, Bruce. *What Hearts.* (M) Gantos, Jack. *Joey Pigza Swallowed the Key.* (M) Le Guin, Ursula. *Wizard of Earthsea.* (M) Littman, Sarah Darer. *Confessions of a Closet Catholic.* (M) Salisbury, Graham. *Lord of the Deep.* (M) Spinelli, Jerry. *Maniac Magee.* (I, M)
Coming of age: self-acceptance, morality, ability to face problems and responsibilities; awareness of one's destiny	Babbitt, Natalie. *Tuck Everlasting.* (M) Barron, T. A. *The Lost Years of Merlin.* (M) Curtis, Christopher Paul. *Elijah of Buxton.* (M) Erdrich, Louise. *The Birchbark House.* (M) Holt, Kimberly Willis. *When Zachary Beaver Came to Town.* (M) Pullman, Philip. *The Golden Compass.* (M) Sachar, Louis. *Holes.* (M) Voigt, Cynthia. *Dicey's Song.* (M)
Search for freedom	Choi, Sook Nyul. *The Year of Impossible Goodbyes.* (M) Ellis, Deborah. *Parvana's Journey.* (M) Ho, Mingtong. *The Clay Marble.* (M) Holm, Anne. *North to Freedom.* (M) Mikaelsen, Ben. *Red Midnight.* (M) Paterson, Katherine. *Jip: His Story.* (M) Temple, Frances. *Tonight, by Sea.* (M)
Loyalty and honor	Collier, James, and Collier, Christopher. *My Brother Sam Is Dead.* (M) Lowry, Lois. *Number the Stars.* (M) Philbrick, Rodman. *Mostly True Adventures of Homer P. Figg.* (M) Taylor, Mildred. *Roll of Thunder, Hear My Cry.* (M) White, E. B. *Charlotte's Web.* (I, M)
Conflict: good vs. evil	Cooper, Susan. *The Dark Is Rising.* (M) L'Engle, Madeleine. *A Wrinkle in Time.* (M) Lewis, C. S. *The Lion, the Witch and the Wardrobe.* (I, M) Rowling, J. K. *Harry Potter and the Sorcerer's Stone.* (I, M)

(continued)

FIGURE 1.2 *continued*

Theme	Sample Books Featuring the Theme
Personal and social responsibility	Haddix, Margaret Peterson. *Among the Hidden*. (M)
	Naidoo, Beverly. *The Other Side of Truth*. (M)
	Park, Linda Sue. *A Single Shard*. (M)
	Paterson, Katherine. *The Great Gilly Hopkins*. (M)
	Paterson, Katherine. *Lyddie*. (M)
Getting along with others: friendship, family conflicts; accepting differences	Creech, Sharon. *Walk Two Moons*. (M)
	Estes, Eleanor. *The Hundred Dresses*. (I)
	Holt, Kimberly Willis. *My Louisiana Sky*. (M)
	Johnson, Angela. *Toning the Sweep*. (M)
	Lord, Cynthia. *Rules*. (I, M)
	Polacio, R. J. *Wonder*. (M)
	Woodson, Jacqueline. *Feathers*. (I, M)
Quests and adventures	Alexander, Lloyd. *The Black Cauldron*. (M)
	Barron, T. A. *Merlin Effect*. (M)
	Dahl, Roald. *James and the Giant Peach*. (I)
	Farmer, Nancy. *A Sea of Trolls*. (M)
	McKinley, Robin. *The Blue Sword*. (M)
	Paterson, Katherine. *Park's Quest*. (M)

main character, Jonas, ran away because he felt trapped by the unfeeling, suffocating dystopia. Because setting and plot often support each other, understanding time and place in a story contributes to an appreciation of the events.

Authors create a vivid, believable setting in several ways. All elements of the setting need to be consistent, something that is particularly important in historical fiction. To help us walk in the shoes of the Meeker family in *My Brother Sam Is Dead* (Collier and Collier) during the Revolutionary War, the family must be described as wearing clothes, eating foods, and living in dwellings consistent with that period. It is also true in an invented world, such as Narnia in *The Lion, the Witch and the Wardrobe* (Lewis) or Hogwarts in the *Harry Potter* series. If the Gryffindor Tower requires a password for entry, a password must be given every time a character enters the tower.

Picture book illustrations can also enhance readers' or listeners' comprehension of setting. For example, in Lita Judge's *One Thousand Tracings: Healing the Wounds of World War II*, paintings convey an emotional sense of the time period. However, it is the collages of black-and-white photographs, foot tracings, and snippets of letters and postcards that vividly portray the life after the war.

Describing the setting is an art in fiction writing: too much description becomes tedious and leaves nothing to the reader's imagination. But too little description may fail to engage the reader. Readers need enough to help them connect with the story, then they can use their imaginations to fill in the rest.

Style. Quality books need more than characters, plot, theme, and setting; they need good language to knit these elements together. This is the function of style. Authors use language to compose a story using their own distinct voice.

Style is comprised of the writer's creative use of vocabulary, sentence structures, and literary devices that convey a unique voice. Style is not a mechanical skill that follows a prescribed blueprint. Rather, the style must fit the plot, characters, and cultural milieu. Most important, the style must make the story come alive. Just as composers blend tone and rhythm to create a symphony, authors imaginatively fuse elements of language into a compelling voice for their story. Style—the rhythm of the sentences, the vivid descriptions, and the fresh imagery—is what subtly affects a reader's response. Even the youngest children can appreciate finely crafted language that resonates in the ear and mind.

Some fiction writers use a fluid, poetic style in which the language is rhythmical and, at times, alliterative, as seen in *Sarah, Plain and Tall* by Patricia MacLachlan. The flowing descriptions can be contrasted by the short and choppy style of Gary Paulsen's *Hatchet*. Other writers use dialogue as an element of their style. Authors find it a useful technique because it can advance the plot and demonstrate characters' thoughts and feelings in a more immediate way than straight exposition. Jack Gantos skillfully uses internal monologue in *Dead End In Norvelt* to lead readers to make inferences about the characters and events. In an early scene the narrator is invited into an elderly woman's house while she is treating her arthritic fingers with hot wax. Jack wonders, "if she was melting herself down. Mom had always said she was worth her weight in gold" (p. 23). The reader doesn't need to be told explicitly that Jack is an intelligent young boy possessing an overactive imagination.

Some students may have difficulty reading "eye dialect," the phonetic writing of nonstandard English that Taylor uses so effectively, and they may need additional support. There is some controversy about the use of dialect, and this may cause young readers to draw inappropriate conclusions about the characters, such as a lack of intelligence or education (Carr, 1978). Being aware of this potential pitfall will aid teachers in counteracting unintentional negative impressions and turning it to their advantage. The Common Core State Standards suggest that upper-level elementary students should be able to compare and contrast varieties of English, including dialects.

Fiction writers often use figurative language to develop style in their work. Skilled authors invent fresh comparisons that make their work distinctive while still fully developing setting, plot, and characters. When Mildred Taylor describes what Cassie saw after the fire she describes dawn poetically as peeping. Engaging use of dialogue, descriptive vocabulary, and varied sentence structure are all factors in creating an author's style.

Point of View. The perspective from which a story is told is called point of view. First-person narrative (using "I" or "me,") is also a popular point of view in children's fiction, as shown by Cassie's position as the narrator in *Roll of Thunder, Hear My Cry*. When Mildred Taylor wants the reader to know about events that Cassie did not witness, such as the time when a wheel came off Mr. Logan's wagon, she adroitly has Cassie grill her brother for information. Some writers extend the first-person point of view by shifting perspective from one character to another to create revolving perspectives. Paul Fleischman uses this technique in *Bull Run*, a Civil War novel showing 16 perspectives, including those of soldiers, observers, men, and women (some southern, some northern). In *Maggie's Door* (Giff), two characters, one female and one male, recount their experiences traveling from Ireland to America to escape the Irish potato famine.

The omniscient, all-knowing storyteller's voice is often used in fiction. When the author employs this voice, the thoughts and feelings of multiple characters can be revealed. Both *The Lion, the Witch and the Wardrobe* (Lewis) and *Charlotte's Web* (White) are told from this perspective. A limited third-person point of view focuses on the perspective of one character; the story is still told in the third person, but the reader knows the story only through the filter of one perspective as seen in *Bridge to Terabithia* (Paterson).

FIGURE 1.3 Guidelines for Choosing Literature: Evaluating Fiction

Characterization

- Are the characters true to life? Do they seem plausible? Are their actions consistent with their age and cultural background?
- Are the main characters multidimensional? Do they have both strengths and weaknesses?
- Do the characters grow and change? Are the reasons for their actions clear?

Plot

- Does the book tell a good story?
- Is the story line developmentally appropriate for the intended audience? (Are the events understandable and interesting to the children who will read it?)
- Is the plot original yet believable?
- Does the story unfold logically?
- Does the climax seem possible?
- Are controversial issues presented openly and honestly?

Setting

- Does the author make the setting seem real?
- Is the setting appropriate for the story?
- Does the author transport readers to the setting so that they feel a part of it?

Theme

- Is the theme developmentally appropriate and of interest to the book's intended audience?
- Does the theme emerge naturally from story events, or does it override the story?
- Has the author talked down to children or become too didactic in conveying the theme?
- Is the theme relevant for today's children?
- Will the theme help readers grow and change?

Style

- Is the style appropriate for the book's intended audience?
- Is this author's use of literary devices, such as figurative language, fresh yet understandable to the book's intended audience?
- Is the dialogue suited to the characters? Do they sound like real people?

Point of View

- Is the point of view appropriate for the story?
- In a book written in first person, do readers get a sense of how other characters think and feel?
- In a book written in third person, do readers get a sense of how several characters think and feel?

Authors determine which point of view to use based on theme, plot structure, and the manner in which characters are revealed. These decisions, in turn, influence readers' response to the story. When we evaluate fiction, we need to determine who is telling the story and whether the viewpoint is effective.

Illustration. The artwork in children's literature can add significantly to the quality of a book. A picture book is a format using illustrations to tell the story. In novels for older students, cover images may be the only visual. In transitional chapter books, there may be pictures that replicate the text. The impact and evaluation of illustrations are discussed in Chapter 4. Figure 1.3 synthesizes these guidelines to assist educators in selecting quality books.

Awards for Children's Literature

A spectrum of awards spotlights high-quality children's titles. Some awards cut across genres, such as the prestigious Newbery Medal, whereas others focus on literature reflecting diversity (e.g., the Coretta Scott King Award); a specific genre, such as nonfiction (the Orbis Pictus Award); or fantasy (the Mythopoeic Fantasy Award). Awards and Notable Book Lists are excellent resources to locate high-quality books. However, even when adult critics proclaim the "best and brightest," it is still important for teachers to evaluate a book in light of their own students and curriculum.

Children's Choice Awards may be useful selection tools. Most states sponsor contests in which children vote for their favorites from preselected lists; these awards typically highlight popular titles that adults may have dismissed (Bang-Jensen, 2010).

The names of form and genre awards with examples in each category are listed at the end of the book; full lists for each award can be found at the sponsor's Web site. Literature reflecting diversity is embedded throughout this book, and awards for multicultural books are described in the appropriate genre chapter.

Guiding Principles for Creating and Implementing a Literature Program

Teachers' actions, from lesson planning to minute-to-minute classroom management, are guided by foundational beliefs. This section describes five important principles that support decisions for creating and implementing the use of literature in a standards-based curriculum (see Figure 1.4). In each instance, we have stated the principle from both the child's and the teacher's perspective.

Principle 1

- Students need to know the best literature from all genres.
- Teachers need to know how to evaluate and select the highest-quality literature that also appeals to children.

Not all children's books exhibit the same level of quality. Our role and responsibility is to lead students to the best; they will find the popular books themselves. Lesser-quality choices may help students develop a continuing interest in reading, but teachers who know literature and their students can recommend titles so that personal interests are broadened and the ability to respond thoughtfully to books is extended. Fostering the ability to help students make good book choices is an important goal of this book.

Principle 2

- All students need to see their own lives reflected in the literature they encounter.
- Teachers should know literature that is culturally authentic, reflects the lives of their children, and leads readers to be more culturally responsive to others.

Novelist Christopher Paul Curtis admits he was not an avid reader as a child, in part due to the dearth of titles populated by African American boys (Curtis, 2008). The absence of characters with whom he could identify inspired him to write the books he wished he had as a child.

FIGURE 1.4 Principles of Teaching Children's Literature in an Era of Standards

Principle	Students Need To:	Teachers Need To:	Teaching Children's Literature
1	. . . know the best literature from all genres.	. . . know how to evaluate and select the highest-quality literature.	Introduced in Chapter 1, all genre chapters, and throughout the book. See "Awards for Excellence in Children's Literature" at the end of the book
2	. . . see their lives reflected in the literature they encounter.	. . . know literature that is culturally authentic, reflects the lives of their children, and leads readers to be more culturally responsive to others.	Introduced in Chapter 1 and interspersed throughout the book
3	. . . respond to literature in ways that celebrate their diverse interests, learning styles, languages, cultural backgrounds, and developmental levels.	. . . know multiple ways to respond to books that support children's diverse interests, learning styles, languages, cultural backgrounds, developmental levels, and cultural awareness.	Introduced in Chapter 2 and throughout the book
4	. . . be in classrooms where literature is valued and celebrated.	. . . know how to create standards-based literature classrooms.	Introduced in Chapter 3 and throughout the book
5	. . . use technology meaningfully and efficiently to select books, access information about books and authors, and extend their appreciation of literature.	. . . know how to use technology effectively to support children's interactions with literature.	21st-century skills introduced in Chapter 1 and throughout the book

This means that teachers must be diligent about ensuring their classrooms and school libraries include titles that reflect the diversity of their students. Share books with children that portray a range of cultures that not only mirror students' experiences but also expand and enrich their lives beyond their immediate community. All readers can benefit from literature reflecting diversity in text and illustrations regardless of their home culture.

We feel strongly about integrating diverse literature in all chapters and not isolating them into a separate chapter. Therefore, you will discover ways to select and use high-quality titles that reflect diversity throughout this book.

Principle 3

- Students need to respond to literature in ways that celebrate their varied interests, learning styles, languages, cultural backgrounds, and developmental levels.

- Teachers need to know multiple ways to respond to books that support children's varied interests, learning styles, languages, cultural backgrounds, developmental levels, and cultural awareness.

As adults, we are often eager to share an exciting book that we just read. Interacting with and responding to literature is at the heart of literary experiences. When readers have meaningful and sustained engagement with literature, they are likely to become lifelong readers. Response is personal, but it is also cultural, experiential, and emotional. Learning about reader response and ways to support response in the classroom is the topic of Chapter 2.

Principle 4

- Students need to be in classrooms where literature is valued and celebrated.
- Teachers need to know how to create literature-rich classrooms while still addressing the Common Core State Standards.

How do you know you are in a classroom in which literature is valued? You see books readily available to students: on the classroom bookshelves, on windowsills, in baskets and bins, displayed on racks and tables, on student desks, and in the teacher's work area. Additional evidence around the room shows that books play a vital role. Projects, posters, and other kinds of book responses, as well as sign-out sheets and charts of book recommendations, are all evidence that books are part of everyday living. Throughout *Teaching with Children's Literature*, suggestions are offered about creating a literature-based, standards-based classroom.

Principle 5

- Students need to use technology meaningfully and efficiently to select books, access information about books and authors, become critical consumers of information, and extend their response and appreciation of literature.
- Teachers need to know how to use technology effectively to support children's interactions and learning with literature.

Many students today are "digital natives" (Prensky, 2001). They have not known a world without cell phones, customized music play lists, mobile computing, and the Internet. Technology evolves, so students need meaningful ways to interact with technology that enhance literacy and learning. When teachers integrate multiple technologies into teaching and learning, students will be better prepared to be lifelong readers and critical consumers of information regardless of format. Twenty-first-century skills are referenced throughout.

Reconciling Our Principles with the Requirements to Meet Standards

COMMON CORE STATE STANDARD FEATURE #1

Determine Central Ideas or Themes of a Text (CCSS.RL.2)

Expectations for each skill build on one another with increasingly complex understandings by grade level. For example, it is clear how understanding progresses year by year in the Career and College Readiness Anchor Standard's (CCRA in CCSS) Reading Standard for Literature: Key Ideas and Details:

RL.K.2. With prompting and support, identify the main topic and retell key details of a text.

RL.1.2. Identify the main topic and retell key details of a text.

RL.2.2.   Identify the main topic of a multiparagraph text as well as the focus of specific paragraphs within the text.

RL.3.2.   Recount stories, including fables, folktales, and myths from diverse cultures; determine the central message, lesson, or moral and explain how it is conveyed through key details in the text.

RL.4.2.   Determine a theme of a story, drama, or poem from details in the text; summarize the text.

RL.5.2.   Determine a theme of a story, drama, or poem from details in the text, including how characters in a story or drama respond to challenges or how the speaker in a poem reflects on a topic; summarize the text.

RL.6.2.   Determine a theme or central idea of a text and how it is conveyed through particular details; provide a summary of the text distinct from personal opinions or judgments.

RL.7.2.   Determine a theme or central idea of a text and analyze its development over the course of the text; provide an objective summary of the text.

RL.8.2.   Determine a theme or central idea of a text and analyze its development over the course of the text, including its relationship to the characters, setting, and plot; provide an objective summary of the text.

Roll of Thunder, Hear My Cry provides a useful example of how to determine themes and central ideas. This novel presses the reader to empathetically experience racism and, subsequently, to understand the risks of confronting that racism (Brooks & Hampton, 2005). Even with unfriendly visitors, Mrs. Logan teaches her seventh-grade class the bitter history of slavery. She demonstrates that facts alone are not sufficient; teachers must make important lessons of history real. Mildred Taylor's description of her own father's storytelling is echoed in *Roll of Thunder, Hear My Cry*—essential history comes not so much from textbooks but rather through oral traditions. Mrs. Logan continues her history lesson of the classroom by demonstrating that stories are not enough; action is needed.

By comparing and contrasting *Roll of Thunder, Hear My Cry* and *The Watsons Go to Birmingham—1963* (Curtis), teachers could guide students in a discussion of the authors' intended and unintended impact on the readers (Barker, 2010).

Another important feature of the Common Core State Standards is that English language arts skills are considered critical in all content-area and technical subjects as teachers bring their discipline-specific skills to assist students in meeting the standards in reading, writing, speaking, listening, and language.

What is taught should be viewed separately from *how* it is taught. Educators have the freedom to select the instructional strategies based on their own preferences and their students' learning needs. In other words, implementing a standards-based classroom does not necessitate constraining educators' wisdom, decision making, or creativity (Long, 2011).

The Common Core document explicitly states that the standards are a shared responsibility; they are goals, not the methodology for attaining them (Wilhelm, 2012). In this book, we outline instructional strategies using literature that are authentic and appropriate while fulfilling the requirement to cover content outlined in the standards. For example, using quality books when addressing the "Reading Standard for Literature: Key Ideas and Details" listed above will be much more engaging and effective than using dry, watered-down texts.

We believe that the progression of learning never stops—for students or for teachers. Teaching is a complex process, and teaching children is not easier because they are younger. Newly adopted standards, curricular choices, pedagogy, assessment, paperwork requirements, and many other expectations vie for time and attention. In addition, researchers continue to pose relevant and intriguing questions; their published findings present new opportunities or challenges for all educational levels.

Because of the weighty responsibility for children's intellectual, social, and emotional growth, teachers must pursue lifelong learning. All educators should keep intellectually active by being readers themselves—studying professional journals and books, keeping current with children's literature, attending conferences or workshops, joining professional book clubs, subscribing to literacy blogs or listservs, and taking graduate courses. Most schools encourage this growth by committing time and money for professional development. Be prepared to be an active participant by suggesting school or districtwide children's literature topics and fostering collegial discussions (Sailors, 2009, p. 647). Becoming adept with the tools of today's youth, especially those that are technology related, assist educators with motivational and constructivist tools. The Common Core State Standards articulate the expectation that all teachers in all disciplines should focus on reading skills and not be distracted by being too preoccupied with "covering the content."

Not everyone views the Common Core in a positive light. "To think that every student in this country should be made to learn the same things is illogical on its face—it lacks face validity" (Tienken, 2011, p. 60). Eccles and Roeser's (2011) review of current research on adolescents' engagement notes that curriculum is only part of the picture; careful material selection and appropriate and scaffolded learning activities that demonstrate multiple perspectives are much more significant motivators (p. 226).

Other critics worry that the standards were crafted too quickly, that teachers are not involved adequately (Strauss, 2013), that current state standards are superior (Stotsky & Wurman, 2010), or that there is a dearth of attention given reader response (Wilson & Newkirk, 2011). Susi Long (2011) speculates that common standards will lead to inappropriate comparisons, eventually resulting in teachers being compensated on the basis of test scores or other "inappropriate assessment practices" (p. vii).

21st-Century Skills

> Twenty-first-century students need a deeper understanding of the core concepts in the disciplines than they receive now. In addition, students need to be able to design, evaluate, and manage their own work. Students need to be able to frame, investigate, and solve problems using a wide range of information resources and digital tools.
> (Linda Darling-Hammond, quoted in Brown, 2011, para. 6)

The abstract concepts of 21st-century skills expand the content knowledge of the Common Core State Standards into a broad range of literacies, specifically information literacy, critical thinking, communication, and problem solving. These skills move a student from knowing facts into the realm of *doing* and *applying*. This emphasis is not new; it is rooted in Socratic discourse, John Dewey's educational theories, and Bloom's taxonomy, among others, but they are newly emphasized.

The Partnership for 21st Century Skills (2013) constructed a unified framework to help reconceptualize public education by joining core knowledge, new-century themes, media literacy, life and career skills, and support systems. Critics of this vision claim that focusing on the process of learning may detract from foundational disciplinary content. Traditional practices

Middle school student uses Google Earth to evaluation information on immigration patterns he located in a nonfiction book. (Anchor Standard SL. 2)

of requiring simplistic book reports imprison students as passive learners, whereas acquiring 21st-century skills requires that students develop the ability to question, locate, analyze, synthesize, and create.

On this point, Linda Darling-Hammond (in Brown, 2011) stresses that forcing the debate into either/or terms distracts from the much-needed balance between content and process. She assigns a major portion of the negative international image of the United States to widely swinging pendulums of conflicting mandates. To Darling-Hammond, a partial solution lies in providing teachers with the adequate professional development time to align standards, instruction, and assessment. This book strives to meet this need.

Tech Click

The Partnership for 21st-Century Skills Framework has captured the interrelatedness of core subjects, professional development, media, curriculum, standards, and other essential educational components, a perfect lens for the Common Core State Standards.

Common Sense Media is an excellent resource to bookmark. This rich and easy-to-access Web presence contains an array of movie and Web reviews as well as *Graphite*, a free service that "rates for learning potential" apps, games, and Web sites in the core subjects as well as arts and hobbies. *Common Sense Media* is also well known for its cyberbullying and digital citizenship materials.

Integrating Our Principles, Standards, and Exemplary Literature to Meaningfully and Authentically Connect Children and Books

Throughout this book, we address issues related to the teaching of children's literature. In addition, each genre and format chapter contains teaching ideas for populations not specifically addressed in the Common Core State Standards. The teaching and response ideas demonstrate how to bring *all* children and books together while still meeting the mandates of the standards. The following sections provide a brief overview of these students.

Supporting Culturally Diverse Students with Children's Literature

Using quality literature provides an engaging and appropriate instructional strategy that is useful for scaffolding (supporting) the learning of all students. However, teachers should be mindful of how and when to bring "culture" forward in classroom conversations.

Cultural authenticity is sometimes debated when considering literacy that reflects diversity. Mildred Taylor is an author of color writing a historical novel about the Logans, several generations of a free African American family that still carries the fresh memories of slavery. While using this book as part of a standards-based unit, care must be taken that the identity of the author be considered and that students of color not be used as "objects of a lesson on racism for white students" (Ricker-Wilson, 1998, p. 70).

Tech Click

All educators working with diverse students should visit the website of Reading Is Fundamental, the largest nonprofit children's literacy organization in the U.S. For resources, including RIF's activity sheets based on award-winning multicultural books for children, visit www. RIF.org. RIF's mission: RIF is dedicated to motivating young children to read by working with children, their parents, and community members to make reading a fun and beneficial part of everyday life.

Supporting English Language Learners with Children's Literature

In today's classrooms, students not only come from diverse ethnic, racial, and national backgrounds but also arrive speaking multiple languages, often just beginning to speak English. "Nationally, 19 percent of children of immigrants age 5 to 17 were limited English proficient (LEP) in 2006" (Fortuny, Capps, Simms, & Chaudry, 2009, p. 7). Consequently, they need targeted support to build English reading and writing skills.

Much has been learned about the acquisition of languages, and the principles that apply to good language and literacy learning in one language apply to language and literacy learning in second, third, and fourth languages as well (Gersten & Geva, 2003). If you have not had the advantage of specialized training in teaching English language learners (ELLs), applying the theory and experience you have had with native-born English-speaking students will help you negotiate challenges with ELLs. Ask yourself the same types of questions you would pose for good reading and language arts teaching (Cox & Boyd-Batstone, 2009):

- How do I make language learning realistic, authentic, and relevant to learners?
- How do I provide meaningful and realistic practice required for any developing skill?
- How do I find texts that are developmentally appropriate but also meaningful and culturally relevant?
- How do I integrate reading, writing, listening, and speaking in all areas of my school curriculum?
- How can new technologies help me achieve these aims in engaging ways?

Today's technology can be particularly helpful in supporting ELL students as they learn to speak, read, and write English. Many digital texts allow the student to click a word or phrase to hear its pronunciation or definition. Digital texts can hyperlink abstract concepts to background information. A curious ELL student reading an electronic text about an unfamiliar holiday, such as the Fourth of July, might wish to click links to understand fireworks or parades.

Naturally, teachers need to evaluate all resources before using them with students to verify that instructional purposes are met. For example, popular e-readers or online apps offer various modes of interaction; usually, the story can be heard read aloud in a page-by-page, linear format. In other modes, the child has full control over interactive components, both textual (e.g., definitional) and within the illustrations (a click makes the flower buds bloom). Grimshaw, Dungworth, McKnight, and Morris (2007) note that all digital books are not equivalent; educators should differentiate between types to determine their educational benefits.

We believe that this emphasis on critical issues will enhance the potential to transform conversations around books to life-changing ones.

Supporting All Students with Technology

Digital devices and online resources can play an important role in literature investigations. When educators understand the power of leveraging technology-mediated environments to enhance knowledge about books and authors, tech-adept students tend to become more motivated, such as melding technology and popular culture as a vehicle for responding to literature (Castek, Bevans-Mangelson, & Goldstone, 2006) ranging from digital storytelling (Czarnecki, 2009) to writing their own fan fiction (Black, 2009). If technology provides an inviting stepping-stone, we should use it to build students' understanding of literature.

In subsequent chapters, you will discover ideas about using technology in support of literacy and a lifelong appreciation of literature. For example, students could hold virtual book discussions with peers in a different town, state, or even country via e-mail or blogs. They can create podcasts based on books they have "published" in the classroom. Reluctant readers might be motivated by reading a book using an electronic device or listening to a digital story recorded by volunteers. Some groups experience another "world" using virtual experiences based on books appropriate for their age level. Technology can also be a powerful tool for ELLs. Students could also set computer preferences to read aloud Web sites or books as text files.

Some adults feel that today's students have nothing to learn about digital technology, yet the opposite is true. Students in prekindergarten through grade 8 may be voracious tech users, but they still require guidance to learn cognitive strategies for deep research, constructive analysis, and communication and collaborative skills (Carr, 2010).

These new literacies illustrate *intertextuality*, drawing "attention to how learners integrate across texts. Students must contend with both on and offline texts, classmates' postings, and e-mail correspondence. In addition, new technologies allow for inclusion of complex nonverbal arrays within learning environments" (Van Meter & Firetto, 2008, pp. 1090–1091). The new literacies are exciting for most students and can greatly enhance their understanding of literature.

We have established that students need a wide variety of books that are interesting and challenging to them so that they maintain their interest in reading. When funds are scarce, we have several suggestions for bringing more high-quality books into your room. First, visit your local school and public libraries. In addition to maintaining extensive collections, libraries often provide additional services for teachers: longer borrowing periods, additional support in book selection, and a higher number of titles borrowed. Second, with many commercial book clubs, teachers receive bonus points based on the number of books students buy, points that can be used for additional books. Third, grants from a local business or foundation may be available. Even small grants of a few hundred dollars can go a long way when purchasing paperbacks or secondhand books from online booksellers. Check with your local bookstore, as it may offer educational discounts. Some schools maintain a wish list of books that teachers would like so that during book fairs or other events, parents and community members can consult this list and may purchase books for the school as gifts. Other districts sponsor programs for parents to purchase classroom or library books in honor of a child's birthday or in memory of a relative.

Controversial Issue: Movies, Commercialization, and Children's Literature

Movie mogul Walt Disney did much in the 1930s to market—with strict copyright protection—toys, dolls, games, and even toothbrushes based on his studio's version of fairy tales and classic books. "Increasingly, children's consumer culture was part of a separate fantasy world, which children and the merchandisers alone understood and which was designed to stimulate unending desire for more goods—even as it provided children with a measure of autonomy" (Consumer Culture, 2008).

The blatant invasion of mass culture into classrooms includes sticker collections, product-oriented "books," or texts based on blockbuster movies (*Star Wars*), candy (Hershey's Kiss math series), or expensive dolls (American Girl). This growing encroachment works in reverse as well; book publishers reach out to toy companies in order to expand their product lines. A quick Web search reveals proliferating stuffed animals and other toys based on book characters: *Harry Potter* (Rowling), *Frederick* (Lionni), *Lily* (Henkes), *Arthur* (Brown), *Clifford, The Big Red Dog* (Bridwell), *Paddington* (Bond), and *Curious George* (Rey). Daniel Hade (2001) views such merchandizing as a way for the shrinking number of publishers to sell "meaning": "The brand doesn't represent the product, the product represents the brand. Thus, a book becomes one more kind of product that carries the brand's meanings" (p. 162).

The lure of corporate sponsorship may be a special enticement for authors of series books. *The Baby-Sitters Club* characters and plots are featured in a mystery board game, learning adventures, dolls, and collectible card sets. Commercialization of children's books is not just an American phenomenon; Moomins, characters in the charming series by Tove Jansson, have sparked museums, theme parks, and merchandizing specifically in Finland and Japan (Classroom Bookshelf, 2010).

As a related issue, some authors consider portraying a hero or heroine as using a specific brand name or a product line. Teachers can encourage reader discussions regarding the value added by fleshing out characters' personalities or the detraction with commercialization. Motoko Rich (2008) elaborates by comparing how the authors of two preteen books handle the dilemma.

Renowned author-illustrator Uri Shulevitz (2004) notes that an increasing number of books are marketed solely on the author's prior fame and not based on intrinsic worthiness (*Budgie the Little Helicopter* by the Duchess of York, Katie Couric's promotional poetry, or Madonna's preachy *Lotas de Casha*). Often, such books emanate not from an author's compelling desire to craft a fine story but rather as a source of income. Phrases such as "'books as merchandise,' 'blockbusters,' and 'products' resound throughout the country. Children's books are joining mass culture" (Shulevitz, 2004, p. 24). "In our highly commercialized culture, children reading becomes one more instance of children consuming" (Hade, 2001, p. 164).

Remembering that our job is to lead students to quality literature, we may find that reluctant readers will enjoy and appreciate books after they have seen the movie (*Harry Potter*). We are not advocating that a movie adaptation can replace reading literature, but movies do have the potential to stimulate students to read the book. Discussions about similarities and differences can make the reading experience richer. On the other hand, a critical adult eye may disparage "books" whose sole purpose is to promote purchases. For the same reason that we see a place for popular series in children's reading lives, we view books with movie ties as having value when students choose them.

Summary

- ***What is children's literature?*** Children's literature encompasses the world of books and includes materials written by skilled authors who generally specialize in the art of writing for children and by illustrators who add special perspectives. These include formats such as picture books, poetry, and e-books and all genres, such as traditional literature and nonfiction.

- ***Why use literature with children?*** Literature is vital to children's lives as they are entertained and educated. Stories shared with the family, in school settings, or at the library, form an important foundation for literacy and lifelong learning. Using high-quality literature fits well with the Common Core State Standards.

- ***How is children's literature organized?*** Teachers need to gain an understanding and appreciation for the various genres (traditional literature, fantasy and science fiction, contemporary realistic fiction, historical fiction, and nonfiction) and various formats (picture books and poetry). Appropriate examples of each are provided.

- ***What are the basic criteria for evaluating children's literature?*** We outline guidelines for evaluating fiction based on characterization, plot, setting, theme, style, and point of view.

- ***What beliefs and principles guide teachers as they create and implement a standards-based literature program?*** Children should have access to quality books: literature that is personally meaningful and fits their developmental level. They should be able to find people like themselves in illustrations and stories. Professional development is a key element in synthesizing multiple requirements and expanding the realm of books. Technology is part of everyday life, and in teaching and learning about literature, online and other technological resources play an ever-increasing role.

All educators can assist children in thinking critically about what they read and take appropriate action based on their conclusions. Educators need to understand the values of the community in which they work and be prepared to support democracy and critical thinking.

Questions/Activities to Invite Thinking, Writing, and Conversation About the Chapter

1. Think about your childhood experiences with children's literature. Write a "Reading Autobiography" that describes your feelings about books in school or on your own. Alternatively, create a podcast, video clip, or PowerPoint presentation that uses media to communicate your memories.

2. It is important to become actively involved with any set of standards; otherwise, they will feel remote from daily life. Look at the list of the Common Core State Standards in this chapter and unpack them by enumerating what students will need to know (nouns) and what students should be able to do (verbs). Brainstorm the activities that would demonstrate successful mastery. Remember to include teachers in disciplines other than literacy. (We have witnessed students as young as first grade who take responsibility for their own learning by unpacking standards and designing and implementing appropriate activities and products for assessment.)

3. Write "I Believe" statements that addresses the principles summarized in Figure 1.4. At the end of the semester, revisit this piece and make changes based on your new knowledge and understanding.

4. Set up a blog or a wiki to collect ideas from the entire class that link children's literature, media, technology, and the Common Core State Standards. Categorize each idea under a broad topic that makes this collaborative work more useful.

2

Literature Response and Engagement

In this chapter, we discuss ways you can support students as they respond to and become engaged with what they read. Specifically, we address the following questions:

- What are response and engagement with literature, and what roles do readers, texts, and contexts play in response and engagement?
- What are the theories regarding how readers respond to literature, particularly the transactional theoretical perspective?
- How can teachers support efferent, aesthetic, and critical responses to texts?
- What are some general strategies for supporting student responses to books?

Then in Chapter 3, we show how these philosophies, understandings about students, and response strategies are embedded in a literacy program. We discuss specific teaching methods and also present model lesson plans that demonstrate how a commitment to response and engagement with literature can undergird literacy instruction that also meets the mandates of standards.

Three fourth graders chose *Julie of the Wolves* (George) for their literature circle book. The story, set in Alaska, describes the adventures and challenges faced by Julie, a young girl who runs away and eventually lives on the tundra with a wolf pack. When the group first gathered to discuss the book, the teacher was prepared with conversation-starter questions. However, she soon found that she was not able to get a word in. The children were so interested in the story that they spent more than an hour debating Julie's choices, how the actions of each wolf illuminated its personality, and what they thought might happen after the book concluded.

Seven-year-old Haileigh was an advanced reader for her age. Usually, she selected beautiful picture books, poetry, and humorous short chapter books, such as Louis Sachar's *Wayside School* series, to read. One day, she came home with *Maniac Magee* (Spinelli), a complex novel that blends fantasy and realism in a story of a boy who unites a racially divided town. She told her mother that the running feet on the cover had attracted her. However, after reading about one-third of the book, she abandoned it because she said it was boring. One year later, she stayed up all night to devour *Bud, Not Buddy* (Curtis), a book at approximately the same level as *Maniac Magee*. "This is the best book I've ever read," she told her mother, "He [the main character] feels just like me."

These examples of children responding to literature show us how children can connect passionately and thoughtfully to books. If we are to raise highly literate children, we need to know how to help students make these memorable personal connections to books. But how can we do this? How do we nurture positive responses to books, engaging children's minds and hearts so that they become lifelong thoughtful and enthusiastic readers?

Reading is so much more than being able to sound out words, decode and pronounce them, and then read them quickly. Mindful of our long-term goals of creating lifelong readers and highly literate beings, it is not the ability to decode, the mastery of a particular standard, or the score on an achievement test that will send our students back to books as adults. They will choose books on their own because they have fallen in love with them—because of the books they spent time with, enjoyed, and were moved by or those that tickled their imagination and their quest for information. They will seek books because we as teachers have developed our students' curiosity, love of words, love of stories, and love of knowledge. Popular newspaper columnist Anna Quindlen (1991) once stated that she hoped her children grew up to think of decorating as "building enough bookshelves." This is the kind of reader we want to cultivate.

What Is Response and Engagement?

When children make a unique personal connection with a story, poem, or even nonfiction they are reading, the world around them almost disappears as they become totally engrossed in the world created by the author. Through books, they can solve mysteries, go on adventures to distant and magical lands, find information on topics they are curious about, cry when a beloved character dies, and laugh over another's humorous antics. The children described in the incidents at the beginning of the chapter are fortunate because they have experienced the joy of connecting with literature.

As teachers, we want to nurture this positive response to books, engaging children's hearts and minds; this is how we can create lifelong, enthusiastic readers. We also want to help children deepen their engagement, in part, by going back into a book to discover what the author did to create connections with readers. We want to stimulate them to think more deeply or help them discover some new insight about their world. To do all this, we must know children's books. But that is not enough. We must also know our children—how they learn, their life experiences, and what their expectations are for future encounters with books.

Additionally, we need to understand and employ today's technology to facilitate response and engagement with literature (Walsh, 2006). Most of today's students are adept with MP3 players and other types of mobile technology. Thus, we can connect them with e-books or literature that uses multiple technologies. Many middle school students view e-mail as "old fashioned"—they communicate with friends via social networking such as Twitter, Instagram, or Facebook; by texting; or through their blogging accounts. Considering these trends, can we ask students to share book discussions through text messages or Twitter? What about connecting students for book discussions in classrooms from another state or country using free video services? We expect to teach our students important literacy skills. Can we do this by accessing both wonderful books and the new literacies (Coiro, Knobel, Lankshear, & Leu, 2008)?

Comprehension is critical to an understanding of text. However, we contend that good readers go beyond simply understanding (often defined as "comprehension") to creating interpretations, critically examining social issues, and becoming emotionally involved with characters or situations. Essentially, they are actively interacting, or "transacting," with text. This is what we call "response." Response complements and extends comprehension.

This definition of response implies a deeper, more intentional interaction with literature. We call this deeper interaction "engagement." Encisco (1994) defines literary engagement as follows:

> A complex interplay of personal, emotional, visual, evaluative experiences and perceptions that are typically felt privately, but also may be expressed publically among a community of readers who share a variety of purposes, interpretations, and interests in reading. (pp. 172–173)

When students are engaged, they connect viscerally with a book, caring about what happens to the characters, becoming engrossed in the events that unfold or the information presented; they are essentially transported into the story world. They do not typically focus on phonics skills, vocabulary drills, or gathering information to answer a teacher's comprehension questions. Rather, they are reading for personal reward: to find more information on a topic that interests them, to vicariously experience someone else's emotions and dilemmas, and to savor beautiful language. This is an active construction of meaning that is personal as well as social. Engagement can subsequently be enriched and expanded through conversations and other socially oriented activities in conjunction with books.

Reader response then is the engaged interaction that occurs in the minds of readers when they experience literature. We generally discuss this interaction as comprised of three facets: (a) the reader, (b) the text, and (c) the context. In the next section, we discuss how each factor contributes to the response process, although in reality they are interrelated.

Response and Engagement: The Reader

Ask anyone what a "good" book is, and you will get a variety of answers. Everyone has their own definition of "good," and that definition differs based on interests, cultural background, school experiences, and worldview. Age is also a factor. Adults often like nostalgic books, such as Munsch's *Love You Forever* (about a boy whose mom is part of his life well into adulthood) and Silverstein's *The Giving Tree* (about a female tree that gives everything she has to a boy until there is nothing left). In our experience, these are books that children often dislike. Conversely, children love the *Captain Underpants* series (full of broad, lowbrow humor) and R. L. Stine's *Goosebumps* books, which feature predictable plots and gratuitous violence. Adults tend to find these books boring and even offensive.

Everything readers bring to a text influences how they will respond. Who we are, our past experiences with literature and the world, our interests, the books we've read, the places we've been, the people we've known, and our ages affect what we bring to the reading experience and what we take away from it. Response, then, is highly idiosyncratic. Knowing this, we need to carefully observe our students, documenting their understandings about books, their preferences for certain kinds of books, and the connections they make to books. We also need to know where they are developmentally: how they think, what they know about language, and how they view justice and morality. We can then make informed decisions about which books will resonate with them. Let us examine these factors more fully.

Experiential Background. Knowledge obtained from school, family, travel, and other experiences creates a foundation that influences how we respond to everything in our world, including literature. For example, a child who has lived on a farm will have different expectations, perceptions, and understandings when he or she reads E. B. White's *Charlotte's Web* than will an urban child who has never had such experiences. Readers approach the world, including literature, from a personal perspective. Yet stories expand our perspectives. So each reader's knowledge of the world and experience keeps changing and growing.

Children also have different life experiences with books and reading. Past experiences explain to a degree whether a student responds enthusiastically to a wide range of books and related activities or avoids the task. Some come to school having had many pleasurable experiences; they may have been read to frequently, learned to read easily, and were encouraged to voice their opinions in response to their interactions with books. These students are likely to be enthusiastic, confident readers right from the start. In contrast, you may have students who see reading as a race—something to do as quickly as possible so they can move to the next activity or level of the reading series. Worse might be the child who has had frustrating experiences with reading and views any interactions with books negatively or fearfully. And in some instances, children arrive at school with little or no familiarity with books and therefore have no understandings about reading at all. In such cases, teachers need to provide children with positive book experiences right from the start.

Interests. It makes sense that students will respond more positively to literature that interests them than to stories, poems, or nonfiction that they find boring. We hope you have had the experience of becoming so interested and personally involved in a book that you are barely aware of the world around you. Teachers can use students' interests to help select books that will engage them and to which they will positively respond. They can also extend students' interests by observing what they currently enjoy and then help them learn to appreciate a broader range of ideas and topics.

Teachers can discover interests by interviewing their students in whole-class sharing sessions, written surveys, or individual conferences. Older students can create a "reading biography" that details their personal history as a reader, including comments about their favorite books, authors, and topics as well as their less pleasurable experiences with literature. Your school librarian can also help you find ways to connect students with books they might like. For example, in one library we know, a popular display consists of a simple sign with arrows pointing left and right labeled "If you liked this . . ." (points to a current favorite) and ". . . then you might like this . . ." (points to books with a similar theme, related characters, or topics).

Tech Click

McKenna and Kear (1990) developed a comprehensive survey instrument, using Garfield figures, to measure student attitudes toward both self-selected and academic reading. Find the survey by searching for "authors' names + Garfield."

Preferences. Whereas interests are personal and individual, preferences reflect broad patterns across gender, age, or other developmental factors. Student preferences were usually identified in the past through survey research that presented prescribed options. So, for example, if students were asked if they preferred to read a mystery, a romance novel, or an adventure story and they responded "mystery," researchers inferred that students of this age prefer mysteries. However, many student interests were not reflected in traditional preference questionnaires. For example, a child asked to select from the choices outlined in the previous example might have actually preferred fantasy—a choice not offered. Typically, categories such as "gross and gory books" that we now know appeal to many students (particularly boys) were not included on many surveys. Thus, the way these studies were conducted (forced choices, varying methodologies, and differences in student populations) make it difficult to precisely discern patterns in children's preferences for kinds of books.

A few general patterns that seem to have some validity have been identified in these studies, although more recent research somewhat contradicts earlier findings. For example, children enjoy narrative literary forms with plenty of lively action, such as adventure, particularly if there are elements of horror or mystery (Boraks, Hoffman, & Bauer, 1997; Ujiie & Krashen, 2002; Worthy, Moorman, & Turner, 1999). Humorous stories are also popular, as are reading materials associated with television shows and movies. Often, specific authors and titles rather than a specific genre are named when children are given more latitude in their choices (Schatz, Pierce, Ghalambor, & Krashen, 2008; Sturm, 2003).

Gender seems to have some influence on preferences. Many studies show that boys tend to prefer stories about sports, crime investigations, war and spies, as well as other adventurous topics, whereas girls tend to prefer realistic and romantic fiction (Boraks et al., 1997; Coles & Hall, 2002; Davilla & Patrick, 2010; Lynch-Brown, 1977). (Researchers note that many girls also enjoy adventure stories.) Boys rarely enjoy Caldecott and Newbery Award recipients and actually prefer books frequently found on banned book lists (Boltz, 2007). They typically like topics that girls see as "gross," such as books about dinosaur poop or the history of bathrooms. Boys seldom indicate preferences for "girl" books, but girls will read books with male protagonists or those with themes typically considered interesting to boys (Dressman, 1997). The *Harry Potter* books reflect this phenomenon. Author J. K. Rowling has said that she deliberately made the main character a boy to ensure that she captured male readers. Boys also often preferred books that "looked good" (defined as a cover featuring a character engaged in a dangerous, life-threatening activity) or that had easy-to-read print and visual features, such as captions, photographs, cartoon drawings, and similar graphic elements (Farris, Werderich, Nelson, & Fuhler, 2009, pp. 183–184).

Gender preferences for nonfiction seem to have evolved. Past research suggested that as children get older, boys tend to gravitate toward nonfiction, whereas girls maintain their interest in fiction (Monson & Sebesta, 1991). However, research conducted by Kristo, Colman, and Wilson (2008) and Genuard (2005) suggests that it is a myth that boys prefer nonfiction more than girls do and that actually both genders often select nonfiction for their reading. Sturm (2003) also reported that both boys and girls indicated strong preferences for nonfiction, particularly books about animals, sports, science, and biography. Mohr's (2006) work with primary children found that first graders of both genders enjoyed nonfiction, particularly books about animals.

Boys' preferences for reading in general have been extensively studied in recent years because it seemed that they read less than girls, particularly in school (e.g., Brozo, 2002; Cavazos-Kottke, 2006; Farris et al., 2009; Newkirk, 2002; Smith & Wilhelm, 2002; Tatum, 2005, 2009; Zambo & Brozo, 2008). There is overwhelming support from the work of these researchers that boys read less not because they are less proficient at this skill but because the books they like are not typically available to them in many classrooms and school libraries. They also do not see books as relevant to their lives or as concerned with issues that they care about and that honor their identity. These are serious problems, but they can be remedied.

We suspect that gender attitudes toward reading as well as preferences for certain kinds of books might be influenced by social roles and expectations for men and women. For example, boys tend to read what is considered socially acceptable for their male role models: information-oriented texts, such as newspapers and instruction manuals or adventure stories with male protagonists facing challenges or solving problems. They tend to view reading as "something girls do" (Dutro, 2002; Katz & Sokal, 2003; Zambo, 2007). These findings have led to a call for increased sensitivity to the needs and preferences of boys as we select the books we will make available to our students. Jon Scieszka (quoted in Sutton, 2007), popular author and founder of *Guys Read*, a nonprofit literacy initiative, suggests that to help boys become self-initiated, lifelong readers, we must "expand our definition of reading, calling more attention to boy's literacy" and in so doing offer more "boy-friendly" choices in schools, such as comics, joke books, humorous fiction, adventure stories, and other masculine reading materials.

We also need to be sensitive to the importance of using books that are perceived by boys as having useful information for their lives. This is particularly true for African American adolescent boys. Tatum (2005, 2009) demonstrated in his work with adolescent African American males in Chicago that these students engage with books that challenge them to think critically about their contemporary circumstances, providing them with a road map that helps them answer questions like "Who am I?" and "What can I become?" Thus, books such as *Handbook for Boys: A Novel* (Myers), *Narrative of the Life of Frederick Douglass: An American Slave* (Douglass), and *The First Part Last* (Johnson), all stories about young Black men grappling with serious issues in their lives, are excellent choices for these students (Tatum, 2009). Smith and Wilhelm (2002) conducted surveys and conversations with elementary boys and found that they were more likely to view reading positively if they could connect to the topics and characters.

Figure 2.1 provides ideas for selecting books that tend to get boys hooked on reading. We offer this list with a caveat: many girls like the books on this list and should be encouraged to read them if interested.

Tech Click

Jon Scieszka's *Guys Read* Web site targets boys and reading. It provides many useful resources and book suggestions that boys will enjoy.

We tend to be less concerned about selecting books for girls, as they typically read a wider variety of stories, including many of those favored by boys, and they often enjoy the books selected or recommended by teachers. However, it is equally important to expand the horizons of girls, thus we must be sure not to neglect their needs. As girls reach adolescence, their brave, forthright child selves often disappear, replaced by young women who are unsure of themselves or hesitate to voice their opinions or who assume a leadership role. Thus, we want to be sure that girls have the opportunity to encounter active, empowered females in the books they read to build and maintain their self-esteem.

This is not as easy as it sounds. Research by Crisp and Hiller (2011), who analyzed Caldecott Award–winning picture books, revealed that female characters are generally portrayed as "passive, inactive, dependent, submissive, nurturing and emotional" (p. 24). Even female protagonists who transcended traditional qualities associated with their gender often relied on males to resolve

FIGURE 2.1 Sampling of Books Many Boys Like

(Books appropriate for preschoolers are marked *; those with significant culturally diverse elements are marked #.)

Aronson, Mark and Newquist, HP. *For Boys Only: The Biggest, Baddest Book Ever.* (I, M)

Balliett, Blue. *The Calder Game.* (M)

Barry, Dave, and Pearson, Ridley. *Science Fair* (James Bernardin, Illus.). (M)

*Black, Michael Ian. *Chicken Cheeks* (Kevin Hawkes, Illus.). (P)

Blume, Judy. *Tales of a Fourth Grade Nothing.* (I)

*Brown, Calef. *Boy Wonders.* (P)

Card, Orson Scott. *Ender's Game.* (M)

Clements, Andrew. *Frindle.* (I)

Colfer, Eoin. *Artemis Fowl.* (M)

Collins, Suzanne. *Gregor the Overlander.* (M)

#Curtis, Christopher. *Bud, Not Buddy; Elijah of Buxton.* (M)

DiCamillo, Kate. *Mercy Watson* (and others). (P)

#Douglass, Frederick. *Narrative of the Life of Frederick Douglass.* (M)

*Faller, Regis. *The Adventures of Polo.* (P)

Frazee, Marla. *A Couple of Boys Have the Best Weekend Ever.* (P)

Floca, Brian. *Locomotive.* (P, I, M)

*Fucile, Tony. *Let's Do Nothing.* (P)

George, Jean Craighead. *My Side of the Mountain* (and sequels). (I, M)

Guinness World Records. *Guinness World Records 2014.* (P, I, M) (Look for yearly updates.)

Haddix, Margaret Peterson. *Among the Hidden* (and others). (M)

Hobbs, Will. *Go Big or Go Home* (and others). (M)

Horowitz, Anthony. *Stormbreaker* (Alex Rider series). (M)

Jacques, Brian. *Redwall* (series). (M)

Johnson, Peter. *The Amazing Adventures of John Smith, Jr. AKA Houdini.* (I, M)

Key, Walt. *Alabama Moon.* (M)

Kinney, Jeff. *Diary of a Wimpy Kid* (and others). (M)

Klein, Suzy. *Horrible Harry* (series). (P)

*LaReau, Otto. *The Boy Who Loved Cars.* (P)

Macauley, David. *The New Way Things Work.* (P, I, M)

*Marshall, James. *George and Martha.* (P)

Mikaelsen, Ben. *Touching Spirit Bear.* (M)

#Myers, Walter Dean. *Handbook for Boys: A Novel; Monster; The Greatest; Fallen Angels* (and others). (M)

National Geographic Kids. *5,000 Awesome Facts (About Everything!).* (I, M)

Nimmo, Jenny. *Midnight for Charlie Bone.* (M)

Paolini, Christopher. *Eragon* (and sequels). (M)

Parry, Roseann. *Heart of a Shepherd.* (M)

Paulsen, Gary. *Hatchet* (and others). (M)

Pilkey, Dav. *Captain Underpants* (series). (I, M)

Raczka, Bob. *Guyku: A Year of Haiku for Boys* (Peter Reynolds, Illus.). (P, I)

Reeve, Phillip. *Hungry City Chronicles* (series). (M)

Rex, Adam. *Cold Cereal.* (I, M)

Riordan, Rick. *Percy Jackson and the Olympians* (series). (M)

Rowling, J. K. *Harry Potter* (series). (I, M)

Sachar, Louis. *Holes.* (M)

Scieszka, Jon. **Trucktown* (series) (P); *Spaceheadz* (series); *Time Warp Trio* (series). (I)

Schwartz, Alvin. *Scary Stories to Tell in the Dark.* (I, M)

Selznick, Brian. *The Invention of Hugo Cabret.* (M)

*Sherry, Kevin. *I'm the Biggest Thing in the Ocean.* (P)

*Slack, Michael. *Monkey Truck.* (P)

Smith, Jeff. *Bone* (graphic novel series). (M)

Soup, Cuthbert. *A Whole Nother Story.* (I)

Snicket, Lemony. *A Series of Unfortunate Events* (series). (M)

#Taylor, Theodore. *The Cay.* (I, M)

Teague, David. *Franklin's Big Dream.* (P)

Thimmesh, Catherine. *Scaly Spotted Feathered Frilled: How Do We Know What Dinosaurs Really Looked Like?* (I, M)

*Willems, Mo. *Don't Let the Pigeon Drive the Bus.* (P)

Wood, Don. *Into the Volcano.* (M)

#Yee, Lisa. *Bobby the Brave (Sometimes).* (I, M)

conflict and stayed close to home rather than adventuring out into the world. So we need to be careful to provide examples of brave, resourceful, and thoughtful heroines in books.

Figure 2.2 features a sampling of books with female protagonists who take control of their lives, show resiliency in difficult situations, or are heroes (as defined by feminine values). We offer the same caveat as we did for our suggested list of books boys enjoy: if boys are interested in reading the books on this list, they should be encouraged to do so.

FIGURE 2.2 Sampling of Books with Empowered Female Protagonists

(Books appropriate for preschoolers are marked *; those with significantly culturally diverse elements are marked #.)

Adler, David A. *Cam Jansen* (series). (P, I)

#Anderson, Laurie. *Fever, 1793; Chains*. (M)

Avi. *The Secret School* (I); *The True Confessions of Charlotte Doyle*. (M)

Barrows, Annie. *Ivy and Bean* (series). (P)

Blume, Judy. *Are You There, God? It's Me, Margaret*. (M)

#Bridges, Ruby. *Through My Eyes*. (I)

#Coerr, Eleanor. *Sadako*. (I)

Collins, Suzanne. *The Hunger Games Trilogy*. (M)

Colman, Penny. *Spies! Women in the Civil War*. (I)

Colman, Penny. *Adventurous Women: Eight True Stories About Women Who Made a Difference*. (I, M)

Colman, Penny. *Where the Action Was: Women Correspondents in World War II*. (M)

Cooney, Barbara. *Miss Rumphius*. (P, I)

#Curtis, Christopher Paul. *The Mighty Miss Malone*. (M)

Cushman, Karen. *The Ballad of Lucy Whipple*. (M)

Dahl, Roald. *Matilda*. (I)

#Dietz, Heather. *Newbery Girls: Selections from Fifteen Newbery Award–Winning Books Especially for Girls*. (M)

Draper, Sharon. *Out of My Mind*. (M)

#Erdrich, Louise. *The Birchbark House* (and others). (I)

*Falconer, Ian. *Olivia*. (P)

#Fenner, Carol. *Yolonda's Genius*. (I, M)

Gauch, Patricia. *This Time, Tempe Wick?* (I)

Glaser, Isabel. *Dreams of Glory: Poems About Girls*. (I, M)

#Grimes, Nikki. *Meet Danitra Brown* (and others). (P, I)

Hale, Shannon. *The Goose Girl; Princess Academy*. (M)

#Hamilton, Virginia. *Her Stories: African American Folk Tales, Fairytales and True Tales*. (I, M)

Hatke, Ben. *Zita the Spacegirl*. (I)

#Hayes, Joe. *Watch Out for Clever Women*. (I)

*Henkes, Kevin. *Lily's Purple Plastic Purse*. (P)

Hesse, Karen. *Out of the Dust*. (M)

Hest, Amy. *When Jessie Came Across the Sea*. (I, M)

*Hoffman, Mary. *Amazing Grace*. (P)

#Hopkinson, Deborah. *Sweet Clara and the Freedom Quilt*. (P)

Hunt, Lynda Mullaly. *One for the Murphys*. (I, M)

Jonell, Lynne. *Emmy and the Incredible Shrinking Rat*. (P, I)

#Kadohata, Cynthia. *Kira, Kira*. (M)

Koenigsburg, E. L. *From the Mixed Up Files of Mrs. Basil E. Frankweiler*. (I)

#Lee, Milly. *Nim and the War Effort*. (P, I)

LeGuin, Ursula. *The Tombs of Atuan*. (M)

#Lester, Julius. *Pharaoh's Daughter: A Story of Ancient Egypt*. (M)

#Levine, Kristin. *The Lions of Little Rock*. (M)

#Lewis, J. Patrick. *Vherses: A Celebration of Outstanding Women*. (M)

Lowry, Lois. *Number the Stars*. (M)

*McDonnell, Patrick. *Me . . . Jane*. (P, I)

*#McKissack, Patricia. *Flossie and the Fox*. (P)

Messer, Kate. *Eye of the Storm*. (M)

Miller, Kirsten. *Kiki Strike: Inside the Shadow City*. (M)

Munsch, Robert. *The Paper Bag Princess*. (P)

FIGURE 2.2 *continued*

O'Connor, Barbara. *How to Steal a Dog.* (I)

Partridge, Elizabeth. *Restless Spirit: The Life and Works of Dorothea Lang.* (M)

Paterson, Katherine. *Lyddie.* (M)

Pennypacker, Sara. *Clementine* (series). (P, I)

#Phelps, Ethel. *Tatterhood and Other Tales.* (I, M)

#Pinkney, Andrea. *Silent Thunder: A Civil War Story.* (M)

#Ragan, Kathleen. *Fearless Girls, Wise Women and Beloved Sisters: Heroes Around the World.* (I, M)

#Ryan, Pam. *When Marian Sang: The True Recital of Marian Anderson* (P, I); *Esperanza Rising* (M); *Riding Freedom.* (M)

Sturtevant, Katherine. *A True and Faithful Narrative.* (M)

#Tingle, Tim. *Crossing Bok Chitto: A Choctaw Tale of Friendship and Freedom.* (I)

Urban, Linda. *The Center of Everything.* (I, M)

Voigt, Cynthia. *Dicey's Song* (and others). (M)

#Weatherford, Carole. *Moses: When Harriet Tubman Led Her People to Freedom.* (P, I)

*Williams, Vera. *A Chair for My Mother.* (P)

#Yee, Lisa. *Millicent Min, Girl Detective.* (M)

#Yolen, Jane. *Not One Damsel in Distress: World Folktales for Strong Girls.* (I, M)

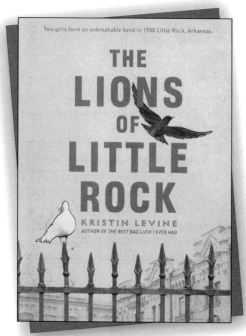

The Lions of Little Rock is a good example of a book with a strong female protagonist.

With the explosion of texts available in digital format, we are likely to see significant changes in children's reading preferences. There is some indication that readers at all levels are less willing to read long texts (Carr, 2010). Several studies already indicate growing preferences for reading text messages and Internet Web sites (Clark & Foster, 2005). In response, some publishers are now using a combination of print and digital formats to attract readers. For example, Scholastic's hugely popular *The 39 Clues* mystery series features online gaming, card collecting, and a wiki to help readers track clues they discover in the books. This combination of print and digital formats seems irresistible to many children. We will likely see dramatic changes in reading preferences as e-books, Twitter, text messaging and other digital formats we cannot even imagine become more popular and available to many children.

Preferences are influenced by not only age and gender but also complex factors, such as cultural expectations, socioeconomic background, and social norms (Dressman, 1997; Summers & Lukasevich, 1983). You probably know girls who never enjoyed romance stories or boys who prefer fantasy over nonfiction. As both boys and girls gain experience with books, their interests and preferences broaden, and they have greater appreciation and enthusiasm for increasingly diverse, more complex types of books (Sturm, 2003). For these reasons, information on children's preferences should be used only to gain a general sense of books students might enjoy. Then individual tastes for certain kinds of books, authors, and print formats become important.

Developmental Characteristics. A child's cognitive, linguistic, moral, and, to a lesser extent, physical development also influence his or her response to books. Just as Haileigh's taste in books (described at the beginning of the chapter) changed as she matured, so do all students' responses change as they are able to produce and understand increasingly complex sentence structures, see multiple perspectives on moral issues, or become more aware of the world beyond their family. In this section, we discuss the influence of children's cognitive, moral, social, and physical development on the books they prefer as well as how they respond to literature.

Ages 3 to 5. Preschool and young kindergarten children are concrete-operational thinkers (Piaget, 1969); they are also egocentric and best relate to stories that focus on concepts within their experience, although they are able to extend their experience with books about animals, seasons, holidays, toys, and other topics close to what they already know. As a result, books such as *Nobody Asked Me if I Wanted a Baby Sister* (Alexander), *Little White Rabbit* (Henkes) (about a rabbit who sets out from home to have an adventure), and *Leaves* (Stein) (which describes a little bear who tried to restore leaves to the trees in the autumn) are popular with this age-group. Although they are beginning to be more independent, they are still closely connected to their families and enjoy stories about family life or young children acquiring a new skill, such as *Little Bear* (Minarik) and *Whistle for Willie* (Keats) (a little boy learns to whistle so that he can call his dog).

Books with repetitive lines and familiar sequences, such as *Chicken Soup with Rice* (Sendak) and *The Very Hungry Caterpillar* (Carle), as well as folktales, such as *The Gingerbread Man*, are also popular because the repetitive features of these books help children keep the story in their minds. Their attention span is increasing; thus, children 3 to 5 years old can listen to longer books than before, although those books do need to be completed in one sitting and should allow for their active participation.

Responses from children in this age-group are typically observable actions, such as pointing, chanting, talking back to characters, and spontaneous acting. Verbal comments often focus on one aspect of the story or an illustration and result from the child's making a personal connection with that aspect of the story.

Ages 5 to 7. Kindergarten and young primary children are also typically concrete-operational thinkers; as with preschoolers, learning is dependent on direct, hands-on experiences. They are beginning to interact with many things beyond their own world, although they are most comfortable with settings, characters, or concepts that are familiar to them. They want independence, but they also need the security of the familiar as they venture out to new experiences. They are beginning to identify with cultural expectations for their gender and are most likely to interact with friends of the same gender, forming true friendships characterized by shared experiences and mutual trust. Thus, stories about family, school, friendships, and other aspects of everyday life are appealing, providing them with new ideas and experiences within familiar settings.

Children this age are also beginning to appreciate the humorous nuances of language, such as multiple meanings and simple wordplay. This is why the *Amelia Bedelia* (Parish) books, featuring a maid who misunderstands cleaning directions such as "dust the furniture" and "put out the lights," are so popular with this age-group.

Morally, they tend to make absolute judgments about right and wrong: they expect bad behavior to be punished and good behavior to be rewarded (Kohlberg, 1981). This explains their continued interest in folktales such as *The Gingerbread Man* and *The Little Red Hen*. However, they are receptive to stories with more ambiguity, and it is appropriate to share stories in which characters wrestle with more subtle moral dilemmas in order to move them to a higher level of thinking and morality.

Although picture books (fiction, nonfiction, and poetry) are important to use with kindergarten and primary grade children, particularly for read-alouds, these students are also learning to read during these years and need stories they can read independently. Easy-reading books have high-frequency vocabulary, familiar settings and situations, and plenty of illustrations to help young children read them successfully. Award-winning books, such as those by Mo Willems, Cynthia Rylant, Kate DiCamillo, and others, are carefully constructed to support the initial efforts of beginning readers while also featuring humor and themes interesting to this age-group. Figure 2.3 features some of the award-winning titles that are particularly well regarded beginning reader texts.

FIGURE 2.3 Sampling of Easy-to-Read Stories

Arnold, Tedd. *I Spy Fly Guy* (and others).

Asch, Frank. *Moonbear* (and others).

Beaumont, Karen. *Move over Rover.*

Bell, Cece. *Rabbit and Robot: The Sleepover.*

Bliss, Harry. *Luke on the Loose* (TOON series).

Campbell, Sarah. *Wolfsnail: A Backyard Predator.*

Dean, James. *Pete the Cat; Pete the Cat and His Four Groovy Buttons* (and others).

DiCamillo, Kate. *Mercy Watson to the Rescue* (and others); *Blink and Gollie.*

Grant, Judyann. *Chicken Said, "Cluck"* (Sue Truesdell, Illus.).

Grey, Mini. *Traction Man and the Beach Odyssey.*

Henkes, Kevin. *Penny and Her Song; Penny and Her Marble; Penny and Her Doll.*

Hoberman, MaryAnn. *You Read to Me, I'll Read to You: Very Short Stories to Read Together* (also fables, fairy tales, and so on).

Howe, James. *Houndsley and Catina: Plink and Plunk* (and others).

Klassen, Jon. *I Want My Hat Back.*

Kvasnosky, Laura. *Zelda and Ivy* (series).

Lin, Grace. *Ling and Ting: Not Exactly the Same.*

Lobel, Arnold. *Frog and Toad Are Friends.*

Long, Ethan. *Up, Tall and High!*

Lunde, Darrin. *Hello, Bumblebee Bat* (Patricia Wynne, Illus.).

Meisel, Paul. *See Me Run.*

McMullan, Kate. *Pearl and Wagner: One Funny Day* (R. W. Alley, Illus.).

Portis, Antoinette. *Not a Box.*

Rylant, Cynthia. *Mr. Potter and Tabby* (series); *Henry and Mudge* (series).

Sayre, April. *Vulture View* (Steve Jenkins, Illus.).

Schneider, Josh. *Tales for Very Picky Eaters.*

Seeger, Laura Vaccaro. *Dog and Bear: Three to Get Ready* (and others); *One Boy; First the Egg.*

Silverman, Erica. *Cowgirl Kate and Cocoa* (and others).

Van Leeuwen, Jean. *Amanda Pig and the Really Hot Day* (Ann Schweninger, Illus.) (and others).

Willems, Mo. *Are You Ready to Play Outside?; Cat the Cat, Who Is That?; Don't Let the Pigeon Drive the Bus* (and others); *I Broke My Trunk; Knuffle Bunny* (and others); *There's a Bird on Your Head; Time to Sleep, Sheep the Sheep!; Today I Will Fly; We Are in a Book; Let's Go for a Drive.*

Wheeler, Lisa. *Jazz Baby* (R. Gregory Christie, Illus.).

Yee, Wong Herbert. *Mouse and Mole: A Winter Wonderland* (and others).

Up, Tall and High is a perfect choice for young readers to dramatize.

Response at this age tends to be physical: children leaning in to comment on stories, chanting a repetitive refrain, or creating a spontaneous dramatization. As they get older, much of this spontaneous behavior becomes more subtle and structured. They will respond to a part of a story that captures their interest—a character's situation or a detail in an illustration or event that connects to their own experience—rather than the story as a whole. Children in this age-group also begin responding through writing as their skills in communicating this way develop. Short summaries or comments in literature journals are typical written responses for this age-group.

Ages 8 to 10. Children in the middle elementary grades are still often concrete-operational thinkers, although their thinking becomes more flexible and abstract as they mature (Piaget, 1969). Their vocabulary knowledge is exploding, and they can both understand and generate complex sentence structures. Additionally, their sense of humor becomes more sophisticated with a growing ability to appreciate subtle wordplay and absurd situations. Thus, a book like *Charlie and the Chocolate Factory*, with its sly mockery of society and exaggerated situations is often a favorite of this age child. Children this age are also increasingly able to consider an individual's intent when deciding if actions are right or wrong so that books like *Shiloh* (Naylor), which presents complex moral issues, are popular, particularly with the older students in this category.

Although there are significant differences in reading ability, many children in this age-group particularly enjoy series books that provide familiar characters, plots, and settings across several books to help scaffold their reading. More advanced readers in this age-group are becoming independent readers and enjoy increasingly longer, more complex plots. They can discuss genres and literary elements in books and create written responses, such as summaries, journal entries, and creative stories, that demonstrate an increasingly sophisticated understanding of literary structures. Additionally, their interest in social relationships makes literature discussions a valuable classroom activity.

Ages 11 to 13. Middle school children can reason logically, grapple with abstractions, view a situation from multiple perspectives, and tolerate ambiguity (Piaget, 1969). This ability to think more abstractly and flexibly enables them to read more complex stories that have multiple plots, advanced vocabulary, and diverse viewpoints. They benefit from experiencing ideas in books where the right decision is ambiguous and dependent on contextual factors, causing disequilibrium in their thinking.

These students also understand and can discuss sophisticated language use, such as subtle figurative language, the way authors select point of view to shape a story's perspective, or methods of creating dialect to make a character seem authentic. Additionally, students in this age-group can analyze character motivation, story structure, and the author's message. Typically, these responses are revealed in discussion or writing, although some students can produce sophisticated art or drama in response to books—and should be allowed to do so. Thus, books such as *The Giver* (Lowry) and *Roll of Thunder, Hear My Cry* (Taylor), with their thought-provoking moral dilemmas, advanced language structures, and complex story lines, are appropriate for these students.

Students this age are searching for their identity. As a result, they enjoy books in which characters must face challenges or explore their own identity. Typically, adults are absent in stories enjoyed by this age-group so that the protagonists must confront and conquer challenges on their own. Thus, many students enjoy "hero quest" books, such as *The Lord of the Rings* (Tolkien), or books with a character alone in a dangerous situation, such as *Hatchet* (Paulson).

As with the studies on reading preferences, we caution you to remember that these are patterns. Growth has wide variations; children change at different rates, and their development is affected by many social, cultural, and biological factors.

Literacy Skills. Students who are proficient readers, enjoy reading, and have advanced literacy skills are likely to enjoy literature and respond positively to it. They can pay attention to subtle nuances in characterization or debate complex issues presented in books. Conversely, children who struggle to comprehend, lack fluency, and have difficulty decoding will be more concerned with the mechanics of reading than grappling with the ideas they encounter in books. However, if less able readers have a strong interest in reading a particular book, this desire can often transcend their reading level (Conniff, 1993; Shapiro & White, 1991; Thames & Reeves, 1994).

In fact, we would argue that for many struggling readers, linking reading instruction with activities that encourage response and engagement makes a critical difference (Gambrell, 1996). It does not help struggling readers to "master" lower-level comprehension competencies before giving them the opportunity to focus on deeper, interpretive responses to texts. Rather, it is the act of reflecting, discussing, and personally engaging with text that actually increases understanding and reading skill (Möller & Allan, 2000).

Ronnie, a fifth-grade student we observed, is a good example of this phenomenon. Classified as a low-achieving reader, he could spell only phonetically, and his response journal entries were typically just a few sentences long. However, he wanted to read Esther Forbes's *Johnny Tremain*, a challenging book set during the American Revolution, with the advanced literature circle group. His teacher encouraged him to try. Ronnie labored for days, taking the book home at night, reading during every free moment, and even getting his reading tutor to help. When he met with his literature group, Ronnie took the lead. He debated ethical issues raised in the book. He shared his extensive personal knowledge of the American Revolution and the Sons of Liberty. In short, he responded in very sophisticated ways to a lengthy, complex novel, far beyond what would normally be expected of him—because he was motivated and interested and had extensive personal background on the historical era depicted in the book.

Another example is a second-grade boy who was reading the 734-page *Harry Potter and the Goblet of Fire* (Rowling). No one would have thought that the fourth book in the series would be appropriate second-grade reading because it is vastly longer than most selections chosen by children that age. However, this child was motivated to read it, and so he did. He was conversant with the details of the first three books, conclusively proving that he read and comprehended them. Who would prevent him from reading a book he wanted to read that much? Remember that the preferences and developmental issues discussed in this chapter do not take the place of a child's passionate desire to read a particular book.

Response and Engagement: The Text

Text Characteristics. Characteristics of the text also affect how a reader responds to a particular book. For example, when we read nonfiction, we tend to approach the experience as a task to gather information. In contrast, when reading a novel, we usually become absorbed in such things as determining relationships among characters, following a sequence of events, and forming opinions about the theme. When we read a picture book, we are continually moving between text and illustration, using information from both to understand the meaning of the story.

Different genres also require different skills to successfully comprehend them. Young children typically have more experience with narrative text structures. Teachers generally read aloud to younger students from narrative text and also often select stories of this type for reading instruction. As a result, children tend to know what to expect when reading fiction on their own, expecting structural elements such as characterization, plot structure, and dialogue. Nonfiction text structure is markedly different from narrative structure. In nonfiction, students must learn how visual features (diagrams, photos, tables, and so on), organizational structures (subheadings, presentation of material, and so on), and other special qualities of nonfiction facilitate a reader's understanding. (These features are discussed in more detail in Chapter 10.) Poetry is structured in yet other ways (stanzas, short lines, and compressed ideas that are subtly stated), creating unique challenges for readers (see Chapter 5).

Online texts also require different skills to read them successfully and with a critical eye. The Internet has provided access to an enormous range of texts, including scholarly articles on genetics, peer-reviewed Wikipedia entries, and "Hey, This Is All About Me" sites. The ability to critically analyze texts for accuracy and bias is particularly crucial for Internet texts. Thus, teachers need to scaffold not only research techniques but also children's ability to evaluate the material they find, how to attribute the information to its source, and how to synthesize all those many facts into something more meaningful so that students successfully comprehend them.

A reader's experience or inexperience with different types of text can influence understanding and engagement. For example, the more experience and interest readers have with nonfiction or Internet texts the more comfortable they will be reading and responding on a complex level. The same can be said for poetry or fiction. Teachers can help their students gain this experience by sharing many different genres of texts.

Text Complexity. Some reading educators believe that text difficulty or readability makes a difference in comprehension and response to a book (Fry, 1978). A formula is used to assign a difficulty or "readability level" by calculating variables such as word and sentence length. This is the basis for ELA-Literacy CCRA Reading: Literature and Reading: Information Standard 10, which states that students will "by the end of the year, read and comprehend literature and [informational texts] in the grade level proficiency band independently and proficiently" (CCSS Initiative, 2010, appendix A). One of the ways in which this "text complexity" is discerned, according to the Common Core State Standards, is through quantitative dimensions of complexity based on word length or frequency, sentence length, and text cohesion, such as the Lexile Framework for Reading (Metametrix), which is the quantitative text difficulty measurement system referenced in the Common Core State Standards.

While the notion of matching students to books and stories that are suited to their ability may be appealing, however it is impossible to accurately measure readability. Moreover, text features such as sentence and word length have never been proven to make reading easy or more difficult. Maurice Sendak's *Where the Wild Things Are*, for example, is popular with young children who can often read or recite the text. However, it is one long sentence that would likely earn a high school or college readability level. And consider the following: *Fahrenheit 451* (Bradbury), the classic novel read by most high school students; *Gossip Girl: A Novel* (von Ziegesar), a chatty romance novel that became the inspiration for a television series; and *Diary of a Wimpy Kid* (Kinney) are all classified within the same Lexile band despite wide differences in literary quality (Miller, 2012). We believe that a readability formula is inadequate because it does not take reader experience and interest into account.

Fortunately, although the Common Core State Standards affirm the usefulness and importance of quantitative text difficulty measures, they also assert that a valid complexity level for any particular child is further dependent on additional, more qualitative factors, such as his or her experiential background, prior knowledge of the content in the story or text, motivation to read it, and engagement with the topic, characters, or events. A text defined as too complex by a quantitatively determined readability score may be relatively easy for a particular child because that child might be highly motivated to read it. The writers of the Common Core State Standards further suggest that these more qualitative, nuanced measures of complexity should confirm or overrule any quantitative analysis of text complexity (appendix A). In short, text complexity has as much to do with the match between book and reader as it does with a mathematically determined complexity level.

As a result, readers who are interested in a book and have some background in a topic will often succeed with one that at first glance might seem too difficult for them. However, we want to encourage such risk taking, as students often become better readers when they read increasingly more difficult books. We also want them to learn how to select books for themselves. A good way to find out if a book is suitable is to let the student try it for a few pages. If it is too difficult, he or she will generally become frustrated and try something else, or an adult or more able reader from another class can provide support.

Text Substantiality. Finally, for response and engagement to be substantive, the text needs to be substantive. There needs to be enough to "chew on"—to question, startle, digest, and critique. Some people believe that children are in need of protection from controversy, injustice, cruelty, and other realities. They contend that we should allow children to read only books that present a happy, bland world, free from conflict or disagreements. However, we believe that children are intelligent. It is a disservice to protect them from complex ideas and the opportunity to grapple with them. We do not mean to imply that a steady diet of horror and bad news is appropriate. However, we do support providing children with substance for their reading. They know much about the world, and they need to see the world reflected in their literature so that they better understand it.

If we want children to respond deeply, passionately, and intellectually to literature—to be fully engaged—we must give them books with the necessary qualities to enable them to make these deeper, more nuanced responses. Thus, they should encounter books that have complex themes, multifaceted characters, and intriguing plots that will inspire critical analysis and reflection.

Response and Engagement: The Context

We have come to understand that although reading is typically a solitary activity, response to reading is often shaped by a social context. Through interaction with others (adults and peers) by negotiating ideas, understandings, and varying perspectives, students develop increasingly more thoughtful, sophisticated responses. They learn how to respond to books by listening to others as well as by getting feedback on their own responses. They also learn to appreciate a wider variety of books. Children in classrooms where books are valued and enjoyed prefer a wider variety of books.

Research also suggests that children who have had many experiences reading and responding to books often exhibit more sophisticated responses than might be expected if one considers just their age or developmental stage. For example, Lehr (1991) found that children in classrooms where they encountered many books and had numerous experiences with literature could understand and discuss more abstract concepts, such as theme and character motivation, than would be expected considering their age. McClure (1990) found that children in classrooms where discussion and writing of poetry were emphasized had more sophisticated responses to that genre than those who were not as familiar with poetry. Kasten and Clarke (in Kasten & Lolli, 1998) found that students in a class that emphasized literature were more articulate about their preferences, citing favorite authors, titles, and genres, than students in classrooms that used mostly commercially published readers with little other supplemental literature.

Peer Influence on Response/Engagement with Books. Peers have a particularly powerful influence on response. "I usually ask people what books they are reading and whether they are good enough" or "I get suggestions from friends because they know what interests me" are the kinds of comments teachers frequently hear from many students for whom talk about books is an important part of friendship (Bang-Jensen, 2010). Anecdotal comments from teachers we know describe their students getting hooked on R. L. Stine's *Goosebumps* horror books, the *Chronicles of Narnia* stories (Lewis), or the *Captain Underpants* series (Pilkey) because those books are passed from child to child. The *Harry Potter* books were virtually unknown until children began recommending them to friends and it became the "cool" thing to read the books, dress like the characters, and wait at bookstores for hours when the latest volume came out. In one sixth-grade classroom, a copy of *Percy Jackson and the Olympians* (Riordan) was so popular that students developed their own waiting list of who would get it next, and the paperback cover was completely worn off from so many readers' hands. The same phenomenon is often seen with *The Hunger Games* trilogy (Collins).

Word-of-mouth peer recommendations made the difference in the popularity of these books. In fact, for many children, the decision about what to read is embedded in their friendships. Children carefully observe the reading choices of their friends and classroom idols and then begin reading these books to strengthen their relationships and status in the classroom. Talk about books becomes a significant part of their interactions (Bang-Jenson, 2010; Guthrie & Anderson, 1999; Pierce, 1999).

Peers help evoke and shape each other's responses to books. Hepler (1982) demonstrated this in a research study showing that in a classroom environment designed to encourage response, a "community of readers" developed that nurtured and supported various response activities. Interactions with peers validated initial responses and provided opportunities for children to try out their initial partially developed responses. Then readers refined those responses through interactions with other readers. Barnes (1976) also reported that talking and writing in groups gave children the opportunity to work through meanings they may not have articulated or had only partially considered.

Teacher Influences on Response/Engagement. Peers are not the only important aspect of social context; teachers also play a major role, particularly in encouraging, nurturing, and deepening response. As teachers, we serve as important models for reading, both as readers ourselves and as the leaders of the reading community in our classrooms. Children often name their teachers' favorite books as their own favorites, demonstrating the powerful influence that teachers have on children's preferences. Teachers help children make significant connections between what was read in the past and what they are currently reading. Teachers also extend students' initial responses through scaffolding: they help students make their own associations and connections with literature and show them how to connect literature with their own experience.

Teachers can also challenge students to examine their previously unchallenged cultural assumptions and broaden their understanding of other cultures through literature. A study by Dressel (2005) with middle school students showed that students developed more positive feelings about multicultural literature when given the opportunity to read and respond to books that focused on diverse cultures. Louie

Boys in Deb White's multiage class examine all parts of a book.

(2005) found that students who developed an understanding of a book's cultural context and were provided with many opportunities to respond to that book developed empathy for characters from a different culture than their own.

Teacher expectations also influence the kinds of responses children make to books. If you always expect students to answer teacher- or publisher-created questions following their reading and if all students must read the same books in lockstep fashion, you will likely find that your students respond superficially and unenthusiastically to books. However, if you surround your students with books and give them time and opportunity to explore many genres, topics, authors, ideas, and cultural perspectives, you will likely discover that your students become enthusiastic readers who are capable of responding to books in increasingly complex, sophisticated ways (Galda, Rayburn, & Stanzi, 2000; Holland, Hungerford, & Ernst, 1993; Kristo, 1993; McClure, 1985; Sipe, 1999).

Time and opportunity for reading and reflecting on that reading are critical. Many of today's children are so used to flitting from page to page online that they have trouble concentrating while reading extended text, such as books (Newkirk, 2012). Slowing down allows more opportunity to attend to the nuances of reading, experiencing the words and meanings as something not to be "processed" but to be enjoyed and savored and allowing us to reflect on what that reading means for the individual reader. "Slow reading" is not only essential for real comprehension but also crucial to the deep pleasure we take in reading and for experiencing the power of reading to change us (Newkirk, 2012).

A teacher's perspective on what constitutes a "good" response makes a critical difference. If you accept only one response to a book or poem as "correct," you will stifle original thought, honest feelings, and personal engagement with books. Sometimes, students have a new way of looking at a book or poem that diverges from what we expect or consider "correct." We can reject these divergent ideas, or we can value them, considering the perspective and thinking that influenced children to construct their opinions. Teachers who value divergent ideas and methods of responding (that can be justified by some aspect of the text) will help their students articulate their thoughts and encourage them to respond in personally satisfying ways, creating an environment that nurtures honest, personal, and thoughtful responses to literature.

This means that teachers should provide opportunities for students to respond in multiple ways. Often, we encourage only written or oral responses. However, Short, Kaufman, and Kahn (2000) discovered that, when children were given alternatives to writing a book response, many children enjoyed incorporating diagrams, sketches, webs, storyboards, and charts into their responses. In fact, these diverse types of responses seem to encourage deeper reflection and analysis. Whitin (2005) found that making sketches to represent literary ideas, supplemented by written commentaries and conversations, resulted in higher-level thought and deeper critical analysis.

Teachers also can nurture engagement with books when they allow students to choose what they read. Research studies overwhelmingly confirm that students prefer to select their own reading materials and that they are more likely to "get lost" in a book they have personally chosen (Clark & Foster, 2005; Johnson & Blair, 2003; Krashen, 1993; Scholastic, 2008; Strommen & Mates, 2004). We recognize that teachers must sometimes assign books to accomplish a particular curricular objective. Sometimes, those assigned books become favorites. However, you should be sure that students have many different kinds of books to choose from in your classroom library, ample opportunities for selecting their own reading, and regularly scheduled opportunities to enjoy their choices.

Classroom Context Influence on Response/Engagement. How teachers organize the classroom can also affect response to books. For example, Sipe (1996) found that close proximity of the classroom library to the read-aloud space facilitated student willingness to connect books with other texts they knew because it was easy to find the connecting books. Morrow and Weinstein (1986) found that "literacy-rich" classrooms that featured books, puppets, materials for spontaneous dramatic play, and other materials related to books supported and deepened children's responses.

School library media specialists can be the literacy teacher's greatest allies, and they will eagerly support your program. Many school libraries have an "open-door" policy that encourages students to drop by if they have a research question or sudden reading urge. Library media specialists can also assemble a themed collection of books for your classroom and often enjoy doing specialized book talks on request. They can produce hard-to-find, must-have titles via interlibrary loan and can help you select appropriate literature for special interest or special reading needs students. A school librarian can also teach online research and reading skills and can provide useful Web resources.

Theoretical Perspectives on Reader Response

Children respond to literature in many ways, and their responses can be examined from different perspectives. This section briefly presents some of the traditional approaches to supporting students as they respond to literature. Afterward, we fully discuss the Literary Transactional Response theoretical model, which can be particularly effective in helping students become fully engaged with books. Finally, we discuss the mandates of the Common Core State Standards and how they influence how teachers can support response and engagement with literature.

Formal Criticism, Generic Perspective, and Intertextual Criticism

You might remember analyzing stories or poems to discern an author's intent or meaning. Your personal response was considered unimportant because it was irrelevant to the relationship of the literary elements to the overall meaning of the work. This approach to response is termed "formal criticism," and this way of responding to books dominated literary study for much of the 20th century. Another approach to literary response is termed the "generic perspective." If you ask students to read biographical pieces about an author's life, essays the author has written about his or her life, or commentary about the historical era in which the author lived, you are encouraging students to respond to a text from the generic perspective. Finally, if you ask students to compare one text with others featuring the same theme, setting, genre, character archetypes, or other literary element, then you are using "intertextual criticism" to facilitate response (Wolf, 2004).

We believe that all these approaches have some validity for facilitating student response to literature. Asking students to consider how an author uses figurative language to create an image or craft a plot to maintain suspense—teaching strategies that are from the formal criticism perspective—are worthy endeavors as long as this is not the only way students are asked to respond to a book. Students often become fascinated by an author's stories or illustrator's images and want to know more about the person behind the work. When this happens, the teacher can provide resources regarding the details of an author's life, along with information on why he or she wrote a story, espoused particular ideas, or used a specific artistic technique (in the case of illustrators). This is effective use of the generic perspective on response. An appropriate activity based on the intertextual criticism perspective might be to link *Shiloh* (Naylor) (a book about a boy who steals a dog to prevent its cruel mistreatment) and *Because of Winn Dixie* (DiCamillo) (a story about a dog who helps a girl cope with her mother's abandonment) to study how themes such as the power of pets to heal and moral decision making are conveyed through stories using complementary or conflicting examples.

Transactional Response Theory

Louise Rosenblatt significantly changed the way educators think about literary criticism and response to literature. In the groundbreaking book *Literature as Exploration* (Rosenblatt, 1995), she transformed our perception of how literature could be taught, providing a theoretical basis for moving beyond the text to consider the perspective of the reader in the response process. This theory of response regards the interaction between text and reader as important in constructing meaning. Rosenblatt asserted that readers are active participants who construct personal responses to literature based on their view of the world. This worldview is created through readers' experiences, conceptions, and perceptions that cause them to distill multiple, personal meanings from what they read.

The text, by virtue of its content, style, and purpose, evokes responses from readers while also guiding and constraining their construction of meaning. Iser (1974) explains that there are many interpretive possibilities in any one text and that one reading event would never exhaust the many possibilities that exist. In reading and responding to text, then, the reader moves back and forth between text and self, forming expectations that are confirmed or rejected as reading progresses. This means that readers often step back and rethink their previous understandings, checking them with what they know about the world, before moving on. It is a process of "reciprocal interaction," of looking forward to the next part of text, then looking back, then forward again (Iser, 1974). Finally, the reader moves out of the world created by the text and considers what has been learned or experienced during reading.

Efferent and Aesthetic Response.   Readers read differently, depending on their purposes. Sometimes, readers want to acquire information; sometimes, they want an emotional experience. Rosenblatt uses the terms "efferent" and "aesthetic stance" to describe the primary purposes readers have as they respond to texts.

For example, the reader may be seeking information (as in reading this book) or directions for action (reading a recipe). In this kind of reading, attention focuses on accumulating something to be taken away from the reading experience. Readers focus on concepts they wish to remember, ideas they want to consider, or actions they plan to take. So they might read *The Tarantula Scientist* (Montgomery) to discover facts about tarantulas. Or they might read *Sarah, Plain and Tall* (MacLachlan) (a lyrically written story about a family living on the prairie) to acquire background knowledge on prairie life or study how the author uses language to create vivid descriptions. Even though one of these books is nonfiction and one is fiction, both can be read from the perspective of gaining information.

Rosenblatt terms this "efferent reading" or "assuming the efferent stance." Readers who respond from an efferent stance focus on information or analysis rather than on the emotional experience of reading. They might retell or summarize the story and evaluate its believability, or they might describe information and facts they learned. Older children might analyze the author's use of various literary elements or text structures (Cox, 1991; Many, 1990; Many & Anderson, 1991). Figure 2.4 shows a literature response entry written from an efferent stance.

FIGURE 2.4 Example of Efferent Response
(*Roll of Thunder*)

Mildred Taylor did a good job developing the character of Cassie [the protagonist] so readers
come to know her and understand why she thinks and acts as she does. The first person point
of view helps a reader know this. Also, the author uses just enough dialect to give us a sense
of how she would really talk while still making sure we know what she is saying. Her voice
seems real and thoughtful without being too grown up or hard to understand.

In contrast, reading with an aesthetic purpose or stance is concerned with what Rosenblatt
terms the "lived through experience" that occurs when readers focus on the sounds and feelings
the text evokes. When readers identify with a story's characters, marvel at the imagery created in a poem, or are moved by the events described in a piece of nonfiction, they are reading
aesthetically. For example, when reading *The Great Fire* (Murphy) (a nonfiction account of the
infamous 1871 Chicago fire that incorporates firsthand accounts, dialogue, and newspaper reports), readers acquire information about this event but are also horrified by the lack of concern
for lower-class people as well as disgusted with the bungled attempts to contain the conflagration. When reading a nonfiction book such as *The Tarantula Scientist* (Montgomery), readers
would be responding from an aesthetic stance if they pondered the bravery of scientists as they
handled these dangerous creatures.

In aesthetic reading, readers draw heavily on their past experiences with reading and the
world. They respond emotionally to the sounds of the words, and they identify with the characters and events as they compare them to their own perspectives and emotions. They focus on
parts of the story or poem that intrigue them (Rosenblatt, 1995). Young children sometimes
talk to characters or add sound effects, particularly if they are responding to a story that has
been read aloud to them (Cox, 1991; Many, 1990; Many & Anderson, 1991). In essence, students
responding aesthetically become involved in sensing, clarifying, structuring, and savoring the
reading as it unfolds. With aesthetic reading, both the mind and the heart are engaged. Figure 2.5
presents a literature response journal entry written from an aesthetic stance.

Although you might think that readers respond to texts with either an efferent or an aesthetic stance, this is not usually the case. Often, reading is a mixture of the two, although readers
typically adopt a dominant stance. Readers sometimes move between efferent and aesthetic,
blending emotion and the search for information as they read a text. Different genres tend to
dictate a dominant stance (i.e., we typically read nonfiction efferently). However, the same text
can be read both efferently and aesthetically. It is the reader's stance that makes the difference.

The Critical Stance. Today's students need to be able to sift through information, critically
analyzing the accuracy, perspectives, and values inherent in a literary work. To account for this,

FIGURE 2.5 Example of an Aesthetic Response

This book is one of the best books I've ever read! Sometimes I cried like when Pa had to
put his fields on fire to save T.J. and when the Logan kids were humiliated by the white bus
driver. Sometimes I laughed at some of the things Little Man did and said. I got really, really
involved with the characters because they seemed so real to me.

scholars have extended Rosenblatt's ideas to include a third stance: the sociopolitical or critical stance. Responding to a text from a critical stance requires the reader to analyze and evaluate a text in terms of whose perspectives, values, and norms are voiced and whose are silenced. Questions of self-efficacy, power, and authority are central to the analysis as the reader attempts to discern hidden assumptions and biased perspectives. Readers are invited to consider alternate perspectives, develop empathy for issues of justice, infer biases in writing, think beyond the text to possible consequences of actions, and consider taking action themselves to make something better. It implies that teachers should provide books and response opportunities that nudge students into intensely exploring more controversial topics and issues.

We believe that the critical stance is a natural outgrowth of the aesthetic stance. Rosenblatt encouraged readers to examine the social implications embedded in the pleasure they take from their [aesthetic] involvement in the text. This suggests that aesthetic reading is not always just pleasurable reading completely detached from the reader's belief system but is likely influenced by the reader's assumptions, expectations, and attitudes (Cai, 2008). Books have the power to change our attitudes, helping us understand perspectives different from our own and giving us insights into social and cultural conflicts. However, readers typically must first experience an individual aesthetic response (e.g., "That character was treated so unfairly" or "Why are only boys allowed to do that?") that is then illuminated and extended by a critical stance or response. Otherwise, they could well resist or misunderstand the sociopolitical issues.

Not all books can or should be considered from a critical stance. However, this stance should also not be ignored. We should regularly encourage students to find and question the cultural story being told and to act on their new awareness. This will help us move away from a curriculum that values conformity toward one that is more accepting of diversity.

Teaching from Transactional and Critical Perspectives

Rosenblatt's ideas suggest, first, that teachers must recognize and support the active role of readers. Readers actively construct images, savor the effect of the language, form opinions, make connections, and pause to reflect; they do this as part of an active search for meaning and personal connection. They are not passive recipients of the information or ideas in a text.

This means that we abandon the notion that there is one correct interpretation of a story or poem. Since readers have different expectations, life experiences, cultural backgrounds, and experiences with literature, they will construct different meanings from reading a text, meanings that are personal to them. Thus, our emphasis should shift from examining a meaning that supposedly resides in the text to examining the many meanings that readers construct as they transact with text. It is this view of reading as a transaction that forms the philosophical basis for the instructional practices we espouse in this book.

Rosenblatt's ideas further imply that we should view response from a broader perspective by encouraging children to use both efferent and aesthetic stances. In particular, the aesthetic stance is often neglected in schools (Rosenblatt, 1995). We must encourage our students to take an aesthetic stance when reading, "savoring the images, words, actions, associations and feelings" (Rosenblatt, 1995, p. 271) evoked by the reading experience. Rosenblatt did not address the critical stance, but we would encourage our students to respond from this perspective as well.

Additionally, children should have opportunities to reflect more deeply on their reading through varied response strategies. There are many ways to encourage and support children's thinking about stories. Many of these can be done immediately after reading to capture initial thoughts and feelings. This might take the form of writing (typically in literature journals or blogs), drawing, and discussion. Or they can be invited to savor and reflect over time through sustained activities that are memorable and engaging, such as drama, discussion, art, or those using technology. Responding in varied, thoughtful ways helps make their responses become more authentic, richer, and more informed. And children are also more likely to become engaged with what they have read.

Supporting students as they respond from a critical stance is referred to as developing critical literacy. Teaching students to examine and question texts from a critical perspective is an essential part of raising students who can participate effectively in a democracy, the fundamental goal of which is equal opportunity for all citizens. So how can we move away from a curriculum that values conformity toward one that is more accepting of diverse ideas and cultures, thus leading to empowerment for all people? How can we teach our children—even young children—to be skeptical of underlying messages in books that might foster attitudes of bias and prejudice?

Lewiston, Leland, and Harste (2007) and Leland, Lewiston, and Harste (2012) proposed four dimensions in teaching critical literacy. The first is teaching in ways that "disrupt the commonplace"; in other words, challenging students to look at everyday life with a new lens by questioning what is accepted fact or tradition. Second, students are encouraged to investigate multiple viewpoints during reading and discussion to discern diverse perspectives, especially those less dominant and less heard. Following these investigations, classroom discussions focus on studying the power relationships within systems and questioning how these relationships can be transformed to promote democratic values. But conversation is not enough. In the final step, children are invited to consider multiple perspectives on an issue and develop an opinion and then encouraged to take action to effect change.

Critical literacy creates exciting opportunities in classrooms for students not only to improve their critical thinking skills but also to engage in meaningful conversations. For example, students can critically examine how history is portrayed in books such as *Johnny Tremain* (Forbes), which espouses a very pro-Patriot vision of the Revolutionary War, with a book such as *My Brother Sam Is Dead* (Collier and Collier), which shows that both Patriots and the British had positive and negative qualities. Or they might respond to a book based in more contemporary times, such as *Smoky Night* (Bunting) (a story set during the Los Angeles riots), in which the protagonist faces dilemmas that cause him to reexamine his beliefs about people from cultures different from his own.

Teachers can encourage reflective, critical responses to books by using purposeful language in book introductions that extends children's thinking about dilemmas, conflicts, and other aspects of a text as they read. Comments such as "What do you notice?," "Whose point of view is shown in the illustration?," "How might the illustrator have shown this scene differently?," or "Is there a different way to think about this situation?" can encourage thoughtful responses in which students consider different perspectives or question the status quo (Labadie, Wetzel, & Rogers, 2012).

Figure 2.6 includes some important questions that are helpful for supporting aesthetic, efferent, and critical responses. Not all questions apply to all texts. However, they are general enough to be applicable for many different genres and themes.

Tech Click

The Partnership for 21st Century Skills (2013) fuses core academic learning with four "Cs": Critical Thinking and Problem Solving, Collaboration, Communication, and Creativity and Innovation. All of these work hand-in-hand with critical literacy. In *Green Thumb* (Thomas), the middle-school protagonist, Grady, is a science genius who attempts to thwart the destruction of a rain forest. Project-based learning groups create a digital KWL concept web and form compelling questions to be researched using reputable online databases. The final product will demonstrate global awareness as well as next steps toward solving the dilemma posed by *Green Thumb*. Other titles and details are available in Clemmons and Sheehy (2011).

FIGURE 2.6 Questions to Support Stances

Efferent Stance

- Can you retell the story?
- Can you summarize the chapter or section?
- How does the author reveal character? What do they do or say that shows their personalities, opinions, and so on?
- What does the main character learn through the story or biography?
- How is the setting significant to the story or text?
- How does the author create suspense (or humor, pathos, and other emotions)?
- How does the author's style compare to other books he or she has written?
- How do the illustrations contribute to the story's meaning? What style of art is used? Is that style appropriate to the story? Is the design and layout of the book effective in presenting the content?
- Do you want to know more about this topic after reading the book?
- What facts do you now know about _____ (topic addressed in the text)?

Aesthetic Stance

- What did you think about the story or the information presented?

- What feelings did you experience as you read?
- Is there a particular part of the story or text that moved you that you would like to share?
- Did you wonder about anything in the story or text?
- Do you agree with the decisions the characters made? If you had the opportunity to talk with a character, what would you say about their decisions?
- What in the reading connects to your experience?
- Does this remind you of any other books, movies, or television programs you have read or seen?

Critical Stance

- Whose viewpoints are expressed? Whose are missing?
- What does the author want us to think?
- Whose voices are silenced? Missing? Discounted?
- How many perspectives are represented?
- What action might you take on the basis of what you have learned from reading this text?
- What might be the consequences of your actions for change, and who might be affected?
- What sources can you use to learn more about other perspectives, cultures, and beliefs?

Response, Engagement, and the Common Core State Standards

The Common Core State Standards for *Reading: Literature and Reading: Information Text* require students to develop skills of literary analysis, such as "reading closely to determine what the text says explicitly," "analyzing the structure of text," "determining central ideas of a text," and "interpreting words and phrases as they are used in a text as the basis for competence in reading." These are skills we associate with Rosenblatt's efferent stance as well as the formal criticism model of response. It is clear that efferent purposes—the ability to take away information related to the literary crafting of a text—are valued in the CCSS and that teachers are expected to ensure that students acquire these competencies.

In contrast, the Common Core State Standards document is essentially silent about the roles of aesthetic response, critical literacy, and engaged reading. These concepts are not easily measured, and this could explain why these important aspects of reading and response are not mentioned and possibly not valued.

We hope we have convinced you in this chapter (with its emphasis on diverse types of responses) and the previous chapter (with its emphasis on authentic teaching and learning based on what we know about children) that supporting students' aesthetic and critical responses as well as facilitating engaged reading are important teaching and learning strategies. We need to be sure that we are not neglecting the "heart or passion or wonder" (Heard, 2011) that are such critical qualities of enthusiastic, lifelong readers. Thus, we contend that encouraging students to respond aesthetically or critically, becoming strongly connected to what they read, can actually undergird the more efferent understandings advocated in the Common Core State Standards document.

Although the Common Core State Standards document does not explicitly address aesthetic response, teachers have the opportunity—indeed, the obligation—to encourage their students to initially respond from this stance. The document clearly states that "standards are not the only thing needed for our students' success." It is expected that teachers will continue to devise lesson plans and tailor instruction to the individual needs of the students in their classrooms, taking charge of their teaching.

Thus, we believe it is imperative that you remain committed to fostering these more personal responses in your classroom. Teachers must ensure that their students have opportunities to respond personally to stories and texts and become deeply interested in what they read before they are asked to complete activities requiring them to "analyze," "interpret," or "closely examine text meaning." Essentially, we want students to first connect with text and then be motivated to learn through text (Long, 2011). This is what we mean by authentic, appropriate practice for teaching reading with literature.

This is a crucial time for teachers. If we believe that it is in the best interests of our students to first become passionately engaged with books as the basis for successfully acquiring the competencies mandated by the Common Core State Standards, then we must believe that we have the freedom to confidently and tenaciously create such a curriculum. Standards do not dictate how teachers must support student learning. They only provide guidelines for what the final learning outcomes should be. It is our responsibility to implement a curriculum that addresses both academic competencies and committed readers.

Opportunities for Children to Respond to Books

Students become more thoughtful readers when they have opportunities to think about books and then express those thoughts in ways they find personally satisfying. Sometimes, this means just savoring a book without being compelled to "do" anything with it. Response does not always have to involve an activity that results in some identifiable or quantitatively assessed product, although there is a place for more academically based responses. Rather, it can be a thoughtful comment, sharing of joy with a peer, or a recommendation to someone—"You gotta read this book. It's awesome!" There's an old saying: "Some books should be tasted, others to be swallowed, and some few to be chewed and digested" (Francis Bacon, 16th-century British lawyer and philosopher in *Of Studies*). We heartily endorse this sentiment. Therefore, we must not overdo requirements to respond to every book read by students. This is not easy in an age of standards and accountability. However, it is critical if we are to help children become engaged readers.

Maybe you may remember that the only way you were allowed to respond to books was writing a book report. Maybe you knew children who completed the assignment by reading the book jacket, writing a quick summary, adding a one-sentence opinion, and turning it in—all without ever reading the book. We think this still happens far too often, and it is counterproductive to our goal of nurturing thoughtful, enthusiastic responses to literature. Consequently, we recommend you do away with traditional book reports or at least revise this activity to make it more meaningful. For example, you might consider having students sign up as an online book reviewer, providing the opportunity to write and polish a piece for a real audience. (Student reviews should be published with initials or pseudonyms for protective reasons.) *Stone Soup*, *KidPub*, and *Launch Pad* also publish student-written book reviews.

Be wary also of commercially produced literature response packets and activity sheets. Providing 50 questions, 10 vocabulary words, and 14 extension activities for a picture book such as Eric Carle's *The Very Hungry Caterpillar* (an actual commercial product) will destroy children's engagement with this delightful book. Scrutinize such materials carefully and use them only as guidelines for starting discussions or as general prompts for journal writing. Do not substitute published materials for your own teacher judgment and response ideas.

Let's now look at the various activities you can use to stimulate both spontaneous and sustained responses to books. All are intended to take students back into a text, extending, enlarging, and challenging their original responses so they grow in their ability to appreciate the crafting involved in creating a great book. In this section, we suggest some general types of response activities. Specific variations within each general activity type are addressed throughout the rest of the book in each of the genre chapters. We suggest that you also encourage students to come up with their own ideas. This will further support your goal of nurturing individual responses to literature.

Writing

Through writing, students can record both initial and subsequently more thoughtful responses to books. Writing provides a permanent way to record thinking as they clarify their understandings, form opinions, and raise questions about their reading. Often, writing in response to books is shared with peers in discussions (such as during literature circles), in writing groups, or with the teacher in a private conference. The response of these listeners to what is shared then shapes and extends the writing. Following are some typical ways elementary and middle grade children can respond to books through writing.

Literature Response Journals or Blogs. Response journals or online blogs are a repository of wonderings, wanderings, speculations, questions, and elaborated thoughts recorded during and/or after reading (Hancock, 2008). Some teachers give children the freedom to write whatever they want about a particular book, whereas others provide general prompts. However, be careful about requiring your students to answer a lengthy list of questions day after day. One child we know read *Hatchet* (Paulson) in middle school. Every night, the boy had to complete a three-page handout of vocabulary and comprehension questions about this coming-of-age novel. Picking up her son's copy of the book, the mother shared the many times she read this book to her sixth graders and everyone sat mesmerized. The middle schooler looked at his mother incredulously, disbelieving that other kids had actually liked the book. Somewhere in 10 sets of three-page handouts, the joy of this very engrossing book had been lost.

Over questioning a book in this manner will kill any true personal response and likely will cause children to dislike it. Instead, we suggest that you invite children to respond at regular intervals as they progress through the reading, noting their predictions, questions, observations, and other personal connections. This helps students remember their responses as the reading progresses while also providing teachers with a record of children's thinking and how their thinking changes over time.

Variations on typical literature journals include *dialogue journals*, where children and teachers or peers write back and forth to each other (often in letter or blog format); *character journals*, where readers pretend to be one of the book's characters, creating a series of journal entries from that person's perspective; and *retelling journals*, where students respond to a specific prompt following the reading (Werderich, 2006). This could also take the shape of Facebook pages.

Double-entry journals are divided into two columns. The reader records quotes, descriptions, events, and other intriguing elements on one side of the page and writes responses to these on the other side. In *sketchbook journals*, children incorporate drawings, charts, and other visuals into the written response. This works particularly well with young children who often need to create a visual image as a prelude to writing and with students who have difficulty expressing themselves in writing.

Written Conversations. Written conversations are characterized by an ongoing, thoughtful correspondence between students and between students and their teachers in which they comment on books they have read. Communication is done entirely through writing. Teachers usually begin this activity with writing mini memos—short letters that introduce and extend initial class work. Then students create responses to teachers and other students in partner dialogue journals, in "write-arounds" (extended written conversations done with small groups), and finally in online forums with students within and outside their own classrooms (Daniels & Daniels, 2013). Using this format allows everyone in a class to think and talk at once instead of one at a time, stimulating higher engagement and response opportunities. The strategy also capitalizes on student interest in the constant writing they do on social media sites.

Writing from Literature Models. Writing activities can also imitate the structure and format of a children's book. For example, children can create a research report on a topic following the format of a nonfiction book they have read (Kristo & Bamford, 2004; Robb, 2004), they can create a poem following the pattern of a favorite poem written by a professional poet, or they can imitate the stylistic techniques of a fiction or picture book writer in their own creative stories, to cite just a few examples. This helps them understand how authors craft their stories and deepens their understanding and awareness of the conventions of various genres.

Tech Click

Sign up for a free account on the Kerpoof or Storybird Web site. These engaging, safe sites allows children to create their own retellings or final chapters with drag-and-drop media. Extend its use with multiclass or multischool story collaboration.

Oral Responses

Responses evoked through informal oral language activities are some of the most common and earliest kinds of responses children exhibit. Comments during read-alouds, such as joining in on repetitive chants or clapping and singing to a beat, are very natural ways that young children, in particular, respond to a book. Children also spontaneously and enthusiastically make comments about their reading or books read aloud to partners or small groups of peers, sharing discoveries, insights, intriguing facts, or illustrations that catch their eye. Teachers should encourage sharing of spontaneous oral responses because these comments offer informative glimpses into children's thinking as their interaction with a book unfolds.

Teachers can also provide opportunities for students to respond orally in more structured and focused ways. Some typical activities follow.

Oral Retelling. Students have a natural affinity for telling stories to others. You have probably seen them at play, making up stories or retelling familiar tales to a classmate or caregiver. This is a valuable activity, particularly for younger children who are not yet adept at creating written responses. Through tellings and retellings, students learn and practice story structure and expand their oral language.

You can encourage this by creating dramatic play centers with puppets, felt board story sets, costumes, toys from popular stories, tape recorders, and props related to specific books and other story-related materials, along with literature books that have been read aloud to the children. Some teachers have a large container in their room full of old hats, scarves, costume jewelry, sheets, tablecloths, shawls, headbands, masks, and other items from people's closets. Students can use these materials as props to help them convey their story.

You can also provide time following read-alouds, shared reading, guided reading, and literature circles for more teacher-directed retellings. This strategy is a significant change from the recall questions typically used by teachers in the past, as it provides opportunities for students to create personal meaning regarding what they have read. In *Read and Retell*, Brown and Cambourne (1987) suggest that teachers engage students in retelling and summarizing text using writing after a read-aloud, a strategy they call "oral-to-written retelling." Students are asked to first orally retell with teacher feedback and prompting and then asked to record their verbal thoughts in writing. This form of retelling is appropriate for all ages of readers and can incorporate drawing into the oral and written responses.

"Say Something". "Say Something" (Harste, Short, & Burke, 1988) is another way children can respond orally to books. It works best with texts that can logically be divided into sections without destroying the continuity of the story. In this strategy, readers read a certain amount of text and then say something to their partner about what was read. These can be predictions, images evoked by the story, questions, connections to their lives, feelings evoked, and so on. Subsequent sections are read in the same way. Once the full reading is completed, students can come together as a class and share their perceptions and understandings with the group. This idea can be adapted to use with Book Buddies, in which an older student reads aloud to a younger one and the two discuss the reading as it progresses.

Book Talks. Students can share "teasers" about the books they have read. Book talks can involve reading aloud favorite passages, hinting at an exciting part, pointing out interesting illustrations, or providing an enthusiastic personal recommendation. Usually, the book talker does not give away the ending because the main purpose is to encourage their peers to read it. Sometimes students dress as a book character or use a prop to help with their talks. A book talk can also be shared in a similar manner while still reading a book.

Book Discussions. Discussions about literature or "grand conversations" (Peterson & Eeds, 2007) is a classroom activity in which students talk together about books. These large- and small-group discussions allow students to share their thoughts about books in a more structured context. During these conversations, children build on each other's ideas, extend their own thinking, and develop richer, more informed responses through talk. Chapter 3 provides extensive information on book discussions.

Choral Speaking. Choral speaking can be done at any age level and with various size groups. It can range from joining in on a repeated refrain from a book read aloud to a four-part reading of a poem. The benefits of these activities are many. Students learn much about interpreting literature as they consider various alternatives for planning their performances. They must closely read and reread, trying out various ways to put words into lines, movements, and interpretations until they find the performance combination that is most appropriate for conveying the meaning of the poem. They also learn how to negotiate and cooperate as they work together to create their reading. Most important, they get the opportunity to savor the rhythms and sounds of language. Since poetry is the most commonly used main genre for this strategy, we discuss specifics for doing choral speaking and poetry performance in Chapter 5.

Tech Click

Podcasting

Podcasting is "basically the creation and distribution of amateur radio" (Richardson, 2010, p. 112). Blogs, wikis, and podcasts are powerful Web tools for classrooms that can be used with all ages of students. For example, we have seen second graders work independently writing, planning, and producing weekly podcasts. Podcasts could also be used for retelling and book talk strategies discussed above.

Tech Click

Recording Performances

Drama and choral speaking performances can be captured with a digital camera. Students could collaborate in producing a movie (iMovie or Windows Movie Maker are free), and in this way plays and poetry can be shared with others or preserved for a digital portfolio. Educators could select one of the videos from the FavoritePoem.com Project as an example. Copyrighted poems should not be posted on the Internet, but original poems could be performed and uploaded to TeacherTube (tagging it "children's poetry") with appropriate school and parental permission. Claymation is a related option for students who want to learn a technique that melds stop-action images with video production.

Drama

Drama activities enhance comprehension and support deep response to what has been read. When students act out the events of a story, many word and sentence meanings, as well as nuances of character, setting, and theme, become clear. Children also tend to identify more closely with characters, and themes are better understood as they work together to re-create a story through drama. The repeated readings that naturally occur as a drama unfolds provide opportunities to develop reading fluency. Furthermore, learners of all abilities can participate in dramatizations, particularly those who have strengths in kinesthetic learning.

Creative or "process drama," the form of drama frequently used for response to literature, often evolves out of spontaneous retelling and storytelling. Often, a quick scene is created to explore a character's dilemma, re-create a favorite folktale, or reread a favorite section of a novel. A finished, polished performance can evolve from a process drama activity. Typically, however, the performance aspect is less important than informally helping children explore stories from multiple perspectives and articulate more thoughtful responses to the book. Children who learn best through physical activity particularly enjoy interacting with books in this way. Following are some recommended ways you can use drama to develop students' responses to literature. The drama strategy you select for use in your classroom depends on the text and what aspects of the story you wish to explore with your students.

Puppetry. Children enjoy using puppets to play out a story. Shy children, in particular, can gain much from the opportunity to retell or create stories while hidden behind a puppet stage. As in other creative drama activities, emphasis should be on creatively acting out a story rather than preparing a formal script.

Students use a large cardboard box for puppet shows, dramatic book responses and even reading spots.

Puppets work well with many genres, although they are particularly effective with folklore and picture books. Selected stories should be short with clear, simple action. It helps to have just one or two main characters to make it easier to manipulate the puppets. Settings and extra objects should be kept simple. While these elements add an appealing visual component, using too many can be confusing to young puppeteers. When preparing a story for puppet performance, it helps to create a story analysis chart of characters, action, and necessary props so that children focus on the main story elements and do not get sidetracked by extraneous details.

Students should be encouraged to "play" their stories several times; this will set the story in their minds. Formal scripts are not necessary and can actually inhibit the flow and spontaneity of the telling. Children then can add puppets, props, music, and other elements to the now familiar story. Puppets can take many forms, from simple shadow and paper bag shapes to more elaborate rod puppets with movable parts.

Folktales, fables, short legends, and learning stories are especially good for creative dramatization and puppet shows because of their simple plots, straightforward characterization, use of repetition, and brevity. Figure 2.7 lists some appropriate stories from traditional literature that work particularly well for dramatization activities.

Storytelling. Storytelling is an excellent way to heighten student interest in books, particularly for stories from traditional literature. Because traditional tales arose from the oral tradition, oral storytelling is a perfect medium for sharing this genre, although short, exciting stories from other genres, such as nonfiction books or historical fiction, can also be adapted for this activity. Not only does storytelling allow for face-to-face, more intimate contact, but the story can be paced and modified to fit the particular audience. Difficult vocabulary and plotlines can be explained and audience participation encouraged.

Selecting the right story is important. Sometimes it helps to begin with family or community stories the children have collected themselves because these are memorable and thus easy to remember. Professional storytellers Hamilton and Weiss (2005) suggest that children begin by telling jokes or short riddle stories, narratives they have created for wordless picture books, or short tales, such as those found in *Stories to Solve* (1985), *More Stories to Solve* (1990), *Still More Stories to Solve* (1994), *True Lies* (1997), and *More True Lies* (2001). Gradually, they can move to more complex stories. These should feature short, simple plots; a minimal number of memorable characters; and predictable action that leads to a logical climax. Repeated phrases and refrains are also helpful because they are easy to remember. Above all, children should love a story before committing to learn it. It sometimes helps if they read several stories, then list their top three to four favorites before choosing a final one.

FIGURE 2.7 Traditional Literature Suitable for Dramatizations and Puppet Show

(Books with significant culturally diverse elements are marked #.)

Aesop. *Aesop's Fables* (Lisbeth Zwerger, Illus.). (P, I)

#Bruchac, Joseph. *Pushing Up the Sky: Seven Native American Plays for Children* (Teresa Flavin, Illus.). (I, M)

Child, Lauren. *Goldilocks and the Three Bears.* (P)

#Demi. *Liang and the Magic Paintbrush* (P); *The Empty Pot.* (P)

#dePaola, Tomie. *The Legend of the Bluebonnet.* (P, I)

#Goble, Paul. *Buffalo Woman.* (I, M)

#Fredericks, Anthony. *American Folklore, Legends and Tall Tales for Readers' Theatre.* (I, M); *African Legends, Myths and Folktales for Readers Theatre.* (I, M); *Mother Goose Readers Theatre.* (P)

Katz, Leon. *The Greek Myths: Puppet Plays for Children from Ovid's Metamorphoses.* (P, I)

#Korty, Carol. *Plays from African Folktales with Ideas for Acting, Dance, Costumes and Music.* (M)

#Lester, Julius. *Sam and the Tigers: A New Telling of Little Black Sambo* (Jerry Pinkney, Illus.). (P, I)

Lobel, Arnold. *Fables.* (P, I)

#Martin, Rafe. *The Rough-Face Girl* (David Shannon, Illus.). (I)

#Perez, Elvia. *From the Winds of Manguito: Cuban Folktales in English and Spanish* (Victor Mora, Illus.). (M)

Sierra, Judy. *Fantastic Theater: Puppets and Plays for Young Performers and Young Audiences* (I, P); *#Multicultural Folktales for Feltboard and Reader's Theatre* (M); *#Nursery Tales Around the World* (P, I); *#Silly and Sillier: Read Aloud Tales from Around the World.* (P, I)

#Sierra, Judy, and Kaminski, Robert. *Twice upon a Time: Stories to Tell, Retell, Act Out and Write About.* (P, I, M)

Wells, Rosemary. *Max and Ruby's First Greek Myths series* (P); *Max and Ruby's Midas.* (P)

Willard, Nancy. *East of the Sun and West of the Moon: A Play* (Barry Moser, Illus.). (I, M)

#Winther, Barbara. *Plays from Hispanic Tales: One-Act, Royalty Free Dramatizations for Young People from Hispanic Stories and Folktales.* (P, I, M)

Once students have selected stories to tell, they must learn them. Tell students that it is not necessary to memorize a story word for word. In fact, this can inhibit the spontaneity and enthusiasm of one's retelling. Professional storytellers typically do not tell a story the same way twice; the same thing is true for novices. Sometimes, it helps to create a story map to help remember the most significant aspects of the story (what Hamilton and Weiss [2005] call its "bones"; p. 56). Students should be encouraged to tell their story to family members, friends on the bus ride home or on the playground, to a mirror—or to anyone else who will listen. Props are also sometimes helpful for supporting children's ability to remember a plot sequence as long as these aids are minimal and relate to the main elements of the story.

Another storytelling strategy is symbolic story representation. In this activity, students make simple hand-drawn icons or bring in small objects that symbolize the characters. When students, especially older, struggling readers, retell the story using these visual symbols, it helps them be more engaged with the story, providing "a means for experiencing what it means for a reader to enter, create and participate in a story world" (Wilhelm, quoted in Christenbury, Bomer, & Smagorinsky, 2009, p. 191). This strategy helps students better understand the plot and characters.

Tech Click

"Storytelling Workshop" with storyteller Gerald Fierst has excellent tips for telling great stories. It includes quality examples as well as extensive suggestions for helping students expand their imaginations.

Pantomime. You can also have children act like a character or re-create a scene without using words. In this technique, the story is conveyed solely through gestures, facial expressions, or other body language. One student can pantomime while another student narrates. This strategy is most effective with short stories that students know well or with picture books. Tableau is a variation of pantomime. After reading a book chapter or other section of a book, small groups of students create frozen, or "tableaux," versions of what they read. The teacher touches each student in a tableau in turn. As each is touched, students, in the role of the characters, describe the thoughts going through their heads.

Reader's Theater. Reader's theater is an informal performance activity where students read from scripts that have been adapted from literature. Usually, the language of the story or poem is closely followed, although sometimes changes are made for smoother scripting and transitions. Lines are not memorized, and costumes are kept to a minimum. Little staging occurs. Rather, it is up to the readers to breathe life into the story through their interpretive reading. Reader's theater is sometimes handled like a radio play behind a screen or hanging barrier. It is popular with students and is known to be an effective strategy for developing fluency in readers, for struggling readers, and for English language learners.

Reader's theater works particularly well with poetry. Adding props, sounds, or movements to the reading of a poem can effectively enhance a characterization, a series of sounds, or images in a poem. For example, students in one classroom planned movement and sounds to accompany their reading of Myra Cohn Livingston's "Street Song" (in Moore, *Sunflakes*), a bouncy, rhythmical poem that celebrates eating potato chips. Part of the group chanted "ch, ch, ch" as the others read the words, everyone snapped their fingers to the beat, and one student walked rhythmically in front of the group while munching potato chips. Many verse novels and picture book collections that focus on poems from different characters' perspectives also work well for reader's theater performances. For example, Eloise Greenfield's *The Friendly Four* features four children who become friends over the course of the summer. Each child's voice is in a differently colored print font, facilitating a performance of the book. Andrea Cheng's *Where the Steps Were* includes poems written from the perspective of various children in a third-grade classroom. Children could take on the perspective of each character and "perform" the book.

Art and Music

Many students enjoy expressing themselves through art and music, creating a painting of a book's pivotal scene, finding music that fits a story's mood, or exploring the style of a favorite picture book illustrator, to name a few examples. Far from being "busywork," these activities require students to go back into the text, verifying that their artistic or musical representation reflects the characters, events, settings, and other elements in their response.

Artistic constructions, in particular, can serve as rehearsals for written and oral responses. Young children, in particular, often must create drawings or constructions before they can respond in other ways. If you allow young children to respond first through art, you may find that their subsequent written and oral responses are more thoughtful and more fully developed.

A well-stocked art center can be a wonderful catalyst for encouraging responses through art. Filling such a center with fabric, yarn, buttons, socks, paper-towel tubes, wire, various kinds of paints, styrofoam, egg cartons, pipe cleaners, empty plastic bottles, doilies, ribbons, glue, tape, stamps (for printing purposes), and miscellaneous objects found around the school or home (pinecones, grasses, packing foam, and so on) can stimulate creative artistic responses to books. Interesting papers, such as grocery bags, construction paper, tissue and textured papers, wallpaper samples, cardboard, oak tag, and cut-up packing boxes, can also stimulate children's imaginations.

Explorations of Illustrators' Media and Style. Students can learn much about the relationship between art and story when they explore the work of a favorite illustrator. With Eric Carle's *The Very Hungry Caterpillar* as an example, children can use watercolors or water-soluble acrylic paints to create decorated papers that are cut up and used to create collages. (Find the charming video of Eric Carle demonstrating his techniques.) Students can use doilies, rubber stamps with raised designs, tissue paper, and watercolors to explore Leo Lionni's style in *Swimmy* or *Frederick*. Other artistic media that children can explore in this way include scratchboard, marbleized paper, handmade paper stencils, and chalk. Titles for exploring various media used in picture books can be found in Chapter 4.

Comic Strips.   A useful and motivating artistic post-reading strategy is to have students create comic strips. Students fold a piece of paper into four frames, then draw any four consecutive scenes from the book or story. As in a real comic strip, readers can add speech balloons to indicate characters talking to each other. Free online and inexpensive software programs can allow for extensive editing by children and still result in a great-looking product.

Sketch-to-Stretch.   This artistic post-reading strategy is one created by individual students after reading a provocative, interesting text. Students are asked to "draw what the story means" to them. Developed at Indiana University (Leland, Lewiston, & Harste, 2012), this strategy enables readers to artistically express some aspect of a story, after which they are invited to orally share.

Response Through Music.   Some students will enjoy finding appropriate background music for dramatizing or reading a story aloud. Some books come with a CD or digital music (legally downloaded from the Internet) that can be played to convey a mood while the book is shared aloud or used to stimulate creative movement in response to a story. Children can also create their own songs and music, such as raps or ballads, or write variations on popular songs for presentations of stories or poetry.

Young children also enjoy singing, then creating new verses in the style of the rhyme for some of their favorite stories that are in the form of songs. Books such as *Oh, A-Hunting We Will Go* (Langstaff), *Down by the Bay* (Raffi & Westcott), *The Hokey-Pokey* (La Prise et al.), and *Mary Wore Her Red Dress* (Peek) are typical books that can be used for this activity.

Responding Through Graphic Organizers

Graphic organizers help students organize and synthesize their understandings and responses to books. A graphic organizer could be as simple as a story web created with crayon and paper or as complex as a free online app or a purchased computer program. *Inspiration* and *Kidspiration* are popular easy-to-use software for this purpose.

Teachers can create graphic organizers as part of a group brainstorming session during which children's ideas are recorded on a large chart or an interactive whiteboard. Alternatively, graphic organizers can be created in small groups, enabling students to benefit from classmates' ideas, compare notes about texts, and challenge each other's thinking. At the conclusion of the activity, each group shares their graphic organizer and explains their reasoning and representations to the class. Sometimes, art is added to extend understanding and increase the visual impact of the display.

You will see numerous ways to use graphic organizers with students throughout this book. Figure 2.8 lists descriptions of some of the most common ones.

Maps and Time Lines

Creating maps of a story setting and time lines of story events or the progression of a character's life are response activities that can make abstract concepts of time and space more concrete for children (Moline, 2011). For example, they can create a map of a character's journey in a historical book or a map of an imaginary land in a fantasy story. They can construct a time line of an individual featured in a biography or how a scientific concept evolved over time in a nonfiction text. These responses help children organize and synthesize their understanding of events and settings.

Tech Click

For geographically inclined students, creating a "Lit [Literature] Trip" with Google Maps would be an exciting book response. See Chapter 9.

Controversial Issue: Are Response Activities Appropriate in the Standards Era?

In this chapter, we have shared many activities that can support responses that children make to the books they read. Research conducted over several decades affirms the viability of active response activities as playing a significant role in supporting critical thinking and generating multilayered interpretations of literature (e.g., Hancock, 2008; Lohfenk, 2006; Long & Gove, 2003; Martens, Martens, Croce, & Maderazo, 2010; Short, Kaufman, & Kahn, 2000; Sipe, 2000, 2002; Whitin, 1996, 2005). Anecdotal evidence from teachers supports this evidence.

However, with the current pressure to obtain high scores on standardized tests, conform to mandated curricula, and teach to standards, some experts contend that such activities are frivolous: how can we justify time devoted to art or drama activities, they say, when we must prepare students for accountability measures that largely require them to read short passages, then respond to this reading through formal writing? For example, because students are not

FIGURE 2.8 Sample Graphic Organizers

Semantic maps. An idea, theme, or concept is placed at the center of the chart with spokes radiating to related words, ideas, or concepts from a text. Some children find writing easier if they web out an idea first. If using a digital program, a simple mouse click will change a web into an outline, making an easier transitioning to writing.

Word webs. A variation of a semantic map in which the concepts related to a particular word are explored and mapped. A key word is placed in the center of a chart and synonyms: definitions or key concepts are connected to the main word to create a weblike graphic.

Venn diagrams. Used to compare two books, characters, themes, or settings. Two overlapping circles are drawn on the chart. Children brainstorm how the two ideas being compared are alike and different. Common qualities are written in the area where the circles intersect; differences are written in the nonintersecting areas of each circle.

Comparison charts. A way to organize thoughts, and talk about several books or about several concepts related to one book. For example, children might compare and contrast books by one author. They might compare variations of one folktale, tracing similarities and differences among characters, action, and resolution of the story. Or, they might compare several biographies of a famous person by different authors.

Plot diagrams. Used to help children see how a plot is structured by charting out the initial problem, events, rising action, climax, and resolution of the story. This could look like a flowchart or diagram.

Story structure maps. These are similar to plot diagrams but also visually depict main and supporting characters, settings, themes, and other story elements.

A fifth grader's sample character map describing characteristics of the protagonist in *Escape from Mr. Lemoncello's Library* by Chris Grabenstein.

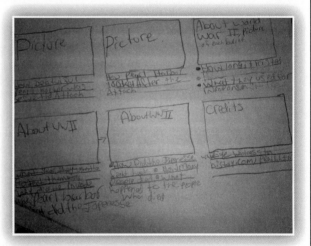

Students use a storyboard in preparation for recreating a movie about a nonfiction book.

tested on their ability to create an artistic piece that expresses a story's theme or their competence in planning a choral reading that demonstrates appreciation for figurative language, are we doing them a disservice if we spend time on more active but untested response activities?

Some support for response activities that use multimodal ways of thinking can be found in the Common Core State Standards. While the standards emphasize writing and discussion tasks as the primary ways students are expected to respond to books, the *ELA-Literacy: Speaking and Listening* Standards cite "visual displays," "multimedia presentations," and "orally reporting on what has been read" as ways to "clarify ideas, thoughts and feelings" in response to books (CCSS, pp. 24–25). Thus, the sample grade-level indicators for ELA-Literacy Standard 4 state the following:

SL.2.4. Tell a story or recount an experience with appropriate facts and relevant, descriptive details, speaking audibly in coherent sentences.

SL.4.4. Report on a topic or text, tell a story, or recount an experience in an organized manner, using appropriate facts and relevant, descriptive details to support main ideas or themes; speak clearly at an understandable pace.

SL.5.4. Report on a topic or text or present an opinion, sequencing ideas logically and using appropriate facts and relevant, descriptive details to support main ideas or themes; speak clearly at an understandable pace.

ELA-Literacy Standard 5 supports the use of visual and multimodal media displays to convey understanding of what has been read, as the following sample grade-level indicators show:

SL.1.5. Add drawings or other visual displays to descriptions when appropriate to clarify ideas, thoughts, and feelings.

SL.3.5. Create engaging audio recordings of stories or poems that demonstrate fluid reading at an understandable pace; add visual displays when appropriate to emphasize or enhance certain facts or details.

SL.5.5. Include multimedia components (e.g., graphics, sound) and visual displays in presentations when appropriate to enhance the development of main ideas or themes.

Clearly, to some degree, the Common Core State Standards recognize the importance of diverse responses to books.

We believe that providing time, advocacy, and opportunities for students to share ideas and understandings about books through movement, talk, writing, drama, online social media, and the arts in ways that are personally engaging and satisfying is critical to helping children respond in richer, multilayered, complex ways. Providing choice in the mode of response builds on pleasure and understanding as children use their preferences for social, kinesthetic, or musical modes of expression to communicate their thoughts and ideas. Not all children learn best through formal writing or discussion experiences. Many need to create a dramatic enactment or construct a graphic organizer of the information first before writing a response commentary or participating in a discussion. Indeed, some children might need to employ an artistic, dramatic, or musical medium as the primary way they respond to a story.

We do need to ensure that any response activities children pursue take them back into the book for a closer look at its structure, literary elements, information, or other elements. Too often, we have seen activities that move students *away* from a book to explore personal feelings or to complete an activity with only tenuous connection (e.g., visiting the zoo after reading a fictional story about gorillas, such as *The One and Only Ivan* [Applegate]). We hope that they will dig deeper rather than move beyond. Additionally, the book on which any activity is based should be worthy of such scrutiny.

Finally, we recommend that response activities be used judiciously, with careful attention to selecting the most salient activities that help students explore the notable aspects of a book while also developing their competence in the Common Core State Standards relevant to their grade level. Variety is important. No single way to respond will be enthusiastically pursued by all students, nor do we advise using the same response activities with many books over time.

Keeping these principles in mind will help us accomplish the goals of meeting our students' individual needs and response preferences, shaping their understandings of how texts work, developing their intellect, and enriching their lives. We are also meeting our responsibility for preparing them to successfully negotiate the demands of national accountability measures.

Summary

Our goal throughout this chapter has been to acquaint readers with the importance, depth, and scope of reader response and engagement, then showing how theories of response and engagement can mesh with the Common Core State Standards.

- Reader response is the engaged interaction that occurs in the minds of readers when they experience literature. This interaction is influenced by the factors of reader, text, and context. Readers bring their experiences, interests, preferences, level of development, and literacy skills to response. Characteristics of texts such as genre, text difficulty, and content can also influence response. Contextual factors such as peers, teacher attitudes and expectations, and room organization are also critical factors.

- Theories of response include the generic perspective, formal criticism, intertextual criticism, and transactional response. Transactional response theory regards the interaction between text and reader as critically important in constructing meaning and ultimately response to literature. This theory describes efferent and aesthetic response as stances that readers assume to achieve their purposes for reading. The critical stance is a way readers approach text to examine text for sociopolitical purposes.

- Teaching from a transactional perspective means that teachers must recognize and support the active role of readers, allowing them choice in book selection and the ways they respond. It means that there is no one correct interpretation of a text. It also suggests that we should encourage children to take aesthetic, efferent, and sometimes critical stances when they respond to books.

- The Common Core State Standards do not mandate the methods teachers must use to help children meet the standards. Thus, we believe that teachers have the freedom to use pedagogically appropriate strategies that help students make memorable connections to literature.

- There are many active ways that students respond to books in thoughtful ways that also engage their interest. These include writing, oral responses, drama, art, music, construction of graphic organizers, maps, and time lines.

Questions/Activities to Invite Thinking, Writing, and Conversation About the Chapter

1. Recall the books that engaged you at various points in your life. Compare your book lists with peers. How are your preferences alike? Different? Do your preferences fit the patterns discussed in the chapter? What conclusions about book preferences can you draw from this activity?

2. Select a popular book appropriate for children in your intended licensure area. Examine online teaching guides for that book. Critique the activities, using questions like "How does each suggested activity help students respond more critically to the book?," "How does each suggested activity help students extend their understanding of the ideas, facts, concepts, or use of literary elements of the book?," "How does each suggested activity support students' aesthetic response to the book?," or "How will the suggested activities help students achieve the academic competencies in reading mandated by the Common Core State Standards?" How would you adapt the activities to achieve these purposes?

3. Plan a storytelling, creative drama, or choral reading of a book. Present the activity to your peers.

3

Strategies for Sharing Literature

This chapter provides you with some tools to teach in ways that meet the mandates of the CCSS while also supporting children in becoming thoughtful, passionate readers who consider reading essential to their lives. As we discuss instructional strategies that feature literature, we address the following questions:

- What is close reading? How can we support students as they learn to study complex texts?

- How can we balance close reading with the goal of developing passionate readers?

- What are interactive read-alouds? How can we implement read-alouds that develop a love for reading and an understanding of how texts are structured or how information is conveyed?

- What is shared reading? How can we develop shared reading lessons that support student awareness of print as well as the ability to re-create text meaning?

- What are literature circles? How can we plan for and implement literature circles that help students develop and practice their ability to respond thoughtfully to books, communicating their ideas orally, artistically, and in writing?

- How can students develop their ability to read and respond to texts independently through reader's workshop?

We also discuss the critical issue of book selection, particularly the effect of censorship on the books we use with our students.

Although we present each strategy separately for better clarity, it is likely that you will integrate multiple strategies as you orchestrate daily literacy experiences for your students. As a professional, you will have the knowledge to determine which strategy works best for a particular purpose. Is your intent to model how to respond thoughtfully to books? Then you might model close reading during an interactive read-aloud or reading strategy lesson. If you want students to develop their own repertoire of reading and response strategies, then you will implement literature circles or reader's workshop.

Several teachers gathered for lunch on a steamy summer day. They had been asked to share their reactions to the Common Core State Standards (CCSS) and the implementation of these standards in their districts. Their enthusiasm was contagious. "I've been doing these things [the skills described in the CCSS] all along," said Peggy who teaches in a parochial school. "Now I can be supported and trusted in my work." Sharon, a lead teacher for literacy in her district, agreed. "The CCSS are going to allow us to do what is best for kids. Now we have the law behind us," added Stella, a teacher of English language learning (ELL). "I've heard people criticize what the CCSS doesn't have but I think we should celebrate what the Standards do require: more sophisticated reading and writing." Sharon agreed, "There is going to be more thinking about texts, more intentional book selection and better scaffolding to help students read harder texts." As an ELL teacher who works with students across several grade levels, Stella also appreciated the organization of the skills matrix. "This will help teachers understand how strategies progress across grade levels. We can better collaborate on how and when skills are taught."

Talk turned to some of the challenges of supporting students and teachers to meet the CCSS. "One of the biggest changes I see is that kids are going to have to learn how to think more intentionally and speak to evidence in the text," said Stella. Peggy agreed, "We will have to delve more into books and show kids explicitly how to have deeper conversations. Like when they make a text-to-text connection, they will now have to tell us what evidence they used to make the connections and how this connection helps us understand the story," added Sharon. They all agreed that teachers would need training and practice on how to teach in the new ways.

When asked how teachers can be helped to understand and embrace the possibilities of the CCSS for guiding students to become thoughtful, passionate readers, everyone agreed this was a chance for teacher empowerment. "This is a great opportunity for us to take responsibility and own the change ourselves," said Sharon. "We need our own book study groups and intentional conversations about teaching. Continuous conversations between teachers that are supported by the district will make a critical difference. It's not about individuals. It's about creating a teaching and learning community where teachers are reflecting on their work and transforming themselves. We need to question our practice; pushing ourselves to critically examine the Common Core State Standards, creating thoughtful lessons for our students, then seeking feedback about our work."

We do need to change our worldview of literacy teaching, taking ownership of a curriculum that supports the needs of our students. This curriculum should be informed by the Common Core State Standards (CCSS) but does not have to be controlled by them. It is an unprecedented opportunity for collaboration: teachers can connect with the best ideas being implemented throughout the country, going beyond their own classrooms and schools to engage in conversations about good teaching with colleagues across the country and the world. The 2012 National Teacher of the Year stated this succinctly in a speech to the National Education Association (NEA), "If we want real change, lasting change, if we want the power, the pride, the soaring achievement that is an exceptional public education, then the revolution begins with us" (NEA, 2012).

Close Reading

Close reading involves students in examining the deep structure of a text: how it is organized, the author's purpose in writing it, the writing style (including vocabulary and figurative language), its key details, arguments, and meanings (Fisher & Frey, 2012; Lapp, Moss, & Rowsill, 2012; McLaughlin & Overturf, 2013). When they are reading closely, students read a text several times, gaining new insights about various literary aspects with each subsequent reading. Teachers ask questions, or students ask questions of themselves to explore increasingly more complex text elements. Close reading can be done with both narrative and informational (nonfiction) texts with the emphasis for narrative texts on literary elements such as character, plot, and theme, whereas the emphasis for informational texts is typically on text structure, organization, and information conveyed.

The teaching of close reading strategies should not be limited to the early grades or English teachers. The CCSS document stresses that non–language arts educators must also be involved in teaching students how to read increasingly varied and complex texts. Cris Tovani (2004) analyzed the procedures good and poor readers use to comprehend text. She noticed that the most effective strategies were those in which students were strategic and interactive as they engaged with texts across various disciplines.

Close Reading and the CCSS

Instruction in close reading is mandated by the CCSS in the Reading: Literature and Reading: Informational Text (RI) Standard 1. The Anchor Standard 1 for Reading: Literature and Reading: Informational Text states the following:

> R.1 (Anchor Standard): Read closely to determine what the text says explicitly and to make logical inferences from it; cite specific textual evidence when writing or speaking to support conclusions drawn from text.

In grades K through 2, students are expected to ask and answer questions to key details in a text. This forms the foundation for more advanced skills required in the upper grades. We believe that kindergarten and primary students can also begin finding evidence in texts to support their answers if provided with sufficient modeling and support. Often, this is done collaboratively in group reading sessions. Beginning in grade 3, however, students are expected to independently analyze and reflect on what they read, providing text evidence for their opinions.

COMMON CORE STATE STANDARD FEATURE #1

Asking and Answering Questions About Texts, Referring to Explicit Evidence (CCSS.RL.1 and RI.1)

Following are sample grade-level competencies for Reading: Literature and Reading: Informational Text Standard 1, showing how this skill evolves:

RL. and RI.1.1.   Ask and answer questions about key details in a text.

RL. and RI.3.1.   Ask and answer questions to demonstrate understanding of a text, referring explicitly to the text as the basis for the answers.

> **RL. and RI.5.1.**   Quote accurately from a text when explaining what the text says explicitly and when drawing inferences from the text.
>
> **RL. and RI.7.1.**   Cite several pieces of textual evidence to support analysis of what the text says explicitly as well as inferences drawn from the text.
>
> While the Reading: Literature and Reading: Informational Text Standard 1 provide the rationale for close reading sessions, student competence in the other Reading: Literature and Reading: Informational Text standards can also be developed through the various types of questions that are asked in these sessions. Additionally, writing and discussion activities completed during close reading support the development of student competence in the Writing and Speaking and Listening Standards.

Key Elements of Close Reading Sessions

Fisher and Frey (2012) identified several key elements that contribute to successful implementation of close reading in K–8 classrooms. These include the following:

- Use of short passages drawn from complex texts
- Limited pre-prereading discussions
- Repeated readings
- Text-dependent questions
- Annotations

We will first discuss the use of each element, then provide an example of how all of them might be incorporated into a close reading strategy session.

Short Passages from Complex Text. Because students are asked to read a passage several times during close reading, we recommend using short passages ranging from a few paragraphs to just a few pages. Selected passages can be an excerpt from a longer text or a short "stand-alone" reading. The key element is complexity; the text should contain concepts, vocabulary, and meanings that are not immediately discernible to your students. Of course, complexity varies by grade level and individual student. Thus, for example, a complex text for first graders will likely be easily understood by third graders, although some third graders might struggle with that same text. More information on text complexity is presented in Chapter 2.

Limited Pre-Prereading Discussions. In the past, teachers often set a purpose for reading and conducted lengthy conversations about what students should expect to find in the text. Or they were directed to activate their own background knowledge about what would be read. Often termed "front loading," these activities were designed to help students make personal connections to a text to facilitate their understanding of it. The CCSS discourages these pre-prereading activities. (You will see later that we do not entirely agree with their opinion on this matter.) Rather, students are encouraged to learn how to make those connections themselves and take on the challenge of figuring out complex meanings without teacher assistance.

Some background building might be necessary to discuss key words that are not readily defined in context or if the text has an unfamiliar or particularly complex structure. However, any front loading in close reading sessions should not detract from the necessity to read the text and should not pull readers too far from the text into their own experiences, according to the CCSS (Fisher & Frey, 2012).

Repeated Readings. Text rereadings foster deeper understandings of the material. Questions that can be answered only through reading the text are posed for each subsequent reading. These questions relate to significant aspects of the text that the teacher believes are worthy of close scrutiny and are guided by the CCSS for a grade level. Questions are typically sequenced to move readers from literal to more inferential, higher-level thinking about text and relate to various competencies outlined in all the Reading: Literature and Reading: Information Text standards.

For example, the first reading of a fictional story with first graders might require them to answer questions about key details in a text (CCSS.RL1.1). A subsequent reading with this group might require them to use illustrations and details to describe characters, settings, or events (CCSS.RL1.7), or identify words and phrases that suggest feelings or appeal to the senses (CCSS.RL.1.4). Similarly, repeated readings of a book appropriate for fifth graders might focus initially on quoting from the text when explaining what is explicitly or implicitly stated (CCSS.RL.5.1). Subsequent readings might focus on determining a theme (CCSS.RL.5.2), determining the meanings of words and phrases as they are used in a text (CCSS.RL.5.4), or analyzing how visual or multimedia elements contribute to the meaning, tone, or beauty of a text (CCSS.RL.5.7).

Text-Dependent Questions. Text-dependent questions are central to close reading. As the name suggests, text-dependent questions are those that can be answered only by referring back to the text. Text-dependent questions usually are open ended; they have many possible answers. Students must return repeatedly to the text to find evidence—words, sentences, passages, illustrations—that supports their answer. So, for example, instead of asking, "What is the main character's name?," an effective text-dependent question might be "What do we know about the protagonist at this point in the story? Use evidence from the story to support your answer." When reading nonfiction texts, an appropriate text-dependent question might be "How did the author structure this text to make the ideas more understandable? How do you know?" Good text-dependent questions are genuine, designed to stimulate student thinking, and capture their interest. They also focus on aspects of text that the CCSS consider important for a particular grade level.

Annotations. "Reading with a pencil," the practice of making notes while reading, is a helpful way to keep track of one's thinking while rereading for specific purposes. It also scaffolds students' ability to contribute meaningfully to book discussions. Additionally, annotations can support writing in response to reading a text as proficient readers often consult their annotations as they create written commentary, arguments, and connections following a close reading session.

Students need to be shown how to use annotations effectively. Figure 3.1 is a suggested developmental sequence that appropriately supports student competence in using annotations for close reading.

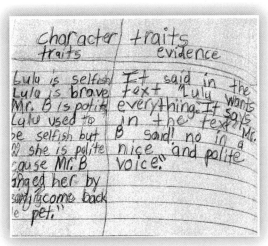

Annotation completed by a second grader documenting evidence for character traits in *Lulu Walks the Dog* by Judith Viorst.

Implementing Close Reading Sessions

There is not one agreed-on sequence for how a series of close readings should unfold. The sequence we suggest is a guideline that is designed to support your planning for sessions that purposefully and effectively scaffold student exploration of a text. You will also vary your sessions based on the specific literary aspects you wish to explore as well as the developmental levels of your students. The following is a sequence we have found useful. It emphasizes teacher questioning, modeling,

FIGURE 3.1 Developmental Sequence for Student Use of Annotations

Grade Level	Annotation Strategies	Annotation Tools
Kindergarten	Use enlarged, predictable texts to create collaborative notes about texts read aloud.	Mark key ideas with Wikki Stix or highlighter tape or highlight ideas in enlarged electronic text.
First	Mark significant aspects of text in personal copies. Compare markings with peers so as to develop understanding of what is useful and appropriate evidence.	Wikki Stix, sticky notes, highlighter tape, and so on to mark key ideas in print copies. Use electronic highlighting tools in electronic text.
Second and third	Record initial responses on sticky notes or other tools and underline key words and ideas or document aspects of text that are confusing directly on text being studied. Organize small-group discussions where students share their thinking and ability to find evidence in texts and support their opinions. Have students then share out in large group.	Writing tools, sticky notes, and comparable electronic tools.
Fourth through sixth	Model more complex annotations by enlarging a section of a grade-appropriate text and then affixing it to a larger paper so that a blank border exists. Show how to resolve confusion as one reads, generate questions, or find text evidence. In addition to marking sections that help students respond to text-dependent questions, ask them to record more in-depth responses, such as their own questions generated during reading, connections to other readings, or more advanced literary understandings. Use more abstract coding markings, such as question marks, arrows (to indicate connections), exclamation marks (to document new insights), and so on. Continue discussions in which students share their evidence and new questions generated while modeling for each other how to do close reading.	Writing tools, sticky notes, different-colored markers for different kinds of coding, and comparable electronic marking tools.
Seventh and eighth	Students should independently know how to annotate texts.	

Source: Adapted from Burke (2012), Fisher and Frey (2012), and Porter-O'Donnell (2004).

and guidance. However, we believe that students should be encouraged to take on increasing responsibility to initiate their own questions as they become more skilled with close reading.

In addition to the following sample sequence, Figure 3.2 suggests sample text-dependent questions at each step that are appropriate for narrative and nonfiction/informational texts.

FIGURE 3.2 Sample Questions for Close Reading Sessions

(It is assumed that Standards RL.1, RI.1, RL.10, and RI.10 are automatically covered in each close reading session. Additional Anchor RL and RI Standards addressed in various close reading sessions are indicated next to the relevant question. Standards for Speaking and Listening as well as Writing are covered in the various activities as well, although we have not delineated them here.)

	Narrative Text	Informational Text
First reading	What do we know about the characters? What evidence supports your conclusions? (RL.3) Where does the story take place? What clues does the author provide to help us know? (RL.5) Retell the story in your own words. (RL.5) What was the moral or lesson in the story? What evidence can you cite to make this conclusion? (RL.2)	What are the key ideas? What are the details that support the main ideas? (RI.2) What is one interesting fact you learned? How is that fact explained in the text? (RI.2) What is the meaning of _____ (key vocabulary word)? (RI.4)
Second reading	Compare two characters. How are they different/alike? Use examples from the text to support your opinions. (RL.3) Describe how the protagonist responds to _____ (major event in the story). (RL.3) Select words, phrases, and use of figurative language that affect the rhythm of the story. (RL.4) From whose point of view is the story told? How does this affect what you know about story events? (RL.6)	What is the most important concept in the text? Find evidence to support your opinion. (RI.2) Explain the relationship between two significant concepts. (RI.9) What is the point of view of the text? Is this perspective biased or neutral? Find examples to support your opinion. (RI.6)
Third reading	How does the author help us know the protagonist? Find specific examples of literary tools (conversations, descriptions, and so on) that help you come to understand that character. (RL.3) How did the author construct the plot to draw you into the story climax? Create a plot diagram that visually shows how the plot unfolds and how the author linked one event with another. (RL.5) How did the author use dialogue and language to enhance your understanding of the _____ (character, setting, plot, and so on). (RL.4) How does the author's use of words, phrases, and figurative language add to the meaning and rhythm of the story? Find examples of this skilled language used in the text. (RL.4)	How did the author help us understand key vocabulary? Find some key words and explore the techniques the author used to help us understand those words. (RI.4) Why did the author use a particular text organizational structure (compare/contrast?, chronological?) to construct this text? Why was this an appropriate structure for this text? (RI.5) Do you notice anything unique or interesting about the author's use of language? How did that add to your understanding of the text? Find examples from the text to support your opinion. (RI.4)

(continued)

FIGURE 3.2 *continued*

	Narrative Text	Informational Text
	How do the illustrations help readers understand the meaning of the story? List specific aspects of the illustrations. (RL.7)	How did the text features, such as illustrations, graphs, sidebars, glossary, and so on, help you understand the meaning? What are specific examples of these text features, and how specifically do they extend meaning? (RI.7)
Fourth reading	Why is the theme of this story significant? (RL.2) What life lessons is the author trying to convey? How do you know this? (RL.2) How do the themes/ideas/literary understandings relate to other stories we have read? (RL.9)	Why is the information in this text important? (RI.9) How does this text relate to other concepts/ideas we have learned about the topic? (RI.9) What was the tone of the text? How do you know? What evidence supports your opinion? (RI.7)

Source: Adapted from Burke (2012) and University of Pittsburgh Institute for Learning (2011).

First Reading: Focus on Key Ideas and Details. The purpose of the first reading is to get the general, literal meaning of a text. A first reading should be completed as independently as possible, although less able readers might need to read with a partner, participate in a group shared reading, or hear the text read aloud. Following this reading, students should share their initial thinking and responses in pairs or small groups as well as the whole class.

Second Reading: Focus on Discerning Significant Literary Aspects and Ideas. During the second reading, students can be asked to identify specific aspects of text that are significant to the overall meaning. For fiction texts, for example, this might be a pivotal plot point, an important revelation about a character, or the central theme. For nonfiction text, students might be asked to state the most significant concepts or identify key vocabulary that supports understanding of important information. As students discover these elements, they are expected to identify evidence from the text that supports their opinions and responses. Annotations help record their thinking for later sharing with others. Opportunities for sharing allow students to compare responses, thus extending their understanding of a text's meaning and the evidence that supports a reader's understanding of that meaning.

Third Reading: Focus on Author's Craft and Text Structure. Students read to answer questions focusing on the author's writing, determining how the choices made in crafting the text influence the overall meaning. Thus, teachers might ask students to focus on how the author uses descriptive or figurative language to create meaning, develops a memorable character, or makes complex ideas understandable. As with the previous readings, students are encouraged to use annotations as a way to record their thinking and the evidence that supports their thinking.

Fourth Reading: Interpretation and Synthesis. Sometimes a fourth reading will occur if the text is complex enough and students are ready for a deeper analysis. Text-dependent questions at this point should stimulate diverse responses, intrigue students, and facilitate understanding of the most complex ideas or literary elements. While additional evidence might be gathered from the text, it is also expected that students will have developed their own opinions and responses to the complex ideas discussed during a fourth reading. They might do some additional annotating at this point but may also synthesize the information from their previous annotations.

Cautions Regarding Close Reading

Close reading sessions can be highly effective in helping students develop competence in discerning how texts are crafted and convey information. Students who possess these understandings ultimately have more informed, more enjoyable reading encounters. *However, we caution you not to overuse this strategy.* Insistence on analyzing and critiquing every text can destroy reading enjoyment. Close reading is a mental process for accessing complex texts; it is not appropriate for all books.

Rather, we suggest that you integrate the strategies involved in close reading in demonstrations, modeling, and guided conversations. For example, in the following sections of this chapter, we discuss other teaching strategies, including interactive read-aloud, shared reading, literature circles, and reader's workshop, all of which use literature at the heart of their approaches. The strategies used in close reading can undergird but should not mandate what occurs in other literature-based reading activities. You might model close reading strategies in read-alouds. You would model and then expect students to practice using close reading strategies during literature circles or while planning a dramatic presentation. You would likely expect students to use close reading strategies independently during reader's workshop.

We also believe there is some value in the practice of background building before teachers ask students to read a text. This is particularly true for younger students who are not yet independent readers and students experiencing reading difficulties. Additionally, some texts might feature complex vocabulary, concepts, or structures that might be difficult for students to successfully comprehend (Beck, McKeown, & Kucan, 2013). Teachers have been successfully scaffolding student reading through background building for decades, and there is significant research supporting this practice (Block & Parris, 2008; Block & Pressley, 2002; Dole, Valencia, Greer, & Wardrop, 1991; Langer, 1984; McKeown, Beck, Sinatra, & Loxterman, 1992; Stevens, 1982; Tovani, 2004; Vaughn & Linan-Thompson, 2004).

Consequently, we do not recommend completely abandoning the strategy of building background before reading. It is a delicate balance: teachers want students to learn to access texts for themselves without assistance. When faced with a challenge, one of the best ways to work through it is to engage, interact, and work through the challenge. However, we do not want students to experience insurmountable obstacles. Thus, we believe that there may be instructional situations where background building is appropriate.

 # Interactive Read-Aloud

Reading books aloud to children is one of the most satisfying and pleasurable aspects of teaching. Your own experiences hearing books read aloud may have been when you were very young or in the primary grades—years that are critical for helping children love books. However, hearing a good book read aloud is something we never outgrow. Reading aloud needs to happen every day for every student at all grade levels. It is that important. In fact, there is a high level of agreement, based on considerable evidence, that the act of reading aloud is "the most foundational piece of a comprehensive literacy program" (Anderson, Hiebert, Scott, & Wilkinson, 1985; Santoro, Chard, Howard, & Baber, 2008). Author Aiden Chambers (1996) said it perfectly:

> Reading aloud to children is essential in helping them become readers. And it is a mistake to suppose that reading aloud is only needed in the early stages (the period people tend to call "learning to read") . . . it has such value, and learning to read is such a long-term process, and the bit we call "learning" such a small part of it, that *reading aloud is necessary all through the school years.* (p. 49)

Jim Trelease, the author of *The Read Aloud Handbook* (2013), considers reading aloud as "seed money": children who experience read-alouds are more likely to read to others and become readers as adults. In the following sections, we discuss how read-alouds can nurture literacy skills, such as knowledge of book language, vocabulary, and complex text structures; develop listening comprehension; provide exposure to many genres and books that children might not select on their own; and ignite a passion for reading (Fisher, Flood, Lapp, & Frey, 2004).

Interactive read-aloud experiences expose children to advanced language structures and rich vocabulary (Barnes, 1992; Lapp & Flood, 2003; Pinnell & Jagger, 2003). Book language differs from spoken language, and the nuances of well-constructed book language come alive when shared aloud. Reading aloud exposes developing readers and writers to these words, thus increasing their vocabulary (Rasinski, 2003). Descriptive phrases, onomatopoeia, alliteration, rhyme, clever wordplay, and dialogue can also be celebrated through reading aloud. As popular children's author Will Hobbs tells us,

> Read alouds are pure magic when you pick a book and read it dramatically for the whole class. Kids need to hear the written word read dramatically to develop and to continually improve their inward ear, so when they turn to their own silent reading, they will model the expression you use. (personal communication, September 1999)

The language development benefits of reading aloud are particularly relevant for English language learners (ELLs). ELL students who hear books read aloud will reap important benefits, including an appreciation for the range of English sounds, sentence structures, vocabulary, and inferential meanings (Britton, 1993), particularly when teachers use gestures and facial expressions while reading. The language skills of ELLs further develop as they participate in conversations during the read aloud, taking cues from other students.

Another important benefit of reading aloud is the development of listening comprehension: the ability to attend to, understand, and retain what one hears. Today's students have weak listening comprehension skills due to a dearth of listening comprehension instruction (Opitz & Zbaracki, 2004). However, listening is a critical competency, and there is evidence that reading both narrative and nonfiction texts aloud to children can increase their listening comprehension skills, particularly if the read-aloud experience is accompanied by activities that ask children to respond to what they have heard (Kraemer, McCabe, & Sinatra, 2012; Morrow & Gambrell, 2002; Opitz & Zbaracki, 2004).

High-quality interactive read-alouds are also a great way to introduce, supplement, wrap up, and connect specific content-area lessons (Sibberson & Szymusiak, 2003). We recommend that teachers at all levels frequently read aloud picture books, parts of longer nonfiction texts, and other resources to scaffold student understanding of the information in a textbook, helping them access that material in a more accessible way. For example, teachers can create short general minilessons with picture books to demonstrate various aspects of the craft of writing or to increase students' knowledge about a science topic before studying it in more depth.

Additional more intangible benefits result from interactive read-alouds. They can ignite a love for literature. They can extend students' literary understandings and tastes. They can introduce students to new genres and demonstrate how readers respond to books in thoughtful ways so that they gain new insights into an author's crafting and meanings. Most important, read-alouds provide the opportunity to talk about important ideas and issues that are relevant for children's lives, to "identify dilemmas, pose solutions, revel in heroes" (Roser, 2010, p. 213).

As a result, teachers who frequently and interactively read aloud observe unintended but powerful and positive changes in their children. They may notice a seemingly disengaged student sharing a connection to a book for the first time or asking for a book by the same author to read at home. They observe students who are often inattentive becoming so engrossed with the read-aloud that they beg to hear "just one more chapter." They see a classroom community evolve as children experience emotionally bonding experiences, such as living through the traumas of Wilbur the pig in *Charlotte's Web* (White) or pondering immortality with Winnie in *Tuck Everlasting* (Babbitt).

Tech Click

Global Read Aloud is an online project in which books for various grade levels are selected for read-alouds and follow-up activities. Students then share their responses to the books with other classes around the world via Twitter, Skype, wikis, e-mail, blogs, or other electronic means.

Interactive Read-Alouds and the CCSS

Daily read alouds require thoughtful selection and careful planning.

Interactive read-alouds are effective for supporting understanding of many concepts delineated in the English language arts CCSS. For example, through read-alouds, teachers can model skills in the Reading: Literature and Reading: Informational Text Standards, such as how to identify themes and trace their development through a text (RL.2 and RI.2) and demonstrate how readers interpret words and phrases as they are used in texts (RL.4 and RI.4). They can show how good readers compare multiple texts (RL.9 and RI.9) or explain how to efficiently evaluate information (RI.8). Teachers can then provide opportunities for students to deepen their understandings of these strategies through their questioning during an interactive read-aloud session.

Interactive read-alouds also support students' developing skills in speaking and listening. According to Speaking and Listening Anchor Standard 1, "students must prepare for and participate in a range of conversations and collaborations with diverse partners, building on others' ideas and expressing their own clearly and persuasively." When interactively reading aloud picture books, competence in Speaking and Listening Anchor Standard 2 ("Integrate and evaluate information presented in diverse media and formats, including visually, quantitatively and orally") can be developed. Ultimately, they are expected to "contribute accurate, relevant information; respond to and develop what others have said; make comparisons and contrasts; and analyze and synthesize a multitude of ideas" (CCSS, p. 22).

Implementing Effective Interactive Read-Alouds

Good read-alouds do not just happen. Careful planning will ensure that your students get the most out of this vital experience. There should be planned, daily times when you and your students enjoy books read aloud simply for the pure pleasure of it. Thus, you need an established, daily time for pleasurable read-alouds that is considered sacred and does not get eliminated when pressures mount to "cover" other curricular objectives. Additionally, when children are waiting for an assembly, settling down after recess, or lining up for lunch, you can share spontaneous read-alouds using short stories, poetry, or brief pieces of traditional literature, such as fables and children's play rhymes.

The following section describes a research-based framework (Fisher et al., 2004) for selecting books and structuring the experience to guide your development of read-aloud sessions that takes advantage of all the benefits this teaching strategy has to offer.

Selecting Books for Read-Alouds. Librarian and teacher Judy Freeman (1995) suggests that teachers carefully select what she calls "books [that] will send kids reeling" (p. 4). Thus, in addition to considering a book's literary qualities, you should consider your students' interests, cognitive understandings, and previous experiences as well as your purposes for reading aloud. Figure 3.3 features suggestions for selecting books for read-aloud sessions.

Tech Click

Check out the numerous Web sites that provide lists of great read-alouds, including those hosted by Jim Trelease, Reading Rockets, Literacy Connections, and Good Reads. Connect online to author Mem Fox's Web site.

FIGURE 3.3 Selecting Books for Reading Aloud

- Share books you personally love and enjoy. That is one of the best ways to generate enthusiasm for books.

- Select enticing examples of books, including picture books from several genres so that students are exposed to a variety. Ask students to browse, select a few, and share why their choices intrigue them.

- Present book talks for three or four books. This should take about 30 minutes and might involve a prop related to the book, a synopsis that highlights intriguing aspects of the book, or a short, exciting section that ends in a cliffhanger. Let the group decide their favorite for the next read-aloud.

- Find books that elevate children's tastes and awareness of literary crafting while also connecting to their interests and life experiences.

- Find books with at least one memorable scene that lingers in one's mind, challenges students to think deeply and analyze a situation, or connects students to other cultures, races, and communities (Freeman, 1995).

- Find award-winning books. (See Appendix A for lists of awards.) These often feature challenging story structure, topics, and vocabulary, so be sure that you read them first to determine the appropriateness for your students.

- Ask parents for their favorites and read those aloud.

- Consult your school librarian, online links, and print resources.

Extra Yarn by Marc Burnett received the 2013 E.B. White Read Aloud Award as the year's best picture book for read aloud sessions.

A Suggested Read-Aloud Sequence. After you have selected a book (whether if be fiction or nonfiction), you should read it yourself so that you are familiar with the content and language. Then you need to think about the ideas, concepts, vocabulary, narrative structure, connections to other books, or other literary aspects you will discuss before, during, and after the read-aloud. Next, create intentional, ongoing questions that are designed to stimulate active response and engagement throughout the read-aloud. In addition to questions that provide opportunities for close reading, you should create questions that invite students to extend, clarify, and restate information. Additionally, you can encourage students to share personal reactions as well as relate concepts from the text to life experiences (Deford, 2003, p. 133).

You also need to plan for discussion of vocabulary that you believe students might not know that could potentially affect their understanding of the text. The words you select should be useful as well as interesting to students (Beck & McKeown, 2001). Words should be discussed as the reading progresses as well as following the reading when a more in-depth discussion of a word's meaning can occur (Beck & McKeown, 2001). This in-depth discussion might include connecting each word's definition to concepts already familiar to the children, sharing examples of how the word is used in various contexts, and asking children to actively use the words in conversations or subsequent academic activities (Beck et al., 2013). The words can also go on a class "word wall" for use in subsequent writing and discussion activities.

When you are ready to read, arrange students so that they can enjoy and benefit from hearing the read-aloud. When sharing a picture book, you must be able to show the illustrations to everyone. So you must consider whether you will hold it so that everyone can see as you read or whether you will read and then show the illustrations. Sometimes, this is a matter of style, but at other times, your purpose will dictate what you do.

Begin by engaging students as you introduce the book, tapping into their prior knowledge or encouraging them to predict the story content unless you are modeling close reading. You might want to have other related material available for developing background knowledge, such as maps, books on a similar topic, newspaper and magazine articles, photographs, or a prop.

For example, if you share a biography about Abraham Lincoln with young children you might introduce the book by showing a penny to the group and discussing whose picture is on it. Or you could create a group chart of all the things the children know about Lincoln and then add some lingering questions they have that might be answered in the subsequent read-aloud. With older students, you might first share photographs, letters, political cartoons, or other memorabilia about the era in which Lincoln lived. If reading a fiction book, you might ask students to share experiences they might have had that are similar to those described in the book or discuss other aspects of the book to help students connect it to their lives.

Then invite interaction during the read-aloud. Research done by Hoffman, Roser, and Battle (1993) indicates that all too often children are not asked to discuss or respond to read-alouds as the reading progresses. Their research shows that such discussions can deepen children's understandings and responses. So it is important to stop at various points to ask for comments, discuss an interesting vocabulary word, examine the literary elements, and pose questions. Or you can describe your own ideas and responses to the book, modeling how this thinking happens. Termed "think-aloud," this combination of questioning and modeling demonstrates how good readers think about texts and makes children more active listeners (Harvey & Goudvis, 2007; Szymusiak & Sibberson, 2001).

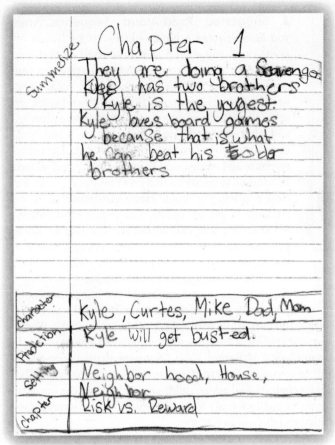

Example of a fifth grader's thinking recorded in a read aloud notebook.

Inviting responses after a read-aloud session is important for extending understanding and encouraging personal, aesthetic response as well as a closer examination of the book's literary qualities. It might be simply a query asking for reactions or an invitation for students to make connections to what they know or other books they have read. Or questioning can be more extensive, asking students to make judgments about the book's structure, the information presented, or how the author developed a particular character. A response could also include writing, artwork, or dramatic experiences that invite students back into the book. You can then revisit the book over several days, deepening students' understanding of plot, information, or vocabulary, depending on what is most relevant for that particular book.

Some teachers have students use *read-aloud notebooks* to record their thinking while listening to a story. These responses help them think about a text more critically and might include jotting down a list of key events, creating ongoing character webs, recording favorite quotes along with their response to those quotes, and other thinking. Teachers facilitate thoughtful comments in these journals by modeling their own thinking both orally and in writing. For example, teacher Karen Terlecky keeps a chart pad next to her during read-aloud time on which she demonstrates plot charts, character webs, and other strategies that support close reading of a story. Once the teacher has modeled a range of possible responses, it is helpful to have students share their notebooks with each other, along with an explanation of what strategies they chose to use and how that strategy helped capture their thinking (Terlecky, 2013).

Figure 3.4 is a sample read-aloud lesson plan for *Roll of Thunder, Hear My Cry*.

Shared Book Experience

Shared book experience, or "shared reading," is a kind of joyous, collaborative instructional reading activity in which students and teachers read selected texts aloud together, usually in enlarged format. Although shared reading provides instructional support from the teacher, the student's role is to also be a reader, actively engaging with the read-aloud experience at his or her developmental level.

During shared reading lessons with young readers, the teacher and a group of children sit close together to read and reread a book that all of them can see. Special enlarged texts, termed "big books," are often used for this purpose, but sometimes teachers take smaller texts and project them on the wall using a document camera or an interactive whiteboard. Because shared reading has its roots in work with young children, attention is focused here on that age-group. However, if the intent is to study and learn from a text together, shared

> **FIGURE 3.4** Sample Read-Aloud Teaching Plan: Chapter 1,
> *Roll of Thunder, Hear My Cry*
>
> *Synopsis:* This fictionalized family story takes place in 1930s Mississippi. In this chapter, readers learn that the African American family owns land—unusual for the historical era. The chapter opens with the African American children walking to school. A school bus of White children careens by and spills mud all over them. When they reach school, they suffer an additional indignity: the books they are given have been discarded by the White school.
>
> *Before Reading: Connecting to History.* Find photographs and other artifacts showing America during the Great Depression. Share these with children and discuss this era of American history. Discuss civil rights during this era, possibly sharing poetry by Langston Hughes, such as "Mother to Son" or "I, Too, Sing America." Locate the setting of the story on a map. Once students have preliminary background about this era and the story setting, ask them, "Based on the title *Roll of Thunder, Hear My Cry* and what you now know about this era, what do you think this book will be about?" Have the group start a prediction chart to record their predictions of story events. You could also share other fictionalized family stories, such as *Pink and Say* or *Katie's Trunk*, to introduce students to this type of fiction.
>
> Due to the length of chapter 1, reading of the chapter would probably be divided into two sections (pp. 1–10 and pp. 11–22).
>
> *Possible Questions to Ask as the Read-Aloud Progresses* (depends on student comments and questions)
>
> *Part I*
> - What does Papa mean when he tells Cassie the land belongs to her?
> - Listen to the description on page 5. What image does this give you of the setting? What are some of the words and phrases Taylor uses to evoke these images in your mind?
> - How did the children feel when they are splashed with mud by the school bus? What are some
>
> actions and comments they make that support your opinions? How do you think the children on the bus felt?
> - After reading the incident where T.J. boasts about lying, ask, "What kind of person is T.J.? How do you know?"
>
> *Part II*
> - Summarize what happened in part I of this chapter.
> - How would you feel if you were given textbooks like those provided to the African American children? How did Little Man, Cassie, and Mama react to being given textbooks that had been discarded by White children? What comments and actions made by the characters support your opinions? What do these actions/comments tell you about their personalities?
>
> *Possible Vocabulary to Discuss During Read-Aloud:* sharecropping (3) mortgage (3) raucous (3) emaciated (4) amiably (7) dubious (14) audible (15) penchant (15) temerity (16) imperiously (22)
>
> *Possible Questions/Activities Following Reading:*
> - What do you know about the characters of Cassie, Stacy, Little Man, and T.J. at this point in the story? Consider their words and actions.
> - Do you think the Night Riders were after the children? What evidence from the story supports your opinion?
> - How does the first-person narration by Cassie influence your understanding of the text?
> - Ask each child to predict what they think will happen next in their prediction journals. Share predictions.
>
> CCSS Standards addressed: Reading Literature Standards: CCRA.RL.1, RL.3, RL.4, and RL.6; Speaking and Listening Standard: CCRA.SL.1; and Writing Standards: W.1 and W.9.

reading is appropriate for students of all ages (Kristo & Bamford, 2004; Parkes, 2000). This is particularly true for modeling close reading strategies. Shared reading of an enlarged text (particularly poetry) can work well for modeling how readers locate evidence for answering text-dependent questions.

Predictable stories, songs, and poems are often used for shared reading sessions. Predictable texts are those that feature consistent rhythms, rhymes, patterns, and/or sequences that enable children to guess what comes next in a story (Parkes, 2000). They are frequently published in an enlarged format to support their use in shared reading lessons. However, be sure that you examine books carefully before you use them. Even though a book might be in an enlarged format, it may not be the best for shared reading lessons due to a lack of predictability or excessive text on each page that is too difficult to read as a group.

Shared reading has two important purposes. First, this teaching strategy gives young children an enjoyable literature-based literacy experience so that they grow to love stories and become fascinated with the sounds of book language (Laminack, 2009). These pleasurable experiences help children feel confident that they too can become readers and writers.

Second, shared reading experiences systematically show children how print works, supporting them in becoming independent readers and writers. A shared reading experience does not stop with one reading; on the contrary, the group reads and rereads the text, delving into explorations of language, meaning, writing craft, and print features. Shared readings with beginning readers focus primarily on how print works—how words are structured, the function of punctuation, and the connections between letters and sounds—and then add the other types of exploration later. Figure 3.5 features suggestions for exploring print that can be done during a shared reading lesson.

Implementing Shared Book Experiences

Most shared reading lessons last several days (typically a week) and include the following segments.

First Reading. Children become familiar with the story line and language patterns of the text during the first reading of a story. Teachers often ask them to predict what might happen next, invite them to join in on a repetitive refrain, or comment on information presented.

At the conclusion of the first reading, children can be asked to share something they noticed about the book or information they learned if it is a nonfiction text. The comments can help you determine what the children noticed and what interested them. These responses can then set the stage for the next day's rereading.

Shared Rereadings. On subsequent days, repeated readings of a text help children become more confident in their knowledge of how text works while building fluency. It also supports more extensive explorations of text features that you think the children are ready to experience. The strategies and activities you use during these rereadings are based on the children's readiness to attend to the print as well as what you think might help them extend their understanding of the text's meaning, how it is structured, or how the author used literary elements, such as language or characterization.

So, for example, you can hesitate before a word that you think children should know, ask them to supply it, and then discus how they figured it out. You can ask them to clap the rhythm of a repetitive

Students participate in a range of shared reading activities. (Anchor Standard SL.1)

FIGURE 3.5 **Suggested Print Exploration Activities During Shared Reading**

The following activities are not all-inclusive but are ones that we have found work well. They are provided to stimulate your thinking to create other activities that are particularly appropriate for a specific book:

- *Write words and phrases from the story on charts, whiteboards, word cards, sentence strips, and so on.* These can then be used for studying letter–sound patterns and for further writings in response to the story (Combs, 2009). This also helps with one-to-one matching: the strip is held directly beneath the matching line of print, and children point to each word in the text and on the strip. Ask students to make flash cards to use on mobile devices (e.g., using Quizlet).

- *Identify high-frequency "sight words" (simple words children can learn to recognize by sight) and punctuation marks.* Cover words or punctuation marks with colored highlighter tape, re-create words with magnetic letters, and match words on cards to words in the text. Identify the function of various punctuation marks. Word cards using words from the story can be sorted by theme, phonetic elements, or other categories. Identified words can then be added to the class word wall (collection of words the class has been learning to identify that are alphabetically organized on a wall display). Or students can find word wall words they already know in the story.

- *Identify rhyming words.* Cover with similarly colored highlighter tape or re-create with magnetic letters. Children can build new words with magnetic letters that aurally connect to the ones in the text.

- *Mask portions of text.* Use sticky notes, sliders, or correction tape to support children's developing use of context and how it works with initial consonants. Typically, teachers mask all but the beginning letter of a word and then ask children to predict based on that letter as well as what makes sense. The word is revealed and the meaning confirmed. Or they mask punctuation marks and ask children to identify them.

- *Use an interactive whiteboard.* Students can easily reorder phrases and sentences by touching and dragging lines on the board and highlighting words, sentences, or other text features for closer scrutiny (Gill & Islam, 2011). Teachers can save these lessons for future use.

- *Practice using all sources of information to discern meaning.* Ask children to predict what comes next in the story, guess how to say particular words and use what they see as clues on the book's cover to deduce meaning. Challenge them to justify answers by examining the clues in both text and illustrations.

(CCSS.ELA. Reading: Foundational Skills standards are addressed with these activities.)

chant, read character dialogue together, sing a verse from a song, or repeat lines read by the teacher. Or children can be asked to find words used to describe a character, determine the theme of a story, or identify the point of view from which the story is told. With information texts, for example, children can be asked what they learned about the topic that is the focus of the text, connect that information to what they already know, identify text structure, or comment on new vocabulary.

Extending Shared Reading

Following several opportunities for repeated readings of a story or other text, teachers often suggest activities that encourage children to retell and respond to it. These activities can be done in large or small groups or as independent projects. Retelling encourages children to reconstruct the text, whereas responding encourages them to consider their understandings about various literary aspects as well as their personal reactions.

Below are some suggested activities for extending children's responses to a shared reading text; they are intended as catalysts to help you think of new possibilities to fit particular texts.

We have connected each idea to the specific skills addressed in the CCSS for Reading: Literature and Reading: Informational Text. Skills addressed in the Reading: Foundational Skills Standards undergird all the suggested activities as well, although we have not specified them here.

- Retell through puppet shows, creative drama, flannel boards, podcasts, and storyboards (series of pictures from significant aspects of the story). Sometimes, stories that are created during these activities are written down for later independent reading. (CCSS.RL.2,3 and CCSS.RI.2,3)
- Create new versions of the story (termed "text innovations") by emulating text structure, adding more verses or characters, changing the story line, adding new adventures, adding dialogue, or similar activities. The text innovations can be made into individual books or a new class shared reading book, possibly through an interactive digital presentation. (CCSS.RL.5 and RI.5)
- Cut apart text and illustrations for pocket chart activities. Mount illustrations in a pocket chart. Ask children to match text with the illustrations; ask them to re-create the sequence of the story and tell it to a partner. (CCSS.RL.7 and RI.7)
- Create lists of sight words, new vocabulary learned, rhyming words, rhythmic phrases, or other language features. (CCSS.RL.4 and RI.4)
- Write responses to the story in individual journals or blogs. (CCSS.RL.2,3, RI.2,3, and W.2,3)
- Create recordings of the story. These can be placed with copies of the book for rereading in a class library, or digital copies can be stored on computers.
- Artistic extensions might include making new illustrations for the story, a mural or story map of events, paintings, collages, and mobiles. (CCSS.RL.7 and RI.7)
- Read new books that feature similar sight words, language patterns, information, or text structures to the text. (CCSS.RL.9 and RI.9)

Figure 3.6 is a sample shared reading lesson plan for beginning readers that focuses on the skills mandated by the CCSS Reading: Foundational Skills Standard. A shared reading for older students would focus mainly on the literary or nonfiction (informational) features of the text. (See Kristo & Bamford (2004) for how to teach interactive read alouds and shared reading using nonfiction for K-6.)

FIGURE 3.6 Sample Shared Reading Plan

A Suggested Shared Reading Lesson

Text: *Brown Bear, Brown Bear, What Do You See?*, by Bill Martin Jr. and illustrated by Eric Carle

Grade Level: Kindergarten/first grade (depending on development)

CCSS Standards Addressed: *Reading Literature*: RL.1, RL.2, RL.3, RL.6, RL.7, RL.10 *Reading Foundations*: RF.1, RF.2, RF.3, RF.4

Day 1

Introduce the Book: Share poem "Teddy Bear, Teddy Bear" (from *Play Rhymes*, compiled by Marc Brown) in enlarged format on chart paper. Read the poem with the children several times and then add motions for acting out the story. Cover up the rhyming words with sticky notes and then have the children guess the masked words. Reveal words and write each set of rhyming words on the whiteboard. Ask the children to tell what they notice about the words. Have them look for the word *bear* in the poem and match the word card with the word in the text. Discuss how both the poem and the book you are about to read are about bears. Present *Brown Bear, Brown Bear, What Do You See?* Before you discuss the cover and

FIGURE 3.6 *continued*

the title, cover all but the *b* in each occurrence of the word *bear* in the title with a sticky note. Ask students to guess what the masked word is by using the picture and beginning sound. Uncover the word and confirm the guess. Ask, "Predict what the book will be about. What evidence did you use to make that prediction?" Discuss other books they know by Bill Martin Jr. and illustrator Eric Carle. Discuss how the characteristics of books by this author/illustrator team might be replicated in *Brown Bear, Brown Bear.*

First reading of the story: As you read, point to each word with a pointer. Children join in as they are able. Before each page, ask them to predict what will happen next, such as who the bear will encounter next. Encourage them to provide evidence for why they make particular predictions. Following the reading, ask children to retell the sequence of events. Go back and find each animal seen by the bear and create a sequence chart of the story on chart paper or electronic whiteboard. With highlighting tape (or electronic highlighting tool), highlight each time the word *bear* appears in the story.

Tell children you will read the book again tomorrow. Ask them what they will particularly look for in the next reading. Find the word *bear* in other texts around the room or find other words beginning with *b*, including the children's names.

Day 2

Reread the Story, Word Work, Analysis of Text Structure, and Illustrations: Reread the poem "Teddy Bear, Teddy Bear." Identify the word *bear* in the poem and cover with highlighter tape (or electronic highlighter). Highlight rhyming words as children identify them again.

Introduce the story again. Ask children what print elements or text structure they noticed the previous day and suggest they look for those in the current reading. Read the story together, pointing to each word in the text. Also ask them to make predictions and to recall the sequence of events from the previous day's reading.

Following the rereading, provide opportunities for closer study of various text features, such as rhyming words ("see" and "me"); color words; and beginning sounds, such as *b*, *s*, and *m*. (Let them

match a card with the word to the same word in the story and use sticky notes to cover up words except the beginning letter and have children guess the masked word, among other strategies.) Ask them how they figured out the word. Return to the list of story events created the previous day on a whiteboard or on chart paper. Review the sequence with the group and edit as needed. Ask, "What if you just heard the story without the illustrations? Discuss how the illustrations contribute to the story."

Days 3 and 4

Reading, Retelling, and Word Work: Read and act out *We're Going on a Bear Hunt* (Rosen), in enlarged format. Find sight words, consonants, and so on that were previously identified from the *Brown Bear, Brown Bear, What Do You see?* story in the poem (can use Wikki Stix to circle these or use electronic highlighter tool). Use sticky notes to mask these words and have children guess what the masked text segment is.

Reread the story chorally. Children should be taking the lead now, requiring little teacher support. Using stick puppets, have children act out the story or select children to take on roles of various characters and do a drama of the story. Pair children up and have them read small copies of the book together.

Some groups might need more attention to word work. These activities might include re-creating words from the story with magnetic letters, giving partners a set of words to re-create sentences from the story, playing games with word cards based on words from the story, finding target words in other books or around the room, and so on. Create a chart of special words the group wants to remember from the story (i.e., high-frequency words that have become sight words). Write these words on a group chart or on the class word wall.

Day 5

Extension Activities and Review of the Week's Work: Reread the book one more time, possibly letting children take turns pointing to the words. Review the words that were the special focus of study for the week. Write a class "text innovation" that emulates the story's structure, theme, or vocabulary (e.g., "Children, children, What do you see? We see _____.").

Literature Circles

Literature circles are small communities of readers who meet daily or several times a week to discuss books. Group members are determined by their interest in reading a particular book rather than ability level. Typically, the group discusses one book they have read in common, although sometimes several books linked by a common element (genre, author, or theme) are the focus of the discussion. Both teacher and children read and reflect on the chosen selection and then meet to discuss what they feel, know, or want to know about the book (Daniels, 2002; Hill, Noe, & King, 2003; Peterson & Eeds, 1990; Schlick Noe & Johnson, 1999; Short, Harste, & Burke, 1996). For example, students might choose to share favorite passages about the story, commenting on the literary qualities that made that passage memorable or how it is critical to the narrative. They might share questions from their response journal or request clarification on a confusing aspect of plot. Everyone has the opportunity to share their reactions to the text and to respond to other group members' questions, ideas, and interpretations.

Literature circles offer many benefits to students. First, they promote a love of literature and reading. Rather than using short selections from an anthology or programmed reader, children read complete books, allowing them to become fully engaged with a complex, longer story that requires effort and persistence to discover its meanings. Extensive and intensive reading naturally evolves with discussions often becoming catalysts for further independent reading as children share insights about their books with others or seek out more books by the author of a literature circle book they have grown to love (Szymusiak, Sibberson, & Koch, 2008).

Second, participating in literature circles allows readers to structure understandings for themselves, constructing interpretations of text in light of their own intents (Peterson & Eeds, 1990). "Interpretation" is the critical word. It occurs when readers deliberate over the meaning of a text, consciously shaping their understanding and using all their experiential background, personal reading history, and purposes for reading the story to create their own meaning.

Recall Rosenblatt's transactional response theory discussed in Chapter 2, and you will see how literature circles naturally evolve from Rosenblatt's ideas. The possibilities for both aesthetic and efferent responses are encouraged when communities of readers in literature circles are allowed to create their own interpretations. Readers have the chance to deepen their aesthetic response because they engage with a longer text that builds these responses over time. Efferent responses are supported as readers return to stories during their discussions to answer questions, explore how a character develops over time, or summarize what they have read so far.

Third, literature circles support thoughtful interaction and collaboration as children share their individually constructed interpretations and responses to books and then help each other clarify ideas, discover new insights, and explore a range of additional possible responses to books (Brabham & Villaume, 2000). It makes use of the natural friendship connections that are part of children's lives. Teachers hear children exclaim, "I never thought about _____ that way before Jessica shared her ideas" or "I read a whole book for the first time and talked about it with _____." Children learn to thoughtfully explore their own ideas and responses while also learning from and valuing those constructed by others. The teacher's role is to create an environment in which interactions flourish, where students help each other share and extend their responses (Hill, Johnson, & Noe, 1995).

Finally, literature circles nurture responsibility in children. They are trusted to choose books that are interesting yet challenging. They are expected to read, reflect, construct their own interpretations and responses, and then actively participate in the group (Daniels, 2002). Encouraging this level of responsibility for their own learning is an important step toward children becoming independent, self-motivated readers.

Literature Circles and the CCSS

Literature circles are a particularly appropriate teaching strategy for meeting the mandates of the CCSS. This is because the focus of discussions in literature circles (following aesthetic response) often is on how authors effectively use literary and nonfiction text elements, such as characterization, theme, story plotting, and text structure—concepts that are integral components of the CCSS Reading: Literature and Reading Informational Text Standards. The Reading: Literature and Reading: Informational Text Standards also require students to understand how authors use language and vocabulary to craft fictional stories, poetry, and informational text—all concepts discussed in this teaching strategy. Thus, it seems that literature circles are a pedagogically sound and developmentally appropriate way to facilitate student competence in these standards.

COMMON CORE STATE STANDARD FEATURE #2

Collaborative Conversations and Oral Presentations (CCSS.SL.1, SL.2, and SL.4)

As with read-alouds, the CCSS Speaking and Listening Standards, which mandate that students participate in discussions regarding a range of grade-appropriate topics, are also addressed through literature circles. Following are the relevant speaking and listening anchor standards:

SL.1. (Anchor Standard): Prepare for and participate effectively in a range of conversations and collaborations with diverse partners, building on others' ideas and expressing their own clearly and persuasively.

SL.2. (Anchor Standard): Integrate and evaluate information presented in diverse media and formats, including visually, quantitatively, and orally.

SL.4. (Anchor standard): Present information, findings, and supporting evidence such that listeners can follow the line of reasoning and the organization, development, and style are appropriate to task, purpose, and audience.

Planning for and Implementing Literature Circles

Effective literature circles do not just happen; they evolve over time as teachers guide students in acquiring the ability to conduct discussions effectively and with increasing independence. Teachers can support children's competence in creating effective discussions by carefully structuring the experience and also showing students *how* to do it. The following sections provide information on selecting books, establishing ground rules, showing students how authentic discussions develop, how to structure time, the role of book extensions, and the use of literature strategy lessons.

Choosing Books for Literature Circles. Authentic literature circles happen when the text being discussed has substance. It should have the potential to provide an intellectual challenge through thought-provoking themes, complex character development, rich language, intriguing information, and other exemplary literary aspects—all qualities that can lead to lively, substantive discussions. Books that draw readers in from the very first chapter with humor, suspense, or action work well because readers are often compelled to keep reading. This is true for both fiction and nonfiction. For younger children, illustrations that are colorful and support the text help them become interested in a story (Schlick Noe & Johnson, 1999).

Although it is helpful if group members can read the book independently, do not make this the determining factor when deciding who will read a particular book. Our experience has shown that literature circle members help each other through the process of reading and understanding books. We have seen students who have been relegated to lower reading levels throughout their school careers successfully read much more complex books because they are motivated to contribute to the discussion and feel supported by other group members. If a child is truly struggling with a book but is highly motivated to read it, that child can read with a partner or a parent aide or listen to the book read electronically.

A more important consideration is to select books that appeal to a range of interests and both genders. It is also good to select books from diverse genres, including poetry and nonfiction. Younger children can discuss picture books and short, transitional chapter books. Sometimes, you might want to relate literature circle books to topics of study in social studies or science. This is appropriate as long as the emphasis is placed on enjoying the literary aspects of the book as well as on its content and curricular connections. For example, literature circles can become discovery circles using nonfiction books (Kristo & Bamford, 2004).

Once you have selected four or five viable books, allow students to choose which book they wish to read and create groups for each book. The opportunity for choice is critical in motivating students to read and enthusiastically discuss. Many teachers give students the opportunity to browse through several choices of books and create a ranked list of the ones that interest them. You can then rotate the books so that students ultimately read several from the choices offered.

Establishing Ground Rules. It helps to develop general guidelines about the number of pages to be read before each discussion session, how literature response journals will be completed, the rules for interrupting a circle that is in session, and other housekeeping matters (Daniels, 2002). Additionally, the importance of bringing books and response journals to the group meeting as well as the necessity for active participation from all students should be communicated right from the start.

It also helps to work collaboratively with students to develop charts of appropriate discussion behaviors, such as "disagree respectfully," "look at the person speaking," and "build on others' ideas." Most students just beginning to participate in circles have no idea how to conduct an effective discussion. Discussing and then modeling appropriate behaviors helps them understand what behaviors support productive interactions.

Helping Students Prepare for Discussions. The best discussions evolve from authentic questions and observations that intrigue, mystify, or connect to readers. However, often students do not initially know how to pose these questions. Thus, teachers need to provide some guidance and scaffolding when first using literature circles. For example, you can suggest that students find one section that particularly resonated with them and one genuine question. Or the group can generate questions together that subsequently are the focus of the discussion. Some teachers initially provide prompts, similar to questions posed in close reading sessions, to stimulate and guide student thinking. Prompts should gradually be unnecessary as students gain more experience with literature circle discussions. The idea is to show students how to prepare for discussions and then continually encourage their own observations and insights so that more natural, authentic discussions evolve.

Literature response journals or online book blogs are other strategies that help prepare students so that discussions are productive. In journals and blogs, children document their predictions, interpretations, and questions about a book as they read. The entries are then used for discussions, giving children the confidence to meaningfully contribute. Prompts such as "I wondered . . .," "My evidence for . . .," "I made a connection to . . .," or "I was surprised by . . ." (Mills & Jennings, 2011) can be provided, or students can be encouraged to create their own prompts. Drawing should be considered valid preparation, as should other strategies, such as creating character webs, question/answer graphs, diary or blog entries (from the perspective of a character), and plot diagrams. We have found that many children, particularly those who might normally be shy about offering their ideas, do so because they have thought through their ideas before attending the discussion.

ELLs may require additional support if asked to use response journals. They might need to write their responses initially in their native language. Or teachers can listen to a student's verbal response and write the entry for that child. Asking additional probing questions can extend these verbal and subsequent written responses. Teachers can also create charts of prompts, key words, pictures, or other cues to refer to as an ELL student is writing a journal entry (Williams, 2009).

When teachers write responses to these entries, they validate and extend children's ideas. Werderich (2006) found that effective teachers used visual aids, modeling, questioning/ requesting, and specific feedback to scaffold students' written literary conversations in response journals, particularly dialogue journals. Sometimes, the teachers' comments focused on developing literary understandings in their students; at other times, the teachers contributed to the written discussion as an equal, allowing students more freedom in their responses. The kind of teacher commentary varies according to the needs of the students and the teacher's instructional objectives, making journals an effective way to support the development of literary understandings.

Students can also be encouraged to annotate passages they want to remember. Bookmarks with space for recording page numbers and a comment also help students return to a particular section during a discussion for evidence that supports a comment or to find a particular passage they wish to share. E-books often feature bookmarking and note-taking capabilities in electronic format that can be used for this purpose.

Helping children prepare for circles in which nonfiction books or articles are the focus is somewhat different, although there are similarities. Instead of prompts about literary elements, such as characterization or theme, teachers often ask students to think about the information in the text: What surprised readers? How did the text structure help readers understand the meaning? What are the most important facts or concepts presented? What did readers know about the topic before reading that was confirmed or extended? Some teachers also change the format of circles based on the difficulty of a nonfiction text, particularly one with challenging vocabulary or complex information. So the students might read text together, taking notes, making annotations, and discussing the content for several days. They then have a "meeting day" where they discuss the reading, using their notes, annotations, and journal entries to guide the conversation (Candler, 2013).

The teacher should read the book in order to plan questions, observations, and other responses. This is not to make you the expert. Rather, it helps you become a knowledgeable group member—one who can keep the discussion going, modeling good questioning and interactions while encouraging students to turn to each other as conversational partners. As children become more adept at sharing their ideas, the teacher can gradually turn the leadership role over to them.

Some teachers initially find it useful to have students assume various roles in literature circles. This helps students learn different ways to examine a story within a predictable structure (Daniels, 2002). Roles rotate each time a group meets so that students get the chance to experience different kinds of interpretations. Figure 3.7 lists some roles that teachers often use for getting discussions started. Most teachers find that once students conduct several group discussions using roles, they are often ready to abandon this structure and participate in a lively discussion drawn from their own reflections and journal entries (Daniels, 2002).

What if, despite all your efforts, discussions falter? This sometimes happens and certainly does not mean that literature circles have failed. First, look at the book. Is it a book with substance and content worth discussing? Is it engaging to the group? Did students choose it, or was it assigned?

FIGURE 3.7 Sample Literature Circle Assigned Roles*

Role in Circles Using Fiction	Description of Role	Role in Circles Using Nonfiction
Discussion leader	• Develops questions that group might discuss • Leads discussion	Discussion leader
Setting recorder	• Locates setting in real world (if appropriate) • Develops questions that relate to the setting and its role in the story	
Vocabulary master	• Hunts for interesting words that stand out, words that others might not know meaning of, or words that are critical to understanding the text • Helps others locate words in the text • Assists group members with figuring out the meanings of selected words	Vocabulary master
	• Finds facts that are important to remember in the text • Organizes facts in some visual display	Fact finder
Literary critic	• Finds interesting, puzzling, humorous passages that the group might discuss in more depth • Creates questions to support discussion of the selected passages	
Illustrator	• Draws a picture, diagram, cartoon, map, and so on related to the reading • Leads discussion on significance of the illustration	Illustrator
Connector	• Makes connections between the book and life, other books, other events, and so on and finds new information related to the text • Creates questions to help group members make their own connections	Researcher
Synthesizer/summarizer	• Listens to the discussion and creates a summary of what was said and shares with group for verification	Synthesizer/summarizer

*Select the roles that are appropriate for your students' grade level and familiarity with doing literature circles.
Source: Adapted from Daniels (2002).

If you think the book is a good choice, then go back to the children and ask them to generate ideas for improving their conversations. Questions such as "What went well today?" and "How can we make our discussion go more smoothly?" can facilitate this analysis. The class may also need to review the rules and guidelines established when you first implemented circles. They can create a self-evaluation checklist based on the qualities of an effective circle and use this as a guideline for improving future sessions. Students can also watch professional videos of effective literature circles or observe videos of their own sessions in order to analyze the quality of their responses and interactions. Mills and Jennings (2011) found that this was an effective way to deepen the power and effectiveness of their students' discussions.

Tech Click

On their Web site, the Partnership for 21st Century Skills (2013) offers a tool kit that aligns their learning framework with the CCSS. One of the English Language Arts (ELA) examples suggests that fourth-grade students record a series of open-ended discussions during literature circles. In small groups, students analyze the conversation for the depth of insights and the effectiveness of arguments. After balancing for each member's participation, students edit and publish as a podcast. An added benefit of having a series of podcasts is that they serve as exemplars or models of how discussions can unfold. The skills addressed are critical thinking, collaboration, communication, information literacy, and informational literacy skills.

Book Extensions. Extension projects can enhance literature circles, providing additional opportunities for students to deepen their interpretation of a book. Completed by individuals, partners, or the group, they continue conversations or help students explore new aspects of a story. When projects are then shared, the audience members are often motivated to read the book themselves.

Selected projects should be those that encourage students to return to the book, generating critical thinking and additional reflection. Many of the response ideas presented in Chapter 2, as well as those featured in the genre chapters, are suitable for this purpose and can easily align with the CCSS competencies. We caution you not to overuse extensions. They should be among the many ways students respond to books. The annotations recorded on sticky notes, journal entries, and teacher observation of children's contributions to circle sessions are also appropriate assessment tools that can be used to document student understandings.

Literature Strategy Lessons. Some teachers like to present literature strategy lessons in conjunction with literature circles. Literature strategy lessons are sessions in which teachers discuss response strategies, literary elements such as those addressed in the CCSS, compare how texts are structured (e.g., the ways nonfiction texts are organized), or teach other reading skills. Sometimes, particularly when just beginning to implement literature circles, teachers will conduct strategy lessons on behavioral expectations and effective discussion strategies. Or they will use this time to celebrate student successes. The best strategy lessons arise from your observations of what the students need to know. However, they can also be planned to meet the mandates of standards.

Literacy strategy sessions are usually brief (around 10 minutes) and focus on one strategy, skill, or piece of information. The concept should be quickly introduced and then illustrated with specific examples to make the idea clear. Next, you can briefly model how to apply the strategy or provide the opportunity for children to practice its use. Brevity and simplicity are important to a teacher's success with strategy lessons (Avery, 1993). The focus should be on giving students a significant nugget of information to help them attain more substantive, enjoyable book discussions. Some teachers have their students keep "Reading Strategy" sections in their response journals to record what they learned in a strategy lesson.

Tech Click

With today's technology, it's easy to "push out the walls" of your classroom and extend literature discussions to other classes, grades, schools, and even countries. For example, we have seen a successful literature circle on *Number the Stars* (Lowry) function between fifth graders and undergraduates.

 *Tech Click*

In2Books is an online program that matches students with adult mentors who discuss books together via electronic pen pal letters. Both students and mentors read the same book and share their ideas via the letters. Students first discuss the book in class with peers and their teacher to lay a foundation of understanding and then deepen their understanding through the written interactions with their mentors.

Structuring Time. Literature circles require time for reading, reflecting in journals, creating extension projects, and discussions. A daily schedule might include 10 to 15 minutes for record keeping and strategy lessons; 40 to 60 minutes for reading, writing, and circle meetings; and then 10 minutes at the conclusion for sharing purposes. Typically, teachers meet with each circle group two or three times a week. Younger children may need to meet more frequently than this schedule suggests, whereas middle school readers might meet less frequently or more frequently but without the teacher as a regular group member.

A Suggested Literature Circle Planning Guide

Figure 3.8 features a sample teacher discussion guide that shows how a teacher might tentatively plan for a literature circle, particularly for students who are just beginning to discuss more thoughtfully. The items on the discussion guide are designed to help teachers support the discussion while allowing opportunities for students to share their own thinking and guide the discussion in a way that is meaningful to them.

 *Tech Click*

Visit the Literature Circles Resource Center online for additional teaching ideas on implementing literature circles in your classroom.

Independent Reading: Reader's Workshop

In a reader's workshop (also sometimes called individualized reading), students are held accountable for reading independently with deep understanding. This teaching strategy is most often used with upper elementary and middle school students who are typically ready for independent reading (Atwell, 1998, 2007; Miller, 2009; Robb, 2000). However, primary teachers can also use reader's workshop, although they usually need to provide more guidance with time management, reading strategies, and book selection for these younger students (Taberski, 2011).

Teachers have traditionally used independent reading time, or sustained silent reading time, in their classrooms as a way to provide daily opportunities for students to read on their own. This was often scheduled after recess or other "spare" moments in the day and involved a specific time in which students and teacher did nothing but silently and independently read self-selected books. The emphasis was on enjoyment and reading practice—two worthy goals.

Interestingly, research on this common practice did not consistently find sufficient evidence to support its continuation as it was originally implemented (Allington, 2006; Bryan, Fawson, & Reutzel, 2003; Cunningham, 2001; Edmondson & Shannon, 2002; National Institute

FIGURE 3.8 Sample Literature Circle Teacher Discussion Guide for "The Cheese Touch," "Costumes," and "The Bleeding Scream" (Chapters from *Wonder* by R. J. Palacio)

Synopsis: Wonder is the story of Auggie, a fifth-grade boy who was born with a deformed face. Homeschooled all his life, he attends regular school for the first time. Most students shun him, whereas some, such as Julian, bully him. His only friends are Summer and Jack—that is, until Halloween, when, dressed in a costume that hides his identity, Auggie overhears Jack tell Julian that he does not really like Auggie.

A discussion guide is constructed as a support for the teacher, who can interject speculations, thoughts, and ideas. Students should guide the discussion themselves as much as possible.

Note: Students will be using a response journal and vocabulary bookmark (bookmark with spaces to record tricky words and page numbers on which the words are found). They will also have started character webs for some of the main characters (Auggie, Jack, Julian, and Summer).

Student Tasks Before Meeting: Students will be asked to respond in literature journals. Possible prompts are the following: Put yourself in Auggie's shoes. How would you have reacted to overhearing your best friend say he doesn't really like you? How does Auggie react? What evidence can you share that supports your opinion of his feelings? Also: record any words on your vocabulary bookmark for which you are unsure about the meanings. Predict what you think the word means based on the context of its sentence. Write the prediction on your bookmark.

Question Focusing on Literary Crafting: What does Palacio do as a writer to make you feel that you are in the story with Auggie?

Teacher Planning Before Meeting: Mark passages with sticky notes. Circle words that you think are critical to understanding the chapter. Generate possible questions to ask. These might include the following (Note: You would probably not ask all these questions. You would just need to be prepared to ensure that students understood the main ideas of the chapters and were able to cite evidence from the story.):

- How does Auggie's perspective influence your understanding of the events in this chapter? What does he say that tells you how he feels about what other children say and do to him?

- What does Auggie mean when he says he is like the Cheese Touch in *Diary of a Wimpy Kid*? Cite evidence from the story to support your opinion.

- Why does Auggie love his Halloween costume so much? What does this tell you about him? How do you know? How do his feelings change?

- Why do you think Jack said he really did not like Auggie? (He's anonymous in a costume too? He wants to fit in? He is scared of Julian?)

- How does Julian have the power to control people's opinions? What kind of person is he? What evidence in the story supports your opinion?

- How do the references to other children's books enhance the story? Why do you think the author did this?

- You might plan a readers' theater reading of the pivotal scene in "Bleeding Scream" where Auggie overhears Jack.

Vocabulary That Might Need to Be Discussed (depending on students and the words they selected for bookmarks): This book does not have difficult vocabulary. However, some students might be unfamiliar with names of *Star Wars* characters referenced in the story. Thus, these might need to be discussed, particularly their significance to character development.

End-of-Discussion Suggestions:
- Do you think the boys' friendship can be repaired after this incident? What do you know about each boy's personality to support your opinion?

- Add new personality qualities to character webs for Auggie, Jack, and Julian.

CCSS Standards addressed: Reading: Literature Standards: CCRA.RL.1, RL.3, RL.4, RL.6, and RL.10; Writing Standards: CCRA.W.1 and W.9; and Speaking and Listening Standard: CCRA.SL.1.

of Child Health and Human Development, 2000; Robertson, Keating, Shenton, & Roberts, 1996; Stahl, 2004; Worthy & Broadus, 2002). These researchers criticized the teaching strategy for sustained silent reading for its lack of teacher guidance in helping students select appropriately challenging books, the evidence of little or no teacher interaction or feedback to students about the quality or quantity of their reading, and no sense of accountability on the part of students (Reutzel, Jones, Fawson, & Smith, 2008).

Does this mean that silent reading of self-selected books is an ineffective strategy? No. We have repeatedly asserted that allowing students the opportunity to engage in extended, self-selected, and independent silent reading practice increases students' reading motivation, engagement, and achievement. Students become avid, engaged, and competent readers when that reading is meaningful to them, they expect to be successful, and they are taught the critical skills and strategies needed to achieve competency (Cambourne, 1988; Gambrell, 1996; Guthrie & Wigfield, 1997; Krashen, 2006; Shaw, 2006). These goals are the purpose of reader's workshop. In this teaching strategy, students independently read self-selected books but are held accountable for that reading. Teachers provide individualized and group instruction to ensure that students are successfully using strategies to understand and thoughtfully respond to what they read (Atwell, 2007; Miller, 2009).

Reader's Workshop and the CCSS

The reader's workshop is an effective teaching strategy for helping students meet the mandates of the CCSS. Teacher/student individual conferences and group literature strategy lessons provide the opportunity to learn reading strategies and acquire knowledge of literary elements or informational text structures in authentic contexts, which are the basis for the Reading: Literature and Reading: Information Text Standards. The use of literature response journals in reader's workshop also provides the opportunity to use writing as "a way of offering and supporting opinions," "respond analytically to literary and informational sources," and "adapt the form and content of writing to accomplish a particular task and purpose," supporting all aspects of the CCSS Writing Standard (CCSS, p. 18).

Finally, and most important, reader's workshop develops student competence in reading critically, deeply, and independently. Our ultimate goal for all students is for them to read independently with enjoyment and understanding as they choose books from a variety of increasingly sophisticated topics and genres. The CCSS mandate this competence in the Reading: Literature and Reading: Information Text Standard 10, which states that children should be able to "read and comprehend complex literary and informational texts independently and proficiently." The standard further states that students "must read widely and deeply from among these texts" so they "acquire the habits of reading independently and closely" (CCRA Anchor Standard 10). Reader's workshop provides the structure and opportunity for students to develop these competencies and lifelong habits.

Implementing Reader's Workshop

The main components of reader's workshop are the opportunity for students to choose their own books, time to read and respond to selected books, teacher conferences with individual children, and opportunities to share responses to one's reading and literature strategy lessons. Each component is described in the following sections.

Self-Selection of Books. Similar to literature circles, self-selection of books is a critical component of this teaching strategy. When allowed to choose books that address their interests, students are more likely to be engaged during the independent reading time. They are also more likely to read more challenging books. Middle school teacher Donalynn Miller (2009)

FIGURE 3.9 Helping Students Make Informed Independent Book Choices

- Create Book Talks. Share three or four good books in a 30-minute session that are good choices for independent reading. This builds student background knowledge for reading certain books that might be challenging while also piquing interest.

- Write personal messages on sticky notes to children, recommending books you think they might enjoy. Put the note on the book and give it to the child or share it during conference time.

- Have a system where students can write recommendations to each other on sticky notes, a class database, a Web site, or a chart with categories such as "Name of recommender," "Recommending to_____," or "Why I recommend this book to you" (Miller, 2009).

- Bring in a collection of books favored by students from previous classes and share why they were popular. Place the set of books in the class library.

- Use read-alouds to stimulate interest in a particular author, genre, or subject. You can put the current read-aloud on display along with enticing, related titles.

- Collaborate with the library media specialist on an exhibit of teachers' favorite books and then have students match books with childhood snapshots of the teachers.

- Explicitly teach children how to find "just right" books. Some teachers use the "five-finger" strategy (Allington, 2006), in which students read selected pages from different parts of the book and raise a finger for each difficult word they encounter. If five fingers go up on one page, they suggest the child try a different book. Primary teachers Gail Boushey and Joan Moser suggest a strategy they call I PICK (**I** choose a book, What is my **p**urpose?, Am I **i**nterested in it?, Can I **c**omprehend it?, Do I **k**now most of the words?). This shifts the emphasis from only readability to include the child's interest in and understanding of the book (Boushey & Moser, 2006).

- Organize the classroom library to support purposeful book selection. Many teachers put books on high-interest topics (e.g., "mysteries," "class favorites," "humorous stories," or "animals") or those written by popular authors in labeled bins so that their students can easily find these books. Placing books so that covers face out is also important. Some teachers organize the classroom library by reading levels. We caution you to do this carefully so that children are not restricted from reading high-level books that interest them. Puppets, stuffed animals, games, and other toys related to books can be added to heighten student interest.

requires her students to read at least 40 books a year in a variety of genres. This often seems initially daunting. However, Miller maintains high expectations for the completion of this requirement and celebrates their steps to achieving this goal.

However, teachers cannot assume that students will choose wisely and find those "just right" books that will interest but also challenge them. Thus, teachers need to demonstrate effective book selection procedures. Figure 3.9 features some suggestions for helping children make informed book selections.

Work Time: Reading and Responding to Books. Once they have selected their books, children need significant uninterrupted time to read and respond. Forty-five to 60 minutes of time is normally scheduled for this purpose. During this time, students read and are held responsible through writing responses in literature response journals, and working on extension projects (see the response activities discussed in Chapter 2 as well as the CCSS features in Part II for more discussion on these activities). Students might also record challenging vocabulary words or mark

A classroom library organized to support purposeful selection of books for reader's workshop.

examples of character development, writing style, and other text elements for later sharing with others. The teacher also uses this time to hold individual conferences and periodically monitor the room to ensure that students are using time productively.

In order for students to successfully read independently, many teachers explicitly model what independent reading "looks like," including "finding a good spot," "staying in that spot," "reading and writing the whole time," and other appropriate behaviors (Sanden, 2012).

Conferences. Conferences are the heart of reader's workshop. Teachers conference with each student at regular intervals for approximately 10 minutes each (some are shorter and some longer, depending on student needs). Typically, the teacher first asks children to retell the story or answer questions about their book. Sometimes, the child will read aloud a section of the book so that the teacher can assess reading fluency. Students might be asked to discuss words that were confusing or difficult in the reading. Teachers can also discuss the crafting of the book, posing questions similar to those used in close reading sessions. Conferences with younger or less advanced readers might include brief instruction on a reading skill or strategy the child seems to be struggling with based on the teacher's observations. Figure 3.10 features a form for recording information gained from these conferences.

Sharing. Sharing extension projects, journal responses, and popular book titles is another important component of readers's workshop and usually occurs during the last 10 to 15 minutes. Sharing provides the opportunity for students to model exemplary responses and projects to their peers. Sometimes, students read aloud favorite passages, the "lead" that got them hooked into their book or another exciting part. Teachers also can share new books, authors, or interesting ideas about books that have been previously shared to broaden students' awareness of possible independent book choices.

Sharing is often conducted in a large group. However, students can also be organized into smaller groups if they are reading several books by the same author or books that feature a similar theme. This provides more opportunities for students to share.

Literature Strategy Lessons. As with literature circles, many teachers using reader's workshop believe that they need to provide time to teach students how to read critically and skillfully. Literature strategy lessons can be regularly scheduled to accomplish this goal. Literature Strategy Lessons are more fully discussed later.

Structuring Time and Expectations. Establishing a regular daily routine for reader's workshop is critical. If students know what to expect and the routine is consistent, they are more likely to focus on important tasks, such as reading and response rather than wondering what they are expected to do. Many teachers start workshops with a "Status of the Class" (Atwell, 1998) check in which they quickly ask children where they are in their reading as well as their goals for the day's work. Because many classrooms have laptops or other mobile technologies, this daily check could be conducted silently with students recording status of the class and goals

FIGURE 3.10 Reader's Workshop Conference Form

Reading Conference Record

Name of Student _____   Date _____

Name of Book _____   Approximate Level _____

Appropriateness of book for child: Good   Too Easy   Too Hard

<u>**Child's general comments about the book**</u>—(enjoyment, difficult parts, connections to other books, etc.)

Following oral reading of passage from the book:

Oral Reading	Circle One			Circle One	
	E (Excellent)	**C (Competent)**	**P (Poor)**	**T (Teacher Models/ Initiates)**	**S (Student)**
Fluency	E	C	P	T	S
Rate	E	C	P	T	S
Phrasing	E	C	P	T	S
Word Solving	E	C	P	T	S
Attention to Punctuation	E	C	P	T	S
Correction of Errors	E	C	P	T	S
Risk taking on challenging words	E	C	P	T	S

<u>**Comments:**</u>

Comprehension: Retelling

	Circle One			Circle One	
Retelling (includes) characters, plot, theme, setting <u>or</u> if non-fiction, retells facts, main ideas	E	C	P	T	S
Retelling: analyzes, summarizes text	E	C	P	T	S

Comprehension: Strategies (Teacher asks questions; evaluates student response)

	Circle One			Circle One	
Schema: "Is there some part of this story that reminds you of something in your life?	E	C	P	T	S
Questioning: Were there parts of the text/story you were curious or confused about? What did you do when that happened? Show me these parts.	E	C	P	T	S
Inferring: Were there places where you had to bring in your own ideas to make inferences? Show me where this happened.	E	C	P	T	S
Synthesizing: Tell me what the text/story is about in just a few sentences. What evidence in the text/story causes you to say this? Was there a place where your thinking changed? How did your thinking change? What do you think is most important to remember about this story/text?	E	C	P	T	S

<u>**Comments:**</u>

<u>**Vocabulary**</u>

Challenging words listed by child:

What strategies did you use to figure out the meanings of these challenging words?

_____ context   _____ picture clues   _____ guess

_____ ask someone   _____ sound it out   _____ other

<u>**Next Steps:**</u> What will child do next with current book? What strategies will he/she focus on as reads? What's the next book he/she will read?

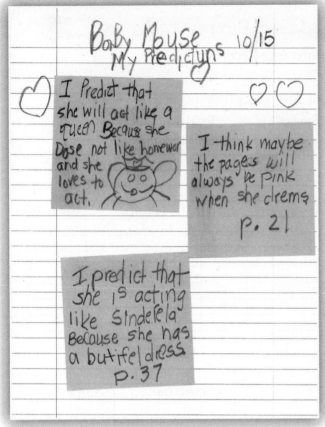

Page from a first grader's reader's workshop notebook with predictions, which was written before reading a section of *Baby Mouse: Queen of the World* by Jennifer Holm.

on a remote site. A literature strategy lesson often follows. Children then complete independent reading and writing activities while the teacher conferences with individuals or instructs small groups. Time for sharing usually concludes the workshop time.

To help students stay organized, some teachers provide a list of suggested activities or guidelines that students keep in the front of a reader's workshop notebook. Other sections of the notebook might include lists of books read, responses to their reading, plans for the day's activities, vocabulary lists, and other materials to document their work. These notebooks help keep students focused and purposeful as they proceed through a workshop session. Time is provided at the beginning of the workshop for students to record this important thinking.

Most workshops last approximately an hour, with 10 to 15 minutes allotted for housekeeping and strategy lessons, 30 to 45 minutes for work time, and 10 to 15 minutes for sharing. Teachers of younger children may need to start with a shorter time block that increases as children develop more reading stamina, or they might break up the workshop time into smaller chunks. These teachers might also need to spend more time teaching reading skills or working with their students in small-group sessions.

Tech Click

The Web site "10 Best Websites with Book Reviews for Children's Books" is an excellent resource for finding books to create a classroom library that supports reader's workshop.

 ## Literature Across the Curriculum

Integrating literature with the study of content areas such as science, social studies, mathematics, health, and the arts has many benefits for students. Beautifully illustrated, well-written texts engage children's interest and draw them into learning about many aspects of the world. Stories of exciting historical events, scientific discoveries, or details about how things work can motivate them to read deeply and widely on topics of personal interest. Additionally, the opportunity to read more than one book on a topic can help them gain diverse perspectives on that topic—something that just does not usually occur with a textbook.

So how can you integrate the use of children's books into your content-area instruction? All the teaching strategies we discussed in this chapter are appropriate for exploring both fiction and nonfiction texts. Reading aloud is one of the easiest and most rewarding ways to bring literature into the study of content areas. Both fiction and nonfiction can be used for literature circle discussions. Children can be encouraged to select from nonfiction texts for reader's workshop. Fiction and nonfiction picture books, because of their brevity and well-crafted writing, work particularly well for close reading sessions. We suggest that you use trade books judiciously and purposefully to provide students with the most current, engaging, and well-written information on the topics in your curriculum.

Therefore, where appropriate, we have included suggested books and specific teaching strategies to integrate literature with instruction in the content areas. For example, a section in Chapter 6 shows how understanding a culture's traditional literature can illuminate one's understanding of its history, geography, and values. Chapter 5 describes how poetry can enhance the study of mathematics, science, and social studies. Chapter 8 is organized to facilitate the study of history through literature. Chapter 10 is an entire chapter devoted to the many excellent nonfiction books to support learning in all aspects of the curriculum.

Controversial Issue: Book Selection

Finding the most engaging, well-written books to support the teaching strategies discussed in this chapter is critical. If a student cannot connect to a book or truly dislikes it, it is unlikely that any instructional strategy will be successful. Thus, many teachers believe that it is important to provide a wide array of materials for students from books to magazines to Internet articles. Considering all the factors influencing book selection discussed in Chapter 2, this is likely a wise decision. Of course, not all materials are classroom appropriate—and what you decide to include in your classroom library must be developmentally appropriate as well. We call this *book selection*.

Some adults do not believe that children should be allowed to read all that is available to them. They contend that it is important to protect children from influences perceived as harmful. The issue becomes complicated because what is considered "harmful" depends on one's perspective and on the developmental age of the reader.

Censorship is not new. As long as books have been available, people have found some inappropriate and should be banned. Their reasons vary, from the potential of books to corrupt youth to the fact that society is in moral decay—and books are the cause. The arguments and intent are remarkably similar from generation to generation. Louisa May Alcott's *Little Women* was once thought scandalous at the turn of the 20th century because Jo, the protagonist, was rebellious and thus a poor role model for young women (Hentoff, 1992). Mark Twain's *The Adventures of Huckleberry Finn*, first published in 1885, is still being challenged because some readers believe that Twain willfully ignored women and disrespected African Americans. These concerns can result in requests for removal of books from classrooms and libraries and is termed *censorship*.

The issue becomes murkier when Internet content is involved, where there are fewer clues regarding whether the author is reliable or a scammer. Children need significant support to guide their ways through the Web, independently learning to judge veracity, reliability, bias, and appropriateness. In the wide-open online world, students must become intelligent information consumers and producers. But where do we draw the line? How do we help children achieve these goals without exposure to questionable content?

We believe that teachers have a responsibility to *select* interesting, high-quality literature that challenges them to explore new and different concepts. We also believe that students should be allowed to choose what they want to read—and teachers have the responsibility to provide a range of materials from which those choices are made. We must also help them critically examine the ideas they encounter in their reading so that they will think for themselves, developing judgment, imagination, and a sense of responsibility (McClure, 1995, p. 5).

If we ask the children, they usually express a desire to have full access to whatever books they want to read. A study by Isajlovic-Terry and McKechnie (2012) found that children had a good idea of their own reading preferences and wanted to have access to books they were interested in reading. They often paid no attention to the issues adults thought might affect them, such as references to same-sex relationships (as in *And Tango Makes Three* [Richardson & Parnell], which is a frequently censored book for this reason) or paranormal content (as in the *Twilight* series). It should come as no surprise, then, that "banned books" are often at the top of children's preference lists. However, they did recognize that some content, particularly that which is violent and frightening, was inappropriate and accepted the role of adults in restricting their access to such content.

Yet we cannot deny the very real concerns of parents as to the values they wish to instill in their own children. Many reasonable, intelligent adults believe that some young children are not ready for the graphic sex described in *Forever* (Blume) or the supposedly alternative family arrangement portrayed in *And Tango Makes Three*. They have the right to determine what their own children might read. We contend that they do not have the right to decide for other students.

So how can you balance intellectual freedom (the right to read) with the legitimate concerns of parents? First, be sure that the books you select are of high literary quality and have content worth exploring. Then you should know how to respond if a parent or community member challenges a book you are using and asks that it be removed from the classroom or the school library. Following are some suggestions for how to diffuse a potential censorship situation:

- Be proactive. Communicate information to parents about the books you are using. Share why you think a book is appropriate for the class or their child and the literary qualities you think make it a distinguished choice. Some teachers create rationales for books that detail the objectives and standards they can meet by using the book. The National Council of Teachers of English Web site has some excellent examples of these.

- Schedule meetings where parents read and discuss books their children will read. This helps parents understand your purposes for teaching the book and encourages them to read the entire text rather than isolated passages out of context.

- Know how to respond to challenges. Most districts have formal procedures to follow if challenges occur. These generally include the steps in the review process, the people responsible for each step, and an appeal procedure. The person or group making the complaint should be asked if they have read the book and should submit a detailed statement regarding objections (or complete a district form).

Challenges to books should be treated respectfully and professionally. A reasoned, thoughtful response can often diffuse most situations. But be prepared to have your statements taken out of context, misconstrued, or twisted to support a censor's agenda, particularly if the objection comes from an organized group.

Tech Click

Click on the YouTube video of "Huckleberry Finn and the 'N' Word" for a provocative discussion of the controversy surrounding this famous book.

 *Tech Click*

Support for educators regarding their book selection is available from the Intellectual Freedom Office of the American Library Association, which provides book rationales, strategies to fight book challenges, lists of banned books, and many other resources. The National Council of Teachers of English also has excellent resources to help teachers.

Looking Ahead

We have provided you with the philosophical and theoretical principles that guide our thinking about literature and its place in children's lives. We have also shown you ideas for connecting books and children in meaningful and authentic ways.

The next set of chapters will provide you with specific knowledge about literature: the wealth of books within each genre as well as teaching strategies for exploring books in each genre that connect to the CCSS. The teaching ideas incorporating the CCSS are considered stepping-stones. We anticipate that they will stimulate you to create new activities that work particularly well with a specific genre and also help you discover how the ideas presented here might work effectively across multiple genres. Most important, we hope you will be enticed into exploring many of the books we describe in more depth and then sharing the ones you love with children so that they will become lifelong readers and lovers of literature.

 ## Summary

- Close reading, interactive read-alouds, shared reading, literature circles, and reader's workshop are all appropriate strategies for helping students respond to literature purposefully, critically, and with enjoyment. Teachers must carefully plan these experiences for them to be effective. Many literacy CCSS can be addressed through these strategies, notably the Reading: Literature and Reading: Information Text Standards.

- Judicious book selection is also critical to an effective literacy program with literature as the basis. If parents object to the books selected for use in your classroom, several strategies were offered to resolve these situations.

 ## Questions/Activities to Invite Thinking, Writing, and Conversation About the Chapter

1. There is some debate about the appropriateness of close reading for elementary students. Have a discussion with your peers on this topic. Are they developmentally ready to explore texts in this manner? Will close reading activities destroy student enjoyment of books and reading? What can we do as teachers to ensure that students learn how to explore texts closely while also learning to enjoy reading?

2. Think back to your most memorable school experiences with books. What did the teacher do to make that experience memorable? What can you do as a teacher to make experiences with books memorable as well as productive learning experiences?

3. Select one of the teaching strategies described in this chapter. Create a lesson plan for that strategy for a book you have read. Compare and critique your plan with peers who selected the same strategy.

Recommended Book Lists

(Books appropriate for preschoolers are marked *;
those with significant culturally diverse elements
are marked #.)

Sampling of Nonfiction Books for Read-Alouds

(There are many books and Web sites that recommend
good fiction books to read aloud. Nonfiction books that
work well for read-alouds are more difficult to find. See
chapter 10 for excellent nonfiction titles. This is a sample
list of ideas to stimulate your thinking.)

Abouraya, Karen Leggett. *Hands Around the Library:
Protecting Egypt's Treasured Books* (Susan L. Roth,
Illus.). (P)

#Adler, David A., and Adler, Michael, S. *A Picture Book of
Cesar Chavez* (Marie Olofsdotter, Illus.). (I)

Bishop, Nic. *Frogs.* (P)

#Brimmer, Larry. *Birmingham Sunday.* (I, M)

DeCristofano, Carolyn. *A Black Hole Is Not a Hole*
(Michael Carroll, Illus.). (I, M)

Deedy, Carmen. *14 Cows for America* (Thomas Gonzalez,
Illus.). (P, I)

Deem, James M. *Bodies from the Ice: Melting Glaciers and
the Recovery of the Past.* (M)

Dussling, Jennifer. *Deadly Poison Dart Frogs* (Gross-Out
Defense series). (I)

George, Jean Craighead. *The Wolves Are Back* (Wendell
Minor, Illus.). (P, I)

#Erdrich, Louise. *Sacajawea.* (I, M)

Goldish, Meish. *Fossa: A Fearsome Predator* (Uncommon
Animals series). (M)

Harwood, Jessica. *Should We Drill for Oil in Protected
Areas?* (M)

Hewitt, Sally. *Smell It!* (Let's Start! series). (P)

#Hill, Laban Carrick. *Dave the Potter: Artist, Poet, Slave*
(Bryan Collier, Illus.). (P, I)

Hillman, Ben. *How Strong Is It? How Weird Is It?* (I, M)

Jenkins, Steve, and Page, Robin. *Dogs and Cats; How
Many Ways Can You Catch a Fly?* (P, I)

#Johnson, Jen Cullerton. *Seeds of Change: Planting a Path
to Peace* (Sonia Lynn Sadler, Illus.). (I)

Jones, Charlotte Foltz. *The King Who Barked: Real
Animals Who Ruled* (Yayo, Illus.). (I)

Kerley, Barbara. *The Extraordinary Mark Twain (According
to Suzy)* (Edwin Fotheringham, Illus.). (I, M)

#Krull, Kathleen. *Wilma Unlimited* (David Diaz, Illus.).
(I, M)

Levinson, Nancy Smiler. *Rain Forests* (Diane Dawson
Hearn, Illus.). (P)

Llewellyn, Claire. *Ask Dr. K. Fisher About Creepy Crawlies*
(Kate Sheppard, Illus.). (P)

Macken, JoAnn Early. *Flip, Float, Fly: Seeds on the Move*
(Pam Paparone, Illus.). (P)

McDonald, Patrick. *Me Jane.* (M)

Messner, Kate. *Over and Under the Snow* (Christopher
Silas Neal, Illus.). (P)

Miller, Debbie. *Survival at 40 Below* (Jon Van Zyle,
Illus.). (P, I)

Miller, Edward. *Fireboy to the Rescue: A Fire Safety
Book.* (P)

Montgomery, Sy. *The Quest for the Tree Kangaroo; The
Man-Eating Tigers of Sundarbans; The Snake Scientist;
Kakapo Rescue: Saving the World's Strangest Parrot*
(Nic Bishop, Photographer). (I, M)

Newman, Mark. *Polar Bears.* (P)

#Pinkney, Andrea Davis. *Sit-In: How Four Friends Stood
Up by Sitting Down* (Brian Pinkney, Illus.). (I)

Settel, Joanne. *Exploding Ants.* (P, I)

Stewart, Melissa, and Young, Allen. *No Monkeys,
No Chocolate* (Nicole Wong, Illus.). (I)

Sweet, Melissa. *Balloons over Broadway: The True Story of
the Puppeteer of Macy's Parade.* (P, I)

Swinburne, S. R. *Whose Shoes? A Shoe for Every Job.* (P)

#Van Wyk, Chris (Ed.). *Nelson Mandela: Long Walk
to Freedom* (The Official Picture Book of His
Best-selling Autobiography). (Paddy Bouma,
Illus.). (I, M)

Walker, Richard. *Ouch! How Your Body Makes It Through
a Very Bad Day.* (I, M)

Wick, Walter. *A Drop of Water: A Book of Science and
Wonder.* (P, I)

Sampling of Predictable Books for Shared Reading Sessions

(See also Chapter 6 [sections on playground games and
folksongs].)

Brown, Ruth. *A Dark, Dark Tale.*

Carle, Eric. *The Very Busy Spider; The Very Quiet Cricket;
The Very Hungry Caterpillar.*

Cowly, Joy. *Mrs. Wishy Washy* (Elizabeth Fuller, Illus.);
In a Dark, Dark Wood; The Farm Concert.

Eastman, P. D. *Are You My Mother?*

Guarino, Deborah. *Is Your Mama a Llama?*

Hogrogian, Nonny. *One Fine Day.*

Hutchins, Pat. *Rosie's Walk.*

Keats, Ezra Jack. *Over in the Meadow.*

Kraus, Robert. *Whose Mouse Are You?*

Martin, Bill. *Brown Bear, Brown Bear, What Do You See?*; *Polar Bear, Polar Bear, What Do You Hear?*; *Chicka Chicka Boom, Boom* (Eric Carle, Illus.).

McCleland, Linda. *I Know an Old Lady.*

Riley, Linnea. *Mouse Mess.*

Sendak, Maurice. *Chicken Soup with Rice.*

Ward, Cindy. *Cookie's Week.*

Westcott, Nadine. *Peanut Butter and Jelly: A Play Rhyme.*

Williams, Sue. *I Went Walking*; *Let's Go Visiting* (Julie Vivas, Illus.).

Wood, Audrey and Don. *The Napping House.*

Sampling of Recommended Novels for Literature Circles

(These are classroom-tested titles that have been used successfully in many classrooms.)

Bunting, Eve. *Fly Away Home* (Ron Himler, Illus.); *#Smoky Night* (David Diaz, Illus.). (P)

Cleary, Beverly. *Ramona the Pest*; *The Mouse and the Motorcycle.* (P, I)

Creech, Sharon. *Ruby Holler.* (I)

#Curtis, Christopher, Paul. *The Watsons Go to Birmingham*; *Bud, Not Buddy.* (I, M)

Dahl, Roald. *James and the Giant Peach*; *The Witches.* (I)

DiCamillo, Kate. *The Tale of Despereaux.* (P, I)

Gardiner, John. *Stone Fox.* (I)

George, Jean. *Julie of the Wolves*; *My Side of the Mountain.* (I)

Henkes, Kevin. *Chrysanthemum*; *Sheila Rae the Brave* (and others). (P)

Howe, James. *Bunnicula.* (P)

Juster, Norton. *The Phantom Tollbooth.* (I,M)

Lord, Cynthia. *Rules.* (I)

Lowry, Lois. *Number the Stars* (I); *The Giver.* (M)

MacLachlan, Patricia. *Sarah, Plain and Tall.* (I)

#Myers, Walter Dean. *Scorpions*; *Monster.* (M)

Naylor, Phyllis. *Shiloh.* (I)

#O'Dell, Scott. *Sing Down the Moon.* (I)

Palacio, R. J. *Wonder.* (I, M)

Paterson, Katherine. *Bridge to Terabithia.* (I)

#Ryan, Pam. *Esperanza Rising.* (I)

#Sachur. Louis. *Holes*; *The Boy in the Girls' Bathroom.* (I, M)

Scieszka, John. *The True Story of the Three Little Pigs.* (P)

Selznick, Brian. *The Invention of Hugo Cabret.* (I, M)

White, E. B. *Charlotte's Web.* (P, I)

#Williams, Vera. *A Chair for My Mother.* (P)

Part II
The Forms and Genres of Children's Literature

Picture Books

(Literary Form)

In this chapter, we address the following questions in relation to picture books:

- What are picture books?

- What is the role of picture books in children's lives?

- How do we choose high-quality picture books?

- What are some types of picture books?

- How do we use picture books to meet the mandates of national standards as well as the needs of our diverse students?

Travor, a first grader, was at a table with a listening center. Using headsets, he could hear a dramatized recording of *Chicka Chicka Boom Boom* (Martin), a playful picture book in which the capital letters of the alphabet climb a tree, only to collapse in a heap at the bottom. He was oblivious to everything around him. He was standing up, hips swaying back and forth, twirling around as far as the earphones would let him. All the teacher could hear was Travor singing the words "Chicka chicka boom boom," and his hips accentuated each "boom." This 6-year-old was lost in the delight of a book, responding to the rhythm and the appealing language of a high-quality picture book.

Fifth graders Kristi and Erin sat intently reading and talking about *The Secret World of Walter Anderson* (Bass). "Look at how the inside of the cover has different colors of purple and blue that look so soft, you want to touch it," shared Kristi. Erin added that "even the first two pages had some of those same colors and that maybe the artist [E. B. Lewis] used them to get people thinking of living near water because the story has a lot to do with that." As with Travor, these fifth graders were also lost in a high-quality picture book, but this one was a biography of artist Walter Anderson, whose story is told using words combined with beautiful watercolor paintings.

Many adults fondly remember the first picture books that were read aloud, such as *Goodnight Moon* (Brown), *Mike Mulligan and His Steam Shovel* (Burton), *Corduroy* (Freeman), *The Tale of Peter Rabbit* (Potter), *Where the Wild Things Are* (Sendak), and many other classics. These first interactions with picture books often begin at home or in a child care center and continue in the early grades as teachers share them aloud for pure enjoyment and connections to the curriculum. However, picture books should be a part of the lives of older children as well. Many picture books are sophisticated in both content and pictures, making them more appropriate for older students. In fact, some writers of nonfiction purposely use this format to accompany complex text about a topic.

What Are Picture Books?

An article by Allyn Johnston and Caldecott Honor recipient Marla Frazee captures the essence:

> What is a picture book, anyway? In the most basic, classic, and very best sense, you could say it's a story for young children told in both words and pictures that unfolds over thirty-two or so printed pages that are sewn together at the spine and housed within . . . covers. And this story, when read aloud, will cast a spell over all who are present to hear it and look at it; and, with luck, it will go straight into their hearts and never be forgotten. (Johnston & Frazee, 2011, p. 10)

Picture books come in various formats, including pop-ups and interactive books, and different types, such as alphabet and counting books. *Picture storybooks* provide plot support with the illustrations; *wordless books* contain few words or none at all. Children's literature critic Leonard S. Marcus (2002) states, "A picture book is a dialogue between two worlds: the world of images and the world of words" (p. 3). As a format, picture books can be found in all genres; there are picture books with a fantasy story line, historical fiction stories, and illustrated poetry as well as nonfiction and biography.

A picture book typically starts with a story idea, and the text is created first. Sometimes the author creates the illustrations and the writing. At other times, an author and illustrator closely collaborate. In many circumstances, however, once a publisher accepts a manuscript, the art director selects an illustrator. Although the arrangement of a writer and an artist working separately may seem odd, it is important for each to have their own vision of the book. Most picture books have 32 pages, usually unnumbered, and have four parts (signatures of eight pages) sewn together to form a book. Nonfiction picture books usually are paginated and may have over 32 pages.

In contrast to the picture books described above, titles such as *The Velveteen Rabbit* (Williams) and *Charlotte's Web* (White), are novels in which text outweigh pictures in telling the story. These are not called picture books.

There are also books that blaze trails beyond the standard definition of a picture book. Several have the thick appearance of a novel but are, in fact, picture books, such as two books by Shaun Tan. *The Arrival*, the highly celebrated wordless book of 128 pages, relates an immigrant's experiences, and *Tales from Outer Suburbia* are short stories set in Australian suburbs.

Brian Selznick, another groundbreaking author, was awarded the Caldecott Medal and listed on the American Library's Association's Top Ten Best Young Adult Books for *The*

The Invention of Hugo Cabret by Brian Selznick is a good example of a highly sophisticated picture book that is combined with elements of a novel, making it appropriate for older children.

Invention of Hugo Cabret. Jonathan Hunt (2008) in reviewing this book described Selznick's "innovative feat of bookmaking and storytelling, featuring illustrations and book design that seem to be an amalgamation of novel, graphic novel, picture book, movie storyboard, and silent film" (p. 423). Selznick's grand creation *Wonderstruck*, a tome of over 600 pages, is another impressive example of his creative and groundbreaking style. Selznick imaginatively combines words and pictures to tell an unforgettable story of the human need for connection and purpose.

The world of picture books offers readers of any age an impressive array of choices in terms of format and content. Innovations in the picture book format open an exciting world of reading and imagination.

Elements of Picture Books

One important way to increase appreciation of the picture book format is learning the specialized vocabulary used in discussing illustrations. We describe the essential elements: the visual aspects or elements of art, design, artistic style, and media.

The Art of the Picture Book. Elements including line, color, shape, texture, design, style, and medium are essential visual aspects in the art of the picture book. Although described separately, artists combine these elements to successfully convey their vision and overall design of the book.

Tech Click

The Picturing Books Web site contains additional information about these elements and a slideshow on various book parts as well as a glossary and a list of authors' birthdays.

Line. The illustrator's use of line is a key element. Depending on the artist's purposes or vision, lines can be created to reveal a range of emotions to show action or mood or to focus the reader's attention in some way. The artist may use a combination of styles and types of lines. The direction of the line can be diagonal, vertical, or horizontal while varying width and length, and style of the line could be wiggly, straight, or curved, depending on what the artist wishes to convey. For example, in *Where the Wild Things Are*, Maurice Sendak uses cross-hatching on the inside of the book covers (end pages) and throughout the book for emotional appeal.

In *Kitten's First Full Moon*, Kevin Henkes uses bold black lines to accentuate the kitten and the moon. In *Don't Let the Pigeon Drive the Bus* (Willems), simple lines dominate. Uncomplicated drawings show a pale blue pigeon outlined in bold black crayon-style lines. The simple variations in the pigeon's eyes signal his fervent desire to drive the bus. The lines of the wings emphasize movement as they express coyness, disappointment, frustration, and complacency in this delightfully funny story with limited text.

Line is also used to show contrasts in size or perception. In *Into the Outdoors* (Gal), the story is told through words and pictures across double-page spreads, using charcoal and digital collage that bleeds (images that seem to run off the edge of the page). Effective use of line shows a city far below the family as they drive higher into the mountains. Looming trees appear so large that they tower over the car, bleeding off the page with their tops out of view. In Caldecott recipient *Owl Moon* (Yolen), illustrator John Schoenherr uses line to depict texture in the feathers of a large owl and to highlight its grand presence on a high branch. In the 2004 Caldecott Medal winner, *The Man Who Walked Between the Towers*, Mordicai Gerstein takes the reader to the World Trade Center in 1974 to watch a daring Frenchman walk a tightrope. Gerstein captures the awe of spectators with his ingenious use of horizontal and vertical lines to show distance, height, and perspective in this true account of a magnificent feat.

Color. One of the most powerful elements in picture books is color, often combined with effective use of line. For example, in Caldecott Honor book *All the World*, Marla Frazee beautifully complements the author's poetic style by melding strong lines and luminous watercolors across double-page spreads. Readers can feel the lively use of color and intriguing combination of computer illustration, paintings on wood, and collage in another 2010 Caldecott Honor book, *Red Sings from Treetops: A Year in Color* (Sidman), illustrated by Pamela Zagarenski. Although brilliant colors dominate, Zagarenski masterfully uses a variety of media to make Sidman's beautiful poetry a rich visual experience.

Color can also effectively capture emotions. In *Grump Groan Growl* by bell hooks [*sic*], illustrator Chris Raschka captures the very essence of grumpiness on the front cover by using large childlike letters for the title in thick black paint. Two children glare at each other with angry, cantankerous expressions. A dog is tucked into the corner of the word GROAN in the title. On the back cover, the two children sit back to back with warm, peaceful expressions on their faces. The endpapers are done in broad vertical brushstrokes of orange, green, and yellow hues. Readers can predict what happens in the book by noticing what is portrayed on the dust jacket. Across the copyright and title pages is a black-framed, double-page spread; childlike finger painting depicts an angry dog and an angrier child who fills the entire space. Raschka uses a wide paintbrush to apply watercolor paints. With only a few well-chosen words throughout the book, bell hooks captures this bad-mood day with the overall message that anger will dissipate. The last word is painted with large letters that sweep gently across both pages.

In *When Sophie Gets Angry—Really, Really Angry*, another book about strong emotion, Molly Bang uses bright bold red and yellow paint that seems to explode throughout the book. In contrast, illustrator Henry Cole depicts the warm feelings of sharing, love, and acceptance in *The Kiss Box* (Verburg) with beautiful watercolor washes of lavender, shades of green, yellow, and brown.

Dianne Goode, illustrator of the Caldecott Honor book *When I Was Young in the Mountains* (Rylant), captures a sense of place from the author's happy childhood reminiscences of life in rural Appalachia in warm, almost soft-to-the-touch pictures using a palette of light-hued colored pencils.

In the award-winning nonfiction picture book *Dave the Potter: Artist, Poet, Slave* (Hill), illustrator Bryan Collier's masterful use of light and subtlety earth-toned watercolor collages complement the eloquent text. The combination of light and color skillfully draws the eye to Dave, a slave, his strong hands masterfully transforming clay into large jars and pots on which he inscribed lines of poetry.

In Dave the Potter: Artist, Poet, Slave the writing and the illustrations work in perfect harmony.

Shape. Artists consider different uses of shape as another essential element of art that serves several functions. For example, shape can support and extend a reader's understanding of mood, emotions, and setting. As with line, shape can also suggest anger, peacefulness, playfulness, or form, such as letters of the alphabet.

David Wiesner creatively and playfully challenges the notions of space and shape in *The Three Pigs*. On some pages, he uses multiple frames in comic strip fashion. Speech balloons violate the margins by overlapping the frames, causing them to pop from the page. Pigs peek out from behind another illustration and play with pages seemingly torn from the book. Elsewhere, the pigs fold book pages into a paper airplane and fly around on their handiwork. Their delightful mischief continues throughout the book.

Lois Ehlert is a master of color, shape, design, and simplicity, making her many books popular particularly with young children. In *Color Farm* and *Color Zoo*, she uses die-cut squares, revealing a series of animal faces. Other titles, such as *Red Leaf, Yellow Leaf*, combine Ehlert's love for nature with informational text and lively art that includes collage and found objects. *Waiting for Wings*, a 12-inch-high by 10-inch-wide book with a vertical title running down the edge of the cover, introduces readers to the life cycle of a butterfly. Ehlert's use of bold, beautiful colors, cut paper and shapes, and graduated half-page books intrigue children.

Texture. When an artist creates a sense of texture in illustrations, readers want to reach out and touch the pages. Texture adds variety and can enrich a reader's appreciation, imagination, and realistic reading experience. The impression of a textured surface is created with the skillful use of a medium, such as paint, pencil, or collage, and applied with varied strokes. For example, in the 1995 Caldecott Medal winner, *Smoky Night* (Bunting), illustrator David Diaz creates scenes depicting a city and its people during the aftermath of a riot, using acrylic paint combined with photographed objects to frame each illustration. These collages are so realistic that the objects seem attached to the surface of the pages.

The Trouble with Cauliflower (Sutton) is an endearing and humorous story about Mortimer, who believes that eating cauliflower causes bad luck. This presents a dilemma when his best friend, Sadie, makes cauliflower stew for him. Jim Harris's illustrations are fun and whimsical, and the variety of textures works in perfect tandem with the story.

Design. Design is the term used to describe the way the artist achieves an overall effect—it is essential. Discussing a book's design encompasses major elements—line, color, shape, and texture. When these elements work harmoniously throughout a book, it creates a positive and pleasurable reading experience. Popular author John Scieszka (1998) elaborates:

> Design is an essential part of any picture book. It is the first aspect of a book that a reader judges. It is the framework for the text and illustration. It is the subtle weave of words and pictures that allows both to tell one seamless tale. (p. 196)

Michael Hall, in *Perfect Square*, starts an adventure with a square that transforms itself into something different—from a fountain to a garden and more. This book is simple, elegant in design, and satisfying as it successfully achieves a sense of unity.

In *Mouse & Lion* (Burkert), unity of design is accomplished in more complex ways. This exquisitely designed retelling of Aesop's fable presents detailed and lavish illustrations with every aspect carefully planned and accomplished. The setting of an African savannah is depicted from various perspectives, including that of a mouse. The illustrations show unit, balance, and a sense of harmony. Thoughtful decisions in the book's planning leave nothing to chance; illustrations expressing action are balanced with blue pages representing past action or no action. These design factors contribute to readers' positive response to the book.

The key factors for achieving unity of design include balance and *emphasis*—the way the illustrator draws the eye to the most important aspects of the page. For example, an artist might use contrasting colors to signify importance or repetition of shapes to illustrate a predictable rhythm. Tomie dePaola is a master of symmetry and design and has earned numerous accolades for his recognizable use of color, line, and overall composition. Readers can easily find excellent examples of the ways dePaola uses symmetry to achieve balance in *Strega Nona, Let the Whole Earth Sing Praise, The Art Lesson*, and *The Night Before Christmas*.

Children's book critic Barbara Elleman (2009) shares her thoughts about dePaola's popular style:

> "His stories sometimes bubble up with laughter, sometimes simmer with sly wit, and sometimes burst with outright silliness. Cleverly, he matches image to mood. The pages, punctuated often with his signature hearts and white birds, are warmed with lively lines and vibrant colors, giving an upbeat feeling that pleases." She furthers remarks that in *Strega Nona*, who is a grandmother witch creating potions and magic cures with her helper, Big Anthony, "Through facial and body expressions, Tomie deftly pictures the hilarious results of Big Anthony's meddling." (p. 105)

Popular author-illustrator Jan Brett is also known for excellent design and meticulous detail. Many of her books include main illustrations framed by intricately decorated borders that provide insights and opportunities to predict the plot. Her style is recognizable in books such as *The Mitten*, *The Hat*, *Gingerbread Baby*, and *Goldilocks and the Three Bears*. *The 3 Little Dassies*, a retelling of "The Three Little Pigs," is set in southern Africa with small guinea-pig-like animals as the characters. It includes Brett's decorative borders as well as side panels showing a parallel story of the Agama Man, who tries to rescue the dassies.

Tech Click

It is easy to find videos and podcasts of picture book authors and illustrators by visiting publishers' sites or by conducting a search of proper names. Prolific author-illustrator Jan Brett maintains an extensive Web site with information about her life and work as well as numerous free literature activities and downloads. Look for the video in which she discusses the creation and design of *The 3 Little Dassies*. In a *Reading Rockets* video interview, illustrator E. B. Lewis explains why he uses the term *artistrator* and talks movingly about the events that changed his life. (Note: Some schools use a firewall to block videos, so work with your school librarian or technical coordinator to gain access or find a viable work around.)

Intriguing and intricately designed borders and panels are effective in helping to tell the story of the *3 Little Dassies* by Jan Brett.

Artistic Style and Media. *Artistic style* is a term we use to describe the characteristics that distinguish one person's work from another. Readers readily recognize a book by Tomie dePaola from one by Jan Brett. Some picture book art reflects characteristics of a formally recognized style, whereas others combine aspects of formal styles, creating a signature style (see Figure 4.1).

Some artists have a favorite medium to create their illustrations, such as watercolor paint, acrylics, ink, colored pencils, or collage, whereas other artists use mixed media, a combination of more than one medium. The media should complement some aspect of the book, such as the content, emotional tone, the time period, setting, or the audience for whom the book was written. So, an illustrator might use a watercolor wash in a book about the ocean or a foggy day, while the author of a nonfiction book about a science topic or a person's life might use photographs as the medium. Figure 4.2 is a sample of artistic techniques and examples of books for each medium.

It is often challenging to determine which medium an artist used. Sometimes, there is a description of the technique(s) on the copyright page or occasionally on the jacket or in the back matter. Look for an illustrator or author note that often provides intriguing

FIGURE 4.1 Artistic Styles in Picture Books

(Books appropriate for preschoolers are marked *; those with significant culturally diverse elements are marked #.)

Naive Art and Folk Art—Naive art is often distinguished by the use of a lot of color, some distortion in figures, and a preponderance of detail and lack of perspective. Some self-taught artists are associated with naive art, drawing from their background and experiences. Folk art often uses motifs and symbols associated with a particular culture with similar characteristics as naive art.

#*Example of naive art:* *Sing to the Sun* by Ashley Bryan.

#*Example of folk art:* *The Whispering Cloth* by Pegi Dietz Shea and illustrated by Anita Riggio.

Cartooning—This style is highly popular and often distinguished by its simplicity, playfulness, and exaggeration.

Examples: *Is Your Mama a Llama?* by Deborah Guarino and illustrated by Steven Kellogg; *No, David* by David Shannon; *It's Disgusting and We Ate It!* by James Solheim and illustrated by Eric Brace.

Impressionist Art—In this style, the artist effectively plays with light and color in interesting ways, sometimes depicting objects with a more abstract look using many tiny bits of color.

Examples: *Mirette on the High Wire* by Emily Arnold McCully; *Mr. Rabbit and the Lovely Present* by Charlotte Zolotow and illustrated by Maurice Sendak.

Realistic or Representational Art—This style reflects reality and what we actually see in real life.

Examples: *The Wolves Are Back* by Jean Craighead George and illustrated by Wendell Minor; *Scorpions!* by Laurence Pringle and illustrated by Meryl Henderson; *Owl Moon* by Jane Yolen and illustrated by John Schoenherr; *Rapunzel* by Paul Zelinsky.

Surrealistic Art—Characteristic of this style is the imaginative incongruity of images on the page.

Examples: *Jumanji* by Chris Van Allsburg; *Me and You* by Anthony Brown; *Art & Max* by David Wiesner.

insights into the writing, creation, and design of the book. Check author and illustrator Web sites for additional information. It is worth the effort, as it can increase appreciation of the book. It may also lead to students wanting other books by the same author or illustrator to compare and contrast styles, design, and writing.

 *Tech Click*

Explore Eric Carle's friendly Web pages to find delightful videos that make visitors feel that they are friends with this jovial and talented author-illustrator. Several engaging clips demonstrating his collage techniques are well worth viewing.

Looking Closely at the Writing in Picture Books

Next, we discuss the writing in picture books and how literary aspects are used. Review Chapter 1 for additional evaluation criteria for fiction; Chapter 10 delves deeper into nonfiction evaluation. Picture book authors and artists need to do more showing than telling.

Well-Written Prose. Well-developed, readable, and appealing language is an expectation for all writing, including picture books. Look for characteristics such as well-organized text, clarity and coherence, good explication of ideas, use of figurative language, appropriate tone, and emotional involvement or voice (McClure, 2003). For example, the 2013 Orbis Pictus winner, *Monsieur Marceau: Actor Without Words* (Schubert, DuBois, Illus.), uses evocative writing. Marceau is described as "the superstar of silence, the maestro of mime."

FIGURE 4.2 Examples of Media Used in Picture Books

(Books appropriate for preschoolers are marked *; those with significant culturally diverse elements are marked #.)

Painterly Techniques

Acrylics (has synthetic base that dissolves in water)

Ashman, Linda. *Starry Safari* (Jeff Mack, Illus.).

Bates, Costa. *Seaside Dream* (Lambert Davis, Illus.).

#Brown, Tameka Fryer. *Around Our Way on Neighbors' Day* (Charlotte Riley-Webb, Illus.).

#Cunnane, Kelly. *Chirchir Is Singing* (Jude Daly, Illus.).

Fraser, Mary Ann. *Heebie-Jeebie Jamboree.*

Hall, Michael. *Perfect Square* (acrylic monotype ink prints).

#Krosoczka, Jarrett J. *Ollie.*

Sarcone-Roach, Julie. *Subway Story.*

Wilson, Karma. *Bear's Loose Tooth* (Jane Chapman, Illus.).

Acrylic and Oil Pastel

#Heller, Linda. *How Dalia Put a Big Yellow Comforter Inside a Tiny Blue Box and Other Wonders of Tzedakah* (Stacey Dressen McQueen, Illus.).

Acrylic and Colored Pencils

Juan, Ana. *The Pet Shop Revolution.*

Perl, Erica S. *Chicken Butt's Back!* (Henry Cole, Illus.).

Gouache (pronounced "gwash"; opaque watercolor paint)

Bloom, Suzanne. *Feeding Friendsies* (gouache and pencil).

#Bridges, Shirin Yim. *Ruby's Wish* (Sophie Blackall, Illus.).

Edwards, Pamela. *While the World Was Sleeping.*

Fleming, Candace. *Clever Jack Takes the Cake* (G. Brian Karas, Illus.).

George, Lindsay Barrett. *That Pup!*

Kurtz, Jane. *Trouble* (Durga Bernhard).

#Lin, Grace. *Thanking the Moon: Celebrating the Mid-Autumn Moon Festival.*

#Qiong, Yu Li. *A New Year's Reunion* (Zhu-Liang Cheng, Illus.).

Russo, Marisabina. *I Will Come Back for You: A Family in Hiding During World War II.*

Tempera (similar to watercolor but mixed with a base, such as egg yolk)

Sendak, Maurice. *Where the Wild Things Are.*

#Spivey Gilchrist, Jan. *My America* (Jan Spivey Gilchrist and Ashley Bryan, Illus.).

Stanley, Diane. *Mozart the Wonder Child: A Puppet Play in Three Acts* (painted on gessoed wooden panels).

Ward, Lynd. *The Silver Pony.*

Oils (colored pigment mixed with linseed oil)

Hills, Tad. *How Rocket Learned to Read* (oil paint and colored pencil).

Ray, Mary Lyn. *Welcome, Brown Bird* (Peter Sylvada, Illus.).

Sheldon, Dyan. *The Whales' Song* (Gary Blythe, Illus.).

Van Allsburg, Chris. *The Polar Express.*

Wood, Audrey. *Heckety Peg; King Bidgood's in the Bathtub* (Don Wood, Illus.).

Wood, Douglas. *No One But You* (P.J. Lynch, Illus.).

Watercolor (color pigment mixed with water)

Beard, Alex. *Monkey See, Monkey Draw.*

Bemelmans, Ludwig. *Madeline.*

Buonanno, Graziella Pacini. *Dancing on Grapes* (Gina Capaldi, Illus.).

dePaola, Tomie. *Strega Nona.*

Gore, Leonid. *The Wonderful Book* (watercolor and ink).

Lobel, Anita. *Nini Lost and Found* (watercolor and gouache).

Ludwig, Trudy. *My Secret Bully* (Abigail Marble, Illus.).

#Manna, Anthony L., and Mitakidou, Soula. *The Orphan: A Cinderella Story from Greece* (Giselle Potter, Illus.).

McAllister, Angela. *Little Mist* (Sarah Fox Davies, Illus.) (watercolor and pencil).

Obed, Ellen Bryan. *Who Would Like a Christmas Tree?* (Anne Hunter, Illus.).

Orloff, Karen Kaufman. *I Wanna New Room* (David Catrow, Illus.) (watercolor and pencil).

Sayre, April Pulley. *If You're Hoppy* (Jackie Urbanovic, Illus.) (watercolor and ink).

Shuleviz, Uri. *Dawn.*

Stead, Phillip. *Jonathan and the Big Blue Boat* (also collage).

Verburg, Bonnie. *The Kiss Box* (Henry Cole, Illus.) (watercolor and pencil).

#Woodson, Jacqueline. *Pecan Pie Baby* (Sophie Blackall, Illus.).

Yolen, Jane. *Owl Moon* (John Schoenherr, Illus.).

Collage (fabrics, wood, paper, and other found objects glued to create a three-dimensional design)

Alko, Selina. *Every-Day Dress-Up* (gouache and collage).

> ### FIGURE 4.2 *continued*

Aston, Dianna. *Dream Something Big: The Story of the Watts Towers* (Susan Roth, Illus.).

#Bunting, Eve. *Smoky Night* (David Diaz, Illus.).

Carle, Eric. *The Very Hungry Caterpillar.*

Craig, Lindsey. *Farmyard Beat* (Marc Brown, Illus.) (hand-painted papers and collage).

*Keats, Ezra Jack. *Snowy Day* (and others).

Lewis, J. Patrick. *The Fantastic 5&10¢ Store: A Rebus Adventure* (Valorie Fisher, Illus.) (mixed-media collage).

Mavor, Sally. *Pocketful of Posies* (hand-sewn fabric relief collages).

#Ramsden, Ashley. *Seven Feathers* (Ed Young, Illus.).

Drawing Techniques

Pencil

#Feelings, Tom. *The Middle Passage.*

Milway, Katie Smith. *The Good Garden: How One Family Went from Hunger to Having Enough* (Sylvie Daigneault, Illus.).

Rylant, Cynthia. *The Relatives Came* (Stephen Gammell, Illus.).

Van Alsburg, Chris. *Jumanji; The Garden of Abdul Gasazi; The Mysteries of Harris Burdick.*

Printmaking Techniques

*Brown, Marcia. *Once a Mouse* (woodcut).

Elliott, David. *In the Wild* (woodblock printing).

#McKissack, Patricia. *The Dark Thirty: Southern Tales of the Supernatural* (Brian Pinkney, Illus.) (scratchboard).

#Pinkney, Brian. *The Ballad of Belle Dorcas* (scratchboard).

Stead, Phillip. *A Sick Day for Amos McGee* (woodblock printing and pencil).

Swanson, Susan. *The House in the Night* (Beth Krommes, Illus.) (scratchboard).

Mixed Media (combining two or more media)

Dowson, Nick. *North: The Amazing Story of Arctic Migration* (Patrick Benson, Illus.) (watercolor, pen, and pencil).

*Fleming, Denise. *In the Tall, Tall Grass; Lunch; underGROUND* (cotton rag fiber and paint).

#Guy, Ginger Foglesong. *¡Bravo!* (René King Moreno, Illus.) (pastels, watercolors, and pencils).

Lionni, Leo. *Swimmy, Frederick* (collage and watercolors).

Lloyd-Jones, Sally. *How to Get a Job by Me, the Boss* (Sue Heap, Illus.) (acrylic, paint, crayons, and felt-tip pen).

Lorenz, Albert. *The Exceptionally Extraordinarily Ordinary First Day of School* (pen and ink, watercolor, and colored pencil).

Moore, Inga. *A House in the Woods* (watercolor and pencil).

Raschka, Chris. *A Ball for Daisy: Daisy Gets Lost: The Hello, Goodbye Window* (ink, watercolor, and gouache).

Stein, David Ezra. *Interrupting Chicken* (watercolor, water, soluble crayon, china marker, pen, opaque white ink, and tea).

Digital and Digital Combined with Other Media

Aylesworth, Jim. *Little Bitty Mousie* (Michael Hague, Illus.) (drawn in pencil and then scanned and colored in Photoshop).

Bradford, Wade. *Why Do I Have to Make My Bed?* (Johanna van der Sterre, Illus.) (watercolor and digitally finished in Photoshop).

Codell, Esmé Raji. *Fairly Fairy Tales* (Elisa Chavarri, Illus.).

Crum, Shutta. *Mine!* (Patrice Barton, Illus.) (pencil sketches created digitally).

Esbaum, Jill. *Tom's Tweet* (Dan Santat, Illus.).

Gal, Susan. *Into the Outdoors* (charcoal on paper and digital collage).

Krull, Kathleen. *Boy Who Invented TV: The Story of Philo Farnsworth* (Greg Couch, Illus.) (acrylic wash with colored pencil and dry brush; schematics, diagrams, and print images added using digital overlay in Photoshop).

Savage, Stephen. *Where's Walrus?* (title type hand lettered by Stephen Savage) (Adobe Illustrator).

Shaw, Hannah. *School for Bandits* (pen and ink, printmaking techniques, and Photoshop).

*Willems, Mo. *Knuffle Bunny Free: An Unexpected Diversion* (rendered by hand in ink and then colored and composited in digital collage).

Willems, Mo. *That Is Not a Good Idea!* (pencil and watercolor, including digital color).

Prolific author Bill Martin Jr. wanted children to fall in love with the sounds of language. Good writing in picture books can be smooth and connected or clipped and jumpy, depending on the desired effect. In Martin and Archambault's *White Dynamite and Curly Kid*, the writers use a staccato effect to enhance the rodeo feeling.

Another feature of effective, well-developed prose is repetition, a key aspect of oral story-telling that appropriately finds its way into some texts. In Cynthia Rylant's sentimental journey *When I Was Young in the Mountains*, each page begins, "When I was young in the mountains," and then expresses a different element of rural Appalachian life. The repetition feels calming, like a recurring, familiar lullaby.

Repetition is handled subtly in *My Great-Aunt Arizona* (Houston). Based on a longtime schoolteacher, Gloria Houston's real-life, great-aunt Arizona, the story takes readers through one woman's lifetime. Several times, Houston repeats a simple description of Arizona's clothing—her dresses, petticoats, shoes, and apron. This phrase is repeated as Arizona grows older, suggesting a constancy and steadfastness of the character as well as her impression on the author.

Figurative Language. Language that is not literal is called *figurative*. Skilled writers use metaphoric language adeptly. For example, in *Migrant* (Trottier), a traveling Mennonite family moves from Canada to Mexico; one character feels like a bird, "her family is a flock beating its way there and back again." Pam Muñoz Ryan, author of the 2011 winner of the Pura Belpré Award, imaginatively describes how a sick boy attempts to focus on his homework: "The twos and threes lifted from the page and waved for the others to join them. . . . They held hands in a long procession of tiny figures, flew across the room, and escaped through the window crack" (p. 2).

Voice. A writer's voice refers to the author's signature style—the combination of all aspects of writing that convey unique characteristics that identify the author. In the same way that readers recognize the artistic style of illustrators, they also become familiar with the writing style of authors. For example, Byrd Baylor has a consistently soft, poetic voice in her books, such as *I'm in Charge of Celebrations*, *The Way to Start a Day*, *When Clay Sings*, *Hawk, I'm Your Brother*, and *Your Own Best Secret Place*.

Some authors adopt a childlike writing voice. Bernard Waber does this adeptly in *Ira Sleeps Over* when the pesky sister talks with a whiny voice. Similarly, Judith Viorst applies this technique in *Alexander and the Terrible, Horrible, No Good, Very Bad Day* and *Alexander, Who Used to Be Rich Last Sunday*. Even Viorst's book title sounds like something a child might say. In *Alexander, Who's Not (Do You Hear Me? I Mean It!) Going to Move*, Alexander calls his brother Nick "puke-face." Childlike prose often helps readers easily identify with characters who think and talk as they do.

Understatement. Sometimes a writer faces the difficult choice of deciding when too much has been said and when it is not enough. Experienced authors have learned this balance—that not everything needs to be explained: sometimes *less* is *more*. Good writers trust their readers to make the connection and fill in between the lines as needed.

In Patricia Polacco's *The Keeping Quilt*, short statements are packed with references to significant changes. As the story passes through multiple generations, Polacco writes about how men and women acted at family weddings with simple statements. These brief sentences clue the reader to the cultural changes that occurred in the author's family. These understatements trust readers to infer and develop insights.

Plot. In picture books, plots are generally simple and straightforward, without complexities or subplots. Typically, the main character is about the age of the intended audience. Often, the plot unfolds from the narration of a third party, an implied or anonymous storyteller. In

Falconer's *Olivia Forms a Band*, the anonymous storyteller relates Olivia's adventures in her imagined world. Readers feel that they are peeking in—another popular way to relate a story's plot. Falconer (2003) shares why he enjoys creating children's books:

> I've always felt that children's books are for the most part condescending toward children and miss how smart children are. Their little hands and mouths may not be able to articulate what is going on in their sharp little brains. Writing children's books is an opportunity to express this, and it seems to be appreciated by both children and adults. (para. 10)

Leads. Writers know that the opening lines of a book are critical. Leads set a mood or tone and may foreshadow events. The little fish in Jon Klassen's 2013 Caldecott winner starts some ripples with, "This hat is not mine. I just stole it." This shocking statement grabs readers' attention, causing them to wonder how the little fish will rationalize the theft and what will happen to him.

Mary Bahr begins *My Brother Loved Snowflakes* with, "Snowflakes liked my brother, Willie. And why not? Nobody cared about them the way he did." This language suggests a story about a character's relationship and fascination with snow.

Characters. Memorable and believable characters in picture book stories are as carefully created as those in longer books, such as novels. Unforgettable characters in classic series, such as Clifford the Big Red Dog (Bridwell), Arthur the aardvark (Brown), and Babar the elephant (de Brunhoff), leave readers with lasting memories of main characters. Appealing characters such as these are brought to life through art and words working in complementary fashion—readers come to know a character's personality, emotions, and key actions that move the plot ahead within limited space.

Dialogue. Many picture books use dialogue effectively to demonstrate insights about the characters. In *One Cool Friend*, author Toni Buzzeo and illustrator David Small collaborate in conveying the dialogue:

> "I think I'll have a bit of a soak," Elliot's father announced.
> "Wait!" Elliot said. "I left my penguin in there."
> "I'll set him on the hamper and do my best not to splash."

In this brief exchange, readers understand the adaptability of the father. Or is it gullibility? This book is a superb example for older students in punctuating dialogue.

In Rachel Isadora's *Yo, Jo!*, the urban theme is conveyed in both illustrations and dialogue. Instead of conventional quotation marks, Isadora uses large colorful fonts for dialogue and black font in between.

Setting. The setting of the book must also be established within the first few pages. This is especially important when it is critical to the plot. For example, in Byrd Baylor's *The Desert Is Theirs*, the setting is essential to the story because she describes the life and beliefs of the Tohono O'odham, indigenous people of Arizona's Sonoran Desert. Similarly, *Thanks to the Animals* (Sockabasin) portrays a winter setting during a time of Passamaquoddy Native American migration. In *The Boy Who Held Back the Sea* (Hort & Locker), the setting is a dike in Holland that prevents flooding; it becomes the crux of the plot as a boy attempts to save his village. In *Pippo the Fool* (Fern), illustrator Pau Estrada re-created medieval Florence, the setting of the story about the architect who first calculated how to build a dome.

Naturally, setting is greatly enhanced and enriched by illustrations that extend the reader's understanding of the story. For Baylor's book, artist Peter Parnall painted wistful watercolors in the hues of the desert. For Locker, the Flemish style of his oils gives a feeling of old Holland and the art of Dutch Masters such as Rembrandt. Language also contributes to the setting in a good book. Estrada details the Italian architecture and crowded feeling of medieval Florentine streets.

The Role of Picture Books in Children's Lives

David Wiesner says this about the importance of picture books in the lives of children: "The first art that most children see is in picture books" (quoted in Marcus, 2012, introduction).

Author Laura Backes (2011) shares the importance of picture books in the lives of her children:

> In our house, picture books—with their vivid, concise text and new illustrations waiting around each page-turn—offered my son an opportunity to become the characters in the story. He'd roll his eyes, gnash his teeth and leap about the room with Maurice Sendak's *Where the Wild Things Are*, complete with his own Wild Rumpus chant (ooga booga ooga booga eeek eeek).
>
> Picture books are family touch points. Seeing the cover immediately brings us back to a specific time and place in our lives. Turning the pages, even years later, elicits shared looks and smiles that don't need explanation. They are priceless memories bound in dust jackets, ready to be pulled off the shelf any time we get the urge to relive them.

The language and memories attached to picture books are powerful influences on the development of a love of reading and writing. "No kind of writing lodges itself so deeply in our memory, echoing there for the rest of our lives, as the books that we met in our childhood," William Zinsser (1998) explains; "when we grow up and read them to our own children, they are the oldest of old friends. Their spell is woven so simply and in so few words that anyone might think they were simple to write" (p. 3). Children enthusiastically remember beloved picture books, especially if they were repeatedly read aloud. For many children, such experiences lead the way to becoming lifelong readers. In early elementary classrooms, teachers share picture books aloud, discussing them and planning interesting and meaningful ways for children to respond through drama, writing, and art. Alluring language, memorable stories, and intriguing information, combined with beautiful illustrations, capture children in ways that remain with them always.

In this chapter and the ones that follow, examples of picture books are provided for each genre with titles appropriate for intermediate and older students. Figure 4.3 gives examples of picture books with themes or topics that are appropriate for older students.

Tech Click

The Mysteries of Harris Burdick (Van Allsburg) continues to fascinate readers of all ages. A popular activity for students revolves around sharing their own Burdick-inspired stories with readers around the world. (For additional details, consult the Harris Burdick Project Web site at harrisburdickproject.weebly.com.)

The Partnership for 21st Century Skills (2011) tool kit lists a Harris Burdick activity for fourth graders, representing the four Cs: creativity, collaboration, communication, and critical thinking (also called information literacy). Compare, contrast, and categorize stories in *The Chronicles of Harris Burdick: Fourteen Amazing Authors Tell the Tales*. Check out the *Who Is Harris Burdick?* video, in which Lemony Snicket "bugs" famous authors, such as Kate DiCamillo and Sherman Alexie, to get to the bottom of the mystery.

FIGURE 4.3 Sample Picture Books with Themes or Topics That Are Appropriate for Older Students

(Books with significant culturally diverse elements are marked #.)

Becker, Aaron. *Journey* (I). Intricate fantasy journey in a wordless format.

Browne, Anthony. *Willy's Pictures* (P, I, M). Art; fiction; famous masterpieces of art are parodied.

Cronin, Doreen. *Click, Clack, Moo, Cows That Type* (P, I). Humorous story; use of understatement.

Daywalt, Drew. *The Day the Crayons Quit* (I) (Oliver Jeffers, Illus.). Humorous and sophisticated parody.

Gallico, Paul. *The Snow Goose* (Angela Barrett, Illus.) (M). Battle of Normandy.

Greenberg, Jan, and Jordan, Sandra. *Action Jackson* (P, I). Art; award-winning biography of Jackson Pollack.

Morpurgo, Michael. *The Best Christmas Present in the World* (M). World War I.

#Myers, Walter Dean. *Blues Journey* (I, M). Poetry; African American theme.

Scieszka, Jon. *Science Verse; Math Curse* (all). Combination of science or math and poetry verses with related illustrations; humorous with much to ponder.

Wiesner, David. *Flotsam* (P, I). Wordless; excursion under the sea and through time.

Like all good literature, picture books take readers on safe adventures without leaving their chairs. Picture books are for all seasons, for all reasons, in all genres, and for all students. Today's picture books are found not only in the nursery but also on the shelves of school libraries and in classrooms at every grade level.

Criteria for Evaluating Picture Books

The criteria below support the evaluation and selection of high-quality picture books. These items take into account not only the artwork but also its interaction with literary aspects. Important considerations also include age and developmental appropriateness and learning outcomes or curricular goals. When choosing picture books, also apply the criteria for writing, characterization, and other literary qualities found in each genre chapter.

1. Do the artistic elements (line, color, shape, and texture) help to interpret and extend appreciation and understanding of the text?
2. Does the artist's choice of medium, style, and design complement the text?
3. Do the illustrations complement or work effectively with the text?
4. Do the art and text present accurate and nonstereotyped or culturally biased images and views?
5. Are the illustrations and text accurate in presenting factual information?
6. Are the text and illustrations developmentally appropriate?

Types of Picture Books

Genre and Thematic Connections

In this section, we discuss various types of picture books; however, not all picture books fall neatly into these types. Some authors use the picture book format for science-related topics or for a fictional story about the past. Some authors write biographies using the picture book format. Others showcase poetry with beautifully illustrated books. Writers may also choose the picture book format for stories with a magical theme (fantasy or science fiction), folktales, myths, or fables (traditional literature), or for stories that could actually happen in our time and in our world (contemporary realistic fiction).

Concept Books

Concept books are among the first picture books shared with children. Young children love to learn about their world, and concept books are ideal for parents and caregivers to build the foundation for simple concepts. These books help foster understanding about specific topics, such as counting, the alphabet, time, seasons, shapes, and pets. Many are illustrated using a variety of media, whereas others use photographs to closely relate to what children see. Concept books are often classified as nonfiction, and we include additional discussion in Chapter 10. Figures 4.4 and 4.5 provide examples of concept books and counting books.

FIGURE 4.4 **Examples of Concept Books (All Primary)**

(Books with significant culturally diverse elements are marked #.)

Bond, Felicia. *Big Hugs, Little Hugs.*

Boyd, Lizi. *Inside, Outside.*

Carle, Eric. *My Very First Book of Colors.*

Fisher, Valorie. *Everything I Need to Know Before I'm Five.*

Freymann, Saxton. *Food for Thought: The Complete Book of Concepts.*

Gravett, Emily. *Blue Chameleon.*

Hoban, Tana. *Black on White Cubes*; *Cones, Cylinders, & Squares*; *Shapes, Shapes, Shapes* (and others).

Horacek, Peter. *Animal Opposites: A Pop-Up Book.*

Hutchins, Hazel. *A Second Is a Hiccup: A Child's Book of Time.*

Intriago, Patricia. *Dot.*

Miller, Margaret. *Where Does It Go?*; *Who Uses This?*

Rosenthal, Amy. *I Scream Ice Cream: A Book of Wordles*; *Question Mark.*

Seeger Vaccaro, Laura. *First the Egg*; *Lemons Are Not Red.*

#Thong, Roseanne. *Round Is a Tortilla: A Book of Shapes.*

FIGURE 4.5 **Examples of Counting Books (All Primary)**

(Books with significant culturally diverse elements are marked #.)

Anno, Mitsumasa. *Anno's Counting Book.*

Baker, Keith. *1, 2, 3 Peas*; *Big Fat Hen.*

Bang, Molly. *Ten, Nine, Eight.*

Barnett, Mac. *Count the Monkeys* (Kevin Cornell, Illus.).

Berkes, Marianne. *Over in the Forest: Come and Take a Peek.*

Boldt, Mike. *123 versus ABC* (counting and alphabet book).

Browne, Anthony. *One Gorilla.*

Carle, Eric. *The Very Hungry Caterpillar.*

Dillon, Leo, and Dillon, Diane. *Mother Goose Numbers on the Loose.*

Ehlert, Lois. *Fish Eyes: A Book You Can Count On.*

Falconer, Ian. *Olivia Counts* (board book).

Hague, Kathleen. *Ten Little Bears: A Counting Rhyme.*

Holub, Joan. *Zero the Hero* (Tom Lichtenheld, Illus.).

Hutchins, Pat. *The Doorbell Rang.*

Keats, Ezra Jack. *Over in the Meadow.*

Kitamura, Satoshi. *When Sheep Cannot Sleep: The Counting Book.*

Lewison, Wendy. *Raindrop Plop* (Pam Paparone, Illus.).

Martin, Bill, Jr. *Ten Little Caterpillars*; *Chicka, Chicka, 1, 2, 3* (Lois Ehlert, Illus.).

O'Keefe, Susan Heyboer. *One Hungry Monster: A Counting Book in Rhyme Board Book.*

Root, Phyllis. *One Duck Stuck.*

Rosenthal, Amy Kraus. *Wumbers* (Tom Lichtenheld, Illus.).

Sayre, April. *One Is a Snail, Ten Is a Crab.*

Sendak, Maurice. *One Was Johnny.*

Sierra, Judy. *Counting Crocodiles.*

Smith, Nikki. *Five Little Speckled Frogs.*

#Walsh, Ellen Stoll. *Mouse Count* (*Cuenta de raton*, bilingual).

Womell, Christopher. *Teeth, Tails, & Tentacles: An Animal Counting Book.*

Alphabet Books

An alphabet book uses letters to carry the theme. While some are purposefully designed to teach the alphabet, others use the alphabet format as an organizational structure around a specific topic. Because they communicate information about a place, an event, or an idea, some alphabet books are nonfiction. For example, *L Is for Lobster* (Reynolds) provides facts about the state of Maine. Other ABC books are considered concept books, such as *G Is for Googol* and *Q Is for Quark*, both by Schwartz. Some books organized alphabetically tell a story, such as *Just in Case: A Trickster Tale and Spanish Alphabet Book* (Morales).

On one end of a reader continuum is *The Dr. Seuss ABC*, intended to help the youngest children learn their letters. On the other hand, Jerry Pallotta's variety of nonfiction ABC books are geared for more sophisticated readers. Some of these include *The Icky Bug Alphabet Book*, *The Vegetable Alphabet Book*, and *The Dinosaur Alphabet Book*. Mordicai Gerstein's *The Absolutely Awful Alphabet Book* combines macabre humor, alliteration, and playful language but it is not intended for beginning readers. Figure 4.6 provides examples of alphabet books.

Easy-to-Read Books

In the 1950s, a new category of illustrated books emerged with the classic *The Cat in the Hat* (Seuss). This type of book was deliberately written with a limited number of simple words to support developing readers. Although not technically considered picture books because the intent and formats vary from the definition, these illustrated texts have been very successful. Seuss went on to write other favorites, such as *One Fish, Two Fish, Red Fish, Blue Fish*, *Green Eggs and Ham*, and many more. Seuss, whose real name was Theodor Seuss Geisel, had a gift for playing with the sounds of language, creating nonsense words in his stories, and appealing to children's

---

FIGURE 4.6 **Examples of Alphabet Books (All are Primary and Preschool)**

(Books with significant culturally diverse elements are marked #.)

Base, Graeme. *Animalia.*

Bataille, Marion. *ABC3D* (pop-up alphabet book).

Carle, Eric. *Eric Carle's ABC.*

Carter, David. *Alphabugs.*

Catalanotto, Peter. *Matthew A.B.C.*

Cleary, Brian P. *Peanut Butter and Jellyfishes: A Very Silly Alphabet Book* (Betsy E. Snyder, Illus.).

Ehlert, Lois. *Eating the Alphabet.*

Ernst, Lisa. *The Turn Around, Upside Down Alphabet Book.*

Fleming, Denise. *Alphabet Under Construction.*

Hoban, Tana. *26 Letters and 99 Cents.*

#Hudes, Quiara. *Welcome to My Neighborhood: A Barrio ABC.*

Johnson, Stephen P. *Alphabet City.*

Joyce, Susan. *ABC Nature Riddles.*

Lear, Edward. *A Was Once an Apple Pie* (Suse Macdonald, Illus.).

Lobel, Anita. *On Market Street.*

Martin, Bill, Jr., and Archambault, John. *Chicka Chicka Boom Boom.*

McDonald, Suse. *Alphabatics.*

McLeod, Bob. *Superhero ABC.*

McLimans, David. *Gone Wild.*

McMullen, Kate. *I Stink.*

McNamera, Margaret. *Apples A to Z.*

Pelletier, David. *The Graphic Alphabet.*

Rose, Deborah. *Into the A, B, Sea* (Steve Jenkins, Illus.).

Thurbly, Paul. *Paul Thurbly's Alphabet.*

Van Allsburg, Chris. *The Z Was Zapped.*

#Weill, Cynthia, and Basseches, K. B. *ABeCedarios: Mexican Folk Art ABC's in English and Spanish.*

Wood, Audrey. *Alphabet Mystery* (Bruce Wood, Illus.).

natural sense of humor. *Up, Tall and High!* (Long), winner of the 2013 Theodor Seuss Geisel Award for beginning readers, is both a concept book and an easy reader.

Other writers were also successful using this easy-to-read format. You may remember the set of characters in Arnold Lobel's *Frog and Toad* series or *Amelia Bedelia* (Parish), the maid who took everything literally and made constant but lovable mistakes. When Amelia was asked to "put out the lights," she hung them on the clothesline. These easy-to-read books satisfy young children's desire to read on their own.

Wordless and Almost Wordless Picture Books

Wordless picture books contain primarily illustrations, although some contain just a few words. The detail in the art tells the story. For example, the 2013 Caldecott winner, *A Ball for Daisy* (Raschka), conveys the simple story of losing a favorite toy, a common event for young children. The joy and sadness of playful Daisy is captured with impressionistic colors and curly lines but no words.

Another example is David Wiesner's *Tuesday*, depicting a nighttime fantasy in which frogs fly through the air on lily pads as they invade a village with hilarious results. Figure 4.7 lists examples of wordless and almost wordless picture books. Search for others by the same illustrators or use the search term "stories without words."

Predictable Patterned Language Books

These are picture books written with predictable language and repeating patterns. Predictability can be the result of obvious patterns, use of rhyme, or text that closely follows illustrations. For example, after just hearing the title, young listeners can easily guess what happens in *Don't Slam the Door!* (Chaconas). Reminiscent of the classic *Goodnight Moon* (Brown), Peggy Rathmann's nearly wordless *Good Night, Gorilla* brings out a giggle and a prediction from even the most reluctant young listener. These books play a critical role in early reading because

---

FIGURE 4.7 **Examples of Wordless or Almost Wordless Picture Books**

Anno, Mitsumasa. *Anno's U.S.A.* (P, I)
Bang, Molly. *The Grey Lady and the Strawberry Snatcher.* (P, I)
Banyai, Istvan. *The Other Side*; *Zoom.* (P, I)
Becker, Aaron, *Journey.* (P, I)
Briggs, Raymond. *The Snowman.* (P, I)
Catalanotto, Peter. *Dylan's Day Out.* (P)
Collington, Peter. *A Small Miracle.* (P, I)
Crews, Donald. *Night at the Fair.* (P)
Day, Alexandra. *Carl's Summer Vacation.* (P)
dePaola, Tomie. *Pancakes for Breakfast.* (P)
Goodall, John. *Story of an English Village.* (P, I)
Hutchins, Pat. *Changes, Changes and Rosie's Walk.* (P)

Judge, Lita. *Red Sled.* (P)
Lee, Suzy. *Wave.* (P)
Lehman, Barbara. *The Red Book.* (P)
Mayer, Mercer. *Frog Goes to Dinner.* (P)
Nolan, Dennis. *Sea of Dreams.* (P)
Pinkney, Jerry. *The Lion and the Mouse.* (P)
Raschka, Chris. *A Ball for Daisy*; *Daisy Gets Lost.* (P, I)
Rodriguez, Béatrice. *The Chicken Thief.* (P)
Savage, Stephen. *Where's Walrus?* (P)
Thomson, Bill. *Chalk.* (P)
Turkle, Brinton. *Deep in the Forest.* (P)
Van Allsburg, Chris. *Ben's Dream.* (P, I)
Wiesner, David. *Flotsam*; *Free Fall*; *Sector 7.* (P, I)

their predictability helps ensure reader success and bolsters students' understanding of how language works. Chapter 3 lists examples of picture books with predictable and patterned language.

Pop-Up Books

Pop-up books use paper engineering. As each page opens, stiff cutouts unfold to create three-dimensional scenes. For example, Matthew Reinhart and Robert Sabuda crafted intricate pop-up pictures of various magical creatures in *Encyclopedia Mythologica: Fairies and Mythical Creatures*. Queen Titania (from Shakespeare's a *Midsummer Night's Dream*) springs up on luminous silver wings. Another page features flowers unfolding and rearranging their petals, turning into delicate flower fairies.

Fresh and intriguing ideas often take the form of pop-up books. The holographic cover image of *ABC3D* (Bataille) flashes one of the letters A, B, C, or D, depending on the angle of light. When opened, letters of the alphabet pop up with intriguing twists: a mirrored page makes V appear as W. With bright colors, a retro look, and superb paper engineering, *Popville* (Boisrobert and Rigaud) offers an interesting blend of picture book types: wordless books, pop-ups, and interactivity. Figure 4.8 lists examples of pop-up books.

As with all children's books, the quality of the text or the story in pop-up books still matters. The paper engineering should not overshadow the words. Movable parts should serve a purpose, not just be attention grabbers, as Lisa Boggiss Boyce (2011) so astutely demonstrates with the use of intriguing spatial relationships and deceptively simple plot sequencing in *Haunted House* (Pieńkowski).

Interactive Books

These books may contain some paper engineering but are less complex than pop-up books. These simple stories invite readers to lift, open, flip, or pull flaps of paper. Alternately, various items are inset that beg to be touched, heard, or smelled. In a classic series about a dog named *Spot* (Hill), readers are invited to lift flaps to see hidden characters or find an object mentioned in the story. A similar, simple favorite, *Dear Zoo* (Campbell), is celebrating 25 years of popularity. Newer titles include *Press Here* (Tuller) and *We Are the Book* (Willems).

Eric Carle's popular books, such as *The Very Busy Spider*, offer things to touch (the emerging web done in raised relief) or something to hear: when a page is turned in *The Very Quiet Cricket*, a sound chip chirps like a cricket.

FIGURE 4.8 Examples of Pop-Up Books

(Books with significant culturally diverse elements are marked #.)

Baum, Frank L., and Sabuda, Robert. *The Wonderful Wizard of Oz: A Commemorative Pop-Up.*

Carter, David A. *Yellow Square.*

Carter, David A. *Blue 2: A Pop-Up Book for Children of All Ages.*

Pledger, Maurice. *Sounds of the Wild: Ocean* (see additional titles in this series).

#Reinhart, Matthew (reteller). *The Jungle Book.*

Sabuda, Robert. *The Little Mermaid.*

Santoro, Lucio and Meera. *Predators: A Pop-Up Book with Revolutionary Technology; Wild Oceans: A Pop-Up Book with Revolutionary Technology.*

The *Very Hungry Caterpillar* by Eric Carle is an outstanding example of a picture book that invites readers' interactions.

Out of all of Eric Carle's books, *The Very Hungry Caterpillar* is one of his best-known and most popular books and a true classic in the field of children's literature. Carle invites young children into the very hungry and active caterpillar's day through his distinctive collage style. Die-cut pages where the caterpillar has "eaten" through them are just the right size to fit a child's tiny finger. Through the sequence of illustrations combined with simple text, readers are treated to the caterpillar's transformation into a beautiful butterfly.

Eric Carle's books are just right to share aloud with young children. For example, when sharing *The Very Hungry Caterpillar*, consider the many opportunities to extend a child's appreciation of the book by using movement to show the life cycles as well as increasing knowledge of concepts such as counting, identifying the variety of food the caterpillar eats, naming the days of the week, and understanding the metamorphosis from caterpillar to butterfly.

Graphic Novels

Graphic novels are stories told through the format of sequential art and are longer than a comic book. Some graphic novels have more than 50 pages and depend on the written content and targeted age. *Graphic novel* is the accepted term in the field and incorporates both fiction and nonfiction.

Botzakis (2009) notes that formerly "comic books were strictly taboo in classrooms, stuck between the pages of a textbook and read when the teacher was not paying attention. In more recent times, these types of texts have been expanded and called graphic novels" (p. 15). Some people associated graphic novels with violence and inappropriate material. Over time, however, the graphic novel has matured in literary quality and is no longer limited to superheroes and violent fantasy.

Teachers and librarians new to graphic novels may wonder to what extent children should read them. The National Council of Teachers of English (2008) issued a statement asserting that comic-style reading may develop comprehension in the same way that picture books support the mental imaging experienced by proficient readers. One critical element of reading is making inferences. In formats with complex pictures that deepen and extend text, readers must construct an understanding about characters and situations as they attend to details and subtleties (McCloud, 2006). Further, enthusiasts believe that graphic texts may be an entrée into deeper literature. Botzakis suggests that, "what can be difficult for students to do with simple text can be more easily accomplished when reading visually oriented materials" (p. 16). Figure 4.9 lists examples of graphic novels.

Postmodern Picture Books

Over the past two decades, picture book authors and illustrators have stretched the boundaries of conventional definitions of picture books; content and illustrations have taken decidedly interesting directions. Some picture books that are considered postmodern present inconsistencies in text and pictures (Sipe & Pantaleo, 2008). Other postmodern picture books do not conform to typical picture book conventions in their layout, design, and presentation. For example, the Ahlbergs' *The Jolly Postman* received a great deal of attention when it was published in 1986. Children enjoyed opening the envelopes and reading the cards and letters, each one told from a different folktale character's point of view.

Probably the most cited example of the postmodern picture book is David Macaulay's *Black and White*. The book contains four stories, each positioned in a different corner of the

FIGURE 4.9 Selected Graphic Novels

Abadzis, Nick. *Laika.* (M)
Bliss, Harry. *Luke on the Loose* (and other Toon books). (P, I)
Bogaert, H. M. van den. *Journey into Mohawk Country* (George O'Connor, Illus). (M)
Cammuso, Frank, and Lynch, Jay. *Otto's Orange Day.* (P, I)
Castellucci, Cicil & Rugg, Jim. *Plain Janes.* (M)
Chabot, Jacob. *The Mighty Skullboy Army* (series). (M)
Craddock, Erik. *Deep-Space Disco.* (I, M)
Davis, Eleanor. *Stinky.* (P)
Gaiman, Neil. *Coraline* (P. Craig Russell, Illus.). (M)
Giarrusso, Chris. *G-man: Learning to Fly.* (I)
Gownley, Jimmy. (2010). *Amelia Rules* (series). (I)
Guibert, Emmanuel. *Sardine in Outer Space* (series) (Joann Sfar, Illus.). (I, M)
Hale, Shannon, and Hale, Dean. *Rapunzel's Revenge* (Nathan Hale, Illus.). (M)
Haspiel, Dean, and Lynch, Jay. *Mo and Jo Fighting Together Forever.* (P)
Hayes, Geoffrey. *Benny and Penny in Just Pretend* (P); *Benny and Penny in the Big No-No!* (P)
Hergé. *Red Rackham's Treasure* (Adventures of Tin Tin series). (M)
Hosler, Jay. *Clan Apis.* (M)
Kibuishi, Kazu. *The Stonekeeper* (Amulet series). (M)
Kovac, Tommy, and Liew, Sonny. *Wonderland.* (I)
Krosoczka, Jarrett, J. *Lunch Lady* series. (I)
Loux, Matthew. *The Legend of Old Salty* (Salt Water Taffy series). (I, M)
Lutes, Jason, and Bertozzi, Nick. *Houdini: The Handcuff King.* (I, M)
McKeever, Sean. *Spider-Man Loves Mary Jane* (Takeshi Miyazawa, Illus.). (M)
Phelan, Marr. *The Storm in the Barn.* (M)
Rosenstiehl, Agnès. *Silly Lilly and the Four Seasons.* (P)
Runton, Andy. *Owly* (Vol. 1). (I, M)
Selznick, Brian. *The Invention of Hugo Cabret.* (M)
Siegel, Siena Cherson. *To Dance: A Ballerina's Graphic Novel* (Mark Siegel, Illus.). (I, M)
Smith, Jeff. *Little Mouse Gets Ready.* (P)
Spiegelman, Art. *Jack and the Box.* (P)
Tan, Shaun. *The Arrival.* (I, M)
Townsend, Michael. *Kit Feeny: On the Move.* (I)
Trondheim, Lewis. *Tiny Tyrant* (Fabrice Parme, Illus.). (I, M)

FIGURE 4.10 Examples of Postmodern Picture Books

Ahlberg, Allan and Janet. *The Jolly Postman.*
Browne, Anthony. *Voices in the Park.*
Burningham, John. *Come Away from the Water, Shirley.*
Child, Lauren. *Who's Afraid of the Big Bad Book?*
Clement, Rod. *Just Another Ordinary Day.*
French, Vivian. *Once upon a Time* (John Prater, Illus.).
Gerstein, Mordicai. *A Book.*
Gravett, Emily. *Wolves; Spells.*
Justin, Norton. *Neville* (G. Brian Karas, Illus.).
Lehman, Barbara. *The Red Book.*
Lester, Mike. *A Is for Salad.*
Lindenbaum, Pija. *Boodil, My Dog* (Gabrielle Charbonnet, Illus.).
Macaulay, David. *Black and White; Shortcut.*
Muntean, Michaela. *Do Not Open This Book!*
Van Allsburg, Chris. *Bad Day at Riverbend; Two Bad Ants.*
Wiesner, David. *The Three Pigs.*

double-page spreads. Each exudes a different artistic style. These multiple stories can be read in differing order, breaking from the tradition that a story must unfold in a linear manner.

The challenge of "reading" such a book demonstrates a key aspect of what defines postmodern picture books. Events are often shown from multiple perspectives and with various styles, leaving the reader to meet these challenges in multiple ways as they rely on their own experiences and background knowledge to move forward (Anstey, 2002). Postmodernism is a trend to follow, as it tests the notion that picture books are only for young children. Figure 4.10 lists examples of postmodern picture books.

Teaching Strategies

Connecting to the Common Core State Standards

COMMON CORE STATE STANDARD FEATURE #1

Understanding How Illustrations Interact with Text (CCSS.RL.7)

The Common Core State Standards (CCSS) have identified integration and evaluation of knowledge and ideas presented in diverse formats as a critical skill for readers. Picture books are an excellent form to assist children in developing competence with this key reading standard, as described in CCSS.RL.7:

CCSSELA_Literacy. CCRA (Anchor Standard): RL.7: Integrate and evaluate content presented in diverse media and formats, including visually and quantitatively, as well as in words.

RL.1.7. Use illustrations and details in a story to describe its characters, setting, or events.

RL.2.7. Use information gained from the illustrations (e.g., maps, photographs, and words in a print or digital text) to demonstrate understanding of its characters, setting, or plot.

RL.3.7. Explain how specific aspects of a text's illustrations contribute to what is conveyed by the words in a story (e.g., create mood, emphasize aspects of a character or setting).

Using picture books to address the CCSS can show students how illustrations interact with text to describe and understand character, setting, plot, and mood. Because picture books depend on both text and illustrations to tell a story, children must attend to all the visual information (interior illustrations, cover, endpapers, charts, graphs, and so on) if they are to fully understand its meaning. Since characters play a significant role in stories, we describe how they are developed by illustrators. However, the same principles also apply to setting, mood, plot, and theme.

Characters are often developed in illustrations through the artist's skillful use of line and color. Research suggests that children are interested in exploring the thoughts and motivations of characters in stories, and illustrations are a rich source of this information (Prior et al., 2012; Sipe, 2008). Teachers can help students become attuned to the artistic techniques that develop character by inviting observation and comments during interactive read-alouds.

For example, when reading aloud *Don't Let the Pigeon Drive the Bus* (Willems), a teacher could show children how Willems uses simple lines to show the pigeon's various expressions and body postures as he begs and pleads to be allowed to drive the bus. When the pigeon doesn't get his way, he erupts into a tantrum on a double-page spread full of writhing feathers and popping eyeballs—all conveyed with artfully placed simple lines (Yokota & Teale, 2005). Similarly, Susan Meddaugh uses simple lines in *Martha Speaks* to show how Martha the dog who can speak after swallowing alphabet soup, has become so cunning that she can dial the phone to order her favorite meat. A single well-placed line for her mouth and a combination of thin and fat lines for her eye convey that Martha has become quite sly.

Illustrators also often use color to show characters' feelings or their relationship to other characters in a book. For example, in *Hello, Goodbye Window* (Juster), illustrator Chris Raschka uses energetic and bright yellows, greens and oranges for simple, childlike illustrations that suggest a world of fun and family love. This use of color is very appropriate for this story, which describes a young girl's enjoyable experiences visiting her grandparents. In contrast, Molly Bang uses oranges and yellows (along with reds and purples) to convey quite a different aspect of character in *When Sophie Gets Angry, Really Really Angry*. The colors are used to outline Sophie's body, bent over in an angry stance, clearly conveying her mood. When Sophie eventually calms down, her body is outlined in cooler colors to indicate her change in mood.

How can teachers help students develop an appreciation for the visual features of picture books? First, find picture books with richly developed characters whose physical characteristics, emotions, and actions are fully conveyed in the illustrations. We have shared some examples here. Then study these books with an illustrator's eye to discern how information about character is conveyed. Questions like the following might be helpful in guiding and informing this process:

- What information in the art is not available in the text?
- What colors are used? Why do you think the author selected these colors? How do the colors support character development? Do the colors change? What is the significance of these changes?
- How do lines communicate meaning about character movement, emotions, and relationships with others?
- Where are various characters placed on the page? What does this say about the role of that character at a particular point in the story?
- What do the body positions of characters tell readers?
- What are some of the symbolic devices used by the illustrator (an erupting volcano is shown when Sophie gets mad in Molly Bang's book)? What meaning do these add to the story?
- What additional visual information is conveyed on the book's cover and endpapers? (adapted from Prior et al., 2005; Martens et al., 2012)

Teachers can then ask children these same questions during read-alouds. We have found new insights arise in discussions, particularly following multiple readings of a story. Exploring visual information can yield deep understandings of the important role pictures play in understanding the complex and rich meanings of stories. The teacher could ask what clues a reader sees before even opening the book. For example, by looking carefully at the title, author and illustrator, and the cover illustration, a reader gets a sense of the type of book or the personalities of the main characters. Students may note a familiarity with the author or illustrator from books previously read. This leads to predictions about the plot, setting, and characters.

Many teachers use picture books pertinent to a core subject theme with older students, such as weather, geography, metaphors, or global awareness (21st Century Skills) to assist with the comprehension of topics. Figure 4.11 lists picture books to build understanding of the Great Depression. Figure 4.12 suggests ways to integrate novels and picture books.

Tech Click

A Web 2.0 tool that is worth investigating is *Glogster*. This is a collaborative online space in which students can demonstrate the RL Standard 7 listed above as well as the four Cs of the 21st Century Skills.

FIGURE 4.11   Suggested Picture Books to Build Understanding of the Great Depression

Booth, David. *The Dust Bowl* (Karen Reczuch, Illus.). (P)

Harper, Jo and Josephine. *Finding Daddy: A Story of the Great Depression* (Ron Mazellan, Illus.). (P, I)

Lied, Kate. *Potato: A Tale from the Great Depression* (Lisa Campbell Ernst, Illus.). (P, I)

Mackall, Dandi Daley. *Rudy Rides the Rails: A Depression Era Story* (Chris Ellison, Illus.). (I, M)

Stewart, Sarah. *The Gardener* (David Small, Illus.). (Note how the endpapers set the mood and time period of this book.)

FIGURE 4.12   Example of Lesson Planning Ideas and Process

1. Work with others to create a plan for incorporating picture books for a unit of study designed for upper elementary or middle school students. Consider your topic, appropriate titles, and why they were chosen, and ways you would engage students with these books. For example, there are historical fiction picture books depicting life during the Great Depression (Figure 4.11). High-quality historical fiction and historical nonfiction picture books (see Chapter 10) help students gain a deeper understanding through stories and pictures about life during a particular time period. If your upper elementary or middle level students are reading *Roll of Thunder, Hear My Cry*, review the list of picture books listed in the Historical Fiction chapter. Which ones do you determine to be appropriate for upper elementary or middle level students, and why? Find additional appropriate picture books to add to your list.

2. A sample activity using these books to incorporate within a unit of study on *Roll of Thunder, Hear My Cry* is to select two picture books from your list to share aloud and then ask students to compare and contrast them with *Roll of Thunder*. Create a Venn diagram (two interconnecting circles) as an effective visual for students to compare differences between or among the books. To prepare for this activity, choose two picture books and design questions to ask about the differences in each book, such as comparing how the illustrators depict the setting, the circumstances of the characters, and the outcome of each story.

Students will no doubt come up with additional questions. Before sharing the books aloud, discuss the purpose of creating a Venn diagram and how this will extend appreciation and understanding of the books. After reading, invite students to note differences on the outer parts of the circles and common aspects in the intersection of the circles.

3. An alternative to a Venn diagram is to create a comparison/contrast chart identifying the ways to compare the books across the top of the chart and listing the picture book titles down the left side of the chart. This alternative method allows for more books to be compared.

4. Another suggestion is to choose picture book titles prior to reading *Roll of Thunder, Hear My Cry* as an excellent way to prepare students to read or listen to the novel read aloud. Prepare background information to introduce each book before reading aloud to set the stage for listening and understanding, such as having a map ready to show story locations, share sound tracks of music from the 1930s, or discuss an aspect of interest about the author or illustrator.

5. Design ways you would plan these activities for younger students. For example, select age-appropriate picture books by one author or illustrator and have students compare them as to plots, writing style, and artistic style. This is good preparation for students to write and illustrate their own picture book.

Tech Click

An interesting strategy is to modify the KWL chart (*know, want* to know, and *learned*). This digital file can be started with whole class and provides the teachers with baseline information about what students bring to a topic of study. Richards and Anderson (2003) modified the KWL strategy to STW to help students focus on illustrations by asking, "What do I *see*?," "What do I *think*?," and "What do I *wonder*?". Richards and Anderson observed that students often do not focus on aspects of illustrations that are important for understanding because they may focus on tiny details without seeing the whole.

Another practice is an interactive read-aloud. To address the CCSS, consider planning a brief think-aloud over some aspect of the standard, such as "What do you think about this character's personality based on the cover illustration?" (RL.1.7). Plan for an interactive session by jotting down ideas for questions about the illustrations and story on sticky notes and placing them on the pertinent pages as signals to stop and pose the question(s). Explain the process of stopping at certain spots to give students an opportunity to think independently or to "turn and talk" to a partner for a quick "buzz" session before sharing with the class. Read-aloud sessions that are designed for learning outcomes need to be planned in advance, as these sessions should focus on supporting an understanding of literary elements, such as plot, events, characters, and setting.

A preliminary strategy is to *think aloud* how to tell a story from a wordless picture book—showing, not telling, is the key. First, model taking a picture walk through the pages of the book to get a sense of the story and then go back and tell a story based on the illustrations. Talk about the differences between simply describing each picture and linking ideas together into a story. Figure 4.7 lists suggestions for wordless or almost wordless books. Sharing and learning from wordless picture books is not only for primary students. They are excellent tools for helping students tell a cohesive story with a beginning, middle, and ending. Even more fun is when students and the teacher create stories independently from the same book and then come together to share. What you might expect is that children will share the nuances in the various versions based on their experiences and background—an excellent lesson on comprehension.

Share a picture book with a story line, such as the 2011 Caldecott Honor book *Interrupting Chicken* (Stein). Chicken cannot help herself from interrupting her bedtime stories. She continually interrupts Papa's reading because she wants to save the fairy-tale characters in the story. Plan an interactive read-aloud for this book with questions that will draw attention to the interesting aspects of the plot and invite discussion about the main character. In addition, see the section in this chapter on English language learners and read about the STW strategy (Richards & Anderson, 2003), which teaches students how to focus on illustrations by asking, "What do I *see*?," "What do I *think*?," and "What do I *wonder*?".

Teach children to be critical thinkers by asking open-ended questions, such as "Why do you think a character did what she did?" Look at the book's illustrations and ask children to describe how they think the characters feel in certain situations. Ask how they think they might feel in a similar situation or if they have ever felt that way themselves.

Tech Click

Candlewick Press's Web site hosts a hilarious book trailer for *Interrupting Chicken*. Use this as a potential model for older students' book responses.

Supporting Culturally Diverse Learners with Picture Books

Books are mirrors in which children see themselves reflected. When children are represented in literature and other media, they begin to see themselves as valuable and worthy of notice. Conversely when children do not see accurate representations of themselves, they may internalize the message that they are not worthy of notice. (Multi-Cultural Bibliography Resource, 2010, p. 3)

Jacqueline Woodson's *Each Kindness* provides a wonderful example in which socioeconomic differences bring to the forefront the theme of kindness at the same time that the illustrator, E. B. Lewis, depicts multiple ethnicities.

Choose culturally relevant and accurate picture books—two fundamental values for selecting diverse picture books for reading aloud and independent reading. These key aspects apply to evaluating and selecting culturally diverse literature across all genres. The criteria for selecting high-quality books in each genre also should be incorporated in making the best choices to share with children. Figure 4.13 lists a sample of culturally diverse picture books.

FIGURE 4.13 **Examples of Culturally Diverse Picture Books**

(Additional examples are included in subsequent chapters.)

Ada, Alma Flor. *I Love Saturdays y domingos* (Elivia Savadier, Illus.). (P)

Altman, Linda Jacobs. *Amelia's Road* (Enrique O. Sanchez, Illus.). (I)

Boelts, Maribeth. *Those Shoes.* (P, I)

Bourdeau, Jan. *SkySisters* (Brian Deines, Illus.). (P)

Brown, Monica. *Chavela and the Magic Bubble.* (P, I)

Bridges, Shirin Yim. *Ruby's Wish* (Sophie Blackall, Illus.). (I)

Chocolate, Debbi. *El Barrio* (David Diaz, Illus.). (P)

Cumpiano, Ina. *Quinito's Neighborhood* (José Ramirez, Illus.). (P)

Diakité, Penda. *I Lost My Tooth in Africa* (Baba Wagué Diakité, Illus.). (P)

Goldin, Barbara Diamond. *A Mountain of Blintzes* (Anik McGrory, Illus.). (P)

Harjo, Joy. *The Good Luck Cat* (Paul Lee, Illus.). (P)

Khan, Rukhsana. *Big Red Lollipop.* (P, I)

Kurtz, Jane. *Trouble* (Durga Bernhard, Illus.). (P)

Look, Lenore. *Uncle Peter's Amazing Chinese Wedding* (Yumi Heo, Illus.). (P, I)

Mora, Pat. *Gracias/Thanks* (John Parra, Illus.). (P)

Morales, Yuyi. *Just a Minute: A Trickster Tale and Counting Book.* (P)

Nelson, Kadir. *Heart and Soul: The Story of America and African Americans.* (I)

Reynolds, Aaron. *Back of the Bus* (Floyd Cooper, Illus.). (P)

Ringgold, Faith. *Tar Beach.* (P, I, M)

Rockliff, Mara. *Me and Momma and Big John* (William Low, Illus.). (P, I)

Rumford, James. *Silent Music: A Story of Baghdad.* (P, I)

Sandoval, Sam. *Beaver Steals Fire: A Salish Coyote Story.* (P)

Schaefer, Carole Lexa. *Dragon Dancing.* (P)

Smith, Cynthia Leitich. *Jingle Dancer* (Cornelius Van Wright and Ying-Hwa Hu, Illus.). (P, I)

Swamp, Jake. *Giving Thanks: A Native American Good Morning Message* (Erin Printup Jr., Illus.). (P, I)

Sockabasin, Allen. *Thanks to the Animals* (Rebekah Raye, Illus.). (P)

Tafolla, Carmen. *Fiesta Babies.* (P)

Tafolla, Carmen. *What Can You Do with a Paleta?* (Magaly Morales, Illus.). (P)

Tonatiuh, Duncan. *Dear Primo: A Letter to My Cousin.* (P)

Wheeler, Lisa. *Jazz Baby.* (P)

Woodson, Jacqueline. *Show Way* (Hudson Talbott, Illus.). (P)

Yamate, Sandra S. *Char Siu Bao Boy* (Carolina Yao, Illus.). (P)

Supporting English Language Learners with Picture Books

Carol Rasco, speaking on behalf of Reading Is Fundamental, visits with parents across the country to share how they can contribute to their children's education. They often meet with parents who do not feel confident speaking English, who do not read English and more often than not feel powerless to assist their children with the skill most critical for the children's education.

> But a picture book can be what brings parents into that education process. The book can bring smiles to not only their children's faces but to the parents' faces as well. No longer must the parent have a command of the English language; no longer must they be proficient readers even in their native language. They can use their voices in the pure joy of conveying story stimulated by the pictures. (Rasco, 2011, paras. 1 and 2)

Picture books are an excellent choice for English Language Learners (ELLs). When choosing culture-specific picture books, relevancy and accuracy apply, as does considering purpose for making selections. When making evaluation and selection decisions, consider what you know about your learners in terms of age and developmental characteristics, experiences learning English, interests, and an understanding of their academic needs.

Depending on these factors, books that have predictable, patterned text, and books in which there is a good match between pictures and words will be helpful for students in making predictions about new vocabulary, characters' actions, and plot. An example is Mo Willems's *That Is Not a Good Idea!* This book has clear and uncluttered humorous pictures with predictable text that is not culture specific. Many children will be able to relate to the humorous plot and may figure out the ending twist.

 *Tech Click*

Unite for Literacy offers excellent, free resources for read alouds in many different languages. Their goal is to "leverage fast growing mobile networks to provide 'book abundance' for families everywhere. . . . The books may be enjoyed on computers, tablets and most smartphones."

Controversial Issue Using Picture Books: The Trend of Digital Picture Books

Some parents prefer having their children flip through the pages of a tangible book. They feel that the bonding of parent and child combined with the delight of turning pages would be lost with a digital text (Richtel & Bosman, 2011). Authors, publishers, and experts in the field of children's literature vary in their opinions on picture books converted to digital formats. Junko Yokota (2013), director of the Center for Teaching Through Children's Books at National Louis University, believes that the physical texture and experience of a tangible book cannot be replicated in bits and bytes. However, some in the book industry regard electronic books as simply another format in which nothing is substantially lost in translation.

However, digital picture books are not without their supporters. E-readers, such as Sony Reader, Kindle Fire, and Nook, allow children to listen to or read picture books independently. While some educators find the click-and-play interactivity distracting, others note features that are excitingly educational. Children typically know words by sound long before they can read them. When reading a digital book, unknown words can be heard simply by tapping or clicking—fast access to new vocabulary. Many e-readers have built-in dictionaries and bookmarks, allowing for additional support. Digital books can inspire students to select familiar titles during free reading or choose others by the same author. A small study of third graders "suggests that the electronic format combined with the opportunity for choosing books was a highly motivating factor for children to read" (Jones & Brown, 2011, p. 18).

Although it is preferable to have a real person interacting with books and children, there are many students who have no one to read to them outside of school. Teachers can find effective ways to use digital books (Doty, Popplewell, & Byers, 2001; Dresang, 2008; Elleman, 2009). Digital books can provide support for independent reading that does not require an adult.

Tech Click

To celebrate picture books, November has been designated as National Picture Book Month to raise awareness and appreciation for the importance of picture books in the lives of children. The Web site picturebookmonth.com provides more information.

There also appears to be confusion over what picture books are and controversy about who should read picture books. Some parents, for example, consider picture books to be strictly for young children learning to read. Some believe that once children learn how to read, they can be challenged only by selecting chapter-length books and should be discouraged from engaging with picture books. We advocate that classroom libraries across the grade levels include books from all genres, including those in picture book format, that are age and interest level appropriate for the grade level. Karen Lotz of Candlewick Books says that "without loving picture books, kids are less likely to grow up to love chapter books or graphic novels, and so on" (quoted in Rubin, 2011).

Summary

- Picture books are a literary format, not a genre. They rely on both pictures and words to tell the story. However, some picture books contain illustrations with few or no words. Books in which the illustrations are subsidiary to the story, no matter how lovely they are, are not considered picture books.

- Picture books are stepping-stones in becoming a competent and lifelong reader. Carefully crafted visuals can convey much information, whereas high-quality text supports student engagement and motivation for reading. There is a range of types and formats that are highly appealing and can be shared with all ages.

- When choosing high-quality picture books, determine whether artistic elements, design, and media interpret and extend appreciation of the text. Choose picture books with illustrations and text that present accurate and nonstereotyped or culturally biased material. Use criteria for each genre to assist in choosing picture books.

- Types of picture books include concept books, counting books, alphabet books, easy-readers, predictable and patterned books, pop-ups and interactive books, graphic novels, and postmodern picture books.

- Strategies that meet the mandates of several CCSS and support diverse students in your classroom include instructional and interactive read-alouds, using wordless picture books, picture walks, and the KWL/STW strategy. Digital technology has the potential to provide support for all types of readers.

Questions/Activities to Invite Thinking, Writing, and Conversation About the Chapter

1. Brainstorm all the ways you would celebrate National Picture Book Month with an age/grade level of your choice. Also consider ways to celebrate and help students grow in their knowledge and appreciation of picture books all year long. Share *The Very Hungry Caterpillar* and others by Eric Carle with one child or a small group. Carefully listen and watch the ways children react to the books and share your observations with others. Consider additional responses, such as engaging children in creating their own collage pictures. Or help children create a giant class caterpillar to display on the wall. Ask them to think of words that begin with "C" and then post those around the caterpillar.

2. Choose other examples of interactive books to share with children to compare and contrast in different ways and record their responses on chart paper. Or compare two books and create a Venn diagram (two intersecting circles) to note how the books are similar and different. In what ways are interactive books engaging for children? Create a list of interactive books and ways to share them with parents and caregivers.

3. Prepare older students to read aloud a picture book with a small group of younger children or a reading buddy at an earlier grade level. How would you plan to do this? Also consider how reading aloud to someone else can help older students become better readers.

4. How would you explain to parents or caregivers of upper elementary or middle level students the reasons why you display, read aloud, and encourage students to read picture books. Also be prepared to explain this to the students themselves. Often, older students believe that picture books are just for babies or younger children. Choose from the list of books at the end of the chapter designated for older students or find other titles and determine the complexities of, for example, the plot, the illustrations, or theme that make these books more suitable for older rather than for younger audiences. Talk about the value you see in picture books as an adult.

Recommended Picture Books

(Books with significant culturally diverse elements are marked #.)

Selected Picture Books for Primary Children
Amato, Mary. *The Chicken of the Family* (Delphine Durand, Illus.). (P)
Arnosky, Jim. *Babies in the Bayou.* (P)
Asch, Frank. *Mooncake.* (P)
Averbeck, Jim. *In a Blue Room* (Tricia Tusa, Illus.). (P)

Baker, Jeannie. *Home; Window* (wordless). (P)
Barton, Chris. *Shark vs. Train* (Tom Lichtenheld, Illus.). (P)
Bean, Jonathan. *At Night.* (P)
Bemelmans, Ludwig. *Madeline.* (P)
Brett, Jan. *The Mitten.* (P)
Brown, Marc. *Arthur's Eyes.* (P)
Brown, Margaret Wise. *Goodnight Moon.* (P)
Brown, Peter. *Mr. Tiger Goes Wild.* (P)

Burkert, Rand. *Mouse & Lion* (Nancy Ekholm Burkert, Illus.). (P)

Burningham, John. *There's Going to Be a Baby* (Helen Oxenbury, Illus.). (P)

Cannon, Janell. *Stellaluna.* (P)

Carle, Eric. *The Artist Who Painted a Blue Horse* (P); *The Very Hungry Caterpillar.* (P)

Carlstrom, Nancy White. *Jesse Bear, What Will You Wear?* (Bruce Degen, Illus.). (P)

Crews, Donald. *Freight Train.* (P)

Day, Alexander. *Good Dog, Carl.* (P)

Daywalt, Drew. *The Day the Crayons Quit* (Oliver Jeffers, Illus.). (P)

dePaola, Tomie. *Nana Upstairs, Nana Downstairs* (P, I); *Strega Nona* (P); *The Art Lesson.* (P)

Donaldson, Julia. *The Highway Rat* (Axel Scheffler, Illus.). (P)

#Dorros, Arthur. *Abuela* (Elisa Kleven, Illus.). (P)

Dr. Seuss. *Fox in Socks; Green Eggs and Ham* (and others). (P)

Ehlert, Lois. *Color Farm; Color Zoo; Feathers for Lunch.* (P)

Emberley, Ed. *Go Away, Big Green Monster.* (P)

Falconer, Ian. *Olivia* (and others). (P)

Fisher, Valorie. *Everything I Need to Know Before I'm Five.* (P)

Fleming, Denise. *In the Tall, Tall Grass.* (P)

Fogliano, Julie. *If You Want to See a Whale* (Erin E. Stead, Illus.). (P)

Foley, Greg. *Don't Worry Bear* (and others). (P)

Foley, Greg. *Willoughby & the Moon.* (P)

Fox, Mem. *Hello Baby!* (Steve Jenkins, Illus.) (P); *Koala Lou* (Pamela Lofts, Illus.) (P); *Wilfrid Gordon McDonald Partridge* (Julie Vivas, Illus.). (P)

Frazee, Marla. *The Boss Baby.* (P)

Freeman, D. *Corduroy.* (P)

Guarino, Deborah. *Is Your Mama a Llama?* (Steven Kellogg, Illus.). (P)

Henkes, Kevin. *A Good Day* (P); *Birds* (Laura Dronzek, Illus.) (P); *Chrysanthemum* (P); *My Garden; Penny and Her Marble.* (P)

Hines, Anna Grossnickle. *I Am a Backhoe.* (P)

Idle, Molly. *Flora and the Flamingo.* (P)

Jeffers, Oliver. *Stuck.* (P)

Jenkins, Emily. *What Happens on Wednesdays* (Lauren Castillo, Illus.). (P)

Johnson, Crockett. *Harold and the Purple Crayon.* (P)

Joyce, William. *George Shrinks.* (P)

Kasza, Keiko. *Ready for Anything.* (P)

Keats, Ezra Jack. *The Snowy Day* (P); *Whistle for Willie.* (P)

Kellogg, Steven. *Best Friends* (P); *Prehistoric Pinkerton.* (P)

Klassen, Jon. *I Want My Hat Back* (P); *This Is Not My Hat.* (P)

Kraus, Robert. *Leo the Late Bloomer* (Jose Aruego, Illus.). (P)

Krauss, Ruth. *The Carrot Seed.* (P)

Leaf, Munro. *The Story of Ferdinand.* (P)

Lobel, Anita. *Hello, Day!* (P)

Lobel, Arnold. *On Market Street.*

Martin, Bill, Jr. *Brown Bear, Brown Bear, What Do You See?* (Eric Carle, Illus.); *Polar Bear, Polar Bear, What Do You Hear?* (Eric Carle, Illus.) (P)

Martin, Bill, Jr., and Archambault, John. *Chicka Chicka Boom Boom* (Lois Ehlert Illus.). (P)

Mayer, Mercer. *What Do You Do with A Kangaroo?; Frog Goes to Dinner.* (P)

McCloskey, Robert. *Blueberries for Sal* (P); *Make Way for Ducklings.* (P)

McDonald, Megan. *Hen Hears Gossip* (Joung Un Kim, Illus.). (P)

#Mora, Pat. *Here, Kitty, Kitty! ¡Ven, Gatita, Ven!* (Maribel Suarez, Illus.). (P).

Noble, Trina Hakes. *The Day Jimmy's Boa Ate the Wash.* (P)

Numeroff, Laura. *If You Give a Mouse a Cookie* (and others) (Felicia Bond, Illus.). (P)

Nyeu, Tao. *Bunny Days.* (P)

Ormerod, Jan. *Moonlight; Sunshine* (wordless). (P)

Oxenbury, Helen. *Good Night, Good Morning; Mother's Helper.* (P)

Piper, Watty. *The Little Engine That Could* (George and Doris Hauman, Illus.). (P)

Polacco, Patricia. *The Keeping Quilt.* (P)

Potter, Beatrix. *The Tale of Peter Rabbit* (and others). (P)

Raschka, Chris. *Little Black Crow.* (P)

Ray, H. A., and Ray, Margaret. *Curious George.* (P)

Savage, Stephen. *Where's Walrus?* (P)

Seeger, Laura Vaccaro. *First the Egg.* (P)

Sendak, Maurice. *Where the Wild Things Are.* (P)

Shannon, David. *No, David!* (and others). (P)

Slobodkina, Esphyr. *Caps for Sale.* (P)

Smith, Charles R., Jr. *Dance with Me* (Noah Z. Jones, Illus.). (P)

#Soto, Gary. *Too Many Tamales* (Ed Martinez, Illus.). (P)

Stead, Philip C. *A Sick Day for Amos McGee* (Erin E. Stead, Illus.). (P)

Stein, David Ezra. *Pouch!* (P)

Thompson, Kay. *Eloise.* (P)

Underwood, Deborah. *The Quiet Book* (Renata Liwska, Illus.). (P)

Viorst, Judith. *Alexander and the Terrible, Horrible, No Good, Very Bad Day* (and others) (Ray Cruz, Illus.). (P)

Waber, Bernard. *Lyle, Lyle, Crocodile.* (P)

Wells, Rosemary. *Edward Unready for School.* (P)

Willems, Mo. *City Dog. Country Frog* (Jon J. Muth, Illus.) (P); *Don't Let the Pigeon Drive the Bus* (P); *Hooray for Amanda and Her Alligator!* (P); *Knuffle Bunny Free: An Unexpected Diversion; That Is Not a Good Idea!* (P)

Williams, Karen Lynn. *A Beach Tail* (Floyd Cooper, Illus.). (P)

Williams, Vera. *A Chair for My Mother.* (P)

Wood, Don and Audrey. *The Little Mouse, the Red Ripe Strawberry and the Big Hungry Bear.* (P); *The Napping House.* (P)

Selected Picture Books for Older Children

#Baker, Jeannie. *Where the Forest Meets the Sea.* (I)

Base, Graeme. *Animalia.* (I, M)

Borden, Louise. *The Greatest Skating Race: A World War II Story from the Netherlands* (Niki Daly, Illus.). (I, M)

Browne, Anthony. *Into the Forest.* (I, M)

Bunting, Eve. *The Wall* (Ronald Himler, Illus.). (I, M)

Bunting, Eve. *The Memory String* (Ted Rand, Illus.). (I, M)

Close, Chuck. *Face Book.* (I, M)

Judge, Lita. *One Thousand Tracings: Healing the Wounds of World War II.* (I, M)

Jukes, Mavis. *Like Jake and Me* (Lloyd Bloom, Illus.). (I)

Kerley, Barbara. *The Extraordinary Mark Twain (According to Susy)* (Edwin Fotheringham, Illus.). (I, M)

#Lee-Tai, Amy. *A Place Where Sunflowers Grow* (Felicia Hoshino, Illus.). (I, M)

#Levine, Ellen. *Henry's Freedom Box: A True Story from the Underground Railroad* (Kadir Nelson, Illus.). (I, M)

Locker, Thomas. *The Boy Who Held Back the Sea; Where the River Ends.* (I, M)

Mathias, Sharon Bell. *The Hundred Penny Box* (Leo and Dianne Dillon, Illus.). (I, M)

McGill, Alice. *Molly Bannaky* (Chris Soenpiet, Illus.). (I, M)

#Pinkney, Andrea Davis. *Boycott Blues: How Rosa Parks Inspired a Nation* (Brian Pinkney, Illus.). (I, M)

#Polacco, Patricia. *Pink and Say* (I, M); *Thank You, Mr. Falker* (I); *The Butterfly* (and others). (I, M)

Rosenthal, Amy Krouse. *Exclamation Mark.* (I)

Siegel, Siena Cherson. *To Dance: A Ballerina's Graphic Novel* (Nathan Hale, Illus.). (I, M)

Sis, Peter. *The Wall: Growing up Behind the Iron Curtain.* (I, M)

#Tan, Shaun. *The Arrival* (wordless). (I, M)

#Tsuchiya, Yukio. *The Faithful Elephants: A True Story of Animals, People, and War* (Ted Lewin, Illus.). (I, M)

Van Allsburg, Chris. *The Mysteries of Harris Burdick.* (I, M)

#Wisniewaki, David. *Golem.* (I, M)

#Yoo, Paula. *Sixteen Years in Sixteen Seconds: The Sammy Lee Story.* (I, M)

Selected Picture Books for K–5

Allard, Harry, and Marshall, James. *Miss Nelson Is Missing.* (P, I)

Aston Hutts, Dianna. *A Rock Is Lively; An Egg Is Quiet; A Seed Is Sleepy* (Sylvia Long, Illus.). (P, I)

Becker, Aaron. *Journey.* (P, I)

Brown, Don. *All Stations! Distress!: April 15, 1912: The Day the Titanic Sank* (Actual Times Series). (P, I)

Bryant, Jen. *A River of Words: The Story of William Carlos Williams* (Melissa Sweet, Illus.). (P, I)

#Bunting, Eve. *One Green Apple* (Ted Lewin, Illus.). (P, I)

Burton, Virginia Lee. *The Little House.* (P, I)

Byrd, Robert. *Electric Ben: The Amazing Life and Times of Benjamin Franklin.* (P, I)

Carrick, Laban. *Dave the Potter: Artist, Poet, Slave* (Bryan Collier, Illus.). (P, I)

Cooney, Barbara. *Miss Rumphius.* (P, I)

Cooper, Elisha. *Farm.* (P, I)

#Cooper, Floyd. *Willie and the All-Stars.* (P, I)

Cutbill, Andy. *The Cow That Laid an Egg* (Russell Ayto, Illus.). (P, I)

#Deedy, Carmen Agra. *Martina the Beautiful Cockroach: A Cuban Folktale* (Michael Austin, Illus.). (P, I)

dePaola, Tomie. *Nana Upstairs, Nana Downstairs.* (P, I)

Fleming, Candace. *Boxes for Katje.* (Stacey Dressen-McQueen, Illus.). (P, I)

Fleming, Candace. *Papa's Mechanical Fish* (Boris Kulikov, Illus.). (P, I)

Graham, Bob. *April and Esme: Tooth Fairies* (P, I); *How to Heal a Broken Wing.* (P, I)

Greenberg, Jan, and Jordan, Sandra. *Ballet for Martha: Making Appalachian Spring* (Brian Floca, Illus.). (P, I)

#Harrington, Janice. *The Chicken-Chasing Queen of Lamar County* (Shelley Jackson, Illus.). (P, I)

Heide, Florence Parry. *Princess Hyacinth (The Surprising Tale of a Girl Who Floated)* (Lane Smith, Illus.). (P, I)

#Hoffman, Mary. *Amazing Grace* (Caroline Binch, Illus.). (P, I)

Holub, Joan. *Little Red Writing* (Melissa Sweet, Illus.). (P, I)

#Howard, Elizabeth Fitzgerald. *Virgie Goes to School with Us Boys* (E. B. Lewis, Illus.). (P, I)

Johnson, D. B. *Palazzo Inverso.* (P, I)

#Joose, Barbara. *Grandma Calls Me Beautiful.* (P, I)

Kearney, Meg. *Trouper* (E.B. Lewis, Illus.). (P, I)

Lionni, Leo. *Frederick* (and others). (P, I)

#Manning, Maurice J. *Kitchen Dance.* (P, I)

Markle, Sandra. *Hip-Pocket Papa* (Alan Marks, Illus.). (P, I)

#Napoli, Donna Jo. *Mama Miti: Wangari Maathai and the Trees of Kenya* (Kadir Nelson, Illus.). (P, I)

Palatini, Margie. *Piggie Pie!* (P, I)

Pennypacker, Sara. *Pierre in Love* (Petra Mathers, Illus.). (P, I)

Perkins, Lynne Rae. *Pictures from Our Vacation.* (P, I)

Quigley, Mary. *Granddad's Fishing Buddy* (Stéphane Jorisch, Illus.). (P, I)

Rappaport, Doreen. *Eleanor, Quiet No More* (Gary Kelley, Illus.). (P, I)

#Reibstein, Mark. *Wabi Sabi* (Ed Young, Illus.). (P, I)

Ringgold, Faith. *Tar Beach.* (P, I)

#Roth, Susan, L., and Trumbore, Cindy. *The Mangrove Tree: Planting Trees to Feed Families.* (P, I)

Rylant, Cynthia. *When I Was Young in the Mountains* (Diane Goode, Illus.). (P, I)

#San Souci, Robert. *The Talking Eggs: A Folktale from the American South* (Jerry Pinkney, Illus.). (P, I)

#Say, Allen. *Grandfather's Journey* (and others). (P, I)

#Say, Allen. *The Favorite Daughter.* (P, I)

Scieszka, Jon. *The True Story of the Three Little Pigs.* (P, I)

Schulman, Janet. *Pale Male: Citizen Hawk of New York City* (Meilo So, Illus.). (P, I)

Scieszka, Jon and Barnett, Mac. *Battle Bunny* (Matthew Myers, Illus). (P, I)

Shulevitz, Uri. *How I Learned Geography.* (P, I)

Slate, Jenny, and Fleischer-Camp, Dean. *Marcel the Shell with Shoes On.* (P, I)

Smith, Lane. *Grandpa Green.* (P, I)

Smith, Lane. *It's a Book.* (P, I)

Steig, William. *Sylvester and the Magic Pebble*; *Doctor De Soto.* (P, I)

#Steptoe, John. *Mufaro's Beautiful Daughters.* (P, I)

Stewart, Melissa. *Under the Snow* (Constance R. Bergum, Illus.). (P, I)

Sweet, Melissa. *Balloons over Broadway: The True Story of the Puppeteer of Macy's Parade.* (P, I)

Thomas, Peggy. *For the Birds: The Life of Roger Tory Peterson* (Laura Jacques, Illus.). (P, I)

Van Allsburg, Chris. *Jumanji* (P, I); *The Polar Express.* (P, I)

Wiesner, David. *Art and Max*; *Mr. Wuffles!* (wordless). (P, I)

Winter, Jeanette. *Follow the Drinking Gourd.* (P, I)

#Woodson, Jacqueline. *Each Kindness* (E. B. Lewis, Illus.) (P, I); *The Other Side* (E. B. Lewis, Illus.). (P, I)

Yolen, Jane. *Owl Moon* (John Schoenherr, Illus.). (P, I)

#Young, Ed. *Lon Po Po.* (P, I)

#Young, Ed. *My Mei Mei.* (P, I)

#Young, Ed. *The House Baba Built: An Artist's Childhood in China.* (P, I)

Zelinksy, Paul O. *Rumpelstiltskin.* (P, I)

5

Poetry

(Literary Form)

This chapter addresses some of the important ideas related to poetry, helping you discover ways to bring children and poetry together. We examine the following ideas:

- What is poetry?
- What is the role of poetry in children's lives?
- How do we choose high-quality poetry?
- What are the categories of poetry?
- How do we use poetry to meet the mandates of national standards as well as the needs of our diverse students?

Fifth-grade teacher Judy Markham loves sharing poetry with her students. She reads poems aloud every day, encouraging her children to listen for powerful descriptive words, feelings, and interesting rhythms. She has memorized poems to share at opportune moments. The children immerse themselves in hundreds of poetry books, sharing their favorites with each other and compiling personal anthologies. They also write their own poetry in poetry journals; Kelly's "Please Pass the Poetry" was created during a series of these daily writing sessions. Eleven-year-old Kelly (the poet) describes how the poem evolved: "As I looked at more and more poem books, I just fell in love with real poems. So I decided to write a poem about this." Here is the final version of Kelly's poem:

Please pass the poetry
On the platter over there.
Not all the stories loaded
Up with fat.
Not the songs with a
Lifetime supply of sugar.
Not the rhymes overcooked
And hard
But poetry, a warm feast
To delight in.

—Kelly, Grade 6

Living the joys of poetry: that is what Judy Markham has her children do every day as she involves them in many positive, enjoyable, and memorable experiences with this genre. Commitment and enthusiasm are the key. We suggest that you think about poetry as one of the major entrées on the literary buffet table. Invite your students to sample from a feast of savory morsels served up by the skilled wordsmiths of poetry.

 ## What Is Poetry?

Poetry is musical language. It skips, it sings, it tugs at you with an insistent voice that rings through your head. Poets love the harmony of sound and rhythm that words create. They get inside and around words, going beyond surface definitions to discover their sounds, textures, rhythms, and connotative qualities. They hope this exploration will help them use words to capture the precise emotions and images they want to convey. J. Patrick Lewis characterizes poetry as "a circus for the brain . . . ten pounds of excitement in a nine pound bag" (quoted in Vardell, 2011). We think this is an excellent way to describe the possible explosive effect of poetry on the senses.

It is also interesting to consider children's definitions of poetry. Fisher (1994) found that children in second through fifth grades typically do not understand what poetry is or how it differs from narrative forms of literature. When asked to define poetry, the children in this study made statements such as, "It just is . . ." or "It needs more adjectives to be a poem." Some focused on the superficial aspects of how poetry is written: "It has capitals on every line, and it's printed in the center and it's short." They had no understanding of the differences among poetic forms or how a poem's lines and phrasing can make a critical difference (Fisher, 1994).

In contrast, children who have been exposed to many examples of good poetry and have written poetry on their own possess a remarkable understanding of the genre. When one group of first- and second-grade children who had extensive experience with poetry were asked to define the genre, they said things such as "Poetry is like a picture taken without a camera," "Poems grab me because they are so nice and comfortable . . . they give me a good feeling," and "Poetry has a satisfaction to it that books don't have" (McClure, 1990, p. 45). These children have a keen sense of what poetry is all about; they know it should nourish the heart and mind as well as the ear. They know this because they have been exposed to many examples of the best this genre has to offer.

For our purposes, we define poetry as the written form that results from the exquisite polishing of words. Poetic language is crafted so that words are chosen carefully and concisely to say just what the poet had in mind. However, crafting is not enough. Skillful poets also often express a unique truth or make an observation that invites us to look at our world in a new way. It is the combination of the two that makes memorable poetry.

The Literary Elements of Poetry

Just as narrative and nonfiction writers use various literary elements to craft their pieces, poets use sound (rhyme, alliteration, and assonance and onomatopoeia), rhythm, figurative language, shape, emotional intensity, and fresh insight to create poetry that is imaginative, evocative, and unique. Writers of other genres use these elements as well. However, in well-crafted poetry, these tools are the essence of the writing. Even though contemporary poets are constantly breaking rules and pushing the boundaries, these elements still make up the palette from which poets draw for their work, particularly when writing for children.

Sound. The sounds of poetic language are what make it musical to the ear. Experienced writers of poetry are wordsmiths. They delight in playing with how language sounds—in the rhythm and rhyme of well-turned phrases and artfully orchestrated words. They are crafters of language, carving and polishing their words until they create just the right image and sound. That is why poetry is so often at its best read aloud. The sounds are what contribute to that pleasing sensation that tickles your ear and tongue.

Rhyme. One of the most salient aspects of sound in poetry for children is rhyme. The appeal of rhyme helps explain the attraction of Mother Goose, jump-rope chants, and other kinds of simple verse that children love. Consider the following poem by J. Patrick Lewis:

> **Sand House***
> I built a house
> One afternoon
> With bucket, cup
> And tablespoon,
> Then scooped a shovel-
> ful of shore
> On top to add
> The second floor.
> But when the fingers
> Of the sea
> Reached up and waved
> A wave to me,
> It tumbled down
> Like dominoes
> And disappeared
> Between my toes.
> —J. Patrick Lewis, in *Earth Verses and Water Rhymes*

Rhymes provide unity by linking the words with each other, creating a pleasant, musical effect. Sometimes, the rhymes are at the ends of lines as they are in Lewis's "Sand House" poem.

---

*Copyright 1991 by J. Patrick Lewis. Reprinted by permission of Curtis Brown, Ltd.

At other times, they are inside the lines (termed "internal"), meaning that the rhymes are within rather than at the end of a line. The rhymes must always fit the meaning of the poem rather than be used merely for the rhyming effect.

Unrhymed poems are pleasing to the ear in a different way; the music is more subtle and sometimes discordant but nevertheless has a memorable effect on the listener. Read aloud "Caterpillar" and consider how this unrhymed poem sounds in contrast to "Sand House":

> *Fog*
> The fog comes
> on little cat feet.
>
> It sits looking
> over harbor and city
> on silent haunches
> and then moves on.
> —**Carl Sandburg.**

Alliteration, Assonance, and Onomatopoeia. Alliteration is the repetition of similar consonant sounds, whereas assonance involves repeating an internal vowel sound that provides a partial rhyme. Say the excerpt from the following poem by Rebecca Kai Dotlich aloud and notice the effect of the alliterative repeating "s" sound:

> *Lemonade Sun**
> We pour
> its liquid sweetness
> from a tall
> glass pitcher,
> splashing
> sunshine
> on frosty squares of ice.
> —**Rebecca Kai Dotlich, in** *Lemonade Sun*

Assonance is the musical effect that occurs when similar vowel sounds are repeated close to one another so as to create an internal rhyming within phrases or lines of poetry. For example, note the repetition of the "long e" sound in the following line from "Lone Dog" by Irene Rutherford MacLeod: "I'm a m**ea**n dog, a k**ee**n dog, a wild dog and lone." In the simple rhyme, "as **I** was going to St. **Ives, I** met a man with seven **wives**," the "long I" sound is repeated to create rhythm and a pleasant, memorable sound.

When words in a poem imitate actual sounds, the poet is using *onomatopoeia*; words such as "smash," "oink," or "clink" are all examples of this use of sound. David McCord's "Pickety Fence" (from *One at a Time*) is an example of onomatopoeia: the clicking sound a stick makes as it is dragged along a wooden fence makes up the entire poem.

Rhythm. Rhythm is the heartbeat of a poem. Young children naturally respond to rhythm: even before they can understand language, they respond to songs and poems with rhythmic movement. Poets use rhythm in different ways. Sometimes, the words and lines are organized so that the rhythm propels the poem forward, as in this excerpt from Karla Kuskin's "Spring":

Lemonade Sun by Rebecca Kai Dotlich. Reprinted by permission of Boyds Mills Press.

Spring*
I'm shouting
I'm singing
I'm swinging through trees
I'm winging sky-high
With the buzzing black bees.
I'm the sun
I'm the moon
I'm the dew on the rose.
I'm a rabbit
Whose habit
Is twitching his nose.

—**Karla Kuskin**, *In the Middle of the Trees*

Poets also use repetition to develop the rhythm of a poem. This repetition can be as simple as repeating one word at the beginning of the line, or it can involve a more complex pattern where the poet repeats stanzas or weaves repetitive words and lines throughout the poem. The effect can be hypnotic and comforting, such as when Robert Frost repeats several lines in his familiar *Stopping by Woods on a Snowy Evening*. Or the repetition can create unity in the poem that results in a satisfying pattern, such as Karla Kuskin's repetition of "I'm" in "Spring."

Acrostic poem and picture by second grader.

Figurative Language. Poets create interesting, unusual images through figurative language. When writers compare one thing to another, using "like" or "as" to connect them, they have created simile. Metaphor, on the other hand, is a direct comparison (without "like" or "as"). It is important that the image resulting from the comparison be unique, providing us with a new perspective on the objects being compared. For example, in "Polliwogs" by Kristine O'Connell George, polliwogs are described as "chubby commas." The comparison is fresh and causes readers to say, "I never thought of frogs quite that way before."

Personification is a comparison in which an inanimate object is described as having human qualities. Figurative language helps show children how poetry can give us a fresh view of the world through an imaginative juxtaposition of images.

Shape. Shape is a poem's visual display on the page: how the words are written, how many are placed per line, and the meaning of the whole poem in relation to its indentations and punctuation. Some poems begin each line with a capital letter and have an orderly succession of lines; others have words scattered all over the page or use punctuation in creative ways for emphasis and to extend the poem's meaning. Shape is important: it affects how you read a poem, defining the rhythm as well as the pace at which the poem unfolds.

*Copyright © 1958, renewed 1980 by Karla Kushkin. Used by permission of Scott Treimel NY.

Poetry's emotional impact is evident with these second grade students.

Poets use print creatively to emphasize particular letters or words, as when "SPLASH" is written in capitals to denote the loud sound a wave makes as it crashes against the beach during a storm. Some poets create a visual image that mirrors their meaning. For example, "Swing" (Burg) is written in a shape that suggests the arc made by a swing as it moves back and forth. Although how a poem looks usually is not its driving force, shape can nevertheless have a significant influence on its meaning and effect.

Emotional Impact. The elements of poetic crafting are of little significance, however, unless they work together to create a response in the reader. Many poems focus on evoking emotion from the reader. They start with a feeling, then the other elements work together to convey that feeling. One poet described this coordination of craft and feeling in the following way: "A poem should fill you up with something and make you swoon; stop you in your tracks, change your mind or make it up; a poem should happen to you like cold water or a kiss" (Heard, 1989, p. 74).

Insight. Although all the elements discussed so far contribute to a good poem, a poem does not always linger in our minds after we initially experience it unless it startles us with its insight. These insights do not have to be sophisticated and complex; sometimes, they amaze us with their simplicity, such as when Deborah Chandra describes skin as like "a canvas tent/that's stretched/from bone to bone" (in "Tent," from *Balloons and Other Poems*). It is the sense that the poem has given you a new perspective or made you feel differently about something that is evoked in truly fine poetry.

Genres and Forms of Poetry for Children

Poetry is also defined by its genres and forms. Two genres of poetry that are appropriate for children are narrative and lyric. Poetic forms include free verse, limerick, ballad, haiku, concrete, acrostic, and poetry novels. Figure 5.1 defines these genres and forms and provides specific examples of each.

We do not recommend that you drill students on defining poetic genres and forms or have them write poems in a particular form. For example, many teachers introduce students to poetry by having them write haiku because it seems like such an easy form to emulate. However, haiku is very complex. The strict numbers of lines and syllables are difficult to get right and still make sense. Because of haiku's brevity, ideas are implied, and connections are often symbolic.

FIGURE 5.1 Common Poetic Forms Used with Children

Narrative

Tells stories. Can rhyme or be in free verse. Can be humorous, sad, or adventurous. Many of the popular traditional ones are now available in picture book format. Most popular form with children.

Examples: *Ernest Lawrence Thayer's Casey at the Bat*, by Christopher Bing; "The Cremation of Sam McGee," by Robert Service (from *Collected Poems*); *Now We Are Six*, by A. A. Milne; much of the poetry by Jack Prelutsky and Shel Silverstein; *Brown Honey in Broomwheat Tea*, by Joyce Carol Thomas; *Meet Damitra Brown*, by Nikki Grimes.

Lyrical

Melodious; focuses on descriptions or observations, conveying an image, feeling, or insight. Most children's poetry is written in this form.

Examples: *Out in the Dark and Daylight*, by Aileen Fisher; *Heartland* and *Cave*, by Diane Siebert; *Splash* and *When Whales Exhale and Other Poems*, by Constance Levy; *Sun Through the Window*, by Marci Ridlon; *Advice for a Frog*, by Alice Schertle; *Lemonade Sun: And Other Summer Poems*, by Rebecca Kai Dotlich; *Honey I Love*, by Eloise Greenfield; *Stopping by Woods on a Snowy Evening*, by Robert Frost.

Free Verse

Nonrhyming; usually has rhythm, although it is not always patterned or consistent. Typically not as popular with students until they gain some background with poetry.

Examples: *Love Letters*, by Arnold Adoff; *All the Small Poems*, by Valerie Worth; *The Dream Keeper*, by Langston Hughes; *Confetti: Poems for Children*, by Pat Mora; *19 Varieties of Gazelle: Poems of the Middle East*, by Naomi Shihab Nye; *Animal Poems* by Valerie Worth.

Limerick

Five lines; thought to be Irish in origin. Humorous nonsense poems with an aabba rhyme scheme. Fifth line is usually a humorous concluding statement. Rhythm also follows prescribed rules. Popular with students.

Examples: *The Hopeful Trout and Other Limericks*, by John Ciardi; *Uncle Switch: Looney Limericks*, by

X. J. Kennedy; *A Lollygag of Limericks*, by Myra Cohn Livingston; work by Edward Lear; *A Pocketful of Nonsense* by James Marshall; *The Book of Pigericks* by Arnold Lobel.

Ballad

Poems with a strong plot and minimal character development. Focuses on dark side of specific dramatic event, conflict, or problem. Written in four-line stanzas with a specific rhyme scheme. Feature steady, predictable rhythm. Examples: *Casey at the Bat* by Ernest L. Thayer; *The Midnight Ride of Paul Revere* by Henry Wadsworth Longfellow.

Haiku

Ancient Japanese three-line form. First and third lines have five syllables; second line has seven syllables. Most haiku poems make an observation about nature and a statement of mood. Students tend not to like haiku until they have extensive experience with poetry.

Examples: *Cool Melons—Turn to Frogs!*, by Matthew Golub; *Black Swan, White Crow*, by J. Patrick Lewis; *Cricket Never Does: A Collection of Haiku and Tanka*, by Myra Cohn Livingston; *Stone Bench in an Empty Park*, by Paul Janeczko; *Don't Step on the Sky: A Handful of Haiku*, by Miriam Chaikin; *A Pocketful of Poems* by Nikki Grimes; *If Not for the Cat* by Jack Prelutsky; *Least Things* by Jane Yolen; *Short Takes* by Charles R. Smith; *Wabi Sabi* by Mark Reibstein; *Guyku* by Bob Raczka; *The Year Comes Round: Haiku Through the Seasons*, by Sid Farrar.

Concrete Poetry

Written in the shape of the poem's subject. Can be rhymed or free verse. Purpose is to be seen as well as heard.

Examples: *Outside the Lines*, by Brad Burg; *Summersaults*, by Douglas Florian; *Splish Splash* and *Flicker Flash*, by Joan Bransfield Graham; *A Poke in the I: A Collection of Concrete Poems* by Paul Janeczko; *Meow Ruff* by Joyce Sidman; *Doodle Dandies—Poems That Take Shape* by J. Patrick Lewis; *A Curious Collection of Cats* by Betsy Franco; *Technically It's Not My Fault* by John Grandits.

(continued)

FIGURE 5.1 *continued*

Acrostic

Form in which a word is written vertically on a page; each letter of the word begins a line of the poem.

Examples: *Winter; Spring; Summer; Fall,* by Stephen Schnur; *African Acrostics: A Word in Edgeways* by Avis Harley; *Silver Seeds* by Paul Paolilli & Dan Brewer.

Poetry Novels

Series of poems (usually free verse) that tell a continuous story. Typically, characterization, theme, setting, and other elements of fiction are important elements in the poetry.

Examples: *Out of the Dust,* by Karen Hesse; *Girl Coming In for a Landing,* by April Wayland; *Becoming Joe DiMaggio,* by Maria Testa; *Where the Steps Were* by Andrea Cheng; *What My Mother Doesn't Know* by Sonia Sones; *A Fire in My Hands* by Gary Soto; *Zorgamazoo* (Weston); *Make Lemonade* (Wolff); *Home of the Brave* by Katherine Applegate; *Hurricane Dancers* by Marguerite Engle; *Inside Out and Back Again* by ThanhhaLai; *Pearl Verses the World* by Sally Murphy.

No wonder most surveys of children's poetry preferences list haiku as the most disliked poetic form. Rather, we recommend that you expose students to many poetic genres and forms so that they can discover what they enjoy and expand their appreciation for a wide variety of poetry.

The Role of Poetry in Children's Lives

When children read, write, and listen to poetry, they become more aware of the world. They are more likely to take the time to closely observe everyday phenomena, discovering new insights and new ways of perceiving things that most people ignore. They also become better writers. Children exposed to poetry often naturally create prose that is more poetic. They learn to say what they mean in a few words—to be concise. They understand the importance of selecting the precise, most appropriate word to express a meaning. Poetry becomes a source of pleasure and a resource for response (McClure, 1989).

Children's Poetry Preferences

Children have some strong opinions about what they like in poetry; survey after survey consistently confirms this (Fisher & Natarella, 1982; Fulmer, 2012; Ingham, 1980; Kutiper & Wilson, 1993; Terry, 1974). The results of these surveys tell us the following:

- Children prefer narrative and limerick poetic forms. Haiku and free verse are the most disliked forms.
- Poetry that is humorous and focused on familiar experiences and animals is most popular.
- The elements of rhyme, rhythm, and sound are enjoyed, whereas complex visual imagery and figurative language are less enjoyed.
- Younger children enjoy poetry about imaginative events and people.
- Younger children prefer contemporary poems.

These results are somewhat discouraging, as it seems that children can enjoy only a very limited kind of poetry. Is this inevitable? Are children capable of appreciating only light, humorous poetry? What would happen to student poetry preferences if they were introduced to a steady diet of increasingly complex poetry by teachers who were knowledgeable about the genre and enjoyed it themselves?

If children are continually exposed to high-quality poetry through read-alouds, discussions, and choral readings; allowed to read poetry extensively on their own; and encouraged to write poetry, their preferences change. Although they do not abandon the light, humorous material, their preference for poetry that features unusual imagery, carefully selected words, and complex meanings is significant. They become familiar with a wider variety of poetry and also seem more appreciative of elements such as figurative language and abstract forms such as haiku (Krogness, 1995; Lenz, 1992; McClure, 1985; Perfect, 1999; Siemens, 1996).

Criteria for Evaluating Poetry

Figure 5.2 lists criteria to help you discover the best examples of this genre.

FIGURE 5.2 Criteria for Evaluating Poetry

- Is it pleasing to your ear? Is it enjoyable to say aloud?
- When the poem has rhythm and rhyme, are these elements in a form that is likely to appeal to students? When it is free verse, does it have some quality—usually imagery, topic, or interesting word choice—that will appeal to children?
- When the poetry rhymes, are the rhymes interesting and fresh, or are they predictable and contrived? Do the rhymes enhance the meaning or get in the way?
- Is it poetry your students will be able to understand and connect to? Be cautious of poetry written many years ago: it might be pleasurably nostalgic to you but seem irrelevant to your students because of archaic vocabulary and references.
- Are the images created by the poet fresh and interesting to children yet still true to life?
- Is the figurative language relevant to students' lives, and does it make comparisons that children can understand?
- Does the content relate to students' lives?
- Does the poem appeal to students yet extend their taste of what they consider "good" poetry?

Categories of Poetry

Poetry can be categorized in several ways: by theme, academic focus, and format. To give you a sense of the diversity in poetry, we discuss some of the best in each of these categories. Further examples of books in each category can be found in the various figures in the chapter as well as in the lists at the chapter's conclusion.

Thematic Poetry

There is an increasingly wider and more sophisticated range of topics and themes in poetry for children. This is great news for those of us who want children to become engaged with poetry and make it part of their daily lives; we can find poems that will appeal to literally every child's interests or life issues. In the following sections, we discuss some of the major themes in poetry that are of high interest to children, according to preference studies. We also highlight the poets who tend to write poetry focusing on that theme. The lists at the end of this chapter feature many excellent poetry books for exploring various themes.

Humor and Wordplay. Humorous verse is perennially the most widely read poetry for children. The popularity of Shel Silverstein, Jack Prelutsky, Douglas Florian, and other poets who write humorous verse (many reach the upper ranks of the *New York Times* best-seller lists) shows that children naturally gravitate to these books.

Edward Lear is one of the best-known traditional poets who wrote nonsense verse and limericks. Known for inventive language and delight in the sounds of words, his most famous poem is "The Owl and the Pussycat," which employs creative language, such as a "runcible spoon," and rhythmic rhyming phrases, such as "They danced by the light of the moon,/The moon,/the moon,/They danced by the light of the moon." An excellent edition of Lear's *A Book of Nonsense* (originally published in 1846) has been reissued and includes Lear's original drawings.

John Ciardi is a 20th-century poet whose use of inventive wordplay and humor has long delighted children. For example, his "Mommy Slept Late and Daddy Fixed Breakfast" was the top choice in one poetry preference study. Ciardi's *You Read to Me and I'll Read to You* and *You Know Who* contains many of his best poems.

Douglas Florian is a contemporary children's poet known for his playfully humorous observations of animals, nature, and the seasons. Florian believes there should be no rules when writing poetry. In his opinion, words can be played with and adapted to whatever meanings we choose. Puns, bad grammar, inventive spellings, and wordplays abound in his poetry.

Florian's creative wordplay and zany humor capture the essence of animals in *Mammalabilia*, *Beast Feast*, *On the Wing*, *In the Swim*, *Insectlopedia*, *UnBEElievables*, and *Zoo's Who*. His collections of poems about seasons—*Summersaults*, *Autumnblings*, *Winter Eyes*, and *Handsprings*—are more serious, although his inventive wordplay is still evident. *Poetrees* cleverly explores trees from coconut palms to banyans. His longer books of general fun and nonsense—*Bing, Bang, Bong* and *Laugh-eteria*—further showcase his talent as a master of humorous wordplay.

Fans of Douglas Florian also often enjoy the humorous poetry of X. J. Kennedy and J. Patrick Lewis. *Exploding Gravy: Poems to Make You Laugh* is a compilation of Kennedy's work. The subjects of his poems range from lessons on not playing with your food to "Mingled Yarns," in which favorite rhymes and stories are intermingled. Kennedy's *Brats* and *Fresh Brats* are poetry collections about mischievous children, some of whom meet a horrible demise but many who get away with their antics. Lewis writes on a variety of topics. His poetry is characterized by sly, often tongue-in-cheek humor and inventive wordplay. You will see many of his works cited throughout this chapter.

Poetry About Nature and the Seasons. Although poems about nature are not always initially children's favorites, they often learn to love the elegant imagery and imaginative references to the world around them when introduced to nature poetry by enthusiastic teachers. Many traditional poets, such as Robert Frost and Carl Sandburg, wrote poetry about nature that contemporary children enjoy. Frost's most memorable poems, such as "Stopping by Woods on a Snowy Evening," "The Pasture," and "Dust of Snow," have been collected for children in *You Come Too*. Single poems, such as "Stopping By Woods . . ." and "Birches," have also been issued in beautiful picture book editions. Carl Sandburg's poetry, including "Buffalo Dusk" (an ode to the vanishing American prairie), "Summer Grass" (that "aches and whispers" for rain), and "Arithmetic" (where numbers are compared to birds that flit in and out of one's consciousness), were collected in *The Sandburg Treasury: Prose and Poetry for Young People*.

Aileen Fisher created deceptively simple but superbly crafted poems that captured a child's perspective on nature and the everyday world. *I Heard a Bluebird Sing* features Fisher's most popular poems, as determined by votes from children across the United States. *Sing of the Earth and Sky: Poems About Our Planet and the Wonders Beyond*, *Out in the Dark and Daylight*, and *Anybody Home* are collections that include many of her most beloved poems.

Constance Levy is also a keen observer of nature. Levy's *A Crack in the Clouds* uses mostly free verse images that encourage children to look closely at the small details of everyday things, such as the music of rushing water in the forest, how rain spills out of a crack in the clouds, or how feet sound as they walk ("gravel crackles, grass squeaks, sneaker slaps/on hard concrete"*). *Splash!* (Levy) celebrates the wonders of water in its many forms.

Many other poets celebrate nature in their work. Kristine O'Connell George is an astute observer who creates magical imagery from ordinary things in *Old Elm Speaks: Tree Poems* and *Hummingbird Nest: A Journal of Poems*. Joyce Sidman celebrates the colors associated with seasons in *Red Sings From Treetops*.

Poetry About Children's Everyday Lives. Children particularly enjoy poetry that mirrors their own lives. Poems about families, feelings, pets, school, and similar topics help them connect to poetry and see its relevance to the people and issues they face every day.

Mary Ann Hoberman's poems resound with the sounds and rhythms of children's everyday lives while also offering fresh insights into their world. One of Hoberman's best-known poems, *A House Is a House for Me*, is published in picture book format. This book uses repetition, rhythm, and a predictable rhyme scheme to describe houses in creative ways, including describing a house as a home for one's "hand or a pen that houses ink." Hoberman's skill with wordplay, particularly the harmony of sound and rhythm, is particularly evident in *The Llama Who Had No Pajama: 100 Favorite Poems*, which brought together her most popular poems about everyday childhood experiences. The collection is an excellent introduction to poetry for young children because it develops an affinity for rhythm and rhyme while addressing appealing topics.

A significant part of children's everyday lives is discovering who they are and where they fit in the world. Feelings, dreams, gender identity, and dealing with conflict—all are issues children must resolve as they grow to adulthood. Several poetry collections focus on these issues. Sara Holbrook, in particular, writes poetry that captures the emotions resulting from the changes and choices children face as they try to balance the tightrope between youth and adulthood in *Which Way to the Dragon!*, *Am I Naturally This Crazy?*, *I Never Said I Wasn't Difficult*, and *Walking on the Boundaries of Change*. Several collections focus on helping both boys and girls celebrate their gender. *More Spice Than Sugar* (Morrison) showcases poems about historical heroines, such as Sojourner Truth, and offers encouragement to active, bold, brave girls who dare to be different. *VHERSES: A Celebration of Outstanding Women* (Lewis) and *All by Herself: 14 Girls Who Made a Difference* (Paul) have similar themes. Issues of male identity are addressed in books such as *A Fury of Motion* (Ghigna), *Tough Boy Sonatas* (Crisler), and *You Don't Even Know Me: Stories and Poems About Boys* (Flake).

Poetry About School. Many collections comment on this important aspect of children's lives in inventive and often humorous ways. Kristine O'Connell George addressed the challenges and joys of navigating "upstream" while finding one's own place in the middle school "wilderness" in *Swimming Upstream: Middle School Poems*. Issues such as locating your locker, finding a place to sit at lunchtime, figuring out where you fit in, and getting to classes are all accurately yet sympathetically portrayed. *Speak to Me (and I Will Listen Between the Lines)* (English) appeals to a younger audience and is another book that addresses children's feelings about navigating the challenges of school.

*From "Feet Talk" in *A Crack in the Clouds and Other Poems* by Constance Levy. Copyright © 1998 by Constance Kling Levy. Used by permission of Marian Reiner for the author.

Organized like a dinner menu, the poems by Lewis and the illustrations by O'Brien are sure to produce a smile.

English's poetic descriptions and perceptive insights draw readers into the world of six inner-city third graders who talk about their school day as well as the challenges of their lives outside of school.

In contrast, Kalli Dakos writes poetry about the funny, silly, and crazy daily life in elementary schools, demonstrating keen insight into classroom situations. For example, "show-and-tell" is a typical classroom routine. However, in Dakos's *If You're Not Here, Please Raise Your Hand*, the routine is enlivened by one child who brings in a worm—then proceeds to eat it. Similar hilarious and poignant incidents, related in both rhymed and free verse poems, are featured in Dakos's *The Goof Who Invented Homework*, *Put Your Eyes Up Here and Other School Poems*, and *Don't Read This Book Whatever You Do*.

Poets have also created specialized poetry collections that focus on the joys of reading and the importance of books in people's lives. Poems on this topic are interspersed throughout many general anthologies as well as specialized anthologies by individual poets. We encourage you to begin collecting these poems, as they are wonderful to share with children during spontaneous moments as well as on special occasions, such as Book Week or Poetry Month. *Wonderful Words: Poems About Reading, Writing, Speaking and Listening*, *I Am the Book*, and *Good Books, Good Times* (all by Hopkins) celebrate the magic of language and the power of words to make literature come alive for students.

Poetry About Animals.   Preference studies indicate that children enjoy poems about animals, both real and imaginary. Cats and dogs are particularly popular pets, and many poets enjoy writing about these animals. *Little Dog Poems* and *Little Dog and Duncan* (George) recount the quiet adventures of a little girl, her puppy, and a very large overnight visitor. Poems in *The World According to Dog* (Sidman) and *A Dazzling Display of Dogs* (Franco) comment on dog behavior and how dogs interact with humans. Cats are the focus of collections such as *Cat Poems* (Crawley), *A Curious Collection of Cats* (Franco), *Meow Ruff: A Story in Concrete Poetry* (Sidman), and *Cat, What Is That?* (Johnston).

Paul Fleischman is known for well-crafted, imaginative poetry about bugs that is full of interesting language and unusual imagery. *Joyful Noise: Poems for Two Voices* is a collection celebrating the "Booming/boisterous/joyful noise"* of the insect world. Alliteration, repetition, and other poetic elements are used to create vivid portraits of insects ranging from fireflies to cicadas to book lice. Each poem is written to be read aloud by two voices, bringing the various insects to life. Fleischman's *I Am Phoenix* is also written to be read aloud by two voices but focuses on the callings of birds.

Some poets have created collections focused on imaginary or mythical animals. *Yellow Elephant: A Bright Bestiary* (Larios) features animals in unusual, brilliant hues, such as "Red Donkey" and "Silver Gull." Marilyn Singer uses a carnival setting to introduce each imaginary character in *Creature Carnival*, which also includes poems about creatures from mythology and literature. *Behold the Bold Umbrellaphant* (Prelutsky) imagines animals that are combined with inanimate objects, such as an elephant and umbrella (hence the title) or a clock with an octopus (clockopus). Prelutsky uses a similar theme for *Sardines Swim High Across the Sky*.

---

*From *Joyful Noise* by Paul Fleischman. Text copyright © 1988 by Paul Fleischman. Used by permission of Harper-Collins Publishers.

Poetry and Content-Area Studies

Many wonderful poetry books are available to support the teaching of science, social studies, and mathematics. Using poetry across the curriculum provides a unique aesthetic dimension that helps children look beyond the "facts" they might learn in their textbooks to discover the rich nuances and textures that underlie a topic. It is not essential, but it makes the whole experience richer and more memorable.

So, when studying American history, for example, students could experience *Hand in Hand: An American History in Poetry* (Hopkins), *The Great Migration: Journey North* (Greenfield), *Mississippi Mud: Three Prairie Journals* (Turner), and Christopher Bing's picture book version of *Paul Revere's Ride*. Children studying geography could explore *A World of Wonders* (Lewis), which uses poetry to explore various geographic features around the world, or *Sacred Places* (Yolen), which has the same purpose but focuses on places that are sacred to various cultures and religions.

Science is another content area that can be greatly enriched by the inclusion of poetry. Joyce Sidman is particularly adept at creating scientifically accurate poems that are also well crafted. *Song of the Water Boatman and Other Pond Poems* (Sidman) combines science facts with vivid poems to describe pond life through the seasons. *Butterfly Eyes and Other Secrets of the Meadow* (Sidman) uses poetic riddles to explore the plants and animals of meadows, whereas *Dark Emperor and Other Poems of the Night* (Sidman) celebrates the nocturnal world of the forest.

A study of animals would be greatly enhanced by sharing *Animal Sense* (Ackerman), which uses startling, original imagery to describe the unique ways animals explore the world. These poems could be compared with *Animal Poems of the Iguazu* (Alarcon), which takes readers on a journey to the rain forest; *What's for Dinner? Quirky, Squirmy Poems from the Animal World* (Hauth), which poetically describes scientific concepts, such as symbiosis and mutualism; and *Ubiquitous: Celebrating Nature's Survivors* (Sidman), which describes how certain species have survived over time. In contrast, a humorous perspective on science is found in Jon Scieszka's *Science Verse*, that relates information about topics such as precipitation, the food chain, and food additives.

Some books on counting and mathematical concepts are written in verse. For example, *Ten Times Better* (Michelson) poetically describes multiples of 10, whereas *Echoes for the Eye: Poems to Celebrate Patterns in Nature* (Esbenson) uses free verse and exquisite language to describe spirals, polygons, circles, and other interesting mathematical patterns in the world of nature. Greg Tang combines his love of mathematics, words, art, and games as he tries to make mathematics interesting and fun in *The Grapes of Math*, *Math Appeal*, *The Best of Times*, *Math Fables*, and *Math-terpieces*. *Math Curse* (Scieszka) begins with a teacher announcing, "You know you can think of almost everything as a math problem." What follows is one student who becomes afflicted with a "math curse" that compels her to find math everywhere.

Figure 5.3 features a sampling of poetry books that can be used to supplement content-area study. Just remember to also enjoy a poem for its artistry and music, not only for its content connection.

Poetry in Different Formats

Poetry can also be categorized by format, including anthologies, books by individual poets, and picture book editions of single poems.

FIGURE 5.3 Poetry Across the Curriculum

(Books appropriate for preschoolers are marked *; those with significant culturally diverse elements are marked #.)

Social Studies

#Altman, Susan, and Lechner, Susan (Eds.). *Followers of the North Star: Rhymes About African American Heroes, Heroines and Historical Times* (Bryon Wooden, Illus.). (I, M)

Chandra, Deborah, and Comora, Madeleine. *George Washington's Teeth* (Brock Cole, Illus.). (P)

#Frank, John. *How to Catch a Fish* (Peter Slyvada, Illus.). (I)

#Gilchrist, Jan Spivey. *My America* (Ashley Bryan, Illus.). (P)

Harrison, David. *Cowboys*. (I)

Hines, Anna Grossnickle. *Peaceful Pieces: Poems and Quilts About Peace*. (I, M)

Hopkins, Lee Bennett (Ed.). *America at War* (M); *Behind the Museum Door* (Stacey Dressen-McQueen, Illus.) (I, M); #*Days to Celebrate: A Full Year of Poetry, People, Holidays, History, Fascinating Facts & More* (I, M); *Got Geography* (Philip Stanton, Illus.) (I, M); *Home to Me: Poems Across America* (Stephen Alcorn, Illus.) (I); #*Lives: Poems About Famous Americans* (Leslie Staub, Illus.) (I); #*My America: A Poetry Atlas of the United States* (Stephen Alcorn, Illus.) (I, M)

Katz, Bobbi. *Trailblazers: Poems of Exploration* (Carin Berger, Illus.) (I, M); #*We the People: Poems* (Nina Crews, Illus.). (I, M)

Katz, Susan. *A Revolutionary Field Trip: Poems of Colonial America* (R. W. Alley, Illus.) (P, I); *The President's Stuck in the Bathtub: Poems About the Presidents* (Robert Neubecker, Illus.). (P, I)

Janeczko, Paul. *Requiem: Poems of the Terezin Ghetto*. (M)

Lewis, J. Patrick. *Monumental Verses* (I, M); *The Underwear Salesman and Other Jobs for Better or Verse* (Serge Bloch, Illus.) (I); *A World of Wonders: Geographic Travels in Verse and Rhyme* (Alison Jay, Illus.) (I, M); *A Burst of Firsts* (Brian Ajhar, Illus.) (P, I, M); #*When Thunder Comes: Poems for Civil Rights Leaders* (various illus.). (I, M)

#Meltzer, Milton (Ed.). *Hour of Freedom: American History in Poetry* (Marc Nadel, Illus.). (M)

Salas, Laura. *Tiny Dreams, Sprouting Tall: Poems About the United States*. (I)

#Schertle, Alice. *We* (Kenneth Addison, Illus.). (I)

#Shange, Ntozake. *Freedom's a-Callin' Me* (Rod Brown, Illus.). (all)

Siebert, Diane. *Heartland* (Wendell Minor, Illus.) (P, I); *Tour America* (Stephen Johnson, Illus.). (P, I)

Singer, Marilyn. *Monday on the Mississippi* (Frane Lessac, Illus.) (P, I); *Rutherford B. Hayes: Who Was He? Poems About the Presidents*. (I, M)

Turner, Ann. *Mississippi Mud: Three Prairie Journals* (Robert J. Blake, Illus.). (I, M)

Volavkova, Hana (Ed.). *I Never Saw Another Butterfly: Children's Drawings and Poems from Terezin Concentration Camp, 1942–1944*. (M)

Wong, Janet. *Declaration of Interdependence: Poems for an Election Year*. (I, M)

Yolen, Jane. *Sacred Places*. (David Shannon, Illus.) (I, M); *Water Music* (Jason Stemple, Illus.). (I, M)

Zimmer, Tracie Vaughn. *Steady Hands: Poems About Work* (Megan Halsey and Sean Addy, Illus.). (M)

Math

*Baker, Keith. *Quack and Count*. (P)

Crawley, Dave. *Reading, Rhyming and 'Rithmetic* (Liz Callen, Illus.). (I, M)

Esbensen, Barbara. *Echoes for the Eye: Poems to Celebrate Patterns in Nature* (Helen K. Harper, Illus.). (I, M)

Franco, Betsy. *Counting Our Way to the 100th Day!* (Steven Salerno, Illus.) (P, I); *Mathematickles!* (Steven Salerno, Illus.); *Bees, Snails & Peacock Tails: Patterns and Shapes . . . Naturally* (Steve Jenkins, Illus.) (P); *Counting Caterpillars and Other Math Poems*. (P)

*Holub, Joan, Dunneck, Regan, and Boyd, Heather. *Riddle-Iculous Math*. (P)

Hopkins, Lee Bennett. *It's About Time* (P, I); *Marvelous Math: A Book of Poems* (Ken Barbour, Illus.). (I, M)

*Hutchins, Hazel. *A Second Is a Hiccup: A Child's Book of Time* (Kady MacDonald Denton, Illus.). (P)

FIGURE 5.3 *continued*

Kay, Jackie, Nichols, Grace, and Agard, Jon. *Number Parade: Number Poems from 0–100.* (P, I)

Lewis, J. Patrick. *Arithme-tickle: An Even Number of Odd Riddle-Rhymes* (Frank Remikiewicz, Illus.) (P); *Edgar Allan Poe's Pies: Math Puzzles in Classic Poems* (Michael Slack, Illus.). (M)

McGrath, Barbara. *Teddy Bear Patterns* (and others) (Tim Nihoff, Illus.). (P)

Michelson, Richard. *Ten Times Better* (Leonard Baskin, Illus.). (P)

Sandburg, Carl. *Arithmetic* (Ted Rand, Illus.). (I, M)

Siegen-Smith, Nikki. *First Morning: Poems About Time* (Giovanni Manna, Illus.). (I, M)

Tang, Greg. *The Grapes of Math: Mind Stretching Math Riddles* (Harry Briggs, Illus.) (P, I) (and others).

Yolen, Jane. *Count Me a Rhyme* (Jason Stemple, Photog.). (P)

Ziefert, Harriet. *Mother Goose Math* (Emily Bolam, Illus.). (P)

Science

(Science poetry about animals can be found in the "Recommended Thematic Poetry" list [animals] at the end of the chapter).

Asch, Frank. *Sawgrass Poems: A View of the Everglades* (Ted Lewin, Photog.) (I, M); *Song of the North* (Ted Levin, Photog.) (I, M); *Cactus Poems* (Ted Levin, Photog.). (I, M)

Beach, Judi. *Names for Snow* (Loretta Krupinski, Illus.). (P)

Blackaby, Susan. *Nest, Nook & Cranny* (Jamie Hogan, Illus.). (I, M)

Brenner, Barbara. *The Earth Is Painted Green: A Garden of Poems About Our Planet* (S. D. Schindler, Illus.). (P, I, M)

Cassedy, Sylvia. *Zoomrimes: Poems About Things That Go* (Michele Chassare, Illus.). (P, I)

Coombs, Kate. *Water Sings Blue: Ocean Poems* (Meilo So, Illus.). (P, I)

Dotlich, Rebecca. *In the Spin of Things* (Karen Dugan, Illus.) (P, I); *What Is Science?* (Sachiko Yoshikawa, Illus.). (P)

*Elliott, David. *In the Sea.* (P, I)

Fisher, Aileen. *Sing of the Earth and Sky: Poems About Our Planet and the Wonders Beyond* (Karmen Thompson, Illus.) (P, I); *The Story Goes On* (Mique Moriuchi, Illus.). (P)

Florian, Douglas. *Comets, Stars, the Moon and Mars: Space Poems and Paintings* (I, M); *Dinothesaurus: Prehistoric Poems & Paintings* (P, I); *UnBEElievables: Honeybee Poems and Paintings.* (P, I)

Fox, Karen. *Older Than the Stars* (Nancy Davis, Illus.). (P)

George, Kristine. *Old Elm Speaks* (Kate Kiesler, Illus.). (P)

Gerber, Carole. *Winter Trees* (Leslie Evans, Illus.). (P)

#Harrison, David L. *Sounds of Rain: Poems of the Amazon* (Doug Duncan, Photog.). (I, M)

Hoberman, Mary Ann, and Winston, Linda (Eds.). *The Tree That Time Built: A Celebration of Nature, Science, and Imagination* (Barbara Fortin, Illus.). (M)

Hopkins, Lee Bennett. *Blast Off: Poems About Space* (Melissa Sweet, Illus.) (P); *Click, Rumble, Roar: Poems About Machines* (Anna H. Audette, Illus.) (I); *Sky Magic* (Stawarski, Mariusz, Illus.) (P); *Spectacular Science: A Book of Poems* (Virginia Halstead, Illus.) (P, I); *Weather: Poems for All Seasons* (Melanie Hall, Illus.). (P)

Hubbell, Patricia. *Earthmates: Poems* (Jean Cassels, Illus.). (I)

Johnston, Tony. *An Old Shell: Poems of the Galapagos* (Tom Pohrt, Illus.). (I, M)

Katz, Susan. *Looking for Jaguar and Other Rain Forest Poems* (Lee Christiansen, Illus.). (I)

Lesser, Carolyn. *Storm on the Desert* (Ted Rand, Illus.). (P, I)

Lewis, J. Patrick. *Scien-Trickery: Riddles in Science* (Frank Remkiewicz, Illus.) (P, I); *Swan Song: Poems of Extinction* (Christopher Wormell, Illus.). (I, M)

Livingston, Myra Cohn. *Earth Songs* (Leonard Everett Fisher, Illus.) (I); *Roll Along: Poems on Wheels* (I, M); *Sea Songs* (Leonard Everett Fisher, Illus.) (I); *Space Songs* (Leonard Everett Fisher, Illus.) (I); *Light and Shadow* (Barbara Rogasky, Photog.). (I)

(continued)

FIGURE 5.3 *continued*

Locker, Thomas. *Cloud Dance* (P); *Mountain Dance* (P); *Water Dance.* (P)

#Mora, Pat. *Listen to the Desert* (Francisco X. Mora, Illus.) (P); *This Big Sky* (Steve Jenkins, Illus.). (I)

Nichols, Judith. *The Sun in Me: Poems About the Planet* (Beth Krommes, Illus.). (I)

Ode, Eric. *Sea Star Wishes: Poems from the Coast.* (P, I)

Peters, Lisa Westberg. *Earthshake: Poems from the Ground Up* (Cathie Festead, Illus.) (I); *Volcano Wakes Up!* (Stephen W. Jenkins, Illus.). (I)

Preus, Margi. *Celebetrees: Historic and Famous Trees of the World* (Rebecca Gibbon, Illus.). (P, I)

Salas, Laura Purdie. *And Then There Were Eight: Poems About Space* (P, I); *Seed Sower, Hat Thrower: Poems About Weather.* (P, I)

Schaefer, Lola M. *This Is the Rain* (Jan Wattenberg, Illus.). (P)

Scieszka, Jon. *Science Verse* (Lane Smith, Illus.). (I)

Shields, Carol D. *Brainjuice: Science Fresh Squeezed!* (M)

Sidman, Joyce. *Butterfly Eyes and Other Secrets of the Meadow* (Beth Krommes, Illus.) (P, I); *Eureka: Poems About Inventions* (K. Bennett Chavez, Illus.) (M); *Just Us Two: Poems About Animal Dads* (P); *Song of the Water Boatman and Other Pond Poems* (Beckie Prange, Illus.) (P, I); *Ubiquitous: Celebrating Nature's Survivors* (Beckie Prange, Illus.) (I, M); *Dark Emperor and Other Poems of the Night* (Rick Allen, Illus.). (P, M)

Siebert, Diane. *Cave* (Wayne McLoughlin, Illus.) (P, I); *Mojave* (Wendell Minor, Illus.). (P, I)

Singer, Marilyn. *Central Heating: Poems About Fire and Warmth* (Meilo So, Illus.) (I, M); *Footprints on the Roof: Poems About the Earth* (Meilo So, Illus.) (I, M); *A Strange Place to Call Home: The World's Most Dangerous Habitats and the Animals That Call Them Home* (Ed Young, Illus.). (I, M)

Sklansky, Amy. *Out of This World: Poems and Facts About Space* (Stacy Schuett, Illus.). (P, I)

Swinburne, Stephen. *Ocean Soup: Tide Pool Poems* (Mary Peterson, Illus.) (P); *Safe, Warm and Snug* (Jose Aruego and Ariane Dewey, Illus.) (P); *Boxing Rabbits, Bellowing Alligators: Courtship Poems from the Animal World* (M); *Unbeatable Beaks* (Joan Paley, Illus.). (P)

Wallace, Nancy Elizabeth. *The Sun, the Moon and the Stars.* (P)

Wassenhove, Sue Van. *The Seldom-Ever-Shady Everglades: Poems and Quilts.* (P)

Weeks, Sarah. *Crocodile Smile: 10 Songs of the Earth as the Animals See It* (Lois Ehlert, Illus.). (P)

Yolen, Jane. *An Egret's Day* (I); *Horizons: Poems As Far As the Eye Can See* (Jason Stemple, Illus.) (I, M); *Mother Earth, Father Sky: Poems of Our Planet* (Jennifer Hewitson, Illus.) (I, M); *A Mirror to Nature: Poems About Reflections* (Jason Stemple, Photog.) (I, M); *Shape Me a Rhyme: Nature's Forms in Poetry* (Jason Stemple, Photog.) (I, M); *Welcome to the Sea of Sand* (Laura Regan, Illus.) (P, I); *Wild Wings: Poems for Young People* (Jason Stemple, Illus.) (I, M); *Bird Watch.* (I, M)

Zaharas, Wade. *Big, Bad, and a Little Bit Scary: Poems That Bite Back.* (P, I)

Comprehensive Anthologies. Comprehensive anthologies serve as the backbone of a poetry collection. These usually are divided into themed sections with many poems on each topic and often feature a balance of contemporary and traditional poets. Figure 5.4 lists some excellent anthologies that will provide you with many poems on a variety of topics for classroom use.

Single-Poet Collections. In contrast to general anthologies, which typically feature the work of diverse poets, many collections focus on the work of a single poet, such as Jack Prelutsky or J. Patrick Lewis. Getting to know some poets and their trademark styles, themes, and forms will enable you to select poetry from their books to match the needs of your children and your curriculum.

Single Poems in Picture Book Format. Some individual poems are published in standard 32-page picture books, printed line by line and accompanied by beautiful illustrations, making these poems accessible and engaging to today's children. These books can also

FIGURE 5.4 Poetry Anthologies

(Books appropriate for preschoolers are marked *; those with significant culturally diverse elements are marked #.)

#Adoff, Arnold. *I Am the Darker Brother: An Anthology of Modern Poems by Black Americans.* (M)

Agard, John (Ed.). *Under the Moon & Over the Sea.* (I, M)

Andrews, Julie, and Hamilton, Emma. *Julie Andrews' Collection of Poems, Songs and Lullabies; Julie Andrews' Treasury for All Seasons: Poems and Songs to Celebrate the Year.* (I, M)

Attenborough, Liz. *Poetry by Heart.* (P, I)

#Booth, David. *'Til All the Stars Have Fallen: Canadian Poems for Children.* (I, M)

Cleary, Brian. *Rainbow Soup* (Neal Layton, Illus.). (I, M)

#Clinton, Catherine. *I, Too, Sing, America: Three Centuries of African-American Poetry* (Stephen Alcorn, Illus.). (I, M)

Cole, Joanna. *A New Treasury of Children's Poetry; Old Favorites and New Discoveries.* (P, I, M)

#Cooling, Wendy (Ed.). *Come to the Great World: Poems from Around The Globe.* (P)

Cullinan, Bernice. *A Jar of Tiny Stars: Poems by NCTE Award-Winning Poets* (Andi MacLeod, Illus.) (I, M) (also *Another Jar of Tiny Stars*). (P, I, M)

dePaola, Tomie. *Tomie dePaola's Little Book of Poems.* (P)

de Regniers, Beatrice Schenk. *Sing a Song of Popcorn.* (P, I)

*Dyer, Jane. *Animal Crackers.* (P)

Dunning, Stephen, et al. *Reflections on a Gift of Watermelon Pickle and Other Modern Verses.* (I, M)

Foster, John. *My First Oxford Book of Poetry.* (P)

*Fox, Mem. *Ten Little Fingers and Ten Little Toes.* (P)

Hall, Donald. *Oxford Book of Children's Verse in America.* (P, I)

Hopkins, Lee Bennett. *People, Holidays, History, Fascinating Facts and More* (I, M); *Side by Side: Poems to Read Together.* (P, I)

*Hoberman, Mary Ann. *Forget Me Nots: Poems to Learn by Heart.* (P, I)

Janeczko, Paul. *The Music of What Happens: Poems That Tell Stories* (M); *The Place My Words Are Looking For* (I, M); *Preposterous Poems of Youth* (M); *Seeing the Blue Between* (M); *Wherever Home Begins: 100 Contemporary Poems.* (M)

*Kennedy, Caroline. *A Family of Poems: My Favorite Poetry for Children* (P, I); *Poems to Learn by Heart.* (all)

*Kennedy, X. J., and Kennedy, Dorothy. *Knock at a Star: A Child's Introduction to Poetry* (P, I); *Talking Like the Rain: A First Book of Poems.* (P, I)

Lansky, Bruce. *A Bad Case of the Giggles: Kids' Favorite Funny Poems.* (I)

*Lewis, J. Patrick. *Countdown to Summer: A Poem for Every Day of the School Year* (Ethan Long, Illus.); *National Geographic Book of Animal Poetry.* (I, M)

Martin, Bill, Jr. *The Bill Martin Big Book of Poetry.* (I)

Moore, Lilian. *Sunflakes: Poems for Children.* (P, I)

National Geographic Books. *National Geographic Book of Animal Poetry: 200 Poems with Photographs That Squeak, Soar and Roar* (Edited by J. Patrick Lewis). (all)

#Nye, Naomi Shihab. *The Space Between Our Footsteps: Poems and Paintings from the Middle East* (M); *The Tree Is Older Than You Are: A Bilingual Gathering of Poems & Stories from Mexico.* (M)

*Prelutsky, Jack. *The Random House Book of Poetry* (P, I); *The 20th Century Children's Poetry Treasury.* (P, I, M)

#Sullivan, Charles (Ed.). *Here Is My Kingdom.* (M)

#Vardell, Sylvia, and Wong, Janet. *The Poetry Friday Anthology: Poems for the School Year with Connections to the Common Core.* (P, I, M)

*Yolen, Jane. *Here's A Little Poem: A Very First Book of Poetry* (Polly Dunbar, Illus.) (P); *Switching on the Moon: A Very First Book of Bedtime Poems* (Andrew Peters, Illus.) (P); *Wee Rhymes: Baby's First Poetry Book.* (P)

help visually oriented students find more meaning in a poem. For example, Susan Jeffers created hauntingly evocative illustrations for Robert Frost's "Stopping by Woods on a Snowy Evening." Charles R. Smith Jr. used compelling photographs of African Americans to illustrate Langston Hughes's tribute to *My People*. Chris Raschka's colorful, abstract illustrations reflect the exuberance of the story in Nikki Giovanni's *The Genie in the Jar* and bell hooks's *Happy to Be Nappy*.

Poetry for Young Children

If you are working with preschoolers and kindergartners, you need some poetry books that are appropriate just for them. Young children have a natural affinity for poetry; they love play rhymes, raps, and playground chants. If you watch them play, you will see them make up their own rhymes or create variations on familiar verses. You can capitalize on this by sharing much excellent poetry with them and providing them with poetry books they can read themselves. Although some people consider these more verse than poetry, we believe that they deserve a place in your poetry collection because they provide a wonderful entrée for young children into the world of poetry. *Wiggle Waggle Fun: Stories and Rhymes for the Very Very Young* (Mayo) is just such a collection. It is full of action rhymes, counting poems, and other traditional verse along with new poems, all sure to delight younger children.

Many of the anthologies as well as collections focusing on an individual poet's work that we have already described feature poems suitable for younger children. We have listed these in the various figures and text sets throughout this chapter, including those marked with an asterisk in the lists in this chapter. We have found the following anthologies particularly useful in our work with younger children: *Here's a Little Poem: A Very First Book of Poetry* (Yolen), *Knock at a Star: A Child's Introduction to Poetry* (Kennedy), *Talking Like the Rain: A First Book of Poetry* (Kennedy), *Ten Little Fingers and Ten Little Toes* (Fox), and *Animal Crackers: A Delectable Collection of Pictures, Poems, and Lullabies for the Very Young* (Dyer).

One traditional poet you will want to introduce to younger children is A. A. Milne. Author of *Winnie the Pooh*, Milne also wrote two books of poetry that have been collected into one volume, *The World of Christopher Robin*. Poems such as "Halfway Down," which captures a child's thoughts while sitting in a favorite spot on the stairs; "Teddy Bear," which comments on the "tubbiness" of a teddy that looks like Pooh; and "Us Two," which celebrates friendship between teddy bear and child, continue to delight contemporary children.

Some poetry books are written specifically for beginning readers. These feature simple vocabulary and sentence structures on topics appealing to young children. Lee Bennett Hopkins has created several excellent ones, including *Surprises* and *Hamsters, Shells and Spelling Bees: Poems About School*, *More Surprises*, *Questions*, and *Sports! Sports! Sports!* Jack Prelutsky has created several beginning reader poetry books to share at holiday time: *It's Thanksgiving*, *It's Halloween*, and *It's Valentine's Day*.

Teaching Strategies

Connecting to the Common Core State Standards

COMMON CORE STATE STANDARD FEATURE #1

Identifying Figurative and Other Nonliteral Language in Poetry Conversations (CCSS.RL.4)

The Reading: Literature Standards of the Common Core State Standards (CCSS) frequently mention poetry as a genre that students should appreciate and understand. Poetry, with its emphasis on careful language crafting, is particularly appropriate for developing skill in CCSS.ELA-Literacy.CCRA.R.4. The Anchor Standard states the following:

CCRA (Anchor Standard) R.4: Interpret words and phrases as they are used in a text, including determining technical, connotative, and figurative meanings, and analyze how specific word choices shape meaning or tone.

Sample Grade-Level Competencies for This Standard Are the Following:

RL.1.4.   Identify words and phrases in stories or poems that suggest feelings or appeal to the senses.

RL.3.4.   Determine the meaning of words and phrases as they are used in a text, distinguishing literal from nonliteral language.

RL.5.4.   Determine the meaning of words and phrases as they are used in a text, including figurative language such as metaphors and similes.

RL.7.4.   Determine the meaning of words and phrases as they are used in a text, including figurative and connotative meanings; analyze the impact of rhymes and other repetitions of sounds (e.g., alliteration) on a specific verse or stanza of a poem or section of a story or drama.

To support student understanding of the concepts described in this standard, we recommend that you read poetry aloud and then follow these readings with poetry conversations that help children develop a deeper appreciation of how the poet crafted that poem so as to make it an enjoyable experience for the listener. If poetry is a natural part of children's daily classroom experiences and is read aloud both purposefully and spontaneously throughout the day, children will naturally develop the understandings described in Reading: Literature Standard RL.4. Although we have chosen to focus on Standard RL.4 in our discussion, the principles can be applied to the study of any poetic elements mandated in the Literature standard of the CCSS.

Choosing the poetry you will read to your children for this purpose is an important decision. It is often helpful to begin with sharing poetry children easily enjoy, such as the humorous pieces written by Silverstein, Prelutsky, and Lewis that feature clever wordplay, consistent rhythms, and clear rhymes. Gradually, you will want to introduce poetry that stretches their literary tastes so that they develop an appreciation for more sophisticated language use.

Reading several poems on the same topic or theme often works well for helping children initially explore how various poets use language to describe the same phenomena. Using the topic of dogs, for example, you could first read aloud some light, humorous poems about dogs and then read "Lone Dog" (McLeod, from *Favorite Poems, Old and New*, edited by Helen Ferris). This poem is popular with children but also is a great example of how a poet uses compelling rhythm and internal rhyme to convey the feel of a tough, stray dog on the run. This poem can be contrasted with other poems portraying dogs, such as "Dog," from *All the Small Poems* (Worth), which uses slow, languid language that describes a dog that lolls on a porch, and those in *The Hound Dog's Haiku* (Rosen), a collection of poems that use language imaginatively to describe a variety of dogs.

Puzzle and riddle poems can also help children develop an appreciation for how poets skillfully use language. For example, omitting the title while reading "Safety Pin" from *All the Small Poems* (Worth) or "Balloons" from *Balloons and Other Poems* (Chandra) causes children to look closely at words and explore how the poet has conveyed meaning. You can ask children to guess what the poet is describing and state which words or phrases caused them to make that guess. Showing the object after guessing and then reading the poem again will heighten the effect of the words and should stimulate thoughtful discussion of how poets carefully select their words to accurately yet creatively describe the subject. Some helpful collections for this purpose are *Riddle Road: Poems in Puzzles and Pictures* and *With One White Wing* (Spires), *The House with No Door* (Swann), *My Head Is Red and Other Riddle Poems* (Livingston), *Riddlelightful* and

Riddleicious (Lewis), *All the Small Poems* (Worth), *Just Beyond Reach* (Nims), *Riddle Rhymes* (Gorton), and *When Riddles Come Rumbling: Poems to Ponder* (Dotlich).

Poetry conversations following a read-aloud help children deepen their appreciation of a poem and what makes it meaningful to a listener. We do not suggest analyzing a poem in the traditional sense of finding the "hidden meaning." Rather, delight or aesthetic response should come first. Questions such as the following can facilitate initial aesthetic poetry responses with children: "What appealed to you in the poem?," "How did the poem make you feel?," and "What did the poem make you think about?" (McClure, Harrison, & Reed, 1990).

Once children have shared their aesthetic responses, they can begin to consider how language makes a poem memorable for them. Explorations could include discerning how the poet has selected just the right words, carefully connected sounds to produce a musical phrase, or constructed a perfect metaphor. Sometimes, it helps to have partners turn to each other and discuss these elements. Or a class can be divided into smaller groups to explore a poem in this way. Figure 5.5 lists poems that will lead naturally into discussions of language use.

Again, we caution you not to overdo this. Enjoyment should be the focus, then help children deepen their enjoyment by exploring the crafting of a poem so the enjoyment is more informed.

FIGURE 5.5 Suggested Poems for Poetry Conversations

Rhyme	Figurative Language	Rhythm
"Sneeze," by Maxine Kumin (from Moore *Sunflakes: Poems for Children*)	"Comma in the Sky," by Aileen Fisher (from *In the Woods, in the Meadow, in the Sky*)	"Street Song," by Myra Cohn Livingston (from *A Tune Beyond Us: A Collection of Poetry*)
"Mice" by Rose Fyleman (from Prelutsky, *The Random House Book of Poetry for Children*)	"Rags," by Judith Thurman (from *Flashlight, and Other Poems*)	"The Swing," by Robert Louis Stevenson (from *A Child's Garden of Verse*)
"The Furry Ones," by Aileen Fisher (from Fisher and Cullinan, *I Heard a Bluebird Sing*)	"The Toaster," by William Jay Smith (from Dunning, *Reflections on a Gift of Watermelon Pickle and Other Modern Verse*)	"Hello and Goodbye," by Mary Ann Hoberman (from *The Llama Who Had No Pajama: 100 Favorite Poems*)
"Keep a Poem in Your Pocket," by Beatrice Schenk de Regniers (from Goldstein, *Inner Chimes: Poems of Poetry*)	"Steam Shovel," by Charles Malam (from Dunning, *Watermelon Pickle*)	"Spring," by Karla Kuskin (from *Dogs and Dragons, Trees and Dreams*)
"Whisper," by Myra Cohn Livingston (from *Whispers and Other Poems*)	"December Leaves," by Kaye Starbird	"Pickety Fence," by David McCord (from *One at a Time*)
"Poem to Mud," by Zilpha Snyder (from *Today Is Saturday*)	"Pollliwogs," by Kaye Starbird (from *Don't Ever Cross a Crocodile*)	"Honey, I Love," by Eloise Greenfield (from *Honey, I Love, and Other Poems*)
"This Is My Rock," by David McCord (from Kennedy and Kennedy, *Talking Like the Rain: A First Book of Poems*)	"Fueled," by Marci Hans (from Dunning, *Watermelon Pickle*)	"Dog," by Valerie Worth (from *All the Small Poems*)
"Catalog," by Rosalie Moore (from Dunning, *Reflections on a Gift of a Watermelon Pickle*)	"Autumn Leaves," by Deborah Chandra (from *Balloons and Other Poems*)	"Cloud Dragons," by Pat Mora (from *Confetti: Poems for Children*)
	"Paper Clips," by Rebecca Kai Dotlich (from Hopkins, *School Supplies: A Book of Poems*)	"The Tide," by Lanston Hughes
	"Becoming the Tea," by Joyce Carol Thomas (from *Brown Honey in Broomwheat Tea*)	
	"Cat Kisses," by Bobbi Katz	

COMMON CORE STATE STANDARD FEATURE #2

Developing Fluency with Poetry Performance (CCSS.RF.1, 2)

The CCSS also emphasize the importance of fluency. From grades 3 to 5, the Reading Foundations Standards state the following:

RF.1.3; 2.3–5.3   Read grade-level prose and poetry orally with accuracy, appropriate rate, and expression.

Poetry is an excellent genre for developing fluency. The brevity of the form and natural rhythms that support a reader's inital attempts make it an excellent resource for practicing fluency. Poetry performances are particularly appropriate for supporting the development of fluency. Figure 5.6 features many ways to design poetry performances, along with suggested poems that work particularly well for each type of performance. You will also find Tech Clicks that describe resources for finding materials to use in poetry performance activities.

Reader's Theater (described in Chapter 2) can also be used to develop fluency. Poetry café is an adaptation of reader's theater in which children present a series of poetry readings to an audience. Some teachers create a café atmosphere complete with jazz music and refreshments for this activity, whereas others have a more formal presentation for parents or other classes.

FIGURE 5.6 Choral Speaking and Poetry Performance with Children

Organizational Format	Description	Suggested Literature
Call/refrain	One person (teacher or student) reads a verse or section of the poem. The others join in on a refrain or repeating line, or they repeat each line after the leader.	"Went to the Corner" (Greenfield, in *Honey, I Love*); "Homework, Oh Homework" (Prelutsky, in *Where the Sidewalk Ends*); "Whispers" (Livingston, in *A Song I Sang to You*)
Line by line	Children take turns reading consecutive lines. Works best for poems that are "lists" of items, comments, observations, or descriptions.	"I Brought a Worm" (Dakos, in *If You're Not Here, Please Raise Your Hand*); "Junk Food" (Dunn, in *Butterscotch Dreams*); "When I Misbehave" (Greenfield, in *Nathaniel Talking*); "Rules" (Kuskin, in *Moon, Have You Met My Mother?*); "Full Blast" (Holbrook, in *Wham! It's a Poetry Jam*); "What Is Science?" (Hopkins, in *Spectacular Science*); "Places to Hide a Secret Message" (Merriam, in *Tomie dePaola's Book of Poems*)

(continued)

FIGURE 5.6 *continued*

Organizational Format	Description	Suggested Literature
Two voices	Two columns of words are placed side by side. Two readers (or groups of readers) take turns reading the columns; sometimes the voices alternate, and sometimes they are joined.	*Joyful Noise: Poems for Two Voices* and *I Am Phoenix* (Fleischman) *Big Talk: Poems for Four Voices* (Fleischman) *Farmer's Garden: Rhymes for Two Voices* (Harrison) *Messing Around on the Monkey Bars* (Franco) "Two Voices in a Tent at Night," from *Toasting Marshmallows* (George) *Side by Side* (Hopkins) *You Read to Me, I'll Read to You* (Hoberman) and others in series *Seeds, Bees and Butterflies* (Gerber) (In addition, stories and poems written in Spanish with English words written on the facing page work well for two-voice reading.)
Cumulative	A few students read the first line or verse, and then additional children join in on the subsequent lines until everyone speaks at the end of the poem. Or everyone can start and then drop out until only a few voices remain at the end of the reading.	"Snow" (Hoberman, in *The Llama Who Had No Pajama*); "Snowfall" (Chandra, in *Balloons and Other Poems*); "Eraser" (Phillips, in Hopkins's *School Supplies*)
Poetry slams	A group poetry-sharing activity in which students take turns spontaneously reading poetry aloud as they find connections among their favorite poems based on common themes, poetic devices, characters, or other qualities. Reach a wider poetry slam audience by participating in *The Favorite Poem Project: Americans Saving Poems They Love.*	These include poems with common themes, such as school, pets, weather, nature, and so on, so that students can easily make connections across multiple poems from different authors or collections. For example, one child might read aloud Constance Levy's poem "Fog" (from *Splash! Poems of Our Watery World*), which compares walking through fog to walking through clouds. A second child might link into the concept of clouds or fog by next sharing Sandburg's "Fog," which describes fog as coming "on little cat feet." A third child might then pick up on the concept of a cat walking stealthily and read "Cat," by Karla Kuskin (from *Near the Window Tree*), which includes the line "The cat comes and goes on invisible toes."

Tech Click

Audio Poetry Performances: Audience, Readers, and Writers

Add an extra dimension to poetry listening by hosting "author visits" to your classroom with CDs from your local library. Audio Bookshelf, Listening Library, HarperCollins, and Weston Woods are well-known producers of quality recordings for children. These auditory treats can be offered for full-class listening, as classroom "stations" with headsets, or as rainy-day recess enrichment.

Also available are audio books, such as *Poetry Speaks to Children*, which features readings of both contemporary and traditional poems (some by the original poets), and *Hip Hop Speaks to Children: A Celebration of Poetry with a Beat* (Giovanni, 2008), which highlights hip-hop, rap, and African American poetry. Search engines have become so intuitive that simply searching for a poet's name quickly retrieves video and audio performances. Other than searching individual poets, there are other valuable methods for locating other poetry resources.

Additional opportunities for presenting poetry read-alouds can be found on authors' home pages. A few examples are the following:

- Joyce Sidman in "To Manga, My Hamster" ponders what wishes pets might have. Listen to other poems on her site.

- Chant along with Ashley Bryan's captivating cadences in "Rain Coming" from Poems & Folktales on *Kids Learn Out Loud*.

- Kristine O'Connell George offers "Swimming Upstream: Middle School Poems," "River Messages," and "Music Class."

- Janet Wong has audio clips for "In Mother's Shadow," "Coin Drive," and "Bubble Troubles."

- Publishers often provide author samples. For example, Scholastic's *Writing with Writers: Poetry* includes audio files of Jack Prelutsky's "Louder Than a Clap of Thunder" as well as free print resources.

- With an iTunes account and 99 cents, your students can immediately hear Shel Silverstein's squishiest, slurpest sounds in "The Squishy Touch" from *A Light in the Attic*.

- YouTube is a rich resource for poetic multimedia. For example, *National Geographic* pairs stunning animal and habitat images with lines from J. Patrick Lewis's "Make the Earth Your Companion." However, many schools block YouTube because of inappropriate content. If educators consult fair use copyright guidelines and use tools such as Download Helper or Flashgot (a browser plug-in), it is possible to view videos safely while offline.

- The Library of Congress Archives provides webcast excerpts from titles such as *Red Hot Salsa: Bilingual Poems on Being Young and Latino in the United States*. With a little cuing up, students can listen to Maxine Kumin or Jack Prelutsky reading many of his favorites as part of his acceptance as the country's first children's poet laureate. This is one of many webcasts archived at the Library of Congress, and it can be found through a site search.

- Fantastic Online Professional Resources (search by title):
  - America's Favorite Poem Project
  - American Library Association (see YA and Children's Services page)
  - Blogspot: Syliva Vardell's blog
  - Joyce Sidman's list of poetry ideas and basic poem starters for younger and older writers (her blog "Out & About" is worth visiting)

- The New York Public Library's National Poetry Contest (on Twitter), "Little Poems, Big Thoughts"
- Poetry Out Loud (national recitation contest)
- Poetry Slam, Inc.
- Public domain poetry: eMule's Poetry Archive and American Verse Project
- *ReadWriteThink*'s multiple resources, including directions for making your own magnetic poetry, a useful idea starter for students who think that they cannot write poetry

Children can be encouraged to create their own recordings of favorite poems using free software such as Audacity or Power Sound Editor. Many smartphones include audio recording apps that make this process even easier. Buffy Hamilton (2009) called her experience with podcasting poetry readings "one of the most memorable experiences of my 17-year career as an educator" (p. 26). Details can be found in her article "Poetry Goes 2.0." This activity addresses the 21st Century Standard Skill in Communication and Collaboration:

> Utilize multiple media and technologies, and know how to judge their effectiveness a priori as well as assess their impact.

Students' own poetry can find audiences beyond the classroom walls in venues such as print magazines (*Cricket*) or online sites, such as The Children's Poetry Archive, which includes students reading their poems. Web 2.0 tools, such as Voice Thread, allows creative poets to use audio, video, images, and text. Public listeners can add oral or written commentary that can be moderated by the teacher and used as an "assessment of impact" (21st Century Standards) by the student poets.

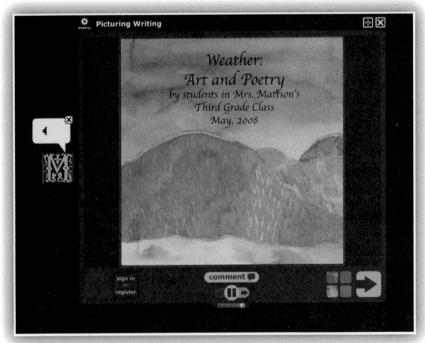

Third graders write and illustrate poetry in Voice Thread, inviting viewers to comment verbally or in text.

Good Luck Gold by Janet Wong is a classic multi-cultural poetry collection that celebrates Asian-American experiences.

Supporting Culturally Diverse Students with Poetry

Diverse voices have traditionally been underrepresented in children's poetry. African American poet Nikki Grimes (2000) describes how this lack of representation felt to her as a child:

> When I was growing up, I rarely found beautiful images of myself in the pages of a book, and that's precisely why I chose to write books for young people like me. I wanted them to meet girls like Zuri and Danitra in *Danitra Brown* . . . boys like Damon and men like Blue in *My Man Blue*. . . . These were people whose stories I knew and wanted to tell, people who looked and felt like me. (p. 32)

In recent years, more collections written by diverse voices have been published. The best poetry that celebrates diversity portrays a particular culture honestly and accurately while giving us insights into what it is like to be a part of that culture. At the same time, this poetry addresses universal themes, emotions, and experiences familiar to all children so that the poetry creates connections across cultures. Contemporary poets write from many cultural perspectives, including African American, Latino, Native American, and Asian, as well as international perspectives, such as Middle Eastern, African, and Caribbean. Figure 5.7 lists poetry from several culturally diverse perspectives.

FIGURE 5.7 Poetry from Diverse Voices

(Books appropriate for preschoolers are marked *.)

African American

Adoff, Arnold. *All the Colors of the Race* (John Steptoe, Illus.) (I); *Black Is Brown Is Tan* (Emily McCully, Illus.) (I); *I Am the Darker Brother* (Benny Andrews, Illus.) (M); *In for Winter, Out for Spring* (Jerry Pinkney, Illus.) (P, I); *Roots and Blues: A Celebration* (R. Gregory Christie, Illus.). (M)

Alexander, Elizabeth, and Nelson, Marilyn. *Miss Crandall's School for Young Ladies*; *Little Misses of Color* (Floyd Cooper, Illus.). (HF) (M)

Bradby, Marie. *More Than Anything Else* (Chris Soentpiet, Illus.) (I); *Once upon a Farm* (Ted Rand, Illus.). (P)

Brooks, Gwendolyn. *Bronzeville Boys and Girls* (Faith Ringgold, Illus.). (I)

*Bryan, Ashley. *Ashley Bryan's ABC of African American Poetry*; *Sing to the Sun*. (P, I)

*Clinton, Catherine. *I Too Sing America: Three Centuries of African American Poetry* (Stephen Alcorn, Illus.). (P, I)

Dove, Rita. *On the Bus with Rosa Parks: Poems*. (M)

Dunbar, Paul Laurence. *Jump Back, Honey*. (P, I)

Feelings, Tom, (Illus.). *Soul Looks Back in Wonder*. (P, I)

(continued)

FIGURE 5.7 *continued*

Forman, Ruth. *Young Cornrows Callin' Out the Moon* (Cbabi Bayoc, Illus.). (P)

Giovanni, Nikki. *Spin a Soft Black Song* (George Martins, Illus.); *The Sun Is So Quiet* (Ashley Bryan, Illus.); *Hip Hop Speaks to Children*. (P)

Grady, Cynthia. *I Lay My Stitches Down: Poems of American Slavery* (Michele Wood, Illus.). (I, M)

*Greenfield, Eloise. *Honey, I Love* (Leo and Diane Dillon, Illus.) (I, M); *Under the Sunday Tree* (Amos Ferguson, Illus.) (P); *Night on Neighborhood Street* (Jan Spivey Gilchrist, Illus.) (P, I); *Nathaniel Talking* (Jan Spivey Gilchrist, Illus.) (I); *The Great Migration: Journey to the North*. (I, M)

Grimes, Nikki. *A Dime a Dozen* (Angelo, Illus.) (M); *It's Raining Laughter* (Myles Pinkney, Illus.) (P, I); *My Man Blue* (Jerome Lagarrigue, Illus.) (I); *Meet Danitra Brown* (Floyd Cooper, Illus.) (and other Damitra Brown volumes). (P)

Hubbell, Patricia. *Black All Around* (Don Tate, Illus.). (P)

Hudson, Wade. *Pass It On: African American Poetry* (Floyd Cooper, Illus.). (P, I, M)

Hughes, Langston. *My People* (Charles Smith, Photog.) (P, I); *The Dream Keeper and Other Poems* (J. Brian Pinkney, Illus.) (I, M); *The Negro Speaks of Rivers* (E. B. Lewis, Illus.) (I, M); *I, Too, Sing America* (B. Collier, Illus.). (I, M)

Johnson, Angela. *Running Back to Ludie* (M); *The Other Side*. (M)

Lewis, J. Patrick. *When Thunder Comes: Poems for Civil Rights*. (I, M)

Medina, Tony. *DeShawn Days* (R. Gregory Christie, Illus.). (P)

Myers, Walter Dean. *Here in Harlem: Poems in Many Voices* (M); *Jazz* (Christopher Myers, Illus.) (I, M); *Blues Journey* (Christopher Myers, Illus.) (M); *We Are America: A Tribute from the Heart*.

Nelson, Marilyn. *Carver: A Life in Poems* (M); *Fortune's Bones: The Manumission Requiem* (M); *The Freedom Business: The Life of Venture Smith* (M); *A Wreath for Emmett Till* (Philippe Lardy, Illus.) (M); *How I Discovered Poetry* (Hadley Hooper, Illus.). (M)

Newsome, Effie Lee. *Wonders: The Best Children's Poems of Effie Lee Newsome* (Lois Mailou Jones, Illus.). (P)

Norman, Lissette. *My Feet Are Laughing* (Frank Morrison, Illus.). (P, I)

Rempersand, Arnold, and Blount, Marcellus (Eds.). *Poetry for Young People: African American Poetry*. (I, M)

Smith, Charles. *Brick by Brick*. (P)

*Steptoe, Javaka. *In Daddy's Arms I Am Tall*. (P)

Strickland, Michael. *My Own Song and Other Poems to Groove To*. (M)

Thomas, Joyce Carol. *Brown Honey in Broomwheat Tea* (Floyd Cooper, Illus.) (P, I, M); *Gingerbread Days*; *The Blacker the Berry*; *Crowning Glory*; *A Mother's Heart, A Daughter's Love: Poems for Us to Share*.

Weatherford, Carole Boston. *Remember the Bridge: Poems of a People* (M); *Birmingham, 1963*. (M)

Asian American

Mado, Michio. *The Magic Pocket* (Anno Mitsumasa, Illus.). (P)

Mak, Kam. *My Chinatown: One Year in Poems*. (P, I)

Park, Linda Sue. *Tap Dancing on the Roof: Sijo Poems* (Istvan Banyai, Illus.). (P. I)

Wong, Janet. *Good Luck Gold and Other Poems* (M); *Knock on Wood: Poems About Superstitions* (Julie Paschkis, Illus.) (I); *Night Garden: Poems from the World of Dreams* (Julie Paschkis, Illus.) (I, M); *The Rainbow Hand: Poems About Mothers and Children* (Jennifer Hewitson, Illus.) (M); *A Suitcase of Seaweed and Other Poems*. (I, M)

Young, Ed. *Beyond the Mountains: A Visual Poem About China*. (P, I)

Latino

Ada, Alma. *Yes! We Are Latinos* (David Diaz, Illus.). (I, M)

Alarcón, Francisco X. *Poems to Dream Together/ Poemas Para Sonar Juntos* (Paula Barragan, Illus.) (I); *From the Bellybutton of the Moon and Other Summer Poems* (Maya Christina Gonzales, Illus.) (P, I, M); *Iguanas in the Snow and Other Winter Poems* (Maya Christina Gonzalez, Illus.) (P, I); *Laughing Tomatoes and Other Spring Poems*; *Angels Ride Bikes and Other Fall Poems* (Maya Christina Gonzalez, Illus.). (I)

FIGURE 5.7 *continued*

Argueta, Jorge. *A Movie in My Pillow/Una pelicula in mi almohada* (Elizabeth Gomez, Illus.); *Guacamole: Un Poema Para Cocinar/A Cooking Poem* (Margarita Sada); *Tamalitos: Un Poema para cocinar/A Cooking Poem.* (I, M)

Brown, Monica. *My Name Is Gabito: The Life of Gabriel Garciá Márquez/Me Llamo Gabito* (Raul Colon, Illus.). (P)

Carlson, Lori. *Cool Salsa; Sol a Sol; Red Hot Salsa: Bilingual Poems on Being Young and Latino in the United States.* (M)

Carlson, Lori M. *Red Hot Salsa: Bilingual Poems on Being Young and Latino in the United States.* (M)

Durango, Julia. *Under the Mango Moon.* (I, M)

*Harris, Jay. *The Moon Is La Luna: Silly Rhymes in Spanish and English* (Matthew Cordell, Illus.) (good for pairs). (P, I)

Herrera, Juan. *Calling the Doves/El Canto de las Palomas* (Elly Simmons, Illus.). (P)

Herrera, Juan. *Laughing Out Loud, I Fly: Poems in English and Spanish* (Karen Barbour, Illus.). (M)

Johnston, Tony. *My Mexico-México Mio* (John Sierra, Illus.). (P, I)

*Luján, Jorge. *Colors! ¡Colores!* (Piet Grobler, Illus.). (P)

Medina, Jane. *My Name Is Jorge on Both Sides of the River* (I, M); *The Dream on Blanca's Wall/El Sueno Pegado en la Pared de Blanca* (Robert Casilla, Illus.). (M)

Mora, Pat. *Confetti: Poems for Children* (Enrique O. Sanchez, Illus.) (I, M); *Love to Mama: A Tribute to Mothers* (Paula S. Barragan, Illus.) (P); *This Big Sky* (Steve Jenkins, Illus.) (I); *Yum! Mmmm! Qué Rico! Americas' Sproutings* (Rafael Lopez, Illus.). (P, I)

Nye, Naomi S. *The Tree Is Older Than You Are: A Bilingual Gathering of Poems and Stories from Mexico.* (M)

Orozco, José-Luis. *Fiestas: A Year of Latin American Songs of Celebration* (Elisa Kleven, Illus.). (P, I, M)

Soto, Gary. *Neighborhood Odes* (David Diaz, Illus.) (M); *Canto Familiar* (Annika Nelson, Illus.); *A Fire In My Hands* (James M. Cardillo, Illus.) (M); *Fearless Fernie: Hanging Out with Fernie and Me.* (M)

Native American

Begay, Shonto. *Navajo: Visions and Voices Across the Mesa.* (I, M)

*Bierhorst, John. *On the Road of Stars: Native American Night Poems and Sleep Charms* (Judy Pederson, Illus.) (P, I); *In the Trail of the Wind.*

Bruchac, Joseph. *No Borders; Thirteen Moons on Turtle's Back: A Native American Year in Poems* (Thomas Locker, Illus.) (P, I); *Four Ancestors: Stories, Songs, and Poems from Native America; The Earth Under Sky Bear's Feet: Native American Poems of the Land.*

Flood, Nancy. *Cowboy Up! Ride the Navajo Rodeo.* (P, I)

Franco, Betty. *Night Is Gone, Day Is Still Coming: Stories and Poems by Native American Teens and Adults.* (M)

Jones, Hettie. *The Trees Stand Shining: Poetry of the North American Indians.* (P, I)

McLaughlin, Timothy. *Walking on Earth and Touching the Sky: Poetry and Prose by Lakota Youth at Red Cloud Indian School.* (I, M)

National Museum of the American Indian. *When the Rain Sings: Poems by Young Native Americans.* (I, M)

Philip, Neil (Ed.). *Earth Always Endures: Native American Poems* (Edward S. Curtis, Photog.). (I, M)

Sneve, Virginia Driving Hawk (Ed.). *Dancing Teepees: Poems of Native American Youth* (Stephen Gammell, Illus.). (P, I, M)

Swann, Brian. *Touching the Distance* (Maria Rendon, Illus.). (I, M)

Tapahonso, Luci. *Songs of Shiprock Fair* (Anthony Chee Emerson, Illus.). (I)

Turcotte, Mark. *Songs of Our Ancestors: Poems About Native Americans.* (I, M)

Wood, Nancy C. *Spirit Walker* (Frank Howell, Illus.) (M); *Dancing Moons* (Frank Howell, Illus.). (M)

Supporting English Language Learners with Poetry

Poetry is a particularly appropriate genre for helping English language learners (ELLs) develop their English language skills. With its emphasis on language cadences, rhyme, repetition, and vivid imagery, poetry provides opportunities for all students to learn new vocabulary, practice fluency and pronunciation, and have opportunities to read in a supportive, appealing context (Vardell, Hadaway, & Young, 2006). The brevity of poetry makes this genre easily accessible to all ages of students and all levels of competency in English. As students hear poetry read aloud, they are exposed to excellent modeling of English language rhythms and pronunciations. As they read poetry themselves, they practice pronunciation, intonation, and fluency. Additionally, poetry tends to focus on one topic or image. This assists ELLs by providing support for clarifying vocabulary and subtle aspects of meaning, such as puns, colloquial expressions, and humor.

Vardell et al. (2006) suggest several guidelines for selecting poetry to use with ELLs. First, teachers should select poems that will resonate with these children and have some relevance to their lives. Topics such as school, family, and animals have universal appeal and connect across cultures. Or poetry can be chosen that relates to something shared within the classroom, such as a science or social studies topic. Selecting poems with these connections will help ELLs more readily understand the vocabulary, concepts, and meanings in a poem. Poems reflective of their culture will also help children connect to the read-alouds and subsequent activities. Thus, children whose cultural heritage is Mexican may enjoy *From the Bellybutton of the Moon and Other Summer Poems* (Alarcon). Students from Middle Eastern cultures might particularly enjoy *19 Varieties of Gazelle: Poems from the Middle East* (Nye).

Poems for ELLs, particularly when students are first encountering poetry, should also feature rhyme and consistent rhythm. This helps children discern language patterns and then use their predicting abilities to actively interact with and understand the poem. Additionally, teachers should be sensitive to the fact that ELLs may not be familiar with many of the subtleties of language that native speakers take for granted. For example, they may misunderstand the puns, sly humor, and sarcasm found in the poetry of Jack Prelutsky or Douglas Florian that make these poets so popular with American children. These linguistic nuances may need to be explained.

Some poetry collections feature each poem in both the alternative language (often Spanish) and English or embed words from another language into the English text. For example, Tony Johnston's *My Mexico/Mexico Mio* features a poem in Spanish on the left-hand page with the same poem in English on the facing page. In contrast, *Confetti/Confetti* (Mora) and *Canto: Familiar* and *A Fire in My Hands* (Soto) incorporate "code switching" in which Spanish words are integrated with a largely English text, providing the flavor of Spanish culture and language while also making the poetry accessible to English speakers. Excellent poetry books for children are also available that are written entirely in other languages. Collections such as these are particularly supportive of students learning to speak English.

ELLs can actively and joyfully participate in activities with poetry. Following are some suggestions for adapting your activites to support these students and their explorations with language:

- When you initially introduce a poem, read aloud it aloud many times. This scaffolding step is critical for ELLs, as it familiarizes them with how the words should sound and engages them with the rhythm and cadences of English (Hadaway, Vardell, & Young, 2001). Encouraging all students to read the poem with you provides excellent practice with English in a supportive context. Poems with repeated lines or those written in a call/response structure are particularly well suited for this since all voices can blend together.

- Show an enlarged version of the words of a poem as it is read aloud. This oral/visual connection assists ELLs with expanding their vocabulary and comprehension of English.

Concrete poems are particularly good for this as their shape supports the meaning (Vardell et al., 2006).

- Provide recordings of poetry readings along with printed texts of each poem featured in the recording. These can be created by poets reading their own work or those made by the teacher, volunteers, or classroom peers. Many publishing houses post sample podcasts or vodcasts (using video) of children's poets performing their favorites. Recordings provide excellent models of language as well as opportunities for ELLs to practice their English.

- Partner ELLs with a native speaker during discussions. Provide time to let partners turn to each other and discuss what they think a poet is saying and then share their ideas with the group. Ask ELLs to translate their favorite poems into their native language and then share with the class.

- Encourage ELLs to communicate their responses to a poem through art or moviemaking. This helps them think more deeply about a poem using a response mode that may be more comfortable. Explaining an artistic response is another way to practice English language skills.

- Encourage students to incorporate physical involvement as they choral read or act out poems. Acccording to Ada, Harris, and Hopkins (1993), representing the actions of a poem and the feelings in the poem, allowing even for silent participation, is very helpful for children acquiring English.

- Using Georgia Heard's *The Arrow Finds Its Mark* as a model, encourage ELLs to collect and combine Twitter feeds, advertisements, and other English texts into "found poems" (poems created by combining words, phrases, and so on from other sources). Word processing programs or blogs can be used to facilitate the manipulation of these texts into poems.

Controversial Issue: Close Reading of Poetry

Young children love poetry. Watch babies and toddlers interact with their mothers as they hear favorite nursery rhymes. Or catch children on the playground chanting advertising jingles, jump-rope rhymes, or nonsense songs.

However, when we ask our own young adult students for their opinions about poetry, we get disturbing responses. A few are ambivalent, but most intensely dislike the genre. When asked about the cause for their negative attitudes, these students cite memorizing, reciting, and then analyzing poems to determine their meanings (like dissecting a frog in biology class) as practices they disliked. For most of them, poetry was a cryptic word puzzle in which poets hid their meaning or put it into a structural code that could be deciphered only through an orderly process of deductive analysis. And the teacher was usually the only one who could do it successfully.

The result of these practices is that students often grow to hate poetry. It is no wonder that just as that frog dissected in biology class is dead, so is the dissected poem devoid of energy and life. The opinions of our students are corroborated by research. Surveys reveal that these approaches create intense dislike of the genre (Benton, 1992; DeLawter, 1992; Fletcher, 2002; Lockward, 1996; Sloan, 2003).

However, the CCSS for Reading: Literature affirm that students must learn how to read poetry closely. Standard 1 requires that students must be able to cite evidence from text that supports an analysis of what the text states explicitly as well as inferences drawn from the text by grade 8. Although this standard does not delineate the genres of literature that should be the focus of this analysis, it is assumed that students must be able to apply this skill to all genres, including poetry. Several standards mention poetry specifically. Standard 5, for example, mandates that students be able to "explain major differences between poems, drama, and prose and refer to the structural elements of poems (e.g.; verse, rhythm, meter) . . . when writing or speaking about a text by Grade 4. By Grade 5, students must explain how a series of chapters, scenes or stanzas [in poetry] fit together to provide the overall structure of a particular story, poem or text." Other standards specifically mention poetry in relation to identifying theme, figurative language, and the impact of rhymes and alliteration on specific aspects of a poem.

So how can we reconcile the CCSS mandates regarding close reading of poetry with the importance of showing students how to delight in the pleasurable language experiences that can be experienced through this genre? We believe that students should always first be asked to respond aesthetically to poetry, experiencing initial delight in the language play, imagery, and sounds that good poems offer us. However, we also contend that children can deepen their enjoyment of a poem by exploring how a poet has used language to create an image, connect sounds in musical ways, or distill a complex idea to its essence. Reading poems to children on topics that are close to their direct experience and that also capture their imagination and senses can lead naturally to such explorations (see CCSS teaching strategy 1).

Children can enjoy looking closely at a poem, developing appreciation for the craftsmanship the poet has used to create a unique work that pleases the ear, the heart, and the mind. It is the combination of aesthetic response first, followed by a more analytical look, that seems to be effective in deepening both understanding and delight. The discussion of poetry conversations earlier in this chapter explained how to accomplish this balance.

Summary

- Poetry is musical language that is crafted so that each word is carefully chosen to express a unique truth or observation about the world. Poets use rhyme, rhythm, figurative language, shape, emotional force, and insight to craft their poems. Poetry can also be categorized by its genres (narrative and lyric) and its forms, including free verse, ballad, limerick, concrete, haiku, acrostic, and verse novel.

- When children read, write, and listen to poetry, they become more aware of the world. They also become better writers. Children have very specific opinions about what they like and dislike in poetry. However, children exposed to high-quality poetry enjoy more complex poems.

- Poetry must be enjoyable to say aloud. Poetic elements must be used in unusual ways or make references to things within the experience of students. Several awards are given for excellence in poetry writing.

- Poetry is categorized by theme, academic focus, and format. Poetry particularly appropriate for young children is also available.

- Poetry is a particularly appropriate genre for supporting student understanding of CCSSRL.4 and RF.4. Poetry by diverse voices has become more available and should be used with all students to develop an understanding of diverse cultures. ELLs can particularly benefit from hearing and reading poetry as they learn English. Many poetry books are available in English/Spanish editions or wholly in other languages, particularly Spanish.

Questions/Activities to Invite Thinking, Writing, and Conversation About the Chapter

1. What were your experiences with poetry in school? Share these with your peers, then create a list of books and activities you could use with children to develop a lifelong love for poetry.

2. Survey several grade levels of students regarding their favorite poets, favorite poetic forms, preferred topics, and likes/dislikes for specific poems. Share results with your peers. Create a group analysis of what contemporary children enjoy/dislike in poetry.

3. Create an online poetry notebook. Examine anthologies, single-poet collections, and other resources to find poems you love that you hope to share with your students. Create electronic files of these poems organized by theme, content area, or other category useful to you. Consider using images or presentation software such as Prezi. An online search for "multimedia poetry projects" presents creative ways to extend and to help you organize your collection.

4. Find Web sites of poets described in the chapter who intrigue you. Become familiar with that person's work. Share what you learned about that poet along with some of his or her poems that have become your favorites with your peers.

Recommended Poetry Books by Themes

(Books appropriate for preschoolers are marked *; those with significant culturally diverse elements are marked #. See also Figure 5.7.)

Everyday Experiences

#Alarcon, Francisco. *Poems to Dream Together/Poemas Para Sonar Juntos* (Paula Barragan, Illus.). (I)

Baird, Audrey. *Storm Coming!* (Patrick O'Brien, Illus.). (P, I)

Dotlich, Rebecca Kai. *Lemonade Sun* (Jan Gilchrist, Illus.). (P, I)

#Flake, Sharon. *You Don't Even Know Me: Stories and Poems About Boys.* (M)

Franco, Betsy. *Things I Have to Tell You: Poems and Writing by Teenage Girls.* (M)

Ghigna, Charles. *A Fury of Motion: Poems About Boys.* (M)

Glaser, Isabel. *Dreams of Glory: Poems Starring Girls* (Pat Lowery Collins, Illus.). (I, M)

Gray, Rita. *One Big Rain: Poems for Rainy Days* (Ryan O'Rourke, Illus.). (P, I)

Harrison, David. *Vacation: We're Going to the Ocean* (Rob Shepperson, Illus.). (I)

Heidbreder, Robert. *Noisy Poems for a Busy Day* (Lori Smith, Illus.). (P)

Holbrook, Sara. *Am I Naturally This Crazy?* (Reuben Martin, Illus.) (I); *By Definition: Poems About Feelings* (Scott Mattern, Illus.) (M); *I Never Said I Wasn't Difficult* (M); *Walking on the Boundaries of Change: Poems of Transition.* (M)

Hollyer, Belinda. *She's All That: Poems About Girls.* (I, M)

Hopkins, Lee Bennett (Ed.). *Amazing Faces* (Chris Soentpiet, Illus.) (I, M); *Oh No! Where Are My Pants? And Other Disaster Poems* (Wolf Erlbruch, Illus.). (I, M)

*Kuskin, Karla. *Any Me I Want to Be* (P, I); *Dogs and Dragons, Trees and Dreams* (I); *Moon, Have You Met My Mother?* (Sergio Ruzzier, Illus.); *Near the Window Tree.* (P, I)

Levine, Gail. *Forgive Me, I Meant to Do It: False Apology Poems* (Matthew Cordell, Illus.). (P, I)

Levy, Debbie. *Maybe I'll Sleep in the Bathtub Tonight and Other Funny Bedtime Poems* (Stephanie Buscema, Illus.). (P)

Lewis, J. Patrick, and Yolen, Jane. *Take Two: A Celebration of Twins.* (I)

*Merriam, Eve. *Blackberry Ink* (Hans Wilhelm, Illus.) (P); *You Be Good and I'll Be Night: Jump on the Bed Poems* (Karen Lee Schmidt, Illus.). (P)

Raczka, Bob. *Guyku: A Year of Haiku for Boys.* (I, M)

*Rosenthal, Amy Krause. *The Wonder Book* (Paul Schmid, Illus.). (P)

*Salas, Laura. *A Fuzzy Fast Blur: Poems About Pets.* (P)

Sidman, Joyce. *This Is Just to Say: Poems of Apology and Forgiveness; What the Heart Knows: Chants, Charms and Blessings* (Pamela Zagorenski, Illus.). (I, M)

*Singer, Marilyn. *A Stick Is an Excellent Thing: Poems Celebrating Outdoor Play* (LeUyen Pham, Illus.). (P)

Stevenson, James. *Corn Chowder* (P); *Candy Corn* (P); *Corn Fed; Cornflakes: Poems* (P); *Just Around the Corner* (P, I); *Popcorn* (P, I); *Sweet Corn.* (P, I)

#Thomas, Joyce Carol. *Gingerbread Days* (Floyd Cooper, Illus.). (P)

Vestergaard, Hope. *I Don't Want to Clean My Room: A Mess of Poems About Chores* (Carol Koeller, Illus.). (P, I)

Viorst, Judith. *If I Were in Charge of the World and Other Worries: Poems for Children and Their Parents* (Lynne Cherry, Illus.) (I); *Sad Underwear and Other Complications* (Richard Hull, Illus.). (P, I)

#Weatherford, Carole. *Sidewalk Chalk: Poems of the City.* (I, M)

Poetry About School and the Joys of Reading

Bruno, Elsa Knight. *Punctuation Celebration* (Jenny Whitehead, Illus.). (I, M)

Calmenson, Stephanie. *Kindergarten Kids: Rebuses, Wiggles, Giggles and More!* (Melissa Sweet, Illus.). (I)

Dakos, Kalli. *Don't Read This Book Whatever You Do* (G. Brian Karas, Illus.) (M); *The Goof Who Invented Homework* (Denise Brunkus, Illus.) (I, M); *If You're Not Here Please Raise Your Hand* (G. Brian Karas, Illus.) (I, M); *Put Your Eyes Up Here and Other School Poems* (G. Brian Karas, Illus.). (I, M)

Franco, Betsy. *First Food Fight This Fall & Other Zany Poems* (Sachiko Yoshikawa, Illus.) (I); *Messing Around the Monkey Bars & Other Poems for Two Voices* (Jessie Hartland, Illus.). (I)

George, Kristine O'Connell. *Swimming Upstream: Middle School Poems* (Debbie Tilley, Illus.). (M)

Harrison, David. *Somebody Catch My Homework* (Betsy Lewin, Illus.). (I, M)

Holbrook, Sara. *The Dog Ate My Homework.* (I, M)

Hopkins, Lee Bennett. *School Supplies* (Renee Flower, Illus.) (P, I); *Wonderful Words: Poems About Reading, Writing, Speaking and Listening* (Karen Barbour, Illus.) (I, M); *I Am the Book.* (P, I)

Kennedy, Dorothy. *I Thought I'd Take My Rat to School: Poems for September to June* (Abby Carter, Illus.). (I, M)

Lewis, J. Patrick. *Countdown to Summer: A Poem for Every Day of the School Year* (Ethan Long, Illus.) (I, M); *Please Bury Me in the Library* (Kyle M. Stone, Illus.) (P, I); *Spot the Plot.* (P, I)

#Medina, Jane. *My Name Is Jorge on Both Sides of the River.* (I, M)

Nesbitt, Ken. *Revenge of the Lunch Ladies: The Hilarious Book of School Poetry* (Mike and Carl Gordon, Illus.); *When the Teacher Isn't Looking and Other Funny School Poems.* (P, I)

Prelutsky, Jack. *I Like It Here at School* (I); *There's No Place Like School* (Jane Manning, Illus.) (I); *What a Day It Was at School* (Doug Cushman, Illus.). (P)

Rich, Mary Perrotta (Ed.). *Book Poems—Poems from National Children's Book Week.* (I, M)

*Salas, Laura. *Bookspeak: Poems About Books.* (P)

Salas, Laura. *Do Buses Eat Kids? Poems About School* (I, M); *Stampede: Poems to Celebrate the Wild Side of School.* (I, M)

Shields, Carol Diggory. *Almost Late to School and More School Poems* (Paul Meisel, Illus.). (I, M); *Lunch Money and Other Poems About School* (Paul Meisel, Illus.). (I, M)

Singer, Marilyn. *All We Needed to Say: Poems About School from Tanya and Sophie* (I); *First Food Fight This Fall and Other Zany Poems* (Sachiko Yoshikawa, Illus.). (I)

Whitehead, Jenny. *Lunch Box Mail.* (P)

Poetry About Sports and Movement

Adoff, Arnold. *The Basket Counts* (Michael Weaver, Illus.). (I, M)

Esbensen, Barbara. *Dance with Me* (Megan Lloyd, Illus.). (I, M)

Florian, Douglas. *Poem Runs: Baseball Poems and Paintings.* (I, M)

Ghigna, Charles. *Score! 50 Poems to Motivate and Inspire* (Julia Gorton, Illus.). (I, M)

Hopkins, Lee Bennett. *Extra Innings* (Scott Medlock, Illus.) (I, M); *Opening Days* (Scott Medlock, Illus.) (I, M); *Song and Dance: Poems* (Cheryl M. Taylor, Illus.) (P); *Sports! Sports! Sports! A Poetry Collection* (Brian Floca, Illus.). (I, M)

#Hoyte, Carol-Ann, and Roemer, Heidi. *And the Crowd Goes Wild: A Global Gathering of Sports Poems.* (I, M)

Janeczko, Paul. *That Sweet Diamond* (Carole Katchen, Illus.). (I, M)

Kennedy, X. J. *Olympics* (Graham Percy, Illus.). (P, I)

Low, Alice. *The Fastest Game on Two Feet and Other Poems About How Sports Began* (John O'Brien, Illus.). (I)

#Mathis, Sharon Bell. *Red Dog Blue Fly: Football Poems* (Jan Spivey Gilchrist, Illus.). (I, M)

Morrison, Lillian. *At the Crack of the Bat* (Steve Cieslawski, Illus.) (I, M); *Rhythm Road: Poems to*

Move To (I); *The Sidewalk Racer and Other Poems About Sports and Motion.* (M)

Preller, James. *Mighty Casey* (Matthew Cordell, Illus.). (P)

Prelutsky, Jack. *Good Sports: Rhymes About Running, Jumping, Throwing and More* (Chris Raschka, Illus.). (P, I)

Smith, Charles R., Jr. *Hoop Queens* (I, M); *Rimshots: Basketball Pix, Rolls and Rhythms* (M); *Short Takes: Fast-Break Basketball Poetry.* (M)

Thayer, Ernest Lawrence. *Casey at the Bat: A Ballad of the Republic Sung in the Year 1888.* (Christopher Bing, Illus.). (I, M)

Wong, Janet. *Twist: Yoga Poems* (Julie Paschkis, Illus.). (I, M)

Humorous Poetry

Agee, Jon. *Orangutan Tongs: Poems to Tangle Your Tongue.* (I)

Ashman, Linda. *M Is for Mischief: An ABC of Naughty Children* (Nancy Carpenter, Illus.). (P)

*Bodecker, N. M. *Hurry, Hurry, Mary Dear* (Erik Blegvad, Illus.). (P)

Brown, Calef. *Dutch Sneakers and Flea Keepers* (I, M); *Flamingos on the Roof* (I, M); *Polkabats and Octopus Slacks* (P, I); *Soup for Breakfast* (I, M); *We Go Together: A Curious Selection of Affectionate Verse.* (P, I)

Ciardi, John. *The Hopeful Trout and Other Limericks* (Susan Meddaugh, Illus.) (P, I); *The Reason for the Pelican* (Mark Corcoran, Illus.) (P); *You Know Who* (Edward Gorey, Illus.) (I); *You Read to Me and I'll Read to You* (Edward Gorey, Illus.). (P, I)

Cleary, Brian. *Rhyme and PUNishment: Adventures in Wordplay.* (I)

Cole, William. *Oh, What Nonsense!* (Tomi Ungerer, Illus.) (I); *Poem Stew* (Karen Ann Weinhaus, Illus.). (I)

Florian, Doug. *Bing, Bang, Bong* (P, I); *Laugh-eteria.* (I, M)

#Harris, Jay. *The Moon/La Luna: Silly Rhymes in English and Spanish* (Matthew Cordell, Illus.). (P, I)

Hirsch, Robin. *FEG: Ridiculous [Stupid] Poems for Intelligent Children* (Ha, Illus.). (P, I, M)

*Hollyer, Belinda. *The Kingfisher Book of Family Poems* (Holly Swain, Illus.). (P, I, M)

Katz, Alan. *Oops* (Edward Koren, Illus.) (I); *Uh-Oh* (Edward Koren, Illus.) (I); *Poems I Wrote When No One Was Looking.* (P, I)

Kennedy, X. J. *Brats* (James Watts, Illus.) (I, M); *Exploding Gravy: Poems to Make You Laugh* (Joy Allen, Illus.) (I); *Fresh Brats* (James Watts, Illus.). (I)

*Lear, Edward. *The Complete Nonsense Book* (P, I); *The Jumblies* (Edward Gorey, Illus.) (I); *Of Pelicans and Pussycats: Poems and Limericks* (Jill Newton, Illus.). (P, I)

*Lee, Dennis. *Alligator Pie* (Frank Newfield, Illus.) (P, I); *Dinosaur Dinner (with a Slice of Alligator Pie)* (Debbie Tilley, Illus.) (P, I); *The Ice Cream Store* (David McPhail, Illus.) (P, I); *Jelly Belly* (Juan Wijngaard, Illus.). (I)

Lewis, J. Patrick. *Good Mousekeeping and Other Animal Home Poems* (Lisa Desimini, Illus.) (P, I); *A Hippopotamus't* (Victoria Chess, Illus.) (P, I); *Riddle-Lightful: Oodles of Little Riddle-Poems*; *Riddleicious* (Debbie Tilley, Illus.).

*Merriam, Eve. *Higgle Wiggle: Happy Rhymes* (P, I); *Poem for a Pickle* (Sheila Hamanaka, Illus.) (I); *If You Were a Chocolate Mustache.* (all)

Moss, Jeffrey. *Butterfly Jar* (Chris Demarest, Illus.). (I, M)

Nesbitt, Ken. *The Tighty Whitey Spider*; *My Hippo Has the Hiccups* (Ethan Long, Illus.). (P, I)

Prelutsky, Jack. *Behold the Bold Umbrellaphant* (Carin Berger, Illus.) (P, I); *For Laughing Out Loud: Poems to Tickle Your Funny Bone* (Marjorie Priceman, Illus.) (P, I); *It's Raining Pigs and Noodles* (James Stevenson, Illus.) (P, I); *The New Kid on the Block* (James Stevenson, Illus.) (P, I); *A Pizza the Size of the Sun* (James Stevenson, Illus.) (P, I); *Poems by A. Nonny Mouse* (Henrik Drescher, Illus.) (P, I); *A. Nonny Mouse Writes Again* (Marjorie Priceman, Illus.) (P, I); *Scranimals* (Peter Sis, Illus.) (P); *Something Big Has Been Here* (James Stevenson, Illus.) (P, I); *I've Lost My Hippopotamus* (P, I); *Sardines Swim Across the Sky and Other Poems* (Carin Berger, Illus.). (P, I)

*Schertle, Alice. *Button Up!* (Petra Mathers, Illus.). (P)

Shannon, George, and Brunelle, Lynn. *Chicken Scratches: Poultry Poetry and Rooster Rhymes* (Scott Menchin, Illus.). (P, I)

Silverstein, Shel. *A Light in the Attic* (P, I, M); *Where the Sidewalk Ends.* (P, I, M)

Singer, Marilyn. *Creature Carnival* (Gris Grimly, Illus.). (P)

Smith, William Jay. *Laughing Time* (Juliet Kepes, Illus.). (I)

*Webb, Steve. *Tanka Tanka Skunk.* (P)

Nature and the Changing Seasons

Adoff, Arnold. *In for Winter, Out for Spring* (Jerry Pinkney, Illus.). (P, I)

#Alarcon, Francisco X. *From the Bellybutton of the Moon and Other Summer Poems* (Maya Christina Gonzalez, Illus.) (P, I, M); *Iguanas in the Snow* (Maya Christina Gonzalez, Illus.). (P, I)

Baird, Audrey. *Storm Coming!* (Patrick O'Brien, Illus.) (P, I); *A Cold Snap: Frosty Poems* (Patrick O'Brien, Illus.). (P, I)

Bernhard, Durga. *Earth, Sky, Wet, Dry.* (P)

#Bryan, Ashley. *Sing to the Sun.* (P, I)

*Bunting, Eve. *Sing a Song of Piglets: A Calendar in Verse* (Emily Arnold McCully, Illus.). (P)

*Davies, Nicola. *Outside Your Window: A First Book of Nature.* (P)

Farrar, Sid. *The Year Comes Round: Haiku Through the Seasons.* (P)

Fisher, Aileen. *I Heard A Bluebird Sing* (Jennifer Emery, Illus.) (P, I); *Out in the Dark and Daylight* (Gail Owens, Illus.) (P, I); *Sing of the Earth and Sky: Poems About Our Planets and the Wonders Beyond* (Karmen Thompson, Illus.). (P, I)

Florian, Douglas. *Autumnblings* (P, I); *Handsprings* (P, I); *Poetrees* (I, M); *Summersaults* (P, I); *Winter Eyes.* (P, I)

Frank, John. *A Chill in the Air* (Mike Reed, Illus.). (P, I)

George, Kristine O'Connell. *The Great Frog Race and Other Poems* (Kate Kiesler, Illus.) (P, I); *Old Elm Speaks: Tree Poems* (Kate Kiesler, Illus.) (P); *Hummingbird Nest: A Journal of Poems* (Barry Moser, Illus.). (P, I)

Havill, Juanita. *I Heard It from Alice Zucchini and Other Poems About the Garden* (Christine Davenier, Illus.). (P, I)

Hines, Anna Grossnickle. *Winter Lights.* (P)

Hopkins, Lee Bennett. *Sharing the Seasons: A Book of Poems.* (P, I)

*Jacobs, Leland. *Just Around the Corner: Poems About the Seasons* (Jeff Kaufman, Illus.). (P, I)

Kurtz, Jane. *River Friendly, River Wild* (Neil Brennan, Illus.). (I, M)

Levy, Constance. *A Crack in the Clouds* (Robin Corfield, Illus.) (I, M); *I'm Going to Pet a Worm Today* (Ronald Himler, Illus.) (P, I); *A Tree Place and Other Poems* (Robert Sabuda, Illus.) (I); *Splash! Poems of Our Watery World* (David Soman, Illus.) (I, M); *When Whales Exhale* (Judy LaBrasca, Illus.). (I, M)

Lewis, J. Patrick. *Earth Verses and Water Rhymes* (Robert Sabuda, Illus.). (I)

#Lin, Grace, and McKneally, Ranida. *Our Seasons.* (P)

Livingston, Myra Cohn. *Calendar* (Will Hillenbrand, Illus.) (P); *A Circle of Seasons* (Leonard Everett Fisher, Illus.) (P, I); *Earth Songs* (Leonard Everett Fisher, Illus.) (I); *Sea Songs* (Leonard Everett Fisher, Illus.) (I); *Sky Songs* (Leonard Everett Fisher, Illus.). (I)

Mordhorst, Heidi. *Pumpkin Butterfly: Poems from the Other Side of Nature* (Jenny Reynish, Illus.). (M)

Nichols, Judith. *The Sun in Me: Poems About the Planet* (Beth Krommes, Illus.). (I)

O'Garden, Irene. *Forest, What Would You Like?* (Pat Schories, Illus.). (P)

Otten, Charlotte. *January Rides the Wind: A Book of Months* (Todd L. Doney, Illus.). (P, I)

Paolilli, Paul, and Brewer, Dan. *Silver Seeds: A Book of Nature Poems* (Paul Paolilli and Dan Brewer, Illus.). (P, I)

Rogasky, Barbara. *Leaf by Leaf: Autumn Poems* (Marc Tauss, Illus.) (I, M); *Winter Poems* (Trina Schart Hyman, Illus.). (I, M)

*Salas, Laura. *Shrinking Days, Frosty Nights: Poems About Fall.* (P)

Saltzberg, Barney. *All Around the Seasons.* (P)

Schnur, Steven. *Autumn: An Alphabet Acrostic* (Leslie Evans, Illus.) (P); *Spring: An Alphabet Acrostic* (Leslie Evans, Illus.) (P); *Summer: An Alphabet Acrostic* (Leslie Evans, Illus.) (P); *Winter: An Alphabet Acrostic* (Leslie Evans, Illus.). (P)

*Shannon, George. *Busy in the Garden* (Sam Williams, Illus.). (P)

*Sidman, Joyce. *Red Sings from Treetops: A Year in Color* (Pamela Zagarenski, Illus.). (P)

Vanderwater, Amy. *Forest Has a Song* (Robbin Gourley, Illus.). (P, I)

Van Laan, Nancy. *When Winter Comes* (Susan Gaber, Illus.). (P)

*Wolff, Ashley. *When Lucy Goes Out Walking.* (P)

Yolen, Jane. *Color Me a Rhyme* (Jason Stemple, Photog.) (P); *Least Things: Poems About Small Natures* (Jason Stemple, Illus.) (P, I); *Once upon Ice* (Jason Stemple, Photog.) (P, I); *Ring of Earth* (John Waller, Illus.) (I, M); *Snow, Snow: Winter Poems for Children* (Jason Stemple, Photog.) (P); *Songs of Summer; Water Music* (Jason Stemple, Photog.) (I, M); *Weather Report* (Annie Gusman, Illus.) (M); *What Rhymes with Moon: Poems About the Moon* (Ruth Tietjen Councell, Illus.). (P, I)

*Zolotow, Charlotte. *Seasons* (Erik Blegvad, Illus.). (P)

Family Life

#Adoff, Arnold. *Black Is Brown Is Tan* (Emily McCully, Illus.). (I)

#Berry, James. *Isn't My Name Magical? Sister and Brother Poems* (Shelly Hehenberger, Illus.). (P, I)

Dotlich, Rebecca. *A Family Like Yours* (Tammie Lyon, Illus.). (P)

Fletcher, Ralph. *Relatively Speaking* (Walter Krudop, Illus.). (M)

George, Kristine. *Emma Dilemma: Big Sister Poems.* (P, I)

Greenfield, Eloise. *Night on Neighborhood Street* (Jan Spivey Gilchrist, Illus.) (P, I); *Brothers and Sisters: Family Poems* (Jan Spivey, Illus.). (P)

Gunning, Monica. *A Shelter in Our Car.* (P)

#*Griego, Margo. *Tortillitas Para Mama* (Barbara Cooney, Illus.). (P)

#Grimes, Nikki. *Hopscotch Love: A Family Treasury of Love Poems* (Melodye Rosales, Illus.); *Oh, Brother* (Mike Benny, Illus.). (P)

Hittleman, Carol and Daniel. *A Grand Celebration: Grandparents in Poetry* (Kay Life, Illus.). (P, I)

Hoberman, Mary Ann. *Fathers, Mothers, Sisters, Brothers: A Collection of Family Poems* (Marilyn Hafner, Illus.). (P)

#Hopkins, Lee Bennett. *Amazing Faces* (Will Terry, Illus.). (P, I)

Livingston, Myra Cohn. *Poems for Mothers* (Deborah Ray, Illus.) (P, I); *Poems for Fathers* (Robert Casilla, Illus.). (P, I)

Merriam, Eve. *Daddies at Work* (Eugenie Fenandes, Illus.). (P)

#Mora, Pat. *Love to Mama: A Tribute to Mothers* (Paula S. Barragan, Illus.). (P)

*Sidman, Joyce. *Just Us Two: Poems About Animal Dads.* (P)

#Steptoe, Javaka. *In Daddy's Arms I Am Tall.* (P)

#*Strickland, Dorothy and Michael. *Families: Poems Celebrating the African American Experience* (John Ward, Illus.). (P, I)

#Thomas, Joyce Carol. *Brown Honey in Broomwheat Tea* (Floyd Cooper, Illus.) (P, I, M); *A Mother's Heart, a Daughter's Love: Poems to Share.* (I, M)

#Wong, Janet. *The Rainbow Hand: Poems About Mothers & Children* (Jennifer Hewitson, Illus.). (M)

Yolen, Jane, and Stemple, Heidi. *Dear Mother, Dear Daughter: Poems for Young People* (Gil Ashby, Illus.). (M)

Animals

Ackerman, Diane. *Animal Sense* (Peter Sis, Illus.). (I, M)

Alarcon, Francisco X. *Animal Poems of the Iguazu* (Maya Christina Gonzalez, Illus.). (I, M)

*Ashman, Linda. *Stella Unleashed* (Paul Meisel, Illus.). (P)

Bouchard, David. *Voices from the Wild*: An Animal Sensagoria. (M)

Bulion, Leslie. *Hey There, Stink Bug!* (Leslie Evans, Illus.) (I, M); *At the Sea Floor Café: Odd Ocean Critter Poems.* (P, I)

Carter, Anne. *Birds, Beasts and Fishes: A Collection of Animal Poems* (Reg Cartwright, Illus.). (I, M)

*Crawley, Dave. *Cat Poems* (Tamara Petrosino, Illus.). (P, I)

*Ehlert, Lois. *Lots of Spots.* (P)

*Elliott, David. *In the Wild*; *In the Sea*; *On the Farm.* (P)

Farber, Norma. *Never Say Ugh! to a Bug.* (P, I)

*Fisher, Aileen. *Feathered Ones and Furry* (Eric Carle, Illus.). (P)

Fleischman, Paul. *Joyful Noise: Poems for Two Voices* (Eric Beddows, Illus.); *I Am Phoenix* (Ken Nutt, Illus.). (I, M)

Florian, Douglas. *Beast Feast* (I); *Bow Wow Meow Meow: It's Rhyming Cats and Dogs* (P, I); *In the Swim* (P, I); *Insectlopedia* (P, I); *Lizards, Frogs and Polliwogs* (P, I); *Mammalabilia* (P, I); *On the Wing: Bird Poems and Paintings* (P, I); *Zoo's Who* (P, I); *UnBEElievables: Honeybee Poems and Paintings.* (P, M)

*Franco, Betsy. *A Curious Collection of Cats*; *A Dazzling Display of Dogs.* (P, I)

Frost, Helen. *Step Gently Out* (Rick Lieder, Illus.). (P, I)

*George, Kristine. *Little Dog Poems* (June Otani, Illus.). (P, I)

*Gibson, Amy. *Around the World in Eighty Legs: Animal Poems.* (P, I)

Grimes, Nikki. *When Gorilla Goes Walking* (Shane Evans, Illus.). (P, I)

*Hauth, Katherine. *What's for Dinner? Quirky, Squirmy Poems from the Animal World.* (P, I)

Heard, Georgia. *Creatures of Earth, Sea, and Sky: Poems* (Jennifer Owens Dewey, Illus.). (P)

Held, George. *Neighbors: The Yard Critters Too* (Joung Un Kim, Illus.). (P)

*Hoberman, Mary Ann. *Bugs!* (P, I)

Hopkins, Lee Bennett. *Hoofbeats, Claws & Rippled Fins: Creature Poems* (Stephen Alcorn, Illus.) (P, I); *Dinosaurs* (Murray Tinkelman, Illus.) (P); *Nasty Bugs.* (P)

Jackson, Rob. *Animal Mischief* (Laura Jacobsen, Illus.). (P, I)

Johnston, Tony. *The Barn Owls* (Deborah Kogan Ray, Illus.) (P); *It's About Dogs* (Ted Rand, Illus.). (P, I)

Katz, Susan. *Oh, Theodore! Guinea Pig Poems* (Stacey Schuett, Illus.). (P, I)

Kiesler, Kate. *Wings on the Wind: Bird Poems.* (P, I)

Lang, Diane. *Vulture Verse: Love Poems for the Unloved.* (P)

Larios, Julie. *Yellow Elephant: A Bright Bestiary* (Juli Paschkis, Illus.) (P, I); *Imaginary Menagerie: A Book of Curious Creatures* (Juli Paschkis, Illus.). (I, M)

Levy, Constance. *When Whales Exhale and Other Poems* (Judy LaBrasca, Illus.). (I, M)

Lewis, J. Patrick. *National Geographic Book of Animal Poetry: 200 Poems with Photographs That Squeak, Soar, and Roar!*; *Face Bug: Poems* (Frederic Siskind, Photos). (P, M)

Maddox, Marjorie. *A Crossing of Zebras: Animal Packs in Poetry* (Philip Huber, Illus.). (I, M)

Prelutsky, Jack. *Tyrannosaurus Was a Beast: Dinosaur Poems* (Arnold Lobel, Illus.) (P, I); *The Beauty of the Beast* (Melio So, Illus.) (P, I); *Behold the Bold Umbrellaphant* (Carin Berger, Illus.) (P, I); *If Not for the Cat* (Ted Rand, Illus.) (P); *Sardines Swim High Across the Sky* (Carin Berger, Illus.). (P, I)

Rosen, Michael. *The Cuckoo's Haiku and Other Birding Poems* (Stan Fellows, Illus.) (P, I); *The Hound Dog's Haiku and Other Poems for Dog Lovers* (Mary Azarian, Illus.). (P)

Ryder, Joanne. *Mouse Tail Moon* (Maggie Kneen, Illus.) (P, I); *Toad by the Road: A Year in the Life of These Amazing Amphibians* (Maggie Kneen, Illus.). (P)

Schertle, Alice. *I Am the Cat* (Mark Buehner, Illus.) (P); *How Now, Brown Cow?* (Amanda Schaffer, Illus.) (P, I); *Advice for a Frog* (Norman Green, Illus.). (P, I)

*Sidman, Joyce. *Meow Ruff: A Story in Concrete Poetry* (Michelle Berg, Illus.) (P); *The World According to Dog.* (M)

Sierra, Judy. *Antarctic Antics: A Book of Penguin Poems* (Jose Aruego and Ariane Dewey, Illus.). (P, I)

Singer, Marilyn. *Twosomes: Love Poems from the Animal Kingdom* (P, I); *Every Day's a Dog's Day: A Year in Poems* (Miki Sakomoto, Illus.). (P)

Worth, Valerie. *Pug and Other Animal Poems* (Steve Jenkins, Illus.). (I, M)

Yolen, Jane. *Animal Fare* (Janet Street, Illus.) (P, I); *Bird Watch* (Ted Lewin, Illus.) (P, I); *Least Things: Poems About Small Natures* (Ted Lewin, Illus.) (P, I); *Birds of a Feather Friends* (P); *Raining Cats and Dogs* (Janet Street, Illus.) (P, I); *Bug Off: Creepy, Crawly Poems.* (P, I)

*Zimmer, Tracie Vaughn. *Cousins of Clouds: Elephant Poems.* (P)

Puzzles, Riddles, and Unusual Twists

Brown, Calef. *Boy Wonders.* (P, I)

Chandra, Deborah. *Balloons and Other Poems* (Leslie W. Bowman, Illus.) (I); *Rich Lizard* (Leslie W. Bowman, Illus.). (I, M)

Dotlich, Rebecca Kai. *When Riddles Come Rumbling: Poems to Ponder* (Karen Dugan, Illus.). (I)

Esbenson, Barbara. *Who Shrank My Grandmother's House? Poems of Discovery* (Eric Beddows, Illus.)

(P, I); *Words with Wrinkled Knees* (John Stadler, Illus.). (P, I)

Fletcher, Ralph. *Ordinary Things: Poems from a Walk in Early Spring* (Walter Lyon Kudrop, Illus.). (M)

Frank, John. *Keepers: Treasure Hunt Poems* (Ken Robbins, Illus.). (I)

*Gorton, Julia. *Riddle Rhymes* (Charles Ghigna, Illus.). (P)

*Grimes, Nikki. *A Pocketful of Poems* (Javaka Steptoe, Illus.). (P)

Heard, Georgia. *The Arrow Finds Its Mark: A Book of Found Poems* (Antoine Guillope, Illus.). (I, M)

*Hoberman, Mary Ann. *A House Is a House for Me* (Betty Fraser, Illus.). (P)

Jensen, Dana. *A Meal of the Stars: Poems Up and Down.* (P, I)

*Lewis, J. Patrick. *Riddlelightful: Oodles of Little Riddle Poems*; *Riddlelicious.* (P)

McGill, Marci Ridlon. *Sun Through the Window* (Tim Gillner, Illus.). (I, M)

Merriam, Eve. *Fresh Paint: New Poems* (David Frampton, Illus.) (I, M); *Jamboree: Rhymes for All Times.* (P, I)

Mitchell, Stephen. *The Wishing Bone and Other Poems* (Tom Pohrt, Illus.). (I, M)

*Nims, Bonnie. *Just Beyond Reach* (George Ancona, Photog.). (P, I)

Schertle, Alice. *Keepers* (Ted Rand, Illus.). (I, M)

Singer, Marilyn. *Mirror, Mirror*; *Follow, Follow: A Book of Reverso Poems.* (P, I)

*Spires, Elizabeth. *Riddle Road: Puzzles in Poems and Pictures* (Erik Blegvad, Illus.) (P, I); *With One White Wing: Puzzles in Poems and Pictures* (Erik Blegvad, Illus.). (P, I)

Worth, Valerie. *All the Small Poems*; *Peacock and Other Poems.* (all)

Yolen, Jane, and Dotlich, Rebecca. *Grumbles from the Forest: Fairy-Tale Voices with a Twist* (Matt Mahurin, Illus.). (P, I)

Traditional Literature

(Literary Genre)

In this chapter, we explore the following questions regarding the genre of traditional literature:

- What is traditional literature?
- What is the role of traditional literature in children's lives?
- What are the criteria for evaluating traditional literature?
- What are the categories of traditional literature?
- How can we use traditional literature to meet the mandates of national standards as well as the needs of our diverse students?

"Do you know why chipmunks have stripes?" "Why do we have thunder and lightning?" Fifth-grade teacher Kevin poses these questions to his students as he begins their investigation of pourquoi stories, a type of traditional literature. "I start with "pourquoi stories" (short traditional tales that explain the origins of everyday phenomena) because these stories are short and often humorous. This makes them really appealing to my students." So he begins by reading aloud several pourquoi stories from different cultures, such as *How Chipmunk Got His Stripes: A Tale of Bragging and Teasing* (Bruchac and Ross, Native American), *Why Mosquitoes Buzz in People's Ears* (Aardema, Africa), and *The Story of Lightning and Thunder* (Bryan, Nigeria). "Following each reading, I ask the kids questions like 'What is the moral of this story,' 'What types of characters are in this story?,' and 'How do these stories compare to other traditional tales we've read?'" The class then creates a chart describing the key qualities of pourquoi stories identified through these discussions, editing it as they became familiar with many examples. Kevin also shares background information about the culture and geographic area from which each tale originated, then leads discussions about the animals that are indigenous to the region, moral lessons imparted, and geographical references that relate to each story's cultural origin.

First graders are proud of their stick puppets to be used for reenacting a traditional literature story.

"I then encourage them to read pourquoi stories on their own, using post-it notes to mark favorite passages or stories they particularly enjoyed. The books are passed from child to child with each adding new post-it notes or commenting on someone else's responses. It's amazing how the kids get into sharing the stories with each other and making their friends guess the ending. Eventually, they wrote their own stories in the style of pourquoi tales, incorporating the elements of traditional tales they discovered through their reading and discussions." These are illustrated, using *Story Jumper*, an online digital story book tool and posted on the class Web site as well as the Internet.

Traditional stories, whether oral or written, are part of every culture; wherever there are people, there are stories. Kevin's students are doing what people have always done: learning about the old stories that have been enjoyed for generations.

Early research suggested that interest in folktales, fables, nursery rhymes, and other shorter forms of traditional literature was strong in the early elementary grades and then tended to decline after approximately age 8 (Favat, 1977). At this age, interest in longer stories, such as epics, myths, and legends, was thought to increase. However, our practical experience suggests that, in fact, younger children often enjoy the conflict and adventure found in mythology and epics such as *Odyssey* or the Gilgamesh cycle, particularly in picture book or short chapter book formats. Conversely, older children are often better able to grasp the subtle morals of fables and the hyperbole of tall tales. Thus, we suggest that you introduce students of all ages to a wide range of traditional literature from many different cultures because these stories can teach them about life issues from many cultural perspectives.

What Is Traditional Literature?

Traditional literature is the body of stories that are part of the oral tradition of a culture, including such diverse forms as nursery rhymes, myths, epics, legends, songs, and folktales. Traditional stories mirror the values and customs of the culture from which they arise and serve many functions. Some stories explain the unknown, such as the origin of geographical features. Others preserve significant events that define a group and shape its culture, teach values and the foundations of cultural beliefs to the young, or entertain (Campbell, 1988). As stories were told, each teller likely recrafted them to fit the audience or the context of the telling (Rosenberg, 1997).

How did these stories evolve? Many anthropologists believe that as early people observed the natural world—the rising and setting of the sun, the changing seasons, and the miracle of a seed turning into food—they speculated about nature, spiritual forces, and human behavior. These speculations became stories. So, for example, when early peoples observed the moon and its changing phases, they created stories such as *Anansi the Spider* (McDermott, Ashanti), *The Tale of Rabbit and Coyote* (Johnston, Mexican), and *The Woman in the Moon* (Rattigan, Hawaiian). All these stories are about the same phenomena. However, they are also significantly different because they are shaped by the geography, climate, language, and social context as well as how the people of that culture were affected by the course of historical events.

Yet there is something that transcends differences in culture, something that seems to be a quality of the human psyche that causes people from many cultures to create fundamentally similar stories. Thus, it is likely that these stories also arose from universal concerns, needs, and aspirations that resonate with all humans. Because the stories have been handed down through time, they have no known author. Rather, stories of this sort have always been part of everyday life, entertaining people while also transmitting cultural values and codes of behavior (Jaffe, 1996).

Elements of Traditional Literature

Traditional stories are characterized by many of the same literary elements found in all fiction, including plot, setting, character, style, and theme. However, because of the origins of traditional stories, these elements often possess unique qualities that help distinguish this genre from others. In this section, we explore how the literary elements of traditional stories are similar to those of fiction but also possess unique qualities.

Plot. Plots in traditional literature are usually simple. Most are sequential, although a few are cumulative, cyclical, or chained (meaning that each event links to the next). Characters, setting, and conflict are described, and then the action begins. Once the story is told, it is concluded swiftly with a brief phrase, such as "and they lived happily ever after" or "snip, snap, snout, my tale's told out." A typical plot in Western traditional literature involves a journey in which the main character has a quest to fulfill, an innocent child goes out into the world, or a royal figure disguised as a peasant is forced into humble circumstances and must reclaim a rightful position. Plots in longer legends or epics are often episodic; that is, the hero goes on a series of adventures or episodes.

Setting. Settings in traditional literature are often deliberately vague, using descriptions such as "Once upon a time," "In the dreamtime," "Long ago and far away," or "In a beautiful castle by the sea." More specifically delineated times and places occur in some tales (particularly longer stories) because they are important to the story's events, as in the King Arthur hero tales or many of the American tall tales. Settings of stories from a specific cultural group often make reference to the indigenous plants, animals, weather, and terrain of the area when these are relevant to the tale.

Characterization. Characters in traditional stories are frequently symbolic and are rarely developed as realistic people with strengths, weaknesses, personalities, and idiosyncrasies. Rather, they tend to be stereotypes: all good, all evil, all wise, or all foolish, depicting fundamental human qualities. Thus, poor people are often kind and helpful, whereas the rich are often portrayed as mean-spirited, miserly, and selfish. Heroes are strong, brave, and kind. Stepmothers are mean and ill-tempered, whereas the young heroine is virtuous, humble, and beautiful. This tends to be true even if the main character is based on a historical figure.

Characters in longer epics and legends are often more fully developed because the longer story form permits this. However, even these characters are often portrayed as symbolic, representing heroic or evil qualities rather than being developed as complex individuals.

Style. Traditional stories arose from oral storytelling; thus, they provide readers with the opportunity to hear the cadences and common expressions of the culture from which the story originated. Some tales include imitations of animal sounds or use musical, repetitive language to enhance the telling and delight the ears. Thus, in *Why Mosquitos Buzz in People's Ears*, a retelling of an African tale, Verna Aardema describes the slithering of a python into a rabbit's hole as "wasawasu." Margaret Hurst uses Caribbean dialect in *Grannie and the Jumbie* to enhance the storytelling quality of this story:

> Emmanuel a very small child. He hear about ghost, spirit, and Jumbie once in a while.
> Grammie, she tell him the spirit story so he minds; like keepin' your cap on the right ju
> all the time. (unpaged)*

Dialect can make a story sound authentic and help children become familiar with the rhythms, colloquial expressions, and vocabulary of a culture's language.

Theme. Because the purpose of traditional stories is not only to entertain but also to instruct, these stories usually have themes important to the culture from which they originated. For example, kindness, humility, concern for the downtrodden, courage, and hard work are values in many traditional cultures; thus, these virtues are usually depicted in stories. Often, the powerless triumph through perseverance, hard work, and intelligence.

Motifs. Literary elements that recur across many stories are called motifs. They can be characters, objects, plot elements, or other aspects important to the culture from which the story originated. For example, the plot motif of transformation (an animal taking on human form or the reverse) can be seen in stories such as *Beauty and the Beast* (France), *The Crane Wife* (Japan), and *The Girl Who Loved Wild Horses* (Native American). Examples of other plot motifs include journeys, quests, foolish bargains, long sleeps, and the possession of magical powers. A character motif found in numerous stories is the "trickster." For example, "Coyote" is featured as a trickster in stories from the American Southwest and Latin America. Anansi the Spider is a popular African trickster, whereas Brer Rabbit is a favorite wily character in stories arising from the African American tradition. Other character motifs include stepmothers, magical beings (fairy godmothers, witches, giants, and fairies), fools, and the youngest child who must solve a problem or complete a task.

Variants and Versions. Many of the world's traditional stories surprisingly resemble each other: similar characters, episodes, and plots appear across many cultures. Yet each culture leaves its unique mark on a story, sometimes changing major characters or plot elements to more closely suit the perspective of that culture.

A story is considered a *variant* of a tale if it has some similarities but differs in terms of significant details, such as character names, plotlines, setting, or motifs. For example, *Cendrillan: A Caribbean Cinderella* (San Souci) tells the traditional Cinderella story from the perspective of the "godmother," a poor washerwoman who had been left a magic wand by her mother. She uses it to transform breadfruit into a coach and six agoutis (Caribbean rodents) into horses to help her beloved goddaughter attend her true love's birthday celebration. Caribbean language and culture are prominently featured in the story that has many elements of the Perrault version (with which you are probably most familiar) but also differs significantly because of the Caribbean setting. Studying variants can help children identify similar elements in folktales across cultures while also seeing the influence of a culture on the telling of a tale.

---

*From *Grannie and the Jumbie* by Margaret M. Hurst. Text copyright © 2001 by Margaret Hurst. Used by permission of HarperCollins Publishers.

In contrast, *versions* are stories that only slightly differ from each other. Sometimes, these differences are in the style an illustrator uses for the pictures of a story. In other instances, minor details of a story have been altered. You might know several endings to the story of the *Three Little Pigs*; in one the wolf is eaten, and in another his life is spared. These stories are different versions of the tale.

Teaching children about motifs and variants can help them identify common threads across traditional stories from one culture as well as understand how stories are similar across multiple cultures. This helps them develop a deeper understanding of a culture's norms and values as well as a sense of the universality of humanity. Figure 6.1 lists variants of several traditional stories identified as folktales. *Can You Guess My Name*? and *Nursery Tales Around the World* (Sierra) are excellent resources for finding story variants.

FIGURE 6.1 Folktale Variants Across Cultures

Cinderella

Climo, Shirley. *The Egyptian Cinderella* (Ruth Heller, Illus.). (I) (Egypt); *The Korean Cinderella* (Ruth Heller, Illus.). (P) (Korea); *The Persian Cinderella* (Robert Florczak, Illus.). (I) (Middle East)

Coburn, Jewell. *Domitila* (Connie McLennan, Illus.) (I) (Mexico); *Jouanah* (Anne Sibley O'Brien, Illus.). (I) (Hmong)

Compton, Joanne. *Ashpet: An Appalachian Tale* (Kenn Compton, Illus.). (P, I) (South, United States)

d'Aulaire, Ingri and Edgar. "The Maid on the Glass Mountain," in *East of the Sun, West of the Moon*. (I, M) (Norwegian)

Ehrlich, Amy. *Cinderella* (Susan Jeffers, Illus.). (P) (Germany)

Hickox, Rebecca. *The Golden Sandal: A Middle Eastern Cinderella* (Will Hillenbrand, Illus.). (P, I) (Middle East)

Huck, Charlotte. *Princess Furball* (A. Lobel, Illus.). (I) (Germany)

Jaffe, Nina. *The Way Meat Loves Salt: A Cinderella Tale from the Jewish Tradition* (Louise August, Illus.). (P, I) (Jewish)

Jagendorf, M. A. "Cinderella of New Hampshire," in *New England Bean-Pot*. (I, M) (New England, United States)

Lock, Kath. *Little Burnt Face* (David Kennett, Illus.). (P) (Native American)

Louie, Ai Ling. *Yeh-Shen* (Ed Young, Illus.). (I) (China)

Lum, Darrell. *The Golden Slipper*. (P, I) (Vietnam)

Martin, Rafe. *The Rough-Face Girl*. (I, M) (Native American)

Mayer, Marianna. *Baba Yaga and Vasilisa the Brave* (K. Y. Craft, Illus.). (I) (Russia)

Mehta, Lila. *The Enchanted Anklet* (Neela Lilmur, Illus.). (P, I) (India)

San Souci, Robert. *Cendrillon* (Brian Pinkey, Illus.) (P) (Caribbean); *Sootface: An Ojibwa Cinderella* (P, I) (Native American); *The Talking Eggs* (Jerry Pinkney, Illus.). (P) (South, United States)

Sierra, Judy. *The Gift of the Crocodile* (Reynold Ruffins, Illus.). (P) (Indonesia)

Rumpelstiltskin

Ernst, Lisa Campbell. *The Three Spinning Fairies*. (P) (Germany)

Hamilton, Virginia. *The Girl Who Spun Gold* (Leo and Diane Dillon, Illus.). (P, I) (West Indies)

Moser, Barry. *Tucker Pfeffercorn: An Old Story Retold*. (I, M) (South, United States)

Ness, Evaline. *Tom Tit Tot*. (P, I) (England)

Sierra, Judy. *Can You Guess My Name? Traditional Tales Around the World* (Stefano Vitale, Illus.). (P, I) (various countries)

Stewig, John. *Princess Florecita and the Iron Shoes* (K. Wendy Popp, Illus.). (P) (Italy)

White, Carolyn. *Whuppity Stoorie* (S. D. Schindler, Illus.). (P, I) (Scotland)

Zelinsky, Paul O. *Rumpelstiltskin*. (P, I) (Germany)

Zemach, Harve. *Duffy and the Devil* (Margot Zemach, Illus.). (P) (England)

Red Riding Hood

Araujo, Frank. *Nekane, the Lamina and the Bear* (Xiao Jun Li and Hsiao-Chun Li, Illus.). (P) (Basque)

(continued)

FIGURE 6.1 *continued*

Artell, Mike. *Petite Rouge* (Jim Harris, Illus.). (P, I) (Cajun)

Daly, Nikki. *Pretty Salma: A Red Riding Hood Story from Africa*. (P) (Africa)

Grimm, Brothers. *Little Red-Cap* (Lisbeth Zwerger, Illus.). (P, I) (Germany)

Hyman, Trina Schart. *Little Red Riding Hood*. (P, I) (Germany)

McKissack, Patricia. *Flossie and the Fox* (Rachel Isadora, Illus.). (P) (African American)

Pinkney, Jerry. *Little Red Riding Hood*. (P) (African American)

Shannon, George. *A Knock at the Door* (Joanne Caroselli, Illus.). (M) (various countries)

Souhami, Jessica. *No Dinner*. (P) (India)

Young, Ed. *Lon Po Po*. (P, I) (China)

The Role of Traditional Literature in Children's Lives

Exposure to traditional stories can provide children with a fascinating glimpse into other cultures. They come to understand much more than the standard social studies topics, such as a culture's government, economic output, and geography. Rather, they learn what people in a culture value, what is considered humorous, and what they scorn, fear, and desire (Young and Ferguson, 1995, p. 491). This knowledge helps students move beyond a focus on their own worldview to an interest in peoples and cultures different from themselves. As a result, cultural barriers are transcended, and stereotypes can be shattered. Students come to understand that peoples around the world have universal needs, challenges, and joys while also possessing unique characteristics.

Familiarity with traditional literature also builds understandings about our mainstream culture, particularly the literary culture that students will encounter later in school and, ultimately, their lives. Our everyday speech and much of our literature makes reference to these stories. You have probably heard the phrases "it's just sour grapes" or "going up against Goliath" or heard someone referred to as "having a Cinderella complex." These references directly allude to characters or plots in traditional literature.

Additionally, many contemporary stories, particularly in the fantasy genre, feature references to myths, legends, and folktales and also incorporate plot structures and character archetypes that originated in traditional stories, such as tricksters, hero quests, cruel stepmothers, and faithful companions, to name a few. Readers who have encountered these allusions and plot elements in traditional literature will develop the background to successfully appreciate nuances of character and plot in fiction.

Stories from traditional literature further teach children what has traditionally been considered acceptable as well as unacceptable behavior in a culture. For example, for centuries, children in western European/American cultures have been told the story of "Little Red Riding Hood" to show them that disobedience can have disastrous consequences. Fables such as "The Tortoise and the Hare" and "The Ants and the Grasshopper" teach values such as perseverance, hard work, and saving for future hard times. The Jatakas (stories from the Buddhist tradition), told by people in China and India, celebrate the power of compassion, love, wisdom, and kindness. Traditional stories are a significant force for transmitting these values because they simplify situations. Characters are clearly drawn and tend to be all good or all evil, making the dichotomy between appropriate and inappropriate behavior clear.

Some adults have voiced concerns about violent themes and scenes in traditional stories, fearful that reading these stories might influence children to commit violent acts. Consequently, they advocate rewriting a tale such as "The Three Little Pigs" so that the wolf is not eaten at the end. In one sanitized version, the wolf sits down to a feast (supposedly vegetarian) with the pigs. "Little Red Riding Hood" has been revised so that neither the girl nor the grandmother gets eaten—and the wolf's life is spared.

We believe that these fears are unwarranted. Because frightening story elements such as wicked witches and big bad wolves are far removed in both place and time from the lives of contemporary children, they are often less frightening than realistic stories. When evil beings are destroyed, children find comfort in the knowledge that the danger is not lurking somewhere. Additionally, the hero always triumphs and vanquishes evil in traditional literature, providing hope that it is possible to persevere and succeed in vanquishing the foes of life.

Other adults are concerned about the stereotypes depicted in the stories (Tatar, 2003). In tales from many cultures, women heroines wait passively for supernatural assistance when faced with a crisis rather than relying on their own resources. Think back to the fairy tales and traditional stories you remember from childhood, such as *Cinderella*, *Snow White*, and *The Sleeping Beauty*. These stories are so much a part of our culture that we do not realize the values they convey to girls: that they should be passive, unambitious, subservient, and eager to marry.

We suggest that, rather than keeping students from reading these stories, teachers can use traditional literature as a resource for discussing issues of gender and its relationship to power. Consider questions such as "Whose perspective dominates these stories?," "What values regarding what it means to be 'male' or 'female' are being espoused?," "Do men always have to be the strong 'rescuer'?" (think of the kinds of pressures that this expectation places on boys), "How does that make you feel?," and "What do these stories tell us about the importance of beauty?" These are important questions that can prompt deeper analysis of the stories as to how they affect our students' self-esteem and identity.

Ultimately, these tales provide a template for how to become mature individuals. Children see many examples of heroes and heroines who go out in the world, face successful challenges, and find their destiny. A traditional story can offer road maps, helping us answer important questions, such as "How can I gain control of my own life and become independent?," "What is the source of happiness, and how can I achieve it?," and "How can I cope with those who would use their superior powers against me?" Children learn that nothing of lasting value comes easily. Rather, it is only through determination and perseverance that we obtain our goals (Rosenberg, p. xxii, 1997).

Most important, traditional literature is entertaining. The rhythmical repetition of language patterns is pleasurable to the ear. The plots that feature plenty of action, heroes who overcome powerful adversaries, and directly stated themes are tailored for the developing attention spans and moral development of children.

Criteria for Evaluating Traditional Literature

Since traditional literature has evolved from so many cultures, it is difficult to evaluate, and it is challenging to apply the same criteria to all stories. Each tale is situated in the culture from which it is derived; thus, expectations for plot structure, characterization, and style are culturally bound and must be authentic in terms of the traditions, geography, animal references, and other qualities unique to the culture in which the story originated. One way to help ensure that a study is authentic in depicting the sacred values, beliefs, and culture of a group is to check the source notes that often accompany retellings of traditional tales. Anthologists, storytellers, and artists are including this information more frequently to validate their work.

Another important consideration is whether the story is considered sacred by the culture. There are many stories for which this judgment differs, depending on the listener's point of view. When a story or myth comes from one's own religion or culture, it is sometimes considered sacred

FIGURE 6.2 Guidelines for Evaluating Traditional Literature: Cultural and Literary Considerations

Authenticity	Author is an insider or is shown to have appropriate credentials that demonstrate extensive study of the cultural group. Does the retelling have local community support or endorsement? (Source notes regarding a story's origin are particularly helpful for judging this.)
Art/illustration	People of the culture are portrayed as individuals. Artifacts in illustrations are accurate. Illustrations enhance the story. Illustration style and media reflect the story's cultural origins.
Narrative	Story is told in a style that seems authentic yet accessible to those outside culture. Language is respectful and reflects culture's narrative style.
Plot	The plot is well structured, so both readers and listeners can follow it.
Theme	The theme reflects the culture and is relevant to contemporary children.
Setting	The setting is authentic to the culture in which the story originated.

by members or "insiders" of that culture. An "outsider" might find the story interesting yet not hold it in an esteemed position. Thus, we think that it is important to ask if the person presenting the story (orally or in writing) is also a member of that culture. Or, if not, we might ask if he or she has firsthand knowledge of that culture and its stories and has permission to tell that story.

We should also be wary of judging stories by contemporary standards. Because traditional literature reflects attitudes, gender roles, and class systems from the past, the content of some stories might surprise or offend today's readers. In addition to worries about violence depicted in these stories, some adults express concern about the universal optimism these stories appear to advocate, where good always triumphs over evil, because this does not always happen in real life. Still others worry about the racial stereotypes that are often portrayed. These are valid concerns. However, we believe that you can discuss these issues with children. We do not advocate changing the stories to make them reflect contemporary values, as this practice makes the stories less culturally authentic.

Figure 6.2 outlines considerations for evaluating a selection of traditional literature. We also recommend that you search for recommendations from book reviews, Web sites, professional societies, and knowledgeable members of the culture from which the tale arose.

Categories of Traditional Literature

Before we discuss the categories of traditional literature, you should understand that the ways they have been defined and categorized were devised by scholars to facilitate the study of the various forms. Storytellers did tell these tales for the purpose of categorizing them. All stories will not fall neatly into a particular category; some have elements that could place them in several categories. We have highlighted a few exemplary examples in each category. More complete lists of titles are included in the section "Recommended Traditional Literature Books" at the end of the chapter.

Pajaro Verde/Green Bird by Joe Hayes is an award winning folktale from the Latino tradition.

Folktales

Folktales are stories that focus on the customs, beliefs, and traditions of ordinary humans and describe how people cope with the events of everyday life. There is usually a crisis or conflict to be faced and resolved. As the stories were told, various tellers modified them so that over time they acquired a cumulative authorship. Eventually, these stories were collected and written down by individuals such as Jacob and Wilhelm Grimm, Charles Perrault, and Joseph Jacobs. Many of the stories that you are likely familiar with—*Cinderella, The Sleeping Beauty, The Little Red Hen*, and *Little Red Riding Hood*—were documented and published by these people.

There is an important distinction between folktales and stories that resemble this literature but that were written by known authors. For example, people often think of stories written by Hans Christian Andersen as traditional literature. However, Andersen's stories originated in written form and were not part of the tradition of stories that were told orally, although he borrowed from some of the popular traditional literature of his time. His work is discussed in Chapter 7.

Figure 6.3 lists several subgenres of folktales, a brief definition of each, and sample titles. The categories are somewhat arbitrary (you will notice that some stories might fit in more than one). They are provided to help you see the diversity of possible characteristics associated with this type of traditional literature.

FIGURE 6.3 Folktale Subgenres

Folktale Subgroup	Definition	Sample Titles
Cumulative/chain stories	Humorous accumulations or linked chains of repeated rhymes and/or actions. Sometimes, a chase ensues in which an accumulating line of characters join to pursue an escaping character.	• *There Was an Old Woman Who Swallowed a Fly* (various authors/illus.) • *Trouble* (Kurtz) (Eritrea) • *The Gingerbread Boy* (Galdone; Aylesworth) (Germany) • *Why Mosquitos Buzz in People's Ears: A West African Tale* (Aardema) (Africa)
Trickster stories	Tricksters are usually powerless creatures who ultimately triumph using cunning and trickery. Anansi the Spider is a popular African trickster. African American tricksters (e.g., Brer Rabbit) often evolved as a way for slaves to feel a sense of control. Tricksters from Asian cultures are small but cunning and trick larger, more powerful adversaries.	• *Anansi the Spider: A Tale from the Ashanti* (McDermott) (Ghana) • *The Tales of Uncle Remus* (Lester) (United States) • *Coyote and the Winnowing Bird; Coyote and Little Turtle* (Sekaquaptwa) (Native American) • *Love and Roast Chicken: A Trickster Tale from the Andes* (Knutson) (South America) • *Brother Rabbit: A Cambodian Tale* (Ho and Rosen) (Cambodia) • *The Jack Tales* (Chase; Hicks) (United States)

(continued)

FIGURE 6.3 *continued*

Folktale Subgroup	Definition	Sample Titles
Stories of fools and simpletons	Tales that feature a silly character often referred to as a noodlehead. The character's poor judgment and/or comical actions lead to unforeseen and often dire consequence, such as a porridge pot that boils over uncontrollably or his capture by an evil or mischievous being.	• *It Happened in Chelm: A Story of the Legendary Town of Fools* (Freedman) (Jewish, Europe) • *Juan Bobo Goes to Work: A Puerto Rican Folktale* (Montes) (Puerto Rico) • *Lightening the Load* (Turkish, European) • *Noodlehead Stories: World Tales Kids Can Read and Tell* (Hamilton and Weiss) (various countries)
Fairy or wonder tales	Tales with supernatural beings, such as giants, fairies, dragons, and wicked witches. Typically, a mortal character has to cope with a supernatural presence, or magical powers are bestowed on ordinary people. Sometimes, transformations occur in which people or objects are changed from one shape to another. Virtues such as kindliness, courage, and humility are rewarded, whereas cruelty, greed, and evil are punished.	• *Cinderella*, "*Beauty and the Beast*, and *Rumpelstiltskin* • *Hansel and Gretel* • *The Frog Prince* (and others) (these stories have variants across many cultures) • *The Arabian Nights; Tales Told by Sheherazade* (Alderson) (Middle East) • *The Funny Little Woman* (Mosel) (Japan) • *Pajara Verde: The Green Bird* (Hayes) (New Mexico, United States) • *The People Could Fly* (Hamilton) (African American, United States) • *Favorite Fairytales from Around the World* (Yolen) (various countries)
Beast tales	Stories in which animals that talk and act like people are main characters. Animals used are indigenous to the culture of the story (spiders, monkeys, and lions in African tales or tigers and crocodiles in tales from India). Human weaknesses are often the focus so as to teach lessons about morality and cultural values.	• Panchantranto tales (India) • *Puss in Boots* (England) • *The Three Billy Goats Gruff* (Norway) • *The Little Red Hen* (England) • *Beautiful Blackbird* (Bryan) (Caribbean)

Excellent folktale anthologies include *Favorite Fairy Tales from Around the World* (Yolen), *From Sea to Shining Sea: A Treasury of American Folklore and Songs* (Cohn), and *Golden Tales from the Arabian Nights* (Soifer and Shapiro). Many folktales have also been beautifully illustrated in picture book editions. Figure 6.4 features some award-winning folktale picture book titles that we think are particularly intriguing to children.

FIGURE 6.4 Award-Winning Folktale Picture Books

(Books with significant culturally diverse elements are marked #.)

#Aardema, Verna. *Rabbit Makes a Monkey Out of Lion* (Jerry Pinkney, Illus.) (P); *Why Mosquitoes Buzz in People's Ears* (Leo and Diane Dillon, Illus.). (P)

Aylesworth, Jim. *The Gingerbread Man* (Barbara McClintock, Illus.) (see also editions by Galdone, Egielski, and McCafferty). (P)

Beneduce, Ann. *Jack and the Beanstalk* (Gennady Spirin, Illus.). (P)

Brett, Jan. *Goldilocks and the Three Bears* (also editions by Clark, Aylesworth, Marchall, and others). (P)

Brown, Marcia. *Cinderella*. (P)

#Bruchac, Joseph, and Ross, Gayle. *The Story of the Milky Way: A Cherokee Tale* (Virginia Stroud, Illus.). (P, I)

#Bryan, Ashley. *Beautiful Blackbird*. (P)

Burkert, Nancy. *Snow White and the Seven Dwarfs*. (I)

#French, Fiona. *Jamil's Clever Cat: A Folktale from Bengal*. (P)

#Goble, Paul. *The Girl Who Loved Wild Horses* (I); *The Legend of the White Buffalo Woman*. (I)

#Gonzalez, Lucia. *The Bossy Gallito* (Lulu Delacre, Illus.). (P, I)

Grimm, Brothers. *Hansel and Gretel* (Paul O. Zelinsky, Illus.) (see also edition by Jeffers, Isadora, Zwerger, and Moses). (P, I)

Grimm, Jacob and Willhelm. *Rumpelstiltskin* (Paul O. Zelinsky, Illus.). (P, I)

#Hamilton, Virginia. *Brer Rabbit and the Tar Baby Girl* (James Ransome, Illus.). (P, I)

#Hayes, Joe. *Dance, Nana Dance* (Mauricio Trenard Sayago, Illus.). (I)

#Hayes, Joe. *Pajaro Verde/Green Bird* (Antonio Castro, Illus.). (P, I)

Hyman, Trina. *Little Red Riding Hood* (see also editions by Priceman, Bing, Goodall, and Marshall) (P); *The Sleeping Beauty*. (P)

#Kurtz, Jane. *Pulling the Lion's Tail* (Floyd Cooper, Illus.). (P)

#Maddern, Eric. *The Fire Children: A West African Folk Tale* (Frane Lessac, Illus.). (P, I)

#Martin, Rafe. *The Rough Face Girl* (David Shannon, Illus.). (P, I)

#McDermott, Gerald. *Pig Boy: A Trickster Tale from Hawaii* (P, I); *Raven: A Trickster Tale from the Northwest*. (P, I)

#Montes, Marisa. *Juan Bobo Goes to Work: A Puerto Rican Folk Tale* (Joe Cepeda, Illus.). (P)

#Olaleye, Issac. *In the Rainfield: Who Is the Greatest?* (Ann Grifalconi, Illus.). (P, I)

#Paterson, Katherine. *The Tale of the Mandarin Ducks* (Leo and Diane Dillon, Illus.). (I)

Perrault, Charles. *Puss in Boots* (Fred Marcellino, Illus.) (P, I) (also version by Jerry Pinkney).

#San Souci, Robert. *The Talking Eggs* (Jerry Pinkney, Illus.). (P, I)

#Sherlock, Philip, and Wright, Petrina. *The Illustrated Anansi: Four Caribbean Folk Tales*. (P, I)

#Steptoe, John. *Mufaro's Beautiful Daughter*. (P, I)

Taback, Simms. #*Kibitzers and Fools: Tales My Zayda Told Me* (P, I); *There Was an Old Lady Who Swallowed a Fly* (P); *This Is the House That Jack Built*. (P)

#Young, Ed. *Lon Po Po: A Red Riding Hood Story from China*. (P)

Zelinsky, Paul. *Rapunzel*. (P, I)

Tech Click

AmericanFolklore.net is an excellent site for finding many cultural variants of folktales.

Fables and Learning Stories

Fables are very short tales designed to teach moral lessons and values in order to transmit a culture's accumulated wisdom. Problems of everyday living are introduced with instruction provided for how to solve those problems. Aesop, a Greek slave who lived around 600 B.C., is most frequently credited with creating these stories, although scholars suspect that several individuals might be responsible for creating the body of fables we know today. Jean La Fontaine later adapted Aesop's fables to verse form.

Fables typically feature animal characters that are referred to simply as "Rabbit," "Mouse," or "Lion." These characters are not fully developed but rather demonstrate qualities of human nature, such as perseverance (the turtle in "The Tortoise and the Hare") or humility (the mouse in "The Lion and the Mouse"). All convey life lessons and present universal truths that are relevant to the lives of children. Sometimes, these lessons are conveyed explicitly: the moral is directly stated at the conclusion of the tale. In others, the lesson must be inferred.

Many collections of Aesop's fables are beautifully illustrated, adding to their appeal. Jerry Pinkney uses vibrant colored pencil and watercolor illustrations to accompany retellings of 61 fables of the stories in his *Aesop's Fables*. The detailed pictures capture the events and morals of the story, making this book particularly appropriate for younger children. *Unwitting Wisdom: An Anthology of Aesop's Fables* (Ward) features two-page spreads that visually introduce each tale, incorporating interesting details that summarize the story's essence. Bader's *Aesop and Company* retells 19 of the most popular fables and also provides an in-depth discussion of their origins, whereas *Aesop's Fables: A Pop-Up Book of Classic Tales* (Moerbeek and others) features magnificently engineered pop-ups, including a lion leaping off the page to liberate himself from his snares.

Beautifully illustrated picture book editions of individual fables are also available for children. Ed Young uses stunning cut-paper illustrations against shiny black backgrounds to illustrate the story of blind mice trying to identify an elephant in *Seven Blind Mice. The Tortoise and the Hare* has been illustrated by several artists, including Janet Stevens, who creates two distinct personas for the main characters in this story, making the moral of "slow and steady wins the race" clearly evident. Other excellent renditions of this fable have been illustrated by Jan Brett, Jerry Pinkney, Eric Carle, Brian Wildsmith, and Giselle Potter.

Some illustrators have chosen to use multicultural settings to portray Aesop's stories or have selected a fable unique to a particular culture to retell. For example, Amy Poole's version of Aesop's *The Ant and the Grasshopper* is set in imperial China. Jerry Pinkney's retelling of *The Lion and the Mouse* is set in the African wilderness and uses spare language to tell the story, letting the magnificent pictures carry the narrative. *Mouse and Lion* (Burkert) is also set in Africa, but in this version, Mouse is the central character and hero. *Head, Body, Legs: A Story from Liberia* is a fable from Africa that describes how various body parts learn to cooperate with each other to acquire food.

Jerry Pinkney's *Lion and the Mouse* is a well deserved winner of the Caldecott Medal.

Apollo
The god of sun, the god of light, the god of prophecy; in many people's delight.

Is loved from sea, is loved from earth, is loved from heaven in mighty bursts.

Handsome, truthful, muscular, strong; Apollo is the god of song.

Playing his golden lyre on Mount Olympus, the people that enjoy are the people that listen.

Lessons in archery, lessons in wrong, His list of worshippers is eternally long.

The son of Zeus you may have guesssed; Apollo was raised by the best of the best.

His twin sister Artemis roams in the forest, with following animals that adore her.

Now his followers do not stop here, Apollo is loved everywhere.

A sixth grader's poem about the god Apollo, written during a unit on Greek mythology.

Learning stories also teach cultural values and moral lessons but are longer, more complex texts that feature both human and animal characters. Morals are not explicitly stated, and different listeners can often gain different insights from a learning story based on their perspectives and the differences in meaning that result from multiple retellings. *Buddha Stories* (Demi) features morality stories that are part of the Buddhist tradition. In this book, each story is followed by a moral that is part of the Buddhist tradition but also universal to all peoples, such as "It is easier to make a promise than keep it" and "When one person tells a falsehood, one hundred repeat it as true."

Myths

Myths are traditional stories that arose to explain specific characteristics of animals, terrain, or climate. Early peoples needed to explain things such as why animals look and behave as they do, how natural phenomena or geographic features evolved, and why humans act in universally similar ways (Hamilton, 1988). Myths have endured not only because they convey sacred beliefs of a culture but also because they are entertaining stories, full of action and intrigue. Although the characters are gods and other sacred beings, they exhibit a range of emotions that provide readers with insight into the human psyche. They also transmit information about basic cultural values.

The most well-known myths in Western culture are those of Greek and Roman origin. *The D'Aulaire's Book of Greek Myths* (D'Aulaire) is a classic collection of these stories that still serves as an excellent resource for introducing children to mythology. The authors never talk down to children and do not edit out the spicy details of love triangles, trysts, and vengeance. *Greek Myths for Young Children* (Amery), with brightly colored oversize illustrations and simply told stories of gods, goddesses, and their magical adventures, is a recommended collection for younger children. *Mythology: The Gods, Heroes and Monsters of Ancient Greece* (Evans) and *Encyclopedia Mythologica: Gods and Heroes* (Reinhart) feature foldout sections, pop-ups, and other interactive features that draw readers into the stories.

Picture book retellings of individual Greek myths are also available for children. *Wings* (Yolen) is a retelling of the story of Daedalus. Other well-told and vividly illustrated individual tales include *Atalanta's Race: A Greek Myth* (Climo), *Cupid and Psyche: A Love Story* (Barth), and *The Arrow and the Lamp: The Story of Psyche* (Hodges). Several graphic novel editions of Greek myths, such as *Psyche and Eros: The Lady and the Monster* (Croall) and *Atalanta* (Fontes), are also now available for students who enjoy this format.

Tech Click

"Myths Around the World," sponsored by the Scholastic Web site, invites students to explore myths from 15 countries. Each story is accompanied by a brief factual paragraph that describes how the story reflects its cultural context.

Creation stories are myths that describe how the world or a specific culture was created. For example, the South American story *Moon Was Tired of Walking on Air* (retold by Natalie Belting) is a tale from the Charote Indians of South America that tells of how Moon desired solid ground to walk on, so he created earth, grass, seeds, and crops. *The Story of the Milky Way* (Ross and Bruchac) is a creation story from the Cherokee peoples that explains how the Milky Way came to be. *In the Beginning: Creation Stories from Around the World* (Hamilton) is an excellent resource for finding creation stories from many cultures.

Pourquoi tales also evolved to explain how things came to be in the natural world. In contrast to myths, these stories focus more on everyday phenomena, describing, for example, how the tiger got its stripes or why rabbits have long ears. Pourquoi stories typically start with a saying, verse, or cadenced invitation to listen. Characters are not developed and are often referred to by generic titles, such as "Deer" or "Hunter." The story is simply structured, presenting a problem, a series of events, and then a solution. The action is fast paced, and conclusions are often humorous (Foster, Theiss, & Buchanan-Butterfield, 2008). For example, *Toad Is the Uncle of Heaven* (Lee, Vietnam) tells of a terrible drought that threatens all the creatures on earth. Toad and the other animals decide to go to the King of Heaven and ask for rain. King tells Toad to just croak when there is a drought, and rain will come, thus explaining why toads croak.

Many pourquoi stories from diverse world cultures are available to children. *The Story of Lightning and Thunder* (Bryan) and *How the Guinea Fowl Got Her Spots: A Swahili Tale of Friendship* (Knutson) are excellent examples from Africa. Joseph Bruchac has collected several pourquoi tales in *Between Earth and Sky: Legends of Native American Sacred Places* and also has picture book editions of single tales, such as *How Chipmunk Got Its Stripes: A Tale of Bragging and Teasing* and *Rabbit's Snow Dance: A Traditional Iroquois Story*. *Tikki Tikki Tembo* (Mosel, China) is an example of a pourquoi tale from Asian cultures.

Tech Click

Scholastic's Web site has examples of pourquoi stories written by children all over the United States.

Legends and Epics

Legends and epics are stories about a person who folklorists are fairly sure actually existed. They differ mainly in their length and narrative style, with epics defined as longer stories that are often written in verse rather than in prose style as legends are. These stories are strongly influenced by cultural aspects of time and setting, as the protagonists must often respond to circumstances as part of their exploits. The main character is often an enduring symbol for an important value in a society or is used as a role model to impart important values to children. The stories of King Arthur are good examples, as they likely evolved when people attempted to hold on to lofty ideals and civilized manners in response to a dark time in Britain's history.

Legends and epics explore complex struggles, decisions, and foibles of human nature in engaging rather than didactic ways to show children why people believed that the qualities highlighted in the stories were important. For example, the story of Gilgamesh, a king who lived over 5,000 years ago in Mesopotamia, examines the abuse of power. Gilgamesh's story is vividly retold for children in *Gilgamesh the Hero* (McCaughreon), *Gilgamesh the King* (Zeman), *The Revenge of Ishtar* (Zeman), and *The Last Quest of Gilgamesh* (Zeman). All are carefully researched picture book renditions of the story that preserve authenticity with full-color illustrations incorporating elements from Sumerian, Assyrian, and Babylonian art. *Lugalbanda: The Boy Who Got Caught Up in a War: An Epic Tale From Ancient Iraq* (Henderson) also recounts an ancient story of heroism, power, and adventure.

Odyssey (Homer), the story of Odysseus and his 10-year journey following the Trojan War, is one of the most famous epics in Western culture. In these tales, Odysseus faces one overwhelming challenge after another, always surviving by wit and cunning. *Tales from the Odyssey* (Osborn) recounts individual adventures of Odysseus in slim volumes that pare down the stories into fast-paced chapters that keep middle-grade readers engaged. A map is included in each book so that children can visualize the events as they unfold. McCaughrean's *The Odyssey* captures the drama and exciting action of Homer's original telling while making the story accessible to older readers. Sutcliff's *Black Ships Before Troy* and *The Wanderings of Odysseus* are retellings of *Iliad* and *Odyssey* for middle school students. In contrast, *The Odyssey: A Pop-Up Book* (Ita) provides readers with magnificent pictures and a graphic novel retelling of the story, making the story appealing to a wide age range.

Stories about King Arthur and his Knights of the Round Table are among the most enduring legends in Western culture. Children's books reflect this interest with many retellings of these popular tales. Talbot's *King Arthur: The Sword and the Stone, King Arthur and the Round Table, Excalibur,* and *Lancelot* are picture books featuring richly detailed watercolor illustrations of costumes, armaments, and characters, bringing Arthur's era to life for younger readers. Robert San Souci created another picture book series detailing the early lives of the legendary Arthurian characters in *Young Merlin, Young Guinevere, Young Lancelot,* and *Young Arthur.* Margaret Hodges retells single tales in *The Kitchen Knight: A Tale of King Arthur* and *Merlin and the Making of a King.*

The legend of the Golem dates back to 16th-century Prague, a time when the Jewish people were heavily persecuted. According to this legend, a rabbi used magical powers to create a Golem from river mud. The Golem then used size and strength to protect the Jewish people when an angry mob attacked the ghetto. Picture book versions of this story by Rogasky and Wisniewski are compelling retellings that bring this legend alive for students.

Legends and epics from African and Asian cultures have also been retold in books for children. For example, Sundiata was a legendary king credited with founding the empire of Mali in West Africa. *Sundiata: Lion King of Mali* (Wisniewski) is a picture book that details how this king defeated his enemies and became the rightful ruler of his people. The Chinese epic poem *Mulan* has traditionally inspired girls of this culture to believe that they are capable of accomplishing the same heroic feats as men. In this story, Mulan dresses up as a man and goes to war in place of her elderly father. *Fa Mulan: The Story of a Woman Warrior* (San Souci) and *The Song of Mulan* (Lee) are carefully researched picture books that respect the cultural origins of Mulan's story in both narrative and illustration.

Ramayana is a famous epic from India that tells of how Rama; his beautiful, virtuous wife Sita; and his brother defeat the evil demon Ravana. *Rama and the Demon King* (Souhami) tells of Rama's adventures in exile and his battle with the evil demon Ravana. *The Ramayana for Children* (Sharma) and *Ramayana: The Epic for Children* (Shastri) retell the entire legendary story.

These world legends and epics are important for the children from the originating cultures to know. However, it is also important for children of all cultures to be familiar with these stories so that they come to understand literary traditions other than their own.

Ghost Stories

Ghost stories that come from the oral tradition are also considered legends. People have always been drawn to the idea that spirits of the dead are with us in some form. Told around campfires, at sleepover parties, and beside cottage hearths, these stories have become an integral part of our culture. *Scary Stories to Tell in the Dark* and others by Alvin Schwartz are among the best-known collections of ghost stories for children. *When the Chenoo Howls* (Bruchac and Bruchac) includes legends about ghosts and monsters from a variety of Northeast Woodland Native American traditions.

Ghost stories are also created by contemporary writers. Because we know the author of tales, these stories are considered fantasy and are discussed in Chapter 7.

Tall Tales

Tall tales are legends with an added element of exaggeration. The stories focus on individuals (usually male) who accomplish impossible tasks using great strength and then become famous for their exploits. This type of story has been documented in cultures around the world, including ancient Greece, China, and Europe. However, it is in the United States where tall tales have flourished. It is likely that the unbelievable strength and outright lies that characterize these stories provided a welcome diversion to those attempting to tame the vast, harsh, and challenging American environment.

Sometimes the stories are based on people whose existence is well documented. For example, "Johnny Appleseed" was actually John Chapman who lived in America during the late 1700s, planting apple seeds as he walked from Massachusetts to Indiana. Davy Crockett and Mike Fink, also the subjects of tall tales, existed as well, although their exploits are highly exaggerated. Other tall tales are based on a composite of "larger-than-life" real persons, such as Paul Bunyan, whose stories describe the exploits of highly skilled lumberjacks, and Sally Ann Thunder Ann Whirlwind Crockett, the fictional wife of Davy Crockett, whose character is undoubtedly a composite of many real-life American frontier women.

Anthologies of several tales are a good way to introduce children to these stories. *American Tall Tales* (Osborne) features nine stories of familiar heroes, such as Crockett and Bunyan, as well as lesser-known ones, such as Stormalong, a giant sailor who was washed onto a Cape Cod beach as a baby. *Larger Than Life: The Adventures of American Legendary Heroes* (San Souci) also chronicles the lives of several male tall tale heroes and one woman (Slue-Foot Sue, who challenged Pecos Bill). Several notable picture book artists have created vibrant renditions of tall tales that heighten children's engagement with these stories. Steven Kellogg uses exuberant, oversize, highly detailed pen and watercolor pictures to capture the larger-than-life antics of *Mike Fink, Paul Bunyan, Pecos Bill, Johnny Appleseed*, and *Sally Ann Thunder Ann Whirlwind Crockett*. Reeve Lindbergh uses a poetic text to chronicle Appleseed's adventures in *Johnny Appleseed: A Poem*.

Tall tale hero John Henry, who raced a steam driven drill with two hammers in each hand, is one of the most popular tall tale heroes. Jerry Pinkney's realistic, oversize watercolor illustrations for *John Henry* (Lester) dominate the pages of the book, reflecting the larger-than-life exploits of this African American hero. Ezra Jack Keats also illustrated a version of this story in *John Henry: An American Legend*. Historian Scott Nelson presents John Henry's story as a mystery to be unraveled, showing students the history behind a tall tale story as well as a glimpse of how historians do research in *Ain't Nothing but A Man: My Quest to Find the Real John Henry*.

Tall tales usually focus on male heroes. However, contemporary anthologists have begun collecting stories about larger-than-life heroines, although this is a challenging task. For example, in researching stories for inclusion in *Cut from the Same Cloth: American Women of Myth, Legend and Tall Tale*, Robert San Souci had difficulty finding stories of strong American women. He speculated that cultural stereotypes of women as nurturers and homebodies rather than "explorers, hunters, warriors and rulers" probably often prevented them from being the main subjects of tall tales. Most tales with strong women that he uncovered were from Native American, African American, Eskimo, and Hawaiian cultures. San Souci's book is considered an excellent collection of tall tale stories featuring strong female protagonists. Others are listed in Figure 6.5, which also includes other types of traditional stories that affirm women.

FIGURE 6.5 Traditional Literature Featuring Positive Portrayals of Women

(Books with significant culturally diverse elements are marked #.)

#Barchers, Suzanne. *Wise Women: Folk and Fairy Tales from Around the World* (Leann Mullineaux, Illus.). (M)

#Gerson, Mary-Joan. *Fiesta Femenina: Celebrating Women In Mexican Folklore* (Maya Christina Gonzalez, Illus.). (I, M)

#Hamilton, Virginia. *Her Stories: African American Folktales, Fairy Tales and True Tales* (Leo and Diane Dillon, Illus.). (I, M)

#Hong, Lily. *The Empress and the Silkworm*. (P, I)

Kellogg, Steven. *Sally Ann Thunder Ann Whirlwind Crockett*. (P, I)

#Lurie, Alison. *Clever Gretchen and Other Forgotten Folktales* (Margot Tomes, Illus.). (I)

#MacDonald, Margaret. *Mabela the Clever* (Tim Coffey, Illus.). (P)

#Mayer, Mariana. *Women Warriors: Myths and Legends of Heroic Women* (Julek Heller, Illus.). (I, M)

#Merrill, Jean. *The Girl Who Loved Caterpillars* (Floyd Cooper, Illus.). (P)

Mills, Lauren. *Tatterhood and the Hobgoblins: A Norwegian Folktale*. (I)

#Oughton, Jerrie. *The Magic Weaver of Rugs: A Tale of the Navajo* (Lisa Desimini, Illus.). (P, I)

Peterson, Julienne. *Caterina, the Clever Farm Girl: A Tale From Italy* (Enzo Giannini, Illus.). (P)

#Phelps, Ethel. *The Maid of the North: Feminist Folk Tales from Around the World* (Lloyd Bloom, Illus.). (M)

Phelps, Ethel. *Tatterhood and Other Tales* (Pamela Baldwin Ford, Illus.). (I, M)

#Ragan, Kathleen. *Fearless Girls, Wise Women and Beloved Sisters: Heroines in Folktales from Around the World*. (I)

#Ragan, Kathleen. *Outfoxing Fear: Folktales from Around the World*. (M)

#Riordan, James. *The Woman in the Moon and Other Tales of Forgotten Heroines* (Angela Barrett, Illus.). (P, I)

#San Souci, Robert. *The Samurai's Daughter* (Stephen T. Johnson, Illus.). (I, M)

San Souci, Robert. *Cut from the Same Cloth: American Women of Myth, Legend, and Tall Tale*. (Brian Pinkney, Illus.). (I, M)

#San Souci, Robert. *Sister Tricksters: Rollicking Tales of Clever Females* (Daniel San Souci, Illus.). (I, M)

#Shelby, Ann. *The Adventures of Molly Whuppie and Other Appalachian Folktales* (Paula McArdle, Illus.). (I, M)

#Shepard, Aaron. *Savitri: A Tale of Ancient India* (Vera Rosenberry, Illus.). (I)

#Tchana, Katrin. *The Serpent Slayer and Other Stories of Strong Women* (Trina Schart Hyman, Illus.). (P, I)

#Uchida, Yoshiko. *Wise Old Woman* (Martin Springett, Illus.). (P, I)

Willey, Margaret. *Clever Beatrice* (Heather Solomon, Illus.). (P, I)

#Yolen, Jane. *Mightier Than the Sword: World Folktales for Strong Boys* (Raul Colon, Illus.). (I, M)

#Yolen, Jane. *Not One Damsel in Distress: World Folktales for Strong Girls* (Susan Guevara, Illus.). (I, M)

Zipes, Jack. *Don't Bet on the Prince: Contemporary Feminist Fairy Tales in North America and England*. (M)

Nursery Rhymes

Children's first introduction to literature is often through the nursery rhymes adults recite while playing with a baby. Their continued popularity might seem surprising as much of the vocabulary in these verses is obscure and dated. However, the rhyme, rhythm, alliteration, and other musical qualities, along with their humor and nonsense, have made these traditional rhymes appealing to generations of children.

Beautifully illustrated traditional nursery rhyme anthologies are available for use with children; many are created by well-known artists, such as Tomie de Paola, Arnold Lobel,

Pio Peep: Traditional Nursery Rhymes by Alma Flor Alda, Isabel Compoy, and Alice Schertle feature traditional Latino nursery rhymes presented both Spanish and English.

James Marshall, and Rosemary Wells. Several provide unusual perspectives on the rhymes. For example, *The Neighborhood Mother Goose* (Crews) has an urban, multiethnic setting; *Baby Goose* (McMullan) includes only the rhymes focused on babies; *The Movable Mother Goose* (Sabuda) has spectacular three-dimensional pop-up illustrations; and a *Pocketful of Posies* (Mavor) features embroidered fabric illustrations that are embellished with buttons, shells, driftwood, and other multidimension materials. Some books feature a single rhyme or a few rhymes on a common theme. They allow focus on one rhyme in depth, encouraging children to particularly pay attention to rhythm, rhyme, wordplay, and theme and how illustrations interpret the rhymes.

Nursery rhyme collections from diverse cultures and languages are also now available. Books such as *Muu, Moo! Rimas de Animales/Animal Nursery Rhymes* (Ada and Campoy), *Tortilla Para Mama* (Cooney), and *Pio Peep! Traditional Spanish Nursery Rhymes* (Ada) introduce children to rhymes from Latin America and the American Southwest. *No Hickory, No Dickory, No Dock: Caribbean Nursery Rhymes* (Agard and Nichols) gives children a glimpse of Caribbean culture through nursery rhymes. *Skip Across the Ocean: Nursery Rhymes from Around the World* (Benjamin), *Classic Nursery Rhymes: Enchanting Songs from Around the World* (Weber), and *Rhymes 'Round the World* (Charo) feature nursery rhymes from a range of cultures.

Ballads and Folk Songs

Ballads are stories from traditional literature that tell of tragic incidents or great exploits. Often, ballads evolved from local events or legends that take on epic significance after being immortalized in the ballad. Heroic deeds are sometimes celebrated in these song/stories, but they also often focus on murder, love gone wrong, feuds, and tragedies. Ballads are typically written in poetic form and are usually sung, distinguishing them from traditional literature, such as legends that are written in prose narrative style. For example, "The Ballad of John Henry" is a version of the John Henry tall tale.

Folk songs are shorter than ballads and are also sung. Many have been illustrated in beautiful picture book editions, making them excellent choices for reading aloud as well as shared reading activities.

Lullabies are among the most enduring folk songs and are excellent resources for introducing preschoolers to traditional literature. Brian Pinkney's illustrations for the lullaby "Hush Little Baby" show a loving African American family playing with their baby. "Twinkle, Twinkle, Little Star" is another familiar lullaby that has been interpreted by illustrators such as Jeanette Winters, Sylvia Long, and Rosemary Wells. Todd and Wayne South created an interactive edition of this lullaby with pop-ups, wheels, and pull tabs. *Hush Songs: African American Lullabies* (Thomas), *Weave Little Stars into My Sleep: Native American Lullabies* (Philip), *Sleep Rhymes Around the World* (Yolen), *Hush, Baby Hush! Lullabies from Around the World* (Henderson), and *Arroraró mi Niño: Latino Lullabies and Gentle Games* (Delacre) are good sources for culturally diverse lullabies.

Spirituals are religious folk songs that are particularly associated with African American traditional literature. *All Night, All Day: A Child's First Book of Spirituals* (Bryan) features beautiful watercolor paintings that glow with the faith emanating from the songs they illustrate. *Let It Shine: Three Favorite Spirituals* (Bryan) uses colorful collage illustrations to illustrate three well-known spirituals. *He's Got the Whole World in His Hands* (Nelson) has strikingly beautiful illustrations of this spiritual, whereas E. B. Lewis shows African American children and their families cheerfully going through their days in *This Little Light of Mine*.

Folk songs also developed as a way to help lighten the burden of difficult, unrelenting physical work. These songs mirrored the rhythm of hammering railroad spikes, laboring farmers in the field, and the spinning wheel's motion. Nadine Westcott used a lively cartoon style to bring the song "I've Been Workin' on the Railroad" alive, whereas Dan Brown used realistic African American characters in his rendition of this song. *The Erie Canal*, with intricately detailed illustrations by Peter Spier, chronicles the hard work of guiding boats through canal locks in the 1800s.

Some songs are just plain nonsense and feature enjoyable language play. For example, "Old McDonald Had a Farm," with its humorous repetitive refrains and descriptive animal sounds, is a perennial favorite that has been illustrated by Glenn Rounds and Carol Jones and reinterpreted in pop-up and interactive versions by David Carter, Frances Cony, and Suse McDonald.

Playground and Other Game-Related Literature

Go outside for recess or listen on city sidewalks where children congregate, and you will see a society with its own songs, riddles, insults, rhymes, and games. You will likely recognize some from your own childhood that are still popular, such as "Teddy Bear, Teddy Bear," "Miss Mary Mack," "One Potato, Two Potato," and "Rock, Paper, Scissors." You will also likely hear jokes and riddles, such as "Why did the chicken cross the road?" or "What's black and white and red all over?"

Many of these popular games, riddles, and playground chants are available in published anthologies. *Miss Mary Mack and Other Children's Street Rhymes* (Cole and Calmenson) includes ball-bouncing chants, counting-out rhymes, teases and taunts, and jump-rope chants. *As the Green Grass Grows All Around* (Schwartz) features sassy, funny, and often naughty songs (e.g., "Mine Eyes Have Seen the Glory of the Closing of the School"). *Mamá Goose: A Latino Nursery Treasury* (Alda and Campoy) is a collection of lullabies, jump-rope songs, riddles, and proverbs from the Spanish-speaking world, whereas *I Saw You in the Bathtub and Other Street Rhymes* (Schwartz) is an "easy-reader" book for young children featuring folk rhymes, taunts, and insults that makes this literature easily accessible to beginning readers.

Some single rhymes are available in picture book format. For example, Jane Cabrera's version of the popular counting-down rhyme *Ten in the Bed* and the hand-motion song *If You're Happy and You Know It* feature brightly colored animals acting out the verses. Anthony Browne's *Animal Fair* has eye-catching pop-up illustrations, as does an edition of Michael Rosen's, *We're Going on a Bear Hunt*.

 # Teaching Strategies

Traditional literature can be used with all ages of children. In primary grades, traditional stories can be the impetus for shared reading experiences or are the stories selected for readers' workshops, especially if the selections have predictable, repetitive story structures. Traditional stories, with their musical language and engaging plots, are also a wonderful resource for reading aloud.

As children mature, they can begin discerning the various forms of traditional stories and appreciate more complex plot structures, such as those in myths, legends, or epics. Middle-level students can assume an anthropological stance toward stories, studying the cultures that produced them and then considering what can be learned about people and their humanity from a culture's stories. They can also consider what these stories tell us about how to live our own lives.

Connecting to the Common Core State Standards

The following activities using stories from traditional literature across cultures support the development of this understanding. (Skills mandated in other Reading: Literature Standards related to characterization, plot analysis, and theme are also developed through these activities.)

COMMON CORE STATE STANDARD FEATURE #1

Comparing Similar Traditional Stories Across Cultures (CCSS.RL.9)

The Common Core State Standards (CCSS) have identified an understanding of how similar stories differ across cultures as an important skill for readers. Traditional literature is specifically mentioned as the genre in which this skill should be learned. The developmental evolution of this understanding over several grade levels is articulated in CCSS.ELA-Literacy Standard RL.9:

CCRA (Anchor Standard) RL.9: Analyze how two or more texts address similar themes or topics in order to build knowledge or to compare the approaches the authors take.

Sample Grade-Level Competencies for This Standard Are the Following:

RL.1.9.   Compare and contrast the adventures and experiences of characters in stories.

RL.2.9.   Compare and contrast two or more versions of the same story (e.g., Cinderella stories) by different authors or from different cultures.

RL.4.9.   Compare and contrast the treatment of similar themes and topics (e.g., opposition of good and evil) and patterns of events (e.g., the quest) in stories, myths, and traditional literature from different cultures.

Folktale Matrix: Comparing Stories Across Cultures: The purpose of this teaching strategy is to identify and compare variants of traditional stories across cultures. This is an excellent strategy for showing children how a culture can leave its unique mark on a story, changing characters, settings, and plot structure of the tale. It can also be used to highlight literary elements and enable students to think more critically about story elements.

Begin by selecting a traditional tale, such as "Cinderella," which has plentiful variants. Collect variants of the story from diverse cultures (see Figure 6.1). After sharing them with your students, begin a matrix on a large sheet of paper with headings such as "Reteller," "Origin of Tale," "Main Character," "Main Character's Foil," "Problem," "Obstacle to the Solution," "Evil Character," "Helpful Character/Guide," and "Ending." The specific categories you use will depend on the story's particular characteristics. For example, if you are comparing variants of a fable, the categories might be "Main Character," "Antagonist," "How the Dilemma Is Solved," and "Moral." Create a column or row every time your students read a new variant, filling in the chart for that story. When the chart is completed, have students examine it for

Students Document Their Understanding of the Various Types of Traditional Literature Through a Comparison Chart

Comparison Chart: Comparing Two Cinderella Stories

Books	Origin	Beginning, Ending, & Moral	Place	Good Characters	Evil Characters	Magic	Similarities	Differences
Mufaro's Beautiful Daughter by John Steptoe	Africa	*"A long time ago"* Never take off without your dad's supervision; Listen to the advice of others	*"In a certain place in Africa"*	Nyasha is kind & good beautiful Father: he loved his daughters equally; he was loyal king: kind	Manyara (sister) is selfish & very mean	King shape shifted into 3 things: the snake, little boy, and old woman	Good Characters Evil Characters No mother Magic: Shape Shifting: Number 3 Quest for a wife	Story Origins Beginnings, Endings, & Moral Where the stories took place Different evil people The king knew who Nyasha was before she knew Prince never met Cinderella before the ball
Cinderella retold by Cynthia Rylant & pictures by Mary Blair	Europe	*"This is a story about darkness and light.* *"They lived happily ever after."* Sometimes your (the good & the sad person's) wishes come true about love.	Somewhere in a kingdom	Cinderella is kind, good, and works hard; did what she was supposed to Fairy Godmother is giving and kind; she made Cinderella beautiful	Cruel stepmother & sisters=3 cruel characters: who want to be rich. They are greedy and jealous of Cinderella	Magic slipper; mice turn into horses; a pumpkin into a carriage		

Two Cinderella stories are compared using a Folktale Matrix.

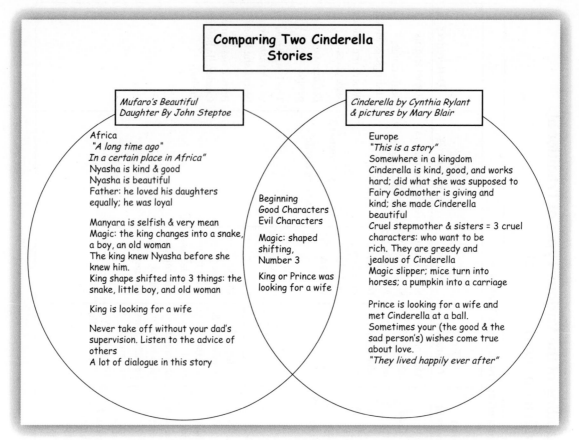

Comparing Two Cinderella Stories

Mufaro's Beautiful Daughter By John Steptoe

Africa
"A long time ago"
In a certain place in Africa"
Nyasha is kind & good
Nyasha is beautiful
Father: he loved his daughters equally; he was loyal

Manyara is selfish & very mean
Magic: the king changes into a snake, a boy, an old woman
The king knew Nyasha before she knew him.
King shape shifted into 3 things: the snake, little boy, and old woman

King is looking for a wife

Never take off without your dad's supervision. Listen to the advice of others
A lot of dialogue in this story

Beginning
Good Characters
Evil Characters

Magic: shaped shifting,
Number 3

King or Prince was looking for a wife

Cinderella by Cynthia Rylant & pictures by Mary Blair

Europe
"This is a story"
Somewhere in a kingdom
Cinderella is kind, good, and works hard; did what she was supposed to
Fairy Godmother is giving and kind; she made Cinderella beautiful
Cruel stepmother & sisters = 3 cruel characters: who want to be rich. They are greedy and jealous of Cinderella
Magic slipper; mice turn into horses; a pumpkin into a carriage

Prince is looking for a wife and met Cinderella at a ball.
Sometimes your (the good & the sad person's) wishes come true about love.
"They lived happily ever after"

Two Cinderella variants are compared and contrasted in a Venn Diagram, a useful strategy for analyzing texts.

similarities and differences. Then lead a discussion on how the values and mores of a culture influenced each variant.

Venn Diagrams: Venn diagrams also give students the opportunity to discuss similarities and differences among stories. The tales compared can be variants of a story, different stories from the same culture, stories that address the same theme across cultures, and so on. Typically, the stories selected for the activity will have something in common along with some significant differences, such as two creation myths or two pourquoi tales from different cultures that explain the same natural phenomenon.

Comparing the Original Versions of Folktales with "Fractured" Versions: Venn diagrams or folktale matrices can also be used to have students compare stories from traditional literature with stories written by contemporary writers that are based on the traditional stories. Often termed "fractured folktales," these stories use elements of the old stories but change them by adding contemporary details or new plot twists, making them particularly useful for studying plot structure in addition to the comparison activity. As these stories are written by known authors, a list of "fractured folktale" books that can be compared to traditional stories is included on the picture book list at the end of Chapter 7. Once students have explored the differences between these stories and their original versions, they can write their own "fractured folktales."

Tech Click

Scholastic's Web site has excellent tips for writing stories in the style of traditional literature. For example, Jane Yolen provides suggestions for brainstorming (including a "Myth Brainstorming Machine") and writing myths. Rafe Martin and Alma Flor Ada provide ideas and models for creating folktales while Jon Scieszka provides ideas for fairy-tale and fable writing. Both sub-sections feature many examples of student writing, organized by writer's age, so your students have many models to inform their own writing.

Tech Click

Students can create a "choose your own adventure" type of fractured fairy tale using presentation software, such as PowerPoint or Keynote. In this type of project, the creator crafts a fractured fairy tale, stopping every so often to ask the reader a question. For example, the student could ask her reader, "Does Snow White buy the apple from the old peddler? Click Yes or click No." Clicking "Yes" may go directly to the traditional story. Clicking "No" could take the reader to an alternative plot point. "Snow White realizes the wicked stepmother will not cease trying to harm her, so she decides to take lessons in self-defense."

COMMON CORE STATE STANDARD FEATURE #2

Comparing How Visual Aspects of a Text Contribute to Story Meaning in Traditional Literature (CCSS.RL.7)

In Chapter 4, we discussed how artists use various artistic elements, media, and their personal style to create a unique literary work. The same is true for those who create movies, Web sites, and other media. The CCSS recognize the importance of these visual elements in CCSS.ELA-Literacy Standard RL.7:

CCRA (Anchor Standard) RL.7: Integrate and evaluate content presented in diverse media and formats, including visually and quantitatively, as well as in words.

Sample Grade-Level Competencies for This Standard Are the Following:

RL.1.7.   Use illustrations and details in a story to describe its characters, setting, or events.

RL.3.7.   Explain how specific aspects of a text's illustrations contribute to what is conveyed by the words in a story (e.g., create mood, emphasize aspects of a character or setting).

RL.5.7.   Analyze how visual and multimedia elements contribute to the meaning, tone, or beauty of a text (e.g., graphic novel, multimedia presentation of fiction, folktale, myth, poem).

RL.6.7.   Compare and contrast the experience of reading a story, drama, or poem to listening to or viewing an audio, video, or live version of the text, including contrasting what they "see" and "hear" when reading the text to what they perceive when they listen or watch.

The following activities can help students develop an understanding of how various visual media can influence one's response to a story.

Analyzing Illustrations in Traditional Literature: An activity that leads to critical analysis and thoughtful discussion involves reading several versions of a story that have strikingly different illustrations. Illustrated versions of a folktale or nursery rhyme work well for this activity. For example, you might share Trina Schart Hyman's *Little Red Riding Hood*, illustrated in a cozy, folklore style with borders framing scenes full of everyday household details, along with Gennady Spirin's version, which features rich, intricate paintings; significant white space; and a spare narrative. The two books convey quite different moods. Hyman's version draws readers in and creates an emotional connection between the realistically portrayed child and the humanlike wolf. This creates subtle tension as readers worry about whether Red Riding Hood will escape from the wolf. In contrast, Spirin's version presents a gentler story: the wolf is large and ferocious but is dressed in a ruffled tunic and feathered hat, and the gorier parts of the story (Red Riding Hood and Grandmother being eaten) are not shown in detail, making this version less dark in tone.

Extend the Little Red Riding Hood comparisons by sharing Jerry Pinkney's rendition, which features illustrations with strikingly different details from the other two. First, Pinkney sets the story in winter, creating an entirely different mood (and also changing some of the story details). The vibrant watercolor illustrations show realistic characters (who also happen to be biracial) and a wolf that is truly a ferocious, wild animal. When the girl is devoured by the wolf, he leaps out of Grandma's bed right at the reader, making the reader almost become the terrified heroine. The contrasts in the illustrations, as well as differences in story details, typically evoke interesting responses from children, helping them understand how illustrations change one's response to a story. Additional versions you could share are Marjorie Priceman's pop-up version, James Marshall's comic book–style rendition, or Ed Young's *Lon Po Po: A Red Riding Hood Story from China*, which uses ancient Chinese panel art combined with a contemporary palette of watercolors and pastels.

Tech Click

Digital versions and iPad apps are also easily obtainable: *Riding Hood* (Boo) (digital version) and *Lil' Red—An Interactive Story* (iPad App). You can easily find multimedia versions of other traditional literature stories, in part because the stories reside in the public domain and do not need copyright clearance.

This activity could also be done with other traditional literature that has been illustrated by multiple artists, such as *Cinderella*, *Snow White*, *The Three Little Pigs*, *The Lion and the Mouse*, *Old McDonald Had a Farm*, and *Old Mother Hubbard*.

Comparing Traditional Literature in Written Form with Movies and Plays: Venn diagrams or other types of comparison charts can be used to facilitate comparison between traditional stories and movies or television series based on those stories. A significant number of media-based adaptations are available for this activity, including "Into the Woods" (a movie that explores the dark psychological side of folktales) and the Disney versions of folktales and television shows, such as *Grimm Once upon a Time*, and *Faerie Tale Theatre*. Students can chart and then discuss how media and book differ in terms of plot details, how characters are developed, or the point of view from which the story is told. They can also consider what has been added, changed, or omitted in the media version and how those changes alter their understanding or response to the story.

Supporting Culturally Diverse Students with Traditional Literature

Using traditional literature from a variety of cultures helps diverse students develop their own cultural identity and understanding of how their heritage has shaped who they are and how they connect to others. Students from mainstream cultures can gain an appreciation for the rich body of traditional stories that contribute to world literature.

Studying the traditional literature of the culturally diverse students in your classroom can help develop these understandings. For example, if you have students from a Mexican cultural background in your classroom, you could conduct a study of Mexican traditional literature, beginning with myths and pourquoi tales. *The Lizard and the Sun: An Old Mexican Folktale* (Ada), *The Tale of Rabbit and Coyote* (Johnston), and *Cuckoo/Cucio* (Ehlert) are appropriate picture book versions of pourquoi tales suitable for primary children. *How We Came to the Fifth World/Como Vinimos al Quinto Mundo: A Creation Story from Ancient Mexico* (Rohmer and Anchondo) is a myth that works well with middle school students. Students could also study Cinderella variants, legends, trickster tales, nursery rhymes, folk songs, and other stories from Mexican traditional literature.

You can use some of the activities we described in Chapter 2 to help students respond to the stories. Storytelling with props or puppets works well with these tales. Dramatizing with readers' theater, pantomime, or short plays can be done by reenacting the stories students have heard or using new stories, such as those found in *Plays from Hispanic Tales* (Winther). Illustrating a story that does not already have pictures in the style of the country's art is a way to study art and story while still respecting a culture's traditional heritage.

Once students have studied the traditional literature of one country or culture, they can compare and contrast stories from many countries. This will show students the unique qualities of various cultures while highlighting universal qualities of all peoples. One of the most efficient ways to do this is to create comparison charts that visually depict the similarities and differences, using categories that are meaningful to students but also applicable to most cultures. Categories we have successfully used include the following:

- Motifs (trickery, magical objects, transformation, and wishes)
- Typical characters (human *and* animal)
- Well-known "archetype" stories
- Typical magical characters
- Common themes
- Stories you have seen in other cultures (variants)
- Important values to the culture that are conveyed through traditional stories

Some teachers have the entire class study the traditional literature of each culture and complete the chart together. Others have small groups study the traditional literature from various cultures, and then meet as a class to make comparisons.

Figure 6.6 features suggested tales from several cultures to support this activity.

Supporting English Language Learners with Traditional Literature

Traditional literature is an excellent genre for supporting the knowledge and use of English of English language learners (ELLs). The brevity of many traditional stories makes them appropriate for ELL students who may not yet possess sufficient English proficiency to read lengthier,

FIGURE 6.6 Traditional Literature from World Cultures

Africa	China	Mexico
Aardema, Verna. *Bringing the Rain to Kapiti Plain* (Beatriz Vidal, Illus.); *Why Mosquitoes Buzz in People's Ears* (Leo and Diane Dillon, Illus.) (and others by Aardema). (P, I)	Bedard, Michael (adapter). *The Painted Wall and Other Strange Tales.* (M)	Aardema, Verna. *Borreguita and the Coyote.* (P) *Ada, Alma Flor. *The Lizard and the Sun: An Old Mexican Folktale* (P); *Pio Peep! Traditional Spanish Nursery Rhymes.* (P)
Anderson, David A. and Sankofa. *The Origin of Life on Earth* (Kathleen Atkins, Wilson, Illus.). (P)	Bouchard, David. *The Great Race.* (I, M)	Bierhorst, John. *Doctor Coyote: A Native American Aesop's Fables.* (I, M)
Arkhurst, Joyce Cooper. *The Adventures of Spider: West African Folktales* (Jerry Pinkney, Illus.). (P, I)	Casanova, Mary. *The Hunter* (Ed Young, Illus.). (P)	Brusca, Maria. *When Jaguars Ate the Moon and Other Stories About Animals and Plants of the Americas.* (P, M)
		Bernhard, Emery. *The Tree That Rains: The Flood Myth of the Huichol Indians of Mexico.* (P)
Badoe, Adwoa. *The Pot of Wisdom: Ananse Stories* (Baba Wague Diakite, Illus.). (I, M)	Chang, Margaret, and Chang, Raymond. *Da Wei's Treasure: A Chinese Folktale.* (P, I)	Coburn, Jewel. *Domitila: A Cinderella Tale from the Mexican Tradition.* (P, I)
Berry, James. *Don't Leave an Elephant to Go and Chase a Bird* (Ann Grifalconi, Illus.) (P); *Spiderman Anancy* (Greg Couch, Illus.). (I)	Chen, Kerstin. *Lord of the Cranes* (Jian Jiang Chen, Illus.). (I)	Delacre, Lulu. *Golden Tales: Myths, Legends, and Folktales from Latin America* (I, M); *Arrorró, Mi Niño: Latino Lullabies and Gentle Games.* (P)
Bryan, Ashley. *Ashley Bryan's African Tales, Uh Huh* (I, M); *The Cat's Purr* (P, I); *Beautiful Blackbird.* (P, I)	Czernecki, Stefan. *The Cricket's Cage: A Chinese Folktale.* (P)	*Ehlert, Lois. *Cuckoo/Cucio.* (P)
Cummings, Pat. *Ananse and the Lizard: A West African Tale.* (P)	Davol, Marguerite. *The Paper Dragon.* (P, I)	Gregor, Shana. *The Fifth and Final Sun: An Ancient Aztec Myth of the Sun's Origin.* (P, I)
*Daly, Nikki. *Pretty Salma: A Red Riding Hood Story from Africa.* (P, I)	*Demi. *Dragon Kites and Dragonflies: A Collection of Chinese Nursery Rhymes.* (P)	Gerson, Mary Joan. *Fiesta Femina: Celebrating Women in Mexican Folktales.* (I, M)
Dayrell, Elphinstone. *Why the Sun and the Moon Live in the Sky* (Blair Lent, Illus.). (P, I)	Heyer, Marilee. *The Weaving of a Dream: A Chinese Folktale.* (P)	Hayes, Joe. *La Llorona/The Weeping Woman: The Day It Snowed Tortillas; The Coyote Under the Table: Folk Tales Told in Spanish and English.* (P, I)

(Books appropriate for preschoolers are marked *.)

FIGURE 6.6 *continued*

Africa	China	Mexico
Diakité, Baba Wagué. *The Hunterman and the Crocodile* (P, I); *The Magic Gourd.* (P, I)	Lawson, Julie. *The Dragon's Pearl.* (P)	Johnston, Tony. *The Tale of Rabbit and Coyote.* (P)
Gerson, Mary Joan. *Why the Sky Is Far Away: A Nigerian Folktale.* (P, I)	Louie, Ai-Ling. *Yeh Shen: A Cinderella Story from China.* (I, M)	Kimmel, Eric. *The Two Mountains: An Aztec Legend.* (I, M)
Haley, Gail E. *A Story, a Story.* (P, I)	Passes, David. *Dragons: Truth, Myth and Legend.* (I, M)	Ober, Hal. *How Music Came into the World: An Ancient Mexican Myth.* (P, I)
*Harrington, Janice. *Busy-Busy Little Chick.* (P)	Pattison, Darcy. *The River Dragon.* (P, I)	*Orozco, Jose Luis. *Diez Deditos and Other Play Rhymes and Action Songs from Latin America; De Colores and Other Latin American Folk Songs.* (P)
Knutson, Barbara. *How the Guinea Fowl Got Her Spots* (P, I); *Sungura and Leopard: A Swahili Trickster Tale* (I, M); *Why the Crab Has No Head: An African Tale.* (P, I)	San Souci, Robert. *Fa Mulan: The Story of a Woman Warrior.* (M)	Philip, Neil. *Horse Hooves and Chicken Feet: Mexican Folktales.* (I, M)
Kurtz, Jane. *Trouble* (Durga Bernhard, Illus.). (P, I)	*Wyndham, Robert. *Chinese Mother Goose Rhymes.* (P)	Winther, Barbara. *Plays from Hispanic Tales.* (I)
Lester, Julius. *How Many Spots Does a Leopard Have? And Other Tales* (David Shannon, Illus.). (I)	Yep, Laurence. *The Shell Woman and the King: A Chinese Folktale; The Junior Thunder Lord.* (P)	
*McDermott, Gerald. *Zomo the Rabbit: A Trickster Tale from West Africa.* (P)	Young, Ed. *Lon Po Po: A Red Riding Hood Story from China; Night Visitors; Little Plum.* (I, M)	
McDonald, Margaret. *Mabela the Clever* (Tim Coffey, Illus.). (P, I)	Yuan, Haiwang. *Princess Peacock: Tales from the Other Peoples of China.* (I, M)	
Medearis, Angela Shelff. *The Singing Man* (Terea Shaffer, Illus.) (I); *Too Much Talk* (Stefano Vitale, Illus.). (P, I)		

(continued)

FIGURE 6.6 *continued*

Africa	China	Mexico
Mollel, Tololwa M. *The Orphan Boy* (Paul Morin, Illus.) (I, M); *A Promise to the Sun* (Beatriz Vidal, Illus.) (P, I); *Rhinos for Lunch and Elephants for Dinner* (Barbara Spurll, Illus.). (P, I)		
Olaleye, Isaac O. *In the Rainfield Who's the Greatest?* (Ann Grifalconi, Illus.). (P)		
Steptoe, John. *Mufaro's Beautiful Daughters: An African Tale.* (I, M)		

more complex texts. Additionally, using traditional literature for drama, storytelling, and writing activities increases the chance that ELL students will be successful because they are able to bring a rich experiential background to response activities.

Finding stories with universal themes and motifs that can be connected across cultures is an excellent way to draw ELLs into read-alouds and discussions about traditional literature. For example, a Cinderella story of European origin can be read and then compared to *Domitila: A Cinderella Story from the Mexican Tradition* (Coburn), *The Korean Cinderella* (Climo), or *Jouanah: A Hmong Cinderella* (Coburn), depending on the background of the ELLs in your classroom.

Songs, chants, lullabies, and other verse forms of traditional literature are excellent resources for supporting the development of English skills while also affirming a child's own culture. Students or their parents can share a song or game from their native language. These can be translated into English, and then both English and native language versions can be put on charts or made into handmade books. Or teachers can access some songs in native languages that are currently in print for this purpose. For example, *De Colores and Other Latin American Folk Songs for Children* (Orozco) and *Diez Deditos and Other Play Rhymes and Action Songs* (Orozco) are two collections that are appropriate for ELL students whose first language is Spanish. Conversely, these are useful for native English speakers learning Spanish.

Storytelling is an excellent way to empower ELL students, help support their growing language skills, and affirm stories from their culture. Some might think that telling a story in a new language might be too intimidating. However, professional storytellers who work extensively with children found that often this is a perfect activity because everyone, including ELL students, must tell a story repeatedly as part of the preparation process (Hamilton & Weiss, 2005, p. 59). This extensive practicing helps reinforce vocabulary and sentence structure.

Students can also be encouraged to tell a story first in their own language and then in English as yet another way to scaffold their use of English. It helps if they use gestures and facial expressions for this activity. Listeners can follow the story in the unfamiliar language by watching the gestures, gaining a new appreciation for the ELL student's native language.

Traditional literature, particularly the shorter folktales, fables, and learning stories, provides an excellent base for doing drama with ELL students. The short, active plots and predictable language of these stories make it easy for children to remember the story and reenact it. Even those with limited English skills can chant repetitive lines, allowing them the chance to participate using just a few words or phrases. They can also act out parts as the teacher reads aloud, improvising action, dialogue, and movement. Connecting physical movement to language helps ELL students expand their vocabulary and comprehension of English through a low-risk activity. Specific strategies for using storytelling and drama activities are discussed in more detail in Chapter 2.

Tech Click

Partnership for 21st Century Skills and the National Council of Teachers of English worked on a "map" containing student outcomes and model projects. Fourth graders read multiple fairy tales (or experience an online quest on global stores) and would use the four Cs when creating a stop-action movie with paper figures or Claymation.

Controversial Issue: The Misappropriation of a Culture's Traditional Literature by Mainstream Cultures

In Chapter 2, we discussed responding to literature from a critical stance. Taking the critical stance asks readers to evaluate a text in terms of whose perspectives, values, and norms are voiced and whose are minimized or silenced. Discussing these issues helps students think more critically about the underlying political and social assumptions and agendas in stories—perspectives that are often a result of years of cultural assumptions that have gone unexamined. It is particularly important to examine traditional literature from a critical stance, as many traditional stories have been marginalized or changed as they were discovered by a mainstream culture.

When stories evolve within a culture, storytellers shape and change those stories to fit their personal style and purposes. This is expected. In some cultures, listeners are invited to add important details if they believe that these are important to the telling. In this way, a communal story evolves through each telling. Because the stories pass down the peoples' religious beliefs, moral values, customs, and history, these alterations matter and must remain true to the spirit and cultural context of the original tale (Reese, 2007, p. 245).

However, sometimes the intent and cultural authenticity of a told story is no longer representative of its culture when it is recorded in written form by a mainstream culture. This often happens because the traditional story must conform to certain publishing and aesthetic expectations, turning a dynamic work into something relatively static. All the significant elements of oral telling—tone, pacing, and gestures—are gone. Additionally, details are sometimes changed to reflect a mainstream culture's values and perspectives.

Tech Click

Oyate.org is a Web site devoted to evaluating stories from Native American cultures regarding cultural authenticity, whereas *The Broken Flute: The Native Experience in Books for Children* (Seale and Slapin) provides extensive reviews of books about Native American culture and lives. Unfortunately, resources for other cultures are very limited.

A good example of this is the publication of Native American stories. Published Native American tales often portray native peoples as romantic, tragic heroes who speak in elaborate poetic language, quite different from the straightforward style that is actually characteristic of the storytelling in many native cultures. For example, *Turkey Girl: A Zuni Cinderella Story* (Pollock) is a story that seems authentic and respectful of the culture from which it originated. The story was favorably reviewed by mainstream literary critics and awarded an Aesop Accolade Award. However, Debbie Reese, a Native American from the Nambe Pueblo tribe, found major cultural misrepresentations in Pollock's book. For example, the writing style is eloquent, romantic prose rather than the straightforward factual style of the Zuni people. The concept of orphanhood, the accumulation of material goods, and status based on wealth and beauty are characteristic of Euro-American rather than Zuni social norms. Essentially, the author changed the story's purpose and meaning so that it is virtually unrecognizable to the Zuni people (Reese, 2007).

Stories from the Inuit peoples of Alaska were similarly transformed in ways that make the stories sometimes unrecognizable to the culture. For example, *Magic Words* (Field) is based on Inuit myths collected by Knud Rasmussen in his travels through the Arctic/Alaskan region in the 1920s. However, Field changed the stories so that the language is distinctly mainstream American in its style, and there are references to events that would not have happened in this culture. Interpreting Inuit lore in this way misrepresents them and is a good example of how what is included and excluded distorts a story's original meaning (Hearne, 1999).

This raises the following questions: From whose perspective is the story being told? Is that perspective an authentic, respectful reflection of the culture from which the story originated? Do the characters in this tale act according to the values and customs of this cultural group? Is the action, moral, or theme reflective of the values of the cultural group? Once students ask these critical questions, they can begin to understand how some cultures have been marginalized and stereotyped through the misrepresentation of their stories.

We believe that these issues must be thoughtfully considered when sharing traditional literature with children. Teachers should continually check the original sources for traditional stories they use whenever possible and see if the notes specifically describe the origin of the story and what the editor or storyteller has changed. This can sometimes be difficult, as publishers often do not want to give space for this information. However, such notes can be useful in documenting authenticity. For example, Gayle Ross, a member of the Cherokee tribe, included detailed, specific notes about her sources—describing the exact contexts in which the story could be found, other storytellers who had recounted the story, and the incorporation of her own family stories—for her retelling of *The Legend of the Windigo: A Tale from Native North America.*

Tech Click

Students could create a blog written from a specific folk character's perspective, such as the miller's daughter pondering the name of that angry little man or, conversely, Rumpelstiltskin gleefully anticipating his new baby. Older students might explore psychological aspects of fairy-tale characters à la Gail Carson Levine or Donna Jo Napoli on a FakeBook page (a site similar to Facebook but for educational use.)

One second-grade teacher we know used Twitter (an online microblogging application) for response activities for traditional literature. Students could simulate Twitter by asking students to visualize what their day would be like, staying in the character of a folktale. For example, Rapunzel might post "used up all shampoo - need to get more," or Prince might post "what kind of impractical woman would have a glass slipper?"

Summary

- Traditional literature is the body of stories that are part of the oral tradition of a culture. These stories reflect the values, beliefs, ways of living, and geographic areas from which the stories arose. Traditional tales are characterized by many of the same elements as fictional stories, but characterization, plotting, and other elements differ due to the brief nature of the stories and as a result of cultural differences. Literary elements that recur across stories are called motifs. Stories that have similar characters, episodes, and plots across cultures but also differ substantially from each other are called variants. Stories that vary in minor details are called versions.

- Exposure to traditional literature provides a glimpse into other cultures, builds an understanding of allusions in mainstream culture, and teaches acceptable and unacceptable behavior norms.

- Traditional literature should be judged on both cultural and literary qualities. Stories should be authentic and faithfully reflect the culture from which they originated. Plots, language, characters, and style should be of high literary quality and also accurately reflect the culture of the story's origin.

- Categories of traditional literature include folktales, fables, myths (including pourquoi stories), legends and epics, tall tales, ballads and folk songs, and children's playground rhymes.

- Traditional literature is particularly appropriate for helping students develop competence in CCSS Standards RL.9 (comparing stories across cultures) and RL.7 (examining the effect of illustrations and multimedia on story). Traditional literature, due to its brevity and connection to many cultures, is an excellent genre to use with culturally diverse students and ELLs. Stories of traditional literature should be examined from a critical perspective, particularly in relation to issues of authenticity.

Questions/Activities to Invite Thinking, Writing, and Conversation About the Chapter

1. Find a traditional story featuring "source notes" that detail the story's origin, how the author adapted it, if he or she received permission from the originating culture to tell it, and so on. Consider how you might use this information with students in a classroom.

2. Construct a study of how a traditional literature tale has been illustrated, using the model provided in the CCSS section of the chapter but with a different story. Share with your peers on a blog or other type of social media and provide commentary on each other's lessons.

3. Collect examples of one category of traditional literature or traditional stories from one culture. Plan how you would organize the study of the books with students in a classroom at the grade level of your intended licensure area.

Recommended Traditional Literature Books

(Books appropriate for preschoolers are marked *; those with significant culturally diverse elements are marked #.)

Folktales (see also titles in Figures 6.3 and 6.4)

#Aardema, Verna. *Rabbit Makes a Monkey Out of Lion* (Jerry Pinkney, Illus.); *Who's in Rabbit's House?* (Leo and Diane Dillon, Illus.). (P)

#Ada, Alma Flor. *The Rooster Who Went to His Uncle's Wedding* (Kathleen Kuchera, Illus.). (P, I)

#Anonymous. *Aladdin and Other Tales from the Arabian Nights* (William Harvey, Illus.). (I, M)

Chase, Richard. *The Jack Tales* (also edition by Hicks). (I)

#*Compestine, Ying Chang. *The Runaway Rice Cake* (Tungwai Chau, Illus.). (P)

#*Compoy, Isabel. *Rosa Raposa*. (P)

#Compoy, Isabel, and Ada, Alma Flor. *Tales Our Abelita Told: A Hispanic Folktale Collection*. (P, I)

#Cummings, Pat. *Ananse and the Lizard: A West African Tale*. (P)

#Dembicki, Matt. *Trickster: Native American Tales: A Graphic Edition*. (M)

*Emberly, Ed. *Chicken Little* (also other editions by other illustrators). (P)

#Goble, Paul. *Return of the Buffaloes; The Girl Who Loved Wild Horses*. (P, I)

Grimm, Jacob and Wilhelm. *The Complete Grimm's Fairy Tales*. (P, I)

#Freedman, Florence. *It Happened in Chelm: A Story of the Legendary Town of Fools* (Nik Krevitsky, Illus.). (P)

#Haley, Gail. *A Story, a Story*. (P)

#Han, Suzanne. *The Rabbit's Judgement; The Rabbit's Escape* (Yumi Heo, Illus.). (P, I)

Kellogg, Steven. *Jack and the Beanstalk*. (P)

Kimmel, Eric. *Baba Yaga: A Russian Folktale* (Megan Lloyd, Illus.); **The Fisherman and the Turtle* (Martha Aviles, Illus.); **The Old Woman and Her Pig* (Gloria Carmi, Illus.). (P)

#Lippert, Margaret, and Paye, Won-Ldy. *Why Leopard Has Spots: Dan Stories from Liberia*. (Ashley Bryan, Illus.). (I)

#Martin, Rafe. *Foolish Rabbit's Big Mistake*. (P)

#McDermott, Gerald. *Coyote: A Trickster Tale from the Southwest*; #*Raven: A Trickster Tale from the Northwest; Jabuti the Tortoise*. (P, I)

*McDonald, Margaret. *The Fat Cat; The Old Woman and Her Pig* (John Kanzler, Illus.). (P)

#Parks, Van Dyke. *Jump! The Adventures of Brer Rabbit* (Barry Moser, Illus.) (also sequels). (I)

Perrault, Charles. *The Complete Fairy Tales of Charles Perrault*. (P, M)

#Pitre, Felix. *Juan Bobo and the Pig*. (P)

#Prose, Francine. *The Angel's Mistake: Stories from Chelm* (Mark Podwall, Illus.). (I)

#*So, Miso. *Gobble, Goggle, Slip, Slop: A Tale of a Very Greedy Cat*. (P)

*Taback, Sims, *The House That Jack Built* (also edition by Bell). (P).

Fables and Learning Stories

Bader. Barbara. *Aesop and Company* (Arthur Geisert, Illus.). (P, I)

#Bierhorst, John. *Dr. Coyote: A Native American Aesop Fables* (Wendy Watson, Illus.). (P, I)

*#Burkert, Nancy. *Mouse and Lion*. (P)

#Demi. *Buddha Stories*. (I, M)

*Moerbeek, Kees, Beatrice, Chris, and Whatley, Bruce. *A Pop-Up Book of Aesop's Fables*. (P)

*Pinkney, Jerry. *Aesop's Fables*; #*The Lion and the Mouse; The Tortoise and the Hare*. (P, M)

Poole, Amy. *The Ant and the Grasshopper*. (P, I)

*#Stevens, Janet. *The Tortoise and the Hare* (also editions by Brett, Carle, Wildsmith, and Potter). (P)

Ward, Helen. *Unwitting Wisdom: An Anthology of Aesop's Fables*. (P, M)

Young, Ed. *Seven Blind Mice*. (P)

General Myths

Amery, Heather. *Greek Myths for Young Children* (Linda Edwards, Illus.). (P, I)

Barth. *Cupid and Psyche: A Love Story*.

Climo, Shirley. *Atalanta's Race: A Greek Myth*. (I, M)

Croall, Marie P. *Psyche and Eros: The Lady and the Monster* (graphic novel). (M)

Curlee, Lynne. *Mythological Creatures: A Classical Beastiary*. (I, M)

Davis, Kenneth C. *Don't Know Much About Mythology*. (I, M)

d'Aulaire, Ingri and Edgar. *D'Aulaire's Book of Greek Myths; Norse Gods and Goddesses*. (I)

Evans, Hestia. *Mythology: The Gods, Heroes and Monsters of Ancient Greece*. (I, M)

#Fisher, Leonard Everett. *Gods and Goddesses of the Ancient Maya*. (I, M)

Fontes, Justine. *Atalanta* (graphic novel). (I, M)

#Gilchrist, Cherry. *Stories from the Silk Road* (Nilesh Mistry, Illus.). (I)

Hodges, Margaret. *The Arrow and the Lamp: The Story of Psyche*. (I, M)

Hoffman, Mary. *A First Book of Myths* (Roger Langton and Kevin Kimber, Illus.). (P, I)

#Jackson, Ellen. *The Spring Equinox: Celebrating the Greening of the Earth* (Jan Davey Ellis, Illus.). (P, I)

Karas, Brian. *Young Zeus.* (P)

Keenan, Sheila. *Gods, Goddesses, and Monsters.* (M)

Lattimore, Deborah Nourse. *Medusa.* (I, M)

Lunge-Larsen, Lisa. *Gifts from the Gods: Ancient Words and Wisdom from Greek and Roman Mythology* (Gareth Hinds, Illus.). (I, M)

Lupton, Hugh, and Morden, Daniel. *The Adventures of Achilles.* (I, M)

#Mama, Raouf. *The Barefoot Book of Tropical Tales* (Deidre Hyde, Illus.). (P, I)

#McCaughrean, Geraldine. *The Bronze Cauldron: Myths and Legends of the World* (Bee Willey, Illus.) (I, M); *The Crystal Pool: Myths and Legends of the World* (Bee Willey, Illus.) (I, M); *Greek Gods and Goddesses* (Emma Chichester Clark, Illus.) (I, M); *Roman Myths* (Emma Chichester Clark, Illus.). (I, M)

Napoli, Donna Jo. *Treasury of Greek Mythology: Classic Stories of Gods, Goddesses, Heroes and Monsters* (Christina Balit, Illus.). (I, M)

#O'Neill, Cynthia. *The Kingfisher Book of Mythology.* (M)

#Philip, Neil. *The Illustrated Book of Myths: Tales and Legends of the World* (Nilesh Mistry, Illus.). (M)

Reinhart, Matthew, and Sabuda, Robert. *Encyclopedia Mythologica: Gods and Heroes Pop-Up.* (I, M)

#Roseni, Michael. *How the Animals Got Their Colors: Animal Myths from Around the World* (John Clementson, Illus.). (I)

Schomp, Virginia. *Myths of the World* (Egypt, ancient Greece, and so on). (M)

Singh, Rina, and Lush, Debbie. *Moon Tales: Myths of the Moon from Around the World.* (M)

Townsend, Mike. *Amazing Greek Myths of Wonders and Blunders.* (I, M)

Turnbull, Ann. *Greek Myths.* (Sarah Young, Illus.). (M)

Vinge, Joan. The *Random House Book of Greek Myths.* (I, M)

Yolen, Jane. *Wings.* (I, M)

Creation Myths and Pourquoi Tales
(All are culturally diverse titles.)

Anaya, Rudolfo. *The First Tortilla: A Bilingual Story* (A. Cordova, Illus.). (P)

Bierhorst, John. *The People with Five Fingers: A Native Californian Creation Tale* (Robert Andrew Parker, Illus.). (P)

Bruchac, Joseph. *Between Earth and Sky: Legends of Native American Sacred Places* (Thomas Locker, Illus.); *How Chipmunk Got Its Stripes; A Tale of Bragging and Teasing* (Jose Aruego and Ariane Dewey, Illus.); *Rabbit's Snow Dance: A Traditional Iroquois Story* (Jeff Newman, Illus.). (P, I)

Bryan, Ashley. *The Story of Lightning and Thunder.* (all)

Burleigh, Robert. *Pandora* (Raul Colon, Illus.). (I, M)

Day, Nancy Raines. *Piecing Earth and Sky Together: A Creation Story from the Mien Tribe of Laos* (Genna Panzarella, Illus.). (P)

Duncan, Barbara. *The Origin of the Milky Way and Other Living Stories of the Cherokee* (Shan Goshorn, Illus.). (I, P)

Gavin, Jamila. *Tales from India: Stories of Creation and the Cosmos* (Amanda Hall, Illus.). (I, M)

Goble, Paul. *Her Seven Brothers.* (P, I)

Hamilton, Virginia. *In the Beginning: Creation Stories from Around the World* (Barry Moser, Illus.). (P)

Hofmeyr, Dianne. *The Star-Bearer: A Creation Myth from Ancient Egypt* (Jude Daly, Illus.). (P, I)

Jackson, Ellen. *The Spring Equinox: Celebrating the Greening of the Earth* (Jan Davey Ellis, Illus.). (P, I)

Keens-Douglas, Richardo. *Mama God, Papa God: A Caribbean Tale* (Stefan, Czernecki, Illus.). (P, I)

Knutson, Barbara. *How the Guinea Fowl Got Her Spots: A Swahili Tale of Friendship.* (P)

*Lee, Jeanne. *Toad Is the Uncle of Heaven: A Vietnamese Folktale.* (P)

Maddern, Eric. *The Fire Children: A West African Creation Tale* (Franc Lessac, Illus.). (P)

Maggi, Maria Elena. *The Great Canoe: A Karena Legend* (Gloria Calderon, Illus.). (P, I)

Mayo, Margaret. *When the World Was Young: Creation and Pourquoi Tales* (Louise Brierley, Illus.). (P, I, M)

McDermott, Gerald. *Musicians of the Sun.* (P, I)

Montileaux, Donald. *Tatanka and the Lakota People: A Creation Story.* (I, P)

*Mosel, Arlene. *Tikki Tikki Tembo.* (P)

Ober, Hal. *How Music Came to the World: An Ancient Mexican Myth* (Carol Ober, Illus.). (I, M)

Oodgeroo Noonuccal. *Dreamtime: Aboriginal Stories* (Bronwyn Bancroft, Illus.). (I)

Powell, Patricia. *Frog Brings Rain* (Kendrick Benally, Illus.). (P)

Ray, Jane. *The Story of the Creation.* (P, I)

Ross, Gayle, and Bruchac, Joseph. *The Story of the Milky Way: A Cherokee Tale* (Virginia A. Stroud, Illus.); *How Turtle's Back Was Cracked.* (P, I)

Strauss, Susan. *When Woman Became the Sea: A Costa Rican Creation Myth* (Cristina Acosta, Illus.). (P)

Yamane, Linda. *When the World Ended: How Hummingbird Got Fire.* (M)

Zhang, Song Nan. *Five Heavenly Emperors: Chinese Myths of Creation.* (I, M)

Legends and Epics

#Bruchac, James and Joseph. *When the Chenoo Howls: Native American Tales of Terror.* (I, M)

#Henderson, Kathy. *Lugalbanda: The Boy Who Got Caught Up in a War: An Epic Tale from Ancient Iraq* (Jane Ray, Illus.). (I, M)

Hodges, Margaret. *The Kitchen Knight: A Tale of King Arthur; Merlin and the Making of a King* (Trina Schart Hyman, Illus.). (I, M)

Ita, Sam. *The Odyssey: A Pop-Up Book.* (I, M)

*Lee, Jeanne. *The Song of Mulan.* (P, M)

#McCaughrean, Geraldine. *Gilgamesh the Hero* (David Perkins, Illus.); *The Odyssey.* (M)

Osborn, Mary. *Tales from the Odyssey; Favorite Medieval Tales.* (P, I)

#Rogasky, Barbara. *The Golem: A Version.* (M)

San Souci, Robert. *Young Merlin; Young Guinivere; Young Lancelot; Young Arthur;* #*Fa Mulan: The Story of a Woman Warrior.* (P, M)

Schwartz, Alvin. *Scary Stories to Tell in the Dark* (and sequels). (P, I)

Shannon, Mark. *Gawaine and the Green Knight.* (David Shannon, Illus.). (I)

#Sharma, Bulbul. *The Ramayana for Children.* (I)

*#Souhami, Jessica. *Rama and the Demon King: An Ancient Tale from India.* (P)

Sutcliff, Rosemary. *Black Ships Before Troy; The Wanderings of Odysseus.* (M)

Talbot, Hudson. *Tales of King Arthur: The Sword and the Stone; King Arthur and the Round Table; Excalibur; Lancelot.* (I)

#Wisniewski, David. *Golem; Sundiata: Lion King of Mali.* (P, I)

#Zeman, Ludmila. *Gilgamesh the King; The Revenge of Ishtar; The Last Quest of Gilgamesh.* (I)

Tall Tales

Keats, Ezra Jack. *John Henry: An American Legend.* (P)

Kellogg, Steven. *Mike Fink; Paul Bunyan; Pecos Bill; Johnny Appleseed; Sally Ann Thunder Ann Whirlwind Crockett.* (P, M)

Lester, Julius. *John Henry* (Jerry Pinkney, Illus.). (P, M)

Lindbergh, Reeve. *Johnny Appleseed: A Poem.* (P, I)

Osborne, Mary Pope. *American Tall Tales* (Michael McCurdy, Illus.). (P, I)

San Souci, Robert. *Larger Than Life: The Adventures of American Legendary Heroes* (Andrew Glass, Illus.); *Cut from the Same Cloth: American Women of Myth, Legend and Tall Tale.* (Brian Pinkney, Illus.). (I, M)

Folk Songs and Games

(All are primary [P] level and also appropriate for preschool.)

#Ada, Alma, and Compoy, Isabelle. *Mama Goose: A Latino Nursery Treasury* (Maribel Suarez, Illus.).

#Bernier-Grand, Carmen. *Shake It, Morena and Other Folklore from Puerto Rico* (Lulu DeLacre, Illus.). (P, I)

Brown, Dan. *The Erie Canal.*

Brown, Marc. *Hand Rhymes.*

Browne, Anthony. *Animal Fair* (pop-up).

#Bryan, Ashley. *All Night, All Day: A Child's First Book of Spirituals; Let It Shine: Three Favorite Spirituals.*

Cabrera, Jane. *Old MacDonald Had a Farm; If You're Happy and You Know It; Ten in the Bed.*

Carter, David. *Old MacDonald Had a Farm.*

Catalano, Dominic. *Frog Went A-Courting: A Musical Play in Six Acts.*

Cauley, Lorinda. *Clap Your Hands.*

Christelow, Eileen. *Five Little Monkeys Sitting in a Tree.*

Church, Caroline Jayne. *Do Your Ears Hang Low? A Love Story.*

Cole, Joanna, and Calmenson, Stephanie. *The Eensy, Weensy Spider: Finger Plays and Action Rhymes* (Alan Tiegreen, Illus.); *Miss Mary Mack and Other Children's Street Rhymes.*

Cony, Frances, and Smyth, Iain. *Old MacDonald Had a Farm.*

Crews, Nina. *The Neighborhood Sing Along.*

#Delacre, Lulu. *Arroz con Leche: Popular Songs from Latin America; Arroraro, mi Niño: Latino Lullabies and Gentle Games.*

Gammell, Stephen. *Once upon MacDonald's Farm.*

Glazer, Tom. *Eye Winker, Tom Tinker, Chin Chopper: Fifty Musical Fingerplays* (Ron Himler, Illus.).

Hale, Sarah Josepha. *Mary Had a Little Lamb* (Bruce McMillan, Photog.).

Hamanaka, Sheila. *The Hokey Pokey.*

#Henderson, *Hush, Baby Hush! Lullabies Around the World.*

Hillenbrand, Will. *Fiddle-I-Fee.*

Hoberman, Mary Ann. *The Eensy Weensy Spider; Miss Mary Mack* (Nadine Bernard Westcott, Illus.).

#Hudson, Wade. *How Sweet the Sound* (Floyd Cooper, Illus.).

Johnson, Paul Brett. *On Top of Spaghetti.*

Kellogg, Steven. *Give the Dog a Bone.*

Kovalski, Maryann. *Take Me Out to the Ballgame; Wheels on the Bus.*

Langstaff, John. *Oh, a Hunting We Will Go* (Nancy Winslow Parker, Illus.).

Lass, Bonnie, and Sturges, Philomon. *Who Took the Cookies from the Cookie Jar?* (Ashley Wolff, Illus.).
Lewis, E. B. *This Little Light of Mine.*
MacDonald, Suse. *Here A Chick, Where A Chick?*
Moss, Marissa. *Knick Knack Paddywack.*
Meyers, Susan. *This Is the Way a Baby Rides* (Hiroe Nakata, Illus.).
#Nelson, Kadir. *He's Got the Whole World in His Hands.*
#Newcome, Zita. *Head, Shoulders, Knees and Toes: And Other Action Rhymes.*
#Orozco, Jose. *Diez Deditos: Ten Little Fingers and Other Play Rhymes and Action Songs from Latin America; Fiestas: A Year of Latin American Songs of Celebration; De Colores and Other Latin American Folk Songs for Children* (Elisa Kleven, Illus.).
#Pinkney, Brian. *Twinkle, Twinkle, Little Star.*
Rae, Mary Maki. *The Farmer in the Dell: A Singing Game.*
Rosen, Michael. *We're Going on A Bear Hunt* (Helen Oxenbury, Illus.).
Rounds, Glen. *Old MacDonald Had a Farm.*
Saport, Linda. *All the Pretty Little Horses.*
Schwartz, Alvin. *I Saw You in the Bathtub and Other Street Rhymes* (Syd Hoff, Illus.); *And the Green Grass Grew All Around* (Sue Truesdell, Illus.).
Schwartz, Amy. *Old MacDonald.*
Scott, Steve. *Teddy Bear, Teddy Bear.*
Sierra, Judy. *Schoolyard Rhymes: Kids' Own Rhymes for Rope-Skipping, Hand Clapping, Ball Bouncing and Just Plain Fun* (Melissa Sweet, Illus.).
Sturges, Philemon. *She'll Be Comin' 'Round the Mountain* (Ashley Wolff, Illus.).
Sweet, Melissa. *Fiddle-I-Fee.*
Taback, Simms. *There Was an Old Lady Who Swallowed a Fly* (also editions by Nadine Westcott and Colin and Jacqui Hawking).
#Thomas, Joyce Carol. *Hush Songs: African American Lullabies* (Brenda Joysmith, Illus.).
Trapani, Iza. *Here We Go Round the Mulberry Bush; I'm a Little Teapot; The Itsy Bitsy Spider; Row, Row, Row Your Boat.*
Warhola, James. *If You're Happy and You Know It.*
Watson, Wendy. *Fox Went Out On A Chilly Night.*
Westcott, Nadine. *I've Been Workin' on the Railroad; I Know an Old Lady Who Swallowed a Fly; The Lady with the Alligator Purse; Skip to My Lou.*
Wood, Jakki. *Fiddle-I-Fee: A Noisy Nursery Rhyme.*
#Yolen, Jane. *Street Rhymes Around the World; Sleep Rhymes Around the World.*
Zelinsky, Paul. *Knick, Knack, Paddy Whack.*

Nursery Rhymes: Anthologies
(All are primary [P] level and also appropriate for preschool.)
#Ada, Alma Flor, and Compoy, F. Isabelle. *Mama Goose* (Maribel Suarez, Illus.); *Muu, Moo! Rimas de Animales/Animal Nursery Rhymes* (Maribel Suarez, Illus.); *Pio Peep! Traditional Spanish Nursery Rhymes* (Vivi Escriova, Illus.); *Ten Little Puppies: Diez Perritos* (Ulises Wensell, Illus.).
#Agard, John, and Nichols, Grace. *No Hickory, No Dickory, No Dock: Caribbean Nursery Rhymes* (Cynthia Jabar, Illus.).
Beaton, Claire. *Mother Goose Remembers.*
#Benjamin, Floella. *Skip Across the Ocean: Nursery Rhymes from Around the World* (Sheila Moxley, Illus.).
#Charo, Kay. *Rhymes 'Round the World.*
Crews, Nina. *Neighborhood Mother Goose.*
dePaola, Tomie. *Tomie dePaola's Mother Goose.*
Dillon, Leo and Diane. *Mother Goose Numbers on the Loose.*
Duffy, Chris. *Nursery Rhyme Comics: 50 Timeless Rhymes from 50 Celebrated Cartoonists* (various artists and illustrators) (graphic novel). (P, I)
Fabian, Bobbi. *Twinkle, Twinkle, an Animal Lover's Mother Goose.*
#Griego, Margot, Bucks, Betsy, Gilbert, Sharon, and Kimball, Laurel. *Tortellitas para Mama and Other Nursery Rhymes* (Barbara Cooney, Illus.).
Hague, Michael. *Mother Goose: A Collection of Classic Nursery Rhymes.*
Lobel, Arnold. *Book of Mother Goose.*
Lucas, Barbara. *Cats by Mother Goose* (Carol Newson, Illus.).
Marshall, James. *James Marshall's Mother Goose.*
Mathers, Petra. *The McElderry Book of Mother Goose: Revered and Rare Rhymes.*
Mavor, Salley. *A Pocketful of Posies: A Treasury of Nursery Rhymes.*
McMullan, Kate. *Baby Goose* (Pascal Lemaitre, Illus.).
Opie, Iona. *My Very First Mother Goose* (Rosemary Wells, Illus.).
Oxenbury, Helen. *Helen Oxenbury Nursery Collection.*
Reinhart, Matthew. *A Pop-Up Book of Nursery Rhymes.*
#Ruesga, Rita. *Cantaba la rana/The Frog Was Singing* (Soledad Sebastian, Illus.).
Sabuda, Robert. *The Moveable Mother Goose.*
Sanderson, Ruth. *Mother Goose and Friends.*
#Weber, Paige. *Classic Nursery Rhymes: Enchanting Rhymes and Songs from Around the World.*
#Wright, Danielle. *My Village: Rhymes from Around the World.*

Nursery Rhymes: Picture Books

(All are primary [P] level and also appropriate for preschool.)

Aylesworth, Jim. *The Completed Hickory Dickory Dock.*

Baker, Keith. *Big Fat Hen.*

Cabrera, Jane. *1, 2 Buckle My Shoe; Old Mother Hubbard.*

Cauley, Lorinda. *The Three Little Kittens.*

dePaola, Tomie. *The Comic Adventures of Old Mother Hubbard and Her Dog.*

Galdone, Paul. *Three Little Kittens.*

Hale, Sarah Joseph. *Mary Had a Little Lamb* (Bruce McMillan, Illus.) (see also edition illustrated by Salley Mavor).

Hines, Anna Grossnickel. *1, 2, Buckle My Shoe.*

Ivimey, John. *Three Blind Mice* (Paul Galdone, Illus.).

Janovitz, Marilyn. *Three Little Kittens.*

Jones, Carol. *Hickory Dickory Dock.*

Kirk, Daniel. *Humpty Dumpty.*

Martin, Sarah Catherine. *Old Mother Hubbard and Her Wonderful Dog* (James Marshall, Illus.).

Mavor, Salley. *Wee Willie Winkie.*

Miranda, Anne. *To Market, To Market.* (Janet Stevens, Illus.).

Muller, Robin. *Hickory Dickory Dock* (Suzanne Duranceau, Illus.).

Pinkney, Jerry. *The Three Little Kittens; Twinkle, Twinkle Little Star* (see also Leslie Harker edition).

Sendak, Maurice. *Hector Protector, and As I Went over the Water: Two Nursery Rhymes with Pictures.*

Spier, Peter. *London Bridge Is Falling Down.*

Stevens, Janet. *And the Dish Ran Away with the Spoon; To Market, to Market.*

Yoon, Salina. *One, Two, Buckle My Shoe: A Counting Nursery Rhyme.*

Fantasy and Science Fiction

(Literary Genre)

This chapter introduces you to the genres of fantasy and science fiction. In this chapter, we address the following questions in relation to these genres:

- What are fantasy and science fiction?
- What is the role of fantasy and science fiction in children's lives?
- How do we choose high-quality fantasy and science fiction?
- What are some common categories of fantasy and science fiction?
- How can we use fantasy and science fiction to meet the mandates of national standards as well as the needs of our diverse students?

It was almost midnight on Friday, July 20, 2007. Hundreds of people stood in line outside the Bunch of Grapes Bookstore in Martha's Vineyard, Massachusetts. Most were dressed like wizards, British school students, and Golden Snitches. Many sported black-rimmed glasses and a lightning bolt "scar" on their foreheads. As midnight approached, the crowds counted down the seconds to midnight, "Ten, nine, eight . . . *finally* . . . one." Shrieks and screams erupted as the door to the bookstore opened and people entered Diagon Alley, a recreated setting straight from the Harry Potter books. Costumed employees passed out copies of *Harry Potter and the Deathly Hallows*, the seventh and final book in the series.

As children received the books, joy and excitement erupted. "This is the best day of my life!" one nine year old was heard to exclaim to his mother. "Oh my god," exclaimed another child, holding the volume straight out, with a dazed look of awe, "I love you." Another girl flipped open her cell phone and began reading Chapter One aloud to her friend on the other end. (Brannen, 2007, p. 10)

This scene was repeated across America and around the world as young readers eagerly awaited the final installment of the *Harry Potter* series. Children dressed as wizards and witches from countries as diverse as England, Australia, Cambodia, Thailand, and India rushed to stores to reserve their copies. As a result of the frenzy, 3 million copies of *Harry Potter and the Deathly Hallows* were sold in 24 hours, making the book a resounding confirmation of the power of fiction to engage and excite young readers.

For many of us, falling in love with books and reading starts with fantasy such as the *Harry Potter* series. Fantasy and science fiction can create intense, deeply felt responses that lead to a lifelong passion for reading. Evidence for this strong affinity for fantasy can be seen on book lists of important and popular books in children's literature. For example, Breen, Fader, Odean, and Sutherland (2000) state that the most frequently listed genres are those from fantasy or science fiction; more than 30 (more if picture books are counted) of the books listed on the 100 Best Books for Children list (Silvey, 2004) are fantasy or science fiction. Best-seller lists (including those by the *New York Times* and *Publisher's Weekly* that chronicle the popularity of books for both children and adults) have consistently listed fantasy/science fiction books such as those in the *Harry Potter*, *Twilight*, and *Hunger Games* series in their top 10 titles.

What Are Fantasy and Science Fiction?

A fictional work is categorized as fantasy when it contains elements that are considered impossible in our world. These could be such disparate elements as talking animals, ghosts, transformations, immortal beings, or the presence of magic. The story might otherwise be totally believable, but the addition of just one magical element categorizes it as fantasy. Sometimes these stories begin in a realistic location and then move to a fantasy realm or an element of fantasy enters the everyday world. Or the story is set in a completely imagined fantasy world that has tenuous or nonexistent connections to our own.

A story is considered science fiction when the elements are based on scientific theory that is not yet possible according to current knowledge. In science fiction, someone may travel forward or backward in time, visit a neighboring planet, or encounter mysteries in the depths of the oceans. Science fiction presents a view of the world that one day might be possible given what we know about science and technology. Thus, discussions of the ethical and societal implications of scientific advancements are also often part of these stories.

Fantasy and science fiction books appeal to many readers because these stories often owe their characters, plots, settings, and themes to our heritage of traditional literature, mingling present-day concerns with roots from the past. Traditional stories have survived for a reason: they reflect our most basic human needs, hopes, and dreams, showing us heroes like ourselves who must survive perilous journeys, assume overwhelming responsibilities, and defeat malevolent foes. Themes of meaningful struggle and "truth" exist in their most undiluted form in traditional literature (Pierce, 1996, p. 180). Fantasy stories are natural inheritors of these traditional themes because they too explore these issues. This is not by accident.

Recurring elements and themes in fantasy and science fiction mirror those from traditional literature because they arise from the universal human psyche. Both traditional literature and fantasy/science fiction tell us that heroes are not born but are created. Choices have consequences. It is necessary to act if the world is to be changed, or saved, or renewed (Johansen, 2005, p. 14). It is important to strive for what is right. It is this connection to basic human needs that makes fantasy stories endure long after more realistic stories are deemed outdated.

Thus, you will see elements of traditional literature in many fantasy and science fiction stories. For example, Gail Levine's *Ella Enchanted* is based on Cinderella, whereas Kate DiCamillo's *The Tale of Despereaux* is based on the traditional plot of a seemingly insignificant hero who, through pluck and wit, saves a princess. The characters, settings, and themes of Greek mythology underlie the books of Rick Riordan's *Percy Jackson and the Olympians* series and Suzanne Collins's *The Hunger Games*. These elements, along with many others, add a deeper dimension to the stories, creating a magical world that parallels our own while also linking us to the literature of our past.

The Role of Fantasy and Science Fiction in Children's Lives

Susan Cooper (1996), author of *The Dark Is Rising*, described the importance of the respite fantasy provides readers in the following way:

> Refreshment, solace, excitement, relaxation, perhaps even inspiration: an escape from reality, and the escape, in turn, brings encouragement, leaving the reader fortified to cope with his own reality when he returns to it. (p. 43)

This is one of the most fundamental values of fantasy: escaping our own world; entering a different, exciting one; and then returning to this world renewed and refreshed.

However, some adults dismiss fantasy as irrelevant or "just pretend." They contend that children need to focus on learning about the real world, reading books that prepare them for this task so that they can successfully navigate the challenges of everyday life. Others object to children reading about imaginary characters such as witches, ghosts, and dragons, believing that children will be influenced to become involved in the occult or will become unable to leave the fantasy world and engage in everyday life.

Yet Lloyd Alexander (1988) tells us, "Imagining and fantasizing are both human functions—not only natural, but necessary" (p. 2). Fantasy pushes us out of our everyday world, helping us see beyond our current reality, and encouraging us to envision alternative ways of thinking and living. Fantasy and science fiction also allow us to mentally play. In order to remain healthy and balanced, our minds must be refreshed; the mind needs to play, the imagination to stretch (Johansen, 2005, p. 13). Fantasy helps us do this.

Additionally, fantasy and science fiction show children universal human truths, such as the importance of loyalty, as when Harry Potter's friends stand by his side while battling Voldemort or how to bravely face incredible danger as Kate DiCamillo's mouse character does in *The Tale of Despereaux*. They can learn that extremism in beliefs, whether from the light or the dark, may be the true cause of evil, as in Susan Cooper's *Dark Is Rising* series. Fantasy shows young readers that such knowledge is not easily gained but often evolves through struggles with external forces as well as through our own internal debates. Rather than being divorced from reality, fantasy sheds light on what is true and gets at the heart of what it means to be human, addressing basic human needs, themes, and issues that speak to us all.

Fantasy also helps empower readers. In the real world, children are allowed little control over their lives. However, in fantasy, the short, unbeautiful, socially awkward, and economically poor characters can triumph, accomplishing important things, such as vanquishing evil, conquering the universe, and achieving control over their destinies. Those normally perceived as unimportant are vital players (Pierce, 1996, pp. 181–182). Control in fantasy and science fiction always comes through persistence and working through obstacles, just as, it is hoped, it does in real life. Weakness is turned to strength, the small become great, and the greatest lessons of life are there to be learned (Ward, 2010). This is intoxicating stuff for young readers, creating hope that they too will grow up to slay the symbolic dragons in their lives.

With fantasy and science fiction, children are responding to something much deeper and older than themselves. They encounter heroic characters and vicariously experience marvelous adventures with them while projecting their own hopes and dreams on these imaginary journeys. The stories mirror the basic desires of all humans: the need for home and safety along with the thirst to break away and establish one's independence while still being able to return to that safe place. In good books from these genres, young readers are exposed to moral dilemmas, elegant language, and lofty ideals, all within exciting adventures.

Criteria for Evaluating Fantasy and Science Fiction

The criteria listed in Chapter 1 (Figure 1.3) are relevant to evaluating the literary quality of fiction. Figure 7.1 lists the additional criteria that are critical for selecting the best fantasy and science fiction for your students.

In fantasy and science fiction, the characters, setting, and plot development must be internally consistent or believable so that readers can easily *suspend disbelief* (i.e., forget that "this isn't real"). They can then become immersed in the story and accept its premises (e.g., animals can talk, dragons are real, or fairies live underground).

FIGURE 7.1 **Guidelines for Choosing Literature: Additional Criteria for Evaluating Fantasy and Science Fiction**

- Has the author made the story internally consistent?
- Is the setting believable?
- Are the characters believable and easy to relate to? Do the characters face significant challenges and develop insights into themselves as the result of facing those challenges?
- Are the fantasy elements logical and consistent throughout the story?
- Does the author remain consistent with established scientific truth while pushing the boundaries of what we accept as "fact" or "truth"? (science fiction)
- Are there important moral or universal truths underlying the fantasy or science fiction?

Characterization

One of the most important ways authors create believability is through the creation of convincing characters who make mistakes, rise to the occasion when faced with challenges, and have emotions that mirror our own. These characters do more than survive. The conflicts they face contribute to a deeper understanding of themselves. Readers then must be able to see ourselves in these characters to believe in them. This is particularly important in fantasy because sometimes the characters are not human.

Setting

A believable setting is also critical to good fantasy and science fiction. While someone is creating a fantasy world, that world should have a context that readers recognize and to which they can relate (Gauch, 1994, p. 164). Some authors achieve believability by describing the setting in minute detail. Madeleine L'Engle does this in *Wrinkle in Time* when she introduces the planet of Comazotz, where Meg's father is believed to be imprisoned. Initially, she sees nothing "strange or different or frightening" in the landscape until they approach a town that is laid out in "harsh, angular patterns" with houses that are exactly alike. The travelers discover that the Comazotz children do everything in rhythm: "All identical. Like the houses. Like the paths. Like the flowers." This detailed description brings the planet of Comazotz into sharp focus, helping readers believe in this fantasy world.

Some authors construct maps to enhance the believability of the world that they create in their stories. Tom Barron has detailed maps of "The Legendary Island of Fincayra" to help his readers connect to the characters' adventures in his *Seven Songs of Merlin* series. Ursula LeGuin created a complex map of Earthsea that is bordered by critical scenes and symbols for the *Wizard of Earthsea*.

Plot

Another important quality of good fantasy is internal plot consistency. Events must follow logically within the boundaries of the plotlines set forth by the author. For example, animals cannot suddenly start talking when they have been mute up to that point in the story. A character cannot read minds or become invisible unless that ability has been previously explained and confirmed. We must be able to believe completely in the world the author has created to become immersed in the fantasy. Internal story consistency is the heart of this believability.

Fantasy plots must also be true by exploring important questions about the human psyche. Memorable fantasy explores the important questions about life: the "key elements of what it means to be human, vulnerable, struggling, searching, making choices, and wholly alive" (Barron, 2012, p. 89).

 # Categorizing Fantasy and Science Fiction

This section describes some of the best books in fantasy and science fiction that are not only of high literary quality but also interesting to children and young adolescent readers. Many of the stories could be categorized in more than one way. The categories are provided as a starting point in learning the possible types of fantasy that can help children develop an appreciation for this genre.

Literary Fairy Tales: Hans Christian Andersen

Literary fairy tales are those that employ many of the themes, motifs, character prototypes, and other elements of traditional literature but are written by a specific author. One of the best-known authors of these stories is Danish writer Hans Christian Andersen, often considered the "father of the modern fairy tale." Andersen wrote gentle, often sad tales with messages meant for adults as well as children. Many reflect the miseries of his own life as a misfit, rejected by society for his odd looks and behavior, winning acclaim only later in life. Some of Andersen's most famous tales include *The Little Mermaid*, *The Ugly Duckling*, *The Emperor's New Clothes*, *The Snow Queen*, and *Thumbelina*. Artists who employ diverse artistic styles to evoke different responses from readers have created beautifully illustrated picture books of Andersen's fairy tales. A sampling of these books are included in the lists at the end of this chapter.

Fantasy Novels Based on Traditional Literature

Some authors expand stories from traditional literature into full-length fantasy novels. These novels use plots, motifs, themes, and characters from traditional stories such as *Cinderella* or *Beauty and the Beast* but go far beyond them to explore some of the psychological issues and character motivations not typically addressed in the short traditional tales.

Cinderella is a particularly popular tale for this type of novel. Gail Carson Levine explores the question of why Cinderella meekly obeyed her stepmother in *Ella Enchanted*. *Glass Slipper, Gold Sandal: A Worldwide Cinderella* (Fleischman) features threads from cultural variants of the *Cinderella* story that are woven into an original cohesive novel. Each culture contributes unique elements so that Cinderella receives a sarong made of gold (Indonesia), diamond anklets (India), and glass slippers (France).

Robin McKinley's *Beauty: A Retelling of the Story of Beauty and the Beast* and *Rose Daughter* go beyond the traditional tale of *Beauty and the Beast* to delve into the complex relationship between a young girl and her seemingly abhorrent suitor. Donna Jo Napoli's *Zel* presents the story of *Rapunzel* as a tale of an overzealous mother who wants only to protect her daughter.

Other authors take elements from traditional literature and weave them into original stories that use fairy tale characters in new settings or make passing references to recognizable plots from traditional literature. For example, in *Where the Mountain Meets the Moon*, Grace Lin draws on Chinese folktales to craft an enchanting story of Minli, a poor peasant girl who sets out to find the Old Man of the Moon so as to bring good fortune to her family. Adam Gidwitz incorporates elements from the Grimm fairy tales, nursery rhymes, and other traditional literature to create a world where Jack and Jill, accompanied by an enchanted frog, embark on a quest to find the Seeing Glass *In a Glass Grimmly*. An omniscient narrator comments on the action and interjects warnings about dark events that will occur as the story unfolds.

Animal and Toy Fantasy

Stories about animals and toys that talk are among the best-loved fantasy tales and are excellent stories for introducing children to this genre. Young children often think that their pets and toys can talk and thus easily accept the fantasy elements in these stories.

Beatrix Potter's delightful adventure stories of Peter Rabbit, written in the early 1900s, are examples of books in which the world is real but the animals are fantastical. Kenneth Grahame's *Wind in the Willows*, the story of Toad, who gets into one scrape after another in the company of his friends Ratty, Badger, and Mole, also endures. These classic fantasies continue to delight many children and are considered important works in our literary heritage.

Mice are often the protagonists in animal fantasy stories. Ralph Mouse in Beverly Cleary's *Mouse and the Motorcycle*, *Runaway Ralph*, and *Ralph S. Mouse* befriends Ryan, a boy who gives him a toy motorcycle. Kate DiCamillo's *The Tale of Despereaux* is ostensibly a story about a very small mouse with very large ears and his quest for a princess. However, a closer reading of this book reveals the exploration of fundamental life questions, such as the difference between the light (good) and the dark (evil), love, honor, and perseverance. Figure 7.2 shows a student's response to this book and *The Miraculous Journey of Edward Tulane*, another book by DiCamillo.

FIGURE 7.2   **A Second Grade Student Compares *The Tale of Despereaux* and *The Miraculous Journey of Edward Tulane*, both by Kate Dicamillo**

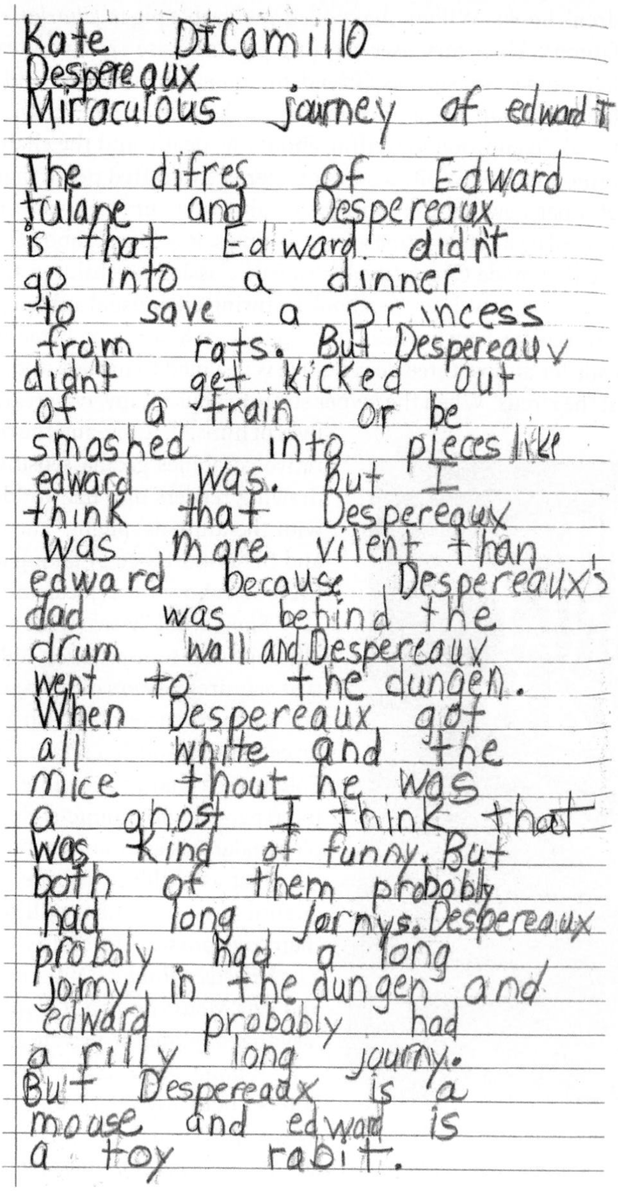

> Kate DiCamillo
> Despereaux
> Miraculous journey of edward t
>
> The difres of Edward tulane and Despereaux is that Edward didn't go into a dinner to save a princess from rats. But Despereauv didn't get kicked out of a train or be smashed into pieces like edward was. But I think that Despereaux was more vilent than edward because Despereaux's dad was behind the drum wall and Despereauv went to the dungen. When Despereaux got all white and the mice thout he was a ghost I think that was kind of funny. But both of them probobly had long Jornys. Despereaux probly had a long Jomy in the dungen and edward probably had a rilly long journy. But Despereadx is a mouse and edward is a toy rabit.

The Cheshire Cheese Cat: A Dickens of a Tale (Deedy) combines history and fantasy in an engaging story of a cat in Victorian London who makes a bargain with the mice who reside in the Cheshire Cheese Inn: he will not eat them as long as they provide him with the delicious cheese for which the inn is named. Their adventures include rescuing a wounded raven, escaping a cruel tomcat, and helping Mr. Charles Dickens write the first line of his new novel, *A Tale of Two Cities*. Well-crafted language and subtle references to Dickens's work are hallmarks of this book.

You might not think that rats would be appealing protagonists. However, *Mrs. Frisby and the Rats of NIMH* (O'Brien) has enchanted generations of young readers. Older children, particularly boys who enjoyed simple stories about rats and mice, often appreciate Brian Jacques's *Redwall*, an epic adventure series featuring rats, mice, and other creatures that inhabit Redwall Abbey and the surrounding Mossflower Woods.

Pigs are another example of an animal that appears as the central character in many children's books. Wilbur, the spoiled yet lovable pig in *Charlotte's Web* (White), is probably the most famous. This story uses a young pig and wise spider to teach us about important qualities of human nature, such as "friendship on earth, affection and protection, adventure and miracle, life and death, trust and treachery, pleasure and pain, and the passing of time" (Welty, 1952, p. 49). In addition to writing about life, death, and the changing of seasons in such a simple yet profound way, White also wrote perfectly crafted prose that captures the rhythmic movements of a barn swing, the sensory delights of a summer's day, and the comical collection of trash stowed by a rat, to name a few examples. It is this combination of human truths and superb writing that made *Charlotte's Web* a true classic that children should know.

A sensitively written book featuring an unusual animal protagonist is *The One and Only Ivan* (Applegate). Ivan has been the "Ape at Exit 8" and star attraction at the Big Top Mall and Video Arcade for almost three decades. He is resigned to his fate until Ruby, a baby elephant, comes to live at the circus. When the owner starts to abuse Ruby, Ivan realizes that it is up to him to change the lives of himself, Ruby, and the other animals. Ivan's first-person narrative combines gorilla sensitivities with humanlike observations, drawing readers into his world and compelling them to empathize with the animals' plight. Themes of friendship, the power of love, and the importance of taking action in the face of injustice elevate this book above the typical animal story.

Flora and Ulysses (DiCamillo) is another unusual animal tale, although the tone is much lighter than *Ivan*. Ulysses is a squirrel that acquires powers of strength, flight, and the ability to write poetry after an encounter with a vacuum cleaner. Flora is a girl who loves comics and is certain that tragedy is around every corner. Following a chance encounter, the two become friends. A narrative interspersed with comic-style graphic sequences and clever wordplay make this a humorous book that appeals to a wide audience.

Just as children ascribe pets and other animals with human qualities, so too are they willing to suspend disbelief and think that their toys possess the ability to talk and have exciting adventures. *The Velveteen Rabbit* (Williams), *The Castle in the Attic* (Winthrop), and *The Mouse and His Child* (Hoban) are classic examples of fantasy that explore the private lives of playthings.

Winnie the Pooh (Milne) stories are among the best-loved books about toy characters. Each chapter features an adventure in which the characters of Pooh ("a bear of little brain"), Eeyore (a gloomy donkey), Owl, Piglet, Rabbit, Kanga, and Roo get into comical predicaments in the 100 Acre Wood. *Return to Hundred Acre Wood* (Benedictus) is a contemporary sequel that continues

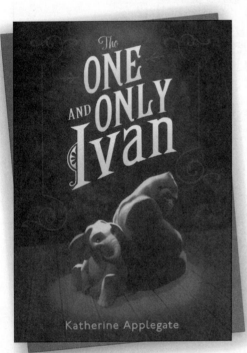

An unusual friendship between a gorilla, a baby elephant, and a dog draws readers into *The One and Only Ivan* by Katherine Applegate.

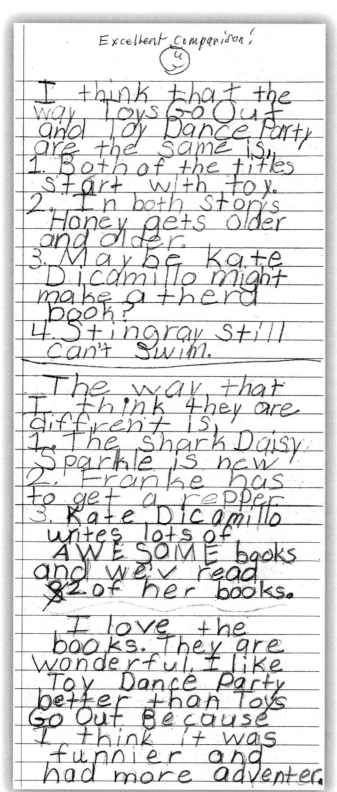

Excellent Comparison!

I think that the way Toys Go Out and Toy Dance Party are the same is,
1. Both of the titles start with toy.
2. In both storys Honey gets older and older.
3. Maybe Kate Dicamillo might make a therd book?
4. Stingray still can't swim.

The way that I think they are diffrent is,
1. The shark Daisy Sparkle is new!
2. Franke has to get a repper.
3. Kate Dicamillo writes lots of AWESOME books and we'v read 82 of her books.

I love the books. They are wonderful, I like Toy Dance Party better than Toys Go Out Because I think it was funnier and had more adventer.

A second grade child compares and contrasts *Toys Go Out* and its sequel *Toy Dance Party* by Emily Jenkins.

the characters' adventures. Kate DiCamillo has created another memorable toy character in *The Miraculous Journey of Edward Tulane*, and Emily Jenkins chronicles the delightful adventures and misadventures of three toys in *Toys Go Out: Being the Misadventures of a Knowledgeable Stingray, a Toughy Little Buffalo, and Someone Called Plastic*.

Ghosts and the Supernatural

Stories from traditional literature that focus on ghosts and other supernatural beings are often the recipients of children's choice awards. They also consistently are ranked near the top in studies of children's favorite books. These stories are popular likely because they seem to satisfy children's curiosity about the unknown without the risk of serious danger or psychological trauma. Readers know that the story's protagonist will triumph, lessening the fear factor.

Mary Downing Hahn is one of the best-known writers of ghost stories for middle-grade children. *Wait till Helen Comes* tells of a ghost named Helen, who waits by a pond to drown children who play with her. In *Deep and Dark and Dangerous* (Hahn), 13-year-old Ali spends time with her aunt in the Maine summerhouse where she meets a strange girl who keeps referring to Teresa, who died under mysterious circumstances many years ago.

Neil Gaiman is also known for writing stories about ghosts and the supernatural, although his work typically appeals to an older audience. *The Graveyard Book* is an inventive, engrossing story of a toddler whose family is murdered. He escapes and toddles into a graveyard where the ghostly inhabitants raise him among the gravestones and monuments. Gaiman blends action, history, humor, horror, and humanity into a tale that attracts children ready for something different. The supernatural takes an unusual twist in *Coraline*, also by Gaiman. In this chilling story, a bored, restless young girl discovers a bricked-up door in her London flat that seems to go nowhere. Finding a key, she unlocks the door, discovering a long, dark hallway that leads to an alternative reality in which a witch mother tries to keep her prisoner.

Many supernatural stories for younger children are humorous, thus lessening the frightening aspect. *Billy Bones: Tales from the Secret Closet* by Christopher Lincoln features a skeleton who lives in a closet in High Manners Manor and keeps the secrets of the manor's unscrupulous occupants. In contrast, *Gossamer* (Lowry) is a gentler story that comments on the healing power of dreams and speculates about the fantasy creatures who bestow them. Like *Gossamer, The Dream Stealer* (Fleischman) is about a dream-stealing creature, this time one who lassos sleepers' nightmares.

Several excellent books from diverse voices provide a unique cultural perspective on the classic ghost story. African American author Virginia Hamilton's *Sweet Whispers, Brother Rush* tells the haunting, engrossing story of 14-year-old Tree, who cares for her sick brother while her mom works. Although readers are often drawn into this book by the supernatural elements, the themes of family unity and finding one's identity lift this book above the typical ghost story. Joseph Bruchac uses traditional Native American ghost tales for the basis of *Skeleton Man, The Dark Pond*, and *Whisper in the Dark*. Tim Tingle also uses a Native American voice for his protagonist in *How I Became a Ghost: A Choctaw Trail of Tears Story*.

Children and Magic

Many fantasy books feature characters that acquire magical powers, come to possess a magical object, or encounter magical beings they assist. These situations typically result in adventures that young readers find irresistible. You may remember books such as *Half Magic, Seven Day Magic*, and *Magic by the Lake* (all by Eager), in which children find magical charms that launch them on exciting adventures. *The Chocolate Touch* (Catling) (in which everything that touches a boy's lips turns to chocolate) and *Chocolate Fever* (Smith) (in which a boy who eats nothing but chocolate breaks out in a mysterious rash) are also entertaining books with magical elements that teachers have long used as read-alouds for drawing children into fantasy.

Some books of this type feature the child protagonist as companion/apprentice to a wizard, witch, or other magical character. For example, in *The Magic Thief* (Prineas), Conn becomes a wizard's apprentice but must find his own "locus magicalicus stone" in order to continue his wizarding studies. Conn's voice is lively and engaging, with exactly the right blend of street smarts and naïveté, making him an endearing character. In other books, it is the child protagonist who possesses magical qualities, such as Mibs in *Savvy* (Law), who is part of a special family in which each person possesses a "savvy"—a special supernatural power that appears at age 13. Mibs is a likable character who matures, learns to appreciate all kinds of people, and discovers that happiness is of one's own making. The sequel, *Scumble* (Law), focuses on Mibs's cousin Milo, who also has difficulties finding his own savvy.

The most famous books in which the young protagonist possesses magical powers are J. K. Rowling's *Harry Potter* books. These stories introduce readers to a magical world of wizards, spells, and wild adventures, all set in a school of magic. Significant issues, such as the nature of heroism, the importance of friendship, the ambiguity involved in moral choices, and the sting of treachery, are explored within the context of a school where students study the care of magical beasts, spell casting, the history of magic, and fortune-telling instead of algebraic equations and Shakespeare. Selling well over 500 million copies and translated into over 60 languages, the series is probably the most popular children's book of the 20th century and, so far, into the 21st.

One reason the books are so popular is because they are filled with humor. Harry and Ron's ill-fated trip to school in a flying car, Hagrid's clumsy efforts to raise a baby dragon, the fumbling Dursleys' attempts to flee the barrage of letters from the wizard community, and a huge troll who comes out of the girl's bathroom are examples of situations that are full of slapstick humor. Abundant wordplay provides more subtle humor for sophisticated readers. All this fun is juxtaposed with scenes of despair, horror, and intense battles against terrifying evil. Thus, the books are genuinely funny and consistently scary, a combination that many readers find irresistible.

It is also likely that the books are popular because Harry is a character with whom we can identify and find something of ourselves. Harry is both a typical adolescent and an epic hero: brutally honest, immensely courageous, and loyal to his friends. He is who we are (and would also like to be), and he is also empowered—qualities that are immensely satisfying to readers.

Alternative Worlds

Many fantasy stories begin in the real world and then quickly move into a new world where links to reality still exist, but the alternative world features implausible characters or events that could not happen in the world as we know it. Thus, when Dorothy is blown away to Oz in the *Wonderful Wizard of Oz* (Baum), she keeps her own personality but meets a talking scarecrow, a cowardly lion, an evil witch, and other magical characters. Alice, in *Alice's Adventures in Wonderland* (Carroll), also encounters an array of bizarre characters in her adventures through Wonderland. Both these classic stories have been reprinted with updated illustrations, appealing formats (including an e-book), and abbreviated story lines to heighten their appeal to contemporary children. For example, in *The Wonderful Wizard of Oz: A Commemorative Pop-Up* (Sabuda), a cyclone actually spins, red poppies seductively wave in the field, and special glasses lead to a hidden message. Baum's text is retold in abridged fashion through minibooks tucked into each page. Robert Sabuda also created intricate three-dimensional images for *Alice's Adventures in Wonderland: A Pop-Up Adaptation*.

The *Chronicles of Narnia* (Lewis) is a classic series that has long engaged readers who love to imagine that an alternative world lies right inside their house. Seven volumes chronicle the adventures of four children who are transported to the magical land of Narnia, where fauns, kings, talking beavers, and an evil Snow Queen reside. Magic helps solve dilemmas, and a fearsome yet gentle lion-God presides over all. In addition to many Christian themes, the *Narnia* series uses motifs, characters, and themes from mythology and fairy tales.

Some readers enjoy identifying these allusions, believing that they enhance their enjoyment of the stories. Others find the Christian references in Lewis' books, inappropriate and "morally loathsome" (Pullman, 1998). Even Lewis's friend J. R. R. Tolkien disliked the *Narnia* books, calling them "outside the range of my sympathy" due to the eclectic mythological references and the motif of time travel between our world and an imaginary realm (Miller, 2008). Young readers are not bothered by these debates but simply enjoy the adventures in which children enter an imaginary kingdom, solve problems, and conquer evil forces.

Younger children are often enchanted with miniature magical worlds. Anyone who has ever wondered where an errant button or postage stamp has gone will appreciate *The Borrowers* (Norton), the story of a miniature family living under the floorboards of an English country house and taking small items from the "human beans" that live there. If one of the Borrowers is seen, disaster erupts. Eventually, the family is "seen" and must flee their home. This event leads to many adventures, chronicled in such sequels as *The Borrowers Afield*, *The Borrowers Afloat*, and others. *The Littles* (Peterson) is another series about a miniature family living among humans.

In some stories of this type, children are on a journey in the real world and then encounter an alternative, magical one through a shipwreck or other mishap. For example, in *The Lost Island of Tamarind* (Aguiar), Maya, Simon, and baby Penny find themselves shipwrecked on an island inhabited with pirates, jungle beasts, mysterious glowing stones, soldiers fighting a war, giants, mermaids, and other magical elements. The children must survive their encounters with all these elements to become reconciled with their parents. September, a girl in Omaha, Nebraska, who longs for adventure, is whisked away to Fairyland by a Green Wind and a Leopard in *The Girl Who Circumnavigated Fairyland in a Ship of Her Own Making* (Valente). Once in this new world, September is sent on a quest by the evil Marquess. Her encounters with various unusual creatures as her journey proceeds, along with beautifully written prose, lead to comparisons of this book to *Alice in Wonderland* and the *Wizard of Oz*. Sequels continue September's adventures.

Fantastic Adventures

Children love exaggeration and over-the-top situations. Thus, they enjoy adventurous fantasy that features memorable characters, such as *Pippi Longstocking* (Lindgren), *Mary Poppins* (Travers), and *Peter Pan* (Barrie). Often, interactions between typical children and these characters lead to marvelous, exciting adventures.

One of the best-loved writers of fantasy involving larger-than-life characters and outlandish adventures is Roald Dahl. Dahl's *Charlie and the Chocolate Factory*, with its sly humor and inventive plot, is one of the most popular books in children's fantasy. Some adults, however, have criticized the book, calling it, in one case, "one of the most tasteless books ever written for children that leaves us poorly nourished with our taste dulled for better fare" (Cameron, 1972). Others rebuked Dahl for calling his factory workers "Ooompa Loompas" and characterizing them as black pygmies. (These references have been deleted in later editions.) Nevertheless, its popularity with children has made the book an enduring classic. Other popular books by Dahl include *James and the Giant Peach*, which describes a boy's travels inside a giant peach accompanied by a group of oversize insects, and *The BFG* (Big Friendly Giant), in which a giant kidnaps a young girl and takes her to Giant County, where "human beans" are the food supply.

Contemporary author Cornelia Funke creates magical, adventurous worlds full of intriguing characters. *The Inkworld Trilogy* (Funke) chronicles the adventures of Maggie Folchart, who has the ability to read herself into a book and bring book characters into the real world. In Funke's *Dragon Rider*, homeless and orphaned Ben becomes the companion of Firedrake, a dragon who is embarking on a dangerous journey to the Rim of Heaven. Although *Dragon Rider* is lengthy with a wide array of characters, middle-grade children who are ready for a challenge enjoy the adventures and sympathize with the dragon, who wants only to fulfill his destiny.

The theme of an orphan left alone to face the challenges of the world is a common theme in fantasy adventure stories. One of the most popular series of this type is *Lemony Snicket's A Series of Unfortunate Events*. This 13-book series, written by Snicket (a pseudonym for writer Daniel Handler), features the adventures of the three Baudelaire orphans. Their nemesis is their uncle, Count Olaf, who dons various disguises to steal the children's fortune. Each sibling has a skill that helps the trio elude their uncle and others out to harm them: one invents things, another discovers new information from books to solve their dilemmas, and the third has especially sharp teeth. The author also functions as a character in that he observes the events and records the Baudelaires' exploits. His commentary provides some comic relief but is also often melancholy, as he constantly warns readers that they might not want to continue reading a book with such dark events. *Splendors and Glooms* (Schlitz) also features orphans left to make their way in a dark world populated with puppets, a manipulative witch, and a malevolent villain. This book is full of suspense and adventure that is interwoven with nuanced explorations of good and evil.

In many contemporary fantasy stories, the children are not orphans but have adventures largely independent of adult intervention. *The Spiderwick Chronicles* (Black and DiTerlizzi) feature the adventures of the three Grace children,

The Mysterious Benedict Society by Trenton Lee Stewart is a popular fantasy series full of villains, unexpected plot, twists and thrilling adventures.

who discover a Field Guide that introduces them to a world of fairies, Bogarts, elves, and other fantastic creatures. A second series, *Beyond the Spiderwick Chronicles*, features new characters whose adventures occur in Florida. The four protagonists in *The Mysterious Benedict Society* (Stewart) are gifted children who are selected by the eccentric Mr. Benedict for an important mission: to infiltrate the Learning Institute for the Very Enlightened, which broadcast messages in order to control the minds of the world's citizens. The children's only chance to defeat the evil forces is to enter the institute and contribute their own unique talents to defeat the evil forces.

Girl power is the focus of the adventures in *Kiki Strike: Inside the Shadow City* (Miller). Kiki, a mysterious new student at Atlanta School, is part Pippi Longstocking, part Russian princess, and part mystery girl. She recruits "The Irregulars," a team of other girls with special skills, such as computer hacking, forging, and lockpicking. This story is smart and sophisticated while avoiding adult content, making it very appropriate for middle school readers, especially girls. The adventures of Kiki and the Irregulars continue in *Kiki Strike: The Empress's Tomb* and *Kikki Strike: The Darkness Dwellers*.

Time Travel Fantasy

Who has not wanted to travel back in time to see what it was really like or travel forward in time to get a glimpse of the future? In addition to exciting adventures, time travel stories often focus on character transformation in which problems or situations are solved by characters who move between the present and a past or future time. These stories also challenge our assumptions about time, suggesting that time might be more fluid and malleable than we commonly think.

Although most characters in time travel fantasies usually jump forward or back in time, in *Tuck Everlasting* (Babbitt) the characters are eternally trapped in the present. This intriguing story centers on young Winnie, who discovers a family that cannot die because they drank from a magical spring that gives everlasting life. Winnie's ultimate choice leads to heated debate among readers, making it an excellent book for introducing middle-grade students to fantasy. Figure 7.3 shows one student's response to this book.

The *Magic Tree House* (Osborne) and *Time Warp Trio* (Scieszka) series books are excellent for drawing younger readers into time travel fantasy. The *Magic Tree House* series features Jack and

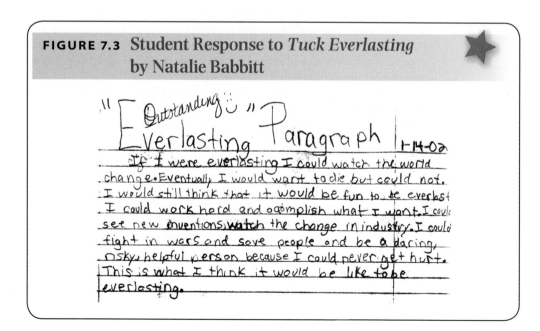

FIGURE 7.3 **Student Response to *Tuck Everlasting* by Natalie Babbitt**

"[Outstanding ☺]" **Everlasting Paragraph** 1-14-02

If I were everlasting I could watch the world change. Eventually, I would want to die but could not. I would still think that it would be fun to be everlast. I could work hard and accomplish what I want. I could see new inventions, watch the change in industry. I could fight in wars and save people and be a daring, risky, helpful person because I could never get hurt. This is what I think it would be like to be everlasting.

Annie, siblings who use a magic tree house to travel back to ancient Egypt, the Ice Age, the Middle Ages, Pompeii, and other significant historical eras. Three boys have wonderfully exciting adventures traveling through time and space in the *Time Warp Trio* series. After accidentally activating "The Book," a strange blue book given to one boy by his magician uncle, the boys are transported to various historical time periods. Dastardly villains, tongue-in-cheek humor, wisecracking wordplay, and swashbuckling action make this series particularly appealing to boys.

When You Reach Me (Stead) is a fascinating time travel fantasy for middle-grade readers. Although the protagonist does not travel in time, she realizes that another character does. Twelve-year-old Miranda discovers mysterious notes from someone who implies that he or she can see events that have not yet happened. The mystery is not solved until the story's unexpected conclusion. Once they know the ending, readers of this book are often motivated to go back and reread it to see how all the pieces fit together.

Heroic Fantasy

Sometimes termed "high fantasy," heroic fantasy usually involves courageous young protagonists who search for their identity as they battle self-doubt along with a threatening external evil. Often, the story takes place in an alternative world that mirrors our own but features landscapes and magical creatures created entirely from the author's imagination. Frequently, the main character has a quest to fulfill or must face challenges that can be completed only through a combination of physical prowess and inner strength with occasional assistance from magical forces. Heroic fantasy stories usually feature characters that must make life-changing decisions based on important truths, such as courage, the importance of friendship and loyalty, the necessity to fight evil forces, and the value of doing the right thing. The tone is typically serious as characters battle evil, pursue dangerous quests, and agonize over difficult decisions.

This type of story is known for using many of the traditional plot motifs you have probably encountered in your previous experiences with literature. For example, a story might follow a hero as a child who is growing up ignorant of his or her real identity embarks on a journey to discover who he or she really is. Or the hero initiates an important quest to fight evil. Helpers often appear, taking the shape of animals, wise mentors, friends, or a magical force. Sometimes, the hero returns home, typically successful in his or her quest but often at great cost: significant sacrifice, loss of a normal life, or loss of special powers (O'Keefe, 2004, p. 164). It is the recognition of one's own struggles, the vicarious thrill of going on dangerous quests from the safety of one's own bedroom, and make-believe worlds that tease and intrigue one's imagination that make heroic fantasy appealing to many readers.

Arguably the most highly regarded fantasies of this type are *The Hobbit* and *The Lord of the Rings* by J. R. R. Tolkien. Many believe that Tolkien's work lifted the quality of children's fantasy to new levels of inventiveness and complexity. Hobbits (Tolkien's invention) are small people who live in a pastoral society where virtues such as honor, loyalty, and valor underlie all codes for behavior. *The Lord of the Rings* was intended as a sequel to *The Hobbit*, but the story became larger and darker in themes and events, making it ultimately a book for older readers, although young adolescents who love *The Hobbit* often become ardent fans of the sequel. In *The Lord of the Rings*, themes are subtler and more complex; the plots are multilayered, ironic, and richly textured; and characters are thoroughly developed with complex personalities (Johansen, 2005, p. 129).

Tolkien's impact on fantasy was not only the telling of a complex, emotionally powerful story. He also created a world that logically and believably incorporated myth, legend, and fairy tale, resulting in a grand epic that both enthralled readers and captured their imaginations. After Tolkien, fully described secondary worlds became more common in children's fantasy, and serious concerns are more frequently part of those worlds. Stories where characters and events from mythology, legend, and other traditional stories enter the "real" world, entwining fantasy and reality, became popular (Johansen, 2005, p. 134). Writers such as Lloyd Alexander, Susan Cooper, and others discussed in this section have been greatly influenced by the themes, characters, settings, and epic plots created by Tolkien.

Percy Jackson and the Olympians (Riordan) is a series based on Greek mythology that works well for enticing middle-grade readers to read heroic fantasy. In book 1, *The Lightning Thief*, Young Percy Jackson (diagnosed with attention-deficit/hyperactivity disorder and dyslexia) discovers that he is the son of Poseidon, god of the sea. Contemporary dialogue infuses the mythology with humor, making these books fun as well as exciting. Riordan's second series is *The Kane Chronicles* (first title: *The Red Pyramid*), in which two children battle figures from Egyptian mythology, eventually learning that they are themselves descended from the gods.

A band of young people, led by Taran (an assistant pig keeper who is really a prince), pursue quests and fight evil in *The Chronicles of Prydain* (Alexander). Several books describe their adventures, culminating in *The High King*, in which the evil forces are finally vanquished. Taran is a wonderful hero for young readers: reckless and impulsive yet courageous, gentle, and eventually wise. The plots of these books feature plenty of action and humor, making them interesting and accessible to a variety of readers, particularly boys.

Will, in *The Dark Is Rising* (Cooper) and its sequels, must battle evil forces that appear in the world. On his 11th birthday, Will learns that he is the youngest of the Old Ones, immortal guardians of the light through the ages. Cooper's books have complex plots with rich connections to British mythology and folklore. Her characters are always real children caught up in supernatural conflicts that test every ounce of their ingenuity and resourcefulness. At the same time, they grow in self-understanding and knowledge of the importance of doing the right thing. These qualities make the books most appropriate for older readers who have had some experience with fantasy.

Robin McKinley writes exciting quest stories in which young women play a central role. McKinley's *The Blue Sword* is set in Damar, an imaginary kingdom of hills and deserts where orphan girl Harry is drawn to the concerns of the Hillfolk and joins them in battle against supernatural invaders. McKinley's *The Hero and the Crown* is a prequel that chronicles Lady Aerin's confrontation with the dragon Maur, an incident that leaves her "not quite mortal."

Both of McKinley's books are thoughtfully written with satisfying plots that demand careful reading. Her heroines are complex individuals who display courage and resourcefulness while also battling personal doubts, making them excellent role models for young women.

Ursula K. Le Guin created a complex imaginary world in *The Wizard of Earthsea*. In this classic tale, young Ged is sent to the island of Roke to become a mage (wizard). When he attempts a spell beyond his skills, he releases an evil gebbeth, or shadow, destined to destroy the world of Earthsea. The concept of shadow is central to this book, as is much of Le Guin's other work. The subsequent books in the *Earthsea* cycle continue Ged's adventures as he grows into a wise, even-tempered mage.

Some authors have taken the themes, events, and ideas from the Arthurian stories and reimagined them, retaining the essence of the original traditional tales while adding new details and perspectives. Tom Barron goes far beyond the traditional King Arthur and Merlin tales in his *The Lost Years of Merlin* epic to explore the early influences that make Merlin the revered wizard he becomes. In *The Seven Songs of Merlin*, *The Fires of Merlin*, and *The Mirror of Merlin* (Barron) and other volumes, Merlin has many adventures, discovering more about himself as well as his destiny as a wizard. In contrast, *Here Lies Arthur* (Reeve) is a powerfully nuanced darker reworking of the Arthurian legends. Reeve's story strips Merlin of his magical powers and portrays him as merely a storyteller with only the power to shape Arthur's rather unremarkable exploits and crude behaviors into legend. Because the heroism and magic of the Arthur stories are no longer evident, this is a novel best appreciated by older middle school students.

The Inheritance Cycle (written by Christopher Paolini when he was 15 years old) includes *Eragon, Eldest,* and *Brisingr.* Set in the fictional world of Alagesia, the books focus on young Eragon and his dragon Saphira. The *Inheritance Cycle* novels are lengthy, with many characters, difficult place-names, and imaginary languages, making them a challenging read even for experienced fantasy readers. Maps and language guides in the later books help readers keep everything straight.

Philip Pullman is considered one of the finest writers of heroic quest fantasy, although he would likely deny the accolade. He has created an intriguing series of alternative worlds and complex, engrossing plots in the *His Dark Materials* trilogy. Inspired by Milton's *Paradise Lost,* Pullman explores issues of spirituality and religion, loss of innocence, the concept of duality in personality, and the nature of good and evil in *The Golden Compass, The Subtle Knife,* and *The Amber Spyglass.* The books feature two inextricably connected plots: a world in peril and two children who are maturing so that they can face an important destiny. A cosmic battle is about to explode, and the children have a pivotal role in ultimately saving Pullman's imagined world. Underlying the story is Pullman's belief that the organized church is a virtual dictatorship that monitors thinking and subverts free will. Only its destruction will free us to become fully conscious and human. This perspective makes the books challenging to read as well as highly controversial.

Science Fiction: Future Worlds

The question of what our world will be like in the future has long intrigued devotees of science fiction. Many novels explore this concept, describing societies in which technology, government control, and societal problems have progressed beyond what we believe is possible. In these worlds, writers often speculate about which essential human qualities will be retained and which will be discarded in response to scientific advancement. These are issues that we hope mature readers will consider so that they will not lose important fundamental values, such as freedom, individuality, love, and empathy, in the face of technological advancement. Exploring these "what ifs" in books leads not only to interesting predictions of the future but possibly, to new perspectives on our current world.

A classic book that focuses on a future utopian society is *The Giver* by Lois Lowry. In Lowry's vision of the future, everything is under control and equal; "sameness" is the rule. Eventually, the protagonist Jonah—and readers—realize that the setting illustrates a dystopia, not a utopia, and he decides to escape so that the people can live with memories again.

Lowry addresses many important themes in this story. One is the importance of connecting meaningfully to other people. Others include the importance of choice—the temptation to succumb to security and sameness versus the risks involved in freedom and diversity—and the importance of individual versus collective good. The book is disquieting yet hopeful, and it typically generates intense discussion.

Lowry's *Gathering Blue* is not intended as a sequel to *The Giver* but rather is a companion book. *Messenger* unites characters from *The Giver* and *Gathering Blue* and explores yet another utopian/dystopian society. This community is based on honesty and openness to strangers, particularly those with disabilities. However, as the story begins, malevolent changes are occurring. The book's conclusion is shocking and memorable, leaving readers with many questions. *Son* completes the saga, returning to *The Giver* to introduce a new character who appears originally in this book but whose destiny intertwines with those in the subsequent books. The concepts of utopia gone wrong and the power of one individual to change the world are issues that young readers will ponder after reading Lowry's work.

Suzanne Collins also portrays a disturbing view of the future in *The Hunger Games*. The protagonist is Katniss, who lives in what remains of the United States following a war between the "capital" and various districts of the country. As part of the districts' surrender terms, each is required to send one boy and one girl to the "Hunger Games," an annual televised event controlled by sadistic game masters. However, the "catch" is that only one contestant survives. The book explores themes such as self-interest versus altruism, survival versus sacrifice, intelligence, and cruelty. However, it is the character of Katniss—her courage, intelligence, determination, and humanity—that resonates with readers long after the book is finished. Mature themes and sometimes brutal scenes make this a book appropriate for sophisticated middle school readers. Katniss's story continues in *Catching Fire* and *Mockingjay* (Collins).

Are you one of the younger children in your family? In the *Among the Hidden* (Haddix) series, you would be kept out of sight because families are allowed only two children in this futuristic authoritarian world. Issues of free will, tyranny, rebellion, the invasion of privacy, and the nature of government are skillfully intertwined with adventure and suspense, making this series popular with middle school readers.

Several other books focus on the future and speculate about which of our societal values will be retained, altered, or abandoned. For example, Nancy Farmer's *The House of the Scorpion* explores the ethics of cloning and how that scientific breakthrough affects our definition of what is human. Farmer's *The Ear, the Eye and the Arm*, set in 2194 Zimbabwe, describes a society that is highly technological. Three children escape from their highly protected enclave, only to be kidnapped and forced to work in a toxic waste dump. *Unwind* (Shusterman) presents a dystopian future in which children before the age of 13 cannot be aborted. However, between the ages of 13 and 18, children can be aborted by their parents as long as their lives do not technically end. The process is called "unwinding" and ultimately means that the young teens' bodies are harvested for organs that are transplanted into adult bodies, making the teens still alive but in a "divided state." Three teens escape this fate but must find somewhere to hide until their 18th birthdays. *Unwind* and its sequels explore important issues of abortion, organ donation, religion, and other serious moral issues of today and the future.

Science Fiction: Space Travel and Beyond

People have long speculated about what exists in space beyond our planet. Is there life on other planets? What might that life be like? Do beings from other planets ever travel to Earth? These and other questions are the basis for many books for children and young adults that focus on traveling through space.

Less complex books that focus on space travel, inventions, and other scientific topics help younger readers become interested in science fiction. For example, *The Wonderful Flight to the Mushroom Planet* (Cameron) details the adventures of two boys who build a spaceship, rocketing to a planet covered with mushrooms. The boys learn that the planet is dying, but they discover a way to solve the problem before returning to Earth.

Jill Paton Walsh's *The Green Book* is another classic science fiction story for younger readers, featuring an accessible plot, interesting characters, and a compelling survival theme. When a group escapes from Earth just before the "Disaster," each traveler is allowed only one book. Although she is ridiculed for her choice, young Pattie chooses to take a blank green book in which she records the history of her community.

Philip Reeve's *Larklight*, *Starcross*, and *Mothstorm* attract middle-grade readers. In Reeve's books, which take place in the mid-19th-century Britain, two siblings live with their father in a house called Larklight, which travels through outer space. When their home is attacked by giant spiders, they join a young pirate and his band of extraterrestrials, investigate incidents at an intergalactic resort, and save the universe from giant moths.

A classic for older readers that tackles themes of space and time travel is Madeleine L'Engle's *A Wrinkle in Time*. L'Engle's heroine Meg Murry, along with her genius younger brother Charles Wallace, must "tesser," or travel, through the universe to the planet Camazotz to rescue her imprisoned father. Camazotz is a completely totalitarian society ruled by a disembodied brain named "IT." On Camazotz, everything is controlled: there is no individuality or love. It is only through Meg's ingenuity and love for her father and Charles Wallace that the family is able to escape and return home.

Picture Books in Fantasy and Science Fiction

Picture books featuring imaginary animals that exhibit human characteristics, toys, and other inanimate objects that come alive and characters that use their imaginations can also help children appreciate fantasy and science fiction. For example, *Click, Clack, Moo: Cows That Type* (Cronin) is a hilarious story of cows that begin negotiating for better working conditions. Younger children enjoy the personified antics of the animals in this story, and older students appreciate the themes of peaceful protest and eventual reconciliation. In *Jumanji* (Van Allsburg), two children find a mysterious board game in the park and take it home. However, when they open it up to play, the jungle comes to life, and soon they have a lion, playfully destructive monkeys, an erupting volcano, and other wild scenarios right in their living room. Many stories of personified animals who find themselves in humorous or adventurous predicaments are also considered fantasy. For example, a contemporary focus on e-books versus old-fashioned print books is the premise of *It's a Book* (Smith), in which a monkey trying to read is continually interrupted by a donkey curious to know how a book's features compare to his digital gadget.

Some authors rewrite traditional folktales so that they are set in contemporary times, the point of view is shifted, the plotline is twisted, or other story elements are manipulated to create a new story. Thus, for example, in *Somebody and the Three Blairs* (Tolhorst), Baby Bear stealthily enters a human dwelling with hilarious results. The perspective in *The True Story of the Three Little Pigs* (Scieszka) changes to the wolf, who proclaims his innocence in all dealings with pigs. A little chicken in *Interrupting Chicken* (Stein) warns various folktale characters what is about to happen to them as he is read bedtime stories. Even the modern classic *Goodnight Moon* (Brown) has been parodied in *Goodnight iPad* (Droyd) and *Goodnight, Goodnight Construction Site* (Rinkey).

The lists at the end of the chapter feature a sampling of fantasy and science fiction picture books that children enjoy. Those particularly appropriate for preschoolers are marked with an asterisk.

Transitional Books in Fantasy and Science Fiction

There are numerous books in these two genres that are appropriate for transitional readers. These shorter, less complex books can help older primary and middle-grade students get hooked on fantasy before they are ready for the longer books. A list of these books is also at the end of the chapter.

Teaching Strategies

Connecting to the Common Core State Standards

COMMON CORE STATE STANDARD FEATURE #1

Discerning Theme (CCSS.RL.2)

The Common Core State Standards (CCSS) have identified an understanding of theme as a critical skill for readers. Fantasy and science fiction are excellent genres for supporting children's developing competence with this literary element as it is described in CCSS Standard for Reading: Literature: RL.2:

CCRA (Anchor Standard) RL.2: Determine central ideas or themes of a text and analyze their development; summarize the key supporting details and ideas.

Sample Grade-Level Competencies for This Standard Are the Following:

RL.1.2. Retell stories, including key details, and demonstrate understanding of their central message or lesson.

RL.4.2. Determine the theme of a story, drama, or poem from details in the text; summarize the text.

RL.5.2. Determine a theme of a story, drama, or poem from details in the text, including how characters in a story or drama respond to challenges.

RL.7.2. Determine a theme or central idea of a text and analyze its development over the course of the text; provide an objective summary of the text.

Following are several activities that will develop children's ability to articulate themes in discussion and in writing. All can naturally and authentically evolve from reading fantasy and science fiction. They can also be incorporated into close reading sessions with these genres.

Initial activities for teaching about theme can require students to do story retellings, creating webs in which students chart the central idea or theme and then listing supporting details or evidence that support this central idea. Or they can create dramatizations in which students act out scenes and then determine the main message. Many of the picture books listed at the end of this chapter work well for story retellings. Groups can then keep "Theme Charts" on which they begin charting all the themes they encounter across many stories (see Chapter 1, Figure 1.2 for ideas of possible themes). Following are some additional activities to help students focus on the theme or central idea of a story.

Two-Word Strategy: Following the reading of a text segment or complete book, students write only two words that reflect what they think are the main ideas or themes. The words are then shared with partners, each student providing evidence from the reading to support why the selected words are appropriate as well as how the words relate to the story and their own lives. A group discussion follows in which all the generated words are shared and a group summary of the group's collective sense of the theme is created.

Triple-Entry Journal: After reading a book of fantasy or science fiction, students can create journal entries in which they summarize what they believe is the theme in one column. In the second column, they state the evidence from the book that supports their opinion of the theme. In the third column, they write their opinion as to whether this value is significant in people's lives today and why. Students then gather in small groups and discuss their responses, eventually creating a chart of the themes they have encountered across different fantasy or science fiction books.

Theme Studies: Select several fantasy books that are examples of a theme, such as "the importance of standing up for justice despite personal peril." Ask students to find examples of how this theme is demonstrated through the thoughts, actions, and words of the central characters as well as through the evolution of each book's plot. The group can then create a concept web (see Chapter 2 for how to create these) that shows how the theme is demonstrated across multiple books.

Sketch to Stretch: We introduced this strategy of sketching ideas related to a book in Chapter 2. It is a particularly useful way to encourage students who express themselves visually to convey their representation of a theme. Ask students to sketch an image, scene, or graphic design that represents their synthesis of a book's central message. The designs are shared with a group who interpret what the image suggests to them. The artist then shares his or her interpretation (Short, Harste, & Burke, 1996).

COMMON CORE STATE STANDARD FEATURE #2

Discerning Plot Structure (CCSS.RL.5)

Plot is another literary element that the CCSS consider important for students to understand. CCSS Reading: Literature Standard RL.5 is the relevant specific standard. It states that students will do the following:

CCRA (Anchor Standard) RL.5: Analyze the structure of texts, including how specific sentences, paragraphs, and larger portions of the text (e.g., a section, chapter, scene, or stanza) relate to each other and the whole.

Sample Grade-Level Competencies for This Standard Are the Following:

RL.1.5. Explain major differences between books that tell stories and books that give information, drawing on a wide range of text types.

RL.2.5. Describe the overall structure of a story, including describing how the beginning introduces the story and the ending concludes the action.

RL.3.5. Refer to parts of stories, dramas, and poems when writing or speaking about a text, using terms such as chapter, scene, and stanza; describe how each successive part builds on earlier sections.

RL.5.5. Explain how a series of chapters, scenes, or stanzas fits together to provide the overall structure of a particular story, drama, or poem.

RL.8.5. Compare and contrast the structure of two or more texts and analyze how the differing structure of each text contributes to its meaning and style.

Fantasy and science fiction stories, particularly heroic tales, often follow the classic plot structure of the hero's journey in which the protagonist leaves home, confronts challenges and dangers, and returns home with a renewed sense of self or new insights on the world. This plot structure is also found in other fiction genres. However, it is typically more explicit in fantasy and science fiction, making these genres particularly appropriate for helping children understand plot structure, particularly the hero's journey structure. Fantasy and science fiction stories can also help students understand the overall structure of "story," including "beginning," "middle," "end," and "chapter" as well as how fiction genres differ from poetry, nonfiction, and drama.

It helps to begin by asking students to retell stories, emphasizing what happens at the beginning, middle, and end. Charts can be completed first as a group and then as individuals, making understanding of these concepts memorable. You can also create a game in which students are asked to match beginnings and endings of stories that they are familiar with. Many of the picture books listed at the end of the chapter work well for these activities because of their simple yet well-defined structure.

Fantasy/science fiction books are also useful for sorting activities in which students must discern the differences between different genres, such as fiction, nonfiction, and poetry. The class can be given a selection of books in several genres and then asked to sort them, skimming through the texts to find the characteristics that distinguish these genres. Charts can then be created that list the similarities and differences. Students could also read aloud from various texts to highlight the differences in structure. You might wish to start these activities with two very different genres, such as fantasy and nonfiction, and then move to discriminating between different fiction genres or the differences between a story and the dramatized version of that story.

Once students have a basic knowledge of plot structure, they can complete more advanced activities, such as the following, to deepen their understandings.

Plot Charts: Plot charts are graphic organizers for visually mapping story elements such as rising action, climax, falling action, and resolution. Stories with well-defined plots, such as those in picture books and transitional books, are best to begin with. Novels can also be explored by plotting individual chapters or sections of a story.

Plot charts can be created as a class, or individuals can chart story elements as a story unfolds. A variation of this activity could involve plotting only the events leading to the conflict in a story, listing how they occur and how they are resolved. Students can then compare their charts—an activity that leads to discussion and deeper understanding as children adjust their own charts in response to comparing with those of their peers. Figure 7.4 is an example of a story element chart that includes charting of plot.

Tech Click

Several online apps, such as Webspiration and BubblUs, have Venn diagrams and chart- and mapmaking capabilities for use with charting activities. ReadWriteThink.org also has interactive plot charts, Venn diagrams, and other graphic maps. Use of these tools also addresses 21st Century Skills of critical thinking, information literacy, and communication. Students can use the tools to color-code concepts, such as the actual laws of physics versus imaginary extraterrestrial characteristics used in a science fiction plot.

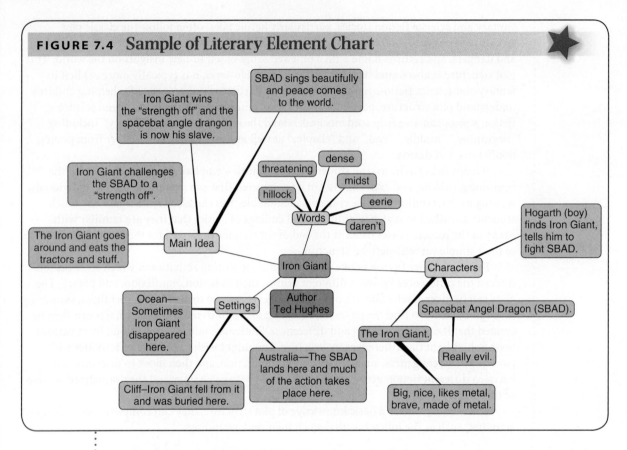

FIGURE 7.4 Sample of Literary Element Chart

Comparing Book and Movie Plots: Many fantasy books have been made into movies, including *The Tale of Despereaux, Harry Potter, The Hunger Games, Charlotte's Web, The Golden Compass,* and *Ella Enchanted.* After reading the book and then watching the movie, have students use a Venn diagram comparing how the plot changes from book to movie (see Chapter 2 for a discussion of Venn diagrams). The group can then discuss why book plots might be adapted when translated into a movie script. Some students may also wish to investigate how computer-generated images contribute to the special effects of a movie.

Writing Prequels and Sequels: Students can also write prequels (a story about events that occurred before the fantasy started) and sequels to their favorite fantasy stories. Writing prequels and sequels requires an understanding of the plot in order to create logical extensions of it. This activity is particularly appropriate for fantasy since authors of this genre often create their own prequels and sequels. *The Giver* (Lowry) is an excellent book to model this activity as readers inevitably speculate about what happens next in this story.

Tech Click

Using themes previously determined by other literature activities (CCSS.RL.5), students can create "postmodern" fantasy or science fiction stories with multiple endings, similar to pick-your-path books. Each twist in the adventure must be explained in terms of character development, moral, or message and supported by the text and visuals.

> *Retelling or writing alternative versions in graphic formats:* Using software such as Comic Life (Mac) or Comic Creator (online at ReadWriteThink.org) or a character-specific cartoon template such as Scholastic's *Charlotte Web* have students reconstruct the story or create a new plot.

Drama and Plot Structure: Drama is an excellent medium for studying a book's plot. Not only do students become aware of a story's structure, but they also develop an understanding of vocabulary associated with plays. When dramatizing plot, students should be involved in selecting the particular aspects of the plot to re-create. Typically, parts with significant action and dialogue work well. Questions such as the following support students as they re-create plots through drama:

- What happens in this scene?
- What are the most important events/interactions in this scene? What is the order of these events?
- What is the mood of this scene?
- How should dialogue be incorporated to advance the plot?
- Is a narrator necessary to "fill in the gaps"? Which parts should be presented through a narrator, and which should be dramatized?

Plot charts can be used to structure student responses to these questions. Then several groups could dramatize the same scene, with discussion afterward about how each group interpreted it. Eventually, several scenes can be developed into a written reader's theater script and presented in sequence.

Tech Click

The 21st Century Skills Map suggests using *The Mysteries of Harris Burdick* (Van Allsburg) or other inspiring story starters to write their own stories that they then record as individual or serial podcasts. Students need not be in the same room, school, or even country to build this type of collaborative literature response.

Supporting Culturally Diverse Students with Fantasy and Science Fiction

It is important to provide fantasy and science fiction books that draw from the cultural and ethnic backgrounds of your diverse learners. This lessens the gap between book and reader's cultural experience, thus making the text more accessible. For example, *Moribito: Guardian of the Spirit* (Uehashi) is a highly recommended fantasy because it draws heavily on Japanese culture to tell a compelling story of a girl's quest to protect a sacred egg, thereby saving the empire from a 100-year drought. Brazilian writer Ana Maria Machado uses fantasy to explore Brazil's history in *From Another World. Where the Mountain Meets the Moon* (Lin) integrates elements from Chinese folklore into a narrative that also has the cadence and cultural elements of Chinese storytelling.

Fantasy/science fiction books featuring characters of color and settings from diverse cultures are not easy to find. Figure 7.5 features some recommended titles. Others are included

FIGURE 7.5 Sampling of Fantasy/Science Fiction Novels with Diverse Main Characters of Color or Set in Diverse Cultures

Allende, Isabelle. *City of the Beasts*; *Kingdom of the Golden Dragon* (South America); *Forest of the Pygmies* (Kenya). (M)

Alexander, Lloyd. *The Remarkable Journey of Prince Jen* (China). (M)

Applegate, K. A. *The Animorphs* (series); *Everworld* (series) (Earth invasion). (I, M)

Bacigalupi, Paolo. *Ship Breaker* (Gulf Coast). (M)

Blackman, Malorie. *Noughts and Crosses Trilogy* (fictional setting). (M)

Bruchac, Joseph. *Skeleton Man*; *Return of Skeleton Man*; *The Dark Pond*; *Whisper in the Dark* (I, M); *Wolfmark* (draws from Native American traditions). (M)

Card, Orson Scott. *Magic Street* (main character of color). (M)

Chabon, Michael. *Summerland* (Clam Island, Washington; diverse characters). (M)

Curry, Jane. *The Black Canary* (biracial main character from the United States; London setting). (I, M)

Dalkey, Kara. *Little Sister* (and others) (Japan). (I, M)

Divakaruni, Chitra Banerjee. *The Conch Bearer* (India). (I, M)

Farmer, Nancy. *The Ear, The Eye, and the Arm*; *The House of the Scorpion* (Zimbabwe, Africa); *A Girl Named Disaster* (Mozambique). (M)

Fishbone, Greg. *Galaxy Games: The Challengers* (connections to Japan). (I)

Gallego Garcia, Laura. *The Valley of the Wolves* (Spain). (I, M)

Goodman, Alison. *Dragoney Reborn* (series) (Asian inspired). (I, M)

Hamilton, Virginia. *Sweet Whispers, Brother Rush*; *The Adventures of Pretty Pearl* (African American characters). (I, M)

Larbalestier, Justine. *Magic or Madness* (trilogy) (Australia; main character of color). (M)

Lin, Grace. *Where the Mountain Meets the Moon*; *Starry River of the Sky* (Chinese). (I, M)

Machado, Ana Maria. *From Another World*; *Me in the Middle* (Brazil). (I, M)

McCall, Guadalupe. *Summer of the Mariposas* (Mexico). (I, M)

McHale, D. J. *Pendragon* (series) (main characters of color). (M)

McKissack, Patricia. *The Dark Thirty: Tales of the Supernatural* (African American characters). (I, M)

McKissack, Patricia. *The Clone Codes* (main character of color). (I, M)

Mlawski, Shana. *Hammer of Witches* (character of Moorish and Jewish heritage; Taino native culture). (M)

Mordecai, Martin. *Blue Mountain Trouble* (Jamaica). (I)

Myers, Walter Dean. *The Legend of Tarik* (Timbukto, Tunisia, and Spain). (I, M)

Norton, Andre. *Dragon Music* (main characters of color). (I, M)

Okorafafor, Nnedi. *Akata Witch* (character lives in Nigeria, born in America); *Shadow Speaker* (Africa). (I, M)

Park, Linda. *Archer's Quest* (main character is Korean American). (I, M)

Pierce, Tamra. *Circle of Magic* (series) (main characters of color). (I, M)

Pratchett, Terry. *The Johnny Maxwell Trilogy* (main character of color). (I)

Rex, Adam. *The True Meaning of Smekday* (main character of color). (I, M)

Sandler, Karen. *Tankborn* (trilogy) (main character of color). (M)

Schodt, Frederick L. *The Astro Boy Essays: Osamu Tezuka, Mighty Atom, and the Manga/Anime Revolution* (graphic novel series) (Japan). (I, M)

Uehashi, Nahoko. *Moribito, Guardian of the Spirit* (and sequels) (Cathy Hirano, Trans.) (Japan). (M)

Wrightson, Patricia. *The Nargun and the Stars* (and others) (Australia aborigine). (I, M)

Yee, Paul. *The Bone Collector's Son* (Vancouver's Chinatown). (M)

Yep, Lawrence. *City of Fire* (trilogy); *The Tiger's Apprentice*; *Dragon of the Lost Sea* (series); *The Magic Paintbrush* (San Francisco; Chinese folklore and culture). (I, M)

on the lists at the end of the chapter. TU Books is an imprint of Lee and Low Publishers that is dedicated to publishing fantasy and science fiction inspired by worldwide cultures. The Barahona Center for the Study of Books in Spanish for Children and Young Adults has databases for books in both Spanish and English with connections to Latino culture. Additionally, they have a list of Newbery Award winners that have been translated into Spanish.

In addition to providing diverse students with books that are written by writers from their culture, all students can benefit from critically examining how culturally diverse characters are sometimes portrayed in fantasy. For example, *The Indian in the Cupboard* (Banks) features a warlike Native American male who talks and acts in stereotypical ways. Early editions of *Mary Poppins* (Travers) feature a Native American character as a "savage" who is shown carrying away a white woman to make her his wife. Willie Wonka's "Oompa Loompas" are from a tribe of miniature pygmies who live in the deepest, darkest part of the African jungle where no white man had ever lived before. Willie pays them in cacao beans and requires them to test various candies that have unfortunate side effects. Important issues to discuss after reading these books are what effect these portrayals have on the students whose cultural backgrounds are being stereotyped and how the attitudes of mainstream students are shaped by these characterizations.

Tech Click

Most presentation software or writing apps have the capacity to include pop-ups and hyperlinks that students can use to gloss key textual details from diverse cultures (CCSS.RL.3.2). Similarly, these features could demonstrate understanding of core scientific principles used in science fiction, juxtaposed with the imagined, futuristic science.

Supporting English Language Learners with Fantasy and Science Fiction

English language learners (ELLs) often enjoy the imaginative, unpredictable, and adventurous stories that are the hallmark of fantasy and science fiction. However, these same qualities can make the genres difficult reading for ELLs; readers must possess a sophisticated understanding of plot structure or extensive background knowledge to successfully read a book that is so unpredictable. In addition, there are relatively few fantasy and science fiction books that feature characters or settings from diverse cultures or that are written in a language other than English. Thus, ELLs have less experiential background knowledge to bring to the reading.

Teachers can help ELLs access books of fantasy and science fiction by building their background and expectation for what they will encounter. It helps to discuss the fantasy elements of a book: characters who do magical things that are impossible to predict, imaginary landscapes that are completely different from reality, or plotlines that subtly introduce fantasy/science fiction elements that might elude a reader not yet proficient in the subtleties of the English language. Sometimes, it helps for a teacher to read aloud the first two or three chapters of a book, discussing how the story line is unfolding and drawing maps of an imaginary setting or creating character charts. These activities will help ELLs access the more subtle, unusual aspects of a fantasy/science fiction story.

When ELL students can read a story independently, encourage them to mark places where understanding breaks down so that they can return to that spot later for clarification. They can also write their ongoing responses and questions about a book in literature response journals, in book blogs, or on graffiti boards (large sheets of paper where children are invited to draw or write their reactions to a book). A teacher can then check these responses and help students work through any misunderstandings.

Picture books and graphic novels with imaginary settings are also useful for helping students build adequate background for successful reading of these genres, as the increased visual support can make books more accessible. Although graphic novels sometimes have complex story lines, the pictures support the plot and are the critical variable that advances the story. Once ELLs become familiar with how authors help readers suspend disbelief, create imaginary settings, and build characters that act and speak in ways that are outside the boundaries of reality in picture books and graphic novels, they are better able to understand these story elements in longer texts.

Controversial Issue: Are Electronic Media Supplanting Book Reading?

Fantasy and science fiction books have become a catalyst for online gaming and fan sites. Featuring characters, themes, and settings from *Harry Potter*, *The Hunger Games*, *Percy Jackson*, and many other books, students are writing online stories, producing videos, composing music, designing role-playing games, and completing a host of other activities (Black, 2009; Curwood, 2013). Often, these activities are pursued outside of school boundaries in online "affinity spaces": physical, virtual, and blended spaces in which people interact around a common interest (Gee, 2004). Spaces such as Mockingjay.net and PanemOctober.com (based on the *Hunger Games* trilogy), Muggle.net (based on the *Harry Potter* books), and the Percy Jackson and the Olympians FanClub at Fanpop.com (based on the series by Rick Riordan) are just a few examples of sites with devoted fans who write fan fiction, create blogs, song parodies, games, art, and online quizzes and conduct discussions about the books using social media. Participants can also participate in virtual reality activities, such as attending Hogwarts on Muggle.net (complete with course work, opportunities to socialize, and participation in virtual Quidditch) or becoming part of a Hunger Games District as in a fan-designed alternative-reality game on PanemOctober.com.

Some adults are alarmed by student obsession with these sites. They contend that Internet content pulls students away from books and into online activities that do not contribute to reading comprehension or critical thinking. A survey by the National Endowment for the Arts (Bradshaw & Nichols, 2004) expresses many of their concerns. This study determined that young adults have transformed from being those most likely to read books to those least likely to read (except for the category of adults aged 65 and older). The reading decline correlates with increased student interaction with electronic media. This is a critical concern, according to the report, because electronic media often require only passive participation, leading to shorter attention spans and a need for accelerated gratification. In contrast, books in print format cultivate "irreplaceable forms of focused attention and contemplation that make complex communications and insights possible" (p. vii). The report concludes that "a cultural legacy is disappearing and that literary reading as a leisure activity will virtually disappear in half a century" (p. xiii).

Is the reading of print books disappearing? Should we be alarmed at the amount of time students spend on Internet sites that are possibly only peripherally related to helping them form knowledgeable, critical responses to books? A growing body of research suggests that the concerns are unwarranted. For example, a study by Curwood (2013) on one adolescent boy's experience with *Hunger Games* trilogy sites found that this student reread each book multiple times and then thoughtfully analyzed the events, themes, characters, and writing style in the books as he engaged with various activities on the sites. A quick perusal of the sites shows that he is not an exception; thousands of fans passionately create "parallel texts," such as stories, podcasts, videos, and other texts that require deep familiarity with the original books. In essence, these online affinity spaces encourage students to read, critique, and then reinvent literature in ways that are personally engrossing to them (Curwood, 2013; Hayes & Duncan, 2012). They are challenged to think creatively and critically as they connect across books and analyze those books to create new parallel texts.

We suggest that the reading of literature is not disappearing. Rather, it is taking new forms. Rather than being limited to one medium (print), reading is being done by students in diverse media, and this can result in improved comprehension, critical reflection, and imagination (Gomez, Schieble, Curwood, & Hassett, 2010). For example, in addition to the fan sites, a good number of current books feature interactive Web sites that combine the reading of print books with games and other activities. Reading then often becomes personally engaging and gratifying, particularly in terms of the social interactions that can occur. Rather than calling this transformation a social crisis, maybe we should view it as a cultural opportunity: a way to invite a wider range of people into the "literary community."

 *Tech Click*

Many books of fantasy and science fiction feature ancillary online materials that extend a book's content into the online environment. For example, students reading *The Search for Wondla* (Diterlizzi) can use a Webcam to get "Wondla Vision" so that they can take an interactive tour through the planet Orbona. *The 39 Clues* series combines reading the books with online gaming and card collecting. *Skeleton Creek* (Carman), a spooky ghost story, allows readers to view online videos of the story events as they unfold. This integration of print and technology can help entice students to read fantasy and science fiction.

 ## Summary

- A fictional work is considered fantasy if it contains elements that are not possible in our world. A story is considered science fiction when the "impossible" elements are based on scientific theory that is not yet considered possible given our current knowledge of science and technology.

- Reading fantasy and science fiction helps children see beyond their current reality, encouraging them to become more imaginative. These genres also show them universal truths within exciting adventures. Additionally, reading fantasy and science fiction provides the opportunity to vicariously experience how a seemingly powerless person can gain control over his or her life.

- All the criteria relevant to fiction (see Chapter 1) apply to fantasy. The additional criteria for fantasy and science fiction are believability of characters, setting and plot, and plot consistency.

- Categories of fantasy include novels based on traditional literature, animal and toy fantasy, ghost stories, tales with magical elements as the focus, stories set in alternative worlds, fantastic adventures, time travel stories, and stories of heroes. Categories of science fiction include stories about future worlds and space travel.

- Theme and plot are important literary elements identified in the CCSS that can be taught through fantasy and science fiction. Teachers can provide books in these genres that come from the cultures of their culturally diverse students (CCSS.RL.2 and CCSS.RL.5). They can also help ELLs read fantasy by building a background for the imaginative and unpredictable plot elements, characters, and settings they will encounter in these genres.

Questions/Activities to Invite Thinking, Writing, and Conversation About the Chapter

1. While many students enjoy and seek out fantasy and science fiction for their reading, some children actively dislike this genre. Considering the grade levels you teach, what are some books and activities you might use to get those students interested in reading books from these genres?

2. Find fan Web sites, such as Muggle.net, HPRan.com (for *Harry Potter*), and TheHungerGamesfansite.com (for *The Hunger Games*). After examining these sites, consider how the use of social media has affected the popularity of these books. Do you think that sites such as these (as well as Facebook, Twitter, and so on) take students away from the books, or do they encourage more reading?

3. Create a read-aloud plan or literature circle discussion guide for a chapter from one of your favorite fantasy/science fiction books. Incorporate attention to plot or theme by using one of the CCSS activities described in the chapter.

4. Select one of the teaching strategies described in the CCSS section of the chapter. Create a plan for using that strategy with one of the books mentioned in the chapter. Share with others in your class.

Recommended Fantasy and Science Fiction Picture Books

(Books appropriate for preschoolers are marked *; those with significant culturally diverse elements are marked #. Also see Figure 7.5 for culturally diverse titles.)

Humor

*Agee, Jon. *My Rhinoceros.* (P)

Bell-Rehwoldt, Bell. *You Think It's Easy Being the Tooth Fairy?* (David Slonim, Illus.). (P, I)

*Brown, Peter. *Children Make Terrible Pets.* (P)

Child, Lauren. *Clarice Bean* (and others). (P, I)

Griffiths, Andy. *The Cat, the Rat and the Baseball Bat* (Terry Denton, Illus.). (P)

Graham, Bob. *April and Esme: Tooth Fairies.* (P)

Gravett, Emily. *Spells* (and other books by Gravett). (P, I)

*Helakoski, Leslie. *Big Chickens* (and sequels) (Henry Cole, Illus.). (P)

Jeffers, Oliver. *The Incredible Book Eating Boy.* (P, I)

Krensky, Stephen. *Big Bad Wolves at School* (Brad Sneed, Illus.). (P)

*Lloyd, Sam. *Mr. Pusskins and Little Whiskers: Another Love Story.* (P)

Meddaugh, Susan. *Martha Speaks* (and other stories). (P, I)

Noble, Trinka. *The Day Jimmy's Boa Ate the Wash*; *Jimmy's Boa Bounces Back* (Steven Kellogg, Illus.). (P)

*Nolen, Jerdine. *Raising Dragons* (Elise Primavera, Illus.). (P)

Palatini, Margie. *Bedhead*; *Sweet Tooth* (Jack E. Davis, Illus.); *Gone with the Wand* (Brian Ajhar, Illus.); *The Web Files* (Richard Egielski, Illus.). (P, I)

Perry, John. *The Book That Eats People* (Mark Fearing, Illus.). (P, I)

Pilkey, Dav. *Dog Breath; Dogzilla; Kat Kong.* (P, I)

*Shannon, David. *Duck on a Bike; No, David.* (P)

*Reynolds, Aaron. *Creepy Carrots.* (P)

Ryan, Pam. *Mice and Beans* (Joe Cepeda, Illus.). (P)

Teague, Mark. *Dear Mrs. LaRue: Letters from Obedience School.* (P, I)

*Willems, Mo. *Don't Let the Pigeon Drive the Bus* (and others); *Knuffle Bunny Books.* (P)

Wisniewski, David. *The Secret Knowledge of Grown-Ups.* (P, I)

Yorinks, Arthur. *Company's Coming* (David Small, Illus.). (P, I)

Characters Using Their Imagination

*Banks, Kate. *Max's Dragon* (Boris Kulikov, Illus.). (P)

Barnett, Mac. *Extra Yarn* (Jon Klassen, Illus.). (P)

*Bently, Peter. *King Jack and the Dragon* (Helen Oxenbury, Illus.). (P)

*Costello, David. *I Can Help.* (P)

Fleischman, Paul. *Weslandia* (Kevin Hawkes, Illus.). (P, I)

Gaiman, Neil. *Crazy Hair* (Dave McKean, Illus.). (I)

Gravett, Emily. *Wolves.* (P, I)

*Henkes, Kevin. *My Garden.* (P)

Horacek, Petr. *My Elephant.* (P)

#*Keats, Ezra. *Dreams.* (P)

Lechner, John. *The Clever Stick.* (P)

*Lee, Suzy. *Shadow.* (P)

*Lucas, David. *Something to Do.* (P)

*Mahy, Margaret. *Bubble Trouble* (Polly Dunbar, Illus.). (P)

*McCarty, Peter. *Jeremy Draws a Monster; The Monster Returns.* (P)

*Petricelli, Leslie. *Faster, Faster.* (P)

Rex, Adam. *Pssst!* (P)

#Ringgold, Faith. *Tar Beach; Aunt Harriet's Underground Railroad in the Sky.* (P)

*Slater, Dashka. *The Sea Serpent and Me!* (Catia Chien, Illus.). (P)

*Snicket, Lemony. *The Dark* (Jon Klassen, Illus.). (P)

*Thompson, Bill. *Chalk.* (P)

*Wing, Natasha. *Go to Bed, Monster* (Sylvie Kantorovitz, Illus.). (P)

Animals with Human Qualities (in addition to classics such as *Very Hungry Caterpillar*, *Corduroy*, *Peter Rabbit*, and so on) (P)

*Becker, Bonny. *A Visitor for Bear* (Kady Denton, Illus.). (P)

Billingsley, Franny. *The Big Bad Bunny* (G. Brian Karas, Illus.). (P)

Breathed, Berkeley. *Pete and Pickles.* (I)

Cronin, Doreen. *Click, Clack, Moo: Cows That Type; Duck for President; Giggle, Giggle, Quack.* (P, I)

DiCamillo, Kate. *Louise, the Adventures of a Chicken* (Harry Bliss, Illus.). (P)

*Falconer, Ian. *Olivia.* (P)

*Fox, Mem. *Koala Lou* (Pamela Lofts, Illus.). (P)

*Henkes, Kevin. *Chrysanthemum; Lily's Purple Plastic Purse; Kitten's First Full Moon; Owen; Sheila Rae the Brave; Penny and Her Song.* (P)

*Hest, Amy. *Little Chick* (Anita Jeram, Illus.). (P)

*Jenkins, Emily. *That New Animal* (Pierre Pratt, Illus.). (P)

Kellogg, Steven. *Pinkerton* (and sequels). (P)

*Klassen, Jon. *I Want My Hat Back: This Is Not My Hat.* (P)

Lionni, Leo. *Frederick.* (P, I)

Marshall, James. *George and Martha* (and others). (P)

*McCarty, Peter. *Hondo and Fabian.* (P)

#McKissack, Patricia. *Flossie and the Fox* (Rachel Isadora, Illus.). (P)

#Morales, Yuyi. *Just in Case: A Trickster Tale and Spanish Alphabet Book.* (P)

*Raschka, Chris. *Hip Hop Dog* (Vladimir Radunsky, Illus.). (P)

*Rathmann, Peggy. *Officer Buckle and Gloria.* (P)

#*Ravi, Anushka. *Tiger on a Tree* (Pilak Biswas, Illus.). (P)

Ryan, Pam. *Nacho and Lolita* (Claudia Rueda, Illus.). (P)

*Rohmann, Eric. *My Friend Rabbit.* (P)

#Soto, Gary. *Chato and the Party Animals; Chato's Kitchen* (Susan Guevara, Illus.). (P, I)

Scotton, Rob. *Russell the Sheep.* (P, I)

Schachner, Judy. *Skippyjon Jones* (and sequels). (P)

*Seeger, Laura. *Dog and Bear: Two Friends, Three Stories.* (P)

Steig, William. *Doctor De Soto; Sylvester and the Magic Pebble.* (P, I)

Stohner, Anu. *Brave Charlotte and the Wolves* (Henrike Wilson, Illus.). (P)

Teague, Mark. *Pigsty.* (P, I)

Vail, Rachel. *Piggy Bunny* (Jeremy Tankard, Illus.). (P)

*#Vamos, Samantha. *The Cazuela That the Farm Maiden Stirred* (Rafael Lopez, Illus.). (P)

Watt, Melanie. *Scaredy Squirrel.* (P)

Wiesner, David. *Mr Wuffles.* (P, I)

Willems, Mo. *City Dog, Country Frog.* (P)

Inventions, Robots

Barnett, Mac. *Oh, No! Or How My Science Project Destroyed the World* (Dan Santat, Illus.). (P, I)

DiPuccio, Kelly. *Clink* (Matthew Myers, Illus.). (P)

Dyckman, Anne. *Boy [+] Bot* (Dan Yaccarino, Illus.). (P)

Gall, Chris. *Dinotrux.* (P)

Jackson, Alison. *Thea's Tree* (Janet Pederson, Illus.). (P, I)

James, Simon. *Baby Brains and RoboMom.* (P)

Kuszyk, Nicholas. *Robot Saves Lunch.* (P)

Riddell, Chris. *Wendel's Workshop.* (P)
Sava, Scott. *Pet Robots* (Diego Jourdan, Illus.). (P, I)
Scieszka, Jon. *Robot Zot* (David Shannon, Illus.). (P)
Slote, Albert. *My Robot Buddy* (Joel Schick, Illus.). (P)
Tougas, Chris. *Mechanimals.* (P)
Varon, Sara. *Robot Dreams.* (P)
Yaccarino, Dan. *If I Had a Robot.* (P)

Fantastic Adventures and Journeys

Banks, Kate. *The Eraserheads* (Boris Kulikov, Illus.); *Max's Dragon.* (P, I)
Bernasconi, Pablo. *Captain Arsenio: Inventions and (Mis)adventures in Flight.* (I)
Burningham, John. *It's a Secret.* (P)
Cecil, Laura. *Noah and the Space Ark* (Emma Chichester Clark, Illus.). (P, I)
Cooper, Helen. *Dog Biscuit.* (P)
#Dorros, Arthur. *Abuela* (Elisa Kleven, Illus.); *Isla* (Elisa Kleven, Illus.). (P)
Fleischman, Paul. *Weslandia* (Kevin Hawkes, Illus.). (P, I)
Gaffney, Timothy. *Grandpa Takes Me to the Moon* (Barry Root, Illus). (P)
Heide, Florence. *Princess Hyacinth: The Surprising Tale of a Girl Who Floated* (Lane Smith, Illus.). (P, I)
Jeffers, Oliver. *The Way Back Home.* (P)
#*Keats, Ezra Jack. *Regards to the Man on the Moon.* (P)
Kirk, Daniel. *Hush, Little Alien.* (P)
Martin, Ruth. *Moon Dreams* (Olivier Latyk, Illus.). (P)
*McCarty, Peter. *Moon Plane.* (P)
McNaughton, Colin. *We're Off to Look for Aliens.* (P)
Metzger, Steve. *Pluto Visits Earth* (Jared Lee, Illus.). (P)
#Morales, Yuyi. *Little Night; Nino Wrestles the World.* (P)
#Myers, Christopher. *Wings.* (P)
*Nolan, Dennis. *Sea of Dreams.* (P)
O'Malley, Kevin. *Captain Raptor and the Moon Mystery* (Patrick O'Brien, Illus.). (P, I)
*Patricelli, Leslie. *Higher! Higher!* (P)
#Pinkney, Brian. *The Adventures of Sparrow Boy.* (P, I)
*Rex, Adam. *Moonday.* (P)
#Ringgold, Faith. *Tar Beach.* (P)
*Rocco, John. *Moonpowder.* (P)
Say, Allen. *A River Dream.* (P)
Schachner, Judy. *Skippyjon Jones Lost in Spice.* (P)
Scieszka, Jon. *Baloney* (Lane Smith, Illus.). (P, I)
*Sendak, Maurice. *Where the Wild Things Are.* (P)
Smallcome, Pam. *Earth to Clunk* (Joe Berger, Illus.). (P)
Teague, Mark. *The Secret Shortcut; Moog Moog Space Barber.* (P)
Van Allsburg, Chris. *Jumanji; The Polar Express; Zathura; The Mysteries of Harris Burdick.* (P, I)
Wiesner, David. *June 29, 1999; Tuesday; Mr. Wuffles.* (P, I)
Yorinks, Arthur. *Hey, Al* (Richard Egielski, Illus.); *What a Trip!* (Richard Egielski, Illus.). (P)

Toys and Inanimate Objects

*Bunting, Eve. *Ducky* (David Wisniewski, Illus.). (P)
*Burton, Virginia Lee. *The Little House; Mike Mulligan and His Steam Shovel.* (P, I)
*Conrad, Pam. *The Tub People* (Richard Egielski, Illus.). (P, I)
*Freeman, Don. *Corduroy.* (P)
Grey, Mini. *Traction Man Is Here.* (P)
Lionni, Leo. *Alexander and the Wind Up Mouse.* (P)
*Long, Loren. *Otis* (and sequels). (P)
*McMullan, Kate. *I Stink!; I'm Dirty!; I'm Mighty!* (Jim MacMullan, Illus.). (P)
*Piper, Watty. *The Little Engine That Could.* (P)
*Rinkey, Sherri. *Good Night, Good Night Construction Site* (Tom Lichtenheld, Illus.). (P)
*Rylant, Cynthia. *Little Whistle* (Tim Bowers, Illus.). (P)
*Scieszka, Jon. *Trucktown* (series); *Garage Tales* (David Shannon, Loren Long, and David Gordon, Illus.). (P)
Yang, James. *PuzzleHead.* (P)

Fractured Folktales

Ada, Alma Flor. *With Love, Little Red Hen* (Leslie Tryon, Illus). (P)
*Ahlberg, Alan. *The Runaway Dinner* (Bruce Ingman, Illus.). (P, I); *Goldilocks Variations.* (P, I)
*Alley, Zoe. *There's a Princess in the Palace: Five Classic Tales* (R. W. Alley, Illus.). (P)
Browne, Anthony. *Me and You.* (P, I)
Child, Lauren. *Beware of the Storybook Wolves.* (P, I)
Cole, Babbette. *Princess Smartypants.* (P, I)
*Elya, Susan. *Rubia and the Three Osos* (Melissa Sweet, Illus.). (P)
Emberley, Michael. *Ruby.* (P, I)
Ernst, Lisa Campbell. *Goldilocks Returns; Gingerbread Girl Goes Animal Crackers.* (P, I)
Forward, Toby. *The Wolf's Story: What Really Happened to Little Red Riding* (Izar Cohen, Illus.). (P, I)
Gerstein, Mordecai. *A Book.* (P)
Kasza, Keiko. *The Dog Who Cried Wolf.* (P)
Levinthal, David. *Who Pushed Humpty Dumpty?: And Other Notorious Nursery Tale Mysteries* (John Nickle, Illus.). (P)
Metzger, Steve. *Detective Blue* (Tedd Arnold, Illus.). (P)
Moerbeek, Kees. *The Diary of Hansel and Gretel.* (P, I)
*Murray, Laura. *The Gingerbread Man Loose in the School* (Mike Lowery, Illus.). (P)
Palatini, Margie. *Gone with the Wand* (Brian Ajhar, Illus.). (P)
Perlman, Janet. *The Penguin and the Pea.* (P)
Scieszka, Jon. *Squids Will Be Squids* (Lane Smith, Illus.). (I)
Scieszka, Jon. *The True Story of the Three Little Pigs; The Stinky Cheese Man; The Frog Prince Continued* (Lane Smith, Illus.). (P, I)
Stanley, Diane. *Rumpelstiltskin's Daughter* (I); *The Giant and the Beanstalk.* (P)

*Stein, David. *Interrupting Chicken*. (P)
*Willems, Mo. *Goldilocks and the Three Dinosaurs*. (P)
Yolen, Jane, and Dotlich, Rebecca. *Grumbles from the Forest: Fairy Tales with a Twist* (Matt Hahurin, Illus.). (P, I)

Transitional Fantasy Books
(Upper Primary, Intermediate)

Angleberger, Tom. *Fake Mustache*.
Bond, Michael. *A Bear Called Paddington* (R. W. Alley, Illus.).
Buckley, Michael. *Nerds; National Espionage, Rescue and Defense Society*.
Byars, Betsy. *Cat Diaries: Secret Writings of the MEOW Society* (Erik Brooks, Illus.).
Cameron, Eleanor. *The Wonderful Flight to the Mushroom Planet*.
Catling, Patrick. *The Chocolate Touch* (Margot Apple, Illus.).
Charles, Veronika. *It's Not About the Pumpkin!* (and others) (David Parkins, Illus.).
Cleary, Beverly. *The Mouse and the Motorcycle*.
Collier, Christopher. *Billy Bones* (Avi Ofer, Illus.).
DiTerlizzi, Tony. *Kenny and the Dragon*.
DiTerlizzi, Tony, and Black, Holly. *The Spiderwick Chronicles*.
Etra, Jonathan, and Spinner, Stephanie. *Aliens for Breakfast*.
Funke, Cornelia. *Igraine the Brave*.
George, Jessica. *Tuesdays at the Castle*.
Gordon, Amy. *Magic by Heart* (Adam Gustavson, Illus.).
Guibert, Emmanuel. *Sardine in Outer Space* (graphic novel series).
Hannigan, Katherine. *Emmaline and the Bunny*.
Horvath, Polly. *Mr. and Mrs. Bunny: Detectives Extraordinaire*.
Howe, James. *Bunnicula*.
Ibbotson, Eve. *The Secret of Platform 13*.

Jenkins, Emily. *Toys Go Out: Being the Adventures of a Knowledgeable Stingray; A Toughie Little Buffalo and Someone Called Plastic* (and sequels) (Paul Zelinsky, Illus.).
Jonell, Lynn. *The Secret of Zoom; Emmy and the Incredible Shrinking Rat*.
King-Smith, Dick. *Pigs Might Fly; Martin's Mice*.
Le Guin, Ursula. *Catwings; Catwings Return* (S. D. Schindler, Illus.).
Lewis, C. S. *Chronicles of Narnia*.
McMullan, Kate. *Dragon Slayers Academy* (Bill Basso and Stephen Gilpin, Illus.).
Moore, Lilian. *I'll Meet You at the Cucumbers* (Shannon Wooding, Illus.).
Morris, Gerald. *Sir Gawaine, the True; The Adventures of Sir Balin, the Ill Fated* (and others) (Aaron Renier, Illus.).
Nimmo, Jenny. *The Snow Spider*.
Osborn, Mary Pope. *The Magic Tree House* (series) (Sal Murdoca, Illus.).
Pearce, Philippa. *A Finder's Magic* (Helen Craig, Illus.).
Pearson, Ridley. *Kingdom Keepers* (Tristan Elwell, Illus.).
Pinkwater, Daniel. *The Hoboken Chicken Emergency* (Tony Auth, Illus.).
Prineas, Sarah. *The Magic Thief* (Antonio Javier Caparo, Illus.).
Riddell, Chris. *Ottoline and the Yellow Cat*.
Riley, James. *Half upon a Time; Twice upon a Time*.
Schlitz, Amy. *The Night Fairy* (Angela Barrett, Illus.).
Snicket, Lemony. *A Series of Unfortunate Events* (series); *"Who Could That Be at This Hour?" (All the Wrong Questions)* (series).
Soup, Cuthbert. *A Whole Nother Story*.
#*The 39 Clues* (series) (various authors).
Vernon. Ursula. *Dragonbreath*.
Viorst, Judith. *Lulu and the Brontosaurus* (Lane Smith, Illus.).
Wrede, Patricia. *Enchanted Forest Chronicles*.

Recommended Fantasy/Science Fiction Novels

(Books appropriate for preschoolers are marked *; those with significant culturally diverse elements are marked #.)

Literary Fairy Tales: Hans Christian Andersen
*Andersen, Hans C. *The Ugly Duckling* (Jerry Pinkney, Illus.) (also versions by Thomas Locker, Robert Ingpen, Steve Johnson, and Lou Fancher). (P)

*Andersen, Hans C. *Thumbelina* (Susan Jeffers, Illus.) (also Adrienne Adams and Brian Pinkney). (P)
*Andersen, Hans C., and Birmingham, Christian. *The Classic Treasury of Hans Christian Andersen*. (P)

Novels Based on Stories from Traditional Literature
Buckley, Michael. *Sisters Grimm: The Fairy Tale Detectives*. (M)

Datlow, Ellen, and Windling, Terri. *Troll's Eye View: A Book of Villainess Tales.* (I, M)

Durst, Sarah Beth. *Into the Wild* (M); *Out of the Wild.* (M)

#Fleishman, Paul. *Glass Slipper, Gold Sandal: A Worldwide Cinderella* (Julie Paschkis, Illus.). (P, I)

Gidwitz, Adam. *A Tale Dark and Grimm; Through a Glass Grimmly; The Grimm Conclusion.* (I, M)

Goldman, William. *The Princess Bride.* (I, M)

Hale, Shannon and Dean. *Rapunzel's Revenge* (Nathan Hale, Illus.) (graphic novel) (I, M); *Goose Girl; Princess Academy* (and sequels). (M)

Holmes, Sara L. *Letters from Rapunzel.* (I, M)

Levine, Gail Carson. *Ella Enchanted* (I, M); *Princess Sonora and the Long Sleep* (I, M); *Fairest* (Snow White). (M)

#Lin, Grace. *Where the Mountain Meets the Moon; Starry River of the Sky.* (P, M)

MacDonald, George. *The Light Princess* (Maurice Sendak, Illus.) (Sleeping Beauty). (I, M)

Mass, Wendy. *Rapunzel: The One with All the Hair* (I, M); *Sleeping Beauty: The One Who Took a Really Long Nap.* (I, M)

McKinley, Robin. *Beauty: A Retelling of the Story of Beauty and the Beast* (M); *Rose Daughter* (Beauty and the Beast) (M); *Spindle's End* (Sleeping Beauty). (M)

Napoli, Donna Jo. *Beast; Bound* (Cinderella) (M); *Zel* (Rapunzel) (M); *Spinners* (Rumpelstiltskin) (M); *The Magic Circle* (Hansel and Gretel) (M); *Crazy Jack.* (I, M)

Pullman, Philip. *I Was a Rat: Or the Scarlet Slippers* (Kevin Hawkes, Illus.) (Cinderella). (M)

Rhodda, Emily. *The Key to Rondo.* (M)

Singer, Marilyn. *Mirror, Mirror: A Book of Reversible Verse* (Josée Massee, Illus.). (I, M)

Stanley, Diane. *Bella at Midnight* (Bagram Ibatoulline, Illus.) (M); *Rumpelstiltskin's Daughter.* (P, I)

Ursu, Anne. *Breadcrumbs* (Snow Queen). (I, M)

Yolen, Jan. *Briar Rose* (Sleeping Beauty). (M)

Stories of Ghosts and the Supernatural

Avi. *The Seer of Shadows* (M); *Strange Happenings: Five Tales of Transformation.* (M)

Billingsley, Franny. *The Folk Keeper.* (M)

#Bruchac, Joseph. *The Dark Pond* (M); *Whisper in the Dark* (M); *Skeleton Man.* (M)

Carman, Patrick. *Skeleton Creek.* (M)

Conrad, Pam. *Stonewords.* (M)

#Compestrine, Ying Chang. *A Banquet of Hungry Ghosts.* (M)

DeFelice, Cynthia. *Ghost Mysteries* (series). (I, M)

#Del Negro, Janice. *Passion and Poison: Tales of Shape-Shifters, Ghosts, and Spirited Women* (Vince Natale, Illus.). (M)

Fleming, Candace. *On the Day I Died.* (I, M)

Gaiman, Neil. *Coraline* (M); *The Graveyard Book.* (M)

Hahn, Mary Downing. *All the Lovely Bad Ones: A Ghost Story* (M); *The Doll in the Garden* (M); *Wait Until Helen Comes.* (M)

#Hamilton, Virginia. *Sweet Whispers, Brother Rush.* (M)

Ibbotson, Eva. *The Beasts of Clawstone Castle.* (M)

Klise, Kate. *Dying to Meet You: 43 Old Cemetery Road.* (I, M)

#Kohara, Kazuno. *Ghosts in the House!* (P)

Lincoln, Christopher. *Billy Bones: Tale from the Secret Closet.* (I)

Lowry, Lois. *Gossamer.* (I)

#McKissack, Patricia. *The Dark Thirty: Southern Tales of the Supernatural* (Brian Pinkney, Illus.). (I, M)

Moser, Lisa. *The Monster in the Backpack* (Noah Z. Jones, Illus.). (P, I)

Ness, Patrick. *A Monster Calls.* (M)

#Reiche, Dietlof. *Ghost Ship.* (M)

Strickland, Brad. *The House Where Nobody Lived* (John Bellairs Mystery) (see additional titles in series). (M)

#Tan, Shaun. *Tales from Outer Suburbia.* (M)

#Tingle, Tim. *How I Became a Ghost: A Choctaw Trail of Tears Story.* (I, M)

Tunage, Sheila. *The Ghosts of Tupelo Landing.* (I, M)

#Yee, Paul. *The Bone Collector's Son; Dead Man's Gold and Other Stories.* (M)

Animal and Toy Fantasy

Adams, Richard. *Watership Down.* (M)

Appelt, Kathi. *The Underneath.* (M)

Applegate, Katherine. *The One and Only Ivan.* (all)

Avi. *Ereth's Birthday; Poppy; Poppy and Rye; Poppy and Ereth; Ragweed; Tales from Dimwood Forest.* (I, M)

Benedictus, David. *Return to Hundred Acre Wood.* (Mark Burgess, Illus.). (P, I)

Bond, Michael. *A Bear Called Paddington.* (I)

Cleary, Beverly. *Mouse and the Motorcycle* (and sequels). (I)

DiCamillo, Kate. *The Tale of Despereaux; The Miraculous Journey of Edward Tulane; Flora and Ulysses.* (I, M)

Deedy, Carmen. *The Cheshire Cheese Cat: A Dickens of a Tale.* (I, M)

Grahame, Kenneth. *Wind in the Willows.* (I, M)

Hoban, Russell. *The Mouse and His Child.* (I)

Holm, Jennifer. *Babymouse: Queen of the World* (and sequels). (I)

Howe. *Bunnicula: A Rabbit Tale of Mystery; The Celery Stalks at Midnight; Nighty Nightmare; Return to Howliday Inn.* (I)

Jacques, Brian. *Redwall* (and sequels). (M)

King-Smith, Dick. *Ace: The Very Important Pig*; *Babe: The Gallant Pig*; *Pigs Might Fly*. (I, M)

Larson, Kirby. *The Friendship Doll*. (I, M)

Milne, A. A. *Winnie the Pooh*; *The House at Pooh Corner*. (P, I)

O'Brien, Robert. *Mrs. Frisby and the Rats of NIMH*. (M)

Peck, Richard. *Secrets at Sea*. (I)

Steig, William. *Abel's Island*. (I)

White, E. B. *Charlotte's Web*. (I)

Williams, Margery. *The Velveteen Rabbit*. (I)

Winthrop, Elizabeth. *The Castle in the Attic*. (I, M)

Children and Magic

Bernstein, Nina. *Magic by the Book* (Boris Kulikov, Illus.). (M)

Catling, Patrick. *The Chocolate Touch*. (I)

Dahl, Roald. *The Witches*. (M)

DiCamillo, Kate. *The Magician's Elephant*. (M)

Eager, Edward. *Half Magic* (and sequels) (N. M. Bodecker, Illus.). (I, M)

Forester, Victoria. *The Girl Who Could Fly*. (M)

Funke, Cornelia. *Inkspell*; *Inkheart*; *Inkdeath*. (M)

Gruber, Michael. *The Witch's Boy*. (M)

Higgins, F. E. *The Black Book of Secrets*. (M)

Law, Ingrid. *Savvy*; *Scrumble*. (M)

Pratchett, Terry. *Wee Free Men*; *A Hat Full of Sky*. (M)

Prineas, Sarah. *The Magic Thief* (and sequels). (M)

Rowling, J. K. *Harry Potter and the Sorcerer's Stone* (and sequels). (I, M)

Smith, Robert K. *Chocolate Fever*. (I)

Ursu, Anne. *The Real Boy*. (I, M)

Alternative Worlds

#Aguiar, Nadia. *The Lost Island of Tamarind*. (M)

#Alexander, Lloyd. *The Chronicles of Prydain*. (I, M)

Baum, L. Frank. *Wonderful Wizard of Oz*. (I, M)

Carroll, Lewis. *Alice's Adventures in Wonderland*. (I, M)

#Chabon, Michael. *Summerland*. (M)

Collins, Suzanne. *The Underland Chronicles*. (I, M)

#de Fombelle, Timothée. *Toby & the Secret of the Tree*. (M)

Edwards, Julie Andrews. *The Last of the Really Great Whangdoodles*. (I, M)

Juster, Norton. *The Phantom Tollbooth*. (I, M)

Lewis, C. S. *The Chronicles of Narnia*. (I, M)

Norton, Mary. *The Borrowers* (series). (I, M)

Pearce, Phillipa. *Tom's Midnight Garden*. (M)

Peterson, John. *The Littles* (Roberta Clark, Illus.). (P, I)

#Pratchett, Terry. *Nation*. (M)

#Sabuda, Robert. *The Wonderful Wizard of Oz: A Commemorative Pop-Up*; *Alice's Adventures in Wonderland*. (P, I)

Stead, Rebecca. *First Light*. (I, M)

Tolkien, J. R. R. *The Lord of the Rings*. (M)

Valente, Catherynne. *The Girl Who Circumnavigated Fairyland in a Ship of Her Own Making*; *The Girl Who Fell Beneath Fairyland*. (M)

Fantastic Adventures

Aiken, Joan. *The Wolves of Willoughby Chase*. (M)

Babbit, Natalie. *The Search for Delicious*. (I)

Barrie, J. M. *Peter Pan*. (all)

Barry, Dave, and Pearson, Ridley. *Peter and the Starcatchers* (and sequels). (M)

Bosch, Pseudonymous. *The Name of This Book Is Secret* (Gilbert Ford, Illus.). (M)

Dahl, Roald. *The BFG*; *Charlie and the Chocolate Factory*; *James and the Giant Peach*. (I, M)

DiTerlizzi, Tony. *The Secret of Wondla*. (I)

Fleming, Ian. *Chitty Chitty Bang Bang*. (I)

Funke, Cornelia. *Inkheart*; *The Thief Lord*; *Dragon Rider*. (M)

Juster, Norton. *The Phantom Tollbooth*. (I, M)

Lindgren, Astrid. *Pippi Longstocking*. (I)

McCaughrean, Geraldine. *Peter Pan in Scarlet* (Scott M. Fischer, Illus.). (M)

Miller, Kristin. *Kiki Strike: Inside the Shadow City* (and sequels). (M)

Nielson, Jennifer. *The False Prince* (and sequels). (I, M)

Schlitz, Laura. *Splendors and Glooms*. (M)

Stewart, Trenton. *The Mysterious Benedict Society* (and sequels). (M)

Travers, P. L. *Mary Poppins*. (I, M)

Whitehouse, Howard. *The Strictest School in the World*; *The Faceless Fiend and the Island of Mad Scientists*. (M)

Time Travel Fantasy

Babbit, Natalie. *Tuck Everlasting*. (I, M)

#Barrett, Tracy. *On Etruscan Time*. (M)

Boston, L. M. *The Children of Green Knowe*. (I, M)

Cooper, Susan. *King of Shadows*. (M)

#Curry, Jane. *The Black Canary*. (I, M)

#Haddix, Margaret. *Running Out of Time*. (M)

Lewis, C. S. *The Lion, the Witch, and the Wardrobe*. (I, M)

Mason, Timothy. *The Last Synapsid*. (M)

#Park, Linda Sue. *Archer's Quest*. (M)

Sauer, Julie. *Fog Magic*. (I)

Stead, Rebecca. *When You Reach Me*. (M)

Yolen, Jane. *The Devil's Arithmetic*. (HF) (M)

Heroic Fantasy

Alexander, Lloyd. *The Chronicles of Prydain*. (M)

Barron, Tom. *The Lost Years of Merlin* (and sequels). (M)

Collins, Suzanne. *Gregor the Underlander* (and sequels). (I, M)

Cooper, Susan. *The Dark Is Rising* (and sequels). (M)

#Divakaruni, Chitra. *The Conch Bearer* (and others). (I, M)

Farmer. Nancy. *The Sea of Trolls* (and sequels). (M)

Le Guin, Ursula K. *The Wizard of Earthsea* (and others). (M)

McKinley, Robin. *The Blue Sword; The Hero and the Crown.* (M)

Paolini, Christopher. *The Inheritance Cycle.* (M)

Pierce, Tamora. *Song of the Lioness; The Immortals; The Circle Opens; A Circle of Magic.* (I, M)

Pullman, Philip. *His Dark Materials: The Golden Compass; The Subtle Knife; The Amber Spyglass.* (M)

Riordan, Rick. *Percy Jackson and the Olympians; The Red Pyramid* (series). (I, M)

Smith, Jeff. *Bone* (graphic novel series). (M)

Tolkien, J. R. R. *The Hobbit; The Lord of the Rings.* (M)

Future Worlds: Utopias and Dystopias

Christopher, John. *The White Mountains* (and sequels). (M)

Collins, Suzanne. *The Hunger Games* (and sequels). (M)

Diamond, Emily. *Raider's Ransom.* (M)

DuPrau, Jeanne. *City of Ember* (and others). (M)

#Farmer, Nancy. *House of the Scorpion; The Ear, the Eye and the Arm.* (M)

Haddix, Margaret Patterson. *Among the Hidden.* (M)

Lloyd, Saci. *The Carbon Diaries, 2015.* (M)

Lowry, Lois. *The Giver; Gathering Blue; Messenger; Son.* (M)

#McKissack, Patricia. *The Clone Codes.* (M)

Nix, Garth. *A Confusion of Princes.* (M)

O'Brien, Robert. *Z for Zachariah.* (M)

Pfeffer, Susan. *Life As We Knew It.* (M)

Shusterman, Neal. *Unwind, Unstrung, Unholy, Unsouled.* (M)

Space Travel and Beyond

Asch, Frank. *Star Jumper: Journal of a Cardboard Genius; Star Jumper; Time Twister.* (P, I)

Cameron, Eleanor. *Wonderful Flight to the Mushroom Planet.* (I)

Card, Orson. *Ender's Game* (and others). (M)

Daley, Michael. *Shanghaied to the Moon.* (M)

Engdahl, Sylvia. *Enchantress from the Stars.* (M)

Hatke, Ben. *Zita the Spacegirl.*

Hughes, Monica. *Invitation to the Game.* (M)

Klass, David. *Stuck on Earth.* (M)

L'Engle, Madeleine. *A Wrinkle in Time.* (I, M)

McCaffrey, Anne. *Dragonriders of Pern.* (M)

Paton Walsh, Jill. *The Green Book.* (I)

Reeve, Philip. *Larklight; Starcross; Mothstorm.* (I)

Rex, Adam. *The True Meaning of Smekday.* (M)

Sleator, William. *Interstellar Pig.* (M)

Teague, Mark. *The Doom Machine.* (M)

8

Historical Fiction

(Literary Genre)

> **In this chapter, we explore the following questions:**
>
> - What is historical fiction?
> - What is the role of historical fiction in children's lives?
> - How do we choose high-quality historical fiction?
> - What are some common categories of historical fiction and examples of good books in those categories?
> - How can we use historical fiction to meet the mandates of national standards as well as the needs of our diverse students?

"Let's put on a play about families going West," announced the students of second-grade teacher Peggy. "I was amazed at their enthusiasm," Peggy told us. "I had taught history with textbooks before, but my children had been so bored and just didn't remember much. This time I used picture books about families traveling West like the *Josephina Story Quilt* (Coerr), *Mississippi Mud* (Turner), and *Aurora Means Dawn* (Saunders) in my literature study groups. I also read aloud more complex books like *Sarah Plain and Tall* (MacLachlan) and *Sing Down the Moon* (O'Dell). We talked a lot about all the hardships people experienced and how we might react to these situations if they happened to us. We also discussed what it would have been like to be Native Americans in this time and place."

Soon, her students wrote *Journey West*, their own play about two families traveling West—one going to California and one to Oregon. "Not only did they include everything that happened to people traveling West, including diseases, snake bites, blizzards and accidents, they also created a large, detailed map that traced each family's journey across the American continent. Their own families were then treated to a performance, complete with two covered wagons created by the children."

"My former students often come back to visit and almost always mention our study of westward expansion as one of their most memorable second grade experiences."

History can be a fascinating focus of study, as it details the human story that has evolved through the challenges and triumphs of real people from the past. However, students often name social studies as their most boring class (Fischer, 1997; Sewall, 2000). We believe that these negative attitudes can be traced to the textbooks used in social studies, particularly history classes. These texts attempt to cover too much material, emphasize sterile facts and dates over human stories, and minimize controversies that make the study of history a fascinating, multifaceted, complex endeavor (Tomlinson, Tunnell, & Richgels, 1992). The result is impersonal, stilted, and difficult-to-read prose that fail to engage readers. Historical fiction, in contrast, provides a compelling look at the people behind those facts and dates. People in the past are much like us today: they struggled against injustice, wrestled with moral dilemmas, loved their families, and faced an unknown and uncertain future. Historical fiction makes these people come alive, showing our students that the past is inextricably connected to the present and that our lives are a result of actions and decisions made by those who came before us. Additionally, the use of present-tense dialogue and multiple characters who embody diverse perspectives in historical fiction lends a sense of immediacy and reality (Tomlinson et al., 1992). Thus, it is important that children have the opportunity to explore history through excellent books available for that purpose.

What Is Historical Fiction?

Books of historical fiction are set in the past and bring together facts with imagination. Writers must piece together facts identified in historical records and then imaginatively fill in the gaps with details and events that could plausibly occur in the historical context. A balance between the qualities of fact and fiction is critical. Too much detail or "fact," and the narrative slows. However, too much imagination leads to a disconnect between the story and its real historical context. As famous author Jill Paton Walsh (1972) tells us,

> The art of [historical] fiction consistently demands that we go beyond the safe, solid footing of the "known to be true" onto the thrilling quagmire of the "might have been." Yet, this dangerous departure is subject to the most exciting constraints. . . . It does not in the least follow that anything goes. (pp. 20–21)

In historical fiction, the characters are usually imaginary, but they often encounter real people who were prominent during the time in which the story is set. The best books in this genre feature young people in difficult, often life-or-death situations that are resolved by their brave, resourceful, or thoughtful actions. Historical fiction writer Laurie Halse Anderson (2010) suggests that we call this genre "historical thrillers" because she believes that the stories are just as exciting and engaging as those from other genres. She sees that her job as a writer is to "have my readers get yelled at by their parents to turn off the light and go to bed but for them to say, 'nooo . . . just one more chapter'" (Anderson, 2010).

Determining where historical fiction ends and realistic fiction begins is tricky. What counts as history to one generation might be "just yesterday" to another. For the purposes of this text, historical fiction is defined as fictional stories set in historical contexts up to the 1970s. However, we recognize that this definition is fluid and will likely shift as time passes and excellent books that focus on historically significant events in the late 1900s and early 2000s are published.

Writers of historical fiction face the challenging task of sifting through the various interpretations of history that they uncover through research. There is much contradictory information from documents of the past because history is composed of stories that are shaded and shaped by individual perceptions and experiences (Aiken, 1996, p. 71). For example, a northern abolitionist will likely create a completely different interpretation of the Civil War than a southern slave owner. Authors must sift through many sources, including both primary (letters, diaries, and newspapers created during the historical era under study) and secondary (publications such as a book or a journal article that interpret and analyze primary documents), to obtain an understanding of their story's complex historical context. Even with all this evidence, gaps remain, and authors must often speculate about how the historical pieces fit together.

The process of constructing this more nuanced view of the past is further complicated because authors invariably write from their own ideological perspectives. For example, Esther Forbes, when writing of *Johnny Tremain* in 1944, consciously drew connections between the American Revolution and attitudes toward war that were widely held in the 1940s during World War II. At that time the prevailing notion was that war was a necessary evil to preserve democracy and freedom (Taxel, 1983). In contrast, Christopher Collier, writing in the 1970s during the waning years of the Vietnam War, created *My Brother Sam Is Dead*, a powerful novel set in the Revolutionary War era that is highly critical of war. Both novels are set in the same era, but each expresses different perspectives on historical events. It is likely that Collier reflected the values of his time just as Forbes did for hers (Sipe, 1997).

Writers also need to ensure that historical details do not become more important than the story itself. They must be skillfully embedded so that the people and place come alive but the reader is totally engrossed in the narrative. Authors do extensive research to ensure authenticity in their books. However, if the reader is impressed with the amount of research, then the writer has failed. Katherine Paterson, author of several award-winning books of historical fiction, states that authors must "bury" their research so that "readers will race to the end of the story to find out what happens to these people" (Paterson, 2005, p. 12).

Some authors add notes at the conclusion of a story to help readers understand more about the historical context discovered in the research process and verify the authenticity of their story. For example, Cynthia Kadohata describes how she researched hunting, tracking, the Vietnam War, and other issues for *A Million Shades of Gray*, her novel about a Vietnamese boy whose family supported the Americans during the war. When the Americans pull out, the villagers are forced to flee the North Vietnamese communists. She also studied Asian elephants and their keepers (her main character is an elephant tender), talked with Special Forces soldiers who served in the conflict, and interviewed Vietnamese refugees (Kadohata, 2010).

Similarly, Sharon Draper wrote *Copper Sun*, the unflinchingly realistic story of an enslaved young woman, after visiting the Ghana slave castles in which thousands of Africans were housed like cattle before being sold as slaves. That experience left an indelible mark on her memory:

> When I crawled through the "door of no return," which led from the darkness of the prison to the incomprehensible vastness of the beach, I knew I had to tell the story of just one of those who had passed that way. (Draper, 2013)

She then spent 10 years researching books, listening to transcripts of slave narratives, and talking to natives of Ghana to ensure that her story was historically accurate.

The Role of Historical Fiction in Children's Lives

Historical fiction provides adventurous narratives and relatable characters that help children vicariously experience the issues, actions, and emotions of people who lived before them. As a result, they begin to understand the course of human events and how those affect both their present and their future lives. The past becomes a tool to illuminate the present. Historical fiction personalizes social studies, helping students realize how their own actions and lives contribute to a history yet to be written (Hickey, 2010).

Historical fiction effectively complements social studies instruction, adding an affective dimension that is infinitely more touching, memorable, and comprehensible than textbook-based lessons. We could read a textbook passage about the southern region of the United States in the 1930s, a time when most African Americans were sharecroppers. We might find the information interesting, but we would likely fail to understand what that experience was really like. Through the artistry of Mildred Taylor in *Roll of Thunder, Hear My Cry*, however, we can feel the rage of Cassie and her brothers, all African American children, when the school bus full of white children not only passes them by but also splashes their new back-to-school clothes with mud in a deliberate act of humiliation.

Historical fiction also helps children see that real people are a critical variable that shapes world history. Most history textbooks describe only prominent people and events. Historical fiction also focuses on important events but adds a layer of everyday humanity—real characters caught in the wars, challenges, and problems of the times—that draws readers into empathizing with and more deeply understanding the influence of historical events on the lives of everyday people.

Additionally, the opportunity to use critical and evaluative thinking naturally evolves with historical fiction. History is not a mere chronological unfolding of events. Rather, it is a human enterprise—one that can be interpreted in multiple ways, depending on one's perspective. It informs us about important moral, ethical, and political issues that people have wrestled with throughout time. Sharing several books of historical fiction that present diverse perspectives on the same event invites children to evaluate characters' actions and decisions and consider what values and perspectives influenced those decisions. They learn to sift evidence, draw conclusions from that evidence, and come to understand that decisions and judgments result from the interplay of complex social, economic, political, cultural, and ideological differences (Levstik, 1992). They can judge the mistakes and triumphs of the past, considering how those events and decisions regarding those events shape their current lives (Blos, 1992). In short, they learn to act like historians. It is the narrative quality of historical fiction that supports this process.

However, we must help children distinguish between fact and fiction when they read historical fiction. We have heard children ask, "Is Martin Luther King real?" and then ask, "Is Delphine [a character in *One Crazy Summer*, a novel set in 1968] real?" They are not always able to separate what is real and what has been constructed from the author's imagination (Zarnowski, 2006). Thus, teachers need to provide multiple examples from history so that students can begin to discern that what they encounter in fiction is not always "truth"—that the historical record is used along with an author's interpretation of that record as well as events devised through the author's imagination. Using this genre with children allows them to feel the emotional and personal impact of history, but we must be sure that they also understand what is considered the accepted historical account.

Historical fiction also helps children develop a better understanding of continuity and change over time. Research studies suggest that even young children have a sense of these concepts but that their understanding is often inexact and dependent on contextual factors

(Barton & Levstik, 1996; Barton, McCully, & Marks, 2004; Heyking, 2004). A more sophisticated understanding of these concepts develops when teachers make the past real and help students make connections between their own lives and those of individuals from the past. Historical fiction can provide these opportunities.

Through historical fiction, readers learn about important human values, such as sacrifice, courage, and resourcefulness, as well as human frailties and failures. They come to understand that times change and power shifts but that basic human needs remain the same, although they are somewhat tempered by cultural values. We all want respect, family ties, human connections, freedom, and love. This is true if we live in 1930s Mississippi, pharaoh-era Egypt, or World War II Germany. Historical fiction helps us acquire a more nuanced understanding of these important truths.

Criteria for Evaluating Historical Fiction

When selecting and using historical fiction, teachers should first apply the criteria outlined in Chapter 1 for evaluating high-quality fictional literature. Using these criteria will help you make initial judgments about quality titles in this genre. The primary additional criterion for evaluating historical fiction is historical authenticity. Are details of the setting authentic? Do characters act and talk in authentic ways considering the era in which the story is set? Does the writing style provide the flavor of how people talked in the era in which the story takes place? These are important questions to ask when evaluating historical fiction stories.

Setting

The historical setting must be accurately described; buildings, streets, and other physical aspects of the setting must have existed during the time the story is set. Events described as part of the story must really have happened and should not contradict historical records. Authors do extensive research to ensure that these details are accurate. Katherine Paterson tells of spending days checking out a historical fact while writing *Lyddie*, a story set in 1846 about a young girl in Lowell, Massachusetts, who fights injustice in the Massachusetts textile mills. She could not verify this detail and thus chose not to include it in her story (Paterson, 2005).

Detailed descriptions of daily life can enhance a story but must also be as authentic as possible. Lois Lowry, for example, interviewed a woman who had grown up in Denmark during the German occupation to enhance the authenticity of *Number the Stars*. The woman described details such as always feeling cold and wearing mittens to bed, the foods she ate, what she wore to school, and what books were in her knapsack—all the small things that gave authentic voice to the perceptions of a frightened child in an occupied country (Lowry, 1994). Including those details in her book made this historical era come alive for Lowry's readers.

Characterization

Characters must also act authentically in accordance with their times. The southern African American characters in *Roll of Thunder, Hear My Cry* (Taylor), a novel set in 1930s Mississippi, could bitterly protest injustice in private, but it would have been unrealistic to have them publicly oppose the actions of their White neighbors. Young women on the frontier might be permitted to run wild as children, but it would have been unlikely that they would have had a choice about their adult conduct. Thus, *Caddie Woodlawn* (Brink), the story of a young girl on the 19th-century Wisconsin frontier, concludes with Caddie receiving instruction on ladylike behavior. This ending is probably historically accurate. In contrast, the young female protagonist in *The Evolution of Calpurnia Tate* (Kelly), a story set in the late 19th century, is permitted to continue pursuing her interest in science as she grows into adulthood. This resolution is also historically accurate for a later, more enlightened historical era.

Writing Style

Creating authenticity in language is a challenging task for writers of historical fiction. Authors can use letters, diaries, and other primary sources as guides when these documents exist. When these documents are not available, they can only speculate. Julius Lester (2000), author of *Pharaoh's Daughter*, an interpretation of the biblical story of Moses, described his struggle with writing dialogue for his book in the following way:

> Writing about a civilization that existed more than three thousand years ago is a challenge. . . .
> For example, ancient Egyptians had no concept of time smaller than an hour. That's why
> no character says, "Wait a minute," and there are no descriptions saying, "She paused for an
> instant." The Egyptians did not have money so I could not have a character use figures of
> speech involving payment, such as "He paid a price for what he did." (p. 169)

Even if authors have a sense of the vocabulary, dialect, and other aspects of speech from a historical era, they have to be careful about using too much of these language elements, or they can lose readers who often cannot connect with characters who speak so differently from themselves. Some writers call this "writing forsoothly" (Sutcliff, 1973). However, too much contemporary language is disconcerting to readers (Blos, 1992) and fails to provide the flavor of the historical vocabulary and speech patterns that add to a story's historical accuracy. Thus, authors often take a middle ground. They incorporate elements of historical language into their story while also ensuring that language is comprehensible to readers. Some write meanings for archaic words into the narrative or provide a glossary at the end of the book.

Another aspect of language that authors must consider is the use of language that is considered offensive by contemporary standards. Words such as "Jap" and "savage" were authentic words in particular historical eras. Should they be used by contemporary authors to develop a character or advance a theme? Authors carefully consider these questions and determine whether using these words is essential to developing a character or theme.

Finally, authors must be careful not to perpetuate stereotypes and myths about historical figures and events. For example, Betsy Ross did not create the first American flag, Marie Antoinette did not say "Let them eat cake," and Christopher Columbus did not believe that he had discovered a new world. All southerners did not support secession from the United States, and native peoples did not easily provide aid to the Puritans. Careful, thorough research helps authors avoid this critical mistake. Figure 8.1 features questions you should consider as you select historical fiction for use in your classroom or library.

Categorizing Historical Fiction: Historical Eras

Although historical fiction features the same significant themes found in most fiction (e.g., coming of age or overcoming adversity) and can be categorized by theme, we have organized our discussion of the books in this genre by the historical era and geographic location in which the book is set. We believe that categorizing in this way will help you become familiar with the range of books from various time periods so that you can select those that are personally interesting to

FIGURE 8.1 Guidelines for Choosing Historical Fiction

Characterization

- Are character actions consistent with their age, time period, and cultural background?
- Do characters (including women and minorities) reflect the time in their speech, values, and attitudes?

Plot

- Does the novel tell a good story that could have taken place in the period of history?
- Are the events tied to the historical era contextualized enough for students to understand what is taking place?
- Are controversial issues presented openly and honestly, consistent with the time period but with characters that illuminate the attitudes of the era?
- Have stereotyping and myths been avoided?

Setting

- Has the historical setting been developed with accurate details?
- Has the author included sufficient detail to provide readers with a sense of the era but not so much that these details overwhelm the story?
- Is the setting free of anachronisms?

Writing Style

- Is the writing comprehensible to the intended audience?
- Has the author captured some of the flavor of language from the historical era while still maintaining readability?

you and effectively complement your social studies curriculum. Within the categories, we also discuss significant themes addressed by these books. You will see that much historical fiction for children occurs in American historical contexts. However, we have discussed some of the best historical stories set in global contexts where they are relevant. Following is a sample of some of the best books this genre has to offer. We first discuss novels, then picture books and series/transitional books.

Ancient Civilizations (up to A.D. 600)

Authors who write stories about ancient times have a difficult task as they research what life was like in ancient cultures. Since few written records are available, they must study the work of anthropologists and archaeologists to acquire a sense of the lives and times of these ancient peoples. One of the most compelling stories set in this era is *Wind Rider* (Williams). Within the context of a prehistoric tribe barely subsisting on the Asian steppes, readers will discover a daring heroine who was the first to domesticate a horse.

Several books blend details of daily life in the ancient cultures of Egypt and Persia with intriguing stories of power, romance, adventure, and betrayal. *The Golden Goblet* (McGraw) and *Mara, Daughter of the Nile* are two stories set in ancient Egypt. *Pharaoh's Daughter: A Novel of Ancient Egypt* (Lester) embellishes an important piece of Jewish/Old Testament history: the story of Moses and the Exodus. *Shadow Spinner* (Fletcher) also imaginatively expands on an ancient story: that of *The Arabian Nights*.

The struggles between the Romans and conquered people of Britain are the focus for the books of Rosemary Sutcliff, one of the most beloved authors of historical fiction. Sutcliff brings this dark and brutal era to life through a skillful blend of fact and fiction along with interesting characters and exciting story lines. Her themes of reverence for the land and the natural world, along with the ebb and flow of power among men, make *The Eagle of the Ninth* (and its sequels, including *The Lantern Bearers*) compelling, well-written books for mature readers interested in this historical era.

The Middle Ages (A.D. 600–1500)

Tales set in the Middle Ages are particularly popular with middle school students. Many stories of this era feature young protagonists who overcome oppression, defy a preestablished destiny, or set out to create their own identity, all themes that resonate with middle-grade readers. For example, in *Catherine, Called Birdy* (set in 1290 England) (Cushman), adolescent Catherine is expected to settle for one of the marriage candidates her father has arranged for her. However, she finds fault with each of them and hatches various schemes to scare them away. Readers identify with the rebellious young woman who dearly wishes to control her own fate in an era when women were considered property.

In contrast, the lives of common people are portrayed in *The Midwife's Apprentice* (Cushman), a story that tells of an orphaned, nameless, and homeless young woman who is rescued from a dung heap by a midwife who feeds her in exchange for work. Gradually, the girl gains some control over her destiny and assumes both a name and a career of her own choosing. Cushman shows young readers the harsh realities of medieval life, particularly medical practices and the debased status of women.

The theme of an orphan set adrift in a cruel medieval society is also explored in *Crispin: The Cross of Lead* (Avi). In this popular adventure story, an orphaned 14-year-old boy knows virtually nothing about his identity and is soon falsely accused of murder. He flees and meets a traveling juggler who protects him, becoming a father figure. In a plot filled with twists and intrigues, the boy finally learns who he really is and eventually, although not easily, becomes someone worthy. Crispin's adventures continue in *Crispin: At the Edge of the World* and *Crispin: The Edge of Time*. The books explore meaningful themes of treachery, religion, and the importance of family, making them popular with upper elementary and middle school readers.

Crispin: The Cross of Lead by Avi combines mystery, adventure, and history in a well crafted story set in medieval England.

Good Masters, Sweet Ladies: Life in a Medieval Village (Schlitz) uses the format of alternating monologues to bring a 13th-century English village to life. In prose and poetry, speakers, such as the lord's daughter, the shepherdess, and the doctor's son, reveal the daily rhythms, superstitions, prejudices, and small joys of this setting. In turns touching, repellant, and humorous, the book provides an intriguing look at this historical time and place.

A few books are set in other world cultures that flourished in the medieval era. *A Single Shard* (Park), set in 12th-century Korea, tells the story of Tree-Ear, a young orphan apprenticed to a master ceramicist. Gradually, he wins his master's trust and is allowed to deliver a pot to the king's emissary. Katherine Paterson explores the culture of feudal Japan in *The Sign of the Chrysanthemum*, a classic coming-of-age novel in which a young man tries to find his father after his mother dies. This is the only way he can claim his rightful heritage and become a man. However, all he knows is that his father is a samurai warrior bearing a chrysanthemum tattoo. *Of Nightingales That Weep* (Paterson) is set during the same period but explores the concerns of Takiko, a young woman who struggles with her identity following the death of her father and her mother's remarriage to someone whom Takiko does not like. The two Paterson novels are useful when read together and can deepen readers' understanding of an unfamiliar culture. *Heart of a Jaguar* (Talbert) is a gripping tale of a 13th-century Mayan boy who agrees to have his heart ripped out to save his village from drought.

North America: Colonial Times and the American Revolution (1600–1800)

Many writers of children's historical fiction have chronicled early American life from the perspective of both European settlers and indigenous peoples. The settlement in Jamestown is a popular setting for books from this era. *The Serpent Never Sleeps* (O'Dell) is a novel for older readers that details the friendship between Pocahontas and Serena Lynn, a young settler. This book can be compared to *Blood on the River: James Town 1607* (Carbone), another interpretation of the Jamestown story, told from the perspective of Captain John Smith's page. Carbone used primary documents, especially personal journals of early settlers, to give this story its authentic feel. Facts, politics, and fictionalized incidents are meticulously interwoven, showing the depth of the cultural differences between colonists and native people—differences that John Smith came to understand but other colonists ignored.

The Salem witchcraft trials are another popular topic for children's historical fiction. One of the most enduring stories set in this era is *Witch of Blackbird Pond* (Speare). In this story, flamboyant teen Kit Tyler moves from Barbados to New England, where she joins her only living relatives. Kit's former, luxurious lifestyle stands in sharp contrast to the Puritan values of her new relatives, and clashes inevitably arise. Then she is accused of witchcraft, resulting in a terrifying trial.

The Revolutionary War has inspired many excellent books for students. While some portray the war from the perspective of the American patriots, others explore important issues affecting both sides of the conflict, including divided loyalties, treachery, the treatment of minorities, and the ravages of war. A classic book about this era is *Johnny Tremain* (Forbes), which is pro-patriot in tone. Other titles present more diverse perspectives. For example, *My Brother Sam Is Dead* (Collier and Collier) depicts a Tory family who has one son fighting for the patriot cause. Told through the eyes of the younger brother, who loves his father (a Tory Loyalist), and his role model teenage brother (who fights with the colonists), the story shows the heartbreaks that come from war no matter where one's loyalties lie. *The Fighting Ground* (Avi) and *Sarah Bishop* (O'Dell) also explore more critical perspectives on the war.

An African American perspective on the Revolutionary War is recounted in *Chains* (Anderson), a story in which Isabel, a young African American girl, is denied her freedom and sold to a cruel Loyalist family. Using the invisibility that comes with her low status as a slave, Isabel becomes a spy for the patriots but soon realizes that they are as untrustworthy as her Tory masters. Isabel's ability to triumph and transcend her emotional and physical "chains" results in a compelling story. *Forge* (Anderson) is the sequel to *Chains* and tells of Isabel's friend Curzon, who escapes from his master and takes refuge by enlisting in the Continental Army. He ends up enduring the cruel conditions at Valley Forge. Both books explore issues such as courage, the abuse of power, and the question of who really is gaining their freedom in this war.

The fledgling country is the setting for *Fever, 1793* (Anderson). Young protagonist Mattie Cook assists her mother in running a small tavern in Philadelphia, by then the nation's capital. Mattie copes with an epidemic of yellow fever that devastates the city. Another "slice-of-life" story from the post-Revolutionary era is Avi's *The True Confessions of Charlotte Doyle*, an exciting tale of a young girl traveling alone from England to America who becomes involved in a mutiny. By necessity, the protagonist grows from being an innocent sheltered flower to a strong, self reliant young woman.

Katherine Paterson's *The Master Puppeteer*, set in 18th-century Japan, shows readers another culture that flourished during the 1700s. A popular form of entertainment at this time was the puppet theater. Young Jiro begins a new life in the theater when he is apprenticed to a master puppeteer but soon finds himself involved in the politics of the era. This exciting novel has been praised for its accurate depiction of Japanese history and culture.

Westward Expansion (1800s)

Stories about American westward expansion before and after the Civil War are among the most popular in children's historical fiction. Movies, songs, and books have romanticized the time of westward expansion. However, settlers faced significant adversity, and actually, indigenous people were often betrayed as the settlers moved west. These more complex issues are increasingly addressed in contemporary children's books set in this era.

Common themes in books about traveling west include the quest for land and self-determination, conflicts between cultures, and the need for families to work together as they made a new life. Many books, particularly those for younger children, depict the experience as full of challenges but also family love and cooperation. The *Little House* books (Wilder), *Caddie Woodlawn* (Brink), and *Our Only May Amelia* (Holm) are examples of books from this perspective. The *Little House* books depict a close-knit family facing many hardships but also celebrating good times as they create a life together. The protagonist in *Caddie Woodlawn* is a tomboy growing up in the 1860s Wisconsin wilderness, while May Amelia in *Our Only May Amelia* and *The Trouble with Amelia* (Holm) must cope with being the only young female in a family of seven brothers as well as her entire Finnish American community. All three books feature vivid details of everyday life.

Sarah, Plain and Tall (MacLachlan) is one of the best-known family stories set on the prairie. In this book, a widowed midwestern farmer with two children advertises for a wife. When Sarah arrives, she is homesick for Maine but eventually falls in love with the family. This loving family experiences some hardships, but on the whole their lives are quiet and contented as the narrative details the rhythms of the seasons and their lives. *Skylark*, *Caleb's Story*, and *More Perfect Than the Moon* (MacLachlan) continue the family's story. All are appropriate for younger readers. In contrast, *Prairie Songs* (Conrad), *Grasshopper Summer* (Turner), and *Beyond the Divide* (Lasky) are excellent stories for older readers that explore the more difficult challenges of daily life on the western prairie.

As people moved west, the native cultures were pushed from their lands and often forced to walk long distances to new reservations. Or their tribes were decimated by European diseases to which they had no resistance. *Sing Down the Moon* (O'Dell) and *Longwalker's Journey* (Harrell) provide an insider's perspective on the "Long Walk," an actual historic event in which southeastern native tribes were forced to walk to reservations in Oklahoma. Native American writer Louise Erdrich crafted a poignant story of life in an Ojibwa tribe decimated by smallpox brought by White settlers in *The Birchbark House*. In this story, 7-year-old Omakayas is the sole survivor of the epidemic but is fortunately adopted by a neighboring tribe. *The Game of Silence*, *The Porcupine Year*, and *Chickadee* (Erdrich) are sequels that continue Omakayas's story as the Ojibwa people try to maintain the rhythms and routines of their lives. Omakayas is a tough, resilient heroine, and her stories are a wonderful celebration of the joys, heartaches, small triumphs, and occasional tragedies that were part of growing up as a Native American female in this era.

Slavery and the Civil War (1800s)

Many excellent books from this historical era portray the horrors of slavery, including slave ships, auction blocks, deplorable living conditions, and the compelling desire to escape. *Never Forgotten* (McKissack) is a lyrical verse novel that incorporates elements of folklore to tell of a young African boy who is kidnapped and sold into slavery. *Ajeemah and His Son* (Berry), *Africa Is My Home: A Story of the Amistad* (Edinger), and *The Captive* (Hansen) feature similar plots. *Day of Tears: A Novel in Dialogue* (Lester) is a fictionalized account of the largest slave auction in the United States that is told from various perspectives, including those of buyers, slaves, and abolitionists.

Nightjohn (Paulsen) is a realistic, emotionally moving account of plantation life seen through the eyes of one slave. Although he is whipped and maimed, Nightjohn persists in teaching other slaves to read. The book is narrated by Sarny, another slave on the plantation who becomes the title character in *Sarny: A Life Remembered* (Paulsen). *Letters from a Slave Girl* and *Letters from a Slave Boy* (Lyons) are written as first-person narratives and based on actual slave diaries. Another harsh, realistic depiction of slavery can be found in *Copper Sun* (Draper). Draper does not flinch from showing the extreme hardships and injustices associated with slavery when, for example, a slave girl is bought at auction as a sexual gift for the master's adolescent son.

In contrast, *Elijah of Buxton* (Curtis) is set in Buxton, an actual Canadian settlement where all villagers were escaped slaves or their children. Elijah is a free African American boy who helps locate escapees seeking a safe place in Buxton. Embedded in the history is an engrossing coming-of-age novel in which the character of Elijah tackles personal and societal challenges, growing up in the process.

The Civil War has been well chronicled in fiction for young people, and many novels use incidents from the war as a backdrop or describe how everyday life was affected by this event. *Shades of Gray* (Reeder) tells the story of Will, orphaned in the Civil War, who is sent to live with his uncle, a man who refused to fight or take sides in the war. Eventually, Will learns to overcome his prejudices and stereotypic views of both Yankees and Confederates. *Across Five Aprils* (Hunt) recounts the lives of a family living in the border state of Illinois who are torn apart by loyalties to both the North and the South. One son joins the Confederate army while his brothers join the Union forces. Protagonist Jethro, as a younger son, is left at home to contend with increased responsibilities as well as taunts and insults from townspeople.

A few novels are set amid Civil War battles. *Bull Run* (Fleischman) is a fascinating look at the first battle of the war as told from the perspective of 16 characters: Blacks, Whites, northerners, southerners, males, and females. The voices appear and then reappear until the inevitable clash occurs. Young Homer in *The Mostly True Adventures of Homer P. Figg* (Philbrick) is trying to find his brother who was sold to the Union army by their guardian uncle. Homer's tendency to embellish a story makes for a humorous account of his adventures until the poignant reconciliation with his brother. *Thunder at Gettysburg* (Gauch), *The Storm Before Atlanta* (Schwabach), and *Which Way Freedom?* and *Red Moon at Sharpsburg* (Wells) are all well-researched, exciting stories of Civil War battles as told by children caught in the middle of major conflicts.

Industrialization, Immigration, and Segregation (Late 19th and Early 20th Centuries)

America changed dramatically in the 19th century as industrialization spread and immigrants continued to arrive from many countries. Although the change in technology was intoxicating, the advent of the industrial revolution brought with it deplorable working conditions in factories and the rise of unions. This was also a time of extensive immigration to America by peoples from all over the world. Books for children and adolescents depict the challenges that people faced in this rapidly changing world.

Lyddie (Paterson) tells the story of a young farm girl who believes that working in a Lowell, Massachusetts, textile mill will be better than life in Vermont. Once there, however, she finds dangerous working conditions, uncaring supervisors, and the beginnings of the labor movement. Paterson paints a vivid image of a strong female protagonist who finds solace in books amidst unrelenting work. Paterson explores labor history again in *Bread and Roses Too*, the fictionalized story of a contentious labor strike that actually took place in Vermont.

Not all books portray industrialization as an evil phenomenon. For example, *Fair Weather* (Peck) shows a family eagerly visiting the 1893 World Columbian Exposition in Chicago. The children are awed by the skyscrapers, a large Ferris wheel, the smooth-surfaced city roads, and the opportunity to see famous people, such as Buffalo Bill Cody. The trip is a backdrop for a humorous story of a loving, close-knit family. A unique look at technology in this era is depicted in *The Invention of Hugo Cabret* (Selznick), in which an orphan boy living in a Paris train station discovers an automaton, a type of early robot. *Hugo Cabret* is a blend of graphic novel and fictional prose narrative, making it particularly appropriate for reluctant readers. Another graphic novel that celebrates technology and innovation in this era is *Around the World* (Phelan). Phelan weaves graphic narrative with first-person accounts as well as those of newspaper reporters of the time to tell of various real-life exploits, such as the first person to bicycle across the United States and the first person to sail solo around the world.

The Evolution of Calpurnia Tate (Kelly) recounts the late 19th-century life of Calpurnia, a young girl from a prosperous Texas family. Calpurnia's mother wants her to be a proper lady. However, Calpurnia is entranced by natural science thanks to her eccentric grandfather. She has never heard of a woman becoming a scientist but aches to be one. This novel communicates a curiosity and passion for science that we rarely see in novels for youth while also exploring Calpurnia's evolution into a young woman capable of deciding her own future. *Family Secrets* (Bolden) and *Crow* (Wright) depict the daily lives of African American children and their families in this era.

Millions of immigrants came to America looking for freedom and economic opportunity. In addition to showing young readers a historical era, books about people who chose to immigrate to America are also survival stories: the characters frequently struggle against societal restrictions, battle the vagaries of chance and bad luck, or face inner conflicts that are resolved with growing maturity.

Beyond the Western Sea (Avi) and its sequels are adventurous stories about three Irish children determined to immigrate to America. Laurence Yep's *Golden Mountain Chronicles* (*Dragon's Gate*, *Dragonwings*, and others) depicts several generations of a Chinese family who immigrate and help construct the transcontinental railroad. Yep weaves interesting cultural and historical details into a compelling story of survival under brutal, almost unendurable conditions. Other excellent stories about immigration in this era include *Esperanza Rising* (Ryan), the story of a pampered, young Mexican girl who flees with her mother to work the fields of California after her father dies; *Nory Ryan's Song* (Giff), a poignant tale of one girl's life during the Irish potato famine that ends with an opportunity to emigrate; and *Letters from Rifka* (Hesse), in which a young Russian Jewish girl battles uncaring officials and countless regulations to be reunited with her family in America.

Rascism was still an integral part of American culture during this era. Gary Schmidt explores the insidious effects of such racism on a small town in *Lizzie Bright and the Buckminster Boy*. This novel centers around Turner, the son of a minister newly assigned to a coastal Maine parish where prejudice and discrimination are accepted as the natural order of things. Turner becomes fascinated by an African American island community, the home of his new friend Lizzie. Unfortunately, the townspeople intend to displace the island residents to create a tourist attraction and will do almost anything to reach that goal. Turner faces a moral dilemma: should an entire historical community be displaced for another town's economic benefit? A tragic conclusion heightens the emotional impact of this compelling book.

Iran in the late 19th century provides the setting for *Anahita's Woven Riddle* (Sayres). Anahita, daughter of a tribal leader, is bethrothed to an old and powerful ally of her father. However, Anahita strikes a bargain that will allow her a voice in choosing her future husband, creating a game in which she makes potential suitors guess the riddle that she weaves into her wedding carpet.

The Great Depression (1930s)

The Great Depression was a particularly difficult time in American history. Many children's books explore the hardships that people experienced during this era, including rampant unemployment, agricultural disasters, and homelessness. One of the most enduring stories set in this era is Mildred Taylor's *Roll of Thunder, Hear My Cry*, which depicts the life of a close-knit African American family in Mississippi during the 1930s. The racism they experience is countered by loving family ties that help them survive. The Logan family's lives are further chronicled in *The Well, Song of the Trees, Let the Circle Be Unbroken, The Friendship*, and the prequel *The Land*.

The Dust Bowl, a time when huge dust storms swept across the American prairies, was a defining event of this era. *Out of the Dust* (Hesse) poignantly chronicles one girl's life in Oklahoma during the Dust Bowl era. Written in a poetic free verse style, this novel illuminates the psychological pain that young Billie Jo endures as she first copes with her mother's death in a fire that Billie Jo caused and then lives with her father's resulting isolation. Played against the constant presence of dust that sneaks through every crack and crevice, the novel has a gritty realism and emotional impact that makes it unforgettable.

Storm in the Barn (Phelan) offers another perspective on the Dust Bowl days. The protagonist, a boy on a Kansas farm beset by drought, tries to be useful to his father by spiritually coaxing the rains. This book of historical fiction breaks convention not only because it is a graphic novel but also because it includes some elements of fantasy. Christopher Paul Curtis's Bud in *Bud, Not Buddy* is an orphan living in Depression-era Michigan. Bud is fed up with the abuse he has endured in various foster homes and runs away to find his long-lost grandfather. Through his own ingenuity and small kindnesses from people along the way, he reaches his goal, only to encounter new challenges. Bud is an endearing hero, full of hope, optimism, and humorous observations on life. *The Mighty Miss Malone* (Curtis) is a sequel that chronicles the challenges faced by Deza Malone, a minor character in *Bud, Not Buddy*, as she travels with her family to find their missing father. Both books capture the desperation that people often felt during the Depression but both also show how communities and individuals helped each other survive.

Moon over Manifest (Vanderpool) is set in Depression-era Manifest, Kansas, a town worn down by drought, sorrow, and the Depression. Twelve-year-old Abilene Tucker is sent there by her father, who lived in Manifest in 1918. Abilene's attempts to uncover the secrets of her past as well as her father's are interwoven with letters, newspaper articles, and stories from 1918. The multiple narratives weave humor and sorrow with adventures involving murders, bootleggers, orphans, and the Ku Klux Klan to create a complex, intriguing story full of colorful characters.

A lighter depiction of small-town life during the Depression is chronicled in *A Long Way to Chicago* (Peck). In this humorous, engaging story, two children leave the city to visit their grandmother in small-town Illinois. Grandma Dowd is "tough as a boot" and devises hilarious schemes to exact revenge against neighbors who have wronged her. Of course, the children become enmeshed in her plans. Each chapter is its own short story, making this book and its sequel, *The Year Down Yonder* (Peck), excellent for read-alouds and for students just getting into chapter books. *Turtle in Paradise* (Holm) also uses a humorous tone to chronicle small-town life during the Depression in which the struggles and deprivations that people experienced during this time are subtly woven into the story events. Turtle is a tough heroine who longs for a happy ending, such as the one in *Little Orphan Annie* comics, although she is savvy enough to realize that life usually does not have Hollywood endings.

Novels that present a unique slice of life from the Depression era are *Al Capone Does My Shirts, Al Capone Shines My Shoes*, and *Al Capone Does My Homework* (Choldenko), which follow the adventures of 12-year-old Moose, who moves to the infamous Alcatraz prison when his father is employed there. Moose and his family are at the center of these stories, but readers also acquire a fascinating glimpse of life on Alcatraz during the gangster era.

World War II (1940s)

World War II is another popular topic for authors of children's historical fiction. Books about the Holocaust, children living their daily lives on the home front in America, and resistance to or escape from occupation help children understand multiple perspectives on this defining event of the 20th century.

A few stories, such as *The Endless Steppe* (Hautzig) and *The Devil's Arithmetic* (Yolen), recount harrowing experiences in concentration camps. However, most titles focus on the trials of families who are forced to hide from the enemy or who narrowly escape to freedom. *Number the Stars* (Lowry) tells the exciting story of Anne Marie, a child living in Denmark during the German occupation who helps a Jewish family escape. *The Upstairs Room* (Reiss) is an emotionally moving account of two Jewish sisters who were successfully hidden by a farm family, whereas *The Island on Bird Street* (Orlev) portrays the experiences of 12-year-old Alex, who eludes detection as he hides in a Polish ghetto. In contrast, *T4* (LeZotte) is a poetic verse novel based on a little-known fact that Hitler also sent disabled people to their deaths in concentration camps. *T4* tells of Paula, a young deaf girl who is successfully hidden and ultimately survives.

Children in Japan and Korea also suffered hardships during this time. Many had to flee from their homes as war closed in around them. *So Far from the Bamboo Grove* (Watkins) recounts the escape of a Japanese family living in North Korea who must flee as the communists take over. Their story continues in *My Brother, My Sister, and I* (Watkins). *When My Name Was Keoko* (Park) is also set in Korea but offers a different perspective in that it describes how two Korean children struggle to survive during the Japanese occupation. *The Year of Impossible Goodbyes* (Choi) also describes the struggles of two Korean children as Japanese forces occupy their country. In this exciting story, the two girls are separated from their family during an escape to South Korea and must complete the harrowing journey on their own.

Books about the American home front during this era typically focus on the effects of war on children. *Stepping on the Cracks* (Hahn) and its sequels show American children going about their everyday lives with the war as a backdrop. *My Friend the Enemy* (Cheaney), written in the first person, features a preteen girl who grows from hating the Japanese to befriending a Japanese American orphan. *Autumn Street* (Lowry), *Lily's Crossing* (Giff), *The Green Glass Sea* (Klages), and *Willow Run* (Giff) all feature young female protagonists who are affected by the war, whereas *On the Wings of Eagles* (Peck) and *The Art of Keeping Cool* (Lisle) have male protagonists.

A number of books help children empathize with Japanese Americans or Japanese Canadians who were interred following the bombing of Pearl Harbor. *Journey to Topaz* (Uchida) is a fictionalized account of the experiences

Wanted Jewish Family Missing!

A wanted Jewish family, The Rosen's, was discovered missing a few days ago.

They lived in Copenhagen, Denmark. They are suspected to be fleeing from Denmark for freedom and hiding from Nazi soliders. It is thought by the Nazi Police that the family was helped by a group called the Resistance.

The Rosen's apartment was searched but all of their belongings were gone.

The Johansen Family was suspected to be involved somehow. They are friends and neighbors of the Rosen's. The Johansen household was searched but no evidence came up.

Police are still searching for many other wanted people of the Jewish Religion. Neighbors say that there was no sign of anyone moving out of or even leaving the apartment building with a lot of belongings.

If you have any information, please call the Copenhagen Nazi Police Headquarters.

Section from a mock newspaper written by a fifth grader in response to Number the Stars by Lois Lowry.

endured by the author's family who were sent to Topaz, an internment center in Utah. *Journey Home* (Uchida) tells of the family's release, only to experience mistrust when they return home.

Weedflower (Kadohata) also provides an in-depth look at prejudice and life in a Japanese internment camp. Sumiko's family is stunned to be removed from their home, knowing that they had never broken a single American law. To be confined to "camp" is difficult, but Sumiko finds meaning in growing flowers as well as in her friendship with an elderly neighbor. The perspective of Louise, a young girl whose best friend, Dottie, is imprisoned, is chronicled in *Best Friends Forever: A World War II Scrapbook* (Patt). Louise's journal along with her friend's letters and other artifacts provide intriguing details into Dottie's life as a prisoner as well as Louise's growing indignation over the injustice of Dottie's imprisonment. Graham Salisbury's *Under the Blood-Red Sun* and *House of the Red Fish* show how Japanese Americans in Hawaii were treated at this time.

Civil Rights, Political Unrest, and the Vietnam War (1950–1970s)

Problems with racism and segregation simmered throughout the 20th century, eventually exploding as the civil rights movement of the 1960s. Several excellent children's books chronicle this tumultuous time in American history. In other stories set in this era, children's everyday lives are chronicled with the mid-20th-century historical setting as a backdrop that influences their lives.

Racism against African Americans in the mid-20th century is vividly conveyed in *The Legend of Buddy Bush* (Moses), a story that describes how 12-year-old Patti Mae's Uncle Buddy is falsely accused of rape and almost lynched. Fortunately, Buddy escapes into the surrounding swamps and heads north. Their story continues in *The Return of Buddy Bush* (Moses) when Patti convinces Buddy to return home, where he is tried and eventually acquitted. Students interested in finding out more about injustices against African Americans, particularly lynchings, can read *A Wreath for Emmett Till* (Nelson), a fictionalized verse novel account of a lynching that actually occurred.

Christopher Paul Curtis uses both humor and pathos to relate the experiences of 10-year-old Kenny as he and his family drive from Detroit to Alabama, where they unwittingly observe the bombing of an African American church in *The Watsons Go to Birmingham—1963*. In *Walking to the Bus Rider Blues* (Robinet), a family finds itself amidst the 1956 Montgomery bus boycott. The effects of school desegregation on children of both races are explored in *The Lions of Little Rock* (Levine) and *Beyond Mayfield* and *Mayfield Crossing* (Nelson).

Racism against Japanese Americans also lingered after World War II. *Bat 6* (Wolff), set in a small town in Oregon in 1949, shows how the prejudices engendered by the war exploded in a girls' community baseball league. Written in alternating voices from the team of girls whose fathers had fought for America in the war and then the opposing team of Japanese American girls, this novel poignantly shows the enmity between those who fought in the American forces and those who were interred. *Kira, Kira* (Kadohata) is a moving story of two Japanese American sisters who move from Iowa to Georgia, where they encounter frank curiosity and outright prejudice. The sisters help each other endure the slurs until the older one dies of leukemia.

The year 1968 was a pivotal one of social and political change for this era: Martin Luther King Jr. was assassinated, the Civil Rights Act was passed, and the Black Panthers formed to promote black power. *One Crazy Summer* (Williams-Garcia) takes readers into the heart of this history through the voice of Delphine, an 11-year-old girl who observes all these events and brings her own perspective to interpreting them. Delphine and her younger sisters are sent to Oakland, California, to stay for a month with their mother, who abandoned the family years

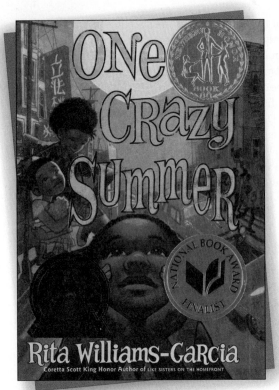

In *One Crazy Summer* by Rita Williams-Garcia, readers vicariously experience what it was like to grow up in the mid 1960s.

ago. They encounter a city in turmoil, far from their dreams of Hollywood and Disneyland. As the girls attend youth programs sponsored by the Black Panthers and tentatively come to understand their mother, they learn much about political revolution as well as the meaning of family. Their story continues in *P.S. Be Eleven* (Williams-Garcia) when the girls return to New York City, only to encounter resistance to their new found independence and assertiveness.

Some books present a slice-of-life perspective on the mid-20th century. Tiger Ann Parker, the protagonist in *My Louisiana Sky* (Holt), struggles to help her mentally challenged parents in Texas of the late 1950s. When given the chance to move in with a glamorous aunt in Baton Rouge, she must decide who and what is important in her life. In *Penny from Heaven* (Holm), Penny must sort out the tensions and prejudices that keep her deceased father's Italian relatives estranged from her mother's family. Lingering prejudices toward Italian Americans that followed World War II are a backdrop for this gentle family story that occurs in New Jersey of the 1950s. *The Loud Silence of Maxine Green* (Cushman) and *The Rising Star of Rusty Nail* (Blume) explore how people's lives were affected by the fear of communism during the 1950s. In all these books, authentic details give young readers a sense of what everyday life was like as well a sense of the social and political issues of this era.

The threat of nuclear war was very real at this time, and a few children's books explore the intense emotions aroused by this possibility. *Countdown* (Wiles) is set just outside Washington, D.C., during the 1960 Cuban missile crisis, a time when people built bomb shelters and children were taught to crouch under their school desks in the event of a nuclear attack. Amidst the threat of war, 11-year-old Franny also contends with family problems and a troublesome best friend. *Dead End in Norvelt* (Gantos) is a more lighthearted look at these fears. Twelve-year old Jack is "grounded for life" in the summer of 1962 and required to dig a bomb shelter for his father. His mom also loans him out to help an elderly neighbor, and Jack becomes enmeshed in adventures featuring Girl Scout cookies, Hell's Angels, molten wax, and murder. Quirky characters and a mystery make this a good book for readers who might not normally read historical fiction.

Social and political issues around the world in the mid-20th century are the context for a few books for children. South African writer Beverly Naidoo explores the violent end of British colonial rule in Kenya in *Burn My Heart*, which focuses on the friendship of Matthew, who is one of the privileged Whites, and Mugo, a native Kenyan. The growing tensions between the White and local inhabitants gradually erupt, and Matthew is faced with an agonizing choice. *Before We Were Free* (Alvarez) is a similarly compelling book for mature middle school readers in which 12-year-old Anna's family is in deadly peril as her father and uncle join the attempt to overthrow the Trujillo regime in the Dominican Republic. When the revolution fails, Anna and her mother must escape the country. Children who were evacuated from Cuba during the 1961 Cuban Revolution are the premise for *90 Miles to Havana* (Floris-Galbes) and *The Red Umbrella* (Gonzalez).

The Vietnam War was another significant event of the mid-20th century. As with historical fiction set in other times of war, many stories set in the Vietnam era tend to focus on American children wrestling with identity issues, the historical details of the war providing a backdrop to the story's main events. For example, *The Wednesday Wars* (Schmidt) humorously recounts the life of Holling Hoodhood, the only boy in his seventh-grade class who remains behind on Wednesday afternoons while the other students attend religion classes. He is convinced that his teacher hates him, particularly when she assigns him Shakespeare to read. Although he initially resists, he gradually falls in love with the plays. Passing references to television broadcasts of war casualties and a classmate who is a Vietnamese refugee, for example, anchor the setting of this book in the late 1960s. *Okay for Now* (Schmidt) is ostensibly a sequel but makes only passing reference to events in *The Wednesday Wars*. Rather, the focus is on Doug Swieteck, a minor player in the first book who must contend with an abusive father, small-town prejudice, and a brother who returns from Vietnam a paraplegic.

Several other books set in this era depict American children contending with issues related to the war, such as absent fathers or older siblings who return from combat forever changed. In *Shooting the Moon* (Dowell), 12-year-old card shark Jamie Dexter yearns to volunteer for service in Vietnam along with her older brother. However, when she starts developing the rolls of film he sends home from the battlefields, Jamie begins to have serious doubts about war and the military. *Almost Forever* (Testa) is a verse novel that explores a young girl's feelings when her father is sent to Vietnam as a medic for a year that seems to last "almost forever."

Few books for elementary and middle school students depict actual Vietnam War battles. Some mature middle school readers might be ready for the graphic language and realistic battle scenes of *Fallen Angels* (Myers), the gripping story of a young man whose platoon battles the Vietcong with devastating results. A book suitable for younger readers is *Cracker!: The Best Dog in Vietnam* (Kadohata), which alternates viewpoints between a young soldier and a dog trained to sniff out land mines. When the soldier is critically injured and sent home, he—and the reader—anxiously await word of the dog's fate. *Letters from Wolfie* (Sherlock) also focuses on a dog that helps soldiers in Vietnam. In this story, 13-year-old Mark volunteers his beloved dog for war service after his older brother enlists. In addition to Wolfie's experiences (chronicled in letters from his soldier companion), readers become aware of the family's growing disillusionment with the war.

Some stories are set in Vietnam or Cambodia and chronicle the experiences of children directly affected by the war. Most show families escaping from the political and economic oppression in Vietnam and Cambodia that resulted from the conflict. *Inside Out and Back Again* (Lai) is a lyrical verse novel that describes the trials of a young girl and her family who narrowly escape to America during the fall of Saigon, only to face new challenges adjusting to life in America. *Escaping the Tiger* (Manivong) tells of 12-year-old Vonlai, who escapes from communist Laos, only to face horrible conditions in a Thailand refugee camp. In contrast, *Never Fall Down* (McCormack) is a fictionalized account of the real peace activist Arn Chorn-Pond, who, as a young Cambodian boy, is captured by the Khmer Rouge to be used as a slave laborer and later a child soldier. He experiences almost unimaginable horrors in a book that haunts the reader long after the reading.

Tech Click

Microblogging with Historical Fiction

Twitter is a text-based microblogging service. Subscribers "follow" their friends via a Web page or mobile device. Your students might enjoy composing "tweets" as if written by the characters in any historical fiction book they have read. They would need to infer a character's daily activities or emotional state and note the historical events likely to happen during the time period. Capturing the cadence and speech patterns of the protagonists would add an extra layer of challenge. Even without a computer or using only small blocks of time, students could simulate fictional characters' tweets.

A second grade child summarizes the story of Yonder by Tony Johnston.

Picture Books in Historical Fiction

Historical fiction picture books typically portray small slices of life from the past. Glimpses of daily routines and human responses to critical historical events or personal dilemmas are simply told through text and illustration. As with novels in this genre, authenticity is critical. Illustrators and writers typically spend considerable time researching details of dress, setting, and language to get everything historically correct. For example, Michael Tunnell and Ted Rand extensively studied historical photographs and documents, including a personal eyewitness account of the child's journey, for *Mailing May*, a delightful story of a little girl who is mailed by railroad to her grandmother in 1914 (Tunnell, 2000). In contrast, *Sky Dancers* (Kirk), an interesting story of the Native American construction workers who helped build the Empire State Building, has one flaw: it includes pictures of bridges that did not yet exist in this era, making it less historically accurate.

Picture books are an excellent medium for drawing primary children into reading historical fiction. For example, *Ma Dear's Aprons* (McKissack) and *The Dream Jar* (Pryor) reveal what life was like at the turn of the 20th century while also showing young readers that family love is timeless. *Boxes for Katje* (Fleming) and *One Thousand Tracings* (Judge) depict American children sending clothing to European children following World War II, demonstrating a value that we hope contemporary children will embrace. *The Sweet Smell of Roses* (Johnson) and *Freedom Summer* (Wiles) introduce young children to some issues surrounding the civil rights movement.

The short, engaging plots and illustrations of historical fiction picture books can bring significant details of setting and events alive for older students as well. *Hiroshima No Pika* (Maruki) shows one family's response to the bombing of Hiroshima. The illustrations and sparse text of this book give readers a more personal understanding of the destructive power of a nuclear bomb and its horrifying effect on people. *The Bracelet* (Uchida) and *Baseball Saved Us* (Mochizuki) are excellent picture books that can introduce students to the internment of Japanese Americans during World War II. *Henry's Freedom Box* (Nelson) is a fictionalized account of Henry Brown, a slave who escaped to freedom by mailing himself in a packing crate. Kadir Nelson cleverly uses cutaways in the book's illustrations to depict how cramped (and sometimes upside down) Henry was as his journey progressed, making his agony and determination emotionally moving. Teachers of older students can use books like these to introduce or complement a unit of study to shed light on complex historical concepts, promote critical

Henry's Freedom Box: A True Story From the Underground Railroad by Ellen Levine depicts the determination of a slave who escapes by mailing himself to the North in a packing crate.

discussions, and make social studies more inviting and accessible (Albright, 2002; Rycik & Rosier, 2009; Wolf, 2004; Youngs & Serafini, 2011). A number of excellent historical fiction picture books for all ages are listed at the end of this chapter.

Series and Transitional Books in Historical Fiction

Series books featuring historical settings and characters are popular with many children. The series *American Girl, Dear America, My Name Is America, American Diaries, Once Upon America, Horrible Histories, Royal Diaries, American Adventures, Roman Mysteries*, and others feature engaging stories set in carefully researched historical contexts. Many are written by award-winning authors such as Patricia McKissack, Karen Hesse, and Jim Murphy, who are already known for their work writing historical fiction or nonfiction based in historical eras.

A few of these series books have been criticized for promoting stereotypes or portraying a too-positive or one-sided perspective on history. Specifically, one of the *Dear America* books, *My Heart Is on the Ground: The Diary of Nannie Little Rose, a Sioux Girl* (Rinaldi), has been criticized for portraying Native Americans in stereotypical and inaccurate ways (Smith, 2006). Most of the books, however, feature short chapters with plenty of historically authentic action and characters who experience interesting challenges and adventures. They are particularly appropriate for enticing younger readers just transitioning into reading chapter books to become interested in the historical fiction genre.

In addition to series books, a number of other historical fiction books feature short chapters, fast-paced plots, and relatable characters set in a historical context that appeals to transitional readers. For example, *Snow Treasure* (McSwigen) is an exciting story set in Norway during World War II in which children must slip $9 million of gold bricks past Nazi guards. They do this by secreting the gold on their sleds. *A Lion to Guard Us* (Bulla) tells the story of three children who sail from London to meet their father, who has already settled in Jamestown. Strong messages of courage in the face of adversity and persistence in reaching one's goals, along with just the right amount of historical detail, make this an excellent book for introducing younger children to historical fiction. A few historical fiction stories are written especially for beginning readers. They often feature young protagonists involved in an adventure in which they play a pivotal role as in *The Boston Coffee Party* by Doreen Rappaport, in which two young sisters tell the story of this actual historical event from their perspective. A list at the end of the chapter features recommended historical fiction books that can engage transitional and beginning readers.

Teaching Strategies

Connecting to the Common Core State Standards

COMMON CORE STATE STANDARD FEATURE #1

Comparing and Contrasting Books on the Same Theme, Historical Era, or Different Genre (CCSS.RL.9 and RI.9)

An important critical reading skill is the ability to move beyond one book and compare various aspects of that book with another one. The Common Core State Standards (CCSS) affirm the importance of this skill in the Reading: Literature Standard and Reading: Informational Text Standards RL.9 and RI.9:

CCRA (Anchor Standard) RL.9 and RI.9 (Anchor Standard): Analyze how two or more texts address similar themes or topics in order to build knowledge or to compare the approaches the authors take.

Sample Grade-Level Competencies for This Standard Are the Following:

RL.1.9, RI.1.9. Compare and contrast the adventures and experiences of characters in stories.

RL.3.9, RI.3.9. Compare and contrast the themes, settings, and plots of stories written by the same author about the same or similar characters (e.g., in books from a series).

RL.5.9, RI.5.9. Compare and contrast the most important points and key details presented in two texts on the same topic.

RL.7.9, RI.7.9. Integrate information from several texts on the same topic in order to write or speak about the subject knowledgeably.

The following strategies help students develop this skill.

Comparison Charts: Creating a chart that visually shows how books are alike and different on selected criteria is an excellent way to help students begin comparing and contrasting books based on literary and historical elements. For example, students could compare historical contexts, themes, character dilemmas, plot conflicts and their resolutions, or other aspects of two or more books set in the same historical era, depending on what literary or historical elements you wish to emphasize. Or charts could be developed to compare how several books develop one element through several eras. For example, the theme of war's effects on children and families could be the focus of a chart of books focused on the American Revolution or the Vietnam War. A historical movement, such as the 1960s struggle for civil rights, or character traits, such as "maintaining one's dignity in face of persecution," are other possible themes. Examples of grids and templates that could be charted in this way can be found on the Internet and in Chapter 2.

Comparing Books in the Same Historical Era Written from Multiple Perspectives: Reading books about the same event that are written from divergent points of view or that feature characters from completely different sides of a conflict can build a deeper understanding of the events or historical era and provide the opportunity to read from a critical stance. For example, when studying the American Revolution, students can create comparison charts or other graphic organizers that compare the attitudes toward the war espoused in *Johnny Tremain* (Forbes) with more critical views in *Chains* (Anderson) and *The Fighting Ground* (Avi). When studying the Holocaust, they could compare *Hide and Seek* (Vos), the story of a Jewish family who goes into hiding, with *Number the Stars* (Lowry), an exciting story of the Danish resistance efforts; *The Boy Who Dared* (Bartoletti), about a German boy who is initially enamored with the Nazis and then joins the German resistance movement; or *Stepping on the Cracks* (Hahn), which provides an entirely different view: the experiences of American children during the war.

Several historical fiction books are written in the form of multiple voices. For example, *Bull Run* (Fleischman) and *Slopes of War* (Perez) feature the perspectives of multiple characters on

Civil War battles. *Voices from the Alamo* (Garland) presents diverse perspectives on this famous battle, whereas *Good Masters! Sweet Ladies: Voices from a Medieval Village* (Schlitz) features the voices of diverse residents of a medieval village, from lord to lowly servant. *New Found Land* (Wolf) is a series of short vignettes of different characters associated with the Lewis and Clark expedition, whereas *Witness* (Hesse) shows the perspectives of many residents in a small town when the Ku Klux Klan attempts to recruit new members into its ranks. These are excellent resources for readers' theater dramatizations. Students can take on the persona of different characters from a book and then create a performance that is followed by a discussion of how each character's perspective influenced their perception of the historical era. (Note: This activity also develops competence in CCSS RL Standard 6: Understanding Point of View.)

Tech Click

The Children's Book Council (CBC) provides a free online book search feature by title, format, genre, and awards. For example, short summary and approximate age level of *A Storm Called Katrina* (Uhlberg) can be found under "Historical Fiction." The CBC also list titles of interest to diverse readers.

Comparing Historical Fiction with Nonfiction Historical Accounts: Students can read a historical fiction book in conjunction with nonfiction texts based on the same historical events to build background knowledge and vocabulary and to scaffold and extend their understanding of the fictional story's historical context. Thus, students could compare the experiences of the Logan family in *Roll of Thunder, Hear My Cry* (Taylor) or Bud in *Bud, Not Buddy* (Curtis) to those of real children and families living through those times as described in *Children of the Great Depression* (Freedman), *Dear Mrs. Roosevelt: Letters from Children of the Great Depression* (Cohen), or *Born and Bred in the Great Depression* (Winter). Using both genres on the same topic provides a more holistic perspective: fiction illuminates the human side, whereas nonfiction adds knowledge of the factual historical record (Soalt, 2005). Additionally, this teaching strategy can build vocabulary as students often explore new vocabulary in multiple contexts; a new word encountered in a nonfiction text may be used in the fictional one. Encountering new words in multiple contexts is critical for deep understanding and retention of those words.

Pairing nonfiction with fiction texts also engages more readers. Children who might normally enjoy only nonfiction might become more interested in a fictional story, whereas those typically more interested in fiction might be motivated to discover "what really happened" in the era of a fictional story they have enjoyed. Students can then consider how the historical fiction author integrated history into the story, determining what is fact and what is fiction. Some sample book pairings for this purpose are listed in Figure 8.2.

Comparing Historical Fiction with Poetic Historical Accounts: Poetic accounts of historical events can add yet another dimension to history. Poetry is often emotional and expressive, drawing readers into exploring intensely personal perspectives on historical events. For example, while studying books on the Holocaust, students could also read selections from *I Never Saw Another Butterfly: Children's Drawings and Poems from the Terezin Concentration Camp* (Volavkova) or selections from *Requiem: Poems of the Terezin Ghetto* (Janeczko). After reading

FIGURE 8.2 Connecting Historical Fiction with Nonfiction

Pilgrims

McGovern, A. *If You Sailed on the Mayflower in 1620.* (NF) (P, M)

Peacock, C. *Pilgrim Cat.* (HF) (P)

Salem Witch Trials

Speare, Elizabeth. *The Witch of Blackbird Pond.* (HF) (M)

Yolen, Jane. *The Salem Witch Trials: An Unsolved Mystery from History.* (NF) (I, M)

American Revolution

Anderson, Laurie Halse. *Forge.* (HF) (M)

Freedman, Russell. *Washington at Valley Forge.* (NF) (M)

Yellow Fever Epidemic

Anderson, Laurie Halse. *Fever 1793.* (HF) (M)

Jurmain, Suzanne. *The Secret of the Yellow Death: A True Story of Medical Sleuthing.* (NF) (M)

Underground Railroad

Hopkinson, D. *Under the Quilt of Night*; *Sweet Clara and the Freedom Quilt.* (HF) (P, I)

Levine, E. *If You Traveled on the Underground Railroad.* (I, M) (NF)

Immigration

Blumberg, R. *Full Steam Ahead: The Race to Build the Transcontinental Railroad.* (I, M)

Freedman, Russell. *Immigrant Kids.* (NF) (I, M)

Hesse, Karen. *Letters from Rifka.* (HF) (I, M)

Yin. *Coolies.* (HF) (I)

The Great Depression

Cohen, Robert (Ed.). *Dear Mrs. Roosevelt: Letters from Children of the Great Depression.* (NF) (I, M)

Curtis, Christopher Paul. *Bud, Not Buddy; The Mighty Miss Malone.* (HF) (I, M)

Freedman, Russell. *Children of the Great Depression.* (NF) (I, M)

Taylor, Mildred. *Roll of Thunder, Hear My Cry.* (HF) (I, M)

Winter, Jonah. *Born and Bred in the Great Depression* (Kimberly Bulcken Root, Illus.). (NF) (P, I)

Dust Bowl Days

Hesse, Karen. *Out of the Dust.* (HF) (M)

Phelan, Matt. *The Storm in the Barn.* (HF) (I, M)

Stanley, Jerry. *Children of the Dust Bowl: The True Story of the School at Weedpatch Camp.* (NF) (I, M)

World War II Japanese Internment

Cooper. Michael. *Remembering Manzanar: Life in a Japanese Relocation Camp.* (NF) (M)

Kadahata, Cynthia. *Weedflower.* (HF) (M)

Sandler, Martin. *Imprisoned: The Betrayal of Japanese Americans During World War II.* (NF) (I, M)

World War II: Holocaust

Fox, A. *Ten Thousand Children: True Stories Told by Children Who Escaped on the Kindertransport.* (NF) (I, M)

Polacco, P. *The Butterfly.* (HF) (I, M)

Thomson, R. *Terezin: Voices from the Holocaust.* (NF) (I, M)

Alcatraz Island Prison

Choldenko, Jennifer. *Al Capone Does My Shirts.* (HF) (M)

Murphy, Claire Rudolph. *The Children of Alcatraz: Growing Up on the Rock.* (NF) (I, M)

Racism: Mid-20th Century

Crowe, Chris. *Getting Away with Murder: The True Story of the Emmett Till Case.* (NF) (M)

Nelson, Marilyn. *A Wreath for Emmett Till* (Philippe Lardy, Illus.). (HF) (M)

Vawter, Vince. *Paperboy.* (HF) (I, M)

Civil Rights

Brimmer, Larry, D. *Birmingham Sunday.* (NF) (I, M)

Curtis, Christopher Paul. *The Watsons Go to Birmingham: 1963.* (HF) (I, M)

School Integration

Levine, Kristin. *The Lions of Little Rock.* (HF) (I, M)

Morrison, Toni. *Remember: The Journey to School Integration.* (NF) (I, M)

The Sweet Smell of Roses (Johnson) or *Freedom on the Menu: The Greensboro Sit-Ins* (Weatherford), two books about the civil rights movement, students could read selections from *When Thunder Comes: Poems for Civil Rights Leaders* (Lewis), which focuses on the ideals and feelings of those who led the protests. Chapter 5 features many excellent titles for this purpose.

COMMON CORE STATE STANDARD FEATURE #2

Analyzing the Connection Between Text and Illustration in Historical Fiction Picture Books (CCSS.RL.7)

Research suggests that supporting children's understandings of the interplay between text and images in picture books of historical fiction builds their understanding of a book's historical era as well as more nuanced interpretations of the story. They can learn to notice how illustrators subtly embed symbolic images in their illustrations, use color to depict mood or highlight character qualities, and employ a visual narrative that complements the written one (Youngs, 2012; Youngs & Serafini, 2011). The CCSS affirm the importance of visual literacy in the Reading: Literature Standard RL.7:

CCRA (Anchor Standard) RL.7: Integrate and evaluate content presented in diverse media and formats, including visually and quantitatively, as well as in words.

Selected Grade-Level Competencies for This Standard Are the Following:

RL.1.7. Use illustrations and details in a story to describe its characters, setting, or events.

RL.3.7. Explain how specific aspects of a text's illustrations contribute to what is conveyed by the words in a story (e.g., create mood, emphasize aspects of a character or setting).

RL.5.7. Analyze how visual and multimedia elements contribute to the meaning, tone, or beauty of a text (e.g., graphic novel, multimedia presentation of fiction, folktale, myth, poem).

Aspects of setting in the illustrations for a picture book can be closely examined to learn about the landscape, characters, architecture, dress, or other elements of a historical era. Children can also learn to notice more subtle elements of illustration, such as color, space, and symbolism. For example, picture book illustrators often use color to convey mood or to emphasize significant visual elements, as Chris Soentpiet did in *So Far from the Sea* (Bunting). In this story, Soentpiet alternates pages in color that depict a present-day setting with those in black and white that show the bleak landscape of a Japanese internment camp in the past. The contrast makes the narrative, which shifts between past and present, clear and dramatic. Sometimes, prominent characters are placed in light to convey their role in the story. *Lisette's Angel* (Littlesugar), the story of a French child who rescues an American paratrooper during World War II, features dark shadows and landscapes. In contrast, the heroine Lisette wears a white nightgown as she bravely hides the man and his parachute from approaching Nazi soldiers. The contrast draws the reader's eye to her and emphasizes the heroism of her acts (Youngs, 2012).

Symbolism in illustrations for historical fiction can particularly enhance the meaning of a story. For example, *The Sweet Smell of Roses* (Johnson), a story of two young African American girls who sneak out to march in a civil rights march, is illustrated completely in black and white with touches of red on symbolic images of freedom, beauty and innocence (e.g., roses), the American flag, and a teddy bear's bow. The symbolic use of red is juxtaposed against the harsh realities they encounter on the march (Youngs, 2012). Outstretched hands form a symbolic bond in *Pink and Say* (Polacco), the story of a friendship between two boys who originally fight on opposite sides of the Civil War. When the boys are wrenched apart by soldiers, their outstretched hands, separated by significant white space, powerfully convey their helplessness in a cruel war.

Supporting Culturally Diverse Learners with Historical Fiction

As with other genres, historical fiction featuring diverse characters provides opportunities for young readers to encounter voices that have been silenced or ignored in traditional historical accounts. These voices are heard and multiple interpretations of events presented. Culturally diverse readers will discover heroes who are lauded for actions that are valued by their culture rather than those perpetuated by the mainstream culture. In turn, readers from mainstream cultures will have their own perspectives broadened as they learn about new ways of looking at the past.

However, appreciation of cultural differences and a sense of pride in the past are not enough. Readers must also encounter books in which diverse characters are empowered, encountering injustices and marginalization and then addressing these inequities. For example, a book such as *Chains* (Anderson), in which a female African American character escapes from slavery through her own initiative, casting off both physical and emotional chains in the process, shows a seemingly ordinary person using courage and ingenuity to gain power over her destiny. *Li'l Dan the Drummer Boy: A Civil War Story* (Bearden), the fictionalized account of a true story in which a young African American slave is freed by northern African American soldiers who in turn saves their lives, affirms the significance of African Americans in American history (Ching, 2005). Books such as these not only develop empathy for their diverse protagonists but also portray these characters as powerful, with the ability to change the course of historical events. We hope that this leads to the willingness of children to critique their own worldviews, particularly with regard to how a dominant group has often marginalized other cultures throughout history (Sipe, 1997).

Historical fiction also helps us reclaim the legacy of women in history. Not only have textbooks marginalized the role of women in history, but their roles have been interpreted through male perspectives and cultural values as well, leading to distorted and inaccurate understandings of these roles. Many of the books described in this chapter feature active, empowered women who significantly influence historical events or gain power to effect change in their lives and those of others they encounter. Reading books such as these gives students of both genders a more accurate and inclusive understanding of history.

Books that feature diverse perspectives on history or diverse characters in significant roles are marked with # in all lists in this chapter.

Tech Click

The International Reading Association's Web site readwritethink.org includes Cube Creator, a simple but interactive tool for English language learners to use in capturing what they know about a historical fiction title.

Supporting English Language Learners with Historical Fiction

Many of the strategies for helping English language learners (ELLs) successfully read other genres are also appropriate for historical fiction. The main additional thing teachers need to be mindful of with this genre is that it is likely that ELL students will not have the background knowledge of historical events that native English speakers often possess. Such knowledge is often assumed by authors as they craft stories with important events as the background or center of the narrative. Thus, teachers must help students develop this knowledge.

Fiction and nonfiction picture books as well as graphic novels that are set in the same era as a novel can provide strong visual cues as well as simple, direct explanations of historical events. Multimedia depictions of various historical eras or events can also help to build this background. For example, the History Channel has many excellent programs that use music, illustration, and narration to bring history vividly to life. Web sites, such as that of the U.S. Holocaust Museum, feature art, actual historical documents (some read aloud on the site), and other artifacts that help make events come alive. Teachers can also bring in historical artifacts from the era of the book's setting, discussing how the artifacts relate to significant aspects of the story.

Once this information is shared, conversations about how this background relates to the story can build English skills as well as an understanding of events and character motivations. The background information can then be recorded visually on time lines, comparison charts, webs, and other graphic displays and placed so that ELL students can easily refer to them as they read the story.

It is also important to build vocabulary knowledge with ELLs. Historical fiction writers sometimes use archaic language to create authenticity. Although this vocabulary may be difficult for many readers, ELL students in particular will likely have no understanding of those words. Additionally, common words, such as *branch*, *stand*, and *party*, have different meanings in history and politics than they do in everyday language, and the specialized meanings for these words may need to be explained. Connecting vocabulary to pictures (drawn or collected by both teachers and students) and word webs that visually display the concepts associated with various words help ELL students develop the vocabulary they need to successfully comprehend stories set in the past.

As with other genres, teachers can use varied strategies to support ELL students as they read a story. Partner reading and readers' theater are effective oral reading strategies. Think-alouds, in which a teacher explains her thinking and evolving understanding of a story as she reads a section of a book, can scaffold the subsequent reading of that story by ELL students. Books on tape can also be used to help ELL students get started with a book, although they should be encouraged as soon as possible to read the book for themselves.

 *Tech Click*

Students are often engaged with online visual representations of what they are learning. Allow students to construct concept webs or vocabulary families using Popplet, Glogster, or Padlet.

 # Controversial Issue: Should All Aspects of History Be Included in Historical Fiction for Children?

Much of history is grim and violent. People do not always act out of noble motives. Sometimes, personal interest, prejudice, or greed rather than concern for the common good were the motivating forces for human actions. People are not all good, nor are they all bad—and thus history is not either. So should we present history to children with all the treachery, bad decisions, and horrific battles (along with the heroic acts and glorious victories) that provide a more complete and realistic picture? Or should they be protected from these realities?

Some adults believe that only the positive aspects of history should be presented to children. Death and war should be reduced to sterile facts and never personalized, they contend. The anticapitalist political beliefs or sexual indiscretions of national icons should not be discussed. (Did you know that Helen Keller was a socialist or that Thomas Jefferson fathered several children with one of his slaves?)

Additionally, some adults contend that profanity and racial epithets should never appear in books for children even if such things are true to the character or realistic for the times. Books like these should be banned from classrooms and libraries. For example, both *My Brother Sam Is Dead* and *The Fighting Ground* are listed in the American Library Association's Top 100 Banned/Challenged Books from 2000 to 2009 due to profanities uttered by some characters (American Library Association, 2010). *Roll of Thunder, Hear My Cry* is also on the list due to racial epithets referring to African Americans that are included in this book and that are historically accurate for its setting.

Attitudes of prejudice and discrimination are also sometimes displayed in historical fiction books. For example, *Little House on the Prairie* has been criticized for including language that is considered derogatory to Native Americans. *Sign of the Beaver*, a story of friendship between a White settler and Native American boy in the Maine wilderness of 1768, includes the following passage in which the White boy describes native characters performing a ceremonial dance:

> He strutted and pranced in ridiculous contortions for the entire world like a clown in a village fair. The line of figures followed after, aping him and stomping their feet in response. (p. 81)

Contemporary stories about the civil rights movement also sometimes show people acting in prejudicial or discriminatory ways, such as in *White Socks Only* (Coman), in which a young African American girl is rudely jerked away from drinking out of a water fountain. Should children be shielded from these attitudes?

We believe that history, with all its glorious achievements as well as its disgraceful parts, should be shared with children. Of course, what is presented must be developmentally appropriate, accurately portray the time period, and be thoroughly discussed. Stories with graphic violence, for example, should probably not be presented to primary grade children. However, children this age can probably grapple with the racial discrimination depicted in picture books or how it must have felt to be a child their age working all day in dangerous factory conditions.

A thoroughly researched, honestly written historical fiction story reflects the values, beliefs, and language of the historical era in which it is set. Author Joyce Hansen (1990) asserts that "the ultimate aim in any book we write for young people should be the heights to which humanity can reach even as we expose the depths to which we can sink" (p. 173). Asking readers of a story to explore why people believed as they did, what factors may have contributed to those beliefs, and then comparing how we think about those issues today are important activities for developing critical thinking and the critical stance. We want students to ask questions such as "How could our country encourage slaves to fight in wars and then not grant them freedom?," "How could factory owners require children to work long hours in unsafe conditions?," or "How could people moving West assume that land was there for the taking?" (Chapter 2 provides more information on taking the critical stance and questioning texts.) We hope that the commonplace is disrupted and that students are moved to think in new ways about issues from the past so that the past informs the present and ultimately the future. A richer, more nuanced presentation of history will help ensure that this thinking occurs.

Tech Click

WebQuests

WebQuests (Dodge, 2001; March, 2007) are an engaging way to integrate resources with close study of historical fiction. Built on existing Web resources, they structure a sequence of learning experiences using preselected links to achieve specific curriculum goals, such as understanding a complex issue or viewing a story from multiple perspectives. For example, several WebQuests for *Number the Stars* (Lowry) ask students to explore World War II history, particularly the Danish resistance. Others might ask students to become a character in the American Revolution with Johnny Tremain (researching the events he participated in) or "escape" with other slaves on the Underground Railroad (locating the best escape routes or other elements of Underground Railroad history).

WebQuests already available on the Internet usually begin with a tantalizing "hook" to immediately grab students and often outline intriguing cooperative roles to be undertaken. Directions for teachers typically include targeted age-level activities, assessment tools, and lists of the curriculum standards addressed. Teachers can use the thousands of existing WebQuests or create their own. (However, be warned that there are many superficial WebQuests online; carefully evaluate any you use.)

Students using WebQuests benefit from exploring reputable sources with rich information that coordinates with classroom curriculum. WebQuests can be individualized so that students can be directed to sources at different reading levels, allowing all students to participate at the appropriate level of challenge. Additionally, the controlled nature of the WebQuests makes it less likely that students will access inappropriate Web sites in the course of their project.

Similar strategies, such as Internet workshops (Leu, 2002) and curriculum webs (Cunningham & Billingsley, 2006), also offer opportunities for high-level engagement and integrating technology, all with focused teacher guidance.

Quality WebQuests apply many 21st Century Skills, specifically fusing core discipline area standards with CCSS and information literary and higher-order thinking. For additional details, access the 21st Century Skills Map that the National Council for Social Studies helped construct: Standards Integration: 21st Century Literacy Skills Media Literacy. Examine how individuals interpret messages differently, how values and points of view are included or excluded, and how media can influence beliefs and behaviors.

Summary

- Historical fiction books are set in the past and portray people and events that could actually have happened. For the purposes of this text, works related to all of recorded time to the 1970s is considered historical fiction.

- Historical fiction helps children experience the past by engaging them with adventurous narratives and relatable characters, adding an affective dimension to social studies instruction. It helps them see that real people like themselves can affect history. Additionally, response to historical fiction develops critical and evaluative thinking skills while also developing an understanding of historical time.

- In addition to the criteria for evaluating fiction discussed in Chapter 1, teachers must particularly consider the authenticity of the setting, characters, and writing style.

- We have chosen to categorize this genre by historical era. Books for children are set in historical eras ranging from ancient times to the Vietnam War era. Historical fiction picture books as well as series/transitional books set in many historical eras are also available.
- Historical fiction is particularly appropriate for developing the ability to compare books on the same theme or historical era or different genres (RL.9 and RI.9) and understanding the effect of illustration on story (RL.7).

Questions/Activities to Invite Thinking, Writing, and Conversation About the Chapter

1. Read two or more books from a particular historical era. Then read a social studies textbook excerpt that focuses on that same era. What aspects of history does each text cover? What does this tell you about the differences between historical fiction and textbooks? How might you use all these texts to teach children about an aspect of history?

2. Select a picture book from the list provided at the end of the chapter. Analyze how the art complements and expands on the story, using the models provided in this chapter.

3. Read a series book of historical fiction. Share your selection with your peers. Together, discuss why these books are so popular and how you might use them to help bridge students into reading more challenging texts.

Recommended Historical Fiction Picture Books

Historical Fiction Picture Books
(Books with significant culturally diverse elements are marked #.)

Ancient and Medieval Times
#Bower, JoAnn. The *Egyptian Polar Bear*. (P, I)
#Brett, Jan. *The First Dog*. (P, I)
#Bunting, Eve. *I Am the Mummy Heb-Nefert* (David Christiana, Illus.). (I, M)
#Clements, Andrew. *Temple Cat* (Kate Kiesler, Illus.). (P)
#Gerrard, Ray. *The Roman Twins*. (P, I)
#Hunt, Jonathan. *Leif's Saga*. (I)
Kurjian, Judi. *In My Own Backyard* (David Wagner, Illus.). (P)
#Lattimore, Deborah. *The Winged Cat*. (P, I)
McCully, Emily. *Beautiful Warrior*. (I, M)
Millen, C. M. *The Ink Garden of Brother Theophane* (Andrea Wisnewski, Illus.). (P, I, M)
#Stoltz, Mary. *Zekmet the Stone Carver: A Tale of Ancient Egypt* (Deborah Nourse Lattimore, Illus.). (I, M)
#Wiesnieski, David. *Rain Player*. (I)
#Winter, Jeanette. *Kali's Song*. (P)

Colonial and Early American History, Pre-1776
Accorsi, William. *Friendship's First Thanksgiving*. (P)
Bowen, Gary. *Stranded at Plimoth Plantation 1626*. (I)
Griffin, Kitty. *The Ride: The Legend of Betsy Dowdy* (Marjorie Pricemen, Illus.). (P, I)
Kimmel, Eric A. *Blackbeard's Last Fight* (Leonard Everett Fisher, Illus.). (I)
Krensky, Stephen. *Hanukkah at Valley Forge* (Greg Harlin, Illus.); *Dangerous Crossing: The Revolutionary Voyage of John and John Quincy Adams* (Greg Harlin, Illus.). (I)
#McGill, Alice. *Molly Bannaky* (Chris Soentpiet, Illus.). (P, I)
#McKissack, Patricia. *Never Forgotten*. (I, M)
Peacock, C. *Pilgrim Cat*. (Doris Ettlinger, Illus.). (P)
Small, David. *George Washington's Cows*. (P, I)
Turner, Ann. *Katie's Trunk* (Ron Himler, Illus.). (I)
Van Leeuwen, Jean. *Across the Wide Dark Sea: The Mayflower Journey*. (P)
#Yolen, Jane. *Encounter* (David Shannon, Illus.). (I, M)

Slavery and Civil War Era (19th Century)
Ackerman, Karen. *The Tin Heart* (Michael Hays, Illus.). (I, M)

Recommended Historical Fiction Picture Books **273**

Armand, Glenda. *Love Twelve Miles Long.* (P, I)

#Bearden, Romare. *Li'l Dan the Drummer Boy: A Civil War Story.* (P)

#Carbone, Elisha. *Night Running: How James Escaped with the Help of His Faithful Dog* (E. B. Lewis, Illus.). (P)

#Cole, Henry. *Unspoken: A Story of the Underground Railroad.* (P, I, M)

#Evans, Freddi Williams. *Hush Harbor: Praying in Secret* (Erin Bennett Banks, Illus.). (I)

#Evans, Shane. *Underground: Finding the Light to Freedom.* (P)

#Grifalconi, Ann. *Ain't Nobody a Stranger to Me* (Jerry Pinkney, Illus.). (P, I)

Fletcher, Susan. *Dadblamed Union Army Cow* (Kimberly Root, Illus.). (P, I)

#Hopkinson, Deborah. *Sweet Clara and the Freedom Quilt* (James Ransome, Illus.) (P, I); *Under the Quilt of Night* (James Ransome, Illus.). (P, I)

#Johnston, Tony. *The Wagon* (James Ransome, Illus.). (I)

Kay, Verla. *Civil War Drummer Boy* (Larry Day, Illus.). (P)

#Levine, Ellen. *Henry's Freedom Box* (Kadir Nelson, Illus.). (I)

Lyon, Kelly. *Ellen's Broom* (Daniel Minter, Illus.). (P)

Lyon, George Ella. *Cecil's Story* (Peter Catalanotto, Illus.). (P, I)

#Medearis, Angela. *The Freedom Riddle.* (P, M)

#Morrow, Barbara Olenyik. *A Good Night for Freedom* (Leonard Jenkins, Illus.). (I)

#Nelson, Vaunda Michaux. *Almost to Freedom* (Colin Bootman, Illus.). (P, I)

#Polacco, Patricia. *Pink and Say*; *Just in Time, Abraham Lincoln.* (I, M)

#Ransom, Candice. *Liberty Street* (Eric Valasquez, Illus.). (P, I)

#Rappaport, Doreen. *Freedom Ship* (Curtis James, Illus.). (I, M)

#Raven, Margaret Theis. *Night Boat to Freedom* (E. B. Lewis, Illus.). (I, M)

#Tingle, Tim. *Crossing Bok Chitto* (Jeanne Bridges, Illus.). (P, I)

Turner, Ann. *Nettie's Trip South* (Ron Himler, Illus.); *Drummer Boy: Marching to the Civil War* (Mark Hess, Illus.). (P, I)

#Walter, Mildred. *Alec's Primer* (Larry Johnson, Illus.). (P, I)

#Weatherfor, Carole. *Moses: When Harriet Tubman Led Her People to Freedom.* (P, I, M)

#Winter, Jeanette. *Follow the Drinking Gourd.* (P, I)

#Woodson, Jaqueline. *Show Way* (Hudson Talbott, Illus.); *This Is the Rope: A Story of the Great Migration* (James Ransome, Illus.). (P, I)

#Wright, Courtni C. *Journey to Freedom: A Story of the Underground Railroad* (Gershom Griffith, Illus.). (I)

19th-Century Life (Primarily American; Some International)

Ackerman, Karen. *Araminta's Paint Box* (Betsy Lewin, Illus.). (P)

Applegate, Katherine. *The Buffalo Storm* (Jan Ormerod, Illus.). (P)

Bedard, Michael. *Emily* (Barbara Cooney, Illus.); *The Divide* (Emily McCully, Illus.). (I)

#Bunting, Eve. *Cheyenne Again* (Irving Toddy, Illus.). (P, I)

Bunting, Eve. *Dandelions* (Greg Shed, Illus.). (P, I)

Bunting, Eve. *Train to Somewhere* (Ronald Himler, Illus.). (I, M)

Christiansen, Candace. *Calico and Tin Horns* (Thomas Locker, Illus.). (I)

Davies, Jacqueline. *Tricking the Tallyman* (S. D. Schindler, Illus.). (P, I)

Fern, Tracey. *Buffalo Music* (Lauren Castillo, Illus.). (P, I)

Floca, Brian. *Locomotive.* (I)

#Garland, Sherry. *The Buffalo Soldier* (Ronald Himler, Illus.). (I, M)

#Goble, Paul. *Death of the Iron Horse.* (I)

Hall, Donald. *Ox-Cart Man* (Barbara Cooney, Illus.). (P)

Hopkinson, Deborah. *Apples to Oregon* (Nancy Carpenter, Illus.). (P, I)

Johnston, Tony. *Sunsets of the West* (Ted Lewin, Illus.). (P)

Lendroth, Susan. *Calico Dorsey: Mail Dog of the Mining Camps* (Adam Gustavson, Illus.). (P, I)

Lowell, Susan. *Elephant Quilt: Stitch by Stitch to California* (Stacey Dressen-McQueen, Illus.). (P, I)

MacLachlan, Patricia. *Warm as Wool.* (P, I)

Park, L. *The Firekeeper's Son* (Korea) (Julie Downing, Illus.). (P)

Sanders, Scott. *Aurora Means Dawn* (Jill Kastner, Illus.). (P, I)

Singer, Marilyn. *Monday on the Mississippi* (Frane Lessac, Illus.). (P, I)

Tunnel, Michael O. *Mailing May* (Ted Rand, Illus.). (P, I)

Turner, Ann. *Dakota Dugout* (Ronald Himler, Illus.). (P, I)

Turner, Ann. *Red Flower Goes West* (Dennis Nolan, Illus.). (P, I)

Van Leeuwen, Jean. *Papa and the Pioneer Quilt* (Rebecca Bond, Illus.) (P); *Going West* (Thomas B. Allen, Illus.). (P)

Wright, Courtni. *Wagon Train: A Family Goes West in 1865.* (I, M)

Immigration, Industrialization (Late 19th and Early 20th Centuries)

#Bartone, Elisa. *American Too* (Ted Lewin, Illus.). (P, I)

Bildner, Phil. *The Greatest Game Ever Played* (Zachary Pullen, Illus.). (P, I)

Chocolate, Debi. *The Piano Man* (Eric Valasquez, Illus.). (P, I)

Cooney, Barbara. *Hattie and the Wild Waves.* (P)

Corey, Shana. *Milly and the Macy's Parade* (Brett Helquist, Illus.). (P, I)

Fleischman, Paul. *The Matchbox Diary* (Barram Ibatoulline, Illus.). (P, I)

#Hall, Bruce. *Henry and the Kite Dragon* (William Low, Illus.). (P, I)

Hest, Amy. *When Jessie Came Across the Sea* (P. J. Lynch, Illus.). (P, I)

Hopkinson, Deborah. *Sky Boys: How They Built the Empire State Building* (James Ransome, Illus.). (P, I)

#Johnson, Angela. *Those Building Men* (Barry Moser, Illus.). (I, M)

#Kirk, Connie. *Sky Dancers* (Christy Hale, Illus.). (P, I)

#Lee, Milly. *Landed* (Yangshook Choi, Illus.). (I, M)

Levinson, Riki. *Watch the Stars Come Out* (Diane Goode, Illus.). (P, I)

McCully, Emily Arnold. *Bobbin Girl*. (I)

#McKissack, Patricia. *Ma Dear's Aprons* (Floyd Cooper, Illus.). (P, I)

Murphy, Claire. *Marching with Aunt Susan*. (P, I)

#Phelan, Matt. *Around the World*. (I, M)

Polacco, Patricia. *The Keeping Quilt*. (P, I)

Pryor, Bonnie. *The Dream Jar* (Mark Graham, Illus.). (P, I)

Rail, Elisa. *What Zessie Saw on Delaney Street*. (I)

#Say, Allen. *Grandfather's Journey*. (P, I)

Shefelman, Janice. *Peddler's Dream* (Tom Shefelman, Illus.). (I)

#Shulevitz, Uri. *How I Learned Geography*. (P, I)

Tavares, Matt. *Mudball*. (P)

*Wells, Rosemary. *Waiting for the Evening Star*. (P)

Woodruff, Elvira. *The Memory Coat* (Michael Dooling, Illus.). (P, I)

#Yin. *Coolies* (Chris Soentpiet, Illus.). (P, I)

The Great Depression: 1930s America

Friedrick, Elizabeth. *Leah's Pony*. (P, I)

#Gonzalez, Lucia. The *Storyteller's Candle*. (P)

#Henson, Heather. *That Book Woman* (David Small, Illus.). (P, I)

Lied, Kate. *Potato: A Tale from the Great Depression*. (P, I)

MacLachlan, Patricia. *What You Know First*. (P)

Santiago, Chiori. *Home to Medicine Mountain* (Doris Lowry, Illus.). (P, I)

Stewart, Sarah. *The Gardener* (David Small, Illus.). (P, I)

World War II: Holocaust, Mid-20th Century

#Adler, David A. *One Yellow Daffodil: A Hanukkah Story* (Lloyd Bloom, Illus.). (I, M)

Aston, Diana. *The Moon over Star* (Jerry Pinkney, Illus.). (I)

Borden, Louise. *Across the Blue Pacific: A World War II Story* (Robert Andrew Parker, Illus.) (M); *The Little Ships: The Heroic Rescue at Dunkirk in World War II* (Michael Foreman, Illus.) (P, I); *The Greatest Skating Race: A World War II Story from the Netherlands* (Niki Daly, Illus.). (I)

#Bunting, Eve. *One Candle* (Wendy Popp, Illus.). (I, M)

#Bunting, Eve. *Terrible Things: An Allegory of the Holocaust* (Steven Gammell, Illus.). (I, M)

#Bunting, Eve. *So Far from the Sea* (Chris Soentpiet, Illus.). (I, M)

#Fleming, Candace. *Boxes for Katje* (Stacey Dressen-McQueen, Illus.). (P, I)

#Herrera, Juan. *Calling the Doves*. (P, I)

#Hesse, Karen. *The Cats in Krasinski Square* (Wendy Watson, Illus.). (I, M)

#Hoestlandt, Jo. *Star of Fear, Star of Hope* (Johanna Kang, Illus.). (I, M)

#Howard, Elizabeth. *Aunt Flossie's Hats (and Crab Cakes Later)* (James Ransome, Illus.); *Mac and Marie and the Train Toss Surprise* (Gail Carter, Illus.). (P)

Innocenti, Robert. *Rose Blanche*. (I, M)

#Johnston, Tony. *The Harmonica* (Ron Mazellan, Illus.). (I, M)

Judge, Lita. *One Thousand Tracings: Healing the Wounds of World War II*. (I, M)

Laminack, Lester. *Saturdays and Teacakes*. (P, I)

Littlesugar, Amy. *Lisette's Angel*. (I)

Lowry, Lois. *Crow Call* (Bagram Ibatouilline, Illus.). (I)

#Maruki, Toshi. *Hiroshima No Pika*. (M)

#Mochizuki, Ken. *Baseball Saved Us* (Dom Lee, Illus.). (I, M)

Nerlove, Miriam. *Flowers on the Wall*. (P, I)

#Oppenheim, Shulamith. *The Lily Cupboard* (Ronald Himler, Illus.). (I)

Paterson, John and Katherine. *Blueberries for the Queen* (Susan Jeffers, Illus.). (P, I)

#Pinkney, Gloria. *Back Home*; *The Sunday Outing* (Jerry Pinkney, Illus.). (P)

#Polacco, Patricia. *The Butterfly*. (I, M)

#Ruelle, Karen Gray. *The Grand Mosque of Paris: A Story of How Muslims Rescued Jews During the Holocaust* (Deborah Desaix, Illus.). (I, M)

Rylant, Cynthia. *When I Was Young in the Mountains*. (P, I)

#Say, Allen. *Home of the Brave*. (M)

Shemin, Margaretha. *The Little Riders* (Peter Spier, Illus.). (I, M)

#Smith, Icy. *Three Years and Eight Months* (Jennifer Kindert, Illus.). (I, M)

Smucker, Anna. *No Star Nights*. (P, I)

#Sneve, Virginia. *The Christmas Coat: Memories of My Sioux Childhood* (Ellen Beier, Illus.). (P)

#Tai, Amy Lee. *A Place Where Sunflowers Grow* (Felicia Hoshino, Illus.). (P, I)

#Tsuchiya, Yukio. *Faithful Elephants: A True Story of Animals, People, & War* (Ted Lewin, Illus.). (M)

Wood, Douglas. *Franklin and Winston: A Christmas That Changed the World* (Barry Moser, Illus.). (I)

#Woodson, Jacqueline. *Coming on Home Soon* (E. B. Lewis, Illus.). (P, I)

#Uchida, Yoshiko. *The Bracelet* (Joanna Yardley, Illus.). (I, M)

#Vander Zee, Ruth, and Sneider, Marian. *Eli Remembers* (Bill Farnsworth, Illus.); *Erica's Story* (Robert Innocenti, Illus.). (M)

Vaughn, Glenda. *Irena's Jar of Secrets* (Ron Mazellan, Illus.). (I, M)

#Williams, Shirley. *Working Cotton*. (P, I)

U.S. Civil Rights Issues: 20th Century

#Bandy, Michael, and Stein, Eric. *White Water* (Shadra Strickland, Illus.). (P)

#Coleman, Evelyn. *White Socks Only* (Tyrone Geter, Illus.). (P, I)

#Cooper, Floyd. *Willie and the All-Stars*. (I)

#Harrington, Janice. *Going North* (Jerome Lagarrigue, Illus.). (I)

#Howard, Elizabeth Fitzgerald. *Virgie Goes to School with Us Boys* (E. B. Lewis, Illus.). (P, I)

#Johnson, Angela. *The Sweet Smell of Roses* (Eric Valasquez, Illus.). (P, I)

#Loribecki, Marybeth. *Sister Anne's Hands* (Wendy Popp, Illus.). (P, I)

#Mason, Margaret. *These Hands* (Floyd Cooper, Illus.). (P, I)

#McKissack, Patricia. *Goin' Someplace Special* (Jerry Pinkney, Illus.). (P, I)

#Mitchell, Maragaree King. *Uncle Jed's Barbershop* (James Ransome, Illus.); *When Grandmama Sings* (James Ransome, Illus.). (P, I)

#Ramsey, Calvin, and Stroud, Bettye. *Belle: The Last Mule at Gee's Bend* (John Holyfield, Illus.). (P, I)

#Reynolds, Aaron. *Back of the Bus* (Floyd Cooper, Illus.). (P, I)

#Stauffacher, Sue. *Bessie Smith and the Night Riders* (John Holyfield, Illus.). (P, I)

#Vander Zee, Ruth. *Mississippi Morning* (Floyd Cooper, Illus.). (M)

#Weatherford, Carole Boston. *Freedom on the Menu: The Greensboro Sit-Ins* (Jerome Lagarrique, Illus.). (P, I)

#Wiles, Deborah. *Freedom Summer* (Jerome Lagarrigue, Illus.). (P, I)

Vietnam War

#Beckler, Rosemary. *Sweet Dried Apples* (Deborah Kogan Ray, Illus.). (P, I)

Bunting, Eve. *The Wall* (Ron Himler, Illus.). (I)

#Garland, Sherry. *The Lotus Seed* (Tatsuri Kiuchi, Illus.). (P, I)

Keller, Holly. *Grandfather's Dream*. (P, I)

#Myers, Walter Dean. *Patrol: An American Soldier in Vietnam* (Ann Grifalconi, Illus.). (M)

#Tran, Khanh. *The Little Weaver of Thai-Yen Village* (Nancy Horn, Illus.). (P)

Trother, Maxine. *The Walking Stick* (Annouchka Galouchko, Illus.). (P)

Historical Fiction Transitional Books
(Series books, such as *Dear America, Royal Diaries, Vietnam, American Girl, Horrible Histories*, and so on, that occur in historical contexts are also transitional books of historical fiction)

Adler, David. *The Babe and I*. (Terry Widener, Illus.).

Avi. *Night Journeys*.

Benchley, Nathaniel. *Sam the Minuteman* (Arnold Lobel, Illus.).

#Bishop, Clare. *Twenty and Ten* (Janet Joly, Illus.).

Borden, Louise. *Sleds on Boston Common: A Story from the American Revolution* (Robert Andrew Parker, Illus.).

Bulla, Clyde. *The Sword in the Tree* (Bruce Bowles, Illus.); *A Lion to Guard Us* (Michelle Chessare, Illus.).

Calkhoven, Laurie. *Daniel at the Siege of Boston, 1776* (and others in the *Boys of Wartime* series).

Cohen, Miriam. *Mimmy and Sophie All Around the Town* (Thomas Yezerski, Illus.).

#Erdrich, Louise. *Chickadee*.

Figley, Marty. *The Schoolchildren's Blizzard* (Shelly Hass, Illus.).

Fritz, Jean. *The Cabin Faced West*.

Gardiner, John. *Stone Fox*.

Gauch, Patricia. *Aaron and the Green Mountain Boys*; *This Time, Tempe Wick?* (Margot Tomes, Illus.).

Lowry, Jeanette. *Six Silver Spoons* (Robert Quackenbush, Illus.).

MacLachlan, Patricia. *Sarah, Plain and Tall* (and sequels).

McSwigan, Marie. *Snow Treasure*.

#Myers, Laurie. *Escape by Night: A Civil War Adventure* (Amy Bates, Illus.).

Peck, Richard. *A Long Way from Chicago*.

Rappaport, Doreen. *The Boston Coffee Party* (Emily McCully, Illus.).

Sandlin, Joan. *The Long Way Westward*.

Stevens, Carla. *Trouble for Lucy* (Ronald Himler, Illus.).

#Stiles, Martha. *Sailing to Freedom*.

Thompson, Kate. *Most Wanted*.

Turner, Ann. *Dust for Dinner* (Robert Barrett, Illus.).

Wilder, Laura Ingalls. *Little House in the Big Woods* (and sequels) (Garth Williams, Illus.).

#Yelchin, Eugene. *Breaking Stalin's Nose*.

Recommended Historical Fiction Novels

(Books with significant culturally diverse elements are marked #.)

Ancient Civilizations
Cowley, Marjorie. *The Golden Bull.* (M)
#Fletcher, Susan. *Shadow Spinner.* (I, M)
Hunter, Mollie. *The Stronghold.* (M)
#Lester, Julius. *Pharaoh's Daughter: A Tale of Ancient Egypt.* (M)
#McGraw, Eloise. *The Golden Goblet; Mara, Daughter of the Nile.* (I, M)
#Napoli, Donna. *Lights on the Nile.* (I, M)
Paton Walsh, Jill. *Children of the Fox.* (I, M)
Sutcliff, Rosemary. *Eagle of the Ninth* (and sequels); *Song for a Dark Queen; Sun Horse, Moon Horse.* (M)
#Williams, Susan. *Wind Rider.* (M)

Middle Ages
Avi. *Crispin: The Cross of Lead* (and sequels). (I, M)
Barnhouse, Rebecca. *The Book of the Maidservant.* (I, M)
Blackwood, Gary. *The Shakespeare Stealer; Shakespeare's Scribe.* (M)
Cushman, Karen. *Catherine, Called Birdy* (I, M); *The Midwife's Apprentice; Will Sparrow's Road.* (I, M)
Marsh, Katherine. *Jep Who Defied the Stars.* (I, M)
McCaffrey, Anne. *Black Horses for the King.* (M)
Namioka, Lensey. *Den of the White Fox* (and others). (M)
#Park, Linda. *A Single Shard.* (M)
#Paterson, Katherine. *The Sign of the Chrysanthemum; Of Nightingales That Weep* (M); *The Master Puppeteer.* (I, M)
Schlitz, Laura. *Good Masters! Sweet Ladies! Voices from a Medieval Village.* (M)
#Talbert, Marc. *Heart of a Jaguar.* (M)
Temple, Frances. *The Ramsay Scallop.* (M)

Early Exploration, Colonial Times, and the American Revolution
#Anderson, Laurie Halse. *Fever 1793; Chains, Forge.* (I, M)
Avi. *The True Confessions of Charlotte Doyle*; #*Sophia's War: A Tale of the Revolution; The Fighting Ground.* (M)
Carbone, Elisa. *Blood on the River: James Town 1607.* (M)
#Collier, James Lincoln and Christopher. *My Brother Sam Is Dead; War Comes to Willie Freeman; Who Is Carrie?; Jump Ship to Freedom.* (M)
#Dorros, Arthur. *Morning Girl.* (I, M)
#Edinger, Monica. *Africa Is My Home: A Child of the Amistad* (Robert Byred Illus.). (I, M)

#Edwards, Sally. *When the World's on Fire.* (I, M)
Forbes, Esther. *Johnny Tremain.* (M)
Fritz, Jean. *Early Thunder.* (I, M)
Hale, Nathan, and Beckerman, Chad. *Nathan Hale's Hazardous Adventures: One Dead Spy* (graphic novel). (I, M)
#O'Dell, Scott. *The Serpent Never Sleeps: A Novel of Jamestown and Pocahantas; The King's Fifth; Sarah Bishop.* (M)
Paulsen, Gary. *Woods Runner.* (M)
Rinaldi, Ann. *A Break with Charity: A Story of the Salem Witch Trials.* (I, M)
Speare, Elizabeth. *The Witch of Blackbird Pond.* (I, M)

Westward Settlements and 19th-Century Life
Avi. *The Barn.* (I)
Brink, Carol Ryrie. *Caddie Woodlawn.* (I)
Conrad, Pam. *Prairie Songs.* (M)
Cushman, Karen. *The Ballad of Lucy Whipple.* (I, M)
#Erdrich, Louise. *The Birchbark House* (and sequels). (M)
#Harrell, Beatrice. *Longwalker's Journey: A Novel of the Choctaw Trail of Tears.* (I)
Holm, Jennifer. *Our Only May Amelia; The Trouble with May Amelia.* (I, M)
Lasky, Kathryn. *Beyond the Divide.* (M)
MacLachlan, Patricia. *Sarah, Plain and Tall* (and sequels). (P, I)
Napoli, Donna Jo. *The Crossing.* (I, M)
#O'Dell, Scott. *Streams to the River, River to the Sea* (M); *Sing Down the Moon.* (I, M)
#Prius, Margie. *Heart of a Samurai.* (M)
Turner, Ann. *Grasshopper Summer.* (I, M)
Wilder, Laura Ingalls. *Little House in the Big Woods* (and sequels). (P, I)
#Wolf, Allan. *New Found Land.* (M)

Slavery and the Civil War
#Berry, James. *Ajeemah and His Son.* (I, M)
#Carbone, Elisa. *Stealing Freedom.* (M)
#Curtis, Christopher Paul. *Elijah of Buxton.* (I, M)
#Draper, Sharon. *Copper Sun.* (M)
#Feelings, Tom. *The Middle Passage.* (M)
Fleischman, Paul. *Bull Run.* (I, M)
Gauch, Patricia. *Thunder at Gettysburg.* (I, M)
#Hansen, Joyce. *Which Way Freedom?* (and sequels). (M)
Hunt, Irene. *Across Five Aprils.* (M)
#Klein, Lisa. *Two Girls of Gettysburg.* (I)
#Lester, Julius. *Day of Tears: A Novel in Verse.* (M)

#Lyons, Mary. *Letters from a Slave Girl*; *Letters from a Slave Boy*. (I, M)

#McKissack, Patricia. *Never Forgotten*. (I, M)

#Paterson, Katherine. *Jip, His Story*. (M)

#Paulsen, Gary. *Nightjohn*; *Sarny: A Life Remembered*. (I)

#Pearsall, Shelley. *Trouble Don't Last*. (I, M)

Philbrick, Rodman. *The Mostly True Adventures of Homer P. Figg*. (I, M)

#Pinkney, Gloria Jean. *Silent Thunder: A Civil War Story*. (I, M)

Reeder, Carolyn. *Shades of Gray*. (I, M)

Rinaldi, Ann. *Numbering All the Bones*. (M)

#Schwabach, Karen. *The Storm Before Atlanta*. (I, M)

#Taylor, Mildred. *The Land*. (M)

Wells, Rosemary. *Red Moon at Sharpsburg*; *Which Way Freedom?* (I, M)

Late 19th and Early 20th Centuries: Industrialization and Immigration

Avi. *Beyond the Western Sea* (and sequels). (I, M)

#Bolden, Tanya. *Finding Family*. (I, M)

Giff, Patricia Reilly. *Nory Ryan's Song*. (I)

#Hesse, Karen. *Letters from Rifka*. (I, M)

Kelly, Jacqueline. *The Evolution of Calpurnia Tate*. (M)

#Kent, Trilby. *Stones for My Father*. (M)

#Lear, Kristin. *The Best Bad Luck I Never Had*. (I, M)

#O'Dell, Scott. *Island of the Blue Dolphins*. (I, M)

Paterson, Katherine. *Bread and Roses, Too*; *Lyddie*. (M)

Peck, Richard. *Fair Weather*. (I, M)

Phelan, Matt. *Around the World*; *Bluffton*. (I, M)

#Ryan, Pam. *Esperanza Rising*. (I, M)

Sayres, Meghan. *Anahita's Woven Riddle*. (M)

#Schmidt, Gary. *Lizzie Bright and the Buckminster Boy*. (M)

Selznick, Brian. *The Invention of Hugo Cabret*. (I, M)

#Simon, Victoria. *Zora and Me*. (I, M)

#Timberlake, Amy. *One Came Home*. (M)

Wright, Barbara. *Crow*. (I, M)

#Yep, Laurence. *Dragon's Gate* (and others). (M)

The Great Depression

Choldenko, Jennifer. *Al Capone Does My Shirts* (and sequels). (I, M)

#Curtis, Christopher Paul. *Bud, Not Buddy*; *The Mighty Miss Malone*. (I, M)

Hesse, Karen. *Out of the Dust*. (I, M)

Holms, Jennifer. *Turtle in Paradise*. (I, M)

#Latham, Irene. *Leaving Gee's Bend*. (I, M)

Peck, Richard. *A Long Way from Chicago*; *The Year Down Yonder*. (I, M)

Phelan, Matt. *Storm in the Barn*. (I, M)

#Taylor, Mildred. *Roll of Thunder, Hear My Cry* (and sequels). (I, M)

Vanderpool, Claire. *Moon over Manifest*. (M)

#Uchida, Yoshiko. *A Jar of Dreams*. (I)

World War II

Bartoletti, Susan. *The Boy Who Dared*. (M)

Cheaney, J. B. *My Friend the Enemy*. (I)

#Choi, Sook Nyui. *Year of Impossible Goodbyes*. (I, M)

#Fitzmaurice, Kathryn. *A Diamond in the Desert*. (I, M)

Flood, Nancy. *Warriors in the Crossfire*. (M)

Giff, Patricia Reilly. *Lily's Crossing*; *Willow Run*. (I)

Hahn, Mary Downing. *Stepping on the Cracks*. (I, M)

Hautzig, Esther. *The Endless Steppe*. (M)

#Kadohata, Cynthia. *Weedflower*. (I, M)

Kerr, Judith. *When Hitler Stole Pink Rabbit*. (I, M)

Klages, Ellen. *The Green Glass Sea*. (M)

#LeZotte, Anne. *T4*. (M)

Lisle, Janet Taylor. *The Art of Keeping Cool*. (I, M)

Lowry, Lois. *Number the Stars*; *Autumn Street*. (I, M)

#Mochiauki, Ken. *Baseball Saved Us*. (I, M)

Orlev, Uri. *The Man from the Other Side*; *The Island on Bird Street*. (M)

#Park, Linda. *When My Name Was Keoko*. (M)

Patt, Beverly. *Best Friends Forever: A World War II Scrapbook*. (I, M)

#Pearsall, Shelly. *Jump into the Sky*. (M)

Peck, Richard. *On Wings of Eagles*. (I)

Reiss, Johanna. *The Upstairs Room*. (M)

Rostoski, Margaret. *After the Dancing Days*. (M)

#Salisbury, Graham. *Under the Blood Red Sun*; *House of the Red Fish*. (I, M)

#Sepetys, Ruta. *Between Shades of Gray*. (M)

Spinelli, Jerry. *Milkweed*. (M)

#Thor, Anika. *A Faraway Island*. (I, M)

#Uchida, Yoshiko. *Journey to Topaz*; *Journey Home*. (M)

Voorhoeve, Anne. *My Family for the War*. (M)

#Watkins, Yoko Kawashima. *So Far from the Bamboo Grove*; *My Brother, My Sister and I*. (M)

#Yolen, Jane. *The Devil's Arithmetic*. (I, M)

#Zusak, Marcus. *The Book Thief*. (M)

Mid-20th Century: Civil Rights and Everyday Life

#Alvarez, Julia. *Before We Were Free*. (M)

Blume, Lesley. *The Rising Star of Rusty Nail*. (I, M)

#Compestine, Ying Chang. *Revolution Is Not a Dinner Party*. (M)

#Curtis, Christopher Paul. *The Watsons Go to Birmingham: 1963*. (I, M)

Cushman, Karen. *The Loud Silence of Maxine Greene*. (I, M)

#Flores-Galbis, Enrique. *90 Miles from Havana*. (I, M)

Gantos, Jack. *Dead End in Norvelt.* (I, M)

#Gonzales, Christina. *The Red Umbrella.* (M)

Grimes, Nikki. *Jazmin's Notebook.* (M)

#Hayles, Marsha. *Breathing Room.* (M)

#Hesse, Karen. *Witness.* (M)

#Holm, Jennifer. *Penny from Heaven.* (I)

Holt, Kimberly. *My Louisiana Sky.* (I, M)

#Levine, Kristen. *The Lions of Little Rock.* (I, M)

#Lord, Bettie. *In the Year of the Boar and Jackie Robinson.* (I)

#Manzano, Evelyn. *The Revolution of Evelyn Serrano.* (M)

#Moses, Sheila. *Legend of Buddy Bush; Return of Buddy Bush.* (M)

#Naidoo, Beverly. *Burn My Heart.* (I, M)

#Nelson, Marilyn. *A Wreath for Emmett Till.* (M)

#Nelson, Vanda. *Beyond Mayfield; Mayfield Crossing.* (I)

#Robinet, Harriet. *Walking to the Bus Rider Blues.* (I, M)

#Russell, Ching Yeung. *Tofu Quilt.* (I)

#Tingle, Tim. *Saltypie.* (I)

Vawter, Vince. *Paperboy.* (I, M)

Wiles, Deborah. *Countdown.* (I, M)

#Williams-Garcia, Rita. *One Crazy Summer; P.S. Be Eleven.* (I, M)

#Wolff, Virginia. *Bat 6.* (I, M)

Vietnam War Era

#Burg, Ann. *All the Broken Pieces.* (I, M)

Dowell, Frances. *Shooting the Moon.* (I, M)

#Ho, Minfong. *The Clay Marble; The Stone Goddess.* (I, M)

#Kadohata, Cynthia. *A Million Shades of Gray; Kira, Kira; Cracker!: The Best Dog in Vietnam.* (I, M)

#Lai, Thanhha. *Inside Out and Back Again.* (I, M)

#Manivong, Laura. *Escaping the Tiger.* (I, M)

#McCormack, Patricia. *Never Fall Down.* (M)

#Myers, Walter Dean. *Fallen Angels.* (M)

Schmidt, Gary. *The Wednesday Wars; Okay for Now.* (I, M)

Sherlock, Patti. *Letters from Wolfie.* (I, M)

Taylor, Theodore. *The Bomb.* (M)

Testa, Marie. *Almost Forever.* (I, M)

Chapter 9

Contemporary Realistic Fiction

(Literary Genre)

This chapter introduces you to the genre of contemporary realistic fiction. We consider the following questions:

- What is contemporary realistic fiction?
- What is the role of contemporary realistic fiction in children's lives?
- How can we choose high-quality contemporary realistic fiction?
- What are some categories of contemporary realistic fiction?
- How do we use contemporary realistic fiction to meet the mandates of national standards as well as the needs of our diverse students?

Fourth-grade teacher Sarah loves literature and wants to develop that same enthusiasm for books and reading in her students. Read-alouds are one of her favorite ways to accomplish this goal. She knew that her students particularly enjoyed reading books of realistic fiction for their independent reading because they could easily identify with the characters and the stories seem real to them. However, they did not always choose the genre's more challenging and complex books. After perusing recently published books for one that would engage her class, she decided on *Wonder* (Palacio) because the writing style presents the story from different points of view. Sarah reasoned that the style, featuring both male and female characters, would help all students connect with the book. She also liked how characters were inspired and transformed by knowing Auggie (the protagonist) and how the author celebrated what truly makes someone beautiful.

She began by showing the class the book's online book trailer, which narrates the compelling opening pages along with the back of Auggie's head. The students were hooked. They asked, "What does Auggie look like?" and "Why hasn't he gone to school since first grade?" They wanted to know more.

Sarah began reading the book daily, covering several chapters in each session. Sometimes, there was more conversation than reading as children clamored to discuss issues such as Jack's betrayal, Auggie's sister Via's feelings of both love and resentment, Julien's bullying of Auggie, and what constitutes a true friend. They were particularly angry with Jack. "Why did Jack want to fit in with Julien? He's a punk!" they angrily stated. This led to reflection on their own behavior as they began asking themselves, "What would I do in this situation?," "Would I have joined in on the bullying?," and "Have I judged others negatively based on their appearance?"

To encourage conversations about bullying and individual differences, Sarah next read aloud *Out of My Mind* (Draper), the story of a brilliant fifth grader with cerebral palsy who cannot speak, write, or walk. The class was just as enthralled with this book, initiating many discussions about how difficult the protagonist's situation was and how other students in her class perceived her. Sarah also began noticing subtle changes in their behavior. She saw more students conversing with her autistic students, particularly in connection with video games, at which the autistic students were quite expert. She saw less negative interactions and more kindness. "These books had such a positive, transformative impact on my students," she said. "I will definitely do this again."

Some readers trace their passion for books back to their discovery of characters who seem like a mirror of themselves. It is the case with realistic fictional stories that people seem so real to us, where we bring our own life to the experience of reading and we can be transformed by the experience. Author Julius Lester (2004) said it perfectly: "At its best, story provides us with ways to see ourselves, ways to affirm our struggles to overcome adversities, ways to help us reach out to others, and forge relationships" (p. 49).

What Is Contemporary Realistic Fiction?

The genre of contemporary realistic fiction includes stories about people and animals that could exist in our current world. Even if the story seems far-fetched, consider whether it happens in the present time without magic or supernatural assistance: if so, then it is contemporary realistic fiction. An important value of this genre is that it offers readers insight into universal human concerns through characters who cope with contemporaneous issues and challenges. Other genres may also offer a similar experience; however, it is in contemporary realistic fiction that readers find stories with both human and animal characters that were created in the authors' imaginations and thus never happened—but they could have.

Reading interest inventories indicate that contemporary realistic fiction is a popular genre for intermediate and middle school students (Monson & Sebesta, 1991). Davila and Patrick (2010) also reported that both genders enjoy fiction, particularly books featuring adventure and humor (p. 207). You can probably guess why this is true: students love to read about others like themselves who are going through life circumstances that are similar to what they are experiencing. They also enjoy vicariously experiencing adventures and situations that are beyond their current reality. These qualities make contemporary realistic fiction popular with students of all ages.

The Role of Contemporary Realistic Fiction in Children's Lives

Ann Cameron (1996), author of *The Most Beautiful Place in the World*, describes her feelings about the value of realistic fiction, which naturally draws readers into books:

> When we help children participate in the stories they read, we're helping them to heal themselves and grow as human beings, to understand the world as it is, and to imagine a better world. (p. 230)

Writers of this genre offer their readers stories with real-life characters who are coping with issues and challenges in their lives. This is one of the key values of contemporary realistic fiction: the potential to help readers see that they are not alone—that characters, much like themselves, have similar life situations, face challenging issues, and grow through the pages of a book. When readers become immersed in just the right book, identify with a character and situation, and imagine a better world or a different way of thinking, they have experienced the power of contemporary realistic fiction to transform humans and help them make sense of their lives.

Authors of high-quality contemporary realistic fiction often depict young protagonists who are faced with seemingly insurmountable challenges. Katherine Paterson's many contemporary realistic fiction books, such as *The Great Gilly Hopkins, Bridge to Terabithia*, and *The Same Stuff As Stars*, are excellent examples of this phenomenon. Her writing explores complicated family and peer situations in a realistic, sensitive, and compassionate manner. Other writers of this genre portray similarly difficult situations in which children are forced by untenable circumstances to assume adult responsibilities, such as becoming caregivers for younger siblings, caring for emotionally collapsed parents, or contending with the foster care system, as in books like *Homecoming* (Voigt), *Waiting for Normal* (Connor), *Almost Home* (Bauer), and *How to Steal a Dog* (O'Connor). In other stories, the protagonist is alone in a forbidding wilderness or must contend with a debilitating disability, as in *Hatchet* (Paulsen) and *Wonder* (Palacio).

Inevitably, the protagonists grow through the course of the narrative, emerging as strong and courageous despite the difficult circumstances in which they find themselves. Many children may not personally encounter such heartbreaking events. However, reading about them can provide vicarious experiences with important values, such as resilience, resourcefulness, loyalty, and the willingness to accept responsibility. Books provide a safe distance to examine how these qualities help others overcome obstacles and significant issues in their lives. Thus, powerfully written contemporary realistic fiction can engage, empower, and inform readers while also providing a sense of hope and confidence in a world that is often unkind to children.

Contemporary realistic fiction also helps readers vicariously understand and then cope with more universally common challenges, such as making and losing friends, moving from one place to another, fitting in while feeling different from others, having a nontraditional family, coming from a different culture, or questioning one's sexuality. Real-life topics such as these are portrayed honestly and sympathetically in contemporary realistic fiction, making books in this genre appealing to many readers. There is a certain comfort that comes from reading about others who have experienced the same issues and feelings and finding out how they solved problems.

Some authors are particularly known for targeting realistic topics with candor and empathy. Their characters make us laugh out loud, cry, or nod in agreement with the familiarity of their actions. You may remember reading every Judy Blume book you could find. Blume's classic titles, such as *Are You There God? It's Me, Margaret*, *Tales of a Fourth Grade Nothing*, and *Blubber* still remain popular for this reason. Blume writes honestly about topics that are important to preteens, including being overweight, contending with friends who have changed, experiencing love for the first time, and questioning one's religion. That fearless realism is what children love about Blume's books and the work of others who write in this genre.

However, there is some debate as to how much realism is appropriate for children. Should they read about stark issues such as child abandonment, drug use, and suicide? Should there always be happy endings? Most realistic fiction writers will assert that it is their responsibility to present real life with all its sadness, frustration, and gritty problems. As writer Stephanie Tolan (1989) asserted,

> The literature we offer [children] should not merely entertain and shelter them. It should provide nourishment for their growing minds and spirits and help give them the strength to meet the future. . . . They sometimes need to see characters who instead of being eventually freed from their problems and saved from pain, gain lasting strength from confronting problems and surviving pain. (p. 14)

Tolan believes that serving a steady diet of books in which all problems are solved is a tremendous disservice to young readers.

Fellow writer Barbara O'Connor (2010) believes that her characters, plots, and settings must be as authentic as she can make them, including all the messy, untidy, imperfect elements. She asserts that the endings of her books should not necessarily be happy, but she should always leave children with hope: a sense that we can learn from our experiences and grow emotionally and that something better is possible. This is realism for O'Connor and many other writers of this genre.

Reluctant readers, in particular, can become enthusiastic about reading when they find just the right book—and that often happens with contemporary realistic fiction. The easily relatable characters, realistic dialogue, and common situations can make literature more accessible to these students, often supporting their first successful foray into longer books.

Contemporary realistic fiction can play a powerful role in children's lives. The books in this genre are often those in which the author's choice of words engages us, makes us want to keep reading, thinking, and wondering and in which the story and the characters remain memorable long after the last page is turned. These titles may become favorite books—the ones that are passed around to friends and prompt the reader to beg for a sequel or another by the same author or with a similar plot. When this happens, we know that our students are hooked on books. That is the most significant and powerful role that contemporary realistic fiction can play in the lives of children.

Criteria for Evaluating Contemporary Realistic Fiction

We discussed the basic criteria for evaluating fiction in Chapter 1. All these criteria are applicable to contemporary realistic fiction. However, the most important additional criterion for this genre is realism: how believable and realistic the plot, characterization, setting, theme, writing style, and point of view are. If any of these elements fail to ring true, then the book will not succeed. In the following section, we discuss how writers develop authentic, realistic, and believable stories in this genre.

Plot

A realistic, believable plot is an essential ingredient for a realistic fiction book. It is what makes children keep asking for one more chapter or, if older, keep reading with a flashlight long after they are supposed to be asleep. In well-written contemporary realistic fiction, the plot must develop logically, with events evolving plausibly from prior action. Plots almost always center on a conflict in which the main characters struggle with a problem or overcome an obstacle. This problem might be a physical setting, such as an unforgiving wilderness, as seen in many of the adventure books. It might be emotional, as when the characters in *Where the Red Fern Grows* (Rawls) must work through grief following the death of their dog. Or it might be a mental challenge, as when the characters must put together the clues of a mystery, like in *The Westing Game* (Raskin) or *The London Eye Mystery* (Dowd).

Some books, particularly those for more mature readers, feature complex, parallel or multiple plots. For example, in *Holes* (Sachar), Stanley's plight of digging senseless holes day after day at a juvenile detention camp is intertwined with an equally engaging plot about how the camp began. The popularity as well as the critical acclaim for this book attest to the author's skill in developing and intertwining both plots so that children can follow them. *Wonderstruck* (Selznick) also unfolds as two intertwining plots, one in pictures and one in words.

Students tend to enjoy realistic fiction plots with plenty of action but minimal description. In particular, cliffhangers at the end of chapters, along with exciting, action-filled events, keep children turning the pages. For example, Gary Paulsen's *Hatchet* features riveting action as the main character, Brian, faces one challenge after another as he struggles to survive in the Canadian wilderness. Paulsen continually reveals Brian's thoughts to his readers, but the emphasis is always on the plot: what happens next.

Characterization

In well-written contemporary realistic fiction, authors create believable main characters who show multiple facets of their personality. Through the course of the story, readers come to know their strengths as well as their flaws and struggles. This is true even if the main character is an animal, such as the lovable dog in Kate DiCamillo's popular *Because of Winn-Dixie*. An author might develop characters by showing their thoughts, creating dialogue with other characters, or portraying how others think about them in order to convey many facets of that individual's personality. Ultimately, each protagonist's individuality (and often that of secondary characters) is portrayed so vividly that these characters come alive for readers.

Author Katherine Paterson (2001) is particularly adept at creating believable characters that resonate with readers. She describes how she accomplishes this in the following way:

> When someone asks me about "building characters," I'm tempted to remind them that characters are people, not models you put together with an erector set. You don't "build" people, you get to know them. . . . When I am beginning a book, the central character is little more than an uneasy feeling in the pit of my stomach. I spend a long time trying to understand who this person is—where he or she was born, when, and from whom. (p. 162)

This close attention to creating fully developed characters helps authors maintain consistency as a story evolves. They must be sure that everything each character says or does is consistent with prior thoughts and actions. The character's behavior should also be congruent with his or her age and the realistic cultural context of the story.

Some authors allow characters to grow across a series, becoming increasingly real and memorable. One example is Beverly Cleary's Ramona, the pesky younger sister of Beezus in *Beezus and Ramona*. Eventually, Ramona is the protagonist in her own books. Readers come to love this active, challenging child to whom they can easily relate because they have grown to know her through her many adventures across multiple books that detail her life over several years.

Theme

Themes for young children in contemporary realistic fiction are typically based on situations, problems, and emotions close to children's own experiences. The theme of picture books such as *When Sophie Gets Angry, Really, Really Angry* (Bang) and *Sometimes I'm Bombaloo* (Vail) is dealing with angry feelings, something that all young children have experienced and can relate to. Themes in books for older readers often focus on growing up, making wise decisions, and accepting the consequences of one's choices, For example, in *The Five Lives of Our Cat Zook* (Rocklin), the protagonist must face the inevitable conclusion resulting from her cat's failing health while also coming to terms with her father's death and her mother's developing relationship with a new man.

Occasionally, themes are explicitly stated, but in most books, readers must think critically in order to uncover a meaningful message. It is particularly important that realistic fiction writers skillfully and subtly embed themes so that an important message does not become didactic or preachy. Rather than being explicitly told the theme statement, a reader's comprehension is developed as the plot unfolds and characters say and do things that convey the theme.

Setting

In contemporary realistic fiction, the setting can be a place that actually exists or one that is invented by the author. In either case, it must be a contemporary setting that could exist within the boundaries of what we know is real. Setting in all fiction—but particularly realistic fiction—is developed through the use of details and rich descriptions. Whether it is the hum of wind, the thundering of trains, the hustle and bustle of a city, or the solitude of the woods, authors choose words and images to evoke the senses and make the story feel real to readers. Because setting and plot often support each other, understanding time and place can contribute to one's appreciation and connection to the events.

Sharon Creech has written many contemporary fiction stories about children searching for identity and their role in the world. In *Ruby Holler* (Creech), the setting is critical in supporting the plot. Twin orphans who trust no one but each other after enduring a string of foster homes are sent to Ruby Holler to assist an eccentric elderly couple. Ruby Holler is a wondrous place, deep in the country, a "basin in the hills . . . where cool breezes drifted through the trees, and where the creek was so clear that every stone on its bottom was visible." Creech's word choices help readers imagine this place of solitude, comfort, and safety: the perfect setting for the protagonists of Ruby Holler to find both peace and their place in the world.

Style

In contemporary realistic fiction, the style must make the story real to readers. Some fiction writers use a poetic style in which the language is rhythmical and at times alliterative. For example, in *Snow Day*, Lynn Plourde's expert use of onomatopoeia taps the senses to what it is like awakening to a snowy day. Patricia MacLachlan is particularly known for this style. For example, in the opening pages of *Journey*, MacLachlan uses active verbs, onomatopoeia, subtle alliteration, rhythmic phrases, and metaphoric images to create a melancholy, wistful tone. At this point in the story the character is reflecting back to the time his mother deserted him and the writing effectively conveys his sadness.

In contrast, some realistic fiction writers use a style with more dialogue and significantly less description. The following passage from *Hoot* (Hiaasen), a story of adventure mixed with humor that is set in Florida, is an example of this. In the passage, Roy, the protagonist, is trapped in a pile of poisonous snakes he has come on in the woods. Suddenly, a voice commands, "Don't move!"

> "Take a deep breath," advised the voice behind him.
> "I'm trying," said Roy.
> "Okay, now step backwards real slow on the count of three."
> "Oh. I don't think so," said Roy.
> "One . . ."
> "Now wait a second."
> "Two . . ."
> "Please!" Roy begged.
> "Three."
> "I can't!"
> "Three," the voice said again.
> Roy's legs felt like rubber as he teetered backward. A hand seized his shirt and yanked him into the thicket of pepper trees. (p. 54)

The terse conversation, with its twinges of humor, is appropriate for this story.

Contemporary realistic fiction writers often use figurative language in their work, inventing fresh comparisons that make their writing distinctive while developing realistic settings, plots, and characters. This style is used particularly well in *Three Times Lucky* (Turnage). Mo Lebeau, the book's protagonist, is a smart, spunky, and precocious heroine who comments perceptively about her fellow inhabitants of Tupelo Landing, North Carolina. Turnage develops the character of Mo as well as those who interact with her by embedding interesting metaphors in Mo's speech. Comments such as "I slept restless and dreamed thin . . . my world spun wobbly, like a worn out top" (p. 193) and "Miss Lana's voice is the color of sunlight in maple syrup" (p. 37) echo the cadences and images of southern speech while also providing insights into Mo's thoughts and feelings. Children do not always like stories with extensive descriptions or "flowery language." However, they can learn to appreciate how figurative language helps make a story seem real if the metaphors relate to their developmental level and experience.

Point of View

Authors of contemporary realistic fiction use various perspectives to tell their stories to fit the characters and make the plot believable. The omniscient, all-knowing storyteller's voice is often used in realistic fiction, revealing the thoughts and feelings of several (or even all) characters.

In contrast, when the reader sees the story only through the filter of one character's perspective, they experience a limited third-person point of view. Jerry Spinelli employs this perspective to begin *Wringer*, the story of a 10-year-old boy who lives in a town where it is traditional for

FIGURE 9.1 Criteria for Evaluating Contemporary Realistic Fiction

- Does the book honestly show contemporary life—the joys as well as the challenges—for readers? Have stereotypes been avoided?

- Are the themes realistic for the age-group? Do the themes overshadow the story, or are they embedded so that they naturally evolve?

- Do the characters act in realistic ways that are consistent with their age? Are they sufficiently developed so that the reader perceives them as real people? Can readers easily empathize with the situations the characters face?

- Does the writing convey the flavor of how real people might talk without using too much dialect that might inhibit a reader's understanding?

- Is the story enduring? Does it have relevance beyond its contemporary setting?

- Are violence or other negative behaviors shown to have consequences?

- Is the setting realistic and authentic? Is it appropriate to the story?

young boys called "wringers" to twist the necks of wounded pigeons shot down during the annual Family Fest Pigeon Shooting Day. The following excerpt demonstrates this point of view:

> He did not want to be a Wringer. This was one of the first things he had learned about himself. He could not have said exactly when he learned it, but it was very early. And more than early, it was deep inside. In the stomach, like hunger. (p. 1)

Sometimes, an author will tell a story using a first-person voice, almost as if the reader enters the character's mind and heart. This perspective provides a sense of realistic immediacy and intimacy that often draws readers into the story. For example, in *Are You There, God? It's Me, Margaret*, author Judy Blume has her character talking directly to God as she worries about moving to a new town and school, drawing readers into the story with a cozy, conversational tone.

Some writers incorporate the limited first-person point into a multiple first-person perspective by shifting the point of view from one character to another as the story progresses, thus creating a revolving first-person perspective. For example, *Wonder* (Palacio) develops the poignant story of Auggie, a boy with a deformed face, by alternating his point of view with those of his friends, sister, and several other characters. Each person adds a piece to the story so that, by the end, the reader understands Auggie and his effect on other people.

Figure 9.1 provides questions that you can use along with the general criteria for fiction discussed in Chapter 1 to select well-written contemporary realistic fiction to share with your students.

Categorizing Contemporary Realistic Fiction

Children's literature professionals categorize fiction in many ways: by content, theme, or use of a particular literary device. The dilemma for contemporary realistic fiction is that books usually fit into more than one category; a family story, for example, might also be a survival story or a mystery. We have organized the books in this genre thematically because teachers frequently create units incorporating these topics. However, children often devise their own ways to categorize books based on personal interests and their purposes for reading. Since children can so easily relate to the characters, plots, themes, and settings of contemporary realistic fiction stories, most find something they enjoy from the many titles encompassing a broad range of topics in this genre.

The following sections describe some of the most well-known books in each category of this genre. Additional excellent titles in each category are included in the lists at the end of the chapter. Picture books and transitional titles are also discussed in subsequent separate sections.

Growing Up: Peer Relationships, Life Changes, and Contending with Problems

As children grow into adulthood, they begin learning that choices have consequences and that they need to accept responsibility for their actions. Sometimes, this means standing up for what you believe in, making difficult decisions, or facing defining moments. Many books of contemporary realistic fiction focus on the process of becoming a mature person who grows emotionally as the story unfolds. Often, an event precipitates this growth, and the main character must work through issues related to this event. For example, Beverley Naidoo's *The Other Side of Truth* tells the story of 12-year-old Jade, who, along with her younger brother, is sent from Nigeria to an uncle in London after her mother is murdered and her father faces imprisonment for criticizing the Nigerian government. Jade must use her wits and determination to help the two of them survive.

In other books, a character encounters some problem: a friendship gone awry, a personal tragedy, a situation that leads to soul-searching, or other real-life issues. Books in this category have been termed "problem novels" because of their focus on issues and tribulations important to students who are exploring who they are.

One of the most important concerns children grapple with as they mature is how to negotiate friendships. Children of all ages are anxious about interacting appropriately with their peers, and books can explore the many issues that children encounter with making and keeping friends. *Bridge to Terabithia* (Paterson) is a classic in this category. This story revolves around 10-year-olds Jess and Leslie, children from different backgrounds who both feel isolated from their families. They create a secret retreat named Terabithia and develop a strong friendship. Other excellent stories that chronicle the satisfaction as well as the challenges in keeping and nurturing friendships are *Summer on the Moon* (Fogelin), *The Kind of Friends We Used to Be* (Dowell), and *The Small Adventures of Popeye and Elvis* (O'Connor). In most instances, the friendships are the backdrop for other "coming-of-age" issues.

Jacqueline Woodson writes realistic stories in which culturally diverse characters explore issues of gender, class, and race within the context of sustaining friends. *After Tupac and D. Foster* (Woodson) tells of three 12-year-old girls whose friendship is framed by the death of a hero (rapper Tupac Shakur) and the plight of one girl's older brother, who is in prison for a hate crime. They are also affected by a third girl, a foster child who yearns for a sense of belonging that the other two girls provide. Authentic dialogue and references to real places and events draws readers into this story. *Miracle's Boys* (Woodson) focuses on three brothers who are raising themselves after the deaths of their parents. Told from the youngest brother's perspective, the novel powerfully and honestly explores the difficulties that result from losing people you love.

Criss Cross and *All Alone in the Universe*, both by Lynn Perkins, tackle coming-of-age issues for girls, particularly those related to negotiating the travails of middle school, including first crushes, friends who abandon you, and fashion disasters. *Criss Cross* is particularly noteworthy because it is written as a series of intersecting vignettes in which poetry is interspersed with narrative. Both books provide a glimpse of young people growing into adulthood and trying to find their place in the world. A similar theme but with a lighter tone is *Each Little Bird That Sings* (Wiles). Ten-year-old Comfort Snowberger's family lives in the local funeral home. She comments humorously on death, her family, and people in her town and initially is worried only about losing her best friend to the "cooler" girls at school. Comfort is then confronted with a crisis that helps her appreciate all that she has in her life: "grief and fear and hope and love somehow woven together . . . all the messy glory" (p. 246).

Chess Rumble (Neri) and *Yummy: The Last Days of a Southside Shorty* (Neri) are stories set in urban environments that focus on middle school boys who are trying to figure out what kind of men they will become. *Freak the Mighty* (Philbrick) also features male protagonists. In this book, two middle school boys—one a mentally challenged giant and one gifted but in leg braces—team up to fight injustice.

Stories About Family Relationships

Stories that explore the relationships among siblings as well as between children and adult family members are also popular in realistic fiction. Many of these portray a relatively happy child with loving parents, doing normal daily activities, such as chores, playing together, squabbling over small issues, and usually having a gentle adventure or two. Lois Lowry's *Anastasia Krupnik* series is an excellent example of these books, as are Beverly Cleary's *Ramona* books and Jeanne Birdsall's books about the Penderwicks. *The Mouse Rap* (Myers) and *Yang the Youngest and His Terrible Ear* (Namioka) feature happy multicultural families.

In other stories, the family experiences problems such as divorce, illness, and poverty or is portrayed as unconventional. Not all children live in safe, nuclear families, and they need to see themselves depicted in the books they read. Typically, the situations are resolved positively, or the authors provide a sense of hope that things will improve. The young protagonists in *Dicey's Song* (Voigt), *Waiting for Normal* (Connor), *Under the Mesquite* (McCall), and *Keeping Safe the Stars* (O'Connor) are forced to grow up quickly and accept enormous responsibilities when parents or caretakers become ill, lose their homes, or suffer other catastrophes. In *A Step from Heaven* (Na), a young Korean girl immigrates with her family to America, the "land of great promise." However, the challenges of language barriers, vastly different cultural expectations, and limited employment opportunities lead her father to become drunk and abusive with disastrous consequences for the family.

Children in the foster care system represent another common situation in realistic fiction. *The Great Gilly Hopkins* (Paterson) and *The Pinballs* (Byars), both featuring foster children, are perennial favorites. *One for the Murphys* (Hunt), *Pictures of Hollis Woods* (Giff), and *Almost Home* (Bauer) are contemporary books in which foster children are taken in by a loving family, begin to trust and love again, and then come to understand the circumstances that affected the breakup of their original family.

Interactions with extended family members, such as grandparents, aunts, and uncles, are often a significant part of children's lives. In children's literature, these adult characters are often unconventional in their behavior. Sometimes, an extended family member raises the child, as in *Becoming Naomi Leon* (Ryan), a story in which Naomi and her brother have been brought up by their grandmother in a trailer park. When their alcoholic mom reappears after 7 years, she sets off a chain of events that lead to Naomi's search for her father and her true identity. Other well-regarded books in which children are raised by extended family members include *Journey, Arthur, and For the Very First Time* (MacLachlan); *Walk Two Moons* (Creech); and *Missing May* (Rylant).

In some books, the older adult is portrayed as a mentor who offers important guidance and support. For example, in *Maniac Magee* (Spinelli), Maniac finds a positive mentor in Grayson, an aging zoo worker who finds the boy in the buffalo pen at the zoo and teaches him how to survive.

In *The Great Wall of Lucy Wu* (Shang), Chinese American Lucy is forced to share her room with a great aunt who has come to visit from China. Initially resentful, she comes to appreciate all the love and knowledge of the family's traditional heritage that her aunt brings to the family.

Animal Stories

Animal stories are classified as realistic fiction if the animal characters act according to their true nature and are not anthropomorphized. In these books, the animal characters play a featured role; however, the human character is often another protagonist and typically matures as a result of interacting with the animal. In fact, some of the best animal stories are as much about the evolution of the human protagonist as about the animal's adventures. You may be familiar with some of the classics in this category, such as *The Incredible Journey* (Burnford), *Lassie Come Home* (Knight), *King of the Wind* (Henry), *Misty of Chincoteague* (Henry), and *Where the Red Fern Grows* (Rawls). These books are still popular with children because of their powerful stories and memorable depictions of both human and animal characters.

Several contemporary realistic fiction animal books have become new classics and are often the catalyst that hooks children into reading. Dog stories are particularly popular. *Shiloh* (Naylor), along with its sequels *Shiloh Season* and *Saving Shiloh*, relates a series of powerful yet poignant stories of an abused dog and the boy who rescues him. *Because of Winn-Dixie* (DiCamillo) tells of a mischievous stray dog who becomes the beloved friend and companion to Opal, a lonely, motherless girl who has just moved to Florida. Winn-Dixie becomes the catalyst for Opal to befriend various eccentric town residents, including Otis, an ex-convict who runs the pet store; Miss Fanny, the town librarian and dispenser of "Litmus Lozenges"; and Gloria Dump, who is almost blind but opens her heart to Opal. When Winn-Dixie runs away in a thunderstorm, everyone helps with the search, and Opal realizes that she is no longer alone. *Little Dog Lost* (Bauer), written in verse novel format, features a series of distinct voices that recount a heartfelt story of a dog who needs a boy and a boy who needs a dog, two lonely people, and a small town. *Zulu Dog* (Ferreira) is a story of a boy and his dog that takes place in South Africa just after apartheid is abolished.

Some books feature compelling tales of animals in danger that are rescued by young people. *Endangered* (Schrefer) is the story of 14-year-old Sophie, who lives on her mother's bonobo sanctuary in the Congo. When war erupts, it is Sophie who must rescue the animals from marauders by caring for them in the jungle. Exciting and compulsively readable, the story shows the importance of courage, resourcefulness, and determination in the face of cruelty and horror. *Our Secret, Siri Aang* (Kessler) is also set in Africa and tells of Namelok, a Maasai girl who commits to protecting a mother rhino and her baby from poachers. The story of her efforts to save the animals is interwoven with her questioning of Maasai tribal rituals, creating a captivating story. *Chained* (Kelly) chronicles the friendship between a young elephant keeper in India and his charge that performs tricks for the circus crowds but is cruelly abused by the owner.

Because of Winn Dixie by Kate DiCamillo is a heartwarming dog story that celebrates friendship, forgiveness, and what it means to be a family.

Adventure and Survival Stories

Students enjoy reading about others their age who use determination and ingenuity to endure incredible challenges and survive on their own. Protagonists in these stories typically face some sort of conflict, survive, and then grow toward maturity. Many of the classic stories of this type feature a character who must survive in a wilderness environment. Often, the character ends up in the situation due to an accident or misfortune and must use wits and determination to figure out how to stay alive. Stories such as *Island of the Blue Dolphins* (O'Dell), *My Side of the Mountain* (and its sequels) (George), and *Julie of the Wolves* (and its sequels) (George) are examples that have endured for decades. These exciting adventures and themes of resilience and self-sufficiency still resonate with children today.

Gary Paulsen's exciting adventure stories typically capture even the most reluctant readers. *Hatchet* and its sequels *The River* and *Brian's Return* depict a young boy surviving alone in the Canadian wilderness with increasing competence.

Will Hobbs also writes compelling adventure stories. In *Far North*, *Downriver*, *Bearstone*, and other books by Hobbs, characters explore wild places and experience heart-stopping escapades while also learning to make positive choices for their lives. Fans of Paulsen and Hobbs also often enjoy *Alabama Moon* (Key), the story of Moon, a young boy who has been living off the land with his antigovernment radical father. When his father dies, he is sent to a group home but uses his survival skills to escape. The story is full of chases, captures, and escapes, with well-paced writing that allows readers to understand Moon and sympathize with his dilemmas.

Although the setting for many survival stories is often in the wilderness or some remote place, books in this category can also be set in more urban environments. Paula Fox's *Monkey Island*, about a young boy living with a group of homeless people in New York City, is an excellent example of this. *Slake's Limbo* (Holman) tells of a 13-year-old, pursued by gangs, who hides in the New York subway system for 121 days. *Ninth Ward* (Rhodes) is set in New Orleans following the devastating Hurricane Katrina. This compelling story features a young girl who feels unworthy because she feels different from others. However, when catastrophe hits, the protagonist Lanesha rescues herself and others, proving that she is capable and resourceful.

Holes (Sachar) depicts both psychological and physical survival as it describes the story of Stanley Yelnats, who is wrongfully sent to a detention center. He initially blames this on a family curse. This plot is interwoven with another plot regarding how the detention center, "Camp Greenlake" (which is a dry desert area with no lake), began existence. Stanley must survive the physical challenges of digging holes day after day with little water while also overcoming the psychological challenge of resignedly accepting what he thinks is his inevitable bad luck. The plots are brought together at the end in a satisfying climax that demonstrates how Stanley has grown physically and has also become an individual who takes control of his destiny. Because many of the events in this book are highly improbable (but still possible), it is considered "magical realism."

Some realistic fiction adventure/survival books explore the theme of young people surviving under oppressive political regimes or contemporary war settings in countries such as Afghanistan, the Sudan, and Lebanon. For example, *A Long Walk to Water* (Park) recounts the compelling story of Salva, whose Sudanese village is attacked by rebel soldiers during civil war. Salva escapes but must endure a year-and-a-half journey to safety that is filled with dangers such as scorpions, crocodiles, lions, and a lack of water. He eventually becomes one of the "Lost Boys of Sudan" who are given new life in America. Nya, a young Sudanese girl who must walk hours to retrieve her family's daily water, alternately narrates the novel. Salva and Nya meet daily when Nay returns to Sudan to help bring clean water to villages in his country. *A Game for Swallows* (Abirached), *Bamboo People* (Perkins), *The Breadwinner* (Ellis), and *Thunder over Kandahar* (McKay) are other well-written books that feature young protagonists facing survival in politically unsettled conditions.

Humorous Stories

Students love to read about characters like themselves who encounter or unwittingly create humorous predicaments. Although many of the titles we have already discussed fall into this category, humorous books are so popular with students that they deserve separate mention.

Beverly Cleary's *Ramona* books are classics that continue to be enjoyed by today's children, as are Judy Blume's stories about Peter and his younger brother, Fudge, in *Tales of a Fourth Grade Nothing* and *Superfudge*. Another perennial favorite is *The Best Christmas Pageant Ever* (Robinson), in which a town's annual pageant is taken over by the Herdmans, the "worst kids in the entire history of the world." The Herdmans swear, rarely wash, and generally disrupt the normally orderly proceedings.

Carl Hiaasen writes humorous adventure stories wrapped around significant ecological issues in *Hoot*, *Scat*, *Flush*, and *Chomp*. Set in South Florida, his books pit adults determined to use the environment for their own nefarious purposes against smart, resourceful kids who are determined to thwart their efforts. These might sound a bit ponderous, but in Hiaasen's hands, the stories are highly entertaining as well as empowering to middle-grade readers. Polly Horvath also writes humorous books that also tackle serious issues, such as dysfunctional families, the trials of growing up, and the necessity of finding your place in the world. *Everything on a Waffle*, *My One Hundred Adventures*, and *The Canning Season*, all by Horvath, offer a skillfully crafted blend of dark and light moments populated with unforgettable characters and resourceful children who often comment on the antics of those around them.

Three Times Lucky (Turnage) features an irresistibly spunky heroine who was abandoned as a baby. Rescued by the Colonel, who names her "Moses," Mo LeBeau grows up in small-town North Carolina surrounded by a truly eccentric cast of characters, including Miss Lana, her surrogate mother who has more costumes and matching wigs than most movie stars, and the Colonel, who suffers from amnesia and talks to Mo in "army lingo." Mo's observations of her life and the people in her life are both poignant and laugh-out-loud funny. A double mystery adds to the appeal of this story.

Many books in this category are intended mainly to be entertaining. Usually, there is a message of some sort, but the emphasis is on hilarious situations either that children comment on or from which they must extricate themselves. The series books starring Judy Moody, Alvin Ho, and Goony Bird Green (Lowry) contain short chapters with easily identifiable characters who get themselves into hilarious predicaments and are designed to lure the transitional reader into books. *The Diary of a Wimpy Kid* books (Kinney) feature drawings and other graphics that add to the humor of a boy trying to navigate middle school angst.

Three Times Lucky by Sheila Turnage features quirky characters and a murder mystery.

Mysteries

Students enjoy reading mysteries because of the suspense and the opportunity to solve the puzzle. Research on children's preferences, described in Chapter 2, confirms that stories of mystery and adventure are consistently at the top of children's preference lists and frequently win awards voted on by children. You may recall reading the *Nancy Drew* and *Hardy Boy* series or the *Encyclopedia Brown* books (Sobol) and working along with the protagonist to solve a mystery or crime. Mysteries are excellent for enticing children to read and are available for all levels of readers, including picture books and transitional books and novels.

Two classic mysteries that keep children guessing right up to the conclusion are *The Mixed Up Files of Mrs. Basil E. Frankweiler* (Koenigsburg) and *The Westing Game* (Raskin). *The Mixed Up Files* chronicles the adventures of two children who run away from home and end up living in New York's Metropolitan Museum of Art. Soon, they are caught up in the mystery of an angel statue that might be the work of Michelangelo. *The Westing Game* is a complex puzzle in which 16 heirs to Samuel W. Westing's fortune must solve the mystery of his murder. The winner inherits his company and $200 million. Quirky characters, unexpected plot twists, and plenty of "red herrings" keep readers guessing until the end of this intriguing story.

Blue Balliet writes similarly smart, engrossing mysteries that feature precocious children on a quest to solve a puzzle. In *Chasing Vermeer* (Balliet), a valuable painting is stolen en route to Chicago. Two children decide to recover the painting but first must decipher a set of pentominos (mathematical puzzles) and a book about unexplainable phenomena. Seemingly random events come together at the end, making this an intriguing intellectual challenge for readers. The children's art-sleuthing adventures continue in *Wright 3* and *The Calder Game*. *The London Eye Mystery* (Dowd) chronicles the disappearance of a boy after riding on the London Eye, an observation wheel overlooking London for miles in every direction. Ted, an autistic boy, solves the mystery, making this a good book to explore individual differences in addition to the reader's challenge of figuring out a puzzling situation. *Escape from Mr. Lemoncello's Library* (Grabenstein) is a mystery full of action, video games, and intricate puzzles as a group of young teens must escape from the town library after spending the night there.

Liar and Spy (Stead) is as much about relationships and finding one's identity as it is about solving a mystery. Seventh grader Georges moves into an apartment building and soon becomes friends and then the first spy recruit of 12-year-old Safer. The two begin tracking another tenant who seems to be acting mysteriously. However, it becomes evident that both boys are hiding their own secrets, and the reader wonders who is the liar and who is the spy. Unexpected twists at the story's conclusion encourage the reader to return to the book to discover the clues that seemed hidden but on reflection are clearly evident.

Laurence Yep's *The Case of the Lion Dance* and *The Case of the Firecrackers* are exciting mysteries that concurrently offer readers a glimpse into Asian American life. *Maximilian and the Mystery of the Guardian Angel* (Garza) is a bilingual mystery novel that also explores elements of Mexican American culture, particularly *lucha libre* (Mexican professional wrestling).

Sports Stories

Sports stories portray the enjoyment as well as individual striving for excellence that are integral values in sports. Few are solely about sports. Rather, the best stories feature solid sports action (often play-by-play accounts) and depict likable protagonists who grapple with life lessons (Schneider, 2011). Issues of how to compete, contend with defeat, negotiate peer relationships, and the like are integrated with the sports action. Writers in this category use lots of sports language, accurately describe the action of the sport, and usually employ many energetic verbs, concrete nouns, and spare sentences (Schneider, 2011).

Matt Christopher is one of sport literature's most prolific writers. His stories feature both team and individual sports with a main character, typically a male, who overcomes some difficulty or challenge so that he can be accepted as part of a team. Mike Lupica is also a popular sportswriter for adults and children with, for example, *Million-Dollar Throw*, *Heat*, *Hot Hand*, and *Miracle on 49th Street*. The latter title appeals to girls because of a basketball-playing female protagonist.

Some books use sport more subtly to convey a theme, develop a plot conflict, or flesh out characters. *The Aurora County All Stars* (Wiles) introduces readers to House Jackson, captain of the baseball team. Lots of baseball action makes this a good sports book, but Jackson also encounters secrets and betrayals in his small town that must be resolved before "the big game." *Taking Sides* (Soto) explores issues of cultural and racial identity in a story about a Hispanic basketball player who moves from a poor to more affluent neighborhood.

School Life

Most children can easily relate to stories about various aspects of school life, including first-day jitters, embarrassing moments, and eccentric teachers. Realistic fiction books about school life can be found for children at all age and interest levels, making these books particularly appropriate for motivating reluctant readers. The best books in this category corroborate the common experiences of school life, showing characters who experience problems or obstacles that they overcome through their own initiative or with the assistance of caring teachers or peers. Although many books have school settings as part of the story, this section discusses those books in which school and school-related issues are the central focus of the story.

A perennial favorite is *Frindle* (Clements), a hilarious story about mischievous fifth grader Nicholas, who invents a new name for a pencil: a frindle. More contemporary books focus on significant issues, such as an inability to read, as in *Bluefish* (Schmatz); moving from being homeschooled to regular school, as in *Ida B* (Hannigan); or reluctant writers, as in *Locomotion* (Woodson) and *Love That Dog* (Creech), both of which describe boys who refuse to write until a caring teacher helps each find his voice.

The Strange Case of Origami Yoda (and sequels) (Angleberger) is an unusually inventive school story involving sixth-grade "loser" Dwight, who talks to his classmates through an origami finger puppet named Yoda. Origami Yoda predicts all kinds of events, such as pop quizzes, while also dispensing sage advice. The mystery for the other kids is whether Origami Yoda is real and, if so, how the puppet can be so wise about life when Dwight is perceived as weird. The class begins conducting scientific experiments to uncover the truth while also negotiating the social dynamics of sixth grade.

Books About People with Physical and Mental Challenges

Children are curious about the differences in people around them. Well-chosen books offer an important opportunity for generating awareness and developing positive regard for those who have physical and mental challenges. Good books in this category should be realistic and accurate, portraying the disability honestly, without showing the disabled person as helpless or pitiable with sugarcoated sentimentally. There should not be a miracle cure; rather, characters should learn to live with the situation in which they find themselves.

A child contending with physical disabilities or illnesses is a common plot in this category. One of the most popular with a wide range of readers is *Wonder* (Palacio), the story of Auggie, the ordinary kid except for his severely deformed face. Homeschooled for 4 years, he enrolls in a public middle school, determined to be just a typical kid. Of course, he is not typical; thus, he endures shocked looks, whispers, and outright bullying. As the year progresses, Auggie learns that although he will probably always be bullied, he can also find true friends. *Out of My Mind* (Draper) is the story of Melody, a brilliant girl with a photographic memory who also has cerebral palsy. As with other books about children with disabilities, the reader comes to know and empathize with gutsy, determined Melody as she learns to communicate and is consequently mainstreamed into a regular classroom, only to be shunned and betrayed by other students. The book shows readers what it is like to be trapped in the mind and body of someone with cerebral palsy. More important, they also learn much more about the misconceptions we have about differently abled people and how we react to them.

Several excellent stories focus on children who have a form of autism. In *Anything but Typical* (Baskin), sixth grader Jason is an autistic boy who writes terrific stories in an online writing forum but fails miserably in real social interactions. The first-person narrative of the book allows readers to experience the world as Jason does, better understanding the obstacles he faces as well as his fierce determination to stay true to himself. *Mockingbird* (Erskine) tells the story of Caitlin, who has Asperger syndrome and is also coping with the murder of her brother. The portrayal of an autistic child is particularly accurate in this book: the way she talks, how she sucks on her sleeve, her obsession with words, and her misinterpretation of social skills. *Rules* (Lord) is told from the perspective of an older sister whose family revolves around her autistic brother. Embarrassed by his behavior, she tries to teach him rules about being normal ("don't put toys in the fish tank," "hug mom but not the video store guy"). When she meets a boy who is a nonverbal paraplegic, she comes to realize that acceptance is more important than social conformity.

The *Joey Pigza* books (Gantos) depict a boy with attention-deficit/hyperactivity disorder who cannot control his behavior. Gantos humorously but honestly captures the significant challenges faced by a child with this disorder.

Lesbian, Gay, Bisexual, and Transgender (LGBT) Literature

LGBT children's literature has gradually expanded since the 1980s and now includes books about children with LGBT parents, children who are themselves LGBT or questioning, homophobia in schools, and gay relatives with AIDS and books about diversity that include LGBT families (Lamme, 2008, p. 209). Most of the LGBT picture books intended for preschool and primary children focus on realistic contemporary families, such as *Best, Best Colors/Los Majores* Colores (Hoffman) in which a young child cannot decide on a favorite color or a best friend until his mammas show him a rainbow flag and he realizes he loves the colors best when they are all together. Novels focusing on this topic allow for greater character development and often explore issues of sexual identity or a family's acceptance of an LGBT member.

Nancy Garden is a groundbreaking author whose work was instrumental in breaking down stereotypes and providing positive portrayals of LGBT characters. *Holly's Secret* by Nancy Garden is a compassionate view of the impact of antigay bias on children with gay parents. Garden is also the author of *Annie on My Mind*, one of the first books to show sexual identity as one aspect of a coming-of-age narrative. This book also was among the first to portray an LGBT love story with a positive ending. Jacqueline Woodson also writes sensitive realistic stories that explore LGBT relationships. For example, *The House You Pass on the Way* (Woodson), invites readers to visit the world of 14-year-old Staggerlee, the daughter of mixed-race parents and the granddaughter of civil rights activists who were killed in a racial bombing. Staggerlee's attraction to her adopted cousin Trout, another 14-year-old girl, is just one part of her search for identity.

In *Country Girl, City Girl* (Jahn-Clough), 13-year-old Phoebe feels an attraction to Melita, a family friend's sophisticated, urban daughter who visits Phoebe's family's home in the country. But Phoebe's same-sex attraction is not the only aspect of her developing identity; she also defines herself as a country girl, preferring her farm in Maine to urban New York City. The search for self is also a theme in *From the Notebooks of Melanin Sun* (Woodson), about a young teen who struggles with his mother's announcement that she is gay.

Aristotle and Dante Discover the Secrets of the Universe (Saenz) recounts a friendship between two teen boys that grows into much more. The two are opposites: Ari feels he is a loner while Dante is sure of who he is, although he faces his own challenges. Issues of family and Mexican identity are integrated with the central theme of sexual identity in this well-written, thoughtful novel.

The Gay, Lesbian, Bisexual, Transgender Round Table and the Social Responsibilities Round Table of the American Library Association have established the "Rainbow Project," an annual list of quality LGBT literature for children. This is a valuable resource for teachers and readers who are looking for books on this topic.

Tech Click

Involve students in the 21st Century Skills of higher-order thinking by discerning top-quality literature and communicating the best to their peers. Students may enjoy categorizing contemporary realistic titles, for example, by developmentally appropriate themes such as those at the end of this chapter. Using simple presentation software such as PowerPoint or Keynote, link book teasers from the menu slide to individual book slides. The resulting product acts as a resource for the teacher and future students, as shown in Figure 9.2 For directions, search for "make PowerPoint or Keynote interactive."

Contemporary Realistic Fiction Picture Books

Realistic fiction picture books provide readers with focused, realistic glimpses into the everyday lives of contemporary children. As with novels in this genre, realism is critical. Characters must act, dress, feel, and live like real people. Plots must focus on events and issues that are important to contemporary sensibilities.

FIGURE 9.2 Interactive Book Recommendations Created with Presentation Software

Many contemporary realistic fiction picture books focus on children interacting with warm, supportive parents or extended family members; squabbling with siblings (or expressing jealousy over a new sibling); learning about family traditions; and other normal everyday family experiences. For example, the protagonist in *What's So Bad About Being an Only Child?* (Best) tries to convince her parents to produce more siblings. In contrast, the only child in *Nobody Asked Me if I Wanted a Baby Sister* (Alexander) is extremely unhappy about an impending new baby. In *The Hello, Goodbye Window* (Raschka), a young child celebrates the kitchen window at her grandparents' house, where they observe the world and also say hello and good-bye to each other. *The Relatives Came* (Rylant) and *We Had a Picnic This Sunday Past* (Woodson) poke gentle fun at family reunions. Inevitably, differences are resolved, family love is affirmed, and happiness prevails in these books, particularly in realistic fiction picture books for the youngest children.

Other everyday occurrences, such as going to school, playing sports, or having a pet, are common plots in contemporary realistic fiction picture books. Many school stories recount first-day jitters, as in *It's My First Day of Kindergarten* (Yee); take children on a school tour, as in *Follow the Line to School* (Ljungkvist); or provide subtle advice on how to make friends, as in *Yo! Yes?* (Raschka). Animal stories commonly focus on children imploring their parents to get a pet or enjoying the pet they have, as in *Posey the Kitten* (Newbery), and the stories about the lovable Rottweiler dog featured in the *Carl* books by Alexandra Day.

Some picture books in this genre address more serious issues, such as appreciating the environment or helping others. For example, both *The Curious Garden* (Brown) and *Something Beautiful* (Wyeth) show children transforming an urban area through gardening. *All the World* (Scanlon) shows a multicultural family appreciating the sun, wind, sea, and the smaller things, such as pebbles and shells that they encounter on a summer day by the sea. *Smoky Night* (Bunting) depicts a family forced to evacuate their apartment during the Los Angeles riots. The event is frightening, but the boy comes to realize the value of working together with his neighbors to rebuild their lives.

The lists at the end of this chapter feature a range of picture book titles that you can use with your children to provide a realistic "slice-of-life" view of other children who live and act like them or those who lead different but contemporary lives.

Contemporary Realistic Fiction Transitional and Series Books

The most popular realistic fiction transitional books are series books, which typically feature multiple volumes populated by the same characters who have similar adventures and challenges across the stories. Realistic fiction series books line the shelves of bookstores and are found frequently heading the national best-seller lists. They are also the most common purchases from children's book clubs (Strickland, Walmsley, Bronk, & Weiss, 1994).

Realistic fiction series books provide a comfort zone for young readers who are just getting into chapter books. The familiarity of realistic characters and plots are also fun for older readers who get similarly hooked on an author's style and consider characters old friends. However, despite the fact that realistic fiction series books seem to weave a special magic for transitional readers as well as those who are ready for more challenging fare, research has found that children view these as the fast food of the literary world: fun to

Thirty-four words convey the blossoming friendship between two boys in *Yo, Yes?* by Chris Raschka.

read but not a substitute for the better literary choices their teachers recommend (Greenlee, Monson, & Taylor, 1996). Thus, it is appropriate for students to read series books even if they can comprehend more complex stories. However, they should be encouraged to move on when they are capable of reading more complex material.

The lists at the end of this chapter provide suggested series book titles that we have found to be popular with children but that are also well written.

Teaching Strategies

Connecting to the Common Core State Standards

Understanding Character

The Common Core State Standards (CCSS.RL 3) have identified an understanding of character as an important skill for readers. Realistic fiction is an excellent genre for supporting children's evolving understanding of characters and how they respond to the events in their lives. The developmental evolution over several grade levels is articulated in CCSS Reading: Literature Standard RL.3:

CCRA (Anchor Standard) RL.3: Analyze how and why individuals, events, and ideas develop and interact over the course of a text.

Sample Grade-Level Competencies for This Standard Are the Following:

RL.1.3.   Describe characters, settings, and major events in a story, using key details.

RL.3.3.   Describe characters in a story (e.g., their traits, motivations, or feelings) and explain how their actions contribute to the sequence of events.

RL.5.3.   Compare and contrast two or more characters, settings, or events in a story or drama, drawing on specific details in the text (e.g., how characters interact).

RL.7.3.   Analyze how an author develops and contrasts the points of view of different characters or narrators in a text.

The following activities using books of realistic fiction can support children's developing ability to understand characters and the ways in which these characters respond to the events they experience. We have organized the suggestions in order of increasing complexity; those described first are appropriate for students just beginning to study characterization, whereas those discussed later are more appropriate for older students.

Character Webs, Maps, and Diagrams: Character webs and diagrams are strategies for illustrating and organizing students' understandings regarding a character in a coherent, easy-to-understand visual arrangement. Depending on their focus, these graphic organizers can help students understand character motivations, the relationships between characters, and a character's role in the overall story. A character web is usually constructed by placing a character name in the middle of the page with spokes radiating out from it. At the end of the spokes, students can write character attributes, such as "Personality Traits," "Feelings," "Appearance," "Likes and Dislikes," "Has a Problem with _____," or other appropriate attributes. Older

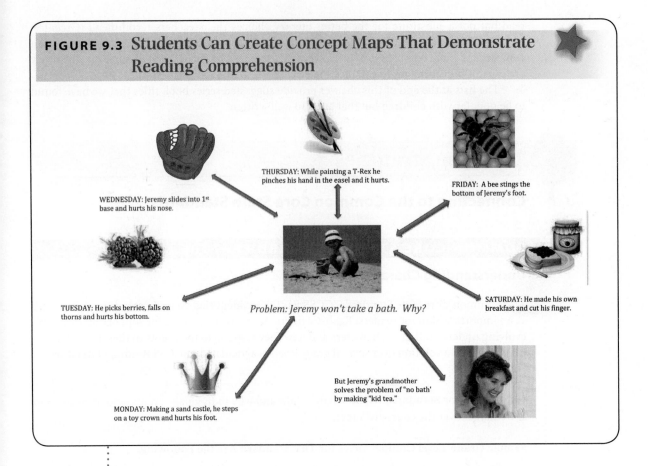

FIGURE 9.3 Students Can Create Concept Maps That Demonstrate Reading Comprehension

WEDNESDAY: Jeremy slides into 1st base and hurts his nose.

THURSDAY: While painting a T-Rex he pinches his hand in the easel and it hurts.

FRIDAY: A bee stings the bottom of Jeremy's foot.

TUESDAY: He picks berries, falls on thorns and hurts his bottom.

Problem: Jeremy won't take a bath. Why?

SATURDAY: He made his own breakfast and cut his finger.

MONDAY: Making a sand castle, he steps on a toy crown and hurts his foot.

But Jeremy's grandmother solves the problem of "no bath" by making "kid tea."

students can be asked to provide evidence from the book, such as quotes, summary of particular passages, or page numbers to support each attribute. Maps for different characters from the same book can be compared.

Venn diagrams, composed of two overlapping circles, are another way to compare two characters. The qualities that two characters share can be written in the intersecting sections of the diagram and the ways the characters are different in the nonintersecting sections. A variation is to compare two characters' perspectives on the same issue. This can be done in pairs, followed by a larger group discussion in which students share their diagrams on various characters' perspectives on a historical event or issue. The discussion that ensures usually deepens their understanding of how the characters respond to events or issues.

Tech Click

Interactive whiteboards can be used to create Venn diagrams, comparison charts, and other graphic organizers. Figure 9.3 shows a sample book response map in which the reader sets up a puzzle for others to guess. A benefit of using this technology is the ability to save files that can be revised or appended at a later date or used in other materials. Some companies offer free printable, online character tools, such as Scholastic's Character Scrapbook.

Tech Click

Some contemporary realistic fiction involves traveling, such as *Runaway* (Van Draanen). Older students could extend their understanding of the story and the protagonist's journal by creating a Google Lit Trip. Quality examples may be posted on the site for other readers to experience. Check out the one for *Walk Two Moons* (Creech), *Lost* (McPhail), or *Are We There Yet?* (Lester). This activity addresses the 21st Century Skill "Create Media Projects" and the CCRA.RL.5.3.

Character Trading Cards: Creating trading cards based on book characters challenges readers to think more deeply about the thoughts, feelings, and motivations of book characters (Giorgis, 2010). The activity is most successful when the cards are based on well-developed characters and students are interested in digging deeper to understand what motivates them. Once students decide on a focus character, they are advised to reread the book to discern critical details, important quotes, significant moments, and important interactions. Sticky notes can be used to record this information. After they have gathered this information, they create a two-sided card. Side 1 is a visual portrait of the character that reveals physical features. Side 2 contains the "vital statistics"—the information gathered about the character in an attractive, readable format. Following the creation of their cards, students can share and discuss how the activity helped them discover more about a particular character (Giorgis, 2010).

Tech Click

Trading Cards is a free iPad app that allows students to create online trading cards. An online link for this purpose is also available at ReadWriteThink.org, but this site requires a Flash plug-in, not yet a standard feature on the iPad.

Time Lines: Students can create individual time lines for the life of one character in a story. They could also be asked to provide specific details or examples related to each event on the time line.

Character Scrapbook: Students can create scrapbook pages for the main character in a book they read. Students can use both writing and illustration to create scrapbook pages highlighting various aspects of a character, including personality traits, responses to story events, interactions with other characters, and other qualities. Students can research the contemporary context of the story and include pages for this information. They can then compare scrapbooks completed for the same character or different characters in the same story to deepen their understandings of these characters.

Tech Click

Students can also create Facebook pages for book characters. They can then use traditional Facebook categories, such as "Friends," "Likes," and "Comments" to organize the information they collected about their character (Giorgis, 2010). Schools that block Facebook can create a similar but static page in Facebook (sponsored by ClassTools).

Letter and Diary Writing: Students can write letters or diary entries from one character's perspective in a book they are reading as the story progresses. These could be compared with letters or diary entries written by a classmate who takes an entirely different perspective on that character (the character's enemy, closest friend, and so on). The challenge is to "stay in character," maintaining the voice and perspective of that person. (This activity also develops skill in another standard: RL.6: Determining Point of View.)

Analysis of Character Response to Events: Using double- or triple-entry journals, students can examine how characters change over the course of a story. They first select a character who is pivotal to the story. In column 1, they summarize various events of the story. In column 2, they describe a character's response to each event as it occurs. In column 3 (for older students), they can analyze how that character grows and changes in response to the events he or she experiences. Students can then summarize how their selected characters responded, grew, and changed throughout the story. Or they can complete this activity by charting how other characters in a story perceive or interact with a main character.

Conversation with a Character: This activity provides another opportunity to analyze a character's actions and motivations in response to historical events. The "conversation" can be held with one character and an interviewer, or two characters (from the same or different books) can converse with each other. In partners, students construct interview questions for the character(s) that they then use to create a dialogue that is presented to the class. Sample interview questions might include the following:

- What are the most important things you accomplished in the story? Why do you think they are important?
- What events or circumstances do you wish were different in the story? Why did you choose these events?
- What was an obstacle you encountered in the story, and how did you overcome that obstacle?
- What is your dream for the future if your story continued?

Tech Click

Word Mover is an iPad app that allows students to create "found poetry." They choose words from a word bank or select their own and then electronically manipulate the words to create a poem about a character or significant story event. This is also linked to ReadWriteThink.org for computers with a flash player.

COMMON CORE STATE STANDARD FEATURE #2

Determining Point of View (CCSS.RL.6)

The CCSS affirm competence in assessing how the point of view from which the story is written affects one's response to what transpires as well as a reader's understanding of the events. Primary grade children are expected to simply identify who is telling a story. By the upper elementary and middle school grades, students are expected to master more subtle aspects of this skill. Following are the Anchor Standard and selected grade-level competencies for this skill, which integrates well with activities related to analyzing character (CCSS.RL.3):

CCRA (Anchor Standard) RL.6: Assess how point of view or purpose shapes the content and style of a text.

Sample Grade-Level Competencies for This Standard Are the Following:
- **RL.1.6.** Identify who is telling the story at various points in a text.
- **RL.3.6.** Distinguish their own point of view from that of the narrator or those of the characters.
- **RL.4.6.** Compare and contrast the points of view from which different stories are narrated, including the difference between first- and third-person narrations.
- **RL.5.6.** Describe how a narrator's or speaker's point of view influences how events are described.
- **RL.7.6.** Explain how an author develops the point of view of the narrator or speaker in a text.

If children are exposed to many stories through interactive read-alouds, literature circles, close reading sessions, and other strategies mentioned in this chapter, they will begin to identify the point of view from which a story is told. One introductory activity to develop an initial understanding of this skill is to ask students to sort books into two categories: those written from the first-person or those written from the third-person point of view. As individuals, with partners, or as a class, they can write sample sentences, examples of dialogue, or summaries that are evidence for the point of view in a story. These can be shared, with students reading their entries in the voice of the characters (Owocki, 2012). A comparison chart can keep the work visible and permanent. This activity works particularly well with picture books but can be easily adapted to longer sections of texts.

Another introductory activity can occur after the class participates in a shared experience (field trip, assembly speaker, and so on). Students write a journal entry describing the event from their own perspectives. These entries can be shared aloud. A discussion could focus on how the same event is viewed in diverse ways.

Following are some additional ideas to support children's developing understandings of point of view in fiction. We have selected realistic fiction to showcase this skill because of the range of books that are written from both first- and third-person perspectives. However, the activities could also be used in conjunction with other types of fiction and with nonfiction.

Character Perspective Charts: This strategy (Yopp & Yopp, 2001) is especially well suited to a book that has two important characters, such as *Bridge to Terabithia* (Paterson) or *The Pain and the Great One* (Blume). Students construct a two-column chart and write the name of each of the two main characters at the top. Listing topics such as setting, problem, goals, attempts to resolve problem, attempts to reach goal, outcomes, and theme, students then write information about these topics from the perspective of the two characters. For example, in *The Pain and the Great One*, the older sister (the "Great One") would consider the problem to be her little spoiled brother. The "Pain," who is the younger brother, would identify the problem as his big sister being too "stuck up."

Dramatizations from Multiple Perspectives: One way to develop understanding of how authors use point of view is to organize opportunities for role-playing characters. Books written from the first-person perspective work particularly well for this activity. Students can create dramatizations that focus on the main character as well as others in the story to understand how each character's perspective changes the reader's understanding of story events.

It helps to first build a sense of the main character by considering questions such as the following:

- What would you look like if you were this character?
- How would this character move and sound?
- How would this character act in response to other characters he or she might encounter?

Several children could become that character and play a scene from the story. The rest of the group can then discuss the differences in each person's interpretation with the emphasis on how the story's point of view informed his or her understanding of this character.

Students can then dramatize the same scene from another character's perspective. They should consider the same questions to develop their understanding of that character, but they will likely have less information, particularly if the book is written from the main character's "first-person" point of view. Following the dramatizations, students can discuss how the events, dialogue, and so on in the same scene from a story could differ based on another character's perspective on the events.

Books in which the point of view shifts also work well for this activity. *Wonder* (Palacio) is an excellent book example because the shifts in perspective are clearly delineated. One character's thoughts are even written entirely in lowercase to distinguish his perspective. Other realistic fiction books that shift points of view and that would work well for this activity are *Same Sun Here* (House and Viswani), *Criss Cross* (Perkins), *Nothing but the Truth* (Avi), and *My Side of the Mountain* and its sequel *Frightful's Mountain* (George).

Tech Click

These dramatizations could be recorded and student edited with simple software, such as iMovie or Windows Movie Maker. Archives of these presentations serve as exemplars for subsequent classes.

Character Monologues: Students could also create character monologues. Each student who has read the book selects a character, dresses as that person, and draws a poster portrait to hang on the wall. Then each student writes a one-page monologue or blog from the character's perspective, introducing the character and his or her perspective on some major plot point in the book. After sufficient rehearsing, students perform their monologues.

Writing Two- or Three-Voice Poems: Students can write poems from different character's perspectives regarding a pivotal point in a book. These poems can be read aloud separately, or students can intertwine the voices. Contemporary realistic fiction novels written in verse that could be used as models for this activity include *Hidden* (Frost), *Where the Steps Were* (Cheng), *Spinning Through the Universe: A Novel in Poems from Room 214* (Frost), *Naked Bunyip Dancing* (Herrick); *What Is Goodbye?* (Grimes), *Minn and Jake* (Wong), and *Amber Was Brave, Essie Was Smart* (Williams).

A variation of this activity is to have students create two-voice dialogues. These are short plays in which characters from one book or different books with similar themes or plots present their perspectives separately or together. For example, a child from Auggie's class in *Wonder* and one from Melody's class in *Out of My Mind* could comment on how they perceive the protagonist in each story.

Supporting Culturally Diverse Learners with Contemporary Realistic Fiction

High-quality contemporary realistic fiction novels and picture books that depict culturally diverse settings or characters can help all readers grow in appreciating, understanding, and respecting the people, places, life experiences, and traditions that are different from their own. Children from diverse cultures should be able to see themselves portrayed in authentic ways both in the books they choose and in those the teacher reads aloud and discusses. These discussions can also help children, no matter their culture or ethnicity, become more aware and appreciative of the many ways in which people are similar and different.

Children from diverse backgrounds seem to particularly connect with "culturally relevant" realistic fiction books (stories that directly reflect their own lives and experiences). It seems that they can more easily construct meaning from a text that contains familiar elements because they can use their background knowledge to make predictions and inferences that lead to better comprehension (Freeman & Freeman, 2004). Following are some questions you can ask to determine if a book is culturally relevant and thus potentially engaging to a particular reader:

- Are the characters like you and your family? Do they talk like you do?
- How close are the characters to you in age?
- Have you had similar experiences to those described in the story?
- Have you lived in or visited the settings of the story? (Freeman & Freeman, 2004)

In addition to examining a book's cultural relevance, you should also look for excellent writing that is age appropriate, true to the culture, and free of stereotyping. For picture books, you should ensure that the illustrations reflect the culture in authentic and genuine ways.

There is some concern regarding authors who write outside of their ethnicity or culture: will their books be authentic and realistic? If this question comes up, conducting a search of the author's background would be appropriate. Quality writing combined with authenticity will endure, but take extra consideration with books that do not pass the test of realistic and accurate writing.

Children have many more choices of books written by culturally diverse authors than in the past—books in which diversity and difference are depicted in authentic ways and in contemporary settings and in which characters, young and old, are featured in realistic situations, sometimes facing incredible challenges. Figure 9.4 features a sampling of culturally relevant picture books from several cultures. Additional books are included in the lists at the end of the chapter.

Supporting English Language Learners with Contemporary Realistic Fiction

Contemporary realistic fiction can be exciting and engaging for all readers, but English language learners (ELLs) may be particularly drawn to this genre (Hadaway & Young, 2010, p. 101). Books with culturally diverse characters can resonate with ELL students, particularly if their first language is included in the story. Readers can more easily see themselves in the stories, resulting in extended conversations that develop their language skills. You can maximize the opportunity to practice their English by connecting the reading experience with listening, speaking, and writing.

Picture books are particularly effective in encouraging interaction and discussion. Students can start by predicting plot based on the title and the cover of a picture book. They can

FIGURE 9.4 Sampling of Culturally Relevant Realistic Fiction Picture Books

(Books appropriate for preschoolers are marked *.)

African American

*Best, Cari. *Red Light, Green Light, Mama and Me.*
Daly, Nikki. *Jamelas's Dress.*
*Diggs, Tony. *Chocolate Me.*
Flournoy, Valerie. *The Patchwork Quilt.*
Greenfield, Eloise. *Grandpa's Face.*
Harrington, Janice. *The Chicken Chasing Queen of Lamar County* (Shelly Jackson, Illus.).
Havill, Jaunita. *Jamaica Is Thankful* (and others about Jamaica).
Hoffman, Mary. *Amazing Grace.*
Hooks, Bell [sic]. *Happy to Be Nappy* (Chris Raschka).
*Keats, Ezra Jack. *The Snowy Day* (and others by Keats).
*Smalls-Hector, Irene. *Jonathan and His Mommy.*
Stoltz, Mary. *Storm in the Night.*
*Tarpley, Natasha. *I Love My Hair.*
*Williams, Vera. *"More, More, More", Said the Baby: Three Love Stories.*
Woodson, Jacqueline. *Our Gracie Aunt; Visiting Day; Each Kindness; *Pecan Pie Baby.*
Wyeth, Sharon. *Something Beautiful.*

Asian American

*Cheng, Andrea. *Goldfish and Chrysanthemums.*
Chim, Karen. *Sam and the Lucky Money.*
*Choi, Sook Nyul. *Yunmi and Halmoni's Trip.*
Choi, Yangsook. *The Name Jar.*
Compestine, Ying Chang. *Crouching Tiger.*
Garland, Sherry. *The Lotus Seed.*
*Irvine, Margaret Chodos. *Best, Best Friends.*
Liang, Cheng. *A New Year's Reunion.*
*Lin, Grace. *Fortune Cookie Fortunes; *Dim Sum for Everyone.*
Look, Lenore. *Uncle Peter's Amazing Chinese Wedding; Henry's First Moon Birthday; Love As Strong As Ginger.*
McDonnell, Christine. *Goyangi Means Cat.*
McKay, Lawrence. *Journey Home.*
Pak, Soyung. *Dear Juno.*
*Park, Linda Sue. *Bee-Bim Bop!.*

Recorvits. Helen. *My Name Is Yoom.*
Sheth, Kashmira. *My Dadima Wears a Sari.*
Wong, Janet. *Apple Pie, Fourth of July; The Trip Back Home; This Next New Year.*
*Yum, Herbert. *The Twins' Blanket.*

Latino/American

Alda, Alma Flor. *I Love Saturdays y Domingos* (Elivia Asvadier, Illus.).
Brown, Monica. *Marisol McDonald Doesn't Match/ Marisol McDonald no combina.*
*Chapra, Mimi. *Sparky's Bark; *Amelia's Show and Tell Fiesta.*
*Cruise, Robin. *Little Mama Forgets.*
*Dorros, Arthur. *Papa and Me.*
Figueredo, D. *When This World Was New.*
*Johnston, Tony. *My Abuelita.*
*Mora, Pat. *Gracias/Thanks; Tomas and the Library Lady; The Rainbow Tulip.*
Perez, Amanda. *My Very Own Room; My Diary from Here to There/Mi diario de aqui hasta alla* (Maya Christina Gonzalez, Illus.).
Soto, Gary. *Too Many Tamales.*
Tafalla, Carmen. *What Can You Do with a Rebozo?; What Can You Do with a Paleta?; *Fiesta Babies.*
Valesquez, Eric. *Grandma's Gift.*

Native American

*Begaye, Lisa. *Building a Bridge.*
Bruchac, Joseph. *Fox Song.*
Lapaca, Kathleen and Michael. *Less Than Half, More Than Whole.*
Miles, Miska. *Annie and the Old One.*
Olsen, Sylvia. *Yetsah's Sweater.*
Sanderson, Esther. *Two Pairs of Shoes.*
Schick, Eleanor. *My Navajo Sister.*
Smith, Cynthia Leitich. *Jingle Dancer.*
Stroud, Virginia. *A Walk to the Great Mystery.*
Tapahonso, Luci. *Songs of Shiprock Fair.*
Waboose, Jan. *SkySisters.*
Wheeler, Bernelda. *Where Did You Get Your Moccasins?*

FIGURE 9.5 Wordless or Nearly Wordless Realistic Fiction Picture Books for ELLs

Baker, Jeannie. *Home; Window; Mirror.* (P, I)

Banyai, Istvan. *The Other Side; Zoom.* (P, I)

Crews, Donald. *Truck.* (P)

Day, Alexandra. *Good Boy, Carl* (and others). (P)

dePaola, Tomie. *Pancakes for Breakfast.* (P)

Fleischman, Paul. *Sidewalk Circus.* (P)

Geisert, Arthur. *Thunderstorm.* (P)

Kim, Patti. *Here I Am* (Sonia Sanchez, Illus.).

Lee, Suzy. *Wave; Shadow.* (P, I)

Liu, Jae Soo. *Yellow Umbrella* (with accompanying CD of classical-style music by Dong II Sheen). (P, I)

Ormerod, Jan. *Moonlight* (P); *Sunshine.* (P)

Raschka, Chris. *A Ball for Daily; Daisy Gets Lost.* (P)

Spier, Peter. *Peter Spier's Rain.* (P)

Vincent, Gabrielle. *A Day, A Dog.* (I, M)

then be invited to talk through a story line either in their own language or in English. This activity is based on enjoyment, but it also reinforces story structure and sequencing of events and stimulates vocabulary growth and oral language development.

Wordless or nearly wordless picture books are also helpful to ELL students because they feature strong visual support while also providing an opportunity to create oral narrative texts. Students can be asked to retell the story using the pictures. Their stories can be written or orally recorded. Many wordless books have a fantasy story line, but the titles we have selected in Figure 9.5 are contemporary realistic fiction. We believe that realistic fiction books are especially appropriate because ELL students can bring their experiential background to the learning experience.

Controversial Issue: Bibliotherapy: Should Books Be Used to Address Life Issues?

Reading can be therapeutic. Avid readers often find themselves enthusiastically jumping into the world of the book, becoming totally involved with the characters and their stories. When they turn the last page, sad that the book is over, they often have new insights to apply to their lives. This experience is the premise for *bibliotherapy*; the practice of sharing books with children so as to help them contend with social issues and developmental challenges associated with growing up (Doll & Doll; 1997; Heath, Sheen, Leavy, Young, & Money, 2005).

Book characters can demonstrate solutions to life challenges, providing a road map to achieving social and emotional maturity. Readers can vicariously experience difficult situations and observe how they are resolved while remaining safe from real conflict. The subsequent discussions that evolve in bibliotherapy sessions provide a sense of community as students realize that they are not alone in their struggles.

It is critical that students identify with characters in order to understand and connect to their challenges. It is easy to make these connections to the contemporary characters and powerful true-to-life stories of contemporary realistic fiction; thus, books from this genre are frequently used for bibliotherapy sessions. For example, *The Recess Queen* (O'Neill), a story of a playground bully who stops bullying when befriended by another child, can be used to help students learn strategies for diffusing this issue. Discussions regarding stealing and whether it is justified naturally arise when reading *Shiloh* (Naylor), a book in which the protagonist witnesses the abuse of a dog and must decide if "rescuing" the animal from the abuse is an ethical choice.

However, critics of the use of bibliotherapy in classrooms and libraries are concerned that those conducting discussions on sensitive issues are "pseudopsychologists" who are not trained to lead therapeutic discussions. Well-meaning teachers and librarians might do more harm than good, these critics assert (Heath et al., 2005; Kanarowski, 2012). Some research has shown that bibliotherapy sessions can be counterproductive, actually reinforcing the negative attitudes and actions that teachers are trying to change (Kanarowski, 2012; Schlenther, 1999). This is particularly a concern if the discussions are brief and few in number and focus on highly sensitive issues that individual students might be facing, such as child abuse, feelings of suicide, or the death of a parent. Others are concerned that books will be "used" rather than appreciated for their engaging story lines, thought-provoking themes, and interesting characters (Chatton, 1988). Will books cease to be enjoyed and used only to instruct or moralize, these critics wonder?

We believe that teachers and librarians are qualified to conduct "developmental" bibliotherapy sessions—those focused on discussing issues associated with general personality development, such as bullying, making friends, social skills, appreciating diversity, and problem-solving strategies (Heath et al., 2005). Teachers and librarians know students well and can use their professional judgment to determine when students are ready to address certain life issues. They are also skilled at building relationships so that children feel comfortable discussing sensitive topics openly and honestly (Ogrenir, 2013) with their teachers. However, trained counselors are best for addressing severe emotional and behavioral issues.

We also suggest that issues be discussed as they naturally occur in the course of reading aloud well-written books that appeal to students. Reading a story purely for its utility in teaching about a value or issue may not lead to the engagement and identification with characters that is critical for effecting change in attitudes and behaviors. Rather, conversations about life issues can arise naturally when students encounter characters with problems or situations that reflect their own or that they are curious about. If we want students to jump wholeheartedly into a story in order to feel empathy for a character's dilemmas and challenges and then learn something about life from the experience, we must always start with great stories.

Not all books that address social issues are appropriate for bibliotherapy discussions. Some offer simplistic or unrealistic solutions that are inadequate for helping students grapple with complex real-life issues (Doll & Doll, 1997). Or there may be so many issues presented in a book that readers cannot focus on what is important, and they may get emotionally overwhelmed (Chatton, 1988). Therefore, it is important to select books that clearly and positively explore an issue you wish to address with your students.

Bibliotherapy can provide an opportunity for students to learn strategies to support their development into socially and emotionally healthy individuals. If used judiciously, as one aspect of a literature program, bibliotherapy sessions can be effective in accomplishing this important goal.

 Summary

- Contemporary realistic fiction includes stories about people and animals that could actually exist, taking part in events that could really happen in the world as we know it.
- Contemporary realistic fiction can vicariously show children how people contend with difficult issues in their lives. They can also learn how others solve common issues and dilemmas.
- Titles in this genre should be evaluated on how well they honestly portray contemporary life and have potential for lasting relevance for the reader. We recommend selecting books

that are realistic yet leave readers with a feeling of resolution, promise, or hope at the end that is authentic and sincere. Books in this genre are written on a range of topics, including issues related to growing up, stories about family relationships, animal stories, adventure and survival stories, mysteries, sports stories, humorous stories, stories about school life, disabilities, and LGBT.

- We offered many teaching ideas that support children's responses to contemporary realistic fiction while also meeting the mandates of CCSS Standards RL.2 and RL.6. We also provided ideas for supporting the use of contemporary realistic fiction with culturally diverse and ELL students.

Questions/Activities to Invite Thinking, Writing, and Conversation About the Chapter

1. Read several books in one category of realistic fiction (e.g., animal stories, adventure/ survival stories, and so on). What are some common themes you discover in the books you read? Compare the themes in your books with those read by your peers in the same category. Then compare your category themes with those discovered by peers who read books in other categories. Create a class chart of themes in books of contemporary realistic fiction.

2. Working with a partner, each selects a different character from one of the contemporary realistic fiction books described in the chapter. Each partner then creates a character monologue or two-voice poem for his or her character that focuses on a pivotal plot point of the book. After sharing the final products, consider how the point of view affected the content of your monologue or poem.

3. Contemporary realistic fiction books for children are often the target of censors. Why do you think this happens? Create a one-page defense for using these books with children at the age level you intend to teach.

Recommended Contemporary Realistic Fiction Picture Books

(Books appropriate for preschoolers are marked *; those with significant culturally diverse elements are marked #. See also Figure 9.4 for additional culturally diverse/relevant picture book titles.)

Family Relationship Stories

*Alexander, Martha. *Nobody Asked Me if I Wanted a Baby Sister*; *When the New Baby Comes, I'm Moving Out*.

*Banks, Kate. *Mama's Coming Home* (Tomek Bogacki, Illus.); *That's Papa's Way* (Lauren Costilla, Illus.); *The Night Worker* (Georg Hallensleben, Illus.).

Best, Cari. *Taxi, Taxi* (Dale Gottleig, Illus.); *What's So Bad About Being an Only Child?* (Sophie Blackall, Illus.).

*Browne, Anthony. *My Mom*; *My Dad*.

Doyle, Roddy. *Her Mother's Face* (Freya Blackwood, Illus.).

Feiffer, Kate. *My Mom Is Trying to Ruin My Life* (Diane Goode, Illus.).

Fox, Mem. *Wilfred Gordon McDonald Partridge*.

#Johnson, Angela. *Tell Me a Story, Mama*.

#Johnston, Tony. *Angel City* (Carole Bayard, Illus.).

*#Joose, Barbara. *Mama, Do You Love Me?*.

Jukes, Mavis. *Like Jake and Me*.

*Keats, Ezra Jack. *Peter's Chair*.

MacLachlan, Patricia. *Mama One and Mama Two* (Ruth Bornstein, Illus.). (I)

Manning, Maurie. *Kitchen Dance*.

Norman, Geoffrey. *Stars Above Us*.

Rocco, John. *Blackout*.

*Saltzberg, Barney. *Cornelius P. Mud, Are You Ready for Baby?*.

Titherington, Jeanne. *A Place for Ben.*

*Turner, Ann. *Through Moon and Stars and Night Skies.*

*Van Camp, Richard. *Little You* (Julie Flett, Illus.).

*Williams, Vera. *A Chair for My Mother*; *More, More, More, Said the Baby*; *Cherries and Cherry Pits*; *Lucky Song.*

Winthrop, Elizabeth. *Squashed in the Middle* (Pat Cummins, Illus.).

Yolen, Jane. *Owl Moon* (John Schoenherr, Illus.); *My Father Knows the Names of Things* (Stephanie Jorisch, Illus.).

Extended Family: Relatives

#Barrett, Joyce Durham. *Willie's Not the Hugging Kind* (Pat Cummings, Illus.).

Best, Cari. *Three Cheers for Katherine the Great* (Giselle Potter, Illus.).

Bunting, Eve. *Going Home* (David Diaz, Illus.).

Caseley, Judith. *Dear Annie.*

dePaola, Tomie. *Nana Upstairs, Nana Downstairs*; *Now One Foot, Now the Other.*

#Faustino, Lisa. *The Hickory Chair* (Benny Andrews, Illus.).

#Garza, Carmen Lomas. *In My Family/En mi familia.*

#Heo, Yumi. *Ten Days and Nine Nights: An Adoption Story.*

#Iqus, Toyomi. *Two Mrs. Gibsons* (Daryl Wells, Illus.).

Lipson, Eden Ross. *Applesauce Season* (Mordicai Gerstein, Illus.).

#Miles, Miska. *Annie and the Old One.*

#Paschkis, Julie. *Mooshka: A Quilt Story*; *Here Comes Grandma.*

Plourde, Lynn. *Thank You, Grandpa* (Jason Cockroft, Illus.). (P, I)

Polacco, Patricia. *Thunder Cake*; *The Keeping Quilt.* (P, I)

#Raschka, Chris. *The Hello Goodbye Window.*

Rylant, Cynthia. *The Relatives Came.* (P, I)

Smith, Lane. *Grandpa Green.*

#Soto, Gary. *Snapshots from the Wedding* (Stephanie Garcie, Illus.); *Too Many Tamales* (Ed Martinez, Illus.).

#Steptoe, Javaka. *The Jones Family Express.*

Stoltz, Mary. *Storm in the Night* (Pat Cummins, Illus.).

Sullivan, Sarah. *Passing the Music Down* (Barry Root, Illus.).

#Wong, Janet S. *Homegrown House* (E. B. Lewis, Illus.).

Wood, Douglas. *Aunt Mary's Rose.*

Woodson, Jacqueline. *We Had a Picnic This Sunday Past* (Diane Greenseid, Illus.).

Everyday Experiences

*Bang, Mollie. *When Sophie Gets Angry, Really, Really Angry.*

Bauer, Marian. *Dinosaur Thunder* (Margaret Chodos-Irvine, Illus.).

Bean, Jonathan. *At Night.*

Brazie, Marla. *A Couple of Boys Have the Best Week Ever.* (P, I)

#Collier, Bryan. *Uptown* (Harlem).

Crew, Donald. *Shortcut.*

*Fogliano, Julie. *And Then It's Spring* (Erin Stead, Illus.).

Gal, Susan. *Night Lights.*

*#Keats, Ezra Jack. *The Snowy Day/Whistle for Willie* (and others).

*Logue, Mary. *Sleep Like a Tiger* (Pamela Zagorenski, Illus.).

Newman, Lesla. *The Best Cat in the World* (Ron Himler, Illus.).

Perkins, Lynne Rae. *Pictures from Our Vacation.* (P, I)

Plourde, Lynn. *Snow Day* (Hideko Takahashi, Illus.); *The Dump Man's Treasures* (Mary Beth Owens, Illus.). (P, I)

Rocco, John. *Blackout.*

Rylant, Cynthia. *When I Was Young in the Mountains*; *All in a Day*; *Night in the Country.* (P, I)

*#Schwartz, Joanne. *Our Corner Grocery Store* (Laura Beinessner, Illus.).

*Shannon, David. *No, David!.*

*Swanson, Susan. *The House in the Night* (Beth Krommes, Illus.).

Vorst, Judith. *Alexander and the Terrible, Horrible, No Good, Very Bad Day* (Ray Cruz, Illus.). (P, I)

Wisniewski, David. *The Secret Knowledge of Grown-Ups.*

School Experiences

Allard, Henry. *Miss Nelson Is Missing.*

Best, Cari. *Shrinking Violet* (Giselle Potter, Illus.).

Bottner, Barbara. *Miss Brooks Loves Books (and I Don't)* (Michael Emberly, Illus.).

#Bunting, Eve. *One Green Apple.* (Ted Lewin, Illus.). (I)

*#Chodos-Irvine, Margaret. *Best Best Friends.*

Cohen, Miriam. *Will I Have A Friend?*; *The New Teacher*; *When Will I Read?* (Lillian Hoban, Illus.).

Grindley, Sally. *It's My School* (Margaret Chamberlain, Illus.).

*#Kirk, Daniel. *Keisha Ann Can!.*

Ljungkvist, Laura. *Follow the Line to School.*

O'Neill, Alexis. *The Recess Queen* (Laura Huliska-Beth, Illus.). (I)

Polacco, Patricia. *The Junkyard Wonders*; *Thank You, Mr. Falker.* (I)

#Rumford, James. *Rain School.*

*Schaefer, Carole Lexa. *Kids Like Us* (Pierr Morgan, Illus.).

Shannon, David. *David Goes to School.*

#Stock, Katherine. *Where Are You Going, Manyoni?.* (I)

#Stuve-Boden. Stephanie. *Elizabeth's School.*
*#Yum, Hyewon. *Mom, It's My First Day of Kindergarten.*

Sports
#Atkins, Jeannine. *Get Set! Swim!* (Hector Lee, Illus.).
Barber, Barbara E. *Allie's Basketball Dream* (Darryl Ligasan, Illus.).
Greene, Stephanie. *Owen Foote: Soccer Star* (Martha Weston, Illus.).
Hicks, Betty. *Swimming with Sharks* (Adam McCauley, Illus.).
Javaherbin, Mina. *Goal!* (A. G. Ford, Illus.).
#Miller, William. *Night Golf* (Cedric Lucas, Illus.).
Tuck, Justin. *Home Field Advantage* (Leonardo Rodriguez, Illus.).

Pets and Other Animals
Castillo, Lauren. *Melvin and the Boy.*
Chall, Marsha. *Pick a Pup* (Jed Henry, Illus.).
Daly, Cathleen. *Prudence Wants a Pet* (Stephen King, Illus.).
Day, Alexandra. *Good Dog, Carl* (and sequels).
*Dockray, Tracy. *The Lost and Found Pony.*
Feiffer, Kate. *Which Puppy?* (Jules Feiffer, Illus.).
George, Jean. *Frightful's Daughter Meets the Baron Weasel* (Daniel San Souci, Illus.). (I)
Graham, Bob. *How to Heal a Broken Wing* (I); *"Let's Get a Pup," Said Kate.*
#Harjoe, Joy. *The Good Luck Cat* (Paul Lee, Illus.).
Hest, Amy. *Charley's First Night* (Helen Oxenbury, Illus.).
*Johnson, Paul B. *Lost* (Celeste Lewis, Illus.).
Newbery, Linda. *Posy the Kitten* (Catherine Rayner, Illus.).
*Radunsky, Vladimir. *You?.*
Raschka, Chris. *A Ball for Daisy.*
*Root, Phyllis. *Scrawny Cat* (Alison Friend, Illus.).
#Sáenz, Benjamin Alire. *The Dog Who Loved Tortillas/ la perrita que la encantaban las tortillas* (Geronimo Garcia, Illus.).
Schoenherr, John. *Bear.* (I)
*Shannon, David. *Good Boy, Fergus!.*
Simont, Marc. *The Stray Dog.*
Sis, Peter. *Madlenka's Dog.*
Viorst, Judith. *The Tenth Good Thing About Barney* (Erik Blegvad, Illus.). (I)
#Uluadluak, Donald. *Kamik: An Inuit Puppy Story.*
Walsh, Barbara. *Sammy in the Sky* (Jamie Wyeth, Illus.).
Wild, Margaret. *Harry and Hopper* (Freya Blackwood, Illus.).

Self-Concept
Becker, Shari. *Maxwell's Mountain* (Nicole Wong, Illus.).
*#Brown, Monica. *Marisol McDonald and the Clash Bash* (Sara Palacios, Illus.).

Child, Lauren. *Clarice Bean, Don't Look Now.*
*Chodos-Irvine, Margaret. *Ella Sarah Gets Dressed.*
#Elliott, Zetta. *Bird* (Shadra Strickland, Illus.).
#Hoffman, Mary. *Amazing Grace.*
Hole, Stan. *Garmann's Summer.*
Lovell, Patty. *Stand Tall, Molly Lou Melon* (David Catrow, Illus.).
Madison, Alan. *Velma Gratch and the Way Cool Butterfly* (Kevin Hawkes, Illus.).
#Recorvits, Helen. *My Name Is Yoon*; *Yoon and the Jade Bracelet* (Gabi Swiatkowska, Illus.).
Raschka, Chris. *Little Black Crow.*
#Robbins, Jacqui. *Two of a Kind* (Matt Phelan, Illus.).
Stott, Ann. *I'll Be There.* (Matt Phelan, Illus.).
Tillman, Nancy. *The Crown on Your Head.*
Wood, Douglas. *No One But You.*

Environmental and Social Concerns
Baker, Jeanne. *Home; Where the Forest Meets the Sea.*
Brown, Peter. *The Curious Garden.*
Bunting, Eve. *Flower Garden* (Kathryn Hewitt, Illus.); *Smoky Night* (David Diaz, Illus.); *Fly Away Home* (Ron Himler, Illus.). (P, I)
Cherry, Lynne. *The Great Kapok Tree.*
Franco, Betsy. *Pond Circle* (Stefano Vitale, Illus.).
Graham, Bob. *A Bus Called Heaven.*
Kitttinger, Jo. *The House on Dirty-Third Street* (Thomas Gonzalez, Illus.).
#Lee, Spike and Tonya. *Giant Steps to Change the World* (Sean Qualls, Illus.). (I)
Ludwig, Trudy. *The Invisible Boy* (Patrice Barton, Illus.).
Lyons, George Ella. *You and Me and Home, Sweet Home* (Stephanie Anderson, Illus.).
Markle, Sandra. *Butterfly Tree* (Leslie Wu, Illus.).
Milway, Katie Smith. *One Hen* (Eugenie Fernandez, Illus.). (I)
McKinley, Cindy. *One Smile* (Mary Gregg Byrne, Illus.). (I)
McPhail, David. *The Family Tree.*
#Pérez, L. King. *First Day in Grapes* (Robert Casilla, Illus.). (I)
Rylant, Cynthia. *All in a Day* (Nikki McClure, Illus.). (I)
#Scanlon, Liz. *All the World* (Marla Frazee, Illus.).
*Stewart, Sarah. *The Gardener* (David Small, Illus.). (I)
#Trottier, Maxine. *Migrant* (Isabelle Arsenault, Illus.).
#Uhlberg, Myron. *A Storm Called Katrina* (Colin Bootman, Illus.). (I)
#Woodson, Jacqueline. *Each Kindness* (E.B. Lewis, Illus.). (I)
#Wyeth, Sharon. *Something Beautiful* (Chris Soentpiet, Illus.). (I)

LGBT Literature
Crawford, Georgina. *The Tales of Zebedy-Do-Dah.*
dePaola, Tomie. *Oliver Button Is a Sissy.*
Garden, Nancy. *Molly's Family.*
*#Gonzalez, Rigoberto. *Antonio's Card/La Tarjeta de Antonio.*
#Hoffman, Mary. *Best Best Colors/Los mejores colores.*
*Newman, Leslea. *Daddy, Pappa and Me; Mommy, Mama and Me; Heather Has Two Mommies; Too Far Away to Touch.*

Oelschlager, Vanita. *A Tale of Two Daddies* (Kristin Blackwood, Illus.).
Polacco, Patricia. *In Our Mother's House.*
Quinlan, Patricia. *Tiger Flowers* (Janet Wilson, Illus.).
Sears, Jessica. *Amazing Mommies.*
Weeks, Sarah. *Red Ribbon.*
Willhoite, Michael. *Daddy's Roommate.*

Recommended Contemporary Realistic Fiction Transitional/Series Books

Adler, David. *Bones* (P, I); *Cam Jansen* (Susannah Natti, Illus.). (P, I)
Allison, Jennifer. *Gilda Joyce Mysteries.* (I, M)
Bloom, Judy. *Fudge.* (I)
Daniels, Angie. *Justin Case* (Matthew Cordell, Illus.). (P, I)
Gifford, Peggy. *Moxy Maxwell* (Valorie Fisher, Illus.). (I, M)
Hicks, Betty. *Gym Shorts* (Adam McCauley, Illus.). (I, M)
Klein, Suzy. *Horrible Harry.* (P)
Lodbell, Scott. *Hardy Boys Graphic Novels.* (I, M)
#Look, Lenore. *Alvin Ho* (LeUyen Pham, Illus.). (P, I)
Lowry, Lois. *Gooney Bird Greene.* (I, M)
Lupica, Mike. *Comeback Kids.* (I, M)

Martin, Ann. *Main Street.* (M)
McDonald, Megan. *Judy Moody* (Peter H. Reynolds, Illus.). (P, I)
#Namioka, Lensey. *Yang.* (I)
Park, Barbara. *Junie B. Jones* (Denise Brukus, Illus.). (P, I)
Pennypacker, Sara. *Clementine* (Marla Frazee, Illus.). (P, I)
Roy, Ron. *Calendar Mystery* (Steven Gurney, Illus.). (I, M)
Sacher, Louis. *Marvin Redpost.* (I, M)
Sobol, Donald. *Encyclopedia Brown.* (I)
Springer, Nancy. *Enola Holmes Mysteries.* (M)
Van Draanen, Wendelin. *Sammy Keyes.* (I)
Warner, Gertrude Chandler. *Boxcar Children* (early readers). (P)

Recommended Contemporary Realistic Fiction Novels

(Books with significant culturally diverse elements are marked #.)

Growing Up
Blume, Judy. *Are You There God? It's Me, Margaret.* (I)
Carmichael, Michael. *Wild Things.* (M)
#Cofer, Judith. *Call Me Maria; The Meaning of Consuelo.* (M)
#Cheng, Andrea. *The Year of the Book.* (I, M)
Dowell, Frances O'Roark. *Chicken Boy; The Kind of Friends We Used to Be.* (I, M)
#Grimes, Nikki. *What Is Goodbye?* (I, M)
Fitzmaurice, Kathryn. *The Year the Swallows Came Early.* (I)
#Flake, Sharon G. *Who Am I Without Him? Short Stories About Girls and the Boys in Their Lives.* (M)

Haworth, Danette. *Violet Raines Almost Got Struck by Lightning.* (I)
Henkes, Kevin. *Junonia.* (P, I)
Henkes, Kevin. *Olive's Ocean; Bird Lake Moon.* (I, M)
Johnson, Peter. *The Amazing Adventures of John Smith Jr., aka Houdini.* (I)
#Lin, Grace. *The Year of the Dog; The Year of the Rat; Dumpling Days.* (I)
#Lopez, Diana. *Confetti Girl.* (M)
#Magoon, Kekla. *Camo Girl.* (M)
Margolis, Leslie. *Boys Are Dogs.* (I)
Messner, Kate. *The Brilliant Fall of Gianna Z.* (I)
Myracle, Lauren. *Ten* (and others). (I, M)
Naylor, Phyllis Reynolds. *Faith, Hope, and Ivy June.* (I, M)

#Neri, Greg. *Chess Rumble*; *Yummy: The Last Days of a Southside Shorty.* (M)

Nichols, Sally. *Ways to Live Forever.* (I, M)

Paterson, Katherine. *The Same Stuff as Stars.* (M)

Pennypacker, Sara. *Summer of the Gypsy Moths.* (I)

Perkins, Lynne Rae. *Criss Cross*; *All Alone in the Universe.* (M)

#Sanchez, Alex. *So Hard to Say.* (M)

Selznik, Brian. *Wonderstruck.* (I, M)

#Sloan, Holly. *Counting by 7s.* (M)

#Smith, Cynthia. *Rain Is Not My Indian Name*; *Indian Shoes.* (I)

Spinelli, Jerry. *Jake and Lily*; *Wringer.* (I)

Springstubb, Tricia. *What Happened on Fox Street.* (I)

Tanshis, Lauren. *Emma Jean Lazarus Fell Out of the Tree.* (I)

Tolan, Stephanie. *Surviving the Applewhites.* (I, M)

Urban, Linda. *Hound Dog True.* (I)

Wiles, Deborah. *Each Little Bird That Sings*; *Love, Ruby Lavender.* (I)

#Woodson, Jacqueline. *Miracle's Boys* (M); *After Tupac and D. Foster*; *Hush.* (I, M)

#Yumoto, Kazumi. *The Spring Tone*; *The Friends.*

Family Relationships

Bauer, Joan. *Almost Home*; *Close to Famous.* (I, M)

Birdsall, Jeanne. *The Penderwicks: A Summer Tale of Four Sisters, Two Rabbits and a Very Interesting Boy* (and sequels). (I, M)

Boyce, Frank. *Cosmic*; *Millions.* (M)

Brooks, Bruce. *What Hearts.* (M)

Byars, Betsy. *The Pinballs.* (I, M)

Cleary, Beverly. *Dear Mr. Henshaw.* (I)

Connor, Leslie. *Waiting for Normal.* (I)

Conway, Celeste. *The Goodbye Time.* (I)

Creech, Sharon. *Ruby Holler*; *Walk Two Moons.* (I, M)

Ellis, Sarah. *Odd Man Out.* (M)

#Fenner, Carol. *Yolanda's Genius.* (I, M)

#Frazier, Sundee T. *Brendan Buckley's Universe and Everything in It.* (I)

Fritz, April. *Waiting to Disappear.* (M)

Giff, Patricia. *Pictures of Hollis Woods.* (I)

Klise, Kate. *Grounded.* (I, M)

Knowles, Jo. *See You at Harry's.* (M)

Lowry, Lois. *Anastasia Krupnik* (and sequels); *A Summer to Die.* (I)

#McCall, Guadalupe. *Under the Mesquite.* (M)

#Moses, Shelia P. *The Baptism.* (M)

#Na, An. *A Step From Heaven.* (M)

O'Connor, Sheila. *Keeping Safe the Stars*; *How to Steal a Dog*; *Sparrow Road.* (I, M)

Paterson, Katherine. *The Great Gilly Hopkins.* (I)

#Peacock, Carol. *Red Thread Sisters.* (I)

Rocklin, Joanne. *The Five Lives of Our Cat Zook.* (I)

#Ryan, Pam Muñoz. *Becoming Naomi León.* (M)

Rylant, Cynthia. *Missing May.* (I, M)

#Salisbury, Graham. *Lord of the Deep.* (M)

#Shang, Wendy. *The Great Wall of Lucy Wu.* (I)

#Smith, Cynthia Leitch. *Indian Shoes.* (I)

#Staples, Suzanne. *Shabanu: Daughter of the Wind.* (M)

Voigt, Cynthia. The Tillerman Family books (*Homecoming*; *Dicey's Song*; and others). (M)

Williams, Carol Lynch. *If I Forget, You Remember.* (M)

Animal Stories

Bauer, Marion. *Little Dog Lost.* (P, I)

Cleary, Beverly. *Strider.* (I)

#Creech. Sharon. *Love That Dog*; *Hate That Cat.* (I)

DiCamillo, Kate. *Because of Winn-Dixie.* (I)

#Ferreira, Anton. *Zulu Dog.* (I, M)

Henry, Marguerite. *King of the Wind*; *Misty of Chintoteague.* (I, M)

Herlong, M. H. *Buddy.* (I)

Howe, Peter. *Waggit's Tale* (and sequels) (Omar Rayyan, Illus.). (I, M)

Jukes, Mavis. *Smoke.* (I, M)

#Kelly, Lynne. *Chained.* (I, M)

#Kessler, Cristina. *Our Secret, Siri Aang.* (M)

Knight, Eric. *Lassie Come Home.* (I)

Lee, Ingrid. *Dog Lost.* (I)

Naylor, Phyllis Reynolds. *Shiloh* (and sequels). (I)

Nelson, Marilyn. *Snook Alone.* (I)

North, Sterling. *Rascal.* (I)

O'Connor, Barbara. *On the Road to Mr. Mineo's.* (I)

Rawls, Wilson. *Where the Red Fern Grows.* (I, M)

#Schrefer, Elliot. *Endangered.* (M)

Taylor, Theodore. *The Trouble with Tuck.* (M)

Adventure and Survival Stories

#Abirached, Zeina. *A Game for Swallows: To Die, to Leave, to Return* (graphic novel). (M)

Clements, Andrew. *A Week in the Woods.* (I, M)

#Compestine, Ying Chang. *Revolution Is Not a Dinner Party.* (M)

Creech, Sharon. *The Wanderer.* (I, M)

#Ellis, Deborah. *The Breadwinner Trilogy*; *No Ordinary Day.* (M)

Frost, Helen. *Hidden.* (M)

George, Jean. *My Side of the Mountain* (and sequels); *Julie of the Wolves* (and sequels). (I. M)

#Hobbs, Will. *Bearstone*; *Downriver*; *Far North* (and others). (M)

#Holman, Felice. *Slake's Limbo.* (M)

Key, Watt. *Alabama Moon*; *Fourmile.* (M)

#Khan, Rukhsana. *Wanting Mor.* (M)

#McKay, Sharon. *Thunder over Kandahar*. (M)
#O'Dell, Scott. *Island of the Blue Dolphins*. (I, M)
#Park, Linda. *A Long Walk to Water*. (I, M)
Paulsen, Gary. *Hatchet* (and sequels); *The Voyage of the Frog*. (I, M)
#Perkins, Mitali. *Bamboo People*. (M)
Petersen, P. J. *Wild River*. (M)
#Rhodes, Jewell. *Ninth Ward*. (I, M)
#Sachar, Louis. *Holes*. (I, M)
Shahan, Sherry. *Death Mountain*. (M)
Smith, Roland. *Peak*. (M)
#Tanaka, Shelley. *Broken Memory: A Novel of Rawanda*. (M)
Thomas, Jane Resh. *Blind Mountain*. (M)
#Whelan, Gloria. *Homeless Bird*. (M)
#Yohalem, Eve. *Escape Under the Forever Sky*. (M)

Humorous Stories

Cleary, Beverly. *Ramona* (and others). (P, I)
Feiffer, Jules. *A Room with a Zoo*. (I)
Gantos, Jack. *I Am Not Joey Pigza* (M); *Jack Adrift: Fourth Grade Without a Clue* (I); *Jack's Black Book*. (M)
Gibbs, Stuart. *Belly Up*. (I, M)
Hiaasen, Carl. *Hoot*; *Scat*; *Flush*; *Chomp*. (I)
Horvath, Polly. *Everything on a Waffle*; *My One Hundred Adventures*; *The Canning Season*. (I, M)
Kinny, Jeff. *Diary of a Wimpy Kid* (and sequels). (P, I)
Klise, Kate. *Regarding the Fountain: A Tale, in Letters, of Liar and Leaks*. (M. Sarah Klise, Illus.) (also others). (I, M)
Korman, Gordon. *Maxx Comedy: The Funniest Kid in America*. (I)
Manes, Stephen. *Be a Perfect Person in Just Three Days!* (Tom Huffman, Illus.). (I)
Meyerhoff, Jenny. *Third Grade Baby* (Jill Weber, Illus.). (P, I)
Mills, Claudia. *How Oliver Olson Changed the World* (Heather Maione, Illus.). (I)
Robinson, Barbara. *The Best Christmas Pageant Ever*. (I)
Turnage, Sheila. *Three Times Lucky*. (I, M)
Viorst, Judith. *Lulu Walks the Dogs* (Land Smith, Illus.). (P, I)

Mysteries

#Ashley-Hollinger, Mika. *Precious Bones*. (I, M)
#Balliett, Blue. *The Calder Game*; *Chasing Vermeer*; *Wright 3*; *The Danger Box*. (M)
Bosch, Pseudonymous. *The Name of This Book Is Secret*. (M)
Broach, Elise. *Shakespeare's Secret*. (M)
Byars, Betsy. *Wanted . . . Mud Blossom*. (I, M)
Cheshire, Simon. *The Curse of the Ancient Mask and Other Case Files: Saxby Smart, Private Detective*. (M)
#Dowd, Siobbhan. *The London Eye Mystery*. (M)
Dowell, Frances O'Roark. *Dovey Coe*. (M)
Duncan, Lois. *Don't Look Behind You* (M); *I Know What You Did Last Summer*. (M)

Fleischman, Sid. *The 13th Floor*. (I, M)
#Garza, Xavier. *Maximilian and the Mystery of the Guardian Angel*. (I, M)
Giff, Patricia. *Eleven*. (I)
Grabenstein, Chris. *Escape from Mr. Lemoncello's Library*. (I, M)
Horowitz, Anthony. *Point Blank*. (M)
Konigsburg, E. L. *From the Mixed-Up Files of Mrs. Basil E. Frankweiler*; *Silent to the Bone*. (M)
Latta, Sara. *Stella Brite and the Dark Matter Mystery* (Meredith Johnson, Illus.). (I)
#Lawrence, Iain. *The Wreckers*. (M)
Paulsen, Gary. *Mudshark*. (I)
Raskin, Ellen. *The Westing Game*. (M)
Runholt, Susan. *Rescuing Seneca Crane*. (M)
#Smith, D. James. *The Boys of San Joaquin*. (M)
Snyder, Zilpha Keatley. *The Egypt Game*. (I)
Sobol, Donald. *Encyclopedia Brown*. (I)
Stead, Rebecca. *Liar and Spy*. (I, M)
Wallace, Barbara Brooks. *Cousins in the Castle*; *Ghosts in the Gallery*; *Sparrows in the Scullery*. (M)
Wynne-Jones, Tim. *The Boy in the Burning House*; *A Thief in the House of Memory*. (M)

Sports Stories

Baskin, Nora Raleigh. *Basketball (or Something Like It)*. (M)
Bledsoe, Lucy Jane. *Hoop Girlz*. (M)
#Brooks, Bruce. *Woodsie, Again*. (M)
Christopher, Matt. *Cool as Ice*; *Football Nightmare*; *Inline Skater* (and others). (I)
#Cochrane, Mick. *The Girl Who Threw Butterflies*. (M)
Jones, V. M. *Out of Reach*. (M)
Koertge, Ron. *Shakespeare Makes the Playoffs*. (M)
Lupica, Mike. *Million Dollar Throw*; *Heat*; *Hot Hand*; *Miracle on 49th Street*. (M)
Mackel, Katherine. *MadCat*. (M)
Northrup, Michael. *Plunked*. (I, M)
Preller, James. *Six Innings*. (I, M)
#Ritter, John. *The Boy Who Saved Baseball*. (I, M)
Scaletta, Kurtis. *Mudville*. (M)
Scieszka, Jon. *Guys Read: The Sports Pages*. (M)
#Soto, Gary. *Taking Sides*. (M)
Spinelli, Jerry. *There's a Girl in My Hammerlock*; *Crash*. (M)
Wiles, Deborah. *The Aurora County All-Stars*. (I, M)

School Life

Angleberger, Tom. *The Strange Case of Origami Yoda*. (I, M)
Bartlett, Susan. *Seal Island School* (Tricia Tusa, Illus.). (I)
#Cheng, Andrea. *Where the Steps Were*. (I)

Clements, Andrew. *Extra Credit* (Mark Elliot, Illus.); *Frindle* (Brian Selznick, Illus.). (I)

Codell, Esma. *Sahara Special.* (I)

Creech, Sharon. *Love That Dog*; *Hate That Cat.* (I)

Daly, Niki. *Bettina Valentino and the Picasso Club.* (I)

Fleming, Candace. *The Fabled Fifth Graders of Aesop Elementary School.* (I)

Frost, Helen. *Spinning Through the Universe.* (I, M)

Hannigan, Katherine. *Ida B . . . and Her Plans to Maximize Fun, Avoid Disaster, and Possibly Save the World.* (P, I)

#Herrick, Stephen. *Naked Bunyip Dancing.* (M)

Holm, Jennifer. *Middle School Is Worse Than Meatloaf: A Year Told Through Stuff.* (I, M)

#Koenigsburg, E. L. *The View from Saturday.* (I, M)

#Myers, Walter Dean. *Darnell Rock Reporting.* (M)

#Pearsall, Shelley. *All of the Above* (Javaka Steptoe, Illus.). (M)

Sachur, Louis. *There's a Boy in the Girls' Bathroom.* (I)

#Schmatz, Pat. *Bluefish.* (M)

Shreve, Susan. *The Flunking of Joshua T. Bates* (Diane de Groat, Illus.). (I)

#Woodson, Jacqueline. *Locomotion.* (M)

Characters with Physical, Mental, and Emotional Differences

Baskin, Nora Raleigh. *Anything but Typical.* (M)

Byars, Betsy. *Summer of the Swans.* (M)

Cheaney, J. B. *The Middle of Somewhere.* (M)

Draper, Sharon. *Out of My Mind.* (I, M)

Erskine, Kathryn. *Mockingbird.* (I, M)

Fusco, Kimberly Newton. *Tending to Grace.* (M)

Gantos, Jack. *I Am Not Joey Pigza*; *Joey Pigza Swallowed the Key* (and other Joey Pigza books). (M)

Greff, Lisa. *The Thing About Georgie.* (I)

Lord, Cynthia. *Rules.* (I, M)

Martin. Ann. *A Corner of the Universe.* (I, M)

Mass, Wendy. *A Mango-Shaped Space.* (M)

Nichols, Sally. *Ways to Live Forever.* (I, M)

Palacio, Rachel. *Wonder.* (I, M)

#Reedy, Trent. *Words in the Dust.* (M)

Selznick, Brian. *Wonderstruck.* (I, M)

Tarshis, Lauren. *Emma Jean Lazarus Fell Out of a Tree.* (I, M)

Zimmer, Tracie Vaughn. *Reaching for Sun.* (M)

LGBT

Burch, Christian. *The Manny Files.* (I, M)

Federle, Tim. *Better Nate Than Ever.* (M)

Garden, Nancy. *Holly's Secret*; *Annie on My Mind.* (M)

Jahn-Clough, Lisa. *Country Girl, City Girl.* (M)

Nelson, Teresa. *Earthshine.* (M)

Peters, Julie. *Between Mom and Jo.* (M)

#Saenz, Benjamin. *Aristotle and Dante Discover the Secrets of the Universe.* (M)

#Sanchez, Alex. *So Hard to Say.* (M)

Talgemier, Raina. *Drama.* (M)

Withrow, Sarah. *Boxgirl.* (M)

#Woodson, Jacqueline. *From the Notebooks of Melanin Sun*; *The House You Pass on the Way.* (M)

Nonfiction

(Literary Genre)

This chapter will help you to evaluate, select, and share the best nonfiction with your students. In this chapter, we address the following topics:

- What is nonfiction?
- What is the role of nonfiction in children's lives?
- How do we choose high-quality nonfiction?
- What are types of nonfiction?
- How do we use nonfiction to meet the mandates of national standards as well as the needs of our diverse students?

Liz McMahon, a library media specialist, enjoys sharing her passion for nonfiction with her middle school students. Educators in her district are committed to the goal of helping students be successful in reading, understanding, and writing nonfiction texts; therefore, the curriculum requires multiple ways to study nonfiction. In fact, Liz is working with elementary-level teachers to increase their awareness of nonfiction as early as possible, not just to ease the transition to middle school but also because today's world is filled with an array of informational sources. It is essential for students to learn the aspects that make nonfiction different from fiction and to be able to distinguish between fact and opinion. Learning about nonfiction can easily begin in the early primary grades (Duke & Bennett-Armistead, 2003; Kristo & Bamford, 2004; Stead, 2002).

Liz works closely with teachers so that lesson plans and experiences using nonfiction (including biography) are consistent, assuring a seamless transition between classrooms and the library. She selects nonfiction books with a common theme or topic, and presents these as a text set (Anderson, 2000; Kristo & Bamford, 2004). Dorfman and Cappelli (2009) describe mentor text sets as "pieces of literature you and your students can relate to, fall in love with, and return to and reread for many different purposes" (p. 2).

A mentor text set can be as small as two books or as large as 10 books, depending on the goals. Liz enjoys selecting and displaying a text set of new, guaranteed hits that will readily appeal to her middle school students. Next, she carefully decides which excerpts to share aloud so that students hear and appreciate good nonfiction: writing that captures the listeners' attention, not like typical textbook language (Freeman, 1997). Liz highlights interesting facts and shows different and eye-catching formats and features. Not surprisingly, these are the very books her students choose to peruse, and that is just what Liz wants. Sometimes, when students are required to conduct "research," they do so unwillingly or without a clear purpose. Liz does not leave the selection of books to chance, as she knows that some students believe that nonfiction is deadly dull.

Liz agrees that the prose in some nonfiction books, especially old titles, can be flat and boring. Worst yet, they may also have out-of-date information. She sees her job of "selling" nonfiction by collecting high-quality, recently published text sets to serve her teaching goals. For example, she selects five or more nonfiction titles in sophisticated picture book format. These will entice students to understand that nonfiction books are not textbooks—they do not look or sound like textbooks. She explains that these nonfiction picture book sets are written for an older audience, not for "little kids." She further notes that the authors made deliberate choices to use photographs and a range of visuals to present information (Moline, 2011). She assembles another text set with books containing superb writing. As she shares excerpts aloud, riveted students hear that well-written nonfiction can rival the best fiction. Liz said, "At one point, the principal joined the group and had a ball!"

Liz's students are captured by engaging narratives, such as those written by Sy Montgomery, who travels the world in search of fascinating topics. Sy shares intriguing information in her books, such as *Spell of the Tiger: The Man-Eaters of Sundarbans* and *Search for the Golden Moon Bear: Science and Adventure in Pursuit of a New Species*. Montgomery masterfully builds suspense and mystery right from the start by her careful word choice and narrative writing style.

Liz's students are also drawn to nonfiction books written in a humorous but factual style, such as *How They Croaked: The Awful Ends of the Awfully Famous* by Georgia Bragg and cleverly illustrated by Kevin O'Malley. They are intrigued with the strange and little-known facts about familiar figures such as Cleopatra, George Washington, and Napoleon. The short chapters lend themselves to brief reading but are long enough to stimulate interest in these famous people. Students seem eager to accept Liz's challenge to find additional facts that verify the information presented so humorously. In Liz's words, "They loved it!"

All through the year, Liz helps her middle school students understand the myriad aspects that make nonfiction special, such as how nonfiction features (e.g., glossaries, captions, time lines, and maps) assist readers. Kristo and Bamford (2004) offer a curriculum for teaching nonfiction beginning in kindergarten that can be adapted for use with the Common Core State Standards (CCSS).

Be familiar with the content of the nonfiction books you share, just as you would with fiction, and be open to the possibility of using nonfiction in picture book format with older students. For example, many of Montgomery's books have outstanding photographs that support and extend the text and can also be appreciated on their own. Her books can be shared successfully at a range of grade levels, depending on content and purposes for selecting them. For example, *Spell of the Tiger: The Man-Eaters of Sundarbans* has an enticing but frightening beginning that is more appropriate for upper elementary and middle level. Other Montgomery books may be used with a wide range of age levels, depending on goals—for reading aloud, for independent reading, as sources for writing, or for teaching about nonfiction features. Sometimes, only a section is shared to match a teaching goal.

The vignette about Liz's work at the middle level could be duplicated in many ways with fourth or fifth graders. The choices she made fit her purposes. She selected nonfiction books that she knew would engage her students right from the beginning, sending the message that nonfiction authors use a variety of ways to write about their topics.

Nonfiction has changed dramatically over the years both in the range of topics and in the ways information is presented. Unfortunately, nonfiction is sometimes equated with textbooks, which can have a dry writing style. After you explore this genre, you will see how interesting and engaging nonfiction can be. In today's world, it is easy to find an array of high-quality nonfiction books on a range of topics, formats, and writing styles.

Engaging nonfiction books will tempt a broad range of ages as well as reluctant readers. Notice the intriguing titles of this sample: *The Spectacular Spider Book* (Davies), *Marcel Marceau: Actor Without Words* (Schubert), *How Weird Is It?* (Hillman), *The Boy Who Invented TV: The Story of Philo Farnsworth* (Krull), *The Case of the Vanishing Golden Frogs: A Scientific Mystery* (Markle), *Are You Afraid Yet? The Science Behind Scary Stuff* (O'Meara), and *Citizen Scientist: Be a Part of a Scientific Discovery from Your Own Backyard* (Burns).

What Is Nonfiction?

Nonfiction books have the potential to spark wonder, joy, and success in learning. These are the books we seek for answering specific questions, for finding information about a particular person or topic, for enjoyment, and for simply browsing. Essentially, these books, sometimes termed "the literature of fact" (Cullinan & Person, 2001; Kristo, Colman, & Wilson, 2008), contain factual information about anything and everything: "real objects, phenomena, events, people, animals and plants" (Latrobe, Brodie, & White, 2002, p. 96).

On the face of it, the term *nonfiction* seems odd. No other genre is defined through negation. The term is even stranger when you realize that we are defining the factual—the actual—things that really happen with an explicit disclaimer that assures the reader that the author did not make it up. Penny Colman (2005), acclaimed author of *Girls: A History of Growing Up Female in America*; *Corpses, Coffins, and Crypts: A History of Burial*; *Rosie the Riveter: Women Working on the Home Front in World War II*; and many others explains how she views the differences between fiction and nonfiction:

> In thinking about definitions, I kept asking myself what is the essence of the difference between fiction and nonfiction. Both can have facts and information. Both can have expository and narrative and descriptive writing. Both can express universal truths. Both can have literary devices. As a writer, I asked myself, what is the difference in terms of what I can or cannot do? The answer is: make up material. With fiction, I can. With nonfiction, I cannot. (p. 9)

The Wolves Are Back is a good example of an illustrated book that is nonfiction.

Although some may use the term *informational book* to mean the same as nonfiction, we prefer to use nonfiction, as it is more precise (Kristo et al., 2008). Note that the CCSS uses the term *informational* to include digital and online resources in addition to print texts.

Sometimes determining if a book is nonfiction is not all that easy. For example, examine a *Magic School Bus* book by Joanna Cole. Is it fiction or nonfiction?

A quick (although not always foolproof) way to discern whether a book is nonfiction is to check the copyright page. Usually found on the reverse of the title page (verso), it is sometimes found at the back of the book. This section typically contains the Library of Congress Cataloging-in-Publication (CIP) data, including the ISBN number (a unique number assigned to every published book), copyright date, and often a summary. Subject headings are usually indicated. These might be your first clues as to whether the book is nonfiction. Look closely at the area where the ISBN is located. If you see "juvenile literature," it is likely that the book is nonfiction. If it is biography, that will be indicated. If it says "juvenile fiction," then you know the book is fiction. Oddly enough, the Library of Congress lists the *Magic School Bus* books sometimes as fiction and other times as juvenile literature, depending on the cataloger. We view these books as blended texts, which are discussed later in this chapter.

Students often believe that books with photographs must be nonfiction, whereas a book illustrated with drawings or paintings could not possibly be nonfiction. The same impression may be true based on the existence of a table of contents or index; children expect to see both in nonfiction. However, not all nonfiction books contain these features. For example, *When the Wolves Returned: Restoring Nature's Balance in Yellowstone* (Patent) and *The Wolves Are Back* (George) both about the same topic do not include these features. Neither has a table of contents. Only *When the Wolves Returned: Restoring Nature's Balance in Yellowstone* has an index, but both are nonfiction. Patent's book is written as a dual-level text, meaning that it contains a statement on one page and an explanatory paragraph on the next page. It includes excellent double-page photographs by Dan Hartman and Cassie Hartman. In contrast, George wrote her book as a narrative with beautiful paintings by Wendell Minor. Because of the illustrations and narrative quality of Jean Craighead George's book, some children may be confused about whether both books are nonfiction unless teachers draw attention to the valuable information on the copyright or verso pages as a first step.

The Role of Nonfiction in Children's Lives

Consider the following scene: The place is a classroom on a summer morning—a literacy clinic for low-achieving readers ages 8 to 12. All are engaged in learning: nonfiction books cover the tables, and students are intensely reading, writing, and talking about their topics. Their teacher, Judy Bouchard, interviewed each student to determine interests and then gathered a variety of nonfiction books from local libraries. She showed them how to browse nonfiction and to judge the usefulness of the books for their topics. Students ultimately created their own nonfiction books.

Ten-year-old Todd disliked school and hated to read, and writing was out of the question. By the end of the summer clinic, he had produced a book on wolves comprised of scanned photos and captions. He proudly declared that this was his first book, and he dedicated it to Mrs. Bouchard, adding excitedly, "Nonfiction makes my brain pump!" Judy will never forget that moment. It demonstrates how knowing students' interests, combined with purposeful teaching and access to quality nonfiction books, can lead to excited and successful learning.

It is a myth that only boys like nonfiction; we know that nonfiction attracts boys and girls of all ages (Kristo et al., 2008). These authors assert, "Teachers we know report that gender differences disappear when their students have access to nonfiction that covers a wide range of topics. For example, sharing nonfiction books about the life cycles and habitats of animals appeals to most everyone" (p. 343).

The tendency to undervalue nonfiction is particularly a problem for boys. Many boys are reluctant readers—they are disengaged from reading and spend less time reading (Brozo, 2010; Zambo & Brozo, 2009). This trend becomes more pronounced as they age. High school boys report less enthusiasm for reading than middle school boys, and middle school boys report less than those in elementary years (Brozo, 2010). However, recent investigations of the kinds of reading that boys enjoy uncovered that they like nonfiction, particularly books with eye-catching visuals (Smith & Wilhelm, 2002). According to Smith and Wilhelm, this is because nonfiction texts connect more directly to readers' lives.

Some children are introduced to nonfiction early in their lives with board books focusing on concepts such as letters, numbers, and simple vocabulary. Many preschoolers and primary-grade children are captivated by such titles as *Mega Trucks: The Biggest, Toughest Trucks in the World!* (Murrell and Gunzi), *Looking for Miza: The True Story of the Mountain Gorilla Family Who Rescued One of Their Own* (Hatkoff), and *The Spectacular Spider Book* (Davies).

Fifth-grade teacher Kerri Doyle agrees that nonfiction is a hit. In fact, many of her students choose nonfiction over fiction at the school library. *How Big Is It: A Big Book All About Bigness* (Hillman); *The Sports Book* (Summers), a tome of over 400 pages with a cover of artificial turf; and *ER Vets: Life in an Animal Emergency Room* (Jackson) were checked out and quickly became popular titles in her room.

Kerri plans ways to attract students to nonfiction, such as creating displays of nonfiction books and a weekly book share called "Mrs. Doyle's Surefire Hits of the Week." She highlights special books she discovers and shares excerpts aloud—just enough to interest her students to explore the books further. School librarian Lynn Mayer works in collaboration with teachers to identify children's interests and then prominently displays nonfiction titles that will surely have instant appeal. Plan thoughtfully for ways that nonfiction becomes an integral and visible part of school life for your students.

We live in a world saturated with information. It comes from all directions and in a multitude of formats, including books, magazines, brochures, podcasts, news clips, and the Internet. Children must become discriminating readers of information and learn to determine fact from fiction. In the next section, we discuss how to evaluate and select high-quality nonfiction books.

Criteria for Evaluating Nonfiction

There are many types of nonfiction books written on a broad range of topics. They are typically judged by the quality of writing and visuals, degree of accuracy and access features, and format and book design. Teachers should select high-quality and up-to-date nonfiction books. It is wiser to have fewer books than to have inaccurate information or dull facts presented in unappealing ways. Outdated books should be discarded, especially those with scientific, biographical, or historical content, and replaced with sources that verify the information. However, depending on teaching purposes, outdated books may be useful as historical resources. However, when mixed with new volumes, obsolete books appear to have equal value to students.

School librarians are usually delighted to help with book selection and will pass along reviews from professional periodicals, such as *The Horn Book Magazine, Language Arts,* and *The Reading Teacher.* Award-winning and recommended nonfiction book lists from Orbis Pictus, Outstanding Science Trade Books for Children, and Notable Trade Books in the Social Studies are available online.

Selection criteria include not only copyright dates and curricular needs but also student interests. Students can be invited to arrange nonfiction titles into topical text sets and design displays that advertise nonfiction. When students catch teachers reading nonfiction just for the pleasure of it, it may not take long for them to do the same. See Figure 10.1 for guidelines for evaluating nonfiction.

FIGURE 10.1 Guidelines for Evaluating Nonfiction

Writing Style

- Is the writing style appropriate for the type of nonfiction? (see types later in the chapter)
- Is the language fresh, vivid, interesting, and appropriate for the content?
- Does the writing style draw readers into the book and stimulate interest?
- Does the author present and use vocabulary within the experience of the intended audience?

Content

- Is the scope of the book appropriate for its intended audience?
- Is content adequately covered without overwhelming readers?
- If projects are included, are they age appropriate? Is adult supervision noted (if needed)? Are directions clear and understandable? Are materials needed easily obtainable?

Organization

- Is the content organized and presented in a clear way?
- To what extend will readers find the organization of text and visual information easy to follow?
- Is the organizational scheme well suited to the content?
- Are the access features, such as table of contents, glossary, and bibliographies informative? To what

extent do they contribute to understanding the content? Are they age appropriate and easy to use?

Accuracy

- Is the author qualified to write on the topic?
- Is the author an acknowledged expert on the topic? If not, were experts consulted or acknowledged?
- Is the information accurate and up to date?
- Are sources and facts documented?
- Is the essential information related to that topic included?
- Has the author clearly distinguished between fact and opinion?
- Are different points of view acknowledged (where appropriate)?

Visual Information, Format, and Design

- Is the overall format and design of the book appealing and age appropriate?
- Does the visual information, such as photographs, diagrams, time lines, maps, and so on, complement the content, clarify, and/or extend the reader's understanding?
- Is the visual information appropriate for the content?
- Are captions or other labels for photographs, drawings, diagrams, and so on easy to understand and informative?

Tech Click

It is vital for our students that they become critical and discerning consumers of information; it makes sense to help them extrapolate from print resources to digital formats. Resources such as Common Sense Media and Rosen's Database for Digital Literacy will provide support in making this transition.

Quality of Writing

Nonfiction writers use various writing tools to create books that are factual yet interesting to read. Some of these tools are similar to those used by authors of fiction, poetry, and traditional literature; others are unique to the nonfiction genre. The following are the most common elements to assess quality of writing.

Style. Writing style in nonfiction has qualities that draw readers into a book and make it memorable. Interesting descriptions, figurative language, and imagery are just as important in a biography or science book as they are in fiction. Many nonfiction writers carefully document facts and present their ideas coherently, but if the expression is dry and boring, it is unlikely that they will ignite readers' enthusiasm for their subject. Robert Burleigh introduces *Chocolate: Riches from the Rainforest* in the following way: "Chocolate. It is that dark, pleasantly bittersweet, creamy, luscious, mouth-watering, impossible-to-forget taste. Mmm." The vivid word choice reaches out to the reader to look for the nearest piece of chocolate. The aspects of style that good nonfiction writers consider are discussed next.

Clarity. A clear, lucid, cohesive text is an essential aspect of style in nonfiction. Authors must carefully order their ideas and support them with explanations and examples without overwhelming readers. Organizational structure, content, language, and style should work together so that writers create an easily understandable context for their information. An example of a well-crafted book is *Bug Hunter*, in which author David Burnie uses a logical ordering of information with straightforward writing.

Organization. Nonfiction authors organize content in various ways. Determining the structure of a book is key in supporting a reader's comprehension of the information (Meyer & Freedle, 1984; Robb, 2004; Tompkins, 2005). Choice of organizational structure usually evolves naturally from the content as well as from the author's purpose. Also, authors often embed one structure within another. Figure 10.2 features typical structures used in nonfiction.

Leads and Conclusions. Successful nonfiction writers usually capture readers right from the start and use a variety of ways to do that—asking a question, starting with a surprising statement, using a poem or song, or creating intriguing chapter titles to generate interest. In *Oh, Rats!: The Story of Rats and People* (Marrin) begins with a poem:

> Rats, rats, and more rats.
> Good rats, bad rats.
> Yummy rats, yukky rats.
> Pet rats, pesky rats.
> Storybook rats, laboratory rats.
> Oh, rats!

FIGURE 10.2 Typical Nonfiction Structures

Structure	Examples
Sequenced—Information is presented in a particular order, usually numerically or alphabetically, such as in counting and alphabet books.	**Counting Books** Marzollo, Jean. *One Gorilla: A Counting Book* by Anthony Browne; *Help Me Learn Numbers 0–20.* #Weill, Cynthia. *Count Me In!: A Parade of Mexican Folk Art Numbers in English and Spanish.* **Alphabet Books** #Das, Prodeepta. *I Is for India.* Zuckerman, Andrew. *Creature ABC.*
Chronological—This narrative structure shows the passage of time, usually a historical event or a person's life, such as a biography.	Byrd, Robert. *Electric Ben: The Amazing Life and Times of Benjamin Franklin.* Ferris, Jeri Chase. *Noah Webster and His Words.* Scott, Elaine. *Buried Alive!: How 33 Miners Survived 69 Days Deep Under the Chilean Desert.*
Enumerative—Survey (or "all-about") books typically use this structure. Individual chapters follow an introductory or overview chapter or section about the topic, each addressing an aspect of the main topic.	Pyers, Greg. *Biodiversity of Wetlands.* Rhatigan, Joe. *White House Kids: The Perks, Pleasures, Problems, and Pratfalls of the Presidents' Children.* Strachan, Bruce. *Ancient Egypt: A First Look at People of the Nile.*
Question and Answer—Highly popular structure using a gamelike or predictable format of a question and answer either on one page or across a two-page spread.	Berger, Melvin and Berger, Gilda. *Scholastic True or False: Amphibians* (and others). Munro, Roxie. *Hatch!* Schwartz, David and Schy, Yael. *What in the Wild?* Stewart, Melissa. *Extreme Rocks & Minerals.*
Narrative—Uses the organizational structure of a story, sometimes blending nonfiction with fictional elements.	#Cole, Joanna. *Ms. Frizzle's Adventures: Imperial China* and *The Magic School Bus Explores the Senses.* Halfmann, Janet. *Star of the Sea: A Day in the Life of a Starfish.* Springett, Martin and Springett, Isobel. *Kate & Pippin: An Unlikely Love Story.*
Compare and Contrast—Information is examined for its similarities and differences.	Kerley, Barbara. *Those Rebels, Tom & John.* Pringle, Laurence. *Scorpions! Strange and Wonderful.*
Cause and Effect—This structure shows how one aspect of a topic influences another and is often embedded within another structure.	Montgomery, Sy. *The Tapir Scientist: Saving South America's Largest Mammal.* O'Neil, Alexis. *The Kite That Bridged Two Nations.* Rosenstock. Barb. *Thomas Jefferson Builds a Library.* Stewart, Melissa. *A Place for Turtles.*
Secondary or Layered Text—This popular structure typically combines simple narrative with more sophisticated facts about the topic.	Butterworth, Chris. *See What a Seal Can Do.* Rusch, Elizabeth. *Volcano Rising.* Sayre, April. *Here Come the Humpbacks!* and *Meet the Howlers!* Stewart, Melissa. *A Place for Turtles.*

(Books with significant culturally diverse elements are marked #.)

Author and illustrator Roxie Munro, well known for her series including *Inside-Outside Dinosaurs*, *Inside-Outside Book of New York City*, and *Inside-Outside Book of Libraries* (Cummins), uses a question-and-answer format for her clever, informative book *Hatch!* She begins with a brief introductory paragraph and a "Did You Know" page about birds and then quickly launches into two-page spreads throughout this giant-size book. The left-hand page poses the question "Can you guess whose eggs these are?" with the answer found on the right-hand page. This is followed by another two-page spread beautifully illustrating the bird in its environment. A succinct but informational paragraph about the bird is included. This pattern is repeated throughout the book, inviting participation by repeating the question "Can you guess whose eggs these are?" *Hatch!* ends with selected sources for more information and a list of "Fun Bird Words to Learn."

In *Bug Hunter*, Burnie uses an invitational writing style that welcomes readers into the intriguing world of bugs and poses basic questions, such as "But what exactly is a bug? Why are they such successful animals?" (p. 4). The focal points of each chapter are indicated at the top of the page, serving to focus readers as to the important content in the section. Additional information about *Bug Hunter* is included under the section on Activity, Craft, Experiment, and How-to Books.

Nonfiction writers often craft transitional paragraphs at the end of chapters to provide a bridge to the next one, compelling the reader to turn the page. Or they might end with a conclusion, leaving the reader either very satisfied or wanting to know more. Author Debbie Miller effectively concludes *River of Life*. The rhythmic description of a world going to sleep for the winter gives the reader a satisfying sense that life will continue when spring arrives.

Language: Sentence Structure and Vocabulary. Nonfiction writers use varied sentence length, alliteration, colorful descriptions, and precise, vivid verbs to make their writing resonate in the mind and the ear. They may choose graceful, elegant language or a more reportlike style, depending on the purpose and type of nonfiction. In *River of Life*, Miller repeats the *s* sound to portray a hushed, still quality. She also varies sentence lengths to establish a rhythm that slows the pace and adds to the quiet feeling. Phrases such as "ice tucks in the whispering river" and "the river rushes to the sea" create vivid pictures in a reader's mind.

Nonfiction writers must carefully use specialized and technical vocabulary so that it is memorable yet understandable. New words need to be introduced, precisely defined, and then embedded in context so that readers retain their meaning. Sometimes, the words are italicized to draw readers' attention, or synonyms are used to clarify meaning. A visual, such as a diagram or photograph, is often used to extend the meaning.

Tech Click

Some students may benefit from a pronouncing dictionary on a mobile device or online; hearing a word sometimes sparks recognition even if the word is above students' reading level.

Figurative Language. Nonfiction writers may use analogies or figurative language as a stylistic device to make their meaning clear and memorable. Freeman (1994) discovered that writers of selected Orbis Pictus Nonfiction Award books were much more likely to use familiar comparisons as well as extended or clustered analogies, adding to the quality of the writing. For example, in *The Forest in the Clouds*, Collard uses simile effectively when he describes "the tropical trade winds blow, sucking up moisture like dry thirsty lungs." Cynthia

Rylant embeds metaphors within the poetic rhythm of *Appalachia: The Voices of Sleeping Birds* that resonate in the mind and paint a vivid picture of this landscape.

Accuracy. Accuracy is one of the most important elements of nonfiction. How do readers know that authors are providing the best and most current information on a topic? One way is to examine the author's credentials, usually found on the jacket flap, in the introduction, or in the "About the Author" section. If someone who is not a recognized authority writes the book, it helps to see if the author consulted and cited experts. Sometimes, a section in the front or back matter will describe the author's research process or include acknowledgments and a list of references. Readers should also check the copyright date because older books may include obsolete or disproven notions. Verifying these details will help ascertain if the author has the expertise to write accurately. Once students research backgrounds and reputations, they can trust what these writers produce. Authors such as Jim Murphy, Penny Colman, Russell Freedman, James Cross Giblin, Laurence Pringle, Sy Montgomery, and Candace Fleming, among others, do impeccable research and have earned the respect of readers.

Questionable explanations can also be double-checked against other informational sources, such as books, Web sites, and local adult authorities. Additionally, teachers should be alert to language and images that may influence children's misconceptions. For example, as Ford (2002) points out, a diagram with colored layers representing layers of the earth may make sense to adults. However, children may perceive these same layers simply as paint stripes.

Educational consultant Alan November (1998) described his nephew Zack's research for a middle school history paper. Zack was thrilled that he had found a relevant Web page, written by a professor, with a domain name "edu." The thesis of Zack's report was that the Holocaust never happened. In shock, the adult queried, "Where did you read that?" Zack blithely responded that he found it on the Internet and that the author was a professor. November's point is that educators have the imperative to teach the lifelong skills of critically evaluating information. The Web allows for the viral spread of misinformation with important repercussions. November adds the postscript that the original link has been removed from the university's Web site. (For interested readers, you can still access many unavailable Web pages by using the Wayback Machine.)

Another facet in the quest for accuracy, particularly for science books, questions whether the author has resorted to anthropomorphism—the attribution of human feelings and behavior to animals, plants, or inanimate objects. Authors must be very careful to avoid this device, or they risk creating an inaccurate portrayal of scientific phenomena.

Tech Click

Extending Literacies into the 21st Century

Higher-order thinking as well as communication skills are evident in the expectation that students need to be critical information consumers. The CCSS expectation that all core disciplines must support English language arts offers the perfect rationale for collaboration. The Partnership for 21st Century Skills provides exciting materials that combine science, social studies, geography, and math with English language arts (ELA). For example, the Science map (2009) highlights information literacy activities for three grade levels, and the ELA map (2008) suggests that students can assume individual responsibility for collaborative efforts around writing a nonfiction textbook with online annotation tools, such as Diigo or Google Notebook.

Visual Information

Illustrations and other visual material are vital aspects of nonfiction. The best are rich in content, clarifying and expanding the topic. Visual features might extend an explanation, provide additional details, or make an abstract idea more concrete. For example, in *Rome: In Spectacular Cross-Section* (Solway), illustrator Biesty used full-color cross-sectional drawings to entice the reader into Rome of A.D. 128. Most of the text occurs as labels and captions on each two-page spread, conveying information in a highly visual way.

Many books feature illustrations ranging from full-color photographs to detailed paintings to intricate computer imagery. The award-winning photographs in *A Drop of Water* (Wick) draw the reader's eye to the intricacies of one magnified drop of water in various settings. In another nature volume, Micucci created detailed drawings to document a year in *The Life and Times of the Honeybee*. Sensational titles, such as *Encyclopedia Horrifica: The Terrifying TRUTH! About Vampires, Ghosts, Monsters, and More* (Gee), present a cover-to-cover array of frightening visuals and text.

Diagrams, maps, tables, captions, and time lines are visual features that play a key role in many nonfiction books. Some are central to the book, as in *Reptiles* (Arlon & Gordon-Harris); *The Way We Work: Getting to Know the Amazing Human Body, Mosque, Building Big, Castle, Pyramid, Underground*, and *The New Way Things Work* (all by David Macaulay); and *Fox's Den* (Phillips). In others, such as *Mission to the Moon* (Dyer) and *Brooklyn Bridge* (Curlee), diagrams clarify and enhance the text. Each page of *Bug Hunter* (Burnie) invites readers to look more closely at the clearly organized visual features—from fascinating photographs with explanatory captions to detailed diagrams.

Captions are explanatory information accompanying maps illustrations, photographs, and diagrams. Effective captions are clearly written and are used to summarize the text, elaborate on it, or provide new information. Sometimes, captions describe two visuals. In this case, words such as *left* and *below* should be clearly indicated. Readers often skip over captions, considering them unimportant, often resulting in missed information not found elsewhere in the book. Books that have clear, well-designed, and helpful captions include *We Shall Overcome: A Song That Changed the World* (Stotts), *Iceberg Right Ahead! The Tragedy of the Titanic* (McPherson), *Behind the Mask: The Life of Queen Elizabeth I* (Thomas), and *Discovering the Inca Ice Maiden: My Adventures on Ampato* (Reinhard).

Maps are another form of visual information found in several content areas. They often orient readers to the content; for example, in *Asteroid Impact* (Henderson) and *Gorilla Walk* (Lewin & Lewin), readers are greeted with a map, setting the stage for the information that follows. Some maps record movement, such as those in *Animals on the Trail with Lewis and Clark* (Patent), showing the various animal species that the explorers encountered. The map in *The Cod's Tale* (Kurlansky) indicates shipping routes for cod, rum, molasses, and slaves.

Authors also convey information with time lines. *The Cod's Tale* offers an interesting example as it continues page to page, documenting historical milestones while the text discusses the importance of cod from early times to the present. A family tree—a different kind of time line—graces the endpapers of *Jack: The Early Years of John F. Kennedy* (Cooper).

Access Features. Access features help readers acquire additional information. The table of contents, glossary, bibliographies, author/illustrator notes, preface, afterword, sidebars, and index are all examples of access features. Not every nonfiction book includes them, but when they are missing, experienced readers can be at a loss locating specific information.

Contemporary nonfiction for children contains an increasing number of these features. In *Popcorn!*, for example, author Elaine Landau includes a list of Web-based resources and sprinkles sidebars of interesting facts throughout the text. *The Environment: Saving the Planet* (Harlow) includes a table of contents, an "About the Book" section that describes each major section, and a bulleted list titled "Remember: Be a Smart Scientist" that describes instructions for experiments and keeping records. Each page is packed with additional visual information, including sidebars, diagrams, and procedures for experiments. These elements work together to help readers access and appreciate the rich information found in nonfiction books. *An Extraordinary Life: The Story of a Monarch Butterfly* (Pringle) is an excellent example of text and illustrative material working together to create an award-winning nonfiction book.

Highly visual nonfiction entices readers. However, some nonfiction books are packed with so many visuals that it is confusing, distracting, or even difficult to know where to start reading. Skilled authors help readers "navigate" the text. For example, the *Magic School Bus* books (Cole & Degen) offer readers a varied mix of interesting, stimulating information with illustrations that cover every inch of the page. Cole and Degen carefully orchestrate text and illustrations so that all information is interrelated; it does not matter what is read first because the concept is mentioned elsewhere on the page. Each piece of information reinforces another (Bamford & Kristo, 2003).

Format and Design

A book's format encompasses all the elements that work as a whole: size and shape, binding, endpapers, and typeface.

Size and Shape. Today's nonfiction has more visual appeal than in the past. Designers create books using shapes and sizes to more precisely reflect the contents. Notice the extra large size of *The Dinosaurs of Waterhouse Hawkins* (Kerley), in which dinosaurs dominate the double-page spreads (Kerper, 2003). In *Talking Walls* (Knight), the endpapers list the word for "wall" in many languages.

The cover of Clive Gifford's *Robots* features an attention-grabbing robot's head and a separate robotic-like piece used to open the book. Each two-page, single-topic spread is filled with sophisticated information presented in boxes, flaps, and pull tabs. In *Leonard's Horse* (Fritz), the book's dome-shaped top reflects the narrative, the tale of a bronze horse that Vinci designed and intended to create.

Robert Sabuda and Matthew Reinhart use ingenious paper engineering to create pop-up books, such as *Dinosaurs: Encyclopedia Prehistorica* and *Young Naturalist Pop-Up Handbook: Beetles*. The creatures are intricately detailed, and feature pullout tabs that are packed with additional visual information. *Beetles* is packaged in a box with a museum-quality paper model. All of these features provide readers with a unique and irresistibly engaging format. The form of other books echoes their content. With *Buzz* (Bingham), even the most bug-phobic reader will delight in the push buttons on the cover to hear the sounds of a bee, mosquito, and cricket. *Pyramids and Mummies* (Bolton), not surprisingly pyramid shaped, features endpapers containing a time line at the front and a game at the back.

Book Covers. Contrary to a popular expression, you can tell something about a book from its cover. Many nonfiction titles feature enticing covers that attract readers. The stunning cover of *Ashley Bryan: Words to My Life's Song* shows a photograph of Bryan, three-time Coretta Scott King award winner, on the beach of his Maine island home. The back cover features, "Praise for Ashley," an artful display of quotes from well-known children's authors and illustrators surrounded by vibrant colors, a hallmark of Ashley Bryan's many books. *A Young Dancer: The Life of an Ailey Student* (Gladstone) dramatically displays an impressive photograph of Iman Bright. *Ask Dr. K. Fisher About Reptiles* (Llewellyn) contains a die-cut hole on the front cover that begs readers to open the book. When they do, they will find a small envelope with a letter from Dr. K. Fisher. In *Chewy, Gooey, Rumble, Plop!: A Deliciously Disgusting Plop-Up Guide to the Digestive System* (Alton), readers are enticed to flip the flap on the cover to feel a tonguelike texture. This pop-up book brings hilarious but informative learning experience to the human digestive system from food "going in" to "going out."

End Pages. Also called endpapers, these often provide visual clues to the book's content. They are most often found glued to the inside front and back covers of hardcover books. They may be decorative, contain pictures, or use color that alert readers to content. In *Sneeze!* (Siy and Kunkel), the end pages are magnifications of neurons; in *Mosquito Bite* (Siy and Kunkel), the end pages look like screens on a door or window. In *Paleo Bugs: Survival of the Creepiest* (Bradley), both the cover and the end pages contain examples of ancient bugs. The wraparound dust jacket identifies some of them. In *A Dictionary of Dance* (Murphy), end pages invite readers into this fun and informative picture book with swirls of color, musical notations, and dancing shoes.

Typeface and Distinctive Markings. Often, designers choose certain typefaces to enhance the appearance of a book. For example, see Jim Murphy's *The Giant and How He Humbugged America*, the story of the Cardiff Giant supposedly discovered in 1869 and proved to be a hoax and one of the most infamous deceptions in the history of the United States. Careful consideration is given to all aspects of this book's design, including the typeface, page color, and historic illustrations and photos. In *Muckrakers: How Ida Tarbell, Upton Sinclair, and Lincoln Steffens Helped Expose Scandal, Inspire Reform, and Invent Investigative Journalism*, author Ann Bausum includes a detailed note on the copyright page, providing testimony to the power of black-and-white photography and the typewriter, two important tools of muckraking. Sections of this book use antique typewriter keys as icons as well as introductory pages for each chapter reflecting the look of a typewritten manuscript. In *B. Franklin, Printer* (Adler), the typeface looks old-fashioned. The copyright page states that "Caslon Antique" font was a typeface frequently used by Franklin himself. Each chapter begins with an interesting symbol or ornament that the copyright page explains came from books printed and sold by Franklin. Features such as these provide evidence of extensive scholarship and research.

Learning about these features of nonfiction is helpful in evaluating and selecting the best books to support your curriculum and match your student interests. Take time to consider what nonfiction books will be the best for sharing aloud and for helping students understand new concepts. These books might be good choices for studying an author's writing style and how information is presented as steps toward students writing their own nonfiction in interesting and exciting ways (Dorfman & Cappelli, 2009; Kristo & Bamford, 2004).

 ## Categorizing Nonfiction

Different types of nonfiction serve different purposes. For example, using the topic of birds, a survey book presents an overall presentation or survey about birds, whereas a specialized book focuses on a unique topic about birds or a particular bird, a biography presents the life or aspects of a person's life who studied birds, a field or identification guide helps to distinguish one bird from another, and a how-to book might show how to make birdhouses. The text set of bird books (Figure 10.3) lists a variety of nonfiction types. Each type is described in the next section of the chapter.

FIGURE 10.3 Types of Nonfiction Books About Birds

(Books with significant culturally diverse elements are marked #.)

Armstrong, Jennifer. *Audubon: Painter of Birds in the Wild Frontier* (biography) (Joseph A. Smith, Illus.). (I, M)

Arnosky, Jim. *Thunder Birds: Nature's Flying Predators* (identification). (I, M)

Burleigh, Robert. *Into the Woods: John James Audubon Lives His Dream* (biography) (Wendell Minor, Illus.). (I)

Davies, Jacqueline. *The Boy Who Drew Birds: A Story of John James Audubon* (biography) (Melissa Sweet, Illus.). (I, M)

Hoose, Phillip. *The Race to Save the Lord God Bird* (specialized). (I, M)

Kalman, Bobbie, and Smithyman, Kathryn. *The Life Cycle of a Bird* (life cycle). (P, I)

León, Vicki. *Parrots, Macaws & Cockatoos* (identification). (M)

Markle, Sandra. *Owls: Animal Predators* (survey). (I)

Montgomery, Sy. *Snowball: The Dancing Cockatoo* (Judith Oksner, Illus.) (specialized). (I, M)

Montgomery, Sy. *Kakapo Rescue: Saving the World's Strangest Parrot* (Nic Bishop, Photog.) (specialized). (I, M)

Pallotta, Jerry. *The Bird Alphabet Book* (concept/alphabet book). (I, M)

Pringle, Laurence. *Crows! Strange and Wonderful* (survey). (P, I)

#Roth, Susan L., and Trumbore, Cindy. *Parrots over Puerto Rico* (Susan L. Roth, Illus.) (specialized). (P, I)

Schwarz, Renee. *Birdhouses (Kids Can Do It)* (how-to/activity book). (I)

Swinburne, Stephen. *In Good Hands: Behind the Scenes at a Center for Orphaned and Injured Birds* (photographic essay). (I, M)

Thomas, Peggy. *For the Birds: The Life of Roger Tory Peterson* (Laura Jacques, Illus.) (biography). (P, I)

Weidensaul, Scott. *National Audubon Society First Field Guide to Birds* (field guide). (M)

Depth and scope are two key terms related to the coverage of a topic and influence the author's choice of what type of nonfiction will best serve to present the content. Depth indicates how far into a topic the author goes, and scope indicates how wide a lens the author uses. The organizational structure of a book is integral to the type of nonfiction selected. These are key aspects for students investigating a topic on their own; the type of nonfiction they choose signals the depth and scope of information presented and how the book is apt to be organized.

Biographies

Today's biographies are written to inform and interest children; many incorporate humor and the interesting foibles of well-known individuals. This is quite a change from the past when biographies were more didactic and formal in their presentations. Biographers not only reveal the lives of individuals but many also highlight events and the historical contexts of the time period. (Sample biographies of Abraham Lincoln are shown in Figure 10.4.) Some authors of contemporary biography choose not only well-known figures in history but also famous people in today's news and increasingly choose to write about the lives of lesser-known individuals.

In biographical writing, there is a delicate balance between the amount of conjecture (based on the facts) authors can use and how much they must adhere to documented records. Biographers have a difficult task: they must make their subject come alive, but they must do so in a way that reflects known actions, speech patterns, and actual events of that person's life. Depending on the completeness of the historical record, this can be a formidable task.

FIGURE 10.4 Exemplary Biographies of Abraham Lincoln

Aylesworth, Jim. *Our Abe Lincoln: An Old Tune with New Lyrics* (Barbara McClintock, Illus.). (P)

Burleigh, Robert. *Abraham Lincoln Comes Home* (Wendell Minor, Illus.). (P, I)

Butzer, C. M. *Gettysburg, the Graphic Novel.* (M)

Cohn, Amy L., and Schmidt, Suzy. *Abraham Lincoln* (David A. Johnson, Illus.). (P, I)

Collier, James Lincoln. *The Abraham Lincoln You Never Knew* (Greg Copeland, Illus.). (M)

Denenberg, Barry. *Lincoln Shot!: A President's Life Remembered* (Christopher Bing, Illus.). (M)

Fleming, Candace. *The Lincolns: A Scrapbook Look at Abraham and Mary.* (M)

Freedman, Russell. *Abraham Lincoln & Frederick Douglass: The Story Behind an American Friendship.* (I, M)

Fritz, Jean. *Just a Few Words, Mr. Lincoln: The Story of the Gettysburg Address* (Charles Robinson, Illus.). (P)

Giblin, James Cross. *Good Brother, Bad Brother: The Story of Edwin Booth & John Wilkes Booth.* (M)

Herbert, Janis. *Abraham Lincoln for Kids: His Life and Times with 21 Activities.* (M)

Holzer, Harold. *Father Abraham: Lincoln and His Sons.* (M)

Hopkinson, Deborah. *Abe Lincoln Crosses a Creek: A Tall, Thin Tale* (John Hendrix, Illus.). (P) (HF)

Jackson, Ellen. *Abe Lincoln Loved Animals* (Doris Ettlinger, Illus.). (P)

Jones, Lynda. *Mrs. Lincoln's Dressmaker: The Unlikely Friendship of Elizabeth Keckley & Mary Todd Lincoln.* (M)

Kalma, Maira. *Looking at Lincoln.* (P)

Lincoln, Abraham. *The Wit and Wisdom of Abraham Lincoln: Book of Quotations.* (M)

Meltzer, Milton (Ed.). *Lincoln in His Own Words* (Stephen Alcorn, Illus.). (M)

Pascal, Janet B. *Who Was Abraham Lincoln?* (John O'Brien, Illus.). (I, M)

Rabin, Staton. *Mr. Lincoln's Boys: Being the Mostly True Adventures of Abraham Lincoln's Trouble-Making Sons, Tad and Willie* (Bagram Ibatoulline, Illus.). (P, I)

Rapport, Doreen. *Abe's Honest Words: The Life of Abraham Lincoln* (Matt Faulkner, Illus.). (I)

Sandler, Martin W. *Lincoln Through the Lens: How Photography Revealed and Shaped an Extraordinary Life.* (M)

St. George, Judith. *Stand Tall, Abe Lincoln* (Matt Faulkner Illus.). (I)

Sullivan, George. *Picturing Lincoln: Famous Photographs That Popularized the President.* (M)

Swanson, James. *Chasing Lincoln's Killer: The Search for John Wilkes Booth.* (M)

Thomson, Sarah L. *What Lincoln Said* (J. E. Ransome, Illus.). (P, I)

Turner, Ann. *Abe Lincoln Remembers* (Wendell Minor, Illus.). (P, I)

Wells, Rosemary. *Lincoln and His Boys* (P. J. Lynch, Illus.). (I, M) (HF)

James Cross Giblin, author of notable biographies such as *The Amazing Life of Benjamin Franklin, The Life and Death of Adolf Hitler,* and *Good Brother, Bad Brother: The Story of Edwin Booth and John Wilkes Booth,* provides evidence of thorough research and accuracy of information by including extensive back matter, detailed source notes, and bibliographies.

In his Newbery acceptance speech for *Lincoln: A Photobiography,* Russell Freedman took a strong stand in favor of sticking to the facts and avoiding any sort of dramatization. Freedman asserted, "It certainly wasn't necessary to embellish the events of [Lincoln's] life with imaginary scenes and dialogue, Lincoln didn't need a speech writer in his own time, and he doesn't need one now" (quoted in Giblin, 2000, p. 418).

Biographies are written in several forms. These are discussed in the next section.

Picture Book Biographies. Illustrations serve an elevated role in describing a person's life in these usually brief accounts. A picture book biography may describe an entire life, a specific part of the subject's life, or only the highlights. *Flying Solo: How Ruth Elder Soared into America's*

Heart (Cummins) presents an episode in the life of a spunky beauty queen who piloted a plane before Amelia Earhart and became a celebrity in 1929. Another picture book biography, *The Tree Lady: The True Story of How One Tree-Loving Woman Changed a City Forever,* is about Kate Sessions, the first woman to graduate with a science degree from the University of California, Berkeley. In *Electric Ben: The Amazing Life and Times of Benjamin Franklin,* author Robert Byrd selected an interesting organization for the text by presenting two-page sections to describe various episodes and subjects related to Franklin's important achievements. David A. Adler is well known for his biographies for young children, such as *A Picture Book of Eleanor Roosevelt* and *A Picture Book of Helen Keller,* whereas Diane Stanley's biographies are particularly well suited for older readers, including *Cleopatra* (with Peter Vennema) and *Leonardo Da Vinci.* Jean Fritz is known for her engaging accounts of famous people and for her talent of portraying the very human, often humorous side of her subjects. Her books, such as *Why Don't You Get a Horse, Sam Adams?* and *And Then What Happened, Paul Revere?* help children see these famous figures as real people exhibiting doubts, worries, and human frailty. Krull's *The Road to Oz: Twists, Turns, Bumps, and Triumphs in the Life of L. Frank Baum* is the first picture book biography of this famous author. Another first is Krull's *The Boy Who Invented TV: The Story of Philo Farnsworth*. Figure 10.5 lists a sample of picture book biographies. More titles are included in the end of chapter list of recommended books.

Partial Biographies. As the name implies, this type of biography is limited to describing a portion of a person's life. For example, in *Dragon Bones and Dinosaur Eggs: A Photobiography of Explorer Roy Chapman Andrews,* author Bausum highlights five of Andrews's fossil-hunting trips to the Gobi Desert. *A Special Fate: Chiune Sugihara, Hero of the Holocaust* (Gold) focuses

FIGURE 10.5 Sampling of Picture Book Biographies

(Books with significant culturally diverse elements are marked #.)

Bass, Hester. *The Secret World of Walter Anderson* (E. B. Lewis, Illus.). (P, I)

Berne, Jennifer. *On a Beam of Light: A Story of Albert Einstein* (Vladimir Radunsky, Illus.). (P, I)

#Bernier-Grand, Carmen T. (2007). *Frida: Viva la Vida: Long Live Life* (Frida Kahlo, Illus.). (P, I)

Bober, Natalie S. *Papa Is a Poet: A Story About Robert Frost* (Rebecca Gibbon, Illus.). (P, I)

#Brown, Monica. *Tito Puente: Mambo King/Rey del Mambo* (Rafael Lopez, Illus.) (P, I)

#Bryant, Jen. *A Splash of Red* (Melissa Sweet, Illus.). (P, I)

Cummins, Julie. *Flying Solo* (Marlene R. Laugesen, Illus.). (P, I)

Heiligman, Deborah. *The Boy Who Loved Math: The Improbable Life of Paul Erdos* (LeUyen Pham, Illus.). (P, I)

#Hill, Laban Carrick. *When the Beat Was Born: DJ Kool Herc and the Creation of Hip Hop* (Theodore Taylor III, Illus.). (P, I)

Hopkins, Joseph H. *The Tree Lady* (Jill McElmurry, Illus.). (P, I) Kalman, Maira. *Thomas Jefferson: Life Liberty and the Pursuit of Everything.* (I)

Kerley, Barbara. *The Extraordinary Mark Twain (According to Suzy)* (Edwin Fotheringham, Illus.). (P, I)

Krull, Kathleen. *Louisa May's Battle* (Carlyn Beccia, Illus.). (P, I)

Markel, Michelle. *Brave Girl: Clara and the Shirtwaist Maker's Strike of 1909* (Melissa Sweet, Illus.). (P, I)

#Nelson, Kadir. *Nelson Mandela.* (P, I) Rappaport, Doreen. *To Dare Mighty Things: The Life of Theodore Roosevelt* (C.F. Payne, Illus.). (P, I)

Rockwell, Anne. *Big George: How a Shy Boy Became President Washington* (Matt Phelan, Illus.). (P, I)

Rusch, Elizabeth. *Electrical Wizard: How Nikola Tesla Lit Up the World* (Oliver Dominguez, Illus.). (P, I)

Tavares, Matt. *Becoming Babe Ruth.* (P, I)

Winter, Jeanette. *Henri's Scissors.* (P, I)

on the humanitarian work performed by Sugihara, a Japanese diplomat, who saved many Jewish lives in Lithuania during World War II. In *Benjamin Franklin*, Kathleen Krull focuses on the science and reasoning behind Franklin's inventions. James L. Swanson's *"The President Has Been Shot!": The Assassination of John F. Kennedy* highlights Kennedy's early years as a naval officer, his marriage, his short-lived presidency, and his assassination. In *The Mad Potter: George E. Ohr, Eccentric Genius*, Jan Greenberg and Sandra Jordan introduce readers to this larger-than-life, highly eccentric artist, more appreciated now than during his lifetime in the late 1800s.

Complete Biographies. A complete biography spans a person's entire life and usually captures in some depth the critical and significant aspects. For example, Russell Freedman's *Babe Didrikson Zaharias: The Making of a Champion* details Babe's early childhood, her various athletic endeavors, her charismatic personality, and her death at a relatively young age. Other examples include Patricia and Frederick McKissack's *Sojourner Truth: A Voice for Freedom*, which could be compared with one of many picture book biographies, such as *A Picture Book of Sojourner Truth* (Adler). Another remarkable and award-winning author, Penny Colman, has also explored little-known figures in history, such as *A Woman Unafraid: The Achievements of Frances Perkins, Secretary of Labor*. Perkins was the first woman to hold a cabinet position.

Collective Biographies. These biographies are themed collections composed of brief sketches about several people. Examples include Krull's humorous *Lives of the Presidents: Fame, Shame (and What the Neighbors Thought)* and *Lives of Extraordinary Women: Rulers, Rebels (and What the Neighbors Thought)*, *Let It Shine: Stories of Black Women Freedom Fighters* (Pinkney), and *Ten Kings and the Worlds They Ruled* (Meltzer).

In *Adventurous Women: Eight True Stories About Women Who Made a Difference*, Penny Colman offers readers a selection of essays about remarkable women, some better known than others, such as Louise Boyd, Arctic explorer, and Mary Gibson Henry, a botanist and plant hunter. Colman shares why she wrote this book: "Because I love true stories, especially about women. I love doing the research and writing about incredible historic women who have so much to offer us" (Colman, 2014, para. 1).

Autobiographies and Memoirs. Typically, the individuals whose lives are depicted in biographies are familiar to readers, yet a growing interest in memoirs offers personal perspectives of major events. Examples include *The Lost Childhood: A World War II Memoir* (Nir) and the picture book *Hidden Child* (Millman); both recount the horrors of living through the Holocaust of World War II. Memoirs may provide more insight into events or a historical period than they do into particular individuals, as seen in Valerie Zenatti's *When I Was a Soldier*, an account of a young girl growing up in Israel.

An excellent addition to classroom collections are biographies of illustrators and authors of children's books, yet the criteria for assessing biographies apply here just as much as they do to any other type. An autobiography or memoir often provides insight into books the author has written. For instance, Gary Paulsen, in *Guts: The True Stories Behind Hatchet and the Brian Books*, recounts his experiences as an emergency ambulance driver. He wrote about a man whose life he tried to save and who became the model for the pilot in *Hatchet*. Paulsen (2001) writes, "I remembered him and his eyes and put him in the plane next to Brian because he was, above all things, real, and I wanted the book to be real" (p. 6). In Paulsen's autobiography, readers learn how he writes, details about his philosophy on writing, and the experiences that shaped his life and writing.

Some biographies of authors, beautifully illustrated, carefully researched, and well documented, are appropriate even for adults. *Tomie dePaola: His Art and His Stories* (Elleman) is highly recommended for understanding the development and sequence of this talented author and artist's life and work. Knowing about the life of an author or illustrator gives students and teachers a view into creative minds and an idea of the range of the person's work. A set of autobiographies may explore different periods in an author's life. In the *26 Fairmount Avenue* series by Tomie dePaola, readers feel as if they are sharing various experiences with him. In the title volume, dePaola includes illustrations of everyone in the book, and a note explains how he decided to write the series.

Biographies of authors and illustrators may include sections on primary sources and artifacts, such as Louise Borden's *The Journey That Saved Curious George: The True Wartime Escape of Margret and H. A. Rey*. In evaluating the book, readers need to consider the extent to which the illustrations, archival photographs, pages of letters, and other artifacts contribute to the understanding of the lives of the individuals and the context of the period in which they lived (Zarnowski, 2006). Some collective biographies of authors and illustrators, such as *Artist to Artist: 23 Major Illustrators Talk to Children About Their Craft*, show readers how a book can be designed using first-person narrative, archival and contemporary photographs, and samples of the artists' work. *Chuck Close: Face Book* is a unique and fascinating interactive autobiography. Readers learn about the artwork of Chuck Close, a most unusual and talented artist who is wheelchair bound and grew up with severe dyslexia and medical challenges. This engaging autobiography uses a question-and-answer format based on questions asked by children and includes a self-portrait flip book section that readers can manipulate to create a host of new faces. See *Chuck Close Up Close* (Greenberg and Jordan) by a well-known author team to learn more about this celebrated artist.

Biography in Poetic Form. This biographical form appeals to many young readers for its concise language and vivid images. Like other biographies, a biography in poetic form can cover entire life of someone, such as *Becoming Billie Holiday* (Weatherford) or a partial biography that highlights one time period. This period may cover a year, as in *Been to Yesterdays: Poems of a Life* (Hopkins) or a shorter period (a trip to the art museum), as in Anthony Browne's *The Shape Game*.

Biographies in poetic form can focus on particular motifs or themes that weave throughout the subject's life. In *Love to Langston*, Tony Medina examines themes that punctuated the life of Langston Hughes in poems touching on individual moments. The poetry in this format does not necessarily rhyme, but the literary images are compact, the language is condensed, the text has rhythm, and the words, phrases, and lines can be repetitive. A combination of these qualities appears in *Twelve Rounds to Glory: The Story of Muhammad Ali* (Smith). In the table of contents, each double-paged chapter is listed as a boxing round and begins with a quotation from Muhammad Ali. Repetitive language appears as cumulative text in such biographies as *The Pot That Juan Built* (Andrews-Goebel) and *The Wright Brothers* (Edwards). The writers' style may be characterized with short, spare sentences, as in *A River of Words: The Story of William Carlos Williams* (Bryant), *Martin's Big Words: The Life of Dr. Martin Luther King, Jr.* (Rappaport), and *Ella Fitzgerald: The Tale of a Vocal Virtuosa* (Pinkney), in which the first-person narrator intersperses poetic language with narrative text.

In examining and selecting biography in poetic form, visual features, such as the time line on the end pages of *The Wright Brothers* (Edwards) or the description of the town in *The Pot That Juan Built* (Andrews-Goebel), are important sources of information. The inclusion of resources, source notes, author notes on the research process, statements of interest, and writing credentials are all key to the assessment of accuracy—critical in selecting biographies because it impacts the reader's understanding of the subject (Wilson, 2006).

Tech Click

Many school and public libraries make audio versions of biographies and other nonfiction books available for download on digital devices. We have found that some students become "hooked" on nonfiction by *listening* to good books first. The OverDrive library project has gained momentum around the United States.

The next section continues with additional types of nonfiction, beginning with concept books.

Concept Books

Concept books typically are a child's first experience with nonfiction. They focus on a specific topic, such as colors, shapes, pairs, opposites, or animals. Concept books also explore more complex ideas, such as telling time, classifying objects, or doing basic tasks. They have minimal text and usually contain simple photographs or drawings. Often, they have durable plastic, cloth, or thick cardboard pages so that even babies and toddlers can safely handle them. Examples include *What Do Wheels Do All Day?* by April Jones Prince, *Everything Goes in the Air* by Brian Biggs, and *It's Time for Preschool!* by Esmé Raji Codell. Some concept books are designed for older children depicting aspects of a culture, such as the homes around the world; games, such as hopscotch, dominoes, or jacks; or a familiar concept. Examples include *I'm Adopted!* (Rotner and Kelly) and *About Insects* by Cathryn Sill.

Alphabet and counting books are specialized types of concept books and typically are sequentially organized. An alphabet concept book provides brief information based on related vocabulary words. Sometimes, the alphabet itself is the concept being taught. If so, usually letters are highlighted along with pictures of items that start with each letter. The most useful books for young children feature both uppercase and lowercase forms and use easily recognized objects that clearly illustrate each letter.

Alphabet books are not necessarily for the very young. Some use sophisticated formats to convey advanced concepts, such as historical eras or scientific classification. Older children will appreciate *A Is for Art: An Abstract Alphabet* (Johnson), *B Is for Baseball: Running the Bases from A to Z* (McGuinness), *Q Is for Quark: A Science Alphabet Book* (Schwartz), *E Is for Extreme: An Extreme Sports Alphabet* (Herzog), and *The Queen's Progress: An Elizabethan Alphabet* (Mannis).

Counting books use a numerical sequence to present facts. Often, a theme will guide the content; thus, children might be asked to count animals or items. Examples of thematic counting books include *Count Your Way Through Egypt* (Haskins and Benson), *Emeka's Gift: An African Counting Story* (Onyefulu), and *Desert Digits: An Arizona Number Book* (Gowan). The concept of *number* is the prime focus, and the objects to be counted should be clear and distinct. For this reason, *Counting Is for the Birds* (Mazzola) and *Count!* (Fleming) are excellent examples of this category. Adults selecting early counting books should avoid potential confusion, such as the number 3 illustrated with a mother cat and three kittens.

Gone Fishing: Ocean Life by the Numbers (McLimans) is an unusual counting book. In this beautifully illustrated book, the shapes of endangered animals are used to form the numbers 1 to 10. A sidebar provides brief information about the classification, habitat, aquatic regions, threats, and status of the animal. In a special section called "Diving Deeper," the author provides informative descriptions of sea life. See also McLiman's first book, a Caldecott Honor Winner, *Gone Wild: An Endangered Animal Alphabet*. Another intiguing and sophisticated counting book is *Lifetime: The Amazing Numbers in Animals Lives* (Schaefer). In this book, children explore the concepts of number and quantity within the world of animals.

Examples of alphabet and counting books include the following (* indicates appropriate for preschool). Additional titles are included on the end of chapter list of recommended nonfiction.

*Beaton, Clare. *One Moose, Twenty Mice.* (P)

Helman, Andrea. *O Is for Orca* (Art Wolfe, Photog.). (P)

*Helman, Andrea. *1, 2, 3 Moose: A Counting Book* (Art Wolfe, Photog.). (P)

*Hruby, Patrick, and Hruby, Emily. *Counting in the Garden.* (P)

Melmed, Laura Krauss. *Capital!: Washington D.C. from A to Z* (Frane Lessac, Illus.). (P, I)

Pallotta, Jerry. *The Construction Alphabet Book.* (P, I)

Schwaeber, Barbie Heit. *Alphabet of Insects—A Smithsonian Alphabet Book* (Sally Vitsky, Illus.). (P, I)

Schwaeber, Barbie Heit. *Alphabet of Dinosaurs—A Smithsonian Alphabet* (Thomas Buchs and Karen Carr, Illus.) (see other Smithsonian alphabet books). (P, I)

Wildsmith, Brain. *Brian Wildsmith's Amazing Animal Alphabet.* (P)

Informational Picture Books. Nonfiction books of this type have a strong story line working in tandem with illustrations. Factual information is interspersed throughout the story. *Pale Male: Citizen Hawk of New York City* (Schulman) is an excellent example of this type of nonfiction. Schulman's beautifully written narrative, in combination with Meilo So's exquisite watercolors, tells the story of a red-tailed hawk that became famous in New York City. The author's note describes Central Park as one of the best places in this country for bird watching and chronicles the discovery of Pale Male.

Another example is *Christmas in the Big House, Christmas in the Quarters* (McKissack and McKissack). This book compares and contrasts how a pre–Civil War Christmas was celebrated by plantation owners and by their slaves. Although the copyright page indicates that this title is juvenile literature (nonfiction), fictional characters are intermingled with historically accurate facts and details. It helps when authors include an explanation of what is factual in the introduction, in the end matter, or set apart so that readers do not confuse what is true with what is made up.

Tech Click

Visit the Web site of nonfiction writer Melissa Stewart, author of *No Monkeys, No Chocolate, A Place for Butterflies,* and *Beneath the Sun.* Video tours of her office and a time line of a book's creation reside near Stewart's musing on how book ideas originate.

Photographic Essays. Nonfiction books illustrated with photographs are not necessarily photographic essays. Rather, photographic essays provide an insider's look into another life, culture or science topic using photographs to document various aspects. Often, these books evoke an emotional response because they feel personal and immediate. Generally, readers go "on-site" with the writer and the photographer through the pages of the book. In *We've Got a Job: The 1963 Birmingham Children's March,* Cynthia Levinson chronicles the critical and powerful role that young people played in the civil rights movement. An example that creates a different kind of emotional response is *Ballerina Dreams* (Thompson), which centers on five young girls who have physical challenges and who want to be dancers. Another excellent example is *Cinco de Mayo: Celebrating the Traditions of Mexico* (Hoyt-Goldsmith). This holiday is an important event for Mexican American families, combining the religious and cultural rituals with a festive celebration. Hoyt-Goldsmith's lively writing, combined with Migdale's stunning photographs, brings the parades and community barbecue to life. In *¡Ole! Flamenco*, award-winning author and photographer George Ancona takes readers to Santa Fe, New Mexico, to meet young Janira Cordova, who studies flamenco dancing. Ancona's beautiful photographs document the preparation of Janira and other students to perform at Santa Fe's annual Spanish market. Ancona also provides a rich look at the history and techniques of flamenco.

Survey Books. Many nonfiction books for children are considered survey or "all-about" books. They focus on a broad main topic, such as insects, birds, ancient Rome, or marine animals. Bamford and Kristo (2000) suggest that readers "think about these as 'all about books,' but not necessarily as in-depth presentations" (p. 27). Breadth of coverage rather than depth is the focus. Often, authors of survey books adopt a particular perspective or stance to make coverage of a broad topic more manageable. For example, they might focus on everyday life to present ancient history, as in *Rome: In Spectacular Cross-Section* (Solway); the characteristics of an intriguing marine mammal, as in *All About Manatees* (Arnosky); the misconceptions about scorpions, as in Laurence Pringle's *Scorpions!: Strange and Wonderful*; or the intriguing world of beavers—their habitat, what they eat, and how they live—as in Gail Gibbons's *Beavers*.

Survey books usually include a table of contents, which is helpful in determining breadth of content as well as organizational structure. For example, in *Reptiles* (Weber), the table of contents is designed in a clever way, with titles of chapters placed on the page in a circular fashion around an armadillo lizard. The introductory chapter, "What Is a Reptile?," is followed by chapters on various reptilian topics, such as "Different Types," "Temperature Control," and so on. This is called an enumerative structure, which typically is the organizational structure used in survey books. An enumerative structure is characterized as having a first or introductory chapter that provides an overview of the topic followed by chapters addressing a variety of subtopics. Teach students how an enumerative structure works by having them first read the introductory chapter to gain an overview of the topic and then select specific chapters of interest. This allows students searching for specific facts to select a particular chapter without reading the entire book. This is particularly helpful for reluctant readers who may shy away from reading a book cover to cover (Kristo & Bamford, 2004). By contrast, a biography generally uses a chronological organization signaling that the entire book should be read cover to cover so as to not lose continuity.

Specialized Books. Nonfiction books of this type are designed to provide information about a specific topic or aspect of a broader subject. They are resources for students with special interests and are likely to be used for intensive rather than extensive study. Many are written in an engaging style that keeps readers engrossed while providing fascinating facts that feed their curiosity. For example, *The Great Fire* (Murphy) weaves survivor accounts with primary sources to create a riveting narrative of the 1871 fire that transformed Chicago into a smoldering wasteland. *What You Never Knew About Beds, Bedrooms and Pajamas* (Lauber) chronicles the development of sleep habits and attire from the Stone Age to the present. Other specialized titles include the fascinating *Corpses, Coffins, and Crypts: A History of Burial* (Colman), and the intriguing account of the ivory-billed woodpecker in *The Race to Save the Lord God Bird* (Hoose).

Journals, Diaries, Sketchbooks, and Documents. Some authors use sketchbooks, journals, or other original documents as the basis for nonfiction books. Virginia Wright-Frierson uses this format for her beautifully illustrated, informative descriptions of various ecosystems in *A Desert Scrapbook*, *An Island Scrapbook*, and *A North American Rainforest Scrapbook*. Each presents entries from an observation notebook, drawings, maps, and detailed watercolors to help readers visualize the habitats.

Some authors incorporate primary sources, such as archival documents, photographs, newspapers, diaries, interviews, letters, and eyewitness accounts. These historical documents function as the main text or are integrated within the body of the book. For example, *Dog of Discovery: A Newfoundland's Adventures with Lewis and Clark* (Pringle) includes entries from the explorers' journals. In *Where the Action Was: Women War Correspondents in World War II*, Penny Colman uses primary sources to meticulously chronicle the experiences of brave World War II journalists. Milton Meltzer inserts letters, diaries, memoirs, interviews, ballads, and newspaper articles to depict the era in *Voices from the Civil War*.

Life Cycle Books. Children's fascination with plants and animals make life cycle books popular. These books typically explain the chronological events of a plant or animal's life over the course of a year or from birth (or sprouting) to death. Often, this type of book shows dramatic struggles with predators or other enemies, adding to the excitement. For example, *A Dragon in the Sky: The Story of a Green Darner Dragonfly* (Pringle) tracks the life of a dragonfly from its hatching in a western New York swamp to a migration of hundreds of miles and finally to a pond in Florida. Each stage of its development, along with the threats it continually faces, is carefully chronicled. In another example, Helen Frost interweaves the life cycle of monarch butterflies with the growth of milkweed plants in *Monarch and Milkweed*.

Activity, Craft, Experiment, and How-to Books. This type of nonfiction acquaints students with ways to become actively involved in their own learning, whether it is conducting a science experiment, baking fudge brownies, planting a window garden, or knitting a hat. These books are designed for readers to thumb through or look up a specific activity rather than read cover to cover. They make good resources for identifying project ideas and fostering hobbies as well as helping students realize that reading can lead to interesting pursuits. Books such as *Checkmate at Chess City* (Harper), *Crafts to Make in the Winter* (Ross), *The Best Birthday Parties Ever!* (Ross), and *Inkblot* (Peot) are examples.

Bug Hunter by David Burnie is a title from the DK Smithsonian Nature Activity Guides series and is perfect for grade 4 students and above. *Bug Hunter* is an example of a how-to book including more than 30 activities inviting readers to explore the fascinating world of bugs, beginning with a description of "Bug Basics."

First, browse through *Bug Hunter* to get a sense of the contents and then more carefully to examine all aspects. These steps will help you prepare your students to become "nonfiction detectives." Every aspect of a nonfiction book is important because each feature that a reader notices provides clues about how to read, enjoy, and use the book.

Next, brainstorm a list of all nonfiction features you identify, beginning with the cover. For example, it is important to note that close to the bottom of the cover, it says, "Explore nature with more than 30 activities." This invitation provides even more information about the book than the title, as it indicates the type of nonfiction it is. Consider how that clue helps size up what to expect as well as how it hints about the organizational structure. Then check out the verso page (back of the title page), also known as the copyright page, and list all significant information you find, such as the copyright date and the boxed information that notes safety tips. Why is that information important for all readers to know before independently using an activity book?

Examine the table of contents page. Notice that the first few topics provide introductory information about the world of bugs and what is needed to examine them in their natural habitats. Teach students to carefully study the introductory chapters of an activity book so as to not miss important information. Use sticky notes to record the nonfiction features you find, such as various kinds of visual information: boxes or sidebars, diagrams, and captions. List access features in addition to the table of contents and consider the ways they help readers.

Using the criteria for nonfiction in this chapter, determine the quality of *Bug Hunter* and the possible challenges your students might encounter using the book and how you would help them. For example, some students may benefit from hearing the strategies you used to read dense information, especially as it is presented in various formats. An activity and how-to book, such as *Bug Hunter*, often leads students to want more books about a specific topic covered in the book. This is a good opportunity to design a text set of books including a variety of types of nonfiction on the topic. For example, this chapter includes a text set on butterflies. Create your own text set of books about another creature featured in *Bug Hunter* locating as many types of nonfiction about the topic you choose.

Identification Books and Field Guides. This type of nonfiction helps readers identify and name examples of a specific class or group. More complex than concept books, these books usually identify an exemplar in a category along with a specific description and often an illustration. Several publishers produce excellent field guides, such as the National Audubon Society's *First Field Guide* series and National Geographic's *My First Pocket Guide* series.

Reference Books. This type of nonfiction provides readers with factual information presented in a succinct format. Books such as atlases, dictionaries, almanacs, and encyclopedias are considered reference books.

Tech Click

Most school libraries carry the current editions of the popular reference books. However, in times of tight budgets, consult the Internet Public Library (IPL2); this site "carries" the electronic versions of your favorite almanac, dictionary, or encyclopedias as well as newspapers, special collections, and myriad other useful resources. IPL2 even sponsors a 24-7 Ask-A-Librarian service for students 13 years old and younger.

Nonfiction Graphic Novels. This popular format, described in the picture book chapter, also can be nonfiction. An example for young readers is *A Day at the Fire Station* (Mortensen), one of the *First Graphics: My Community series*. *To Dance: A Ballerina's Graphic Novel* (Siegel) captures the memories of a young dancer and her lifelong love for dancing.

Nonfiction "graphic novels" can be a satisfying alternative to other kinds of books to develop an understanding and appreciation for important times in history. They have the potential to both capture the essence and powerful drama of historical times and keep readers interested from start to finish. An example is *Anne Frank: The Anne Frank Authorized Graphic Biography* by Sid Jacobson and Ernie Colón. Another is *March: Book One*, the first in a trilogy that tells the story of John Lewis, congressman and legendary civil rights leader. *March* is a collaborative effort between John Lewis, staffer Andrew Aydin, and Nate Powell, a well-known graphic artist. Another graphic novel capturing civil rights is *The Silence of Our Friends*, also illustrated by Powell. *Lewis & Clark* (Bertozzi) is a historically accurate account beginning with President Jefferson's request to explore the western lands to the conclusion of the famous expedition.

Lost on a Mountain in Maine, the true and harrowing story of Donn Fendler, who at 12 years old became separated from his family on a hike up mile-high Mount Katahdin during a storm. This popular survival story is also presented as a graphic novel, *Lost Trail: Nine Days Alone in the Wilderness* by Donn Fendler with Lynn Plourde.

Teaching Strategies

Connecting to the Common Core State Standards

The Common Core State Standards (CCSS) identify the understanding of how to effectively read nonfiction (informational) text as an important skill for students. Learning to be an effective reader of nonfiction presents challenges that are different from reading fiction. By the time children enter the intermediate grades, they typically have had much more experience with fiction than nonfiction, yet they are expected to be able to read and understand content-area textbooks, nonfiction books, and other expository material starting in the intermediate grades. This section focuses on competencies pertaining to the craft and structure of informational text for grades 2 and 4 and the integration of knowledge and ideas pertaining to grade 3, as follows:

There are no separate Anchor Standards for Reading Informational Text.

RI.2.5 Know and use various text features (e.g., captions, bold print, subheadings, glossaries, indexes, electronic menus, and icons) to locate key facts or information in a text efficiently.

RI.3.5 Use text features and search tools (e.g., key words, sidebars, hyperlinks) to locate information relevant to a given topic efficiently.

RI.3.9 Compare and contrast the most important points and key details presented in two texts on the same topic.

RI.4.5 Describe the overall structure (e.g., chronology, comparison, cause/effect, problem/solution) of events, ideas, concepts, or information in a text or part of a text.

Several highly effective teaching strategies support the activities that follow—scaffolding or supporting instruction through teacher think-alouds, reading aloud, using a broad range of nonfiction to provide direct and engaging experiences with literature to meet learner needs, and analyzing, comparing, and contrasting books. Because the activities were designed using these strategies, they can easily be adapted for each of the competencies as well as modified to meet student learning needs and level of knowledge about nonfiction.

COMMON CORE STATE STANDARD FEATURE #1

Knowing Various Text Features

Teaching Nonfiction Features Using Think-Alouds (CCSS.RL.5): Think-alouds are effective in teaching, supporting, and reinforcing new learning before students are expected to work independently. As a first step, it is important to informally assess student knowledge about nonfiction to determine gaps in learning and what skills have been mastered. Create an assessment checklist listing the following important aspects about nonfiction that students are expected to know: nonfiction features, such as those that assist readers in accessing information—table of contents, headings, subheadings, glossaries, indexes, and captions; visual information, such as bolded print, diagrams, maps, and time lines; organizational structures, such as chronological structure, compare/contrast, sequential, and enumerative; and comparing and contrasting information by determining main ideas or key points and supporting details from two texts.

Next, include observable levels of competence for each category. For example, observe whether each student can *point out* a table of contents. Is the student able to *name it* as such?

Is the student able to *describe how to use* a table of contents? Does the student *use a table of contents in reading*? Does the student *use a table of contents in writing*? The results of the assessment checklist provide valuable information about what students already know and what skills need additional teaching. See Kristo and Bamford (2004) for additional information.

Second grade students work in pairs to identify nonfiction features.

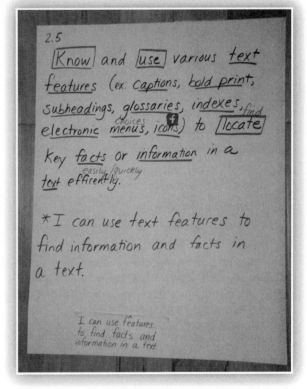

Second-grade teacher Kim Oldenburgh works with students to create a chart of nonfiction features.

Kim unpacks a standard by helping students write it in language they understand.

Examples of adapting the strategies to meet learning needs are integrated within the activities described next.

Second-grade teacher Kim Oldenburgh emphasizes reading and writing nonfiction from the beginning of the school year. She makes thoughtful book selections to plan think alouds (Wilhelm, 2001) in which she shares aloud how she uses strategies to efficiently locate, identify, and use nonfiction features.

In Figure 10.6, Kim offers examples of the various features she highlights and the nonfiction books she selects for planning think-alouds that are integrated into her read-aloud sessions. Note that some titles are labeled as appropriate for intermediate and middle level. Kim identifies only an excerpt or specific feature to share with her students. Since Kim bases her think-alouds on what students need to learn at any given time, the focus of those and the nonfiction books she selects change as needed. She uses the assessment checklist she created to provide guidance on what skills need to be taught and those that need reinforcing.

Tech Click

The Web-based Teaching Channel presents a series of useful (and brief) videos on CCSS topics.

FIGURE 10.6 Using Think-Alouds to Teach Nonfiction Features

Think-Alouds to Model Strategies Used in Reading Nonfiction

When students understand how to "navigate" nonfiction (understand features or aspects of nonfiction that make reading it different from fiction), they are more capable of reading nonfiction on their own:

- Burns, Loree Griffin. *Tracking Trash: Flotsam, Jetsam, and the Science of Ocean Motion.* (I, M)

  Back matter includes glossary, bibliographic notes, and short annotated lists of books and Web sites.

- Markle, Sandra. *Octopuses.* (I, M)

  Follow-up questions, glossary, and suggestions for further readings.

- Montgomery, Sy. *Quest for the Tree Kangaroo: An Expedition to the Cloud Forest of New Guinea.* (I, M)

  Web resources, notes about conservation, and a glossary of Tok Pisin (the language spoken by the team) are appended.

- McClafferty, Carla. *Something Out of Nothing: Martie Curie and Radium.* (I, M)

  Note to readers, source notes, bibliography, illustration credits, index, and recommended Web sites.

- Siy, Alexandar. *Sneeze.* (P, I)

  Web sites, detailed glossary, and fascinating facts about the science and folklore of sneezing.

Think-Alouds to Entice Students to Read Another Book by the Same Author

When students read books by the same author, they learn about a writer's style and how information is conveyed through words, visual information, and access features in ways that will be understandable and interesting to read.

Books by Steve Jenkins, such as the following:

- *Actual Size.* (P, I)

  Colorful cut-paper collages show actual sizes of animals, such as a 36-inch giant Gippsland earthworm. Not all animals can fit on a page, of course, so Jenkins inserts the African elephant's foot or a Siberian tiger's face as a creative way to show size differentiation.

- *Down, Down, Down: A Journey to the Bottom of the Sea.* (P, I)

  This book takes readers to the depths of the ocean where few have ventured. Sidebars on each page show the relative depth in the Marianas Trench where each creature lives.

FIGURE 10.6 *continued*

- *Prehistoric Actual Size.* (P, I)

  In keeping with the same format as *Actual Size*, this book features aspects of prehistoric animals, such as the beak and head of a flying reptile and the Giganotosaurus's huge teeth.

- *Sisters and Brothers*: *Sibling Relationships in the Animal World.* (P, I)

  Presents 19 different species of animal siblings from elephants and beavers to shrews and anteaters. Amazing facts are featured, such as that the nine-banded armadillos are *always* born as identical quadruplets and cheetah brothers hunt together throughout their lives while the sisters separate from their families when they are 2 years old to start their own families.

Books by Catherine Thimmesh, such as the following:

- *Lucy Long Ago: Uncovering the Mystery of Where We Came From.* (I, M)

  This book shows how a pile of 47 bones (Lucy's partial skeleton) changed the way scientists envisioned our ancestors.

- *The Sky's the Limit: Stories of Discovery by Women and Girls* (Melissa Sweet, Illus.). (I, M)

  Over a dozen stories reveal the contributions women have made to science and history.

- *Team Moon: How 400,000 People Landed Apollo 11 on the Moon.* (I, M)

  The space mission that landed a man on the moon told from the perspective of all the contributors who made the historic flight possible.

Think-Alouds to Model Strategies Used in Reading Nonfiction

Using well-planned think-alouds, teachers help students become aware of the strategies experienced readers use to understand nonfiction text:

- Goldish, Meish. *Fossa: A Fearsome Predator.* (P, I)

  Few people have ever seen a Fossa, and most children have never heard of one, making this an excellent choice for thinking aloud throughout the entire book.

- Montgomery, Sy. *The Man-Eating Tigers of Sundarbans* (Eleanor Briggs, Photog.). (I, M)

  Montgomery effectively captures the reader's attention using engaging narrative that becomes a page-turning mystery. Through her word choice, sentence structure, and storytelling style, she builds suspense and tension about certain tigers who quietly and relentlessly attack people, even snatching them from their boats.

Think-Alouds to Challenge Students' Understanding of Nonfiction

It is not always easy to determine whether a book qualifies as nonfiction. It is important for students to know whether what they read is factual, made up, or a combination of both. Some books that appear to be nonfiction have characteristics that confuse readers. Teach students to be "nonfiction detectives" by showing how to carefully examine all aspects of a book, including the dust jacket and verso or copyright page.

  Nonfiction books are often identified as "juvenile literature" on the copyright page. Usually, there is also a brief summary of the book and additional information, such as acknowledgment of experts who were consulted. If this information is missing, it can often be found on the Web page of the publisher. Children as young as kindergarten can be taught to be successful nonfiction detectives. See the copyright page in the following books:

- Davies, Nicola. *One Tiny Turtle* (Jane Chapman, Illus.). (P, I)

  Explains the life cycle of a loggerhead sea turtle from the time she is small to when she mates and lays her own eggs. The author uses a poetic, descriptive narrative style.

- Grimes, Nikki. *Talkin' About Bessie: The Story of Aviator Elizabeth Coleman* (E. B. Lewis, Illus.). (P, I)

  A biography written in poetry from differing points of view about the life of the first black female licensed pilot.

(continued)

FIGURE 10.6 *continued*

- Prap, Lila. *Why?* (P)

  A series of questions set up like a joke book about animals with serious and sometimes silly answers.

Think-Alouds to Share Interesting Access or Visual Features to Entice Students to Read the Book

Reading aloud a particular interesting excerpt, sidebar, or caption is sometimes all it takes to motivate students to take a closer look. Examples follow:

- Borgenicht, David, and Epstein, Robin. *The Worst-Case Scenario Survival Handbook: Junior Edition* (Chuck Gonzales, Illus.). (I, M)

  Embarrassing moments that children can empathize with are covered in this humorous guide. Simply read the contents list, and students will beg to read it.

- Fleischman, Sid. *The Trouble Begins at 8: A Life of Mark Twain in the Wild, Wild West.* (I, M)

  Includes Twain's amazing exploits aboard stagecoaches and steamboats, making and losing fortunes, and trying to find his place in the world. Students will enjoy the photos, cartoons, and samples of Twain's work.

- Guilberson, Brenda Z. *Ice Bears* (Ilva Spirin, Illus.). (P, I)

  A polar bear mother struggles to keep her cubs alive through the harsh conditions of the Arctic.

- Patent, Dorothy Hinshaw. *When the Wolves Returned: Restoring Nature's Balance in Yellowstone* (Dan Harman, Illus.). (I, M)

  The unique organization of the text (brief explanations on the left and longer text on the right) could lead to reading aloud one side of the text with an invitation to students to read the other side.

Structure and Feature Charts: Another way to help children become aware of nonfiction elements is to create feature charts. This activity is adapted from Harvey's (1998) convention/purpose two-column notes idea. This version uses three columns. In one column, students identify a particular nonfiction feature or an organizational structure, such as chronology, sequential, and cause/effect; in the second column, they state how the feature is used or how they determined the organizational structure. In the third column, they indicate the title of a nonfiction book and the page or section that shows the example. These charts show what students understand about nonfiction features or organizational structures and also lists go to books for examples. Also see Figure 10.9 for ideas to extend student understanding of features by creating a chart listing a selection of books on the same topic, examples of features, and how each is used to help learn about the content.

Nonfiction Messages: Nonfiction messages are an enjoyable and informative activity that invites students to look closely at nonfiction for the purpose of locating answers to "messages" (Kristo & Bamford, 2004). This activity can be designed as an informal pre- or post-assessment and reinforces the skill of using nonfiction features to efficiently find information in books.

First, select nonfiction books that contain a variety of visual or access features or both so that there is at least one or more books for each student. Create a question about a visual or access feature for each book and type it on a strip of paper. For example, the messages can focus on specific features of nonfiction, such as finding information from glossaries, indices, and tables of contents. Fold the "messages" and put them in an envelope or container.

Here is an example: What is a *giant vinegaroon*, and where did you find the information?

The answer key: Found on page 24 in the index of *Goliath Bird-Eating Tarantula: The World's Biggest Spider by Meish Goldish*. (The giant vinegaroon is a big arachnid that grows up to 6 inches.)

Students can work in pairs or alone after they select a "message." Carefully observe how they examine the books to locate the answer. Do they struggle and look page by page or do they strategize by first checking the index or table of contents? Give children a reasonable amount of time to do this and then call them back to the group so that each reads the message and shares the book and the answer. Give positive feedback if the student used a good strategy even if the answer is incorrect. Once students understand the procedure, invite them to create their own "nonfiction messages."

Use this activity in flexible ways to meet your needs. For example, if you are teaching about captions, find a selection of books and pose questions that rely on students reading the captions to find the information. This can be modified for finding information from maps, diagrams, and time lines. Another variation is to focus on accuracy and to locate books in which students need to search for clues that speak to the accuracy of the information. Or select a group of fiction and nonfiction books and simply ask students to select a fiction book and one that is nonfiction and record on a sticky note the rationale for determining each. This is an effective variation in determining whether students can differentiate between fiction and nonfiction and provide a rationale for their decision.

Another variation is to select examples of books with clear organizational structures and provide messages with clues to help students identify the structure or type of nonfiction and a rationale. For example, select a survey book and write a message asking students to determine the organizational structure by examining the table of contents. Or, identify the organizational structure as enumerative and ask pairs of students to identify the type of nonfiction. Although this can be a challenging activity, if students understand organizational structure, their comprehension improves (Kristo & Bamford, 2004).

Create a Mentor Set of Nonfiction Books: Select examples of nonfiction books with either exemplars of diagrams, flowcharts, time lines, and other visuals; books with quality access features, such as glossaries, sidebars, and tables of contents; or a selection to show various organizational structures. Refer to Figure 10.2 for examples of typical structures. These sets of books are valuable in serving as useful teaching tools and handy resources. They should be readily accessible for students to share and consult for their nonfiction reading and writing. A sample mentor set is shown in Figure 10.7 and

FIGURE 10.7 Sample Nonfiction Mentor Set

Bird, Bettina, and Short, Joan. *Insects* (Deborah Savin, Illus.). (I) (Table of contents using a main heading and subheadings, diagrams, cross sections, flowcharts, photographs, and captions.)

Chancellor, Deborah. *I Wonder Why Lemons Taste Sour and Other Questions About Senses.* (P, I) (Uses question/answer organizational structure; information on one topic across a two-page spread; use of sidebars and simple diagrams; index.)

Gibbons, Gail. *Horses!* (P, I) (Diagrams, use of labels, summary chart, combination of visuals, illustrations, and text on each page presented in an organized way.)

Lauber, Patricia. *Volcano: The Eruption and Healing of Mount St. Helens.* (I) (Narrative and personal style of writing to use in contrast with the Seymour Simon book.)

Simon, Seymour. *Volcanoes.* (I, M) (Factual style of writing.)

includes aspects and features of science-oriented nonfiction books appropriate for a range of ages with clear examples of several nonfiction features. Each title includes a brief description of its excellent qualities. Also see Figure 10.9 for an example of a content mentor set.

COMMON CORE STATE STANDARD FEATURE #2

Comparing and Contrasting Key Points in Two Texts

RL.3.9   Comparing and Contrasting the Most Important Points and Key Details Presented in Two Texts on the Same Topic

Comparing Biographies: Comparing and contrasting requires students to thoroughly study and analyze at least two different books on the same topic. Select two biographies about the same person for a pair of students to read, analyze, and explore comparisons. This is similar in concept to comparing two folktales as described in the traditional literature chapter and creating a comparison chart or Venn diagram. For example, in comparing two picture book biographies, a Venn diagram can show the comparison of how extensive the coverage is about the person's life in each book. Or students could identify the focus of each book and compare how each author approached writing about that time in the person's life. Illustrations could be compared in terms of how effective the artist was in depicting the person, setting, and time period in each biography. Students could be assisted in locating a biography written many years ago and compare it to a more recently written biography on the same person and then discuss the ways biographies have changed over time. If conflicting information is found, help students find additional books or sources to help settle the conflicting information. Students could use their nonfiction detective skills to compare the nonfiction features in each biography, such as the access or visual features.

Comparing and Contrasting Fiction and Nonfiction on the Same Topic: Figure 10.8 provides a list of sample fiction/nonfiction pairs, including biography. Ask students to either work as pairs or solo to analyze each set of books using a two-column form. Label one column "Fiction"

FIGURE 10.8 Fiction/Nonfiction Pairs

Fiction Titles	Nonfiction Titles
Animal Relationships Bauer, Marion Dane. *A Mama for Owen* (John Butler, Illus.).	Hatkoff, Isabella, Hatkoff, Craig, and Kahumbu, Paula. *Owen & Mzee: The Language of Friendship* (Peter Greste, Photog.). Holland, Jennifer. *Unlikely Friendships: 47 Remarkable Stories from the Animal Kingdom.*
Birds Henkes, Kevin. *Birds* (Laura Dronzek, Illus.).	Sill, Cathryn. *About Birds: A Guide for Children* (John Sill, Illus.).
Butterflies Madison, Alan. *Velma Gratch and the Way Cool Butterfly* (Kevin Hawkes, Illus.).	Bishop, Nic. *Nic Bishop Butterflies and Moths.*

(Books with significant culturally diverse elements are marked #.)

FIGURE 10.8 *continued*

Fiction Titles	Nonfiction Titles
Dinosaurs Edwards, Wallace. *The Extinct Files: My Science Project.* Rennert, Laura. *Buying, Training & Caring for Your Dinosaur* (Marc Tolon Brown, Illus.).	• Barrett, Paul M. *National Geographic Dinosaurs* (Raul Martin, Illus.). • Bishop, Nic. *Digging for Bird-Dinosaurs: An Expedition to Madagascar* (Scientists in the Field series). • Brewster, Hugh. *Dinosaurs in Your Backyard: The Coolest, Scariest Creatures Ever Found in the USA!* (Alan Barnard, Illus.). • Relf, Patricia. *A Dinosaur Named Sue: The Story of the Colossal Fossil: The World's Most Complete T. Rex.*
Dogs Blake, Robert J. *Swift.*	Jenkins, Steve. *Dogs and Cats.*
Food Arnosky, Jim. *Gobble It Up! A Fun Song About Eating.* Napoli, Donna Jo. *Sly the Sleuth and the Food Mysteries.*	• Gibbons, Gail. *The Vegetables We Eat.* • Robbins, Ken. *Food for Thought: The Stories Behind the Things We Eat.* • Souza, D. M. *Look What Mouths Can Do.*
Frogs Ryder, Joanne. *Toad by the Road: A Year in the Life of These Amazing Amphibians* (Maggie Kneen, Illus.).	Bishop, Nic. *Frogs.* Carney, Elizabeth. *National Geographic Readers: Frogs.*
Mosquitos #Aardema, Verna. *Why Do Mosquitoes Buzz in People's Ears?* (Leo Dillon and Diane Dillon, Illus.).	Siy, Alexandra. *Mosquito Bite* (Dennis Kunkill, Photog.).
Snails Avi. *The End of the Beginning: Being the Adventures of a Small Snail and an Even Smaller Ant* (Tricia Tusa, Illus.).	Campbell, Sarah C. *Wolfsnail: Backyard Predator* (Sarah C. Campbell and Richard P. Campbell, Photog.).
Trees Ruelle, Karen G. *The Tree* (Deborah Durland DeSaix, Illus.).	Gibbons, Gail. *Tell Me, Tree: All About Trees for Kids.* Ingoglia, Gina. *The Tree Book for Kids and Their Grown-Ups.*
Weather Plourde, Lynn. *Spring's Sprung* series (Greg Couch, Illus.); The *First Feud Between the Mountain and the Sea* (Jim Sollers, Illus.).	Hannah, Julie and Holub, Joan. *The Man Who Named the Clouds* (Paige Billin-Frye, Illus.).
Amelia Earhart and Eleanor Roosevelt Ryan, Pam Muñoz. *Amelia and Eleanor Go for a Ride* (Brian Selznick, Illus.).	Kelly, Doreen. *Eleanor, Quiet No More: Eleanor's Big Words* (Gary Kelley, Illus.). Tanaka, Shelley. *Amelia Earhart: The Legend of the Lost Aviator* (David Craig, Illus.).

(continued)

FIGURE 10.8 *continued*

Fiction Titles	Nonfiction Titles
The Arctic #Bania, Michael. *Kumak's Fish: A Tall Tale from the Far North.*	Kirkpatrick, Katherine. *The Snow Baby of the Arctic: The Childhood of Admiral Robert E. Peary's Daring Daughter.*
Brooklyn Bridge Johnson, Angela. *Those Building Men* (Barry Moser, Illus.).	Curlee, Lynn. *Brooklyn Bridge.*
Civil Rights #Pinkney, Andrea Davis. *Boycott Blues: How Rosa Parks Inspired a Nation* (Brian Pinkney, Illus.).	#Farris, Christine King. *March On! The Day My Brother Martin Changed the World* (London Ladd, Illus.). #Rappaport, Doreen. *Martin's Big Words: The Life of Dr. Martin Luther King, Jr.* (Bryan Collier, Illus.). #Shange, Ntozake. *Coretta Scott* (Kadir Nelson, Illus.).
Empire State Building Bunting, Eve. *Pop's Bridge* (C.F. Payne, Illus.). Hopkinson, Deborah. *Sky Boys: How They Built the Empire State Building* (James E. Ransome, Illus.).	Mann, Elizabeth. *Empire State Building: When New York Reached for the Skies* (Alan Witschonke, Illus. and Lewis Hine, Photog.).
Middle East and the Importance of Knowledge #Alalou, Elizabeth, and Alalou, Ali. *The Butter Man* (Julie Klear Fiskalli, Illus.). #Heide, Florence Parry, and Heide Gilliland, Judith. *The House of Wisdom* (Mary GrandPré, Illus.). #Lewin, Ted. *The Storytellers.* #Rumford, James. *Silent Music: A Story of Baghdad.*	#Stamaty, Mark Alan. *Alia's Mission: Saving the Books of Iraq* (nonfiction graphic novel). Vogel, Jennifer. *A Library Story: Building a New Central Library.* #Winter, Jeanette. *The Librarian of Basra: A True Story from Iraq.*
Harriet Tubman #Weatherford, Carole Boston. *Moses: When Harriet Tubman Led Her People to Freedom* (Kadir Nelson, Illus.).	#Calkhoven, Laurie. *Sterling Biographies: Harriet Tubman: Leading the Way to Freedom.*
Abraham Lincoln Bryant, Jen. *Abe's Fish: A Boyhood Tale of Abraham Lincoln* (Amy June Bates, Illus.).	Fleming, Candace. *The Lincolns: A Scrapbook Look at Abraham and Mary.*
Negro Baseball League #Johnson, Angela. *Just Like Josh Gibson* (Beth Peck, Illus.). #Lorbiecki, Marybeth. *Jackie's Bat* (Brian Pinkney, Illus.). #Slote, Alfred. *Finding Buck McHenry.*	#Golenboch, Peter. *Teammates* (Paul Bacon, Illus.). #Mellage, Nanette VanWright. *Coming Home: A Story of Josh Gibson, Baseball's Greatest Home Run Hitter* (Cornelius Van Wright and Ying-Hwa Hu, Illus.). #Nelson, Kadir. *We Are the Ship: The Story of the Negro Baseball League.* #Robinson, Sharon. *Promises to Keep: How Jackie Robinson Changed America.*

FIGURE 10.8 *continued*

Fiction Titles	Nonfiction Titles
Tuskegee Airmen #Johnson, Angela. *Wind Flyers* (Loren Long, Illus.).	#Fleischman, John. *Black and White Airmen: Their True History.*
Katharine Wright Yolen, Jane. *My Brothers' Flying Machine: Wilbur, Orville, and Me* (Jim Burke, Illus.).	Maurer, Richard. *The Wright Sister: Katharine Wright and Her Famous Brothers.*
Mary Pope Osborne F/NF Pairs See titles from The Magic Tree House fiction and companion nonfiction research guides by Mary Pope Osborne, such as these examples: Osborne, Mary Pope. *A Good Night for Ghosts* (Sal Murdocca, Illus.). Osborne, Mary Pope. *Revolutionary War on Wednesday* (Sal Murdocca, Illus.). Osborne, Mary Pope. *Dark Day in the Deep Sea* (Sal Murdocca, Illus.).	Osborne, Mary Pope and Boyce, Natalie Pope. *Ghosts: A Nonfiction Companion to A Good Night for Ghosts* (Sal Murdocca, Illus.). Osborne, Mary Pope and Boyce, Natalie Pope. *American Revolution* (Sal Murdocca, Illus.). Osborne, Mary Pope and Boyce, Natalie Pope. *Sea Monsters: A Nonfiction Companion to Dark Day in the Deep Sea.*
Inventions Davis, Eleanor. *The Secret Science Alliance and the Copycat Crook.* Kelly, Katy. *Melonhead* (Gillian Johnson, Illus.). (see others in the series)	Murphy, Glenn. *Inventions.*
Pirates Harrison, David L. *Pirates* (Dan Burr, Illus.).	Gilkerson, William. *A Thousand Years of Pirates.*
September 11, 2001 Cart, Michael, Aronson, Marc, and Carus, Marianne (Eds.). *911: The Book of Help.* Patel, Andrea. *On That Day: A Book of Hope for Children.* Prose, Francine. *Bullyville.* Winter, Jeanette. *September Roses.*	Brown, Don. *America Is Under Attack: September 11, 2001: The Day the Towers Fell.* Fradin, Dennis Brindell. *September 11, 2001.* Gerstein, Mordicai. *The Man Who Walked Between the Towers.*

and the other "Nonfiction" and ask students to compare and contrast each author's treatment of the subject, depending on the genre. To facilitate the process of comparing books with students, teachers can model how readers would approach this task using a think-aloud. Offer the following categories to focus the comparisons: compare and contrast the style of writing; the lead or beginning of each book; the use of visual information, such as illustrations versus diagrams, maps, and other nonfiction visual features; each author's purpose or intention; what ways the two books enrich the experience of reading about the topic; and other possibilities. Ask students for their suggestions and have a follow-up discussion to share findings and conclude with a master summary listing major differences between the fiction and nonfiction titles.

Tech Click

After a topical study, ask students to create an infographic (a visual that collects and displays information) that consolidates the facts from all their resources. Online tools, such as Blendspace, make this an exciting task with professional-looking results.

Supporting Culturally Diverse Learners with Nonfiction

Carefully chosen nonfiction books closely matching the topic of study and developmental level of students, combined with teacher modeling and experiential opportunities to make learning real, will support children's efforts in reading and learning from nonfiction books.

On the first day of school in Kim's second grade, nonfiction books about monarchs, butterflies, and Mexico surround a butterfly habitat containing tiny monarch caterpillars eating their way through milkweed leaves. See Kim's collection of sample nonfiction books on monarch butterflies and Mexico in Figure 10.9. Kim chose from *Caterpillar to Butterfly* (Heiligman) to model for students how she thinks about a book before she decides to read it and what questions she hopes it will answer. She also wants students to understand that a book with drawings and not photographs can be nonfiction. As Kim reads aloud, she takes turns with students to discuss the illustrations and to point out objects in the picture that match with the text. She shares how this helps her to understand what she reads. Modeling what effective readers do supports the efforts of diverse learners.

Kim chose a topic within the experiential range of her students. Creating the butterfly habitat provides opportunities to teach observational skills and to discuss how learners use what they know to help them understand what they read. She teaches students how to track the monarch migration in the fall and spring to and from Mexico. They also participate in a symbolic migration by creating a butterfly that will winter in Mexico and return in late spring (Figure 10.9).

Kim orchestrates each part of her teaching and thoughtfully chooses the books she believes will increase their repertoire of reading strategies. She will later share *National Geographic Readers: Great Migrations Butterflies* (Marsh), which uses photographs and simple labeling and diagrams. Kim reinforces strategies she has modeled until students demonstrate that they can use them independently. She helps each create a "Nonfiction Journal" to keep a record of new learning, such as "I know how to look at the cover of a book before I read it" or "I made these questions because I think the book will give the answer." Using these practices supports culturally diverse students with their learning so that they feel a true sense of accomplishment on their path to becoming effective nonfiction readers.

Tech Click

Journey North (an on-line science education project): Students can track the monarch butterflies migration in the fall and spring to and from Mexico. Classrooms can participate in the symbolic migration by creating a butterfly that will overwinter in Mexico and return in the late spring.

FIGURE 10.9 Text Sets of Exemplary Texts About Monarch Butterflies

Text	Nonfiction Text Feature	What It Helps Us Learn	Example from Book
Monarch and Milkweed (Helen Frost and Leonid Gore)	Author's note	Elaborates on the topic by providing more information that the reader does not learn in the text.	"Each monarch lays hundreds of eggs, usually one egg on each milkweed plant."
A Place for Butterflies (Melissa Stewart, Higgins Bond, Illus.)	Sidebars	Extra information found on the perimeter of a page outside of the main text.	A running narrative about butterflies adorns the pages of this text while each sidebar contains information about a specific butterfly. Some sidebars also contain the life cycle, why butterflies are important, and how we can help butterflies.
The Life Cycle of a Butterfly (Bobbie Kalman)	Table of contents	Helps the reader understand the content of the text as well as the way it is organized.	A reader who is interested in discovering only what a caterpillar eats can immediately turn to page 12 and read about "Hungry Caterpillars."
Monarch Butterfly (Gail Gibbons)	Labeled diagram	A visual representation of the topic is displayed along with labels pointing to parts of the diagram.	A monarch is shown with arrows pointing to its scales, head, proboscis, and so on. New vocabulary is defined right beside the label.
Ask Dr. Fisher About Creepy Crawlies (Claire Llewellyn, Kate Sheppard, Illus.)	Glossaries	Provides definitions of words in the text.	Llewellyn uses easy-to-understand definitions, such as "Nectar: the sugary juice inside flowers."
An Extraordinary Life: The Story of a Monarch Butterfly (Laurence Pringle, Bob Marstall, Paintings)	Further reading	Gives the reader other titles to learn more about the topic. May include books, Web sites, or organizations.	Pringle tells the reader the most valuable resource on the subject as well as other titles to explore.

Supporting English Language Learners with Nonfiction

We have found that everything-ESL, a blog about teaching English language learners (ELLs), is helpful, as it shares effective strategies using nonfiction literature for ELL students. Judie Haynes, author of the blog, shares the following:

English language learners may not be able to ask questions about the author's language or vocabulary in the same way that proficient English native speakers do. However, they can begin to make a habit of questioning and this habit will improve their capacity for

FIGURE 10.10 Recommended Nonfiction Books on Hispanic Culture

Bertrand, Diane Gonzales. *Ricardo's Race/La carrera de Ricardo* (Anthony Accardo, Illus.). (P, I)

Herrera, Juan Felipe. *Calling the Doves/El canto de las palomas* (Elly Simmons, Illus.). (P, I)

Locricchio, Matthew. *The Cooking of Mexico.* (I, M)

Mora, Pat. *A Library for Juana: The World of Sor Juana Ines* (Beatrice Vidal, Illus.). (P, I)

Rau, Dana Meachen. *Fire Safety/Seguridad en caso de incendio* (Safe Kids/Niños Seguros series). (P, I)

Weill, Cynthia. *Opuestos: Mexican Folk Art Opposites in English and Spanish.* (P, I)

Weill, Cynthia, and Basseches, K. B. *ABeCedarios: Mexican Folk Art ABCs in English and Spanish.* (P, I)

Winter, Jonah. *¡Béisbol! Latino Baseball Pioneers and Legends.* (I, M)

understanding and thus support their becoming more proficient readers of English text. It is important to emphasize with ELLs that they need to voice what they don't understand and use reading strategies to figure out answers. (Haynes entry from March 15, 2010)*

Plan instructional read-alouds (Kristo & Bamford, 2004) to help ELL students understand specific aspects of nonfiction. This kind of read-aloud incorporates think-alouds; students listen and observe how the teacher thinks through a strategy as it applies to a nonfiction book. For example, the teacher can model how to make predictions about the content by looking carefully at the cover and title of the book or think aloud; how to figure out new vocabulary; how to read a map, photographs, and captions; and how to use other nonfiction. Think-alouds are particularly helpful for ELL students and others when learning something new and can be followed up with shared reading experiences.

Designing a mentor text set of nonfiction about a specific heritage or culture can help ELL students appreciate and become more knowledgeable about their own cultural history. The content of the books featured in the text set shown in Figure 10.10 focuses on Hispanic culture, but these same strategies can be easily applied to other cultures by identifying appropriate books. (Also refer to the Digital Library of Picture Books in Chapter 4 to access this free resource of books that can be heard in other languages. Identify those that are nonfiction and apply the read-aloud and think-aloud strategies discussed in this section.)

 ## Controversial Issue: Using Blended or Faction Books

Some books look like nonfiction but may be a blended book or "faction" (Avery, 1998)— a book that fuses fact with fiction. Many readers mistake these books for nonfiction. Dorothy Leal (1995) states that informational storybooks with a scientific focus "may indeed be a useful tool for learning science because it may make science information more memorable" (p. 199). She believes that this type of book can be used to engage student interest "as a doorway to a deeper processing of information that comes with expository [nonfiction] text" (p. 199). Blended books can play an important role in the classroom because they may interest children into deeper explorations of a topic (Figure 10.11). However, teachers need to be clear

*From "Part 2 Reading comprehension strategies for ELLs: Asking questions". Retrieved from http://everythingesl-everythingesl.blogspot.com/2010/03/part-2-reading-comprehension-strategies.html. Reprinted by permission of the author, Judie Haynes.

FIGURE 10.11 Sample of Blended Books

Arnosky, Jim. *Turtle in the Sea*. (P)

Bang, Molly, and Chisholm, Penny. *Living Sunlight: How Plants Bring the Earth to Life* (Molly Bang, Illus.). (P)

Bourke, Anthony, and Rendall, John. *Christian the Lion*. (I)

Bowers, Vivien. *Wow, Canada! Exploring this Land from Coast to Coast to Coast* (Dan Hobbs and Dianne Eastman, Illus.). (I)

Flatharta, Antoine. *Hurry and the Monarch* (Meilo So, Illus.). (P)

Franco, Betsy. *Birdsongs* (Steve Jenkins, Illus.). (P)

Lingemann, Linda S. *Survival in the Sea: The Story of a Hammerhead Shark* (Stephen Marchesi, Illus.). (P)

Llewellyn, Claire. *Ask Dr. K. Fisher About Weather* (Kate Sheppard, Illus.). (P)

Lumry, Amanda, and Hurwitz, Laura. *Polar Bear Puzzle* (P); *South Pole Penguins*. (P)

Prosek, James. *A Good Day's Fishing*. (I)

Ryan, Pam Muñoz. *Amelia and Eleanor Go for a Ride* (Brian Selznick, Illus.). (I)

Talbott, Hudson. *Safari Journal: The Adventures in Africa of Carey Monroe*. (I)

that blended books contain both factual and created information. Teachers and librarians play a critical role in helping students distinguish between what is factual and what is fiction in a blended book and how that decision was made. Referring to the copyright page for genre information may be helpful, as will author notes. Teach children to be "nonfiction detectives" to see what they can discover as they browse, carefully scanning the front and back matter as well as the book jacket.

Without guidance, it is easy for students to become confused, especially if the book has the "look" of nonfiction but is not. If children are interested in a blended book because of the topic, use it as a springboard to nonfiction selections on the same topic. Then have students compare the information found in the blended book with that of the nonfiction title.

Summary

- In this chapter, we define nonfiction as the books we use to seek answers for specific questions, for finding information about a particular person or topic, or for simply browsing. These books are sometimes termed "the literature of fact" (Kristo et al., 2008).

- To effectively support children's selection and use of good nonfiction, become committed to reading good nonfiction yourself and know how to select the best titles for your students. The most important elements to use in the evaluation of nonfiction and biography include writing style, organization, accuracy, visual features, format, and design.

- The major types of nonfiction are described: concept books, informational picture storybooks, photographic essays, survey books, specialized books, journals, diaries, sketchbooks, life cycle books, activity books, field guides, and reference books. In considering types of nonfiction, determining the scope and breadth as well as organizational structure are factors in matching the reader's purpose and goals with the type of nonfiction that will be most useful.

- Create effective ways to help all students increase their understanding of nonfiction in active rather than passive ways by teaching about characteristics of nonfiction, such as access and visual features. Help students understand common organizational structures as a key to reading more efficiently and effectively. Students can also learn more about a subject when comparing a variety of books on that topic.

Questions/Activities to Invite Thinking, Writing, and Conversation About the Chapter

1. *Nonfiction/Fiction Think-Pair-Share.* Think about the following statement. Then share with a partner by recording them in two columns: "fiction" on the top of one column and "nonfiction" on the other. Share your list with others.

   - Statement: *Students at all grade levels need to know how fiction is different from nonfiction.*

     Next, refer back to Figure 10.6 containing the fiction/nonfiction pairs. Read several of the pairs and create a Venn diagram or comparison chart to record your responses. Try this with students. How do their responses inform you as to next teaching steps?

   - For an extended example, here is a text set of historical nonfiction to support the reading and class study of *Roll of Thunder, Hear My Cry* (historical fiction). With your partner, choose another historical fiction novel or time period and create a text set of high-quality historical nonfiction. Discuss ways teachers could use this set to support student understanding of a time period.

     - Cooper, Michael L. *Dust to Eat: Drought and Depression in the 1930's.* (I, M)
     - Freedman, Russell. *Children of the Great Depression.* (I, M)
     - Freedman, Russell. *Eleanor Roosevelt: A Life of Discovery.* (I, M)
     - Sandler, Martin W. *The Dust Bowl Through the Lens: How Photography Revealed and Helped Remedy a National Disaster.* (I, M)
     - Stanley, Jerry. *Children of the Dust Bowl: The True Story of the School at Weedpatch Camp.* (I, M)
     - Winter, Jonah. *Born and Bred in the Great Depression* (Kimberly Buicken Root, Illus.). (P, I)

2. Collect a mentor text set of nonfiction books for your class. Create "nonfiction messages" and exchange within a small group. Discuss which questions worked best and why. Then consider: how can you improve this activity?

3. Conduct a classroom nonfiction audit to determine the extent that a classroom is "nonfiction friendly."

   - To what extent does the classroom library include up-to-date and high-quality nonfiction books?
   - What types of books are introduced through book talks, read-alouds, or other means?
   - What genres are on display?
   - Are there any other questions you wish to pose?

Recommended Nonfiction Books

(Books appropriate for preschoolers are marked *; those with significant culturally diverse elements are marked #. To identify titles for a science or social studies curriculum scan at least several categories that follow to select a variety of nonfiction books.)

Find high-quality nonfiction books for K–8 on easily accessible online sources, including National Council of Teachers of English (NCTE), Orbis Pictus Award for Outstanding Nonfiction for Children, Notable Social Studies Trade Books for Young People, Outstanding Science Trade Books for Students K–12, and *The Horn Book Magazine*.

Concept Books

*American Museum of Natural History. *ABC Animals*. (P)

#Chin-Lee, Cynthia, and De La Pena, Terri. *A Is For The Americas* (Enrique O. Sanchez, Illus.). (P)

#Elya, Susan Middleton. *N Is for Navidad* (Joe Cepeda, Illus.). (P)

Fain, Kathleen. *Handsigns: A Sign Language Alphabet*. (P)

Floca, Brian. *The Racecar Alphabet*. (P)

*Franceschelli, Christopher. *Alphablock*. (P)

*Gonzalez, Maya Christina. *My Colors, My World/Mis colores, Mi mundo*. (P)

Kalman, Bobbie. *The ABCs of Continents*. (I)

*Kunhardt, Katharine. *Let's Count the Puppies*. (P)

*Lawler, Janet. *Ocean Counting* (National Geographic Little Kids Series) (Brian Skerry, Photog.). (P)

*Marshall, Natalie. *My Turn to Learn Numbers* (My Turn to Learn Series). (P)

Mayer, Bill. *All Aboard!: A Traveling Alphabet*. (P)

McGuinness, Lisa. *B Is for Baseball: Running the Bases from A to Z*. (P)

McLaren, Chesley, and Jaber, Pamela. *When Royals Wore Ruffles: A Funny & Fashionable Alphabet!* (P, I)

Melmed, Laura Krauss. *Heart of Texas: A Lone Star ABC* (Frané Lessac, Illus.). (I)

Pallotta, Jerry. *The Beetle Alphabet Book* (David Biedrzycki, Illus.). (P)

Raczka, Bob. *3-D ABC: A Sculptural Alphabet*. (P)

#Razzak, Shazia. *P Is for Pakistan* (Prodeepta Das, Photog.). (P)

Riehle, Mary Ann McCabe. *M Is for Mom: A Child's Alphabet* (Chris Ellison, Illus.). (I)

Seeger, Laura Vaccaro. *Green*. (P)

Shoulders, Michael. *The ABC Book of American Homes* (Sarah S. Brannen, Illus.). (P)

#Weill, Cynthia, and Basseches, K. B. *ABeCedarios: Mexican Folk Art ABCs in English and Spanish*. (P, I)

#Whelan, Gloria, and Nolan, Jenny. *K Is for Kabuki: A Japan Alphabet* (Oki S. Han, Illus.). (P, I)

Zuckerman, Andrew. *Creature ABC*. (P)

Chapter-Length and Collective Biographies

Alexander, Sally Hobart, and Alexander, Robert. *She Touched the World: Laura Bridgman, Deaf-Blind Pioneer*. (I, M)

Benjamin, Michelle, and Mooney, Maggie. *Nobel's Women of Peace*. (I, M)

#Bolden, Tonya. *M.L.K. Journey of a King*. (I, M)

#Bolden, Tonya. *Tell All the Children Our Story: Memories and Mementos of Being Young and Black in America*. (M)

Caravantes, Peggy. *Petticoat Spies: Six Women Spies of the Civil War*. (I, M)

Colman, Penny. *A Woman Unafraid: The Achievements of Frances Perkins*. (M)

Fleischman, John. *Phineas Gage: A Gruesome but True Story About Brain Science*. (M)

Fleming, Candace. *Amelia Lost: The Life and Disappearance of Amelia Earhart*. (I, M)

Fradin, Dennis Brindell, and McCurdy, Michael. *The Signers: The 56 Stories Behind the Declaration of Independence*. (I, M)

Freedman, Russell. *Abraham Lincoln & Frederick Douglass: The Story Behind an American Friendship*. (I, M)

Harness, Cheryl. *Rabble Rousers: Twenty Women Who Made a Difference*. (I, M)

Holzer, Harold. *Father Abraham: Lincoln and His Sons*. (M)

#Hoose, Phillip. *Claudette Colvin: Twice Toward Justice*. (I, M)

#Keller, Bill. *Tree Shaker: The Story of Nelson Mandela*. (I, M)

Kirkpatrick, Katherine. *The Snow Baby: The Arctic Childhood of Admiral Robert E. Peary's Daring Daughter*. (I, M)

Krull, Kathleen. *Lives of the Scientists* (Kathryn Hewitt, Illus.) (see other titles in the series). (I, M)

#Maydell, Natalie, and Riahi, Sep. *Extraordinary Women from the Muslim World* (Heba Amin, Illus.). (M)

McGinty, Alice B. *Darwin: With Glimpses into His Private Journal and Letters*. (M)

#Pinkney, Andrea Davis. *Let It Shine: Stories of Black Women Freedom Fighters* (Stephen Alcorn, Illus.). (I, M)

#Pinkney, Andrea Davis. *Hand in Hand: 10 Black Men who Changed America* (Brian Pinkney, Illus.). (I, M)

Weaver, Janice. *Harry Houdini: The Legend of the World's Greatest Escape Artist* (Chris Lane, Illus.). (I, M)

Sandler, Martin W. *Kennedy: Through the Lens.* (I, M)

Picture Book Biographies

Adler, David A., and Adler, Michael S. *A Picture Book of Dolley and James Madison* (Ronald Himler, Illus.). (P, I)

Adler, David A., and Adler, Michael S. *A Picture Book of Harry Houdini* (Matt Collins, Illus.). (P)

Anderson, Laurie Halse. *Thank You Sarah: The Woman Who Saved Thanksgiving* (Matt Faulkner, Illus.). (P, I)

Anderson, Laurie Halse. *Independent Dames: What You Never Knew About the Women and Girls of the American Revolution* (Matt Faulkner, Illus.). (P, I)

Bardhan-Quallen, Sudipta. *Ballots for Belva: The True Story of a Woman's Race for the Presidency* (Courtney A. Martin, Illus.). (P, I)

Barton, Chris. *The Day-Glo Brothers: The True Story of Bob and Joe Switzer's Bright Ideas and Brand-New Colors* (Tony Persiani, Illus.). (P, I)

Bogacki, Tomek. *The Champion of Children: The Story of Janusz Korczak.* (P, I)

Brighton, Catherine. *Keep Your Eye on the Kid: The Early Years of Buster Keaton.* (I)

Brown, Don. *Teedie: The Story of Young Teddy Roosevelt.* (P, I)

#Brown, Monica. *Pelé, King of Soccer/Pelé, El rey del fútbol* (Rudy Gutiérrez, Illus.). (P, I)

#Brown, Monica. *My Name Is Celia: The Life of Celia Cruz/Me Llamo Celia: La Vida De Celia Cruz* (Rafael López, Illus.); *My Name Is Gabito: The Life of Gabriel García Márquez/Me Llamo Gabito: La Vida De Gabriel García Márquez* (Raúl Colón, Illus.). (P, I)

#Bruchac, Joseph. *Jim Thorpe's Bright Path* (S. D. Nelson, Illus.). (P, I)

#Calcines, Eduardo F. *Leaving Glorytown: One Boy's Struggle Under Castro.* (M)

#Capaldi, Gina. *A Boy Named Beckoning: The True Story of Dr. Carlos Montezuma, Native American Hero.* (I)

#Christensen, Bonnie. *Django: World's Greatest Jazz Guitarist.* (P, I)

Christensen, Bonnie. *The Daring Nellie Bly: America's Star Reporter.* (I, M)

Cline-Ransome, Lesa. *Helen Keller: The World in Her Heart* (James Ransome, Illus.). (P)

Cooney, Barbara. *Eleanor.* (P, I)

Corey, Shana. *Mermaid Queen: The Spectacular True Story of Annette Kellerman Who Swam Her Way to Fame, Fortune, & Swimsuit History!* (Edwin Fotheringham, Illus.). (P, I)

#Crowe, Ellie. *Surfer of the Century: The Life of Duke Kahanamoku* (Richard Waldrep, Illus.). (I, M)

#Cunxin, Li. *Dancing to Freedom: The True Story of Mao's Last Dancer* (Anne Spudvilas, Illus.). (I)

#Dray, Philip. *Yours for Justice, Ida B. Wells: The Daring Life of a Crusading Journalist* (Stephen Alcorn, Illus.). (P, I)

#Golenbock, Peter. *Teammates: How Two Men Changed the Face of Baseball* (Paul Bacon, Illus.). (P, I)

Greenstein, Elaine. *The Goose Man: The Story of Konrad Lorenz.* (P)

#Grimes, Nikki. (2008). *Barack Obama: Son of Promise, Child of Hope.* (Bryan Collier, Illus.). (P, I)

#Hopkinson, Deborah. *Michelle* (A. G. Ford, Illus.). (P, I)

#Hubbard, Crystal. *The Last Black King of the Kentucky Derby: The Story of Jimmy Winkfield* (Robert McGuire, Illus.). (P, I)

Hurst, Carol Otis. *Rocks in His Head* (James Stevenson, Illus.). (P, I)

#Ingalls, Ann, and MacDonald, Maryanne. *The Little Piano Girl: The Story of Mary Lou Williams, Jazz Legend* (Giselle Potter, Illus.). (P)

Kerley, Barbara. *What to Do About Alice? How Alice Roosevelt Broke the Rules, Charmed the World, and Drove Her Father Teddy Crazy!* (Edwin Fotheringham, Illus.). (P, I)

Kerley, Barbara. *Those Rebels, John & Tom* (Edward Fotheringham, Illus.). (P, I)

Klier, Kimberly Wagner. *You Can't Do That, Amelia!* (Kathleen Kemly, Illus.). (P, I)

#Krull, Kathleen. *Kubla Khan: The Emperor of Everything* (Robert Byrd, Illus.). (I)

#Krull, Kathleen. *Harvesting Hope: The Story of Cesar Chavez* (Yuyi Morales, Illus.). (P, I)

Kulling, Monica. *It's a Snap! George Eastman's First Photograph* (Bill Slavin, Illus.). (P, I)

Lasky, Kathryn. *Georgia Rises: A Day in the Life of Georgia O'Keeffe* (Ora Eitan, Illus.). (P, I)

#Lord, Michelle. *A Song for Cambodia* (Shino Arihara, Illus.). (I, M)

Lyon, George Ella. *Mother to Tigers* (Peter Catalanotto, Illus.). (P, I)

#McCully, Emily Arnold. *Manjiro: The Boy Who Risked His Life for Two Countries.* (P, I)

#Mora, Pat. *A Library for Juana: The World of Sor Juana Ines* (Beatrice Vidal, Illus.). (P, I)

#Moss, Marissa. *Sky High: The True Story of Maggie Gee* (Carl Angel, Illus.). (P, I)

#Myers, Walter Dean. *Muhammad Ali: The People's Champion* (Alix Delinois, Illus.). (I, M)

Nivola, Claire. *Life in the Ocean: The Story of Oceanographer Sylvia Earle.* (P, I)

#O'Brien, Tony, and Sullivan, Mike. (2008). *Afghan Dreams: Young Voices of Afghanistan* (Tony O'Brien, Photog.). (I, M)

Old, Wendie C. *To Fly: The Story of the Wright Brothers* (Robert Andrew Parker, Illus.). (P, I)

Ottaviani, Jim. *Primates: The Fearless Science of Jane Goodall, Dian Fossey, and Birute Galdikas* (Maris Wicks, Illus.) (nonfiction graphic novel). (M)

#Pinkney, Andrea Davis. *Martin & Mahalia: His Words, Her Song* (Brain Pinkney, Illus.). (P, I)

Plourde, Lynn. *Margaret Chase Smith: A Woman for President* (David McPhail, Illus.). (P, I)

Rappaport, Doreen. *Eleanor, Quiet No More: The Life of Eleanor Roosevelt* (Gary Kelley, Illus.). (P, I)

#Rappaport, Doreen. *Martin's Big Words: The Life of Dr. Martin Luther King, Jr.* (Bryan Collier, Illus.). (P, I)

Rockwell, Anne. *Big George: How a Shy Boy Became President Washington* (Matt Phelan, Illus.). (P, I)

#Reich, Susanna. *José! Born to Dance.* (Raúl Colón, Illus.). (P, I)

#Rubin, Susan Goldman. *Haym Salomon: American Patriot* (David Slonim, Illus.). (P, I)

Schubert, Leda. *Monsieur Marceau: Actor Without Words* (Gerard DuBois, Illus.). (P, I)

Stone, Tanya Lee. *Who Says Women Can't Be Doctors? The Story of Elizabeth Blackwell* (Majorie Priceman, Illus.). (P, I)

#Van Wyk, Chris. *Nelson Mandela: Long Walk to Freedom* (Paddy Bouma, Illus.). (P, I)

Walker, Sally M. *Freedom Song: The Story of Henry "Box" Brown* (Sean Qualls, Illus.). (P, I)

Wargin, Kathy-Jo. *Alfred Nobel: The Man Behind the Peace Prize* (Zachary Pullen, Illus.). (P, I)

#Weatherford, Carole Boston. *Before John was a Jazz Giant: The Song of John Coltrane* (Sean Qualls, Illus.). (P, I)

#Weston, Mark. *Honda: The Boy Who Dreamed of Cars* (Katie Yamasaki, Illus.). (I)

Whitaker, Suzanne George. *The Daring Miss Quimby* (Catherine Stock, Illus.). (P, I)

Winter, Jeanette. *My Name Is Georgia.* (P, I)

#Winter, Jonah. *Barack* (A.G. Ford, Illus.). (P, I)

#Winter, Jonah, and François, Roca. *Muhammad Ali: Champion of the World.* (I, M)

Winter, Jonah. *You Never Heard of Sandy Koufax?!* (André Carrilho, Illus.). (P, I)

#Wise, Bill. (2007). *Louis Sockalexis: Native American Baseball Pioneer* (Bill Farnsworth, Illus.). (P, I)

Yaccarino, Dan. *The Fantastic Undersea Life of Jacques Cousteau.* (P, I)

#Yoo, Paula. *Shining Star: The Anna May Wong Story* (Lin Wang, Illus.). (I)

Zronik, John. *Jacques Cousteau: Conserving Underwater Worlds.* (I, M)

Biographies (Including Autobiographies) of Writers, Poets, and Illustrators

Borden, Louise. *The Journey That Saved Curious George: The True Wartime Escape of Margret and H. A. Rey* (Allan Drummond, Illus.). (I, M)

#Brown, Monica. *Pablo Neruda: Poet of the People* (Julie Paschkis, Illus.). (P, I)

Brust, Beth Wagner. *The Amazing Paper Cuttings of Hans Christian Andersen.* (I, M)

Bryan, Ashley. *Ashley Bryan: Words to My Life's Song* (Bill McGuinness, Photog.). (I, M)

Bryant, Jen. *A River of Words: The Story of William Carlos Williams* (Melissa Sweet, Illus.). (P, I)

Byars, Betsy. *The Moon and I.* (I, M)

Christopher, Dale. *Behind the Desk with . . . Matt Christopher: The #1 Sportswriter for Kids.* (I, M)

#Cooper, Floyd. *Coming Home: From the Life of Langston Hughes.* (P, I)

Cotter, Charis. *Born to Write: The Remarkable Lives of Six Famous Authors.* (I, M)

Crutcher, Chris. *King of the Mild Frontier: An Ill-Advised Autobiography.* (M)

dePaola, Tomie. *26 Fairmont Avenue* (see additional titles). (P, I)

*Ehlert, Lois. *Hands: Growing Up to Be an Artist.* (P)

Ehlert, Lois. *The Scraps Book: Notes from a Colorful Life.* (P)

#Engle, Margarita. *The Poet Slave of Cuba: A Biography of Juan Francisco Manzano* (Sean Qualls, Illus.). (M)

Fleischman, Sid. *The Trouble Begins at 8: A Life of Mark Twain in the Wild, Wild West.* (M)

Fletcher, Ralph. *Marshfield Dreams: When I Was a Kid.* (I)

Giff, Patricia Reilly. *Don't Tell the Girls: A Family Memoir.* (I, M)

Harrison, David L. *Connecting the Dots: Poems of My Journey* (Kelley Cunningham Cousineau, Illus.). (I, M)

Hesse, Karen. *The Young Hans Christian Andersen* (Erik Blegvad, Illus.). (P, I)

Hopkins, Lee Bennett. *Been to Yesterdays: Poems of a Life* (Charlene Rendeiro, Photog.). (I, M)

Kerley, Barbara. *Walt Whitman: Words for America* (Brian Selznick, Illus.). (I, M)

Kerley, Barbara. (2010). *The Extraordinary Mark Twain (According to Susy)* (Edward Fotheringham, Illus.). (P, I)

Krull, Kathleen. *The Road to Oz: Twists, Turns, Bumps, and Triumphs in the Life of L. Frank Baum* (Kevin Hawkes, Illus.). (P, I)

McDonough, Yona Zeldis. *Louisa: The Life of Louisa May Alcott* (Bethanne Andersen, Illus.). (P, I)

Murphy, Jim. *Pick and Shovel Poet: The Journeys of Pascal D'Angelo.* (M)

#Myers, Walter Dean. *Bad Boy: A Memoir.* (M)

Paulsen, Gary. *Woodsong.* (M).

#Perdomo, Willie. *Visiting Langston* (Bryan Collier, Illus.). (P, I)

Pete, Bill. *Bill Pete: An Autobiography.* (I, M)

#Ray, Deborah Kogan. *To Go Singing Through the World: The Childhood of Pablo Neruda.* (I)

Reef, Catherine. *E. E. Cummings: A Poet's Life.* (M)

Reef, Catherine. *Ernest Hemingway: A Writer's Life.* (M)

Richard C. Owen Publishers. *Meet the Author* series (including *Before It Wriggles Away* by Janet S. Wong; *A Letter from Phoenix Farm* by Jane Yolen [Jason Stemple, Photog.]; *See for Your Self* by Douglas Florian; *The Writing Bug* by Lee Bennett Hopkins [Diane Rubinger, Illus.]; *My Writing Day* by David A. Adler [Nina Crews, Illus.]; *Fine Lines* by Ruth Heller [Michael Emery, Illus.]; *Nature! Wild and Wonderful* by Laurence Pringle [Tim Holmstrom, Illus.]; *Surprising Myself* by Jean Fritz [Andrea Fritz Pfleger, Illus.]). (P, I)

Richard C. Owen Publishers. *Author at Work* series (including #*Out of the Dark* by Nikki Grimes; *On the Slant* by Jane Yolen; *Reflections* by Ralph Fletcher; *Essentially M* by Margaret E. Mooney). (I, M)

Scieszka, Jon. *Knucklehead: Tall Tales & Mostly True Stories About Growing Up Scieszka.* (I, M)

Spinelli, Jerry. *Knots in My Yo-Yo String: The Autobiography of a Kid.* (I, M)

Stanley, Diane, and Vennema, Peter. *Bard of Avon: The Story of William Shakespeare* (Diane Stanley, Illus.). (I, M)

Winter, Jeanette. *Beatrix.* (P, I)

Wong, Janet S. *A Suitcase of Seaweed and Other Poems.* (I, M)

Nonfiction Books About the English Language and Communication

Chronicle Books Staff. *L Is for Lollygag: Quirky Words for a Clever Tongue.* (M)

Davies, Nicola. *Talk, Talk, Squawk: A Human's Guide to Animal Communication* (Neal Layton, Illus.). (I, M)

Donoughue, Carol. *The Story of Writing.* (I, M)

Dubosarsky, Ursula. *The Word Snoop: A Wild and Witty Tour of the English Language* (Tohby Riddle, Illus.). (I, M)

Gorrell, Gena K. *Say What? The Weird and Mysterious Journey of the English Language.* (I, M)

Robb, Don. *Ox, House, Stick: The History of Our Alphabet* (Anne Smith, Illus.). (I)

Science Nonfiction Books

Arndt, Ingo. *Best Foot Forward: Exploring Feet, Flippers, and Claws.* (P)

Arnosky, Jim. *Wild Tracks! A Guide to Nature's Footprints.* (P, I)

Bishop, Nic. *Snakes.* (P, I)

Bishop, Nic. *Marsupials.* (P, I)

Carson, Mary Kay. *Beyond the Solar System: Exploring Galaxies, Black Holes, Alien Planets, and More.* (I, M)

DeCristofano, Carolyn Cinami. *A Black Hole Is NOT a Hole* (Michael Carroll, Illus.). (I, M)

Fridel, Ron. *Forensic Science* (Cool Science series). (I, M)

Gray, Leon. *Giant Pacific Octopus.* (P, I)

Heos, Bridget. *Stronger Than Steel: Spider Silk DNA and the Quest for Better Bulletproof Vests, Sutures, and Parachute Rope* (Andy Comins, Illus.) (Scientists in the Field series). (I, M)

Hillman, Ben. *How Strong Is It? A Mighty Book All About Strength.* (I, M)

Jenkins, Martin. *Can We Save the Tiger?* (Vicky White, Illus.). (P, I)

Markle, Sandra. *Insects: Biggest! Littlest!* (Dr. Simon Pollard, Photog.). (P, I)

Montgomery, Sy. *The Tapir Scientist: Saving South America's Largest Mammal* (Nic Bishop, Photog.) (Scientists in the Field series). (I, M)

Rusch, Elizabeth. *The Mighty Mars Rovers: The Incredible Adventures of Spirit and Opportunity.* (I, M)

Sayre, April Pulley. *Here Come the Humpbacks!* (P, I)

Simon, Seymour. *Dolphins.* (P, I)

Simon, Seymour. *A Shipmate's Guide to Our Solar System: Earth.* (P, I)

Simon, Seymour. *Seymour Simon's Extreme Oceans.* (P, I)

Siy, Alexander, and Kunkel, Dennis. *Mosquito Bite.* (I, M)

Turner, Pamela S. *Prowling the Seas: Exploring the Hidden World of Ocean Predators.* (I, M)

Webb, Sophie. *Far from Shore: Chronicles of an Open Ocean Voyage.* (I, M)

Nonfiction Books for Social Studies

#Abouraya, Karen Leggett. *Hands Around the Library: Protecting Egypt's Treasured Books* (Susan L. Roth, Illus.). (P)

#Ancona, George. *Murals: Walls That Sing; ¡Ole! Flamenco.* (I, M)

Bannatyne-Cugnet, Jo. *The Day I Became a Canadian: A Citizenship Scrapbook* (Song Nan Zhang, Illus.). (P)

#Barasch, Lynn. *Hiromi's Hands.* (P)

#Barnard, Bryn. *The Genius of Islam: How Muslims Made the Modern World.* (I, M)

#Brimner, Larry Dane. *Birmingham Sunday.* (I, P)

Colman, Penny. *Thanksgiving: The True Story.* (I, M)

Cooper, Ilene. *Jewish Holidays All Year Round: A Family Treasury* (Elivia Savadier, Illus.). (I)

Hoose, Phillip. *We Were There, Too!: Young People in U.S. History.* (I, M)

Laroche, Giles. *If You Lived Here: Houses of the World.* (P, I)

Lewin, Ted, and Lewin, Betsy. *Balarama: A Royal Elephant.* (I, M)

Macaulay, David. *Built to Last.* (I, M)

#National Geographic. *1001 Inventions & Awesome Facts from Muslim Civilization* (National Geographic Kids series). (I, M)

#Padmanabhan, Majula. *I Am Different: Can You Find Me?* (Global Fund for Children's Books). (P, I)

Rappaport, Doreen. *Beyond Courage: The Untold Story of Jewish Resistance During the Holocaust.* (M)

#Rotner, Shelley, and Kelly, Sheila M. *Shades of People* (Shelley Rotner, Photog.). (P)

Rubin, Susan Goldman. *The Anne Frank Case: Simon Wiesenthal's Search for the Truth* (Bill Farnsworth, Illus.). (M)

#Ruelle, Karen Gray, and DeSaix, Deborah Durland. *The Grand Mosque of Paris: A Story of How Muslims Rescued Jews During the Holocaust.* (I, M)

Sandler, Martin W. *Lincoln Through the Lens: How Photography Revealed and Shaped an Extraordinary Life.* (M)

Sis, Peter. *The Wall: Growing Up Behind the Iron Curtain.* (I, M)

Thomson, Ruth. *Terezin: Voices from the Holocaust.* (I, M)

Tunnell, Michael O. *Candy Bomber: The Story of the Berlin Airlift's "Chocolate Pilot".* (I, M)

#Warren, Andrea. *Escape from Saigon: How a Vietnam War Orphan Became an American Boy.* (M)

Nonfiction Books with Intriguing, Engaging, and Humorous Topics

Aronson, Mark. *If Stones Could Speak: Unlocking the Secrets of Stonehenge.* (I, M)

Boudreau, Hélène. *Crimebusting and Detection.* (I, M)

Bragg, Georgia. *How They Croaked: The Awful Ends of the Awfully Famous* (Kevin O'Malley, Illus.). (I, M)

Butcher, Kristin. *Pharaohs and Foot Soldiers: One Hundred Ancient Jobs You Might Have Desired or Dreaded* (Martha Newbigging, Illus.). (I, M)

Cusick, Dawn. *Get the Scoop on Animal Poop!: From Lions to Tapeworms: 251 Cool Facts about Scat, Frass, Dung, and More!* (P, I)

Davis, Jill. *Orangutans Are Ticklish: Fun Facts from an Animal Photographer* (Steve Grubman, Photog.). (P, I)

Hort, Lenny. *Did Dinosaurs Eat Pizza? Mysteries Science Hasn't Solved* (John O'Brien, Illus.). (P)

Hughes, Susan. *Case Closed?: Nine Mysteries Unlocked by Modern Science* (Michael Wandelmaier, Illus.). (I, M)

Jenkins, Steve. *Never Smile at a Monkey and 17 Other Important Things to Remember.* (P, I)

Jenkins, Steve, and Page, Robin. *Animals Upside Down: A Pull, Pop, Lift & Learn Book!* (P, I)

Lawrence, Ellen. *Man-Eating Plants.* (P, I)

Lucke, Deb. *The Book of Time Outs: A Mostly True History of the World's Biggest Troublemakers.* (I)

Masoff, Joy. *Oh, Yikes! History's Grossest, Wackiest Moments* (Terry Sirrell, Illus.) (I, M); *Oh Yuck! The Encyclopedia of Everything Nasty* (Terry Sirrell, Illus.). (I, M)

Nobleman, Marc Tyler. (2008.) *Boys of Steel: The Creators of Superman* (Ross MacDonald, Illus.). (P, I)

Paley, Rebecca. *Dogs 101: Your Ultimate Guide to Man's Best Friend.* (P, I)

Raab, Brigitte. *Where Does Pepper Come From? And Other Fun Facts* (Manuela Olten, Illus.). (P)

Raum, Elizabeth. *The Story Behind Toilets.* (I, M)

Rondina, Catherine. *Don't Touch That Toad & Other Strange Things Adults Tell You* (Kevin Sylvester, Illus.). (I, M)

Ruffin, Frances E. *Medical Detective Dogs.* (I)

Solheim, James. *It's Disgusting and We Ate It!: True Food Facts from Around the World and Throughout History* (Eric Brace, Illus.). (P, I, M)

Tagliaferro, Linda. *Therapy Dogs.* (I, M)

Walker, Kathryn. *Mysteries of Alien Visitors and Abductions.* (M)

Awards for Children's Literature

Award & Sponsor	Description / Purpose	Selected Winners
Aesop Prize *Sponsor:* Children's Folklore Section of American Folklore Society	Honors English language books for children and adults that provide information about a tale's cultural background and accurately reflect the culture and worldview of the people who originated the story. Books should reflect high artistic standards and should have strong appeal to young readers.	• Hayes, Joe, reteller. *Dance, Nana, Dance.* • Henderson, Kathy, reteller. *Lugalbanda: The Boy Who Got Caught Up in a War: An Epic Tale From Ancient Iraq.* • MacDonald, Margaret Read, reteller. *Mabela the Clever.* • Sierra, Judy. *Can You Guess My Name: Traditional Stories Around the World.*
American Indian Youth Award *Sponsor:* American Library Association	Awarded to high-quality books that reflect in text and artwork the values and world-view of Native cultures.	• Alexie, Sherman. *Absolutely True Diary of a Part-time Indian.* • Fortunate Eagle, Adam. *Pipestone: My Life in an Indian Boarding School.* • Highway, Tomason. *Caribou Song, Atihko Oonagamoon.*
Andre Norton Award for YA Science Fiction & Fantasy *Sponsor:* Science Fiction & Fantasy Writers of America	Recognizes outstanding science fiction and fantasy books (including graphic novels) written in English.	• Black, Holly. *Valiant: A Modern Tale of Faerie.* • Larbalestier, Justine. *Magic or Madness.* • Rowling, J. K. *Harry Potter And the Deathly Hallows.* • Wilce, Ysabeau. *Flora's Dare.*
Boston Globe Horn Book Award *Sponsor:* *Boston Globe* and the *Horn Book Magazine*	Given to titles published in the United States based on three judges appointed by Horn Book editors for Picture books; Fiction/Poetry; and Nonfiction.	• Barnett, Mac. *Extra Yarn.* • DiCamillo, Kate. *Miraculous Journey of Edward Tulane.* • Byrd, Robert. *Electric Ben: The Amazing Life and Times of Benjamin Franklin.*
Caldecott Medal *Sponsor:* American Library Association	For the excellent execution of artistic media and illustration that extends and enhances text.	• Floca, Brian. *Locomotive.* • Pinkney, Jerry. *The Lion & the Mouse.* • Taback, Simms. *Joseph Had a Little Overcoat.* • Wiesner, David. *The Three Pigs.*

Award & Sponsor	Description / Purpose	Selected Winners
Carter G. Woodson Book Awards *Sponsor:* National Council for the Social Studies	Recognizes nonfiction books for young readers that accurately and sensitively depict ethnicity in the United States.	• Asim, Jabari. *Fifty Cents and a Dream: Young Booker T. Washington.* • Watson, Renee. *Harlem's Little Blackbird: The Story of Florence Mills.*
Charlotte Zolotow Award *Sponsor:* Cooperative Children's Book Center & University of Wisconsin	Awarded to the best picture book text published in the United States.	• Foley, Greg. *Thank You Bear.* • Graham, Bob. *How to Heal a Broken Wing.* • Tafolla, Carmen. *What Can You Do With a Paleta?* • Williams, Vera B. *Lucky Song.*
Children's Book Guild Nonfiction Award *Sponsor:* The Children's Book Guild of Washington, DC	Awards an author or author-illustrator whose total work has contributed to the quality of children's nonfiction.	• Candace Fleming • Jan Greenberg and Sandra Jordan • Kathleen Krull • Peter Sis
E.B. White Read Aloud Award *Sponsor:* American Booksellers Association	Given to books that have universal appeal as "terrific" read alouds. Books are selected in two categories: Picture Books and Older Readers.	Picture Books: • Barnett, Marc. *Extra Yarn.* • Becker, Bony. *A Visitor For Bear.* • Klassen, Jon. *I Want My Hat Back.* Older Readers: • Broach, Elise. *Masterpiece.* • Maloy, Meile. *The Apothecary.* • Palacio, R.J. *Wonder.*
Edgar Allan Poe Award *Sponsor:* Mystery Writers of America	Awards for the Best Juvenile novel and the Best Young Adult Novel in the categories of suspense, crime, and mystery.	• Butler, Dori Hillestad. *The Buddy Files: The Case of the Lost Boy.* • Ferraiola, Jack D. *The Quick Fix.* • Hahn, Mary Downing. *Closed for the Season.*
Ezra Jack Keats New Illustrator Award *Sponsor:* Ezra Jack Keats Foundation	Given to multicultural books that display strong families by illustrators who have fewer than four books.	• Collier, Bryan. *Uptown.* • Juan, Ana. *The Night Eater.* • Khan, Rukhsana. *Silly Chicken.* • Thompson, Lauren. *The Apple Pie That Papa Baked.*
Flora Stieglitz Straus Award *Sponsor:* Bankstreet College of Education	Award for a distinguished work of nonfiction serving to inspire children.	• Marrin, Albert. *Flesh and Blood So Cheap: The Triangle Fire and Its Legacy.* • Rappaport, Doreen. *Beyond Courage: The Untold Story of Jewish Resistance During the Holocaust.* • Sweet, Melissa. *Balloons Over Broadway: The True Story of the Puppeteer of Macy's Parade.*

Award & Sponsor	Description / Purpose	Selected Winners
Golden Duck; Eleanor Cameron; Hal Clement Awards *Sponsor:* Super-Con-Duck-Tivity	Purpose is to encourage primarily science fiction but considers fantasy. Good characterization is crucial. Awards given for a picture book (Golden Duck), for a book written for grades 2-6 (Eleanor Cameron), and for young adult (Hal Clement). Special awards occasionally given to a book, author, illustrator, or publisher not fitting into the other categories.	• Applegate, Katherine. *Andalite Chronicles.* • Asch, Frank. *Gravity Buster.* • Farmer, Nancy. *The Ear, the Eye and the Arm.* • Haddix, Margaret Peterson. *Escape From Memory.* • McNaughton, Colin. *We're Off to Look for Aliens.*
Hugo Award *Sponsor:* World Science Fiction Convention ("Worldcon")	Most prestigious award in science fiction.	• Card, Orson Scott. *Ender's Game.* • Gaiman, Neil. *The Graveyard Book.* • Rowling, J. K. *Harry Potter and the Goblet of Fire.*
Jane Addams Book Award *Sponsor:* Women's National League for Peace and Freedom and the Jane Addams Peace Association	Award for a book published the preceding year that most effectively promotes the cause of peace, social justice and world community. There is also a picture book category.	• Levinson, Cynthia. *We've Got a Job: The 1963 Birmingham Children's March.* • Warren, Sarah. *Dolores Huerta: A Hero to Migrant Workers.* • Woodson, Jacqueline. *Each Kindness.*
Jefferson Cup *Sponsor:* Virginia Library Association	This award goes to authors writing about America's past, including historical fiction, biography, and nonfiction.	• Carbone, Elisa. *Blood on the River: James Town 1607.* • Carvel, Marlene. *Sweetgrass Basket.* • Paterson, Katherine. *Preacher's Boy.* • Reeder, Carolyn. *Shades of Gray.*
Kate Greenaway Medal *Sponsor:* Chartered Institute of Library and Information Professionals, UK	Award for illustrations that provide a stimulating and satisfying visual experience.	• Ahlberg, Janet. *Each Peach Pear Plum* • Gravett, Emily. *Wolves.* • Oxenbury, Helen. *Alice's Adventures in Wonderland.* • Pinhold, Levi. *Black Dog.*
Lee Bennett Hopkins Poetry Award *Sponsor:* Pennsylvania Center for the Book (Penn State University)	Presented to American poet or anthologist for the most outstanding new book of poetry published in the previous calendar year. Given annually.	• Mitchell, Stephen. *The Wishing Bone and Other Poems.* • Myers, Walter Dean. *Jazz.* • Schertle, Alice. *Button Up.* • Sidman, Joyce. *Song of the Water Boatman & Other Pond Poems.* • Weatherford, Carole Boston. *Birmingham, 1963.*

Award & Sponsor	Description / Purpose	Selected Winners
Lee Bennett Hopkins Promising Poet Award *Sponsor:* International Reading Association	Given to promising new children's poet who has published no more than two books of children's poetry. Awarded every 3 years.	• Chandra, Deborah. *Rich Lizard and Other Poems.* • Crist-Evans, Craig. *Moon Over Tennessee: A Boy's Civil War.* • George, Kristine O'Connell. *The Great Frog Race and Other Poems.* • Johnson, Lindsay Lee. *Soul Moon Soup.* • Wong, Joyce Lee. *Seeing Emily.*
Mythopoeia Fantasy Award *Sponsor:* Mythopoeic Society	Awarded to a book-length fantasy that exemplifies the spirit of J. R. R. Tolkien and C. S. Lewis.	• Billingsley, Franny. *The Folk Keeper.* • Farmer, Nancy. *Sea of Trolls.* • Funke, Cornelia. *Inkheart.* • Gaiman, Neil. *Coraline.*
National Book Award *Sponsor:* National Book Foundation	Given for books written by Americans that enhance public awareness and encourage reading. One category is awarded to literature for youth.	• Alexander, William, *Goblin Secrets.* • Kadohata, Cynthia. *The Thing About Luck.* • Paterson, Katherine, *The Great Gilly Hopkins.*
NCTE Award for Excellence in Poetry for Children *Sponsor:* National Council of Teachers of English	Honors a living American poet for his or her aggregate work for children, ages 3-13. Awarded every 3 years.	• Arnold Adoff • Aileen Fisher • Nikki Grimes • Mary Ann Hoberman • Lee Bennett Hopkins
Newbery Medal *Sponsor:* American Library Association	Given to the most distinguished American children's book for literary quality, quality of presentation, and interpretation of theme.	• Applegate, Katherine, *The One and Only Ivan.* • DiCamillo, Kate. *Flora & Ulysses: The Illuminated Adventures.* • Sachar, Louis, *Holes.* • Vanderpool, Clare. *Moon Over Manifest.*
Orbis Pictus Award for Outstanding Nonfiction for Children *Sponsor:* National Council of Teachers of English	Promotes and recognizes the best in children's nonfiction for grades K–8.	• Greenberg, Jan and Jordan, Sandra. *Ballet for Martha: Making Appalachian Spring.* • Schubert, Leda. *Monsieur Marceau: Actor Without Words.* • Sweet, Melissa. *Balloons Over Broadway: The True Story of the Puppeteer of Macy's Parade.*

Award & Sponsor	Description / Purpose	Selected Winners
Original Art Lifetime Achievement Award *Sponsor:* Society of Illustrators	Given to a body of work honoring innovative and pioneering contributions to the field of children's book illustration. (Note: Name has been changed to Lifetime Achievement Awards)	• Ashley Bryan • Eric Carle • Barbara Cooney • David Macaulay
Phoenix Award *Sponsor:* Children's Literature Association	Given in recognition for high literary merit and books that touch the imagination and enrich the spirit.	• Hicyilmaz, Gaye. *The Frozen Waterfall.* • Yep, Laurence. *Dragonwings.*
Pura Belpré Award *Sponsor:* American Library Association	Awarded to a writer and illustrator whose work affirms and celebrates Latino culture.	• Medina, Meg. *Yaqui Delgado Wants to Kick Your Ass.* • Montes, Marisa. *Los Gatos Black on Halloween.* • Schmidt and Diaz. Martin de Porres. *The Rose in the Desert.* • Yuyi, Morales. *Niño Wrestles the World.*
Robert F. Sibert Informational Book Medal *Sponsor:* American Library Association	Honors the author(s) and illustrator(s) of the most distinguished informational book published in the United States in English.	• Bartoletti, Susan Campbell. *Black Potatoes: The Story of the Great Irish Potato Famine.* • Giblin, James Cross. *The Life and Death of Adolf Hitler.* • Sheinkin, Steve. *Bomb: The Race to Build—and Steal—the World's Most Dangerous Weapon.*
Scott O'Dell Award for Historical Fiction *Sponsor:* O'Dell Award Committee	First established by Scott O'Dell to encourage and reward writers of historical fiction; award given to an author for a book intended for children or young adults published the prior year.	• Anderson, Laurie H. *Chains.* • Curtis, Christopher P. *Elijah of Buxton.* • Garcia, Rita W. *One Crazy Summer.* • Phelan, Matt. *The Storm in the Barn.*
Theodor Seuss Geisel Award *Sponsor:* American Library Association	Awarded to the most distinguished book for beginning readers.	• Kvasnosky, Laura McGee. *Zelda and Ivy: The Runaways.* • Rylant, Cynthia. *Henry and Mudge and the Great Grandpas.* • Willems, Mo. *Are You Ready to Play Outside?* • Willems, Mo. *There Is a Bird on Your Head!*
Wanda Gag Read Aloud Award *Sponsor:* Minnesota State University	Given for outstanding writing in a children's picture book.	• Kulka, Joe. *Wolf's Coming!* • Smallcomb, Pam. *Earth to Clunk.* • Stower, Adam. *Silly Doggy.*

References

Ada, A. F., Harris, V. J., & Hopkins, L. B. (1993). *A chorus of cultures: Developing literacy through multicultural poetry.* Carmel, CA: Hampton-Brown Books.

Aiken, J. (1996). Interpreting the past: Reflections of an historical novelist. In S. Egoff, G. Stubbs, R. Ashley, & W. Sutton (Eds.), *Only connect: Readings on children's literature* (pp. 62–73). Ontario: Oxford University Press.

Albright, L. (2002). Bringing the ice maiden to life: Engaging adolescents in learning through picture book read alouds in content areas. *Journal of Adolescent and Adult Literacy, 45*(5), 418–428.

Alexander, J. (2005). The verse-novel: A new genre. *Children's Literature in Education, 36*(3), 269–283.

Alexander, L. (1988). Fantasy and the human condition. *The New Advocate, 83*(2), 75–83.

Allington, R. (2002). What I've learned about effective reading instruction from a decade of studying exemplary elementary classroom teachers. *Phi Delta Kappan, 83*(10), 740–747.

Allington, R. L. (2006). *What really matters for struggling readers: Designing research-based programs* (2nd ed.). Boston: Allyn & Bacon.

Allington, R., McGill-Frazen, A., Camilli, G., Williams, L., Graff, J., Zeig, J., et al. (2010). Addressing summer reading setback among economically disadvantaged elementary students. *Reading Psychology, 31*(5), 411–427.

American Library Association. (2010). *Top 100 banned/challenged books from 2000–2009.* Available from http://www .ala.org/books/top-100-bannedchallenged-books-2000-2009

Anderson, C. (2000). *How's it going? A practical guide to conferring with student writers.* Portsmouth, NH: Heinemann.

Anderson, C. A., Hiebert, E. H., Scott, J. A., & Wilkinson, I. A. G. (1985). *Becoming a nation of readers: The report of the Commission on Reading.* Washington, DC: National Academy of Education.

Anderson, L. (2010). Writer Laurie Halse Anderson on her book *Forge and the inspiring American Revolution.* New York: Simon & Schuster. Available from http://www.youtube.com/watch?v=aa-WMxPqTek

Anderson, N. A. (2009). *Elementary children's literature: Infancy through age 13* (3rd ed.). Boston: Allyn & Bacon.

Anderson, R. C., Wilson, P. T., & Fielding, L. G. (1988). Growth in reading and how children spend their time outside of school. *Reading Research Quarterly, 23*(3), 285–303.

Anstey, M. (2002). "It's not all black and white": Postmodern picture books and new literacies. *Journal of Adolescent & Adult Literacy, 45*(6), 444–457.

Arter, L. M., & Nilsen, A. P. (2009). Using Lemony Snicket to bring smiles to your vocabulary lessons. *The Reading Teacher, 63*(3), 235–238.

Atkinson, T. S., Matusevich, M. N., & Huber, L. (2009). Making science trade book choices for elementary classrooms. *The Reading Teacher, 62*(6), 484–497.

Atwell, N. (1998). *In the middle: New understandings about writing, reading, and learning.* Portsmouth, NH: Heinemann.

Atwell, N. (2007). *The reading zone: How to help kids become skilled, passionate, habitual, critical readers.* New York: Scholastic.

Avery, C. (1993). *And with a light touch: Learning about reading, writing and teaching with first graders.* Portsmouth, NH: Heinemann.

Avery, C. (1998). Nonfiction books: Naturals for the primary level. In R. A. Bamford & J. V. Kristo (Eds.), *Making facts come alive: Choosing quality nonfiction literature K–8* (pp. 193–203). Norwood, MA: Christopher-Gordon.

Backes, L. (2011, November 19). Why picture books are important. *Picture Book Month.* Available from http://picturebookmonth.com/2011/11/why-picture-books-are-important-by-laura-backes

Bamford, R. A., & Kristo, J. V. (2000). *Checking out nonfiction K–8: Good choices for best learning.* Norwood, MA: Christopher-Gordon.

Bamford, R. A., & Kristo, J, V. (2003). *Making facts come alive: Choosing and using quality nonfiction literature K–8* (2nd ed.). Norwood, MA: Christopher-Gordon.

Bang-Jensen, V. (2010). A children's choice program: Insights into book selection, social relationships, and reader identity. *Language Arts, 87*(3), 169–176.

Barker, J. L. (2010). Racial identification and audience in *Roll of Thunder, Hear My Cry* and *The Watsons Go to Birmingham—1963. Children's Literature in Education, 41,* 118–145.

Barnes, D. (1976). *From communication to curriculum.* New York: Penguin.

Barnes, D. (1992). *From communication to curriculum* (2nd. ed.). Portsmouth, NH: Heinemann.

Barron, T. A. (2012). Why fantasy must be true. *Horn Book, 88*(4), 85–89.

Barton, K., & Levstik, L. (1996). Back when God was around and everything: Elementary children's understanding of historical time. *American Educational Research Journal, 33*(2), 419–454.

Barton, K., McCully, A., & Marks, M. (2004). Reflecting on elementary children's understanding of history and social studies: An inquiry project with beginning teachers in Northern Ireland and the United States. *Journal of Teacher Education, 55*(1), 70–90.

Beck, I. L., & McKeown, M. G. (2001). Text talks: Capturing the benefits of read-aloud experiences with young children. *The Reading Teacher, 55*(1), 10–20.

Beck, I. L., McKeown, M. G., & Kucan, L. (2013). *Bringing words to life: Robust vocabulary instruction*. New York: Guilford.

Benton, M. (1992). Poetry response and education. In P. Hunt (Ed.), *Literature for children: Contemporary criticism* (pp. 127–134). London: Routledge.

Black, R. (2009). English-language learners, fan communities, and 21st century skills. *Journal of Adolescent and Adult Literacy, 52*(8), 688–697.

Black, R. W. (2009). Online fan fiction, global identities, and imagination. *Research in the Teaching of English, 43*(4), 397–425.

Block, C. C., & Parris, S. R. (Eds.). (2008). *Comprehension instruction: Research-based practices*. New York: Guilford.

Block, C. C., & Pressley, M. (Eds.). (2002). *Comprehension instruction: Research-based best practices*. New York: Guilford.

Blos, J. (1992). Perspectives on historical fiction. In R. Ammon & M. Tunnell (Eds.), *The story of ourselves: Teaching history through children's literature* (pp. 11–17), Portsmouth, NH: Heinemann.

Boltz, R. H. (2007). What we want: Boys and girls talk about reading. *School Library Media Research, 10*. Available from http://www.ala.org/aasl/slmr

Boraks, N., Hoffman, A., & Bauer, D. (1997). Children's book preferences, patterns, particulars and possible implications. *Reading Psychology, 18*(4), 309–341.

Botzakis, S. (2009). Graphic novels in education: Cartoons, comprehension, and content knowledge. In D. A. Wooten & B. E. Cullinan (Eds.), *Children's literature in the reading program* (pp. 15– 23). Newark, DE: International Reading Association.

Boushey, G., & Moser, J. (2006). *The daily five*. Portland, ME: Stenhouse.

Boyce, L. B. (2011). Pop into my place: An exploration of the narrative and physical space in Jan Pieńkowki's *Haunted House. Children's Literature in Education, 42*(3), 243–255.

Brabham, E. G., & Villaume, S. K. (2000). Questions and answers: Continuing conversations about literature circles. *The Reading Teacher, 54*(3), 278–280.

Bradshaw, T., & Nichols, B. (2004). *Reading at risk: A survey of literary reading in America*. Washington, DC: National Endowment of the Arts.

Brannen, K. (2007, July 24). Muggle mothers and many others awaited midnight Potter release. *Martha's Vineyard Gazette*, p. 10.

Breen, K., Fader, E., Odean, K., & Sutherland, Z. (2000). One hundred books that shaped the century. *School Library Journal, 46*(1), 50–58.

Britton, J. (1993). *Language and learning* (2nd ed.). London: Penguin.

Brooks, G., Waterman, R., & Allington, R. L. (2003). A national survey of teachers' reports of children's favorite series books. *The Dragon Lode, 21*(2), 8–14.

Brooks, W., & Hampton, G. (2005). Safe discussions rather than first hand encounters: Adolescents examine racism through one historical fiction text. *Children's Literature in Education, 36*(1), 83–98.

Brown, H., & Cambourne, B. (1990). *Read and retell: A strategy for whole language and natural learning classrooms*. Portsmouth, NH: Heinemann.

Brown, J. (2011, February 11). Literacy forum. *New Haven Independent*, para 6 . Available from http://www.newhavenindependent.org/index.php/archives/entry/literacy_forum_learning_in_the_/

Brozo, W. (2002). *To be a boy, to be a reader: Engaging teen and preteen boys in active literacy*. Newark, DE: International Reading Association.

Brozo, W. G. (2010). *To be a boy, to be a reader: Engaging teen and preteen boys in active literacy* (2nd ed.). Newark, DE: International Reading Association.

Bruckerhoff, C. (1977). What do students say about reading instruction? *The Clearing House, 51*(3), 104–107.

Bryan, G., Fawson, P. C., & Reutzel, R. (2003). Sustained silent reading: Exploring the value of literature discussion with three non-engaged readers. *Reading Research and Instruction, 43*(1), 47–73.

Burke, B. (2012, October 20). *A close look at close reading: Scaffolding students with complex texts*. Paper presented at the Anne Arundel County Reading Council Mini Conference. Available from http://juliekozisek.wikispaces.com

Cai, M. (2008). Transactional theory and the study of multicultural literature. *Language Arts, 85*(3), 212–220.

Cambourne, B. (1988). *The whole story: Natural language and the acquisition of literacy in the classroom*. Auckland: Ashton Scholastic.

Cameron, A. (1996). Imagination and language. In A. McClure & J. Kristo (Eds.), *Books that invite talk, wonder, and play with language* (pp. 226–230). Urbana, IL: National Council of Teachers of English.

Cameron, E. (1972, Dec.). McLuhan, youth, and literature: Part II. *Horn Book, 48*. Available from http://archive.hbook.com/magazine/articles/1970s/dec72_cameron.asp

Campbell, J. (1988). *The power of myth*. New York: Doubleday.

Candler, L. (2013, September 19). *Literature circle models*. Available from http://www.lauracandler.com/strategies/litcircles.php

Carr, N. (2010). *The shallows: What the Internet is doing to our brains*. New York: Norton.

Carr, R. L. (1978, March). *Dialect in children's literature: An issue of importance*. Paper presented at the 10th annual meeting of the Illinois Reading Council of the International Reading Association, Charleston, IL.

Carter, B. (2010). Not the Newbery: Books that make readers. *Horn Book, 86*(4), 52–56.

Castek, J., Bevans-Mangelson, J., & Goldstone, B. (2006). Reading adventures online: Five ways to introduce the new literacies of the Internet through children's literature. *The Reading Teacher, 59*(7), 714–728.

Castleman, M. D. (2011). Alcatraz and Iser: Applying Wolfgang Iser's concepts of implied reader and implied author and reality to the metafictive Alcatraz Smedre series. *Children's Literature in Education, 42*, 19–32.

Cavazos-Kottke, S. (2006). Five readers browsing: The reading interests of talented middle school boys. *Gifted Child Quarterly, 50*(2), 132–147.

Chambers, A. (1996). *Tell me: Children, reading and talk*. York, ME: Stenhouse.

Chatton, B. (1988). Apply with caution: Bibliotherapy in the library. *Journal of Youth Services in Libraries, 1*(3), 334–338.

Ching, S. (2005). Multicultural children's literature as an instrument of power. *Language Arts, 83*(2), 128–136.

Christenbury, L., Bomer, R., & Smagorinsky, P. (2009). *Handbook of adolescent literacy research.* New York: Guilford Press.

Clark, C., & Foster, A. (2005). *Children's and young peoples' reading habits and references: Who, what, why, where and when.* London: National Literacy Trust.

Classroom Bookshelf. (2010, December 19). *The Moomin Books.* Available from http://classroombookshelf.blogspot.com/2010/12/moomin-books.html

Clemmons, K., & Sheehy, C. (2011). Science, technology and YA lit. *Science Teacher, 78*(7), 42–45.

Coiro, J., Knobel, M., Lankshear, C., & Leu, D. J. (Eds.). (2008). *Handbook of research on new literacies.* Mahwah, NJ: Lawrence Erlbaum Associates.

Coles, M., & Hall, C. (2002). Gendered readings: Learning from children's choices. *Journal of Research in Reading, 25*(1), 96–108.

Colman, P. (2005, November). *Writing, selecting, and teaching children's literature: A dynamic model.* Paper presented at Presidential Roundtable, Queens College, City University of New York, Flushing.

Colman, P. (2014). *Penny Colman: Q & A.* Available from http://pennycolman.com/readers-resources/q-a

Combs, M. (2009). *Readers and writers in primary grades: A balanced and integrated approach* (4th ed.). Boston: Pearson.

Common Core State Standards. (2010, 2012). National Governors Association Center for Best Practices & Council of Chief State School Officers. Washington, DC: Author. Available from http://www.corestandards.org

Conniff, C. (1993). How young readers perceive reading and themselves as readers. *English In Education, 27*(2), 19–25.

Consumer Culture. (2008). In *Encyclopedia of children and childhood in history and society.* Available from http://www.faqs.org/childhood/Ch-Co/Consumer-Culture.html

Cooper, S. (1996). *Dreams and wishes: Essays on writing for children.* New York: Margaret McElderry Books.

Cox, C. (1991). The media arts and language arts teaching and learning. In J. Flood, J. Jensen, D. Lapp, & D. R. Squire (Eds.), *Handbook of research in teaching the English language arts* (pp. 542–548). New York: Macmillan.

Cox, C., & Boyd-Batstone, P. S. (2009). *Engaging English learners: Exploring literature, developing literacy and differentiating instruction.* Boston: Allyn & Bacon.

Crisp, T., & Hiller, B. (2011). Telling tales about gender: A critical analysis of Caldecott medal-winning picture books, 1938–2011. *Journal of Children's Literature, 37*(2), 18–29.

Cullinan, B. E., & Person, D. G. (Eds.). (2001). *The continuum encyclopedia of children's literature.* New York: Continuum International.

Cunningham, C. A., & Billingsley, M. (2006). *Curriculum webs: Weaving the Web into teaching and learning.* Boston: Pearson.

Cunningham, J. W. (2001). The national reading panel report. *Reading Research Quarterly, 36*(3), 326–335.

Curtis, C. P. (2008). The literary worlds of Bud, Kenny, Luther, and Christopher: Finding books for me. In S. S. Lehr, (Ed.), *Shattering the looking glass: Challenge, risk, and controversy in children's literature* (pp. 155–159). Norwood, MA: Christopher-Gordon.

Curwood, J. (2013). The Hunger Games: Literature, literacy, and online affinity games. *Language Arts, 90*(6), 417–427.

Czarnecki, K. (2009). How digital storytelling builds 21st century skills. *Library Technology Reports,* 15–19.

Daniels, H. (2002). *Literature circles: Voice and choice in book clubs and reading groups.* Portland, ME: Stenhouse.

Daniels, H., & Daniels, E. (2013). The Best-Kept Secret: How Written Conversations Engage Kids, Activate Learning, Grow Fluent readers . . . K-12. CA.: Thousand Oaks. Corwin Press.

Davila, D., & Patrick, L. (2010). Asking the experts: What children have to say about their reading preferences. *Language Arts, 87*(3), 199–210.

Deford, D. (2003). Interactive read-aloud: Supporting and expanding strategies for comprehension. In G. S. Pinnell & P. Scharer (Eds.), *Teaching for comprehension in reading, grades K–2* (pp. 211–224). New York: Scholastic.

DeLawter, J. (1992). Teaching literature: From clerk to explorer. In J. A. Langer (Ed.), *Literature instruction: A focus on student response* (pp. 131–162). Urbana, IL: National Council of Teachers of English.

Dodge, B. (2001). Five rules for writing a great webquest. *Learning and Leading with Technology, 28*(8), 58.

Dole, J. A., Valencia, S. W., Greer, E. A., & Wardrop, J. L. (1991). Effects of two types of prereading instruction on the comprehension of narrative and expository text. *Reading Research Quarterly, 26*(2), 142–159.

Doll, B., & Doll, C. (1997). *Bibliotherapy with young people: Libraries and mental health professionals working together.* Englewood, CO: Libraries Unlimited.

Dorfman, L. R., & Cappelli, R. (2009). *Nonfiction mentor texts: Teaching informational writing through children's literature, K–8.* Portland, ME: Stenhouse.

Doty, D. E., Popplewell, S. R., & Byers, G. O. (2001). Interactive CD-ROM storybooks and young readers' reading comprehension. *Journal of Research on Computing in Education, 33*(4), 374–384.

Draper, S. (2013). *Copper Sun: Intro, summary and general questions.* Available from http://sharondraper.com/bookdetail.asp?id=20

Dresang, E. T. (2008). Radical change theory, postmodernism, and contemporary picturebooks. In L. R. Sipe & S. Pantaleo (Eds.), *Postmodern picturebooks: Play, parody, and self-referentiatlity* (pp. 41–54). New York: Routledge.

Dressel, J. H. (2005). Personal response and social responsibility: Responses of middle school students to multicultural literature. *The Reading Teacher, 58*(8), 750–764.

Dressman, M. (1997). Preference as performance: Doing social class and gender in three school libraries. *Journal of Literacy Research, 2*(3), 319–361.

Duke, N., & Bennett-Armistead, V. S. (2003). *Reading and writing informational text in the primary grades.* New York: Scholastic.

Dutro, E. (2002). Us boys like to read football and boy stuff: Reading masculinities, performing boyhood. *Journal of Literacy Research, 34*(4), 465–500.

Eccles, J. S., & Roeser, R. W. (2011). Schools as developmental contexts during adolescence. *Journal of Research on Adolescence, 21*(1), 225–241.

Edmondson, T., & Shannon, P. (2002). The will of the people. In R. L. Allington (Ed.), *Big brother and the national reading curriculum: How ideology trumped evidence* (pp. 224–231). Portsmouth, NH: Heinemann.

Elleman, B. (2009). Magic deserves a little caution. In A. Silvey (Ed.), *Everything I need to know I learned from a children's book* (p. 105). New York: Roaring Brook Press.

Enciso, P. (1994). Cultural identity and response to literature: Running lessons from Maniac Magee. *Language Arts, 71*(7), 524–533.

Falconer, I. (2003). Author talk. *Kidsread.* Available from http://www.kidsreads.com.asp1-14.dfw1-2.websitetestlink.com/authors/au-falconer-ian.asp

Farris, P., Werderich, D., Nelson, P., & Fuhler, C. (2009). Male call: Fifth grade boys' reading preferences. *The Reading Teacher, 63*(3), 180–188.

Favat, F. A. (1977). *Child and tale: The origins of interest.* Urbana, IL: National Council of Teachers of English.

Fischer, B. (1997) The bottom line. *NEA Today, 16*(4), 9.

Fisher, C. (1994). Sharing poetry in the classroom: Building a concept of poem. In J. Hickman & B. E. Cullinan (Eds.), *Children's literature in the classroom: Weaving Charlotte's web* (pp. 53–65). Norwood, MA: Christopher-Gordon.

Fisher, C. J., & Natarella, M. A. (1982). Young children's preferences in poetry: A national survey of first, second, and third graders. *Research in the Teaching of English, 16*(5), 339–355.

Fisher, D., & Frey, N. (2012). Close reading in elementary schools. *Reading Teacher, 56*(3), 179–188.

Fisher, D., Flood, J., Lapp, D., & Frey, N. (2004). Interactive read-alouds: Is there a common set of implementation practices? *The Reading Teacher, 58*(1), 8–17.

Fletcher, R. J. (2002). *Poetry matters: Writing a poem from the inside out.* New York: Harper.

Ford, D. J. (2002). More than facts: Reviewing science books. *Horn Book Magazine, 78*(3), 265–271.

Fortuny, K., Capps, R., Simms, M., & Chaudry, A. (2009, August). *Children of immigrants: National and state characteristics.* Washington, DC: Urban Institute.

Foster, K. K., Theiss, D., & Buchanan-Butterfield, D. L. (2008). Pourquoi tales on the literacy stage. *The Reading Teacher, 61*(8), 663–667.

Freeman, J. (1995). *More books children will sit still for: A read-aloud guide.* New Providence, NJ: Bowker.

Freeman, M. (1994). Trope densities, analogy clusters, and metaphor types: Metaphors, similes, and analogues in elementary science textbooks and trade books. *Dissertation Abstracts International, 55*(11), 3436A. (University Microfilms No. AAT9434204)

Freeman, M. S. (1997). *Listen to this: Developing an ear for expository.* Gainesville, FL: Maupin House.

Freeman, Y., & Freeman, D. (2004). Connecting students to culturally relevant texts. *Talking Points, 15*(2), 7–11.

Fry, E. (1978). *Fry readability scale.* Provincetown, RI: Jamestown Press.

Fulmer, A. (2012). *Poetry attitude survey for fourth and fifth graders.* Unpublished master's thesis. California State University, San Marcos.

Galda, L., & Beach, R. (2004). Response to literature as a cultural activity. In R. B. Rudell & N. J. Unrau (Eds.), *Theoretical models and processes of reading* (pp. 852–869). Newark, DE: International Reading Association.

Galda, L., Rayburn, J. S., & Stanzi, L. C. (2000). *Looking through the faraway end: Creating a literature-based reading curriculum with second graders.* Newark, DE: International Reading Association.

Gambrell, L. B. (1996). Creating classroom cultures that foster reading motivation. *The Reading Teacher, 50*(1), 14–25.

Garan, E. M., & DeVoogd, G. (2008). The benefits of sustained silent reading: Scientific research and common sense converge. *The Reading Teacher, 62*(4), 336–344.

Gauch, P. L. (1994). A quest for the heart of fantasy. *The New Advocate, 7*(3), 159–167.

Gee, J. P. (2004). *Situated language and learning: A critique of traditional schooling.* New York: Routledge.

Genuard, M. (2005). *Focus on nonfiction literature: Students' reading preferences and teachers' beliefs and practices.* Unpublished master's thesis. Queens College, City University of New York.

Gersten, R., & Geva, E. (2003). Teaching reading to early language learners. *Educational Leadership, 60*(7), 44–49.

Giblin, J. C. (2000). More than just the facts: A hundred years of children's nonfiction. *Horn Book Magazine, 76*(4), 413–424.

Gill, S. R., & Islam, C. (2011). Shared reading goes high-tech. *The Reading Teacher, 65*(3), 224–227.

Giorgis, C. (2010). Character trading cards. *Journal of Children's Literature, 36*(2), 88–89.

Giovanni, N. (2008). Hip hop speaks to children: A celebration of poetry with a beat. (A Poetry Speaks experience). Sourcebooks; Jabberwocky.

Gomez, M. L., Schieble, M. B., Curwood, J. S., & Hassett, D. (2010). Technology, learning, and instruction: Distributed cognition in the secondary English classroom. *Literacy, 44*(1), 20–27.

Goodman, K. (2005). Making sense of written language: A lifelong journey. *Journal of Literacy Research, 37*(1), 1–24.

Greenlee, A. A., Monson, D. L., & Taylor, B. M. (1996). The lure of series books: Does it affect appreciation for recommended literature? *The Reading Teacher, 50*(3), 216–225.

Greenlee, A., Monson, D., & Taylor, B. (1996). The lure of series books: Does it affect appreciation for recommended literature? *The Reading Teacher, 50*(3), 216–224.

Grimes, N. (2000). The power of poetry. *Book Links, 9*(4), 32–36.

Grimshaw, S., Dungworth, N., McKnight, & Morris, A. (2007). Electronic books: Children's reading and comprehension. *British Journal of Educational Technology, 38*(4), 583–599.

Guthrie, J. T., & Anderson, E. (1999). Engagement in reading: Processes of motivated, knowledgeable, social readers. In J. T. Gutherie & D. E. Alverman (Eds.), *Engaged reading* (pp. 17–45). New York: Teachers College Press.

Guthrie, J. T., & Humenick, N. M. (2004). Motivating students to read: Evidence for classroom practices that increase motivation and achievement. In P. McCardle & V. Chhabra (Eds.), *The voice of evidence in reading research* (pp. 329–354). Baltimore: Brookes.

Guthrie, J. T., & Wigfield, A. (Eds.). (1997). *Reading engagement: Motivating readers through integrated instruction*. Newark, DE: International Reading Association.

Hadaway, N. L., & Young, T. A. (2010). *Matching books and readers: Helping English language learners in grades K–6*. New York: Guilford Press.

Hadaway, N. L., Vardell, S. M., & Young, T. A. (2001). Scaffolding oral language development through poetry for students learning English. *The Reading Teacher, 54*(8), 796–806.

Hade, D. D. (2001). Curious George gets branded: Reading as consuming. *Theory into Practice, 40*(3), 158–165.

Hamilton, B. (2009). Poetry goes 2.0. *Library Media Connection, 28*(1), 26–27.

Hamilton, M., & Weiss, M. (2005). *Children tell stories: Teaching and using stoytelling in the classroom*. Katonah, NY: Richard C. Owens.

Hamilton, V. (1988). *In the beginning: Creation stories from around the world*. San Diego, CA: Harcourt.

Hancock, M. R. (2008). The status of reader response research: Sustaining the reader's voice in challenging times. In S.S. Lehr (Ed.), *Shattering the looking glass: Challenge, risk, and controversy in children's literature* (pp. 91-108). Norwood, MA: Christopher-Gordon.

Hansen, J. (1990). Whose story is it? The creative process. *The New Advocate, 3*(3), 167–173.

Harste, J., Short, K., & Burke, C. (1988). *Creating classrooms for authors*. Portsmouth, NH: Heinemann.

Harvey, S. (1998). *Nonfiction matters: Reading, writing and research in grades 3–8*. York, ME: Stenhouse.

Harvey, S., & Goudvis, S. (2007). *Strategies that work: Teaching comprehension for understanding and engagement*. York, ME: Stenhouse.

Hayes, E. R., & Duncan, S. C. (Eds.). (2012). *Learning in video game affinity spaces*. New York: Peter Lang.

Haynes, J. (2010, March 15). *Part 2 reading comprehension strategies for ELLs: Asking questions*. Available from http://everythingesl-everythingesl.blogspot.com/2010/03/part-2-reading-comprehension-strategies.html

Heard, G. (1989). *For the good of the earth and sun: Teaching poetry*. Portsmouth, NH: Heinemann.

Heard, G. (2011). *Georgia Heard on the Common Core* [podcast]. Available from http://www.choiceliteracy.com/public/1708.cfm

Hearne, B. (1999). Swapping tales and stealing stories: The ethics and aesthetics of folklore in children's literature. *Library Trends, 47*(3), 509–528.

Heath, M., Sheen, D., Leavy, D., Young, E., & Money, K. (2005). Bibliotherapy: A resource to facilitate emotional healing and growth. *School Psychology International, 26*, 563–580.

Hentoff, N. (1992). *Free speech for me—but not for thee: How the American left and right relentlessly censor each other*. New York: HarperCollins.

Hepler, S. (1982). *Patterns of response to literature: A one year study of a fifth and sixth grade classroom*. Unpublished doctoral dissertation. Ohio State University, Columbus.

Heyking, A. (2004). Historical thinking in the elementary years: A review of current research. *Canadian Social Studies, 39*(1), 1–9. Available from http://www2.education.ualberta.ca/css/css391arheykinghistoricalthinkingcurrentresearch.html

Hickey, G. (2010). *Personalizing social studies for young children*. Retrieved from http://www.ednebula.com/index.php/earticles/452-earticle-personalizing-social-studies-for-young-children.htm.?tmpl.=com

Hill, B. C., Johnson, N. J., & Noe, K. S. (1995). *Literature circles and response*. Norwood, MA: Christopher-Gordon.

Hill, B. C., Noe, K. L. S., & King, J. A. (2003). *Literature circles in middle school: One teacher's journey*. Norwood, MA: Christopher-Gordon.

Hoffman, J. V., Roser, N. L., & Battle, J. (1993). Reading aloud in classrooms: From the modal to a "model." *The Reading Teacher, 46*(6), 496–503.

Holland, K., Hungerford, R., & Ernst, S. (1993). *Journeying: Children responding to literature*. Portsmouth, NH: Heinemann.

Hunt, J. (2008). Worth a thousand words. *Horn Book, 84*(4), 421–426.

Ingham, R. (1980). *The poetry preferences of fourth and fifth grade students in a suburban school setting in 1980*. Unpublished doctoral dissertation. University of Houston.

International Reading Association. (2007). *Making every moment count: Maximizing quality instructional time*. Available from http://www.reading.org/Libraries/reports-and-standards/MEMC_070620.pdf

Isajlovic-Terry, W., & McKechnie, L. (2012). An exploratory study of children's views of censorship. *Children and Libraries, 10*(1), 38–43.

Iser, W. (1974). The implied reader: Patterns of communication in prose fiction from Bunyan to Beckett. Baltimore, MD: Johns Hopkins University Press.

Jaffe, N. (1996). Reflections on the work of Harold Courlander. *School Library Journal, 42*(9), 132–133.

Johansen, K. V. (2005). *Quests and kingdoms: A grown-up's guide to children's fantasy literature*. New Brunswick, Canada: Sybertooth.

Johnson, D. (2010). Online magazines for children and teens. *Reading and Writing Quarterly, 20*(1), 103–107.

Johnson, D., & Blair, A. (2003). The importance and use of student self-selected literature to reading engagement in an elementary curriculum. *Reading Horizons, 43*(3), 181–202.

Johnston, A., & Frazee, M. (2011). Why we're still in love with picture books (even though they're supposed to be dead). *Horn Book, 87*(3), 10–16.

Jones, T., & Brown, C. (2011). Reading engagement: A comparison between e-books and traditional print books in an elementary classroom. *International Journal of Instruction, 4*(2), 5–22.

Kadohata, C. (2010). Endnote. In *A Million shades of gray*. New York: Atheneum.

Kanarowski, E. (2012*). The influence of bibliotherapy on children's attitudes toward peers who use augmentative and alternative communication*. Unpublished doctoral dissertation, University of Utah, Salt Lake City.

Kasten, W. C., & Lolli, E. M. (1998). *Implementing multi-age education: A practical guide*. Norwood, MA: Christopher-Gordon.

Katz, H., & Sokal, L. (2003). Masculine literacy: One size does not fit all. *Reading Manitoba, 24*(1), 4–8.

Kerper, R. M. (2003). Choosing quality nonfiction literature: Examining aspects of design. In R. A. Bamford & J. V. Kristo (Eds.), *Making facts come alive: Choosing & using nonfiction literature K-8* (pp. 65–78). Norwood, MA: Christopher-Gordon.

Knobel, M., & Lankshear, C. (2008). Remix: The art and craft of endless hybridization. *Journal of Adolescent and Adult Literacy, 52*(1), 22–33.

Kohlberg, L. (1981). *The philosophy of moral development: Moral stages and the idea of justice.* New York: Harper.

Kraemer, L., McCabe, P., & Sinatra, R. (2012). The effects of read-alouds of expository text on first graders' listening, comprehension and book choice. *Literacy Research and Instruction, 51*(2), 165–178.

Krashen, S. D. (1993). The *power of reading: Insights from the research.* Englewood, CO: Libraries Unlimited.

Krashen, S. D. (2006). *The power of reading: Insights from re-search.* Portsmouth, NH: Heinemann.

Kristo, J. V. (1993). Reading aloud in a primary classroom: Reaching and teaching young readers. In K. Holland, R. Hungerford, & S. Ernst (Eds.), *Journeying: Children responding to literature* (pp. 54–69). Portsmouth, NH: Heinemann.

Kristo, J. V., & Bamford, R. A. (2004). *Nonfiction in focus: A comprehensive framework for helping students become independent readers and writers of nonfiction, K–6.* New York: Scholastic.

Kristo, J. V., Colman, P., & Wilson, S. (2008). Bold new perspectives: Issues in selecting and using nonfiction. In S. S. Lehr (Ed.), *Shattering the looking glass: Challenge, risk, and controversy in children's literature* (pp. 339–360). Norwood, MA: Christopher-Gordon.

Krogness, M. (1995). *Just teach me, Mrs. K: Talking, reading and writing with resistant adolescent learners.* Portsmouth, NH: Heinemann.

Kutiper, K., & Wilson, P. (1993). Updating poetry preferences: A look at the poetry children really like. *The Reading Teacher, 47*(1), 28–35.

Labadie, M., Wetzel, M., & Rogers, R. (2012). Opening spaces for critical literacy. *The Reading Teacher, 66*(2), 117–127.

Laminack, L. (2009). *Unwrapping the read aloud: Making every read aloud intentional and instructional.* New York: Scholastic.

Lamme, L. L. (2008). Literature about lesbian, gay, bisexual, and transgender people and their families. In S. S. Lehr (Ed.), *Shattering the looking glass: Challenge, risk, and controversy in children's literature.* Norwood, MA: Christopher-Gordon.

Langer, J. A. (1984). Examining background knowledge and text comprehensive. *Reading Research Quarterly, 19*(4), 468–481.

Lapp, D., & Flood, J. (2003). Exemplary reading instruction in urban elementary schools: How reading develops, how students learn, and how teachers teach. In J. Flood & P. L. Anders (Eds.), *The literacy development of students in urban schools: Research and policy.* Newark, DE: International Reading Association.

Lapp, D., Moss, B., & Rowsill, J. (2012). Envisioning new literacies through a lens of teaching and learning. *The Reading Teacher, 65*(5), 367–377.

Latrobe, K. H., Brodie, C. S., & White, M. (2002). *The children's literature dictionary: Definitions, resources, and learning activities.* New York: Neal-Schuman.

Leal, D. J. (1995). When it comes to informational learning to read. In A. Jagger & M. T. Smith-Burke (Eds.), *Observing the language learner* (pp. 82–98). Newark, DE: International Reading Association.

Lehr, S. (1991). *The child's developing sense of theme: Responses to literature.* New York: Teachers College Press.

Leland, C., & Fitzpatrick, R. (1994). Cross-age interaction builds enthusiasm for reading and writing. *The Reading Teacher, 47*(4), 292–301.

Leland, C., Lewiston, M., & Harste, J. (2012). *Teaching children's literature: It's critical.* New York: Routledge.

Lenz, L. (1992). Crossroads of literacy and orality: Reading poetry aloud. *Language Arts, 69*(8), 597–603.

Lester, J. (2000). Endnote. In *Pharaoh's daughter: A novel of ancient Egypt.* New York: HarperCollins.

Lester, J. (2004). *On writing for children and other people.* New York: Dial.

Leu, D. (2002). Exploring literacy on the Internet. *The Reading Teacher, 55*(5), 466–472.

Levstik, L. (1992). I wanted to be there. In R. Ammon & M. Tunnell (Eds.), *The story of ourselves: Teaching history through children's literature* (pp. 65–76). Portsmouth, NH: Heinemann.

Lewiston, M., Leland, C., & Harste, J. (2007). *Creating critical classrooms: K–8 reading and writing with an edge.* New York: Routledge.

Lockward, D. (1996). Poets on teaching poetry. *English Journal, 83*(5), 65–70.

Lohfenk, G. (2006). *Responses to postmodern picture books: A case study of a fourth grade book club.* Unpublished doctoral dissertation. Kansas State University, Manhattan.

Long, S. (2011). *Supporting students in a time of core standards: English language arts grades preK–2.* Urbana, IL: National Council of Teachers of English.

Long, T. W., & Gove, M. K. (2003). How engagement strategies and literature circles promote critical response in a fourth grade urban classroom. *The Reading Teacher, 57*(4), 350–361.

Louie, B. Y. (2005). Development of empathetic responses with multicultural literature. *Journal of Adolescent and Adult Literacy, 48*(7), 566–578.

Lowry, L. (1994). Newbery acceptance speech. *Horn Book, 66*(4), 412–421.

Lukens, R. J., Smith, J. J., & Coffel, C. M. (2012). *A critical handbook of children's literature* (9th ed.). New York: Longman.

Lynch-Brown, C. (1977). Procedures for determining children's book choices. *Reading Horizons, 17*(4), 243–250.

Many, J. E. (1990). The effect or reader stance on students' personal understanding of literature. In J. Zutell & S. McCormick (Eds.), *Literary theory and research: Analyses from multiple paradigms.* (pp. 51–63). Chicago: National Reading Conference.

Many, J. E., & Anderson, D. D. (1991). The effects of stance and age level on children's literary responses. *Journal of Reading Behavior, 23*(1), 61–85.

March, T. (2007). Revisiting webquests in a web 2 world: How developments in technology and pedagogy combine to scaffold personal learning. *Interactive Educational Multimedia, 15*, 1–17.

Marcus, L. S. (Ed.). (2012). *Show me a story! Why picture books matters.* Somerville, MA: Candlewick.

Martens, P., Martens, R., Doyle, M., Loomis, J., & Aghalarov, S. (2012). Learning from picturebooks: Reading and writing multimodally in first grade. *The Reading Teacher, 66*(4), 285–294.

Martens, R., Martens, P., Croce, K., & Maderazo, C. (2010). Reading illustrations: Helping readers use pictorial text to construct meaning in picture books. In P. Albers & J. Sardars (Eds.), *Literacy, the Arts and Multimodality* (pp. 187–210). Urbana, IL: National Council of Teachers of English.

McCloud, S. (2006). *Making comics: Storytelling secrets of comics, manga and graphic novels.* New York: Morrow.

McClure, A. (1985). *Children's responses to poetry in a supportive literary context.* Unpublished doctoral dissertation. Ohio State University.

McClure, A. (1989). Poetry in the school: Bringing poetry and children together. In J. Hickman & B. E. Cullinan (Eds.), *Children's literature in the classroom: Weaving Charlotte's web.* Norwood, MA: Christopher-Gordon.

McClure, A. (1990). *Second, third, and fourth grade children's understandings of poetry in supportive literary contexts.* Final research report for the Elva Knight Research grants program. Newark, DE: International Reading Association.

McClure, A. (1995). Censorship of children's books. In S. Lehr (Ed.), *Battling dragons: Issues and controversy in children's literature.* Portsmouth, NH: Heinemann.

McClure, A. A. (2003). Choosing quality nonfiction literature: Examining aspects of writing style. In R. A. Bamford & J. V. Kristo (Eds.), *Making facts come alive: Choosing & using nonfiction literature K–8* (pp. 79–96). Norwood, MA: Christopher-Gordon.

McClure, A., Harrison, P., & Reed, S. (1990). *Sunrises and songs: Reading and writing poetry in an elementary classroom.* Portsmouth, NH: Heinemann.

McDowell, K. (2002). *Roll of Thunder, Hear My Cry*: A culturally specific, subversive concept of child agency. *Children's Literature in Education, 33*(3), 213–225.

McElmeel, S. (1996). *Christopher Collier and James Lincoln Collier.* Available from http://www.mcelmeel.com/writing/collier.html

McGillis, R. (2011). Literary studies, cultural studies, children's literature, and the case of Jeff Smith. In S. Wolf, K. Coats, P. Enciso, & C. Jenkins (Eds.), *Handbook of research on children's and young adult literature* (pp. 345–355). New York: Routledge.

McKenna, M., & Kear, D. (1990). Measuring attitude toward reading: A new tool for teachers. *The Reading Teacher, 43*(9), 626–639.

McKeown, M. G., Beck, I. L., Sinatra, G. M., & Loxterman, S. A. (1992). The contribution of prior knowledge and coherent text to comprehension. *Reading Research Quarterly, 27*(1), 78–93.

McLaughlin, M., & Overturf, B. J. (2013). *The common core: Teaching K–5 students to meet the reading standards.* Newark, DE: International Reading Association.

Meyer, B. J. F., & Freedle, R. O. (1984). Effects of discourse type on recall. *American Educational Research Journal, 21*(1), 121–143.

Miller, D. (2009). *The book whisperer: Awakening the inner reader in every child.* San Francisco: Jossey-Bass.

Miller, D. (2012). *Guess my lexile.* Available from http://blogs.edweek.org/teachers/bookwhisperer

Miller, L. (2008). *The magician's book: A skeptic's adventures in Narnia.* New York: Little, Brown.

Mills, H., & Jennings, L. (2011). Talking about talk: Reclaiming the value and power of literature circles. *The Reading Teacher, 64*(8), 590–598.

Mohr, K. (2006). Children's choices for recreational reading: A three-part investigation of selection preferences, rationales and processes. *Journal of Literacy Behavior, 38*(1), 81–104.

Moline, S. (2011). *I see what you mean: Visual literacy K–8.* Portland, ME: Stenhouse.

Möller, K. J., & Allen, J. (2000). Connecting, resisting and searching for safer places: Students respond to Mildred Taylor's *The Friendship. Journal of Literacy Research, 32*(2), 145–186.

Monson, D. L., & Sebesta, S. (1991). Reading preferences. In J. Flood, J. M. Jensen, D. Lapp, & J. R. Squire (Eds.), *Handbook of research on teaching the English language arts* (pp. 664–673). New York: Macmillan.

Morrow, L. M., & Gambrell, L. B. (2002). Literature-based instruction in the early years. In S. B. Neuman & D. K. Dickinson (Eds.), *Handbook of early literary research* (pp. 348–360). New York: Guilford.

Morrow, L. M., & Weinstein, C. S. (1986). Encouraging voluntary reading: The impact of a literature program on children's use of library centers. *Reading Research Quarterly, 21*(3), 330–346.

Multi-Cultural Bibliography Resource. (2010, November). Anti-Defamation League *No Place for Hate*® *Newsletter.* Available from http://www.austinschools.org/campus/small/counselors/docs/November%20No%20Place%20for%20Hate%202010%20newsletter.pdf

National Council of Teachers of English. (2008). Using comics and graphic novels in the classroom. *Council Chronicle*, September 2005. Available from http://www.ncte.org/magazine/archives/122031

National Education Association. (2012). *National Teacher of the Year: Great teachers lead with both their heads and their hearts.* Available from http://www.nea.org/home/52486.htm

National Governors Association Center for Best Practices & Council of Chief State School Officers. (2010). *Common Core State Standards.* Washington, DC: Author. Available from http://www.corestandards.org

National Institute of Child Health and Human Development. (2000). *Report of the National Reading Panel. Teaching Children to Read: An Evidence-Based Assessment of the Scientific Research Literature on Reading and Its Complications for Reading Instruction* (NIH Publication No. 00-4769). Washington, DC: U.S. Government Printing Office.

Newkirk, T. (2002). *Misreading masculinity: Boys, literacy, and pop culture.* Portsmouth, NH: Heinemann.

Newkirk, T. (2012). *The art of slow reading: Six time-honored practices for engagement.* Portsmouth, NH: Heinemann.

Norton, D. E., & Norton, S. (2010). *Through the eyes of a child: An introduction to children's literature* (8th ed.), Boston: Pearson.

November, A. (1998). Teaching Zack to think. *November Learning*. Available from http://novemberlearning.com/resources/archive-of-articles/teaching-zack-to-think

Nystrand, M. (2006). Research on the role of classroom discourse as it affects reading comprehension. *Research in the Teaching of English, 40*(4), 392–412.

O'Connor, B. (2010). Keeping it real: How realistic does realistic fiction for children need to be? *Language Arts, 87*(6), 465–471.

O'Keefe, D. (2004). Battlefield worlds: Fighting tyranny and chaos. In D. O'Keefe (Ed.), *Readers in wonderland: The liberating worlds of fantasy fiction* (pp. 166–206). New York: Continuum.

Ogrenir, B. (2013). *Teacher's adequacy in applications of bibliotherapy in classrooms.* International Academic Conference Proceedings, January 14–16, 2013, Antalya, Turkey, 40–41.

Opitz, M., & Zbaracki, M. (2004). *Listen hear! 25 effective comprehension strategies.* Portsmouth, NH: Heinemann.

Owocki, G. (2012). *The Common Core lesson plan book: K–5.* Portsmouth, NH: Heinemann.

Parkes, B. (2000). *Read it again! Revisiting shared reading.* Portland, ME: Stenhouse.

Parkinson, S. (2011). Flying kites and chasing white rabbits: Children's literature in functional times. *Horn Book, 87*(5), 52.

Partnership for 21st Century Skills. (2013). Available from http://www.p21.org

Paterson, K. (2001). *The invisible child: On reading and writing books for children.* New York: Dutton.

Paterson, K. (2005). Why historical fiction? *Vermont History, 73,* 5–15.

Paulsen, G. (2001). *Guts: The true stories behind* Hatchet *and the Brian books.* New York: Delacorte.

Perfect, K. A. (1999). Rhyme and reason: Poetry for the heart and head. *The Reading Teacher, 52*(7), 728–737.

Peterson, R., & Eeds, M. (2007). *Grand conversations: Literature groups in action.* New York: Scholastic.

Piaget, J. (1969). *The psychology of the child.* Translated from the French by Helen Weaver. New York: Basic Books.

Pierce, K. M. (1999). I am a level 3 reader: Children's perceptions of themselves as readers. *New Advocate, 12*(4), 359–375.

Pierce, T. (1996). Fantasy. Why kids read it: Why kids need it. In S. Egoff, G. Stubbs, R. Ashley, & W. Sutton (Eds.), *Only connect: Readings on children's literature* (pp. 179–181). Ontario: Oxford University Press.

Pinnell, G. S., & Jagger, A. (2003). Oral language: Speaking and listening in elementary classrooms. In J. Flood, D. Lapp, J. Squire, & J. Jensen (Eds.), *Handbook of research on teaching the English language arts* (2nd ed., pp. 881–913). Mahwah, NJ: Lawrence Erlbaum Associates.

Porter-O'Donnell, C. (2004). Beyond the yellow highlighter: Teaching annotation skills to improve reading comprehension. *English Journal, 93*(5), 82–89.

Prensky, M. (2001). Digital natives, digital immigrants. *On the Horizon, 9*(5). Available from http://www.marcprensky.com/writing

Prior, L. A., Willson, A., & Martinez, M. (2012). Picture this: Visual literacy as a pathway to character understanding. *The Reading Teacher, 66*(3), 195–206.

Pullman, P. (1998, October 1). The darkside of Narnia. *The Guardian,* p. 6.

Quindlen, A. (1991, August 7). Public and private: Enough bookshelves. *New York Times.* Available from http://www.nytimes.com/1991/08/07/opinion/public-private-enough-bookshelves.html

Rasco, C. (2011). Why picture books are important. *Picture Book Month.* Available from http://picturebookmonth.com/2011/11/why-picture-books-are-important-by-carol-rasco

Rasinski, T. V. (2003). *The fluent reader: Oral reading strategies for building word recognition, fluency, and comprehension.* New York: Scholastic.

Reese, D. (2007). Proceed with caution: Using Native American folktales in the classroom. *Language Arts, 84*(3), 245–255.

Reis, S. M., McCoach, D. B., Coyne, M., Schreiber, F. J., Eckert, R. D., & Gubbins, E. J. (2007). Using planned enrichment strategies with direct instruction to improve reading fluency, comprehension, and attitude toward reading: An evidence-based study. *Elementary School Journal, 108*(1), 3–23.

Reutzel, R., Jones, C., Fawson, P., & Smith, J. (2008). Scaffolded silent reading: A complement to guided repeated oral reading that works. *The Reading Teacher, 62*(3), 194–207.

Rich, M. (2008, February 19). In books for young, two views on product placement. *New York Times,* p. E1.

Richards, J. C., & Anderson, N. A. (2003). What do I see? What do I think? What do I wonder? (STW): A visual literacy strategy to help emergent readers focus on storybook illustrations. *The Reading Teacher, 56*(5), 442–444.

Richardson, W. (2010). *Blogs, wikis, and podcasts: Powerful web tools for classrooms.* Thousand Oaks, CA: Corwin.

Richtel, M., & Bosman, J. (2011, November 20). For their children, many e-book fans insist on paper. *New York Times.* Available from http://www.nytimes.com/2011/11/21/business/for-their-children-many-e-book-readers-insist-on-paper.html?_r=1

Ricker-Wilson, C. (1998). When the mockingbird becomes an albatross: Reading and resistance in the language arts classroom. *The English Journal, 87*(3), 67–72.

Robb, L. (2000). *Teaching reading in middle school: A strategic approach to teaching reading that improves comprehension and thinking.* New York: Scholastic.

Robb, L. (2004). *Nonfiction writing from the inside out: Writing lessons inspired by conversations with leading authors.* New York: Scholastic.

Robertson, C., Keating, I., Shenton, L., & Roberts, I. (1996). Uninterrupted sustained silent reading: The rhetoric and the practice. *Journal of Research in Reading, 19*(1), 25–35.

Rosenberg, D. (1997). *Folklore, myths and legends: A world perspective.* Lincolnwood, IL: NCT Publishing Group.

Rosenblatt, L. (1995). *Literature as exploration.* New York: Modern Language Association.

Roser, N. (2010). Policy can follow practices. *Language Arts, 87*(3), 211–214.

Roser, N., Martinez, M., Fuhrken, C., & McDonnold, K. (2007). Characters as guides to meaning. *The Reading Teacher, 60*(6), 548–559.

Rubin, C. M. (2011, November 29). How will we read: Children's books? *Huffington Post.* Available from http://www.huffingtonpost.com/c-m-rubin/how-will-we-read-children_b_1116543.html

Rycik, M., & Rosier, B. (2009). The return of historical fiction. *The Reading Teacher, 63*(2), 163–166.

Sailors, M. (2009). Improving comprehension instruction through quality professional development. In S. E. Israel & G. G. Duffy (Eds.), *Handbook of research on reading comprehension* (pp. 645–657). New York: Routledge.

Sanden, S. (2012). Independent reading: Perspectives and practices of highly successful teachers. *The Reading Teacher, 66*(3), 222–231.

Santoro, L. E., Chard, D. C., Howard, L., & Baber, S. K. (2008). Making the very most of read-alouds to promote comprehension and vocabulary. *The Reading Teacher, 61*(5), 396–408.

Scales, P. (2011). Talking with Phyllis Reynolds Naylor. *Book Links, 20*(4), 15.

Schatz, A., Pierce, K., Ghalambor, K., & Krashen, S. (2008). More on the "literacy crisis": Do children like to read? *Knowledge Quest, 37,* 70–71.

Schlenther, E. (1999). Using reading therapy with children. *Health Libraries Review, 16,* 29–37.

Schlick Noe, K., & Johnson, N. (1999). *Getting started with literature circles.* Norwood, MA: Christopher-Gordon.

Schmidt, G. (1991). The story as teller: An interview with Madeleine L'Engle. *ALAN Review, 18*(2), 10–14.

Schneider, D. (2011). What makes a good sports novel? *Horn Book, 87,* 69–72.

Scholastic. (2008). *2008 Scholastic kids and family reading report.* Available from http://www.scholastic.com/aboutscholastic/news/readingreport.htm

Schooley, F. A. (1994). *Within class ability grouping and its effect on third grade attitudes toward reading.* (ERIC Document Clearinghouse, ED 371–345)

Scieszka, J. (1998, March/April). Design matters. *Horn Book, 74*(2). Available from http://archive.hbook.com/magazine/articles/1998/mar98_scieszka_leach.asp

Sewall, G. (2000). *History textbooks at the new century: A report of the American Textbook Council.* New York: American Textbook Council. (ERIC Document Reproduction Service No ED 441 731)

Shapiro, J., & White, W. (1991). Reading attitudes and perceptions in traditional and nontraditional reading programs. *Reading Research and Instruction, 30*(4), 52–66.

Shaw, M. L. (2006). Sustained silent reading: Another view. *Reading Today, 24*(1), 16.

Short, K. G., Harste, J. C., & Burke, C. (1996). *Creating classrooms for authors and inquirers.* Portsmouth, NH: Heinemann.

Short, K., Harste, J. & Burke, C. (1996). *Creating classrooms for authors and inquirers* (2nd ed.). Portsmouth, NH: Heinemann.

Short, K., Kaufman, G., & Kahn, L. (2000). I just need to draw: Responding to literature across multiple sign systems. *The Reading Teacher, 54*(2), 160–171.

Shulevitz, U. (2004). Children's books: Personal observations and memories of how things were and how they are now. In L. M. Pavonietti (Ed.), *Children's literature remembered: Issues, trends and favorite books* (pp. 21–25). Westport, CT: Libraries Unlimited.

Sibberson, F., & Szymusiak, K. (2003). *Still learning to read: Teaching students in grades 3–6.* Portland, ME: Stenhouse.

Siemens, L. (1996). "Walking through the time of kids": Going places with poetry. *Language Arts, 73*(4), 234–240.

Silvey, A. (2004). *100 Best books for children.* Madison, WI: Demco.

Singleton, E. (2006). *The Girls of Central High*: How a progressive era book series for girls furthered the cause of female interschool sport. *Children's Literature in Education, 37*(3), 211–227.

Sipe, L. R. (1996). *The construction of literacy understanding by first and second graders on response to picture storybook read-alouds.* Unpublished doctoral dissertation. Ohio State University, Columbus.

Sipe, L. R. (1997). In their own words: Authors' view on issues in historical fiction. *The New Advocate, 10*(3), 243–255.

Sipe, L. R. (1999). Children's response to literature: Author, text, reader, context. *Theory into Practice, 38,* 120–129.

Sipe, L. R. (2000). The construction of literary understanding by first and second graders in oral response to picture storybook read-alouds. *Reading Research Quarterly, 35*(2), 252–275.

Sipe, L. R. (2002). Talking back and taking over: Young children's expressive engagement during storybook read-alouds. *The Reading Teacher, 55*(5), 476–483.

Sipe, L. R. (2008). *Storytime: Young children's literary understanding in the classroom.* New York: Teachers College Press.

Sipe, L. R., & Pantaleo, S. (2008). *Postmodern picturebooks: Play, parody, and self-referentiality.* New York: Routledge.

Slavin, R., Lake, C., Cheung, A., & Davis, S. (2009). *Beyond the basics: Effective reading programs for the upper elementary grades.* Baltimore: Center for Data-Driven Reform in Education.

Sloan, G. D. (2003). *Give them poetry: A guide for sharing poetry with children, K–8.* New York: Teachers College Press.

Smith, A. (2006). Paddington Bear: A case study of immigration and otherness. *Children's Literature in Education, 37*(1), 35–50.

Smith, A., & Westberg, K. (2011). Student attitudes toward *Accelerated Reader*: "Thanks for asking." *Current Issues in Education, 14*(2), 1–6.

Smith, C. L. (2006). *Book to avoid: My heart is on the ground.* Available from http://www.cynthialeitchsmith.com

Smith, M. W., & Wilhelm, J. D. (2002). *Reading don't fix no Chevys: Literacy in the lives of young men.* Portsmouth, NH: Heinemann.

Soalt, J. (2005). Bringing together fictional and informational texts to improve comprehension. *The Reading Teacher, 58*(7), 680–683.

Stahl, K. A. D. (2004). Proof, practice and promise: Comprehension strategy instruction in the primary grades. *The Reading Teacher, 57*(7), 598–609.

Stead, T. (2002). *Is that a fact? Teaching nonfiction writing K–3.* Portland, ME: Stenhouse.

Stevens, K. C. (1982). Can we improve reading by teaching background information? *Journal of Reading, 25*(4), 326–329.

Stotsky, S., & Wurman, Z. (2010). *Common Core's Standards still don't make the grade: Why Massachusetts and California must regain control over their academic destinies.* Boston: Pioneer Institute.

Strauss, V. (2013, April 17). Eighth grader designs standardized test that slams standardized tests. *Washington Post.* Available from http://www.washingtonpost.com/blogs/answer-sheet/wp/2013/04/17/eighth-grader-designs-standardized-test-that-slams-standardized-tests

Strickland, D. S., & Morrow, L. M. (1991). Making home-school connections: Using the *Sesame Street Magazine* and *Parents' Guide* with kindergarten children and their parents. *The Reading Teacher, 44*(7), 510–512.

Strickland, D., Walmsley, S., Bronk, G. T., & Weiss, K. (Eds.). (1994). *School book clubs and literacy development: A descriptive study* (Report 2.22). Albany, NY: National Research Center on Literature Teaching and Learning.

Strommen, L. T., & Mates, B. F. (2004). Learning to love reading: Interviews with older children and teens. *Journal of Adolescent and Adult Literacy, 48*(3), 188–200.

Sturm, B. (2003). *The information and reading preferences of North Carolina children.* American Library Association. Available from http://www.ala.org/a/a/mgrps/divs/aas/pubsandjournals/slmrb/slmrcontents/volumbe6

Summers, E. G., & Lukasevich, A. (1983). Reading preferences of intermediate-grade children in relation to sex, community and maturation (grade level): A Canadian perspective. *Reading Research Quarterly, 18*(3), 347–360.

Sutcliff, R. (1973). History is people. In V. Haviland (Ed.), *Children and literature: Views and reviews* (pp. 305–312). Glenview, IL: Scott Foresman.

Sutton, R. (2007). An interview with Jon Scieszka. *Hornbook, 83*(5), 445.

Sutton, R. (2013, June 20). Editorial: Common Core ready? *Horn Book.* Available from http://www.hbook.com/2013/06/choosing-books/horn-book-magazine/editorial-common-core-ready

Sweet, A. P., Guthrie, J. T., & Ng, M. M. (1998). Teacher perceptions and student reading motivation. *Journal of Educational Psychology, 90,* 210–223.

Szymusiak, K., & Sibberson, F. (2001). *Beyond leveled books: Supporting transitional readers in grades 2–5.* Portland, ME: Stenhouse.

Szymusiak, K., Sibberson, F., & Koch, L. (2008). *Beyond leveled books: Supporting early and transitional readers in grades K–5.* Portland, ME: Stenhouse.

Taberski, S. (2011). *Comprehension from the ground up: Simplified, sensible instruction for the K–3 reading workshop.* Portsmouth, NH: Heinemann.

Tan, S. (n.d.). *Picture books.* Available from http://www.shauntan.net/books.html

Tatar, M. (2003). *The hard facts of the Grimms' fairy tales.* Princeton, NJ: Princeton University Press.

Tatum, A. (2005). *Teaching reading to black adolescent males: Closing the achievement gap.* Portland, ME: Stenhouse.

Tatum, A. (2009). *Reading for their life: (Re) building the textual lineages of African American adolescent males.* Portsmouth, NH: Heinemann.

Taxel, J. (1983). The American Revolution in children's fiction. *Research in the Teaching of English, 17*(1), 61–83.

Terlecky, K. (2013). *The power of read aloud notebooks.* Available from https://www.choiceliteracy.com

Terry, A. (1974). *Children's poetry preferences: A national survey of upper elementary grades.* Urbana, IL: National Council of Teachers of English.

Thames, D. G., & Reeves, C. K. (1994). Poor readers' attitudes: Effects of using interests and tradebooks in an integrated language arts approach. *Reading Research and Instruction, 33*(4), 293–308.

Thames, D., Reeves, C., Kazelskis, R., York, K., Boling, C., Newell, K., et al. (2008). Reading comprehension: Effects of individualized, integrated language arts as a reading approach with struggling readers. *Reading Psychology, 29*(1), 86–115.

Tienken, C. H. (2011, Winter). Common Core Standards: The emperor has no clothes, or evidence. *Kappa Delta Pi Record,* 58–62.

Tolan, S. (1989). Happily ever after. *The New Advocate, 2*(1), 9–14.

Tomlinson, C., Tunnell, M., & Richgels, D. (1992). The content and writing of history in textbooks. In R. Ammon & M. Tunnell (Eds.), The *story of ourselves: Teaching history through children's literature* (pp. 51–64). Portsmouth, NH: Heinemann.

Tompkins, G. E. (2005). *Language arts: Content and teaching strategies* (6th ed.). Upper Saddle River, NJ: Merrill/Prentice Hall.

Tovani, C. (2004). *Do I really have to teach reading?* Portland, ME: Stenhouse.

Trelease, J. (2013). *The read aloud handbook.* New York: Penguin.

Trites, R. S. (2007). *Twain, Alcott, and the birth of the adolescent reform novel.* Iowa City: University of Iowa Press.

Tunnell, M. (2000). Endnote. In *Mailing May* (Ted Rand, Illus.). New York: Greenwillow.

Tunnell, M. O., Calder, J. E. & Phaup, E. S. (1991). Attitudes of young readers. *Reading Improvement, 28*(4), 237–243.

Ujiie, J., & Krashen, S. (2002). Homerun books and reading enjoyment. *Knowledge Quest, 31*(3), 36–37.

University of Pittsburgh Institute for Learning. (2011). *Designing open-ended, text-based questions using the patterned way of reading, writing and talking.* Available from http://juliekozisek.wikispaces.com

Van Meter, P. N., & Firetto, C. (2008). Intertextuality and the study of new literacies. In J. Coiro, M. Knobel, C. Lasnkshear, & D. J. Leu (Eds.), *Handbook of research on new literacies* (pp. 1079–1092). New York: Lawrence Erlbaum Associates.

Vardell, S. (2011). *A circus for the brain: The 2011 children's poet laureate speaks.* Available from http://www.poetryfoundation.org/article/242020

Vardell, S., Hadaway, N., & Young, T. (2006). Matching books and readers: Selecting literature for English learners. *The Reading Teacher, 59*(8), 734–741.

Vaughn, S., & Linan-Thompson, S. (2004). *Research-based methods of reading instruction: K–3.* Alexandria, VA: Association for Supervision and Curriculum Development.

Walsh, C. (2006). Beyond the workshop: Doing multiliteracies with adolescents. *English in Australia, 41*(3), 49–57.

Walsh, J. P. (1972). History is fiction. *Horn Book, 48,* 16–23.

Ward, B., & Day, D. (2010). A dozen great books: Blurring genre. *Language Arts, 36*(1), 63–66.

Ward, D. (2010). Unlikely heroes and the lure of fantasy: An author's perspective. *Dragon Lode, 28*(2), 46–54.

Welty, E. (1952, October 19). Life in the barn was very good. *New York Times Book Review,* 49.

Werderich, D. (2006). The teacher's response process in dialogue journals. *Reading Horizons, 47*(1), 47–74.

What Works Clearinghouse. (2010, August). Washington, DC: U.S. Department of Education, Institute of Education Sciences.

Whitin, P. (1996). Exploring visual responses to literature. *Research in the Teaching of English, 30*(1), 114–140.

Whitin, P. (2005). The interplay of text, talk and visual representation in expanding literacy interpretation. *Research in the Teaching of English, 39*(4), 365–397.

Wilhelm, J. (2001). *Improving comprehension with think-aloud strategies.* New York: Scholastic.

Wilhelm, J. D. (2012). Proactivity vs reactivity: Preparing students for success with CCSS. *Voices in the Middle, 20*(1), 68–72.

Williams, M. (2009). *Use anchor charts for English language learners.* Available from http://suite101.com/a/use/-anchor-charts-for-english-language-learners-a121105

Wilson, M., & Newkirk, T. (2011, December 14). Can readers really stay within the standards lines? *Education Week,* 28–29.

Wilson, S. L. (2006). Getting down to facts in children's nonfiction literature: A case for the importance of sources. *Journal of Children's Literature, 32*(1), 56–64.

Wolf, S. (2004). *Interpreting literature with children.* Mahwah, NJ: Lawrence Erlbaum Associates.

Wolf, S. (2004). Using picture books to teach for democracy. *Language Arts, 82*(1), 26–35.

Wooten, D. A., & Cullinan, B. (Eds.). (2009). *Children's literature in the reading program: An invitation to read.* Newark, DE: International Reading Association.

Worthy, J., & Broadus, K. (2002). Fluency beyond the primary grades: From group performance to silent, independent reading. *The Reading Teacher, 55*(4), 334–343.

Worthy, J., Moorman, M., & Turner, M. (1999). What Johnny likes to read is hard to learn in school. *Reading Research Quarterly, 34*(1), 12–27.

Yokota, J. (2013). From print to digital? Considering the future of picturebooks for children. In G. Grilli (Ed.), *Bologna: Fifty years of children's books from around the world.* Bologna: Bononia University Press.

Yokota, J., & Teale, W. (2005). Bringing the best of characters into primary classrooms. In N. L. Roser & M. L. Martinez (Eds.), *What a character! Character study as a guide to literary meaning in grades K–8* (pp. 154–167). Newark, DE: International Reading Association.

Yopp, R. H., & Yopp, H. K. (2001). *Literature based reading activities* (3rd ed.). Boston: Allyn & Bacon.

Young, T. A., & Ferguson, P. M. (1995). From Anansi to Zumo: Trickster tales in the classroom. *The Reading Teacher, 48*(6), 490–503.

Youngs, S. (2012). Understanding history through the visual images in historical fiction. *Language Arts, 89*(6), 379–395.

Youngs, S., & Serafini, F. (2011). Comprehension strategies for reading historical fiction picture books. *The Reading Teacher, 65*(2), 115–124.

Zambo, D. (2007). Using picture books to provide archetypes to young boys: Extending the ideas of William Brozo. *The Reading Teacher, 61*(2), 124–131.

Zambo, D., & Brozo, W. G. (2009). *Bright beginnings for boys: Engaging young boys in active literacy.* Newark, DE: International Reading Association.

Zarnowski, M. (2006). *Making sense of history: Using high-quality literature and hands-on experiences to build content knowledge.* New York: Scholastic.

Zinsser, W. (Ed.). (1998). *Worlds of childhood: The art and craft of writing for children.* New York: Houghton.

Index

Aardema, Verna, 178
ABC3D (Bataille), 125
About Insects (Sill), 333
Absolutely Awful Alphabet Book, The (Gerstein), 123
access features, nonfiction, 325–326
accuracy, nonfiction, 320, 324
Across Five Aprils (Hunt), 255
acrostic poetry, 143, 144–146
activity books, 336–337
Ada, Alma Flor, 192, 197
Adler, David A., 330
adventures
   contemporary realistic fiction, 289–290, 311–312
   fantasy fiction, 222–223, 243
   fiction themes, 16
Adventures of Huckleberry Finn, The (Twain), 5, 101, 102
Adventurous Women: Eight True Stories About Women Who Made a Difference (Colman), 331
Aesop, 185–186
Aesop and Company (Bader), 186
Aesop Prize, 358
Aesop's Fables, 186
Aesop's Fables: A Pop-Up Book of Classic Tales (Moerbeek), 186
aesthetic response, 49–50, 51, 53
Africa Is My Home: A Story of the Amistad (Edinger), 254
African Americans. *See also* civil rights movement; Civil War; cultural diversity; *Roll of Thunder, Hear My Cry* (Taylor)
   ballads and folk songs, 192–193
   book selection, 36
   fantasy and science fiction, 220, 234
   historical fiction, 248, 253, 255, 256, 259, 268, 270
   picture books, 121, 304
   poetry, 152, 155, 161, 163–164, 173
   traditional literature, 178, 180, 183, 184, 190, 191
After Tupac and D. Foster (Woodson), 287
Ain't Nothing but A Man: My Quest to Find the Real John Henry (Nelson), 190
A Is for Art: An Abstract Alphabet (Johnson), 333
Ajeemah and His Son (Berry), 254
Alabama Moon (Key), 290
Al Capone Does My Homework (Choldenko), 257
Al Capone Does My Shirts (Choldenko), 257
Al Capone Shines My Shoes (Choldenko), 257

Alcatraz Versus the Evil Librarians (Sanderson), 10
Alcatraz Versus the Shattered Lens (Sanderson), 10
Alcott, Louisa May, 101
Alexander, Lloyd, 213, 225
Alexander, Who's Not (Do You Hear Me? I Mean It!) Going to Move (Viorst), 118
Alexander, Who Used to be Rich Last Sunday (Viorst), 118
Alexander and the Terrible, Horrible, No Good, Very Bad Day (Viorst), 118
Alice (Naylor), 9
Alice's Adventures in Wonderland (Carroll), 221
Alice's Adventures in Wonderland: A Pop-Up Adaptation (Sabuda), 221
All About Manatees (Arnosky), 335
All Alone in the Universe (Perkins), 287
All by Herself: 14 Girls Who Made a Difference (Paul), 149
alliteration, 142, 284–285
All Night, All Day: A Child's First Book of Spirituals (Bryan), 192
All the Small Poems (Worth), 157, 158
All the World (Frazee), 112, 296
Almost Forever (Testa), 261
Almost Home (Bauer), 281, 288
alphabet books, 123, 333
alternative worlds, fantasy fiction, 221, 243
Amazing Life of Benjamin Franklin, The (Giblin), 329
Amber Spyglass, The (Pullman), 226
Amber Was Brave, Essie Was Smart (Williams), 302
Amelia Bedelia (Parish), 40, 124
American Adventures series, 263
American Diaries series, 263
American Girl series, 263
American Indian Youth Award, 358
American history
   book lists, 266, 272–278
   civil rights movement, 259–261, 266, 275, 277–278, 337
   Civil War, 254–255, 272–273
   colonial times (1600–1800), 253, 266, 272, 276
   Great Depression, 130, 257, 266, 274, 277
   industrialization, immigration, segregation, 255–256, 273–274, 277
   Vietnam War, 259–261, 275, 278
   westward expansion (1800s), 254, 276
   World War II (1940s), 258–259, 266, 274–275, 277, 331

American Library Association, 161, 294
American Revolution, 253, 266, 272, 276
American Tall Tales (Osborne), 190
American Verse Project, 162
America's Favorite Poem Project, 161
Am I Naturally This Crazy? (Holbrook), 149
Among the Hidden (Haddix), 227
Anahita's Woven Riddle (Sayres), 256
Anansi the Spider (McDermott), 177
Anastasia Krupnik (Lowry), 288
ancient civilization, 251–252, 272, 276
Ancona, George, 335
Andersen, Hans Christian, 183, 216
Anderson, Laurie Halse, 246
Andre Norton Award for YA Science Fiction & Fantasy, 358
And Tango Makes Three (Richardson & Parnell), 102
And Then What Happened, Paul Revere? (Fritz), 330
Animal Crackers: A Delectable Collection of Pictures, Poems, and Lullabies for the Very Young (Dyer), 156
Animal Fair (Browne), 193
Animal Poems of the Iguazu (Alarcon), 151
animals
   book lists, 242–243
   fantasy fiction, 216–217
   poetry about, 150, 173–174
   realistic fiction, 289, 309, 311
Animal Sense (Ackerman), 151
Animals on the Trail with Lewis and Clark (Patent), 325
Anne Frank: The Anne Frank Authorized Graphic Biography (Jacobson & Colón), 337
Annie on My Mind (Garden), 294
annotation, as instructional strategy, 73, 74, 91
antagonist, 12
Ant and the Grasshopper, The (Poole), 186
anthologies, poems, 154–156
anthropomorphism, 324
Anybody Home? (Fisher), 149
Anything but Typical (Baskin), 293–294
Appalachia: The Voices of Sleeping Birds (Rylant), 324
Applegate, Katherine, 218
apps for writing, 235
Arabian Nights, The, 251
Are We There Yet? (Lester), 299
Are You Afraid Yet? The Science Behind Scary Stuff (O'Meara), 317
Are You There God? It's Me, Margaret (Blume), 282, 286

Aristotle and Dante Discover the Secrets of the Universe (Saenz), 294
Around the World (Phelan), 256
Arrival, The (Tan), 110
Arroraró mi Niño: Latino Lullabies and Gentle Games (Delacre), 192
Arrow and the Lamp: The Story of Psyche, The (Hodges), 187
Arrow Finds Its Mark, The (Heard), 167
art
    evaluating fiction, 18
    historical fiction, 267–268
    media used, list of, 116–117
    nonfiction texts, 325–326
    in picture books, 111–115
    reader responses, 61–62, 86
    traditional literature analysis, 198
Arthur (MacLachlan), 288
Arthur series (Brown), 27
artistic style, picture books, 114–115
Artist to Artist: 23 Major Illustrators Talk to Children About Their Craft (Eric Carle Museum of Picture Book Art), 332
Art Lesson, The (dePaola), 113
Art of Keeping Cool, The (Lisle), 258
Ashley Bryan: Words to My Life's Song (Bryan), 326
Asian Americans. *See also* cultural diversity
    contemporary realistic fiction, 289, 292
    fantasy and science fiction, 216, 233, 234
    historical fiction, 253, 256, 258–259, 262, 266, 267
    nonfiction, 331
    picture books, 132, 262, 304
    poetry, 145, 163, 164
    traditional literature, 189, 198, 200–201, 207
Ask Dr. K. Fisher About Reptiles (Llewellyn), 326–327
assonance, 142
Asteroid Impact (Henderson), 325
As the Green Grass Grows All Around (Schwartz), 193
Atalanta (Fontes), 187
Atalanta's Race: A Greek Myth (Climo), 187
attitudes about reading, 5–6
Audacity, 161
Aurora County All Stars, The (Wiles), 292
Aurora Means Dawn (Saunders), 245
authenticity, traditional literature, 181–182, 203–204
autism, people with, 293–294, 313
autobiographies, 331–332
Autumnblings (Florian), 148
Autumn Street (Lowry), 258
Avi, 14, 252, 253
awards for children's literature, 19, 358–362
Aydin, Andrew, 337

Babe Didrikson Zaharias: The Making of a Champion (Freedman), 331
Babe the Gallant Pig (King-Smith), 13
Baby Goose (McMullan), 192
Baby-Sitters Club, The (Martin), 9, 27
Backes, Laura, 120

background information, historical fiction, 269
Bacon, Francis, 54
Bahr, Mary, 119
ballads, 144–146, 192–193
Ballerina Dreams (Thompson), 335
Ball for Daisy, A (Raschka), 13, 124
Balliet, Blue, 292
Balloons and Other Poems (Chandra), 157
Bamboo People (Perkins), 290
Bang, Molly, 112, 129
banned books, 101–103, 270
Barahona Center for the Study of Books in Spanish for Children and Young Adults, 235
Barron, Tom, 215, 225
Baseball Saved Us (Mochizuki), 262
Bat 6 (Wolff), 259
Bausum, Ann, 327
Baylor, Byrd, 118, 119
Bearstone (Hobbs), 290
Beast Feast (Florian), 148
beast tales, 184
Beauty and the Beast, 216
Beauty and the Beast (France), 178
Beauty: A Retelling of the Story of Beauty and the Beast (McKinley), 216
Beavers (Gibbon), 335
Because of Winn Dixie (DiCamillo), 49, 283, 289
Becoming Billie Holiday (Weatherford), 332
Becoming Naomi Leon (Ryan), 288
Been to Yesterdays: Poems of a Life (Hopkins), 332
Beezus and Ramona (Cleary), 284
Before We Were Free (Alvarez), 260
Behind the Mask: The Life of Queen Elizabeth I (Thomas), 325
Behold the Bold Umbrellaphant (Prelutsky), 150
Belting, Natalie, 188
Beneath the Sun (Stewart), 334
Benjamin Franklin (Krull), 331
Best, Best Colors/Los Majores Colores (Hoffman), 294
Best Birthday Parties Ever!, The (Ross), 336
Best Christmas Pageant Ever, The (Robinson), 291
Best Friends Forever: A World War II Scrapbook (Patt), 259
Best of Times, The (Tang), 151
Between Earth and Sky: Legends of Native American Sacred Places (Bruchac), 188
Beyond Mayfield (Nelson), 259
Beyond the Divide (Lasky), 254
Beyond the Spiderwick Chronicles (Black & DiTerlizzi), 223
Beyond the Western Sea (Avi), 14, 256
BFG, The (Dahl), 222
B. Franklin, Printer (Adler), 327
bibliotherapy, 305–306
Biggs, Brian, 333
Billy Bones: Tales for the Secret Closet (Lincoln), 219
Bing, Bang, Bong (Florian), 148
Bing, Christopher, 151

biography
    book lists, 353–356
    comparing two texts, 344
    overview of, 9, 328–333
Birchbark House, The (Erdrich), 254
birds, nonfiction book list, 328
Birdsall, Jeanne, 288
bisexual literature, 294, 313
B Is for Baseball: Running the Bases from A to Z (McGuinness), 333
Black and White (Macaulay), 126
Black Ships Before Troy (Sutcliff), 189
blended genres, 10–11, 318, 350–351
Blendspace, 348
blogs
    Blogspot: Sylvia Vardell's Blog, 161
    English language learners, 349–350
    historical fiction microblogs, 261
    literature circles and, 90–91
    reader response activities, 55–56
Blood on the River: James Town 1607 (Carbone), 253
Blubber (Blume), 282
Bluefish (Schmatz), 293
Blue Sword, The (McKinley), 225
Blume, Judy, 282, 291
book covers, nonfiction, 326–327
book lists
    10 Best Websites with Book Reviews for Children's Books, 100
    biographies, 329, 330
    blended books, 351
    books boys may like, 37
    books for reading aloud, 80
    contemporary realistic fiction, 304, 307–313
    easy-to-read stories, 41
    fantasy and science fiction, cultural diversity, 234
    fantasy and science fiction, novels, 241–244
    fantasy and science fiction, picture books, 238–241
    female protagonists, 38–39
    folktales, 179–180, 185
    graphic novels, 127
    Great Depression, 130
    historical fiction, 266, 272–278
    literature circles, 105
    literature for drama and puppet shows, 60
    nonfiction, 322, 328, 343, 350, 351, 353–357
    nonfiction/fiction pairs, 344–347
    picture books, 121–124, 127, 132, 135–138, 185, 330
    poetry, 145–146, 155, 158, 163–165, 169–174
    poetry, choral speaking and performance, 159–160
    poetry across the curriculum, 152–154
    pop-up books, 125
    read-alouds, 104
    shared reading, 104–105
    traditional literature, 191, 200–202, 206–210
Book of Nonsense, A (Lear), 148
book reviews, 55

book selections
controversial books and, 101–103
literature circles, 89–90
reader's workshop, 96–97
book talks and discussions, 57
Bookworm's Feast, The (O'Brien), 150
Borden, Louise, 332
Born and Bred in the Great Depression (Winter), 265
Borrowers, The (Norton), 221
Boston Coffee Party, The (Rappaport), 263
Boston Globe Horn Book Award, 358
Bouchard, Judy, 318–319
Boxes for Katje (Fleming), 262
Boyce, Lisa Boggiss, 125
Boyd, Louise, 331
boys, reading preferences of, 35–39
Boy Who Dared, The (Bartoletti), 264
Boy Who Held Back the Sea, The (Hort & Locker), 119
Boy Who Invented TV: The Story of Philo Farnsworth, The (Krull), 317, 330
Bracelet, The (Uchida), 262
Bradbury, Ray, 44
Bragg, Georgia, 316
Brats (Kennedy), 148
Bread and Roses Too (Paterson), 255
Breadwinner, The (Ellis), 290
Brett, Jan, 114, 186
Brian's Return (Paulsen), 290
Bridge to Terabithia (Paterson), 17, 281, 287, 301
Bright, Iman, 326
Brisingr (Paolini), 226
Brooklyn Bridge (Curlee), 325
Brown, Dan, 193
Brown, Marc, 86
Brown Bear, Brown Bear, What Do You See? (Martin), 86–87
Browne, Anthony, 193, 332
Bruchac, Joseph, 188, 220
Bryan, Ashley, 161, 326
Bud, Not Buddy (Curtis), 13, 257, 265
Buddha Stories (Demi), 187
Budgie the Little Helicopter (H. R. H. The Duchess of York Ferguson), 28
Bug Hunter (Burnie), 321, 323, 325, 336–337
Building Big (Macaulay), 325
Bull Run (Fleischman), 17, 255, 264
Bunyan, Paul, 190
Burleigh, Robert, 321
Burnie, David, 321, 336
Burn My Heart (Naidoo), 260
Butterfly Eyes and Other Secrets of the Meadow (Sidman), 151
Buzz (Bingham), 326
Buzzeo, Toni, 119
Byrd, Robert, 330

Cabrera, Jane, 193
Caddie Woodlawn (Brink), 249–250, 254
Caldecott Medal, 358
fables, 186

female characters in winning books, 36
nonfiction, 333
picture books, 110–112, 113, 119, 124, 131
Calder Game, The (Dowd), 292
Cameron, Ann, 281
Canning Season, The (Horvath), 291
Canto: Familiar (Soto), 166
Can You Guess My Name? (Sierra), 179
Captain Underpants series (Pilkey), 9, 33, 46
captions, nonfiction, 325
Captive, The (Hansen), 254
Career and College Readiness Anchor Standard, 21–22
Carl (Day), 296
Carle, Eric, 40, 55, 62, 86–87, 125–126, 186
Carter G. Woodson Book Awards, 359
Carter, David, 193
cartoons, 115
Case of the Firecrackers, The (Yep), 292
Case of the Lion Dance, The (Yep), 292
Case of the Vanishing Golden Frogs: A Scientific Mystery, The (Markle), 317
Castle (Macaulay), 325
Castle in the Attic, The (Winthrop), 12, 218
Cat, What Is That? (Johnston), 150
Catching Fire (Collins), 227
Caterpillar to Butterfly (Heiligman), 348
Catherine, Called Birdy (Cushman), 252
Cat in the Hat, The (Seuss), 123
Cat Poems (Crawley), 150
cause and effect, nonfiction structures, 322
Cave, The (Plato), 5
Cendrillan: A Caribbean Cinderella (San Souci), 178
censorship, 101–103
Chained (Kelly), 289
Chains (Anderson), 253, 264, 268
chain stories, 183
Chandra, Deborah, 144
chants, 193, 202
Chapman, John, 190
characters
character conversation activities, 300
character journals, 56
character monologues, 302
character perspective charts, 301
character trading cards, 299
character webs, maps, and diagrams, 297–298
elements of fiction, 12–13, 18
historical fiction, 249–250, 251
picture books, 119
realistic fiction, 283–284, 297–302
science fiction and fantasy, 215
traditional literature, 177
Charlie and the Chocolate Factory (Dahl), 42, 222, 235
Charlotte's Web (White), 17, 34, 79, 110, 218, 232
Charlotte Zolotow Award, 359
Chasing Vermeer (Balliet), 292
Checkmate at Chess City (Harper), 336
Cheng, Andrea, 61
Cheshire Cheese Cat: A Dickens of a Tale, The (Deedy), 218

Chess Rumble (Neri), 288
Chewy, Gooey, Rumble, Plop!: A Deliciously Disgusting Plop-Up Guide to the Digestive System (Alton), 327
Chicka Chicka Boom Boom (Martin), 109
Chickadee (Erdrich), 254
Chicken Soup with Rice (Sendak), 40
Children of the Great Depression (Freedman), 265
Children's Book Council (CBC), 265
Children's Book Guild Nonfiction Award, 359
Children's Choice Awards, 19
children's literature
defining, 4–5
genres and forms, 7–11
role of, 5–7
teaching guidelines, 19–24
Children's Poetry Archive, 161
Children's Poetry Archive, The, 161
Chinese Americans. *See* Asian Americans; cultural diversity
Chocolate Fever (Smith), 220
Chocolate: Riches from the Rainforest (Burleigh), 321
Chocolate Touch, The (Catling), 220
Chomp (Hiaasen), 291
choral readings, poetry, 147, 159–160
choral speaking, 57–58
Christmas in the Big House, Christmas in the Quarters (McKissack & McKissack), 334
Christopher, Matt, 292
Chronicles of Harris Burdick: Fourteen Amazing Authors Tell the Tales, The (Van Allsburg), 120
Chronicles of Narnia (Lewis), 46
Chronicles of Narnia, The (Lewis), 221
Chronicles of Prydain, The (Alexander), 225
chronology, nonfiction structures, 322
Chuck Close: Face Book (Close), 332
Ciardi, John, 148
Cinco de Mayo: Celebrating the Traditions of Mexico (Hoyt-Goldsmith), 335
Cinderella stories, 179, 181, 183, 198, 202, 216
Citizen Scientist: Be a Part of a Scientific Discovery from Your Own Backyard (Burn), 317
civil rights movement, 259–261, 266, 275, 277–278, 337
Civil War, historical fiction, 254–255, 272–273
clarity, nonfiction, 321
Classic Nursery Rhymes: Enchanting Songs from Around the World (Weber), 192
classroom environment, reader response, 46–48
Cleary, Beverly, 216, 284, 288, 291
Cleopatra (Stanley), 330
Click, Clack, Moo: Cows That Type (Cronin), 228
Clifford the Big Red Dog (Bridwell), 9, 27
close reading, strategies for, 71–77
Cobblestone, 4
Codell, Esmé Raji, 333

Cod's Tale, The (Kurlansky), 325
cognitive development, readers, 39–43
Cole, Henry, 112
Cole, Joanna, 318
collaboration, literature circles, 88
collective biographies, 331
Collier, Bryan, 112
Collier, Christopher, 247
Collins, Suzanne, 213, 227
Colman, Penny, 317, 324, 331, 336
Colón, Ernie, 337
colonial times, historical fiction, 253, 266, 272, 276
color, picture books and, 112, 267
Color Farm (Ehlert), 113
Color Zoo (Ehlert), 113
comic strips, 62
coming of age, fiction themes, 15–16
commercialization of literature, 27–28
Common Core State Standards (CCSS)
    close reading, 71–77
    contemporary realistic fiction, 297–302
    fantasy and science fiction, 229–233
    historical fiction and, 263–268
    information book, use of term, 318
    information literacy, 324
    interactive read-alouds, 79
    literature, defining, 4–5
    literature, role of, 5–7
    Literature and Reading: Information Standard 10, 44–45, 53–54
    literature circles and, 89
    literature genres and forms, 7–11
    literature programs, guidelines for, 19–24
    nonfiction, 338–347
    picture books, use of, 128–131
    poetry and, 156–162, 167–168
    point of view, activities for, 300–302
    reader response activities, value of, 63–66
    reader's workshop, 96
    Reading Standard for Literature, 21–23
    shared reading activities and, 86–87
    traditional literature, use of, 193–198
    WebQuests, 271
Common Sense Media, 24, 321
compare and contrast, nonfiction structures, 322, 344–347
comparison
    book and movie plots, 232
    comparison charts, 64, 264, 298
    historical fiction, 264
    poetry, 143
complete biographies, 331
Compoy, Isabel, 192
comprehension, text complexity and, 44–45
concept picture books, 122, 333–337, 353
concept webs, 269
concrete poetry forms, 144–146
conferences, reader's workshop, 98, 99
Confetti/Confetti (Mora), 166
conflict, fiction themes, 15–16
construction of meaning, 49–53, 88, 197–198

contemporary realistic fiction
    adventure and survival stories, 289–290
    animal stories, 289
    bibliotherapy, 305–306
    book lists, 304, 307–313
    categories, overview of, 286–287
    connecting to CCSS, 297–302
    culturally diverse learners, 303, 304
    English language learners, 303, 305
    evaluation criteria, 282–286
    family relationships, 288–289
    growing up themes, 287–288
    humorous stories, 290–291
    LGBT literature, 294
    mysteries, 291–292
    overview, 8, 278–281
    people with physical or mental challenges, 293–294
    picture books, 295–296, 303–305
    role of, 281–282
    school life, 293
    sports stories, 292
    transition and series books, 296–297, 310
content, nonfiction, 320
content-area studies, poetry and, 151, 152–154
context, reader response, 45–48
contrast, nonfiction structures, 344–347
controversial books, 101–103
conversations, written, 56
conversations with characters, 300
Cony, Frances, 193
Cooper, Susan, 213, 225
Copper Sun (Draper), 247, 255
copyright, traditional literature, 198
copyright page, 318
Coraline (Gaiman), 219
Corduroy (Freeman), 110
Corpses, Coffins, and Crypts: A History of Burial (Colman), 317, 335
Count! (Fleming), 333
Countdown (Wiles), 260
counting books, 333
Counting Is for the Birds (Mazzola), 333
Country Girl, City Girl (Jahn-Clough), 294
Count Your Way Through Egypt (Haskins & Benson), 333
Couric, Katie, 28
covers, nonfiction books, 326–327
Cracker!: The Best Dog in Vietnam (Kadohata), 261
Crack in the Clouds, A (Levy), 149
craft books, 336–337
Crafts to Make in the Winter (Ross), 336
Crane Wife, The (Japan), 178
creation stories, 188, 207
Creature Carnival (Singer), 150
Creech, Sharon, 284
Cricket, 4, 161
Crispin: At the Edge of the World (Avi), 252
Crispin: The Cross of Lead (Avi), 14, 252
Crispin: The Edge of Time (Avi), 252
Criss Cross (Perkins), 287, 302
critical literacy, developing, 52
critical stance, reader response, 50–51, 53
critical thinking skills, 248

Crockett, Davy, 190
Crockett, Sally Ann Thunder Ann Whirlwind, 190
Crow (Wright), 256
Cube Creator, 268
Cuckoo/Cucio (Ehlert), 199
cultural diversity. *See also* contemporary realistic fiction; historical fiction; traditional literature
    Cinderella stories, 216
    civil rights movement, 259–261, 266, 275, 277–278, 337
    fantasy and science fiction, 233–235
    ghost stories, 220
    historical fiction, 268
    LGBT literature, 294
    literature programs and, 25
    nonfiction, 348
    people with physical or mental challenges, 293–294
    photographic essays, 334–335
    picture books for, 132
    poetry, 163–165
    segregation, historical fiction, 256
    slavery, historical fiction, 254–255, 272–273
cumulative stories, 183
Cupid and Psyche: A Love Story (Barth), 187
Curious Collection of Cats, A (Franco), 150
Curious Garden, The (Brown), 296
Curious George (Rey), 27
curriculum, literature uses, 100–101
Curtis, Christopher Paul, 13, 19, 257, 259
Cut from the Same Cloth: American Women of Myth, Legend and Tall Tale (San Souci), 190

Dahl, Roald, 161, 222
dairy writing activities, 300
Dakos, Kalli, 150
Dark Emperor and Other Poems of the Night (Sidman), 151
Dark Is Rising, The (Cooper), 213, 225
Dark Pond, The (Bruchac), 220
D'Aulaire's Book of Greek Myths, The (D'Aulaire), 187
Dave the Potter: Artist, Poet, Slave (Hill), 112
Davy Crockett, 190
Day, Alexandra, 296
Day at the Fire Station, A (Mortensen), 337
Day of Tears: A Novel in Dialogue (Lester), 254
Dazzling Display of Dogs, A (Franco), 150
Dead End in Norvelt (Gantos), 14, 17, 260
Dear America series, 263
Dear Mrs. Roosevelt: Letters from Children of the Great Depression (Cohen), 265
Dear Zoo (Campbell), 125
De Colores and Other Latin American Folk Songs for Children (Orozco), 202
Deep and Dark and Dangerous (Hahn), 219
dePaola, Tomie, 113, 191, 332
Desert Digits: An Arizona Number Book (Gowan), 333
Desert Is Theirs, The (Baylor), 119
Desert Scrapbook, A (Wright-Frierson), 336

design, nonfiction texts, 326–327
design, picture books, 113–114
Devil's Arithmetic, The (Yolen), 258
diagrams, nonfiction, 325
dialect, in fiction, 17, 178
dialogue, 17, 119
dialogue journals, 56, 91
diaries, nonfiction texts, 335–336
Diary of a Wimpy Kid, The (Kinney), 44, 291
Diaz, David, 113
DiCamillo, Kate, 12, 40, 213, 216, 217, 218, 219, 283, 289
Dicey's Song (Voigt), 288
Dictionary of Dance, A (Murphy), 327
Diez Deditos and Other Play Rhymes and Action Songs (Orozco), 202
digital devices
    literature programs and, 26–27
    online reference books, 337
    OverDrive library, digital downloads, 333
    reading preferences and, 39
digital literacy, 321
digital picture books, 133–134
Dinosaur Alphabet Book, The (Pallotta), 123
Dinosaurs: Encyclopedia Prehistorica (Sabuda), 326
Dinosaurs of Waterhouse Hawkins, The (Kerley), 326
disabilities, people with, 293–294
Discovering the Inca Ice Maiden: My Adventures on Ampato (Reinhard), 325
discussion groups, 88–94
Disney, Walt, 27
distinctive markings, nonfiction, 327
diverse learners. *See also* traditional literature
    critical literacy skills, 52
    fantasy and science fiction, 233–235
    historical fiction, 268
    LGBT literature, 294
    literature programs and, 19–20, 25
    nonfiction, 348
    people with physical and mental challenges, 293–294
    photographic essays, 334–335
    picture books for, 132
    poetry for, 163–165
    traditional literature for, 199–202
DK Smithsonian Nature Activity Guides, 336
documents, nonfiction texts, 335–336
Dog of Discovery: A Newfoundland's Adventures with Lewis and Clark (Pringle), 336
Domitila: A Cinderella Story from the Mexican Tradition (Coburn), 202
Don't Let the Pigeon Drive the Bus (Willems), 111, 128
Don't Read This Book Whatever You Do (Dakos), 150
Don't Slam the Door! (Chaconas), 124
Dotlich, Rebecca Kai, 142
double-entry journals, 56
Down by the Bay (Raffi & Westcott), 62
Downriver (Hobbs), 290
Doyle, Kerri, 319

Dragon Bones and Dinosaur Eggs: A Photobiography of Explorer Roy Chapman Andrews (Bausum), 330
Dragon in the Sky: The Story of a Green Darner Dragonfly, A (Pringle), 336
Dragon Rider (Funke), 222
Dragon's Gate (Yep), 256
Dragonwings (Yep), 256
drama
    fantasy and science fiction, 233
    reader response and engagement, 42, 58–61
    shared reading activities, 86
    teaching strategies, realistic fiction, 301–302
Draper, Sharon, 247
Dream Jar, The (Pryor), 262
Dream Stealer, The (Fleischman), 220
Drop of Water, A (Wick), 325
Dr. Seuss ABC, The (Seuss), 123
Dust Bowl, historical fiction, 257, 266
dystopian societies, 226–227, 244

Each Kindness (Woodson), 132
Each Little Bird That Sings (Wiles), 288
Eagle of the Ninth, The (Sutcliff), 252
Ear, the Eye and the Arm, The (Farmer), 227
easy-reading books, 40–41, 123–124
e-books
    digital picture books, 133–134
    reader engagement and, 32–33
    reading preferences and, 39
    Story Jumper, 176
    traditional literature, multimedia versions, 198
E.B. White Read Aloud Award, 359
Echoes for the Eye: Poems to Celebrate Patterns in Nature (Esbenson), 151
Edgar Allan Poe Award, 359
efferent response, 49–50, 51, 53
Ehlert, Lois, 113
E Is for Extreme: An Extreme Sports Alphabet (Herzog), 333
ELA-Literacy CCRA Reading standards, 44–45
ELA-Literacy: Speaking and Listening Standards, 65
Eldest (Paolini), 226
Electric Ben: The Amazing Life and Times of Benjamin Franklin (Byrd), 330
electronic media, supplemental content, 236–237
elementary school children, 40–42, 121
Elijah of Buxton (Curtis), 255
Ella Enchanted (Levine), 213, 216, 232
Ella Fitzgerald: The Tale of a Vocal Virtuosa (Pinkney), 332
Elleman, Barbara, 114
ELLs. *See* English language learners (ELLs)
Emeka's Gift: An African Counting Story (Onyefulu), 333
emotional impact, poetry, 144
Emperor's New Clothes, The (Andersen), 216
eMule's Poetry Archive, 162
Encyclopedia Brown (Sobel), 291

Encyclopedia Horrifica: The Terrifying TRUTH! About Vampires, Ghosts, Monsters, and More (Micucci), 325
Encyclopedia Mythologica: Gods and Heroes (Reinhart), 187
Encylopedia Mythologica: Fairies and Mythical Creatures (Reinhart & Sabuda), 125
Endangered (Schrefer), 289
Endless Steppe, The (Hautzig), 258
end pages (endpapers), 327
engagement. *See* reader engagement
English language learners (ELLs)
    contemporary realistic fiction, 303, 305
    fantasy and science fiction, 235–236
    historical fiction, 269
    literature circles, 91
    nonfiction, 349–350
    picture books, 133
    poetry, 166–167
    read-alouds, importance of, 78
    support for, 25–26
    traditional literature, 199, 202–203
enumeration, nonfiction structures, 322
environmental issues, book list, 309
Environment: Saving the Planet, The (Harlow), 325–326
epics. *See also* traditional literature
    book list, 208
    heroic fantasy, 224–226
    overview of, 188–189
Eragon (Paolini), 226
Erdrich, Louise, 254
Erie Canal, The (Brown), 193
ER Vets: Life in an Animal Emergency Room (Jackson), 319
Escape from Mr. Lemoncello's Library (Grabenstein), 292
Escaping the Tiger (Manivong), 261
Esperanza Rising (Ryan), 256
Estrada, Pau, 119
ethnicity. *See* cultural diversity
everyday life, poems about, 149, 169–170
everyday life, realistic fiction, 308
Everything Goes in the Air (Biggs), 333
Everything on a Waffle (Horvath), 291
Evolution of Calpurnia Tate, The (Kelly), 250, 256
Excalibur (Talbot), 189
Experiential background, preferences and, 34
experiment books, 336–337
Exploding Gravy: Poems to Make You Laugh (Kennedy & Lewis), 148
extension projects, 93
Extraordinary Life: The Story of the Monarch Butterfly, An (Pringle), 326
Extra Yarn (Burnett), 81
e-zines, 4
Ezra Jack Keats New Illustrator Award, 359

fables. *See also* traditional literature
    book list, 206
    overview, 8, 185–187
    role of, 180

Facebook pages, 299
faction books, 350–351
Faerie Tale Theater, 198
Fahrenheit 451 (Bradbury), 44
Fair Weather (Peck), 256
fairy tales, 184, 216, 241
Fallen Angels (Myers), 261
family life
    contemporary realistic fiction, book
      lists, 307–308, 311
    poems about, 172–173
    realistic fiction, 288–289
Family Secrets (Bolden), 256
Fa Mulan: The Story of a Woman Warrior
    (San Souci), 189
fantastic adventures, book list, 243
Fantastic Online Professional Resources, 161
fantasy fiction
    alternative worlds, 221
    animal and toy fantasy, 216–217
    book lists, 234, 238–244
    cultural diversity, 233–235
    English language learners, 235–236
    evaluation criteria, 214–215
    fairy tales, 216
    fantastic adventures, 222–223
    ghosts and the supernatural, 190, 219–220
    heroic fantasy, 224–226
    magic, 220–221
    overview, 8, 211–213
    picture books, 228, 238–241
    role of, 213–214
    science fiction, 226–228
    supplemental electronic media, 236–237
    teaching strategies for CCSS, 229–233
    time travel fantasy, 223–224
    traditional literature, expansions of,
      216, 228
Farmer, Nancy, 227
Far North (Hobbs), 290
Favorite Fairy Tales from Around the World
    (Yolen), 184
Favorite Poems, Old and New (McLeod), 157
feature charts, nonfiction, 342
female protagonists, book list, 38–39, 191
Fendler, Donn, 337
Fever, 1793 (Anderson), 253
fiction
    elements of, 12–19
    guidelines for choosing, 18
    overview of, 8
field guides, 337
Fighting Ground, The (Avi), 253, 264, 270
figurative language, 17, 118, 143, 323–324
Fink, Mike, 190
Fire in My Hands, A (Soto), 166
Fires of Merlin, The (Barron), 225
First Field Guide (National Audubon
    Society), 337
First Graphics: My Community series, 337
First Part Last, The (Johnson), 36
Fisher, Aileen, 149
Fisher, Dr. K., 326–327
Five Lives of Our Cat Zook, The (Rocklin),
    284
Fleischman, Paul, 17, 150

Fleming, Candace, 324
Flora and Ulysses (DiCamillo), 218
Flora Stieglitz Straus Award, 359
Florian, Douglas, 148
fluency, poetry and, 159–162
Flush (Hiaasen), 291
*Flying Solo: How Ruth Elder Soared into
    America's Heart* (Cummins), 329–330
folk art, 115
folk songs, 192–193, 208–209
folktales. *See also* traditional literature
    book list, 179–180, 185, 206
    fantasy, 233
    matrix for comparison, 194–196
    overview, 8, 183–184
    preschool and kindergarten readers, 40
Follow the Line to School (Ljungkvist), 296
fools, stories of, 184
Forbes, Esther, 247
Forest in the Clouds, The (Collard), 323
Forever (Blume), 102
Forge (Anderson), 253
form, poetry, 144–146
formal criticism, reader response, 48–49
format, nonfiction texts, 326–327
forms of literature, overview, 7–11
For the Very First Time (MacLachlan), 288
Fox, Paula, 290
Fox's Den (Phillips), 325
fractured fairytales, 197
fractured folktales, 196
Frazee, Marla, 110, 112
Freak the Mighty (Philbrick), 288
Frederick (Lionni), 27, 62
Freedman, Russell, 324, 329, 331
freedom, fiction theme, 15
*Freedom on the Menu: The Greensboro
    Sit-Ins* (Weatherford), 267
Freedom Summer (Wiles), 262
free verse, 144–146
Fresh Brats (Kennedy), 148
Friendly Four, The (Greenfield), 61
friendship, fiction themes, 15–16, 287–288
Friendship, The (Taylor), 257
Frightful's Mountain (George), 302
Frindle (Clements), 293
Fritz, Jean, 330
Frog and Toad Are Friends (Lobel), 14, 124
From Another World (Machado), 233
*From Sea to Shining Sea: A Treasury of
    American Folklore and Songs*
    (Cohn), 184
*From the Bellybutton of the Moon and Other
    Summer Poems* (Alarcon), 166
From the Notebooks of Melanin Sun
    (Woodson), 294
Frost, Helen, 336
Frost, Robert, 143, 148, 155
Funke, Cornelia, 222
Fury of Motion, A (Ghigna), 149
future worlds, book lists, 244

Gaiman, Neil, 219
Game of Silence, The (Erdrich), 254
game-related literature, 193, 208–209
Gantos, Jack, 14, 17

Garden, Nancy, 294
Gathering Blue (Lowry), 226
Gay, Lesbian, Bisexual, Transgender Round
    Table, 294
gay literature, 294, 313
Geisel, Theodor Seuss, 123
Game for Swallows, A (Abirached), 290
gender, reading preferences and, 35–39
generic perspective, reader response, 48–49
Genie in the Jar, The (Giovanni), 156
genres, overview of, 7–11. *See also* specific
    genre names
George, Jean Craighead, 318
George, Kristine O'Connell, 143, 149, 161
Gerstein, Mordicai, 112, 123
ghost stories, 189–190, 219–220, 242
*Giant and How He Humbugged America,
    The* (Murphy), 327
Gibbons, Gail, 335
Giblin, James Cross, 324, 329
Gidwitz, Adam, 216
Gifford, Clive, 326
Gilgamesh the Hero (McCaughrean), 188
Gilgamesh the King (Zeman), 188
Gingerbread Baby (Brett), 114
Gingerbread Man, The, 40
Giovanni, Nikki, 156
girls, reading preferences of, 35–39
*Girls: A History of Growing Up Female in
    America* (Colman), 317
Girls of Central High, The series, 9
*Girl Who Circumnavigated Fairyland in
    a Ship of Her Own Making, The*
    (Valente), 221
Girl Who Loved Wild Horses, The (Native
    American), 178
G Is for Googol (Schwartz), 123
Giver, The (Lowry), 14, 16, 42, 226, 232
Giving Tree, The (Silverstein), 33
*Glass Slipper, Gold Sandal: A Worldwide
    Cinderella* (Fleischman), 216
Global Read Aloud, 79
Golden Compass, The (Pullman), 226, 232
Golden Duck; Eleanor Cameron; Hal
    Clement Awards, 360
Golden Goblet, The (McGraw), 251
Golden Mountain Chronicles (Yep), 256
Golden Tales from the Arabian Nights
    (Sofier & Shapiro), 184
Goldilocks and the Three Bears (Brett), 114
Golem, 189
Gone Fishing: Ocean Life by the Numbers
    (McLimans), 333
Gone Wild: An Endangered Animal Alphabet
    (McLiman), 333
Good Books, Good Times (Hopkins), 150
*Good Brother, Bad Brother: The Story of
    Edwin Booth and John Wilkes Booth*
    (Giblin), 329
Goode, Dianne, 112
Good Luck Gold (Wong), 163
*Good Masters, Sweet Ladies: Life in a
    Medieval Village* (Schlitz), 252, 265
Goodnight, Goodnight Construction Site
    (Rinkey), 228
Good Night Gorilla (Rathmann), 124

Goodnight iPad (Droyd), 228
Goodnight Moon (Brown), 110, 124, 228
Goof Who Invented Homework, The (Dakos), 150
Google Lit Trip, 299
Goosebumps (Stine), 33, 46
Goosebumps Gold (Stine), 9
Gorilla Walk (Lewin & Lewin), 325
Gossamer (Lowry), 220
Gossip Girl: A Novel (von Ziegesar), 44
Grahame, Kenneth, 216
Grannie and the Jumbie (Hurst), 178
Grapes of Math, The (Tang), 151
graphic novels, 111, 126, 127, 256, 257, 269, 337
graphic organizers, 63, 64, 298
Graphite, 24
Grasshopper Summer (Turner), 254
Graveyard Book, The (Gaiman), 219
Great Depression, 130, 257, 266, 274, 277
Great Fire, The (Murphy), 50, 335
Great Gilly Hopkins, The (Paterson), 281, 288
Great Migration: Journey North, The (Greenfield), 151
Great Wall of Lucy Wu, The (Shang), 289
Greek Myths for Young Children (Amery), 187
Greenberg, Jan, 331
Green Book, The (Walsh), 227
Green Eggs and Ham (Seuss), 123
Greenfield, Eloise, 61
Green Glass Sea, The (Klages), 258
Green Thumb (Thomas), 52
Grimes, Nikki, 163
Grimm, Jacob, 183
Grimm, Wilhelm, 183
Grimm Once Upon a Time, 198
growing up themes, realistic fiction, 287–288, 310–311
Grump Groan Growl (Hooks), 112
Guts: The True Stories Behind Hatchet and the Brian Books (Paulsen), 331
Guys Read, 36

Hahn, Mary Downing, 219
haiku, 144–146
Half Magic (Eager), 220
Hall, Michael, 113
Hamilton, Buffy, 161
Hamsters, Shells and Spelling Bees: Poems About School (Hopkins), 156
Handbook for Boys: A Novel (Myers), 36
Hand in Hand: An American History in Poetry (Hopkins), 151
Handler, Daniel, 222
Handsprings (Florian), 148
Hansen, Joyce, 270
Happy to Be Nappy (Giovanni), 156
Hardy Boys (Dixon), 9, 291
Harry Potter (Rowling), 5, 13, 16, 27, 28, 35, 43, 46, 211–212, 220–221, 232, 236
Hartman, Cassie, 318
Hartman, Dan, 318
Hat, The (Brett), 114
Hatch! (Munro), 323
Hatchet (Paulsen), 14, 17, 43, 55, 281, 283, 290

Haunted House (Pieńkowski), 125
Hawk, I'm Your Brother (Baylor), 118
Head, Body, Legs: A Story from Liberia (Paye & Lippert), 186
Heard, Georgia, 167
Heart of a Jaguar (Talbert), 252
Heat (Christopher), 292
Hello, Goodbye Window, The (Raschka), 128, 296
Henkes, Kevin, 40, 111
Henry, John, 190
Henry, Mary Gibson, 331
Henry's Freedom Box (Nelson), 262
Henry's Freedom Box: A True Story From the Underground Railroad (Levine), 262
Here Lies Arthur (Reeve), 225
Here's a Little Poem: A Very First Book of Poetry (Yolen), 156
Hero and the Crown, The (McKinley), 225
Heroes of Olympus (Riordan), 10
heroic fantasy, 8, 224–226, 243–244
He's Got the Whole World in His Hands (Nelson), 193
Hesse, Karen, 263
Hiaasen, Carl, 285, 291
Hidden (Frost), 302
Hidden Child (Millman), 331
Hide and Seek (Vos), 264
High King, The (Alexander), 225
Hip Hop Speaks to Children: A Celebration of Poetry with a Beat (Giovanni), 161
Hiroshima No Pika (Maruki), 262
His Dark Materials (Pullman), 226
historical documents, nonfiction, 336
historical fiction
    ancient civilizations (up to A.D. 600), 251–252
    book lists, 266, 272–278
    civil rights, Vietnam War (1950–1970), 259–261
    colonial times, American Revolution (1600–1800), 253
    controversy, what to include, 269–270
    diverse learners, 268
    English language learners, 269
    evaluation criteria, 249–250, 251
    Great Depression, 257
    industrialization, immigration, segregation, 255–256
    Middle Ages (A.D. 600–1500), 252
    overview, 8, 245–247, 250–251
    picture books, 262–263
    role of, 248–249
    series and transitional books, 263
    slavery and Civil War (1800s), 254–255
    teaching strategies, CCSS, 263–268
    WebQuests, 271
    westward expansion (1800s), 254
    World War II (1940s), 258–259
Hobbit, The (Tolkien), 224
Hobbs, Will, 78, 290
Hoberman, Mary Ann, 149
Hodges, Margaret, 189
Hokey-Pokey, The (La Prise), 62
Holbrook, Sara, 149
Holes (Sachar), 283, 290

Holly's Secret (Garden), 294
Holocaust, historical fiction, 258–259, 266
Holocaust, nonfiction, 331
Homecoming (Voigt), 281
homosexuality, 294
honor, fiction theme, 15
hooks, bell, 112
Hoot (Hiaasen), 285, 291
Hopkins, Lee Bennett, 156
Horn Book Magazine, The, 320
Horrible Histories series, 263
Horvath, Polly, 291
Hot Hand (Christopher), 292
Hound Dog's Haiku, The (Rosen), 157
House Is a House for Me, A (Hoberman), 149
House of Scorpion, The (Farmer), 227
House of the Red Fish (Salisbury), 259
House with No Door, The (Swann), 157
House You Pass on the Way, The (Woodson), 294
Houston, Gloria, 118
How Big Is It: A Big Book All About Bigness (Hillman), 319
How Chipmunk Got His Stripes: A Tale of Bragging and Teasing (Bruchac & Ross), 175, 188
How I Became a Ghost: A Choctaw Trail of Tears Story (Bruchac), 220
How the Guinea Fowl Got Her Spots: A Swahili Tale of Friendship (Knutson), 188
How They Croaked: The Awful Ends of the Awfully Famous (Bragg), 316
how-to books, 336–337
How to Steal a Dog (O'Connor), 281
How We Came to the Fifth World/Como Vinimos al Quinto Mundo: A Creation Story from Ancient Mexico (Rohmer & Anchondo), 199
How Weird Is It? (Hillman), 317
Hughes, Langston, 155
Hugo Award, 360
Hummingbird Nest: A Journal of Poems (George), 149
humor
    contemporary realistic fiction, 290–291
    nonfiction book list, 357
    poetry and, 148, 171
    realistic fiction, 312
Hunger Games, The (Collins), 46, 212, 213, 227, 232, 236
Hurst, Margaret, 178
Hush, Baby Hush! Lullabies from Around the World (Henderson), 192
Hush Songs: African American Lullabies (Thomas), 192
hybrid works, 10–11
Hyman, Trina Schart, 198

I Am Phoenix (Fleischman), 150
I Am the Book (Hopkins), 150
Iceberg Right Ahead! The Tragedy of the Titanic (McPherson), 325
Icky Bug Alphabet Book, The (Pallotta), 123

Ida B (Hannigan), 293
identification books, 337
If You're Happy and You Know It
    (Cabrera), 193
If You're Not Here, Please Raise Your Hand
    (Dakos), 150
I Heard a Bluebird Sing (Fisher), 149
Iliad (Homer), 189
illustration. *See also* art
    fiction, 18
    historical fiction, 267–268
    media used, list of, 116–117
    nonfiction, 325–326
    picture books, 111–115
    traditional literature analysis, 198
I'm Adopted! (Rotner & Kelly), 333
I'm in Charge of Celebrations (Baylor), 118
immigration, historical fiction, 255–256,
    266, 273–274, 277
impressionist art, 115
In2Books, 94
In a Glass Grimmly (Gidwitz), 216
Incredible Journey, The (Burnford), 289
independent reading, readers workshop,
    94–100
Indian in the Cupboard, The (Banks), 235
individualized reading, 94–100
industrialization, historical fiction,
    255–256, 273–274, 277
I Never Said I Wasn't Difficult
    (Holbrook), 149
*I Never Saw Another Butterfly: Children's
    Drawings and Poems from the Terezin
    Concentration Camp* (Volavkova), 265
infographics, 348
informational picture books, 334
information book, use of term, 318
information literacy, 324. *See also* Common
    Core State Standards (CCSS)
Inheritance Cycle, The (Paolini), 226
Inkblot (Peot), 336
Inkworld Trilogy, The (Funke), 222
Insectlopedia (Florian), 148
Inside Out and Back Again (Lai), 261
Inside-Outside Book of Libraries
    (Cummins), 323
Inside-Outside Book of New York City
    (Monro), 323
Inside-Outside Dinosaurs (Monro), 323
insight, poetry, 144
Inspiration, 63
instructional strategies
    book lists, sampling of, 104–105
    close reading, 71–77
    contemporary realistic fiction, 297–302
    controversial book selections, 101–103
    fantasy and science fiction, 229–233
    historical fiction, 263–268
    interactive read-alouds, 77–82, 83
    literature across the curriculum,
        100–101
    literature circles, 88–94, 95, 105
    nonfiction, 338–347
    overview of, 69–71
    picture books, 128–131
    poetry, 156–162

reader's workshop, 94–100
    shared book experience, 82–87, 104–105
    traditional literature, CCSS and,
        193–198
interactive picture books, 125–126
interactive read-alouds, 77–82, 79, 83,
    129, 131
International Reading Association, 268
Internet. *See also* Tech Click
    information accuracy, 324
    online literature circles, 93, 94
    online texts, characteristics of, 44
    reading slowly, 47
    Story Jumper, 176
    supplemental content on, 236–237
    WebQuests, 271
Interrupting Chicken (Stein), 131, 228
intertextual criticism, reader response,
    48–49
intertextuality, 27
*In the Beginning: Creation Stories from
    Around the World* (Hamilton), 188
In the Swim (Florian), 148
Into the Outdoors (Gal), 111
Inuit peoples, 204
Invention of Hugo Cabret, The (Selznick),
    111, 256
I PICK, 97
Ira Sleeps Over (Waber), 118
Isadora, Rachel, 119
*I Saw You in the Bathtub and Other Street
    Rhymes* (Schwartz), 193
Island of the Blue Dolphins (O'Dell), 290
Island on Bird Street, The (Orlev), 258
Island Scrapbook, An (Wright-Frierson), 336
It's a Book (Smith), 228
It's Halloween (Prelutsky), 156
It's My First Day of Kindergarten (Yee), 296
It's Thanksgiving (Prelutsky), 156
It's Time for Preschool! (Codell), 333
It's Valentine's Day (Prelutsky), 156
iTunes, 161

Jack: The Early Years of John F. Kennedy
    (Cooper), 325
Jacobs, Joseph, 183
Jacobson, Sid, 337
Jacques, Brian, 218
James and the Giant Peach (Dahl), 222
Jane Addams Book Award, 360
Japanese Americans. *See* Asian Americans;
    cultural diversity
Jefferson Cup, 360
Jeffers, Susan, 155
Jenkins, Emily, 219
Joey Pigza (Gantos), 294
John Henry (Lester), 190
John Henry: An American Legend
    (Keats), 190
Johnny Appleseed (Kellogg), 190
Johnny Appleseed: A Poem (Lindbergh), 190
Johnny Tremain (Forbes), 43, 52, 247, 253,
    264
Jolly Postman, The (Ahlberg), 126
Jones, Carol, 193
Jordan, Sandra, 331

Josephina Story Quilt (Coerr), 245
Jouanah: A Hmong Cinderella (Coburn), 202
journals, activities
    literature circles and, 90–91
    overview, 55–56
    point of view activities, 301–302
    reader's workshop, 96, 98
    triple-entry journal, 229–230
journals, nonfiction texts, 335–336
Journey (MacLachlan), 285, 288
Journey Home (Uchida), 259
Journey North, 348
*Journey That Saved Curious George: The
    True Wartime Escape of Margret and
    H. A. Rey, The* (Borden), 332
Journey to Topaz (Uchida), 258
Journey West, 245
Joyful Noise: Poems for Two Voices
    (Fleischman), 150
Judge, Lita, 16
Julie of the Wolves (George), 31, 290
Jumanji (Van Allsburg), 228
Just Beyond Reach (Nims), 158
*Just in Case: A Trickster Tale and Spanish
    Alphabet Book* (Morales), 123

Kadohata, Cynthia, 247
Kane Chronicles, The (Riordan), 225
Kate Greenaway Medal, 360
Keats, Ezra Jack, 190
Keeping Quilt, The (Polacco), 118
Keeping Safe the Stars (O'Connor), 288
Kellogg, Steven, 190
Kennedy, X. J., 148
key ideas and details, reading standards,
    21–22
KidPub, 55
Kids Learn Out Loud (Bryan), 161
Kidspiration, 63
Kiki Strike: Inside the Shadow City
    (Miller), 223
Kiki Strike: The Darkness Dwellers
    (Miller), 223
Kiki Strike: The Empress's Tomb (Miller), 223
kindergarten readers, 40–42, 156
Kind of Friends We Used to Be, The
    (Dowell), 287
King Arthur and the Round Table
    (Talbot), 189
King Arthur stories, 188, 189, 225
King Arthur: The Sword and the Stone
    (Talbot), 189
King of the Wind (Henry), 289
Kira, Kira (Kadohata), 259
Kiss Box, The (Verburg), 112
Kitchen Knight: A Tale of King Arthur, The
    (Hodges), 189
Kitten's First Full Moon (Henkes), 111
Klassen, Jon, 119
*Knock at a Star: A Child's Introduction to
    Poetry* (Kennedy), 156
Korean Cinderella, The (Climo), 202
Krull, Kathleen, 331
Kumin, Maxine, 161
Kuskin, Karla, 142–143
KWL (know, want to know, learned), 131

labor movement, historical fiction, 255–256
La Fontaine, Jean, 186
Lancelot (Talbot), 189
Land, The (Taylor), 257
Landau, Elaine, 325
language. *See also* vocabulary
  contemporary realistic fiction, 285
  historical fiction, 250, 265, 269
  nonfiction, 323
  poems for English language learners, 166
  pronouncing dictionary, online, 323
  read-alouds, importance of, 78
  writing style, 17
Language Arts, 320
Lantern Bearers, The (Sutcliff), 252
*Larger Than Life: The Adventures of
  American Legendary Heroes* (San
  Souci), 190
Larklight (Reeve), 227
Lassie Come Home (Knight), 289
Last Quest of Gilgamesh, The (Zeman), 188
Latinos. *See also* cultural diversity
  ballads and folk songs, 192, 208
  fantasy and science fiction, 235
  nonfiction, 350
  picture books, 304
  poetry, 161, 163, 164–165
  traditional literature, 183, 192, 193, 200
Laugh-eteria (Florian), 148
Launch Pad, 55
layered text, nonfiction structures, 322
leads, picture books, 119
Lear, Edward, 148
learning stories, 185–187, 206
learning styles, literature programs and,
  20–21
Leaves (Stein), 40
Lee and Low Publishers, 235
Lee Bennett Hopkins Poetry Award, 360
Lee Bennett Hopkins Promising Poet
  Award, 361
Legend of Buddy Bush, The (Moses), 259
*Legend of the Windigo: A Tale from Native
  North America, The* (Ross), 204
legends, 8, 188–189, 208. *See also* traditional
  literature
LeGuin, Ursula K., 215, 225
*Lemony Snicket's A Series of Unfortunate
  Events* series, 10, 222
L'Engle, Madeleine, 8, 215, 228
Leonardo Da Vinci (Stanley), 330
Leonard's Horse (Fritz), 326
LEP (limited English proficient), 25–26. *See
  also* English language learners (ELLs)
lesbian, gay, bisexual, and transgender
  (LGBT) literature, 294, 313
Lester, Julius, 250, 280
*Let It Shine; Stories of Black Women
  Freedom Fighters* (Pinkney), 331
Let It Shine: Three Favorite Spirituals
  (Bryan), 193
Letters from a Slave Boy (Lyons), 255
Letters from a Slave Girl (Lyons), 255
Letters from Rifka (Hesse), 256
Letters from Wolfie (Sherlock), 261
letter writing activities, 300

Let the Circle Be Unbroken (Taylor), 257
Let the Whole Earth Sing Praise (dePaola),
  113
Levine, Ellen, 262
Levine, Gail Carson, 213, 216
Levinson, Cynthia, 334
Levy, Constance, 149
Lewis, C. S., 16, 46, 221
Lewis, E. B., 109, 114, 132, 193
Lewis, John, 337
Lewis, J. Patrick, 140, 141, 148, 154, 161
Lewis & Clark (Bertozzi), 337
LGBT (lesbian, gay, bisexual, and
  transgender) literature, 294, 313
Liar and Spy (Stead), 292
Library of Congress Archives, 161
Life and Death of Adolf Hitler, The
  (Giblin), 329
Life and Times of the Honeybee, The
  (Micucci), 325
life changes, realistic fiction, 287–288
life cycle books, nonfiction, 336
*Lifetime: The Amazing Numbers in Animal
  Lives* (Schaefer), 334
Light in the Attic, A (Silverstein), 161
Lightning Thief, The (Riordan), 225
*Li'l Dan the Drummer Boy: A Civil War
  Story* (Beardon), 268
Lily (Henkes), 27
Lily's Crossing (Giff), 258
limericks, 144–146
limited English proficient (LEP), 25–26. *See
  also* English language learners (ELLs)
Lin, Grace, 216
Lincoln, Abraham, 329
Lincoln, Christopher, 219
Lincoln: A Photobiography (Freedman), 329
Lindbergh, Reeve, 190
line, picture books, 111–112, 267
Lion, the Witch, and the Wardrobe, The
  (Lewis), 16, 17
Lion and the Mouse, The (Pinkney), 186, 198
Lionni, Leo, 62
Lions of Little Rock, The
  (Levine), 39, 259
Lion to Guard Us, A (Bulla), 263
Lisette's Angel (Littlesugar), 267
L Is for Lobster (Reynolds), 123
listening skills, read-alouds and, 78
literacy skills. *See also* instructional
  strategies
  critical literacy, 52
  digital literacy, 321
  information literacy, 324
  reader response and engagement, 43
  reading, rates of, 236–237
literature
  across the curriculum, 100–101
  awards for, 19
  defining, 4–5
  digital devices, use of, 26–27
  diversity, 25
  English language learners (ELLs), 25–26
  fiction, guidelines for choosing, 18
  genres and forms, 7–11
  movies and, 27–28

  role in children's lives, 5–7
  teaching guidelines, 19–24
Literature and Reading: Information
  Standard, 44–45, 53–54. *See also*
  Common Core State Standards
  (CCSS)
Literature as Exploration (Rosenblatt), 49
literature circles, 88–94, 95, 105
literature response and engagement. *See*
  reader engagement and response
literature strategy lessons, 93, 98
Little Bear (Minarik), 40
Little Dog and Duncan (George), 150
Little Dog Lost (Bauer), 289
Little Dog Poems (George), 150
Little House on the Prairie (Wilder), 254, 270
Little Mermaid, The (Andersen), 216
Little Orphan Annie (Gray), 257
Little Red Hen, The, 40, 183
Little Red Riding Hood (Hyman), 198
Little Red Riding Hood, variants of,
  179–180, 183, 198
Littles, The (Peterson), 221
Little White Rabbit (Henkes), 40
Little Women (Alcott), 101
*Lives of Extraordinary Women: Rulers,
  Rebels (and What the Neighbors
  Thought)* (Krull), 331
*Lives of the Presidents: Fame, Shame
  (and What the Neighbors Thought)*
  (Krull), 331
Livingston, Myra Cohn, 61
*Lizard and the Sun: An Old Mexican
  Folktale, The* (Ada), 199
Lizzie Bright and the Buckminster Boy
  (Schmidt), 256
*Llama Who Had No Pajama: 100 Favorite
  Poems, The* (Hoberman), 149
Lobel, Arnold, 124, 191
Locomotion (Woodson), 293
London Eye Mystery, The (Dowd), 283, 292
Long, Sylvia, 192
Long Walk to Water, A (Park), 290
Longwalker's Journey (Harrell), 254
Long Way to Chicago, A (Peck), 257
*Lon Po Po: A Red Riding Hood Story from
  China* (Young), 198
*Looking for Miza: The True Story of
  the Mountain Gorilla Family
  Who Rescued One of Their Own*
  (Hatkoff), 319
Lord of the Rings, The (Tolkien), 5, 12, 14,
  43, 224
Lost (McPhail), 299
*Lost Childhood: A World War II Memoir,
  The* (Nir), 331
Lost Island of Tamarind, The
  (Aguiar), 221
Lost on a Mountain in Maine (Fendler), 337
*Lost Trail: Nine Days Alone in the
  Wilderness* (Fendler), 337
Lost Years of Merlin, The (Barron), 225
Lotas de Casha (Madonna), 28
Lotz, Karen, 134
Loud Silence of Maxine Green, The
  (Cushman), 260

Love That Dog (Creech), 293
Love to Langston (Medina), 332
Love You Forever (Munsch), 33
Lowry, Lois, 14, 16, 226, 249, 288
loyalty, fiction theme, 15
Lugalbanda: The Boy Who Got Caught Up in a War: An Epic Tale From Ancient Iraq (Henderson), 188
lullabies, 192–193, 202
Lupica, Mike, 292
Lyddie (Paterson), 249, 255
lyrical poems, 145

Macaulay, David, 126, 325
Machado, Ana Maria, 233
MacLachlan, Patricia, 17, 285
MacLeod, Irene Rutherford, 142
Ma Dear's Aprons (McKissack), 262
Madonna, 28
Mad Potter: George E. Ohr, Eccentric Genius, The (Greenberg), 331
magazines, 4, 161
Maggie's Door (Giff), 17
magic, fantasy fiction, 220–221, 243
magical realism, 290
Magic by the Lake (Eager), 220
Magic School Bus series (Cole), 9, 318, 326
Magic Thief, The (Prineas), 220
Magic Tree House series (Osborne), 223–224
Magic Words (Field), 204
Mailing May (Tunnell), 262
Mamá Goose: A Latino Nursery Treasury (Alda & Campoy), 193
Mammalabilia (Florian), 148
Maniac Magee (Spinelli), 10, 288
Man Who Walked Between the Towers, The (Gerstein), 112
maps, nonfiction, 325
maps, reader responses, 63
maps for travel stories, 299
Mara, Daughter of the Nile (McGraw), 251
Marcel Marceau: Actor Without Words (Schubert), 317
March: Book One (Lewis), 337
Marcus, Leonard S., 110
Markham, Judy, 139–140
Marshall, James, 192, 198
Martha Speaks (Meddaugh), 128
Martin, Ann, 9
Martin, Bill Jr., 86–87, 118
Martin, Rafe, 197
Martin's Big Words: The Life of Dr. Martin Luther King, Jr. (Rappaport), 332
Mary Poppins (Travers), 222, 235
Mary Wore Her Red Dress (Peek), 62
Master Puppeteer, The (Paterson), 253
math, poems for, 151, 152–153
Math Appeal (Tang), 151
Math Curse (Scieszka), 151
Math Fables (Tang), 151
Math-terpieces (Tang), 151
Maximilian and the Mystery of the Guardian Angel (Garza), 292
Mayer, Lynn, 319
Mayfield Crossing (Nelson), 259
McCord, David, 142

McDonald, Suse, 193
McKinley, Robin, 216, 225
McKissack, Frederick, 331
McKissack, Patricia, 263, 331
McMahon, Liz, 315–316
meaning, construction of, 49–53, 88, 197–198
Medina, Tony, 332
Mega Trucks: The Biggest, Toughest Trucks in the World! (Murrell & Gunzi), 319
Me . . . Jane (McDonnell), 14
Meltzer, Milton, 336
memoirs, 331–332
mental challenges, people with, 293–294, 313
mentor texts, 315–316, 343–344
Meow Ruff: A Story in Concrete Poetry (Sidman), 150
merchandising of literature, 27–28
Merlin and the Making of a King (Hodges), 189
messages, nonfiction activities, 342–343
Messenger (Lowry), 226
metaphor, 143, 284–285
Middle Ages, historical fiction, 252, 272, 276
middle elementary children, developmental characteristics, 42
middle school children, developmental characteristics, 42–43
Midwife's Apprentice, The (Cushman), 252
Mighty Miss Malone, The (Curtis), 257
Migrant (Trottier), 118
Mike Fink (Kellogg), 190
Mike Mulligan and His Steam Shovel (Burton), 110
Miller, Debbie, 323
Million-Dollar Throw (Christopher), 292
Million Shades of Gray, A (Kadohata), 247
Milne, A. A., 156
Minn and Jake (Wong), 302
Minor, Wendell, 318
Miracle on 49th Street (Christopher), 292
Miracle's Boys (Woodson), 287
Miraculous Journey of Edward Tulane (DiCamillo), 217, 219
Mirror of Merlin, The (Barron), 225
Missing May (Rylant), 288
Mission to the Moon (Dyer), 325
Mississippi Mud: Three Prairie Journals (Turner), 151, 245
Miss Mary Mack and Other Children's Street Rhymes (Cole & Calmenson), 193
Misty of Chincoteague (Henry), 289
Mitten, The (Brett), 114
Mixed Up Files of Mrs. Basil E. Frankweiler, The (Koenigsburg), 291
Mockingbird (Erskine), 294
Mockingjay (Collins), 227
modeling, shared book experiences and, 82–85
Monarch and Milkweed (Frost), 336
Monkey Island (Fox), 290
monologues, character, 302
Monsieur Marceau: Actor Without Words (Schubert, Dubois), 115
Montgomery, Sy, 316, 324
Moon over Manifest (Vanderpool), 257

Moon Was Tired of Walking on Air (Belting), 188
morals, 187
More Perfect Than the Moon (MacLachlan), 254
More Spice Than Sugar (Morrison), 149
More Stories to Solve (Hamilton & Weiss), 59
More Surprises (Hopkins), 156
More True Lies (Hamilton and Weiss), 59
Moribito: Guardian of the Spirit (Uehashi), 233
Mosque (Macaulay), 325
Mosquito Bite (Siy & Kunkel), 327
Most Beautiful Place in the World, The (Cameron), 281
Mostly True Adventures of Homer P. Figg, The (Philbrick), 255
Mothstorm (Reeve), 227
motif, traditional literature, 178
motivation for reading, 5–6
Mouse and His Child, The (Hoban), 218
Mouse and Lion (Burkert), 186
Mouse and the Motorcycle (Cleary), 216
Mouse & Lion (Burkert), 113
Mouse Rap, The (Myers), 288
Movable Mother Goose, The (Sabuda), 192
movement, poems about, 170–171
movies, literature and, 27–28, 198, 232
Mrs. Frisby and the Rats of NIMH (O'Brien), 218
Muckrakers: How Ida Tarbell, Upton Sinclair, and Lincoln Steffens Helped Expose Scandal, Inspire Reform, and Invent Investigative Journalism (Bausum), 327
Mulan (San Souci), 189
Munro, Roxie, 323
Murphy, Jim, 263, 324, 327
music, reader responses, 61–62
Muu, Moo! Rimas de Animales/Animal Nursery Rhymes (Ada & Campoy), 192
My Brother, My Sister, and I (Watkins), 258
My Brother Loved Snowflakes (Bahr), 119
My Brother Sam Is Dead (Collier and Collier), 16, 52, 247, 253, 270
My First Pocket Guide series (National Geographic), 337
My Friend the Enemy (Cheaney), 258
My Great-Aunt Arizona (Houston), 118
My Head Is Red and Other Riddle Poems (Livingston), 157
My Heart Is on the Ground: The Diary of Nannie Little Rose, a Sioux Girl (Rinaldi), 263
My Louisiana Sky (Holt), 260
My Mexico/Mexico Mio (Johnston), 166
My Name Is America series, 263
My One Hundred Adventures (Horvath), 291
My People (Hughes), 155
My Side of the Mountain (George), 290, 302
mysteries, realistic fiction, 291–292, 312
Mysteries of Harris Burdick, The (Van Allsburg), 120, 233
Mysterious Benedict Society, The (Stewart), 222, 223

mythology, 187–188, 206–207. *See also* traditional literature
Mythology: The Gods, Heroes and Monsters of Ancient Greece (Evans), 187
Mythopoeic Fantasy Award, 19, 361

Naidoo, Beverly, 260, 287
Naked Bunyip Dancing (Herrick), 302
Nancy Drew (Keene), 291
Napoli, Donna Jo, 216
narrative, nonfiction structures, 322
Narrative of the Life of Frederick Douglass: An American Slave (Douglass), 36
narrative poems, 145
National Book Award, 361
National Endowment for the Arts, 236
National Geographic, 161
National Geographic Readers: Great Migrations Butterflies (Marsh), 348
National Picture Book Month, 134
Native Americans. *See also* cultural diversity
    ballads and folk songs, 192
    contemporary realistic fiction, 304
    ghost stories, 200
    historical fiction, 254, 262, 270
    misappropriation of stories, 202–204
    picture books, 304
    poetry, 165
    stereotypes, 235, 270
    traditional literature, 175, 178, 179, 183, 188, 189, 190, 200, 203–204, 206–208
native art, 115
nature poems, 148–149, 171–172
Naylor, Phyllis Reynolds, 9–10
NCTE Award for Excellence in Poetry for Children, 361
Neighborhood Mother Goose, The (Crews), 192
Nelson, Scott, 190
Never Fall Down (McCormack), 261
Never Forgotten (McKissack), 254
Newbery Medal, 19, 235, 329, 361
New Found Land (Wolf), 265
New Way Things Work, The (Macaulay), 325
New York Public Library's National Poetry Contest, 162
Night Before Christmas, The (dePaola), 113
Nightjohn (Paulsen), 255
19 Varieties of Gazelle: Poems from the Middle East (Nye), 166
90 Miles to Havana (Floris-Galbes), 260
Ninth Ward (Rhodes), 290
Nobody Asked Me if I Wanted a Baby Sister (Alexander), 40, 296
No Chocolate (Stewart), 334
No Hickory, No Dickory, No Dock: Caribbean Nursery Rhymes (Agard & Nichols), 192
No Monkeys (Stewart), 334
nonfiction. *See also* instructional strategies
    access features, 325–326
    biographies, 328–333
    blended (faction) books, 350–351
    book lists, 322, 328, 343, 350, 351, 353–357
    categories, overview, 327–328

concept books, 333–337
    culturally diverse learners, 348
    English language learners, 349–350
    evaluation criteria, 319–327
    fiction/nonfiction pairs, 344–347
    format and design, 326–327
    gender preferences, 35–39
    as literature, 4
    literature circles and, 91
    mentor sets, 343–344
    messages activity, 342–343
    overview of, 9, 315–318
    in poetic form, 332–333
    role of, 318–319
    structure and feature charts, 342
    teaching strategies and the CCSS, 338–347
    text characteristics, 43–45
    think-alouds, use of, 338–344
    visual information, 325–326
    writing quality, 321–324
North American Rainforest Scrapbook, A (Wright-Frierson), 336
Nory Ryan's Song (Giff), 256
Notable Book Lists, 19
Notable Trade Books in the Social Sciences, 320
Nothing but the Truth (Avi), 302
November, Alan, 324
nuclear war, historical fiction, 260
Number the Stars (Lowry), 93, 249, 258, 264, 271
nursery rhymes, 191–192, 209–210. *See also* traditional literature
Nursery Tales Around the World (Sierra), 179

O'Connor, Barbara, 282
Odyssey (Homer), 176, 189
Odyssey, The (McCaughrean), 189
Odyssey: A Pop-Up Book, The (Ita), 189
offensive language, historical fiction, 250
Of Nightingales That Weep (Paterson), 252
Of Studies (Bacon), 54
Oh, A-Hunting We Will Go (Langstaff), 62
Oh, Rats!: The Story of Rats and People (Marrin), 321
Okay for Now (Schmidt), 261
Old Elm Speaks: Tree Poems (George), 149
Old McDonald Had a Farm, 198
Old Mother Hubbard, 198
¡Ole! Flamenco (Ancona), 335
Olivia Forms a Band (Falconer), 119
O'Malley, Kevin, 316
omniscient point of view, 17, 285
Once Upon America series, 263
One and Only Ivan, The (Applegate), 66, 218
One Cool Friend (Buzzeo), 119
One Crazy Summer (Williams-Garcia), 248, 259–260
One Fish, Two Fish, Red Fish, Blue Fish (Seuss), 123
One for the Murphys (Hunt), 288
One Thousand Tracings: Healing the Wounds of World War II (Judge), 16, 262
online texts
    characteristics of, 44
    Global Read Aloud, 79

reading slowly, 47
    written response forms, student, 56
onomatopoeia, 142, 284–285
On the Wing (Florian), 148
On the Wings of Eagles (Peck), 258
oral responses, students, 56–58
Orbis Pictus Award for Outstanding Nonfiction for Children, 19, 115, 320, 323, 361
organization, nonfiction, 320, 321, 322
Original Art Lifetime Achievement Award, 362
Other Side of Truth, The (Naidoo), 287
Our Only May Amelia (Holm), 254
Our Secret, Siri Aang (Kessler), 289
Out in the Dark and Daylight (Fisher), 149
Out of My Mind (Draper), 280, 293, 302
Out of the Dust (Hesse), 10, 257
Outstanding Science Trade Books for Children, 320
Owl Moon (Yolen), 112

Paddington (Bond), 27
Pain and the Great One, The (Blume), 301
Pajaro Verde/The Green Bird (Hayes), 183
Palacio, R. J., 95
Pale Male: Citizen Hawk of New York City (Schulman), 334
Paleo Bugs: Survival of the Creepiest (Bradley), 327
Pallotta, Jerry, 123
pantomime, 61
Paolini, Christopher, 226
Paradise Lost (Milton), 226
Parkinson, Siobhán, 3–4
Parnall, Peter, 119
partial biographies, 330–331
Partnership for 21st Century Skills, 23–24, 52, 93, 120, 203
Paterson, Katherine, 247, 249, 252, 253, 281, 283
patterned language books, 124–125
Paul Bunyan (Kellogg), 190
Paul Revere's Ride (Bing), 151
Paulsen, Gary, 14, 17, 55, 283, 290, 331
Pecos Bill (Kellogg), 190
peers
    contemporary realistic fiction, 287–288
    reader response and engagement, 46
Penny from Heaven (Holm), 260
Percy Jackson and the Olympians (Riordan), 9, 46, 213, 225, 236
Perfect Square (Hall), 113
performance, poetry, 159–160
Perkins, Lynn, 287
Perrault, Charles, 183
personification, 143
Peter Pan (Barrie), 222
pets, 296. *See also* animals
Pharaoh's Daughter: A Novel of Ancient Egypt (Lester), 250, 251
Phoenix Award, 362
photographic essays, 334–335
photographs, nonfiction, 325, 334–335
physical challenges, people with, 293–294, 313

Picture Book of Eleanor Roosevelt, A
(Adler), 330
Picture Book of Helen Keller, A (Adler), 330
Picture Book of Sojourner Truth, A
(Adler), 331
picture books
alphabet books, 122, 123, 124, 125
biographies, 329–330, 354–355
book list for older students, 121
book lists, 122, 123, 124, 125, 135–138,
185, 330
Common Core Standards and, 128–131
concept books, 122, 333–337
contemporary realistic fiction, 284,
295–296, 303–305
digital picture books, 133–134
for diverse learners, 132
easy-to-read, 123–124
elements of, 111–115
for English language learners, 133
evaluation criteria, 121
fantasy and science fiction, 228, 238–241
folktales, 185, 228
for genre and thematic connections,
121–122
graphic novels, 126, 127
historical fiction, 262–263, 267–268, 269
interactive books, 125–126
LGBT literature, 294
media used, list of, 116–117
nonfiction, 316, 319, 333–337
overview of, 7–8, 16, 18, 109–111
pop-up books, 125
postmodern picture books, 126–127
predictable patterned language, 124–125
role of, 120–121
wordless and almost wordless books, 124
writing in, 115, 118–120
Pictures of Hollis Woods (Giff), 288
picture storybooks, 110
Pilkey, Dave, 46
Pinballs, The (Byars), 288
Pink and Say (Polacco), 268
Pinkney, Brian, 192
Pinkney, Jerry, 186, 190, 198
*Pio Peep! Traditional Spanish Nursery
Rhymes* (Ada), 192
Pippi Longstocking (Lindgren), 222
Pippo the Fool (Fern), 119
Place for Butterflies, A (Stewart), 334
Plato, 5
playground traditional literature, 193
Play Rhymes (Brown), 86
plays, traditional literature, 198
Plays from Hispanic Tales (Winther), 199
plot
contemporary realistic fiction, 283
fantasy and science fiction, 230–231
fiction, 18
historical fiction, 251
motifs, traditional literature, 178
overview, 13–14
picture books, 118–120
science fiction and fantasy, 215
traditional literature, 177, 180
variants and versions, 178–179

plot charts, 231–232
plot diagrams, 64
Plourde, Lynn, 284–285, 337
Pocketful of Posies (Mavor), 192
podcasts, 58, 86, 161
Poetrees (Florian), 148
poetry
anthologies and collections, 154–156
book lists, 152–154, 155, 158, 163–165,
169–174
close reading of, 167–168
content-area studies and, 151, 152–154
culturally diverse students, 163–165
English language learners, 166–167
evaluation criteria, 147
genres and forms, 144–146
historical fiction and, 265, 267
literary elements of, 141–144
nonfiction, 332–333
overview of, 8, 139–141
poetry conversations, 158
poetry novels, 144–146
Poetry Out Loud, 162
Poetry Slam, Inc., 162
poetry slams, 160
Poetry Speaks to Children, 161
realistic fiction, 302
role of, 146–147
thematic poetry, 147–150, 169–174
for young children, 156
point of view
activities for CCSS, 300–302
contemporary realistic fiction, 285–286,
300–302
overview, 17–18
Polacco, Patricia, 118
Poole, Amy, 186
Popcorn! (Landau), 325
pop-up books
epics, 189
fantasy fiction, 221
nonfiction, 326, 327
overview of, 125
rhymes, 193
traditional literature, 186, 198
Popville (Boisrobert & Rigaud), 125
Porcupine Year, The (Erdrich), 254
Posey the Kitten (Newberry), 296
postmodern fantasy and science fiction, 232
postmodern picture books, 126–127
Potter, Beatrix, 216
Potter, Giselle, 186
Pot That Juan Built, The (Andrews-
Goebel), 332
pourquoi stories, 175–176, 188, 207
Powell, Nate, 337
Power Sound Editor, 161
Prairie Songs (Conrad), 254
predictable patterned language books,
124–125
preferences of readers, 35–39
Prelutsky, Jack, 148, 150, 154, 156, 161
prequels, 232
prereading discussions, 72, 77
preschool-aged readers, 40, 156
Press Here (Tuller), 125

Priceman, Marjorie, 198
primary school children, developmental
characteristics, 40–42
Prince, April Jones, 333
Princess Diaries, The (Cabot), 9
Pringle, Laurence, 324, 335
print exploration activities, 85
problem novels, 287
professional development, 23
prose, picture books, 115, 118–120
protagonist, 12
P.S. Be Eleven (Williams-Garcia), 260
Psyche and Eros: The Lady and the Monster
(Croall), 187
public domain, poetry, 162
public domain, stories in, 198
Pullman, Philip, 226
puppets, reader response and, 59, 60
Pura Belpré Award, 118, 362
purpose for reading, 49–50
*Put Your Eyes Up Here and Other School
Poems* (Dakos), 150
puzzle poems, 157, 174
Pyramid (Macaulay), 325
Pyramids and Mummies (Bolton), 326

Q Is for Quark: A Science Alphabet Book
(Schwartz), 123, 333
*Queen's Progress: An Elizabethan Alphabet,
The* (Mannis), 333
question and answer, nonfiction
structures, 322
Questions (Hopkins), 156
quest stories, 16, 224–226
Quindlen, Anna, 32

*Rabbit's Snow Dance: A Traditional Iroquois
Story* (Bruchac), 188
race. *See* cultural diversity
Race to Save the Lord God Bird, The
(Hoose), 335
Ralph S. Mouse (Cleary), 216
Rama and the Demon King (Souhami), 189
Ramayana (India), 189
Ramayana for Children, The (Sharma), 189
Ramayana: The Epic for Children
(Shastri), 189
Ramona series (Cleary), 288, 291
Rand, Ted, 262
Ranger Rick, 4
Rappaport, Doreen, 263
Rapunzel, 216
Raschka, Chris, 112, 128, 155, 296
Rasco, Carol, 133
Rasmussen, Knud, 204
Rathmann, Peggy, 124
readability levels, 44–45
read-alouds
book list for, 104
fantasy and science fiction, 235–236
historical fiction, 257
nonfiction, 350
overview, 77–82, 83
picture books, 129, 131
poetry, 147, 166

Read and Retell (Brown and Cambourne), 57

reader engagement and response. *See also* instructional strategies
 after read-aloud sessions, 82
 art and music responses, 61–62
 books boys may like, 37
 books with female protagonists, 38–39
 Common Core Standards and, 53–54
 context and, 45–48
 developmental characteristics and, 39–43
 drama activities, 42, 58–61, 86, 233, 301–302
 graphic organizers, 63, 64, 298
 importance of, 32–33
 literacy skills and, 43
 literature circles, 88–94, 95, 105
 maps and time lines, 63
 oral responses, 56–58
 overview of, 31–33
 poetry, 158
 readers, characteristics of, 33–39
 reader's workshop, 97–98
 shared reading activities, 85–87
 student responses, overview, 54–55
 text characteristics, 43–45
 traditional approaches, 48–49
 transactional response theory, 49–53
 value of reader response activities, 63–66
 written responses, 55–56

readers, characteristics of
 3–5 year olds, 40
 5 to 7 year olds, 40–42
 8 to 10 year olds, 42
 11 to 13 year olds, 42–43
 experiential background, 33–34
 interests of, 34
 literacy skills of, 43
 preferences of, 35–39

reader's theater, 61

reader's workshop, 94–100

reading, rates of, 236–237

Reading Aloud Handbook, The (Trelease), 78

Reading: Foundational Skills Standard, 86–87

Reading Is Fundamental (RIF), 25, 133

Reading Rockets, 114

Reading Standard for Literature. *See also* Common Core State Standards (CCSS)
 key ideas and details, 21–23

Reading Teacher, The, 320

ReadWriteThink, 162

realism, appropriate levels of, 282

realistic art, 115

realistic fiction. *See* contemporary realistic fiction

Recess Queen, The (O'Neill), 305

Red Hot Salsa: Bilingual Poems on Being Young and Latino in the United States, 161

Red Leaf, Yellow Leaf (Ehlert), 113

Red Moon at Sharpsburg (Wells), 255

Red Pyramid, The (Riordan), 225

Red Riding Hood, variants of, 179–180, 183

Red Sings from Treetops: A Year in Color (Sidman), 112, 149

Red Umbrella, The (Gonzalez), 260

Redwall (Jacques), 218

Reese, Debbie, 204

Reeve, Philip, 227

reference books, 337

Reinhart, Matthew, 125, 326

Relatives Came, The (Rylant), 296

religion
 creation stories, 188
 myths, 187–188
 spiritual songs, 192–193

repeated readings, 73

representational art, 115

Reptiles (Arlon & Gordon-Harris), 325

Reptiles (Weber), 335

Requiem: Poems of the Terezin Ghetto (Janeczko), 265

responsibility, fiction themes, 16

retelling, fantasy and science fiction, 229–230, 232–233

retelling, oral responses, 57, 86

retelling journals, 56

Return of Buddy Bush, The (Moses), 259

Return to the Hundred Acre Wood (Benedictus), 218

Revenge of Ishtar, The (Zeman), 188

Revolutionary War, historical fiction, 253

rhyme, poetry elements, 141–142

rhymes, 193, 208–210. *See also* poetry

Rhymes 'Round the World (Charo), 192

rhythm, poetry and, 142–143

Riddleicious (Lewis), 158

Riddlelightful (Lewis), 157

Riddle Rhymes (Gorton), 158

Riddle Road: Poems in Puzzles and Pictures (Spires), 157

riddles, 157, 174, 193

Riordan, Rick, 10, 213

Rising Star of Rusty Nail, The (Blume), 260

River, The (Paulsen), 290

River of Life (Miller), 323

River of Words: The Story of William Carlos Williams, A (Bryant), 332

Road to Oz: Twists, Turns, Bumps, and Triumphs in the Life of L. Frank Baum, The (Krull), 330

Robert F. Sibert Informational Book Medal, 362

Robots (Giffords), 326

role-playing games, 236–237

roles, literature circles, 91–92

Roll of Thunder, Hear My Cry (Taylor), 11–19, 42, 50, 83, 130, 248, 249, 257, 265, 270

Roman Mysteries series, 263

Rome: In Spectacular Cross-Section (Solway), 325, 335

Rose Daughter (McKinley), 216

Rosen, Michael, 193

Rosenblatt, Louise, 49

Rosen's Database for Digital Literacy, 321

Rosie the Riveter: Women Working on the Home Front in World War II (Colman), 317

Ross, Gayle, 204

Rounds, Glenn, 193

Rowling, J. K., 13, 35, 220–221

Royal Diaries series, 263

Ruby Holler (Creech), 284

Rules (Lord), 294

Rumpelstiltskin, variants of, 179

Runaway (Van Draanen), 299

Runaway Ralph (Cleary), 216

Ryan, Pam Muñoz, 118

Rylant, Cynthia, 40, 118, 323–324

Sabuda, Robert, 125, 221, 326

Sacred Places (Yolen), 151

sacred stories, 181–182

Salem witch trials, historical fiction, 266

Salisbury, Graham, 259

Sally Ann Thunder Ann Whirlwind Crockett (Kellogg), 190

Same Stuff As Stars, The (Paterson), 281

Same Sun Here (House & Viswani), 302

Sandburg, Carl, 142, 148

Sandburg Treasury: Prose and Poetry for Young People, The, 148

San Souci, Robert, 189, 190

Sarah, Plain and Tall (MacLachlan), 17, 49, 245, 254

Sarah Bishop (O'Dell), 253

Sardines Swim High Across the Sky (Prelutsky), 150

Sarny: A Life Remembered (Paulson), 255

Saving Shiloh (Naylor), 289

Savvy (Law), 220

"Say Something," 57

Scary Stories to Tell in the Dark (Schwartz), 189

Scat (Hiaasen), 291

Schertie, Alice, 192

Schmidt, Gary, 256

Schoenherr, John, 112

school, poems about, 149–150, 170

school, realistic fiction, 293, 308–309, 312–313

Schwartz, Alvin, 189

science, poems for, 151, 153–154

science fiction. *See also* fantasy fiction
 book lists, 234, 238–244
 cultural diversity, 233–235
 English language learners, 235–236
 evaluation criteria, 214–215
 future worlds, 226–227
 overview, 8, 211–213
 picture books, 228, 238–241
 role of, 213–214
 space travel and beyond, 227–228
 supplemental electronic media, 236–237
 teaching strategies for CCSS, 229–233
 traditional literature, expansions of, 228

Science Verse (Scieszka), 151

Scieszka, Jon, 36, 113, 151, 197

Scorpions!: Strange and Wonderful (Pringle), 335

Scott O'Dell Award for Historical Fiction, 362

scrapbooks, 299

Scumble (Law), 220
search for freedom, theme of, 15
Search for the Golden Moon Bear: Science and Adventure in Pursuit of a New Species (Montgomery), 316
Search for Wondla, The (Diterlizzi), 237
seasons, poems about, 148–149, 171–172
secondary text, nonfiction structures, 322
Secret World of Walter Anderson, The (Bass), 109
segregation, historical fiction, 255–256, 259–261
self-concept, realistic fiction lists, 309
Selznick, Brian, 110–111
semantic maps, 64
Sendak, Maurice, 40, 44, 111
sequels, student writing, 232
sequence, nonfiction structures, 322
series books
    contemporary realistic fiction, 291, 296–297, 310
    historical fiction, 263
    identification and field guides, 337
    overview of, 9–10
Series of Unfortunate Events, A (Snicket), 222
Serpent Never Sleeps, The (O'Dell), 253
Sessions, Kate, 330
setting
    contemporary realistic fiction, 284
    fiction, 14, 16, 18
    historical fiction, 249, 251
    picture books, 119–120
    science fiction and fantasy, 215
    traditional literature, 177
Seven Blind Mice (Young), 186
Seven Day Magic (Eager), 220
Seven Songs of Merlin, The (Barron), 215, 225
sexual orientation, 294
Shades of Gray (Reeder), 255
Shadow Spinner (Fletcher), 251
Shakespeare Bats Cleanup (Koertge), 10
shape, nonfiction books, 326
shape, picture books, 112–113
shape, poetry, 143–144
Shape Game, The (Browne), 332
shared book experience, 82–87, 104–105
Shiloh (Naylor), 42, 49, 289, 305
Shiloh Season (Naylor), 289
Shooting the Moon (Dowell), 261
Shulevitz, Uri, 28
Sidman, Joyce, 149, 151, 161
Sign of the Beaver (Speare), 270
Sign of the Chrysanthemum, The (Paterson), 252
Silence of Our Friends, The (Powell), 337
Sill, Cathryn, 333
Silverstein, Shel, 33, 148, 161
simpletons, stories of, 184
Sing Down the Moon (O'Dell), 245, 254
Singer, Marilyn, 150
Single Shard, A (Park), 252
Sing of the Earth and Sky: Poems About Our Planet and the Wonders Beyond (Fisher), 149

size, nonfiction texts, 326
Skeleton Creek (Carman), 237
Skeleton Man (Bruchac), 220
sketchbook journals, 56
sketchbooks, nonfiction texts, 335–336
sketch-to-stretch, 62, 230
Skip Across the Ocean: Nursery Rhymes from Around the World (Benjamin), 192
Sky Dancers (Kirk), 262
Skylark, Caleb's Story (MacLachlan), 254
Slake's Limbo (Holman), 290
slavery, historical fiction, 253, 254–255, 266, 272–273, 276–277
Sleeping Beauty, The, 181, 183
Sleep Rhymes Around the World (Yolen), 192
Slopes of War (Perez), 264
Small, David, 119
Small Adventures of Popeye and Elvis, The (O'Connor), 287
Smedry, Alcatraz, 10
Smith, Charles R. Jr., 155
Smoky Night (Bunting), 52, 113, 296
Sneeze! (Siy & Kunkel), 327
Snicket, Lemony, 120
Snow Day (Plourde), 284–285
Snow Queen, The (Andersen), 216
Snow Treasure (McSwigen), 263
Snow White, 181, 198
So, Meilo, 334
social issues, book lists, 309–310
social issues, using books as therapy, 305–306
social networks, reader engagement and, 33, 299
Social Responsibilities Round Table, 294
social studies. *See also* historical fiction
    nonfiction book list, 356–357
    poems for, 151, 152
Soentpiet, Chris, 267
So Far from the Bamboo Grove (Watkins), 258
So Far from the Sea (Bunting), 267
software. *See also* Tech Click
    graphic organizers, 63
    plot charts, 231
    presentation software, 295
    writing aps, 235
Sojourner Truth: A Voice for Freedom (McKissack), 331
Somebody and the Three Blairs (Tolhorst), 228
Something Beautiful (Wyeth), 296
Sometimes I'm Bombaloo (Vail), 284
Song of Mulan, The (Lee), 189
Song of the Trees (Taylor), 257
Song of the Water Boatman and Other Pond Poems (Sidman), 151
songs, traditional literature, 192–193, 202
sound, poetry and, 141–142
South, Todd, 192
South, Wayne, 192
space travel, 227–228, 244
Speaking and Listening Standards, 89
Speak to Me (and I Will Listen Between the Lines) (English), 149

Special Fate: Chiune Sugihara, Hero of the Holocaust, A (Gold), 330–331
specialized nonfiction books, 335
Spectacular Spider Book, The (Davies), 317, 319
Spell of the Tiger: The Man-Eaters of Sundarbans (Montgomery), 316, 317
Spiderwick Chronicles, The (Black & DiTerlizzi), 222–223
Spier, Peter, 193
Spinelli, Jerry, 10, 285–286
Spinning Through the Universe: A Novel in Poems from Room 214 (Frost), 302
Spirin, Gennady, 198
spirituals, 192–193
Splash! (Levy), 149
Splendors and Glooms (Schlitz), 222
sports, poems about, 170–171
sports, realistic fiction, 292, 309, 312
Sports Book, The (Summers), 319
Sports! Sports! Sports! (Hopkins), 156
Spot (Hill), 125
Stanley, Diane, 330
Starcross (Reeve), 227
Stead, Rebecca, 10
Step from Heaven, A (Na), 288
Stepping on the Cracks (Hahn), 258, 264
stereotypes, traditional literature, 181
Stevens, Janet, 186
Stevenson, Robert Louis, 1, 4
Stewart, Melissa, 334
Stewart, Trenton Lee, 222
Still More Stories to Solve (Hamilton & Weiss), 59
Stine, R. L., 9, 33, 46
Stone Soup, 55
Stories to Solve (Hamilton & Weiss), 59
Storm Before Atlanta, The (Schwabach), 255
Storm in the Barn (Phelan), 257
storyboards, 86
Story Jumper, 176
Story of Lightning and Thunder, The (Bryan), 175, 188
Story of the Milky Way, The (Ross & Bruchac), 188
story structure maps, 64
storytelling, English language learners and, 202
storytelling, reader response, 59–61
Strange Case of Origami Yoda, The (Angleberger), 293
strategies. *See* instructional strategies
Strega Nona (dePaola), 113
structure and feature charts, nonfictions, 342
STW (see, think, wonder), 131
style
    contemporary realistic fiction, 284–285
    fiction, 17, 18
    nonfiction, 321–324
    traditional literature, 178
substantiality of texts, 45
Subtle Knife, The (Pullman), 226
Summer on the Moon (Fogelin), 287
Summersaults (Florian), 148
Sundiata: Lion King of Mali (Wisniewski), 189

Sunflakes (Moore), 61
Superfudge (Blume), 291
supernatural stories, 219–220, 242
Surprises (Hopkins), 156
surrealistic art, 115
survey books, 335
survival stories, realistic fiction, 289–290, 311–312
Sutcliff, Rosemary, 251
Swanson, James L., 331
Sweet Smell of Roses, The (Johnson), 262, 267, 268
Sweet Whispers, Brother Rush (Hamilton), 220
Swimming Upstream: Middle School Poems (George), 149
Swimmy (Lionni), 62
symbolism, picture books, 268

T4 (LeZotte), 258
table of contents, 338–339
tables, nonfiction, 325
Taking Sides (Soto), 292
Tale of Despereaux, The (DiCamillo), 12, 213, 216–217, 232
Tale of Peter Rabbit, The (Potter), 110
Tale of Rabbit and Coyote, The (Johnston), 177, 199
Tales from Outer Suburbia (Tan), 110
Tales From the Odyssey (Osborn), 189
Tales of a Fourth Grade Nothing (Blume), 282, 291
Talking Like the Rain: A First Book of Poetry (Kennedy), 156
Talking Walls (Knight), 326
tall tales, 8, 190, 208
Tan, Shaun, 110
Tang, Greg, 151
Tarantula Scientist, The (Montgomery), 49, 50
Taylor, Mildred, 11–12, 13, 17, 22, 248, 249, 257
teachers. *See also* instructional strategies
 influence on reader response and engagement, 46–48
 role in promoting literacy, 5–6, 23
 transactional and critical perspectives, 51–53
Tech Click
 Alice (Naylor), 9–10
 AmericanFolklore.net, 185
 author video of writing process, Melissa Stewart, 334
 book sources, 100
 Children's Book Council, book search, 265
 Common Sense Media, 24, 321
 concept webs, 269
 contemporary realistic literature project, 295
 Facebook pages, 299
 Garfield, reading attitudes survey, 34
 Global Read Aloud, 79
 Glogster, 129
 graphic organizers, 298
 Green Thumb (Thomas), 52

Guys Read, 36
historical fiction microblogs, 261
Huckleberry Finn, controversy about, 102
infographics, 348
information literacy, 324
Intellectual Freedom Office of the American Library Association, 103
International Reading Association, Cube Creator, 268
Interrupting Chicken (Stein), 131
Journey North, butterfly migration, 348
KWL and STW, 131
literature circles, 93–94
The Mysteries of Harris Burdick (Van Allsburg), 120, 233
Myths Around the World, 187
National Picture Book Month, 134
online materials, fantasy fiction, 237
online story retelling sites, 56
OverDrive library, digital downloads, 333
picture book creator Web sites, 114, 115
Picturing Books Web site, 111
plot charts, aps for, 231
podcasts, 58
poetry, audio performance, 161
postmodern fantasy and science fiction, 232
pourquoi stories, 188
pronouncing dictionary, 323
read-aloud book lists, 80
Reading Is Fundamental, 25
recording performances, 58
reference books online, 337
Rosen's Database for Digital Literacy, 321
"Storytelling Workshop," 61
trading cards, characters, 299
traditional literature, blogging about, 204
traditional literature, multimedia versions, 198
traditional literature, Native American culture, 203
traditional literature, projects for, 203
traditional literature, writing ideas, 197
travel stories, mapping of, 299
Unite for Literacy, 133
video recording, dramatizations, 302
WebQuests, 271
Word Mover, 300
writing aps, 235
technology. *See also* Tech Click
 audio files, downloading, 161
 audio files, recording of, 161
 digital devices, 26–27
 digital picture books, 133–134
 English language learners and, 26
 graphic organizer software, 63
 literature programs and, 21
 reader engagement and, 32–33
 reader's workshop, 98, 100
 reading preferences and, 39
 reading slowly, 47
Story Jumper, 176
traditional literature, multimedia versions, 198
"Teddy Bear, Teddy Bear," 86–87
Ten in the Bed (Cabrera), 193

Ten Kings and the Worlds They Rules (Meltzer), 331
Ten Little Fingers and Ten Little Toes (Fox), 156
Ten Times Better (Michelson), 151
Terlecky, Karen, 82
text, picture books, 115, 118–120
text characteristics, readers and, 43–45
text complexity, 44–45
text-dependent questions, 73, 75–76
text features, nonfiction, 338–344
text innovations, 86
text substantiality, 45
texture, picture books, 113
Thanks to the Animals (Sockabasin), 119
That is Not a Good Idea! (Willems), 133
theme
 contemporary realistic fiction, 284
 fiction and, 14, 15–16, 18
 thematic poetry, 147–150, 169–174
 theme studies, fantasy, 230
 traditional literature, 178
Theodor Seuss Geisel Award, 124, 362
"The President Has Been Shot!": The Assassination of John F. Kennedy (Swanson), 331
think-alouds, 338–344
39 Clues, The series, 39, 237
This Little Light of Mine (Lewis), 193
3 Little Dassies, The (Brett), 114
Three Little Pigs, The, 179, 198
Three Pigs, The (Wiesner), 112–113
Three Times Lucky (Turnage), 285, 291
Thumbelina (Andersen), 216
Thunder at Gettysburg (Gauch), 255
Thunder over Kandahar (McKay), 290
Tikki Tikki Tembo (Mosel), 188
time lines, nonfiction, 325
time lines, reader responses, 63, 299
time travel fantasy, 223–224, 243
Time Warp Trio (Scieszka), 9, 223–224
Tingle, Tim, 220
Titanic, 14
Toad Is the Uncle of Heaven (Lee), 188
To Dance: A Ballerina's Graphic Novel (Siegel), 337
Tolan, Stephanie, 282
Tolkien, J. R. R., 12, 221, 224
Tomie dePaola: His Art and His Stories (Elleman), 332
Tortilla Para Mama (Cooney), 192
Tortoise and the Hare, The (Stevens), 186
Tough Boy Sonatas (Crisler), 149
toys, fantasy fiction, 216–217, 242–243
Toys Go Out: Being the Misadventures of a Knowledgeable Stingray, a Toughy Little Buffalo, and Someone Called Plastic (Jenkins), 219
trade books, defined, 5
trading cards, characters, 299
traditional literature
 ballads and folk songs, 192–193
 book lists, 179–180, 191, 206–210, 241–242
 Common Core Standards and, 193–198

culturally diverse students and, 199–202
elements of, 177–179
English language learners, 199, 202–203
evaluation of, 181–182
fables and learning stories, 185–187
fantasy and science fiction, use of,
212–213, 216, 228, 241–242
folktales, 179–180, 183–185
ghost stories, 189–190
legends and epics, 188–189
misappropriation of, 203–204
myths, 187–188
nursery rhymes, 191–192
overview, 8, 175–177
picture books, 228
playground and game-related, 193
role of, 180–181
tall tales, 190
transactional response theory, 49–53
transgender literature, 294, 313
transitional books
contemporary realistic fiction, 296–297,
310
historical fiction, 263, 275
travel stories, mapping of, 299
*Tree Lady: The True Story of How One
Tree-Loving Woman Changed a City
Forever, The* (Hopkins), 330
Trelease, Jim, 78
trickster stories, 183
triple-entry journal, 229–230
Trouble with Amelia, The (Holm), 254
Trouble with Cauliflower, The (Sutton), 113
True Confessions of Charlotte Doyle, The
(Avi), 253
True Lies (Hamilton & Weiss), 59
True Story of the Three Little Pigs, The
(Scieszka), 228
TU Books, 235
Tuck Everlasting (Babbitt), 79, 223
Tuesday (Wiesner), 124
Tunnell, Michael, 262
Turkey Girl: A Zuni Cinderella Story
(Pollock), 204
Turnage, Sheila, 291
Turtle in Paradise (Holm), 257
Twain, Mark, 7, 101, 102
*Twelve Rounds to Glory: The Story of
Muhammad Ali* (Smith), 332
21st-Century Skills
digital devices, use of, 26–27
framework for, 23–24
26 Fairmount Avenue (dePaola), 332
Twilight (Meyer), 102, 212
two-word strategy, 229
typeface, nonfiction, 327

Ubiquitous: Celebrating Nature's Survivors
(Sidman), 151
Ugly Duckling, The (Andersen), 216
UnBEElievables (Florian), 148
Underground (Macaulay), 325
understatement, picture books, 118
Under the Blood-Red Sun (Salisbury), 259
Under the Mesquite (McCall), 288
Unwind (Shusterman), 227

*Unwitting Wisdom: An Anthology of Aesop's
Fables* (Ward), 186
Up, Tall and High! (Long), 42, 124
Upstairs Room, The (Reiss), 258
utopian societies, 226–227, 244

values, traditional literature and, 180–181
Van Allsburg, Chris, 228
Vardell, Sylvia, 161
variants, traditional literature, 178–179
Vegetable Alphabet Book, The (Pallotta), 123
Velveteen Rabbit, The (Williams), 110, 218
Venn diagrams, 64, 196, 298, 344
Vennema, Peter, 330
verse novel, 10
versions, traditional literature, 178–179
Very Busy Spider, The (Carle), 125
Very Hungry Caterpillar, The (Carle), 40,
55, 62, 126
Very Quiet Cricket, The (Carle), 125
*VHERSES: A Celebration of Outstanding
Women* (Lewis), 149
video recording, dramatizations, 302
video recording, writing process of Melissa
Stewart, 334
Vietnam war, 259–261, 275, 278
violence, historical fiction, 269–270
violence, traditional literature, 180–181
Viorst, Judith, 118
visual design, nonfiction, 320
visual information, nonfiction, 325–326
visual representation, poetry, 143–144
vocabulary. *See also* language
digital picture books and, 134
historical fiction, 250, 265, 269
nonfiction, 323
nursery rhymes, 191
pronouncing dictionary, online, 323
read-alouds, importance of, 78
shared reading activities, 85, 86
voice, of writer, 118
Voices from the Alamo (Garland), 265
Voices from the Civil War (Meltzer), 336
Voice Thread, 161

Waber, Bernard, 118
Waiting for Normal (Connor), 281, 288
Waiting for Wings (Ehlert), 113
Wait till Helen Comes (Hahn), 219
Walking on the Boundaries of Change
(Holbrook), 149
Walking to the Bus Rider Blues (Robinet),
259
Walk Two Moons (Creech), 288, 299
Walsh, Jill Paton, 227, 246
Wanda Gag Read Aloud Award, 362
Wanderings of Odysseus, The
(Sutcliff), 189
Watsons Go to Birmingham, The (Curtis),
22, 193
Way to Start a Day, The (Baylor), 118
*Way We Work: Getting to Know the
Amazing Human Body, The*
(Macaulay), 325
We Are the Book (Willems), 125

*Weave Little Stars into My Sleep: Native
American Lullabies* (Philip), 192
Web sites. *See also* Tech Click
information accuracy, 324
nonfiction access features, 325–326
OverDrive library, digital downloads,
333
Wednesday Wars, The (Schmidt), 261
Weedflower (Kadohata), 259
We Had a Picnic This Sunday Past
(Woodson), 296
Well, The (Taylor), 257
Wells, Rosemary, 192
We're Going on a Bear Hunt (Rosen),
87, 193
*We Shall Overcome: A Song That Changed
the World* (Stotts), 325
Westcott, Nadine, 193
Westing Game, The (Raskin), 283, 291
westward expansion, historical fiction,
254, 276
*We've Got a Job: The 1963 Birmingham
Children's March* (Levinson), 334
What Do Wheels Do All Day? (Prince), 333
What Is Goodbye? (Grimes), 302
*What's for Dinner: Quirky, Squirmy Poems
from the Animal World* (Hauth), 151
What's So Bad About Being an Only Child?
(Best), 296
*What You Never Knew About Beds,
Bedrooms and Pajamas* (Lauber), 335
When Clay Sings (Baylor), 118
When I Was a Soldier (Zenatti), 331
When I Was Young in the Mountains
(Rylant), 112, 118
When My Name Was Keoko (Park), 258
*When Riddles Come Rumbling: Poems to
Ponder* (Dotlich), 158
*When Sophie Gets Angry—Really, Really
Angry* (Bang), 112, 129, 284
When the Chenoo Howls (Bruchac &
Bruchac), 189
*When the Wolves Returned: Restoring
Nature's Balance in Yellowstone*
(Patent), 318
*When Thunder Comes: Poems for Civil
Rights Leaders* (Lewis), 267
When You Reach Me (Stead), 10, 224
*Where the Action Was: Women War
Correspondents in World War II*
(Colman), 336
Where the Mountain Meets the Moon (Lin),
216, 233
Where the Red Fern Grows (Rawls),
283, 289
Where the Steps Were (Cheng), 61, 302
Where the Wild Things Are (Sendak), 44,
110, 111
Which Way Freedom? (Wells), 255
Which Way to the Dragon! (Holbrook), 149
Whisper in the Dark (Bruchac), 220
Whistle for Willie (Keats), 40
White, E. B., 17, 34, 218
White Dynamite and Curly Kid (Martin &
Archambault), 118
White Socks Only (Coman), 270

Who Is Harris Burdick (Van Allsburg), 120
Why Don't You Get a Horse, Sam Adams? (Fritz), 330
Why Mosquitoes Buzz in People's Ears (Aardema), 175, 178
Wiesner, David, 112–113, 120, 124
Wiggle Waggle Fun: Stories and Rhymes for the Very Very Young (Mayo), 156
Wildsmith, Brian, 186
Willems, Mo, 40, 133
Williams-Garcia, Rita, 259–260
Willow Run (Giff), 258
Wind in the Willows (Grahame), 216
Wind Rider (Williams), 251
Wings (Yolen), 187
Winnie the Pooh (Milne), 156, 218
Winter Eyes (Florian), 148
Winters, Jeanette, 192
witches, 220–221
Witch of Blackbird Pond (Speare), 253
With One White Wing (Spires), 157
Witness (Hesse), 265
Wizard of Earthsea, The (LeGuin), 215, 225
wizards, 220–221
Wolves Are Back, The (George), 318
Woman in the Moon, The (Rattigan), 177
Woman Unafraid: The Achievements of Frances Perkins, Secretary of Labor, A (Colman), 331
Wonder (Palacio), 95, 279–280, 281, 286, 293, 302
Wonderful Flight to the Mushroom Planet, The (Cameron), 227
Wonderful Wizard of Oz (Baum), 221
Wonderful Wizard of Oz: A Commemorative Pop-Up (Sabuda), 221
Wonderful Words: Poems About Reading, Writing, Speaking and Listening (Hopkins), 150

Wonderstruck (Selznick), 111, 283
wonder tales, 184
Wong, Janet, 161, 163
Woodson, Jacqueline, 132, 287, 294
wordless books, 110, 305
Word Mover, 300
wordplay, 148
word webs, 64
World According to Dog, The (Sidman), 150
World of Christopher Robin, The (Milne), 156
World of Wonders, A (Lewis), 151
worldview, traditional literature and, 180
World War II, 258–259, 266, 274–275, 277, 331
Wreath for Emmett Till, A (Nelson), 259
Wright 3 (Dowd), 292
Wright Brothers, The (Edwards), 332
Wright-Frierson, Virginia, 335–336
Wringer (Spinelli), 285–286
Wrinkle in Time, A (L'Engle), 215, 228
write-arounds, 56
writing activities
    letter and diary writing, 300
    shared reading, 85
writing quality, nonfiction, 321–324
Writing Standard, reader's workshop, 96
writing style
    fiction, 17
    historical fiction, 250, 251
    nonfiction, 320
Writing with Writers: Poetry, 161
written conversations, 56
written responses, students, 55–56

Yang the Youngest and His Terrible Ear (Namioka), 288
Year Down Yonder, The (Peck), 257
Yearling, The (Rawlings), 5

Year of Impossible Goodbyes, The (Choi), 258
Yellow Elephant: A Bright Bestiary (Larios), 150
Yep, Laurence, 256, 292
Yo, Jo! (Isadora), 119
Yolen, Jane, 197
You Come Too (Frost), 148
You Don't Even Know Me: Stories and Poems About Boys (Flake), 149
You Know Who (Ciardi), 148
Young, Ed, 186, 198
Young Arthur (San Souci), 189
Young Dancer: The Life of an Ailey Student, A (Gladstone), 326
Young Guinevere (San Souci), 189
Young Lancelot (San Souci), 189
Young Merlin (San Souci), 189
Young Naturalist Pop-Up Handbook: Beetles (Sabuda), 189
You Read to Me and I'll Read to You (Ciardi), 148
Your Own Best Secret Place (Baylor), 118
YouTube, 161
Yo! Yes? (Raschka), 296
Yummy: The Last Days of a Southside Shorty (Neri), 288

Zagarenski, Pamela, 112
Zel (Napoli), 216
Zenatti, Valerie, 331
Zinsser, William, 120
Zoo's Who (Florian), 148
Zulu Dog (Ferreira), 289

Credits

PHOTO CREDITS

Cover, Kzenon/Fotolia. **Cover,** Atikinka2/Fotolia. **Cover,** Monkey Business/Fotolia. **Cover,** Andres Rodriguez/Fotolia. **Cover,** Hallgerd/Fotolia. **Cover,** Diego Cervo/Fotolia. **Cover,** Petro Feketa/Fotolia. **Cover,** Andres Rodriguez/Fotolia. **Cover,** EpicStockMedia/Fotolia.

Chapter Opener background, Maksym Yemelyanov/Fotolia. **Common Core State Standard Feature icon,** Maksim Pasko/Fotolia. **Questions/Activities icon,** Ivan Kopylov/Fotolia. **Recommended Books icon,** Paulista/Fotolia. **Tech Click icon,** Tsiumpa/Fotolia.

CHAPTER 1   p. 5, Tammy Ranger. **p. 7,** Deborah White. **p. 12,** "Roll of Thunder, Hear My Cry" by Mildred D. Taylor. Used by permission of Penguin Group (USA) LLC All rights reserved. **p. 24,** Tammy Ranger.

CHAPTER 2   p. 39, "The Lions of Little Rock" by Kristin Levine. Used by permission of Penguin Group (USA) LLC All rights reserved. **p. 42,** "Up, Tall and High" by Ethan Long. Used by permission of Penguin Group (USA) LLC All rights reserved. **p. 46,** Deborah White. **p. 59,** Deborah White. **p. 64 (bottom),** Tammy Ranger. **p. 64 (top),** Amy McClure.

CHAPTER 3   p. 73, Amy McClure. **p. 79,** Jules Selmes/Pearson Education. **p. 81,** Copyright © 2012 by Mac Barnett, illustrations copyright © 2012 by Jon Klassen. Used by Permission of HarperCollins Publishers. **p. 82,** Amy McClure. **p. 84,** Deborah White. **p. 98,** Amy McClure. **p. 100,** Amy McClure.

CHAPTER 4   p. 111, Cover illustration copyright © 2007 by Brian Selznick from "The Invention of Hugo Cabret" by Brian Selznick, published by Scholastic Press, an imprint of Scholastic. Used with permission. **p. 112,** "Dave the Potter: Artist, Poet, Slave" by Laban Carrick Hill, illustrated by Bryan Collier. Little, Brown and Company, a division of Hachette Book Group, Inc. **p. 114,** "The 3 Little Dassies" by Jan Brett. Used by permission of Penguin Group (USA) LLC All rights reserved. **p. 126,** "The Very Hungry Caterpillar" by Eric Carle. Used by permission of Penguin Group (USA) LLC All rights reserved.

CHAPTER 5   p. 143, Amy McClure. **p. 144,** Kim Oldenburgh. **p. 150,** "The Bookworm's Feast" by J. Patrick Lewis, pictures by John O'Brien. Used by permission of Penguin Group (USA) LLC All rights reserved. **p. 162,** Reproduced with permission of VoiceThread. **p. 163,** From "Good Luck Gold" copyright © 2011 by Janet S. Wong.

CHAPTER 6   p. 176, Deborah White. **p. 183,** Image from "Pajaro Verde / The Green Bird" by Joe Hayes, illustrated by Antonio Castro L. Used by permission of Cinco Puntos Press. **p. 186,** "The Lion and the Mouse" by Jerry Pinkney. Little, Brown and Company, a division of Hachette Book Group, Inc. **p. 192,** Spanish compilation copyright © 2003 by Alma Flor Ada and F. Isabel Campoy. English adaptations copyright © 2003 by Alice Schertle. Illustrations copyright © 2003 by Vivi Escriva. Used by permission of HarperCollins Publishers.

CHAPTER 7   p. 217, Amy McClure. **p. 218,** Copyright © 2012 by Katherine Applegate, illustrations copyright © 2012 by Patricia Castelao. Used by permission of HarperCollins Publishers. **p. 219,** Amy McClure. **p. 222,** "The Mysterious Benedict Society" by Trenton Lee Stewart, illustrated by Carson Ellis. Little, Brown and Company, a division of Hachette Book Group, Inc. **p. 223,** Amy McClure.

CHAPTER 8   p. 252, Avi. From "Crispin: The Cross of Lead." Hyperion Books, an imprint of Disney Book Group, 2005. Copyright © 2002 Hyperion Books, an imprint of Disney Book Group. All rights reserved. Reproduced by permission. **p. 258,** Amy McClure. **p. 260,** Copyright © 2010 by Rita Williams-Garcia. Used by Permission of HarperCollins Publishers. **p. 262 (bottom),** Cover illustration copyright © 2007 by Kadir Nelson from "Henry's Freedom Box" by Ellen Levine, illustrated by Kadir Nelson, published by Scholastic Press, an imprint of Scholastic. Used with permission. **p. 262 (top),** Amy McClure.

CHAPTER 9   p. 289, "Because of Winn-Dixie" Copyright © 2000 by Kate DiCamillo. Reproduced by permission of the publisher, Candlewick Press, Somerville, MA. **p. 291,** "Three Times Lucky" by Shelia Turnage. Used by permission of Penguin Group (USA) LLC All rights reserved. **p. 295 (Adventure icon),** Kokhanchikov/Fotolia. **p. 295 (Animal Stories icon),** Anna Velichkovsky/Fotolia. **p. 295 (Family Relationship icon),** Leremy/Fotolia. **p. 295 (Humor icon),** Adore/Fotolia. **p. 295 (Mystery icon),** Wong Yu Liang/Fotolia. **p. 295 (Peer Relationships icon),** Iostephyit/Fotolia. **p. 295 (Romance icon),** Andrey Kiselev/Fotolia. **p. 295 (School Stories icon),** Rob/Fotolia. **p. 296,** Book cover illustration copyright © 1993 by Chris Raschka from "Yo! Yes?" published by Orchard Books, an imprint of Scholastic. Used with permission. **p. 298 (Friday icon),** Raman Maisei/Fotolia. **p. 298 (Jeremy icon),** Pbrazauskas/Fotolia. **p. 298 (Jeremy's grandmother icon),** Monkey Business/Fotolia. **p. 298 (Monday icon),** Jboy/Fotolia. **p. 298 (Saturday icon),** Matthew Cole/Fotolia. **p. 298 (Thursday icon),** LoopAll/Fotolia. **p. 298 (Tuesday icon),** Yasonya/Fotolia. **p. 298 (Wednesday icon),** Yael Weiss/Fotolia.

CHAPTER 10   p. 318, "The Wolves Are Back" by Jean Craighead George, paintings by Wendell Minor. Used by permission of Penguin Group (USA) LLC All rights reserved. **p. 339 (bottom left),** Kim Oldenburgh. **p. 339 (bottom right),** Kim Oldenburgh. **p. 339 (top),** Kim Oldenburgh.

TEXT CREDITS

CHAPTER 1   p. 3, Reprinted from the September/October 2011 issue of *The Horn Book Magazine* by permission of The Horn Book, Inc., www.hbook.com. **p. 7,** Reprinted from the July/August 2013 issue of *The Horn Book Magazine* by permission of The Horn Book, Inc., www.hbook.com. **p. 21,** © Copyright 2010. National Governors Association Center for Best Practices and Council of Chief State School Officers. All rights reserved. **p. 25,** Reprinted by permission of Reading Is Fundamental.

CHAPTER 2   p. 44, © Copyright 2010. National Governors Association Center for Best Practices and Council of Chief State School Officers. All rights reserved. **p. 65,** © Copyright 2010. National Governors Association Center for Best Practices and Council of Chief State School Officers. All rights reserved.